Business-
Government
Relations
in Canada

BUSINESS-GOVERNMENT RELATIONS IN CANADA

Grappling with Leviathan

W. T. STANBURY

University of British Columbia

 METHUEN

Toronto · New York · London · Sydney · Auckland

Copyright © 1986 by Methuen Publications
(A Division of The Carswell Company Limited)

Canadian Cataloguing in Publication Data

Stanbury, W. T., 1943–
   Business-government relations in Canada

Bibliography: p.
Includes index.
ISBN 0-458-99470-7

1. Industry and state — Canada.   I. Title.

HD3616.C32S73 1986   338.971   C85-099953-7

Printed and bound in Canada
1 2 3 4   86   90 89 88 87

CONTENTS

**3 / Describing Leviathan:
A Governing-Instruments Approach**

8 / Lobbying Techniques and Vehicles: Part 1

9 / Lobbying Techniques and Vehicles: Part 2

12 / Advocacy Advertising

The following table has been prepared to direct students using *Canadian Cases in Business-Government Relations* by M.C. Baetz and D.H. Thain (Methuen, © 1985) to sections in *Business-Government Relations in Canada* by W.T. Stanbury (Methuen, © 1986) that contain information helpful in determining solutions to the cases.

Case from Baetz and Thain	Suggested Reading from Stanbury
1. Hazardous Products Legislation in Canada	Chap. 3 Sec. 4.0 Chap. 4 Sec. 1.0 to 6.4
2. National Meat Packers	Chap. 5 Sec. 7 Chap. 6, Chap. 11 Sec. 4
3. Bell Canada's Corporate Reorganization	Chap. 7 Sec. 10.6 Chap. 9 Sec. 2.5
4. Sherbrooke Life	Chap. 4 Sec. 6.5, 6.6 Chap. 11 Sec, 4
5. FIRA and the Canadian Appliance Industry	Chap. 7 Sec. 2.3
6. Michelin Tires	Chap. 5 Sec. 6
7. Volkswagen Duty Remission Plan	Chap. 9 Sec. 6
8. National Footwear Conference of Canada	Chap. 5 Sec. 6 Chap. 8 Sec. 4.3, 4.5, 4.6
9. Massey Ferguson	Chap. 3 Sec. 6
10. Harry D. Shields Ltd.	Chap. 5 Sec. 7 Chap. 7 Sec. 1 to 6
11. Saskatchewan Potash (A)	Chap. 2 Sec. 4.3, and 5.1 to 5.3 Chap. 5 Sec. 6
12. Saskatchewan Potash (B)	Chap. 8 Sec. 4.1, 4.5, 4.6
13. Saskatchewan Potash (C)	Chap. 11 Sec. 2.1, 2.2
14. Note on Crown Corporations/ Canada Development Corp.	Chap. 3 Sec. 5.7
15. The Canadian Federation of Independent Business and the MacEachen Budget	Chap. 8 Sec. 4.2, 4.4
16. Imperial Oil and the "Bertand Report"	Chap. 12
17. Tier I/Tier II	Chap. 5 Sec. 5.4
18. Northern Telecom and the American Political Process	Chap. 10 Sec. 8.0, 9.0

PREFACE and ACKNOWLEDGMENTS

My interest in business-government relations in Canada was stimulated by my study of the politics of Canadian competition policy published by Carswell/Methuen in 1977. Subsequently, I developed a more general framework within which to analyze interest-group behaviour in Canada — see Stanbury (1978) and Thompson and Stanbury (1979). Fred Thompson and I continued to explore the related issues of incumbency (*Canadian Public Policy* 10, no.1 [1984]) and a contingency theory of the functioning of interest groups in a volume on *Regulatory Regimes in Conflict* (1984). Most recently, I have worked with Jane Fulton extending and applying the model of interest-group–government interaction first published in Baetz and Thain, *Canadian Cases in Business-Government Relations* (1985). We showed the generality of the model by applying it to the lobbying strategies of two organizations in the health-care sector (*Canadian Public Administration* 28, no. 2 [1985]).

Work on the model was stimulated by Mark Baetz's comments and suggestions on the first draft in the summer of 1984. The catalytic event that pushed me to convert lecture notes for my M.B.A. course on "A Strategic Approach to Government Policies Affecting Business," to rewrite various unpublished materials, and to prepare much new material was an invitation I received to give a paper at the Canadian-American Business Conference at Michigan State University in June of 1984. In the six weeks prior to the conference, with the help of research assistants Peter Thain and Martin Dresner, I was able to do a rough draft of over 200 pages.

This study has benefited from the comments of my M.B.A. students and those at the Banff School of Advanced Management who used the next (but still incomplete) version as "required reading" in the spring term of 1985. I have also had the benefit of the comments from anonymous referees retained by Methuen and from Jane Fulton.

I am deeply indebted to Norm Couttie, Susan Jones, Surjeet Rai, and Jeff Richmond, who, for their major project in Commerce 592, took on the subject of "Business and the Media." Parts of their extensive paper, rewritten by me, appear in chapter 11. While engaged in a job search, Norm Couttie did extensive library research and drafted parts of chapter 6. His contribution, as with that of the other authors of the group project, makes it a pleasure to say that those two chapters are co-authored.

I have greatly benefited from the advice and enthusiasm of Herb Hilderley, executive editor of Methuen Publications. He stayed with the project while I doubled the size of the first draft by seemingly endless revisions and extensions in the late summer and fall of 1985.

Karyn MacCrimmon and Andrea Demchuk handled many of the mechanical details of proofing, checking, and re-reading, both carefully and cheerfully. I greatly appreciate their efforts. The out-of-pocket cost of research assistants, typing, and photocopying were met by the funds provided by the UPS Foundation Professorship in Regulation and Competition Policy.

I am deeply grateful to Katie Eliot and to other members of the word-processing staff in the Faculty of Commerce at the University of British Columbia. Lori, Kim, Elaine, Nancy, and Linda all worked on the many drafts as the manuscript evolved. Thank you for executing well what was a difficult task.

Publishing a book involves a high degree of specialization and division of labour. Part of this process involves the use of a copy editor, who, directed by the publisher's policy, gets the final word. While the world has moved from sexism to feminism and now to post-feminism, readers will be surprised to learn that Irving Shapiro, Jack Gallagher, W. O. Twaits, Bill Neville, and Austin Taylor were or are "chairpersons" of their respective boards of directors. Perhaps we should be grateful that they were not referred to simply as "chairs," thereby being converted into inanimate objects.

It is hard to argue that issues of equality for all, no matter what sex, colour, or creed, are not noble pursuits. But when correct usage of the language conflicts with lofty agendas for the future, often an author's voice is lost.

I regret that precision of description of past and present realities has to be sacrificed to the dream of a more egalitarian future.

This study is something of a pioneering effort and therefore will have its share of errors and omissions. In writing it, I was conscious of the proposition that a book is a permanent record of the author's mistakes. For good or ill, responsibility for what follows rests with the author. I would be pleased to receive suggestions for improving subsequent editions.

W. T. STANBURY
Vancouver
April 1986

1

Introduction

- *The extensive interpenetration of business and government makes it difficult to identify areas in which they do not interact. (Aram 1983, 5)*
- *[Managers in a more turbulent environment] will have to learn to operate in a political environment. (Drucker 1980, 220)*
- *It is not who owns the means of production, but who makes the key decisions, that is crucial in evaluating the relative distribution of public and private power. (Weidenbaum 1977, 286)*
- *We have an essentially capitalist economy linked to a democratic political system in a pluralistic society that is governed by interest groups. (J. Fred Weston in Jacoby 1975, 124)*

1.0 THE IMPORTANCE OF GOVERNMENT FOR BUSINESS

Governments have a large amount of influence on economic activity in Canada as in all other Western "mixed economies." They relate to business enterprises in at least the following ways:

- Governments attempt to stabilize the economic environment of business through fiscal, monetary, and income policies.
- They subsidize a wide variety of types of business, including farming, textiles, shoes, clothing, and shipbuilding.
- They promote business abroad through trade fairs, information services, favourable taxation, and advertising.
- They finance a wide range of enterprises through direct loans and loan guarantees and insurance (see Economic Council of Canada [ECC] 1982).
- They are the largest purchaser of goods and services in the economy.
- They are partners in over 300 mixed enterprises with private investors (see Elford & Stanbury 1986).
- Governments regulate virtually every aspect of economic activity of firms in the private sector in some way (see ECC 1981). About one-third of the Gross National Product (GNP) is produced subject to direct regulation, that is, controls over price, output, entry, etc. (see Stanbury & Thompson 1980 and Khemani 1986).

- They tax incomes, the value of goods and services, capital gains, and other sources of revenue. Such tax revenues amount to almost 40 percent of the GNP.
- They directly produce and distribute goods and services on a large scale through nonmarket transactions.
- Through crown corporations, by means of voluntary market exchanges, governments produce and sell large volumes of goods and services — perhaps 8 percent of the GNP.
- They seek to alter the behaviour of firms and individuals in the private sector by means of suasion, that is, without resort to legitimate, legally coercive governing instruments (see Stanbury & Fulton 1984).

In chapter 3 I examine in more detail the size, scope, and growth of governments in Canada.

Given Canadians' demonstrated taste for government intervention (see Howard & Stanbury 1984), it seems unlikely that government activity will shrink noticeably in the foreseeable future despite the recent rhetoric about restraint.[1] John McCallum, now a senior advisor to the Mulroney government in Ottawa, makes the same point when he states: "Managers who hope that government won't get further involved in their activities as the 1980s roll on are destined to be greatly disappointed. It's hard to think of anything in our unfolding business environment that would constrain government from becoming more activist while the pressures in the opposite direction are staggering" (1983, 15).

The expansion of government's role in the United States has created some 90 000 "intermediaries between government policy makers and business executives" focused around regulatory agencies in Washington (Reich 1981, 84). These lawyers, lobbyists, public relations specialists, trade association personnel, and government relations consultants exercise skills that "are for the most part strategic, not substantive." Reich continues, "They know how to 'position' a client to reduce unfavourable exposure, minimize risk, gain a positive image, fend off threats to its autonomy, enlarge its domain, reduce its vulnerability or generally thwart rivals" (1981, 85). These intermediaries provide several types of services for their business clients. They gather information about what the "other side" is doing; represent the client's position in a wide variety of forums, from regulatory hearings to the "rubber chicken" circuit; manipulate administrative procedures to advance the interest of their employers/ clients; and use political pressure, for example, in the form of organizing coalitions of interests, generating "grass roots" lobbying, and conducting and disseminating public opinion polls (Reich 1981, 85).

2.0 THE NEED FOR NEW MANAGERIAL SKILLS

In Canada, Fleck and Litvak (1984, 1) argue that business executives are facing an increasing number of obstacles of greater size in achieving their economic goals. "Many factors in the environment of business — political, economic, social, cultural, technological — can create these obstacles, yet they are outside the control of the firm. In order to reduce or overcome these obstacles, business managers must understand and become involved in the political process."[2] Fleck and Litvak state that there is a "consensus that corporations have certain national and social responsibilities and that reasonably efficient forms of government intervention are acceptable" (1984, 5). Moreover, as the high level of macroeconomic concentration in Canada increases — the 100 largest non-financial enterprises now account for one-half of all corporate assets in Canada[3] — the visibility and impact of the biggest firms guarantee that they will be heavily involved in both political and economic markets. "The large corporation in particular must recognize that it operates in a social-political arena where its existence can only be legitimized by ensuring that its economic performance and social behaviour is perceived as being sensitive to the needs of the community" (Fleck & Litvak 1984, 6).

Thornton Bradshaw, a highly regarded American senior business executive, has explained the logical consequence of greater government influence over the affairs of corporations as follows:

> The more the corporation is expected to expand its functions beyond the economic and the more its total environment is determined by the actions of government, the more pressure there will be for it to act as a political activist. The line between government and business, once sharp and clear, has become more and more shadowy. Economic decisions are no longer clearly distinguished from political ones. (1981, p. xxvi)

Based on their survey of American chief executive officers (CEOs), Steiner et al. have identified those qualities CEOs believe their successors should possess (1981, 12-14): if an individual did embody all fourteen, he or she would be a truly renaissance manager. What is interesting, however, is the emphasis given to the future CEO's ability to deal effectively with the social and political environment of the enterprise. The future CEO:

- must be sensitive to social and political forces that have a major impact upon the firm,
- must be able to appropriately balance the legitimate interests of major constituents of the business,
- must assume personal responsibility for advocacy and activism on behalf of the firm,
- must be a good communicator both internally and externally, and
- "must be able to swim in political waters with as much ease as in the traditional economic and technical environments of the corporation."

Irving Shapiro, former chairperson of E. I. duPont, has argued that "the generation of managers who will direct our evolving private enterprise system . . . will have to be skilled in dealing with government, with the news media, with investors and the general public" (Moore 1980, 1). Professor John Aram echoes the views of the CEOs when he states:

> In the coming decades the greatest challenge to managers may arise from social and political movements — areas not traditionally linked to business success. Managers' effectiveness will depend on their abilities to integrate corporate performance with a broad range of public needs and expectations. . . .
>
> Tomorrow's managers will require a wide range of skills to deal with this public policy environment. A premium will be placed on understanding external issues and inventing adaptive managerial policies. The manager will need to be an active participant in the formulation of public policy. (1983, p. xiv)

At the same time, the future CEO, according to a sample of those who now hold the reins of power, must be profit conscious, have a thorough knowledge of the economic and technical characteristics of the business, be a skilled administrator, set a high moral tone for the organization, and devote more time to strategic management rather than to tactical considerations (Steiner et al. 1981, 12–14).

Therefore, it is desirable that managers of business enterprises understand how (and why) governments act to influence private sector economic activity.[4] The reason for doing so is not merely a matter of intellectual interest. Rather, managers need to understand government to be able to *influence* its behaviour in ways beneficial to their firms.[5] Murray and McMillan state that the subject of business-government relations "has become one of more than practical and everyday relevance; it reflects profound questions about the very nature of the country, the future direction of the economy and the structure of basic political and economic institutions" (1983, 592). Yet David Vogel has argued very cogently that "American businessmen, throughout most of their history and particularly over the last forty years, have proven incapable of understanding adequately the economic and political requirements of the socio-economic system upon whose political stability and economic growth their own social existence rests" (1978, 74). It is obvious, however, that in the future the managers of large business enterprises will have to understand their political, economic, and competitive environments if their enterprises are to be successful.

In her article "Remaking the Management Mind," Marguerite Wente, editor of *Canadian Business*, remarks: "Every business must strike a balance with a variety of constituencies, and that inevitably means interaction with every level of government. Many CEOs still see this process as an intrusive nuisance; [others] define it as a central — and growing part of the job. [Moreover], understanding bureaucrats or politicians is one skill that CEOs don't get a lot of training in."[6] In the same vein, James Gillies remarks that "practitioners and scholars both agree that the great challenges to corporate managers in the next two decades are not going to be found in the traditional management fields — production, marketing, financing and so on — but rather in relating the firm to the environment within which it operates and in maintaining a role for the private sector in the economy" (1981, p. ix). This assessment has particular force in Canada. For many businesses, governments now have the greatest capacity to shape the environment within which business enterprises will operate, and it is governments that will be a major force in determining the size and character of the role the private sector will play in the economy in the future. Governments, however, respond — albeit imperfectly — to public opinion, which in turn is influenced both by forces outside the compass of governments in Canada (e.g., the Organization of Petroleum Exporting Countries [OPEC], shifts in comparative advantage, East-West tensions) and by the actions of governments themselves.

3.0 PURPOSE AND GENERAL APPROACH OF THE BOOK

The purpose of this book is to provide a synoptic view of the relationship between business and government in Canada and to provide advice suggesting how business organizations can be more effective in their dealings with government. This is a daunting task. Over a decade ago Professor Donald Thain (1970a, 25) stated that it was "practically impossible to describe systematically and comprehensively the 'business-government relationship.' " This is so because "Canadian governments . . . are now related to business so deeply and broadly . . . [and because they] permeate all aspects of Canadian national life." In light of this injunction, this study might be described, to use the words of Samuel Johnson, as "the triumph of hope over experience."

The literature on the many aspects of business-government relations in Canada has grown rapidly in the past decade. It is a mixture of description, analysis, and prescription. As yet, however, there exist very few books that try to offer a comprehensive survey and synthesis to be used by business executives (and the students who wish to be their successors) as an aid to dealing with governments in Canada.[7] While this book is not primarily a "how to" manual for firms and trade associations, it does contain a substantial amount of material on how to influence public policy.

This study focuses on two types of situations where business and government interact. First, the book addresses the situation where business actors (individuals, firms, trade associations) initiate efforts to influence public policy and decision-making processes of a government. Typically, some type of lobbying activity is involved, but less-direct methods include contributions to political parties and advocacy advertising. Here government (the executive and/or the legislature) becomes the "target" of actions by business. Much of the book is devoted to strategies business might follow in order to influence government.[8]

Second, this study addresses those situations where a government initiates actions designed to modify the behaviour of individuals and firms in the private sector by means of one or more governing instruments,[9] such as taxes, direct expenditures (including subsidies), "tax expenditures," regulation, mixed enterprises, loans and guarantees, and suasion. Here, business organizations are the object of government's behaviour and they wish to respond to government initiatives by seeking to modify them to make them less onerous.

Although this book focuses on business-government relations, much of it can easily be adapted for use by other interest groups. Indeed, in teaching the M.B.A. course out of which this volume grew, I have had student groups study the lobbying behaviour of such environmental groups as Greenpeace, SPEC, and Project Wolf, as well as groups relating to the abortion issue (both pro and con) and the street prostitution issue, the B.C. Medical Association, the B.C. Agrologists Association, the B.C. Teachers' Federation, and the B.C. Federation of Labour.[10] Their work indicates that the model focusing on targets, vehicles, and timing originally developed in Stanbury (1978) and extended in this volume has equal applicability to nonbusiness groups interested in influencing public policy whether for pecuniary or nonpecuniary objectives. See, for example, Fulton and Stanbury (1985).

The general approach taken in this study has the following characteristics. First, while the study focuses on business-government relations in Canada, a few comparisons with the U.S. are used to illuminate the Canadian experience. Second, much of the discussion is organized around a simple analytic framework (chapter 2) that tries to identify the important variables that influence both the *process* of business-government relations and, to a lesser extent, the *outcomes* that the relationship produces. Third, considerable emphasis is placed on the social, economic, and political parameters that shape the environment within which business organizations and governments interact. For example, I argue that certain elements in Canada's political structure determine the most important targets of lobbying activity (i.e., bureaucrats and cabinet members) and that the different political structure of the United States requires that lobbyists focus their efforts on other targets (notably legislators and committee or subcommittee chairpersons). Fourth, the study focuses almost exclusively on relations between business organizations and the federal government. This is regrettable, since Canadian federalism is characterized by a larger role for the provinces than that accorded to the states in the U.S., but necessary for two reasons. First, there is little literature on the relationship of business to the ten provincial governments. Second, space limitations (not to mention the limited resources of the author) allowed for only passing reference to business's dealings with provincial governments.[11]

This book, like most problems in life, is an exercise in constrained optimization. When I began, I defined the task as writing a reasonably comprehensive treatment of the most important aspects of business-government relations in Canada in about 300 pages. Moreover, I thought that the book should combine theory, analysis, description, and some prescriptive material. In addition, it should contain plenty of examples to illustrate the more general or abstract concepts. As well, the book should be well documented by references to the appropriate literature, not only to support its assertions, but also to acquaint both new and experienced students with the literature of the field so that they may conveniently study the issues in more detail.

In meeting all these constraints, the author should be able to convince most of his readers that his necessarily linear plan of attack has handled well numerous elements that should, ideally, be considered in parallel — see Fig 1-1 below. Are the blocks of material in the right order? Are they connected to each other in an understandable way?

Notwithstanding all of the above, the book should be written in such a way as to sustain the interest of readers — both voluntary and involuntary — as they seek knowledge of the field in general or some specific answers to particular problems they must deal with in the real world. Only the reader can judge whether this book meets these various criteria.

In writing a "textbook," I have been conscious of the fact that, in some ways, it is an unsatisfactory substitute for having the reader deal directly with a wide range of primary sources. In discussing what he thought should be done in courses for business students in public policy or business-government relations, Edward Littlejohn, vice-president of public affairs for Pfizer Inc., argued that no textbook should be used. In his view,

> energy-releasing ideas are more likely to be found in original works, both classical and current. Textbooks are often bland collections of facts and opinions, classified and arranged for easy consumption, and consequently they are often dull and uninspiring. In the books I have in mind, students would encounter the human experience. They would share the intellectual struggle of a man engaged in the adventure of ideas. (1980, 184)

However, a text can provide a helpful structure for a vast, growing body of relevant knowledge that is scattered across several fields of study.

Moreover, given the usual constraints of time and energy, a text may permit readers to gain a more comprehensive grasp of the subject matter.

4.0 A DOUBLE-EDGED SWORD

The mixture of positive and normative analyses in this book reflects the conflicting uses to which a greater knowledge of how to influence government may be put. On the one hand, as the data and discussion in chapter 3 make clear, I am concerned about the enormous size and scope of government in the Canadian economy. On balance, I believe that the average Canadian's standard of living would increase more rapidly if effectively competitive market forces were relied on to a greater extent and if, correspondingly, the constraints imposed by governments (directly and indirectly) on markets were substantially reduced.[12] Therefore, better equipping business executives in their effort to restrain the growth of governments or to actually reduce their size and scope seems highly desirable.

On the other hand, I am acutely aware that a very considerable part of the present high level of government activity is attributable to the past and present efforts of business firms, trade associations, and their allies — see Bliss (1980a). History makes it clear that, on balance, Canadian business people have been favourably disposed toward government intervention in many forms: tariff protection; import quotas and other nontariff barriers to trade; cash subsidies; loans and guarantees; bailouts; protective regulation that controls entry and prices; and government expenditures for transportation and communications infrastructure (Bliss 1982a, 1985). Sophisticated business executives also appreciate that much of the social safety net of income transfer programs shifts to the treasury (and taxpayers in general) costs that might otherwise be the subject of collective bargaining.

Business executives in Canada frequently complain about their lack of influence with government. Their complaints were loudest during the last years of the Trudeau government (Bliss 1982b). Prime Minister Trudeau observed that "business always loves government, of course, when it's spending money to help business and despises it the rest of the time."[13] Yet the evidence, when one reviews the enormous volume of business-oriented tax expenditures, direct subsidies, bailouts, soft loans, and the nontariff forms of protection, suggests that the business community has supped deeply at the public trough (Howard & Stanbury 1984). It is not clear, however, that such assistance has actually raised the nation's standard of living, although it has probably altered the distribution of income.[14] Therefore, Adam Smith's advice, given over 200 years ago, is still relevant:

The proposal of any new law or regulation of commerce which comes from [merchants and manufacturers], ought always to be listened to with great precaution, and ought never to be adopted till after having been long and carefully examined, not only with the most scrupulous, but with the most suspicious attention. It comes from an order of men, whose interest is never exactly the same with that of the public, who have generally an interest to deceive and even to oppress the public, and who accordingly have, upon many occasions, both deceived and oppressed it. (Smith 1937 ed., 250)

Consequently, we have the following conundrum. If business executives become more skilled at influencing government policy, will they use such capabilities to restrain the growth of government and enhance the role of competitive markets? That is, will they seek to have the invisible hand that operates through voluntary market exchanges replace the visible hand of government action? Or will business people simply be able to lobby more effectively for benefits from government at the expense of other groups in society, including the average taxpayer?

The question is of great importance to the nation as a whole, for, as Mancur Olson argues — and many agree with him — "On balance, special-interest organizations and collusions reduce efficiency and aggregate income in societies in which they operate and make political life more divisive" (1982, 47). Moreover, Olson suggests that "distributional coalitions slow down a society's capacity to adopt new technologies and to reallocate resources in response to changing conditions, and thereby reduce the rate of economic growth" (1982, 65). Finally, he argues that "the accumulation of distributional coalitions increases the complexity of regulation, the role of government, and the complexity of understandings, and changes in the direction of social evolution" (1982, 73).

5.0 CHARACTERIZING THE RELATIONSHIP BETWEEN BUSINESS ORGANIZATIONS AND GOVERNMENT

The relationship between business firms and governments in either positive or normative terms cannot be characterized in a single phrase. It is inevitably plural and diverse. Depending upon the industry, the time, the other issues on the public policy agenda, the individuals involved, and what each "side" is seeking to do vis-à-vis the other, the relationship might be characterized as adversarial, cooperative, symbiotic, supportive, or protective.

Proust observed that nothing separates two men more than their adherence to differing ethical systems. So it is with groups and even large-scale organizations. Let us compare and contrast business and government in terms of the assumptions that underlie their role and functions in society.

Business	*Government*
• focus is on the individual and the firm	• focus is on the state or the collectivity
• self-interested behaviour is assumed	• the apparent objective is to advance the public interest, a concept that is hard to define
• exchanges are based on goods/services for money	• loyalty and support of the state is commanded on an involuntary basis (capacity to exercise legitimate means of coercion)
• focus is on production for profit	• focus is on the distribution of income and rights
• hierarchical rewards based on personal characteristics and success in the marketplace	• political equity emphasizes the equality of individuals and concern for the weaker and less successful
• utilitarian perspective	• political perspective of popular sovereignty

This list of comparisons is obviously not complete, but it is sufficient to make the point that business people operate under a different set of assumptions than do politicians and bureaucrats.[15] The workings of popular democracy with its emphasis on equality and a wide range of political rights almost inevitably are a major force for the expansion of the state. The state is the vehicle by which the commitment to equality is made real. David Vogel suggests that "the ideological hostility of business-men toward their state is a function of their state's democratic heritage: the greater the responsiveness of the state to popular interest-group pressures, the more likely it is that businessmen will find increased state authority over economic decisions threatening" (1978, 76).

Kenneth Boulding, a remarkable man whose abilities go far beyond his profession as economist, has summed up his view of business-government relations in verse:[16]

The public fist is thinly gloved:
Business, feeling much unloved,
Thinks Government is out to get it
And if it does we may regret it.

Business, more than in the past,
Feels itself to be harassed.
For power to stop becomes an art
More powerful than the power to start.

When things become a little sour
We call on countervailing power.
And, as the tension slowly mounts,
The countervailing is what counts.

Business meets a messy fate
If it tries to be a State;
Business leaves us in the lurch
When it tries to be a Church;
Business makes itself a fool
When it tries to be a School;
Business drowns in love of self
When it tries to be itself;
Business might as well enjoy
Living as a whipping boy.

The imminent approach of death
Will clear the mind and sweeten breath.
So agencies are most effective
That die on reaching their objective.

Creating crises may be how
We all could learn from Chairman Mao.
So troubles should not much dismay us
Who seek the best amount of chaos!

6.0 MARKET EXCHANGES AS COMPARED TO BUSINESS-GOVERNMENT RELATIONS

The nature of the relationship between business and government can be illuminated if we compare and contrast the relations between a government and an individual business to those between actors in a competitive market. The hallmark of market relations is that they are voluntary,[17] decentralized, and unabashedly self-interested. In general, the interaction is initiated bilaterally and there is a rough parity of power.[18] In the case of business-government interactions initiated by the latter, the state usually is using its wide range of legitimate powers of coercion to alter the behaviour of firms. The fact is that governments have coercive powers (e.g., to tax, to regulate, and, in the case of the federal government, the power to print money) that have no counterpart among firms — even a monopolist.[19] Conversely, where the interaction is initiated by business, it is apparent that, except in unusual circumstances (e.g., the large multinational vis-à-vis a regional government in a small, developing nation), the firm or trade association has the opportunity to *persuade*, but not the power (legitimate or otherwise) to coerce.

Therefore, the business-government relationship, from the perspective of the firm, stands in sharp contrast to the relationship the firm has with its suppliers, customers, shareholders, employees, and creditors to which it is connected by means of markets. The cash nexus, even as modified by the modern administered contract, usually provides both sides of the exchange with alternative suppliers, customers, and employees. In dealing with government, the firm deals with a monopolist, although in a federal state with concurrent jurisdiction, the firm may be able to "play one level of government off against another."[20] The potential dominance of government, being backed by its extensive legitimate powers of coercion, colours its relationship with business regardless of the rhetoric. Both sides know that ultimately government can get its way, subject to the constitutional protections of private property. "We have ways of making you talk!"

Moreover, many of the actions by government that modify the behaviour of business are not aimed at firms per se. Rather, business is an intermediary in a process whose objective is quite different. Specific excise taxes and the corporate income tax are not really levies on particular outputs or on the net income of a particular class of economic actors. Rather, they are the means to achieve other (often ill-defined) social objectives, such as reducing the consumption of a particular product or generating revenues in order to redistribute income to the needy (however defined). Market exchanges are essentially what they seem: goods or services are exchanged for money. Deep psychological symbolism aside, that's about all there is to it. The exchange is not designed to serve some larger purpose, although the existence of well-functioning markets as institutions is of profound significance to society as a whole. Perhaps it was this idea that prompted Lord Keynes to remark that "it is better that a man should tyrannize over his bank balance than over his fellow citizens."

In market exchanges the legitimacy of the actions of the participating firms or individuals is unquestioned and without ambiguity. When business, on the other hand, seeks to influence government by lobbying, the legitimacy of its actions is much more open to question. While the idea that, in a democracy, individuals have the *right* to petition the government for the redress of grievances, the right of corporations — merely *legal* persons — to do so is subject to argument, particularly when the corporation is large and possesses substantial economic power. Moreover, the corporation, where it manifestly has far greater resources with which to try to influence government than the individual, is in an even more ambiguous position. Does it have the right to use all its resources to influence the legislature by legal means? (See chapter 3.)

7.0 TERMINOLOGY

It is necessary to comment on the "tyranny of terminology." The all-encompassing terms *business* and *government* are convenient but often misleading. To simplify and more easily manipulate concepts, we use simple terms that reflect an unfortunate degree of abstractness. Business (or government) is obviously *not* a homogeneous entity as the single word would imply. At the very least, business incorporates individual executives, firms, and various types of trade associations (horizontal, vertical, and industry-specific). Government includes line departments, central agencies, the legislature, independent regulatory bodies, the cabinet, and individual bureaucrats and politicians. In both cases, the intragroup variance often swamps that between business and government. As Whalen remarks, "In some respects the broad categories 'business' and 'government' are quite inadequate for analytical purposes" (1961, 5).

There are particular problems when one writes of the *business community* or simply *business*. There are plenty of conflicting interests among individual firms and industries. As business historian Michael Bliss notes, "One of the little-noticed characteristics of Canadian business opinion is how deeply divided businessmen are in their advice to governments" (1982b, 55), for example, on the size of the deficit, interest rates, the desirability of bailouts, wage and price controls, and the appropriate value of the Canadian dollar.

The reasons for these conflicting interests are not hard to find. First, in any industry the firms are rivals for the same customers and often draw upon the same markets for various inputs (labour, materials, capital). Only under atomistic competition can firms ignore the actions of individual competitors. Second, industries tend to be regionally concentrated. Frequently, regional interests are in conflict and, therefore, firms/industries are bound up in these conflicts (the manufacturing heartland vs. the remote extractive industries). Where political jurisdictions coincide with economic regions, *and* economic regions also exhibit cultural differences, the potential for conflict within the business community is high.

Third, where tariff and nontariff barriers are important, the interests of export-oriented firms/industries are different than the interests of those which sell only in the domestic market and face import competition. The two groups will be in conflict on the appropriate degree of protection and exchange rates at the very least. Also important in Canada is the potential conflict between domestic and foreign-owned enterprises. Here, conflict will not be confined to policies concerning foreign ownership, but would extend to trade policies, taxation, and other issues.

Finally, there is the matter of size. Small and medium-sized firms appear to face special problems as compared with "big business." In Canada, the growing differentiation of the interests of small business has resulted in the creation of the Canadian Federation of Independent Business (CFIB) which now has almost one-half the number of members as the Canadian Chamber of Commerce (CCC) and one of the larger budgets of any trade association in Canada (see Adelson et al. 1985).

The simple reference to *government* can also be simplistic and even misleading. Obviously, there are many governments in Canada: the federal government, ten provincial governments, two territorial governments, and literally hundreds of municipal and regional governments. Moreover, the federal government, for example, is composed of hundreds of departments, agencies, and other crown entities (even if we ignore the almost 300 commercial crown corporations). In fact, the volume entitled *The Organization of the Government of Canada* (1980), which describes briefly the various administrative units, is 635 pages long.

More importantly, despite the trappings of cabinet solidarity in the Westminster model of government, the fact is that governments incorporate a wide variety of disparate objectives, some of which are always in conflict with one another. Indeed, there is as much conflict, rivalry, and jockeying for power within any government as between any government and business organization. (One wag has suggested that an efficient bureaucracy is the greatest threat to the liberty of the individual.) In fact, later in this book I will argue that firms and trade associations could make use of conflict over policy within a government to advance their own interests. The point is that governments are not unified, homogeneous entities acting in a rational manner to achieve their objectives. Virtually all generalizations about governments or a government are treacherous. Yet, in the interests of economy of expression, I speak of governments — as I speak of business — in a more abstract way than is ideal.

8.0 STRUCTURE OF THE VOLUME

A diagram illustrating the structure of this book is given in Figure 1-1. Chapter 2 presents a framework within which to analyze business-government relations in Canada. It consists of three levels of aggregation: a set of social, economic, and political parameters that define the system within which business and government interact; sets of exogenous variables that shape the actions of businesses and governments and sets of variables that both "sides" are able to use to shape their strategies toward each other; and the process of interaction as governments seek to influence the behaviour of business firms and businesses strive — along with other groups — to shape public policy.

The second part of the book, chapters 3 and 4, is designed to develop an understanding of the size and scope of government activity in the Canadian economy and of the policy-making process. In chapter 3, "Describing Leviathan," I also draw out some tentative implications for business of large-scale government involvement in the economy. In chapter 4, in contrast to the traditional descriptive approach to the policy-making process, I offer a public choice perspective on what goes on in political markets. I believe that business executives, by paying heed to the political calculus that lies behind public policy actions, will be better equipped to influence those who make the government policies that affect them. Chapter 4 also explains the myriad ways in which public policy is made, ranging from new legislation to ministerial statements in press releases to decisions of the courts that authoritatively interpret

Figure 1-1
STRUCTURE OF THE BOOK

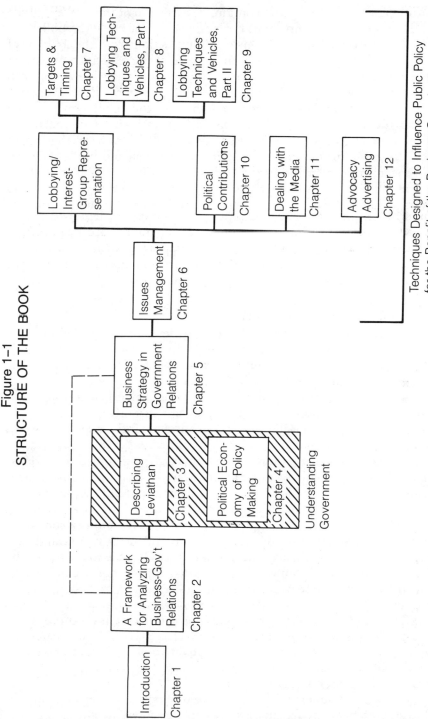

statutes and regulations, and contains a discussion of the concept of the public interest as an important normative concept in public policy.

The role of chapter 5 is to make the transition from the analysis of government in the economy and the nature of the exchange process in political markets to the development of a firm's strategy in dealing with government, which is the focus of the second part of the book. The strategic choices are outlined, the growth of the government relations function in Canada is described, and the goals a firm may choose in seeking to influence government are discussed. In addition, I address the fact of conflicts within the business community over what should be the direction and means of implementing public policy.

Chapter 6 deals with what has immodestly come to be called issues management. It offers a way of classifying both issues and the publics that deal with them. The chapter also includes a discussion of how issues evolve and get on the public policy agenda. Considerable space is devoted to strategies that corporations may use to handle public policy issues.

Chapter 7 is the first of three that focus on lobbying as a specific technique for influencing public policy for the benefit of an interest group. It deals with the targets of lobbying efforts (e.g., bureaucrats, ministers, MPs) and the timing of such efforts.

Chapters 8 and 9 are devoted to a fairly detailed analysis of lobbying techniques and vehicles. Chapter 9 also includes sections on the strategic use of the concept of the public interest in lobbying and the various proposals to regulate lobbying in Canada.

Chapter 10 addresses the difficult problem of political contributions and the role they do or should play in business efforts to influence governments. While it is illegal to try to purchase influence, there seems to be little doubt that campaign contributions serve to "lubricate" business-government relations, although, as I point out in chapter 4, there are several media of exchange between business and government whereby the latter supplies policy initiatives favoured by business.

The news media play an important role in shaping how businesses seek to influence government policy. In chapter 11, I address such matters as the characteristics of the electronic and print media and how these must be taken into account if business is to be able to use the media to its own advantage. Some rather detailed suggestions are offered on how to deal effectively with the media interview.

In chapter 12, I deal with one of the most rapidly growing instruments that business firms and trade associations (not to mention professional groups, unions, and other interest groups) use to try to influence public policy and public opinion: advocacy advertising. Such paid messages are designed to sell ideas with a view to shaping public policy rather than to selling products at a profit.

The book concludes with an extensive bibliography that also contains all the references cited in the text and in the notes.

NOTES

1. For example, the Social Credit government of Premier W. R. Bennett in B.C. has imposed the harshest restraint measures, particularly since its re-election in 1983. Yet, as columnist Marjorie Nichols (Vancouver *Sun*, December 8, 1984, p. 5) has noted, government expenditures and taxes have actually increased over the past few years. Nichols states: "In the three years of restraint, the B.C. government has introduced a dozen new provincial taxes that have raised more than $1.2 billion for the treasury. . . . The total provincial debt has increased . . . from $11.3 billion in 1982 to this year's anticipated total of $15 billion. . . . Their own figures show that annual health and social service spending has increased $450 million between 1982 and 1984, but new health taxes will raise $150 million this year and about $204 million next year." More generally, see Dobell (1984). The latest effort by the Mulroney government on regulatory reform, for example, was announced on February 13, 1986. See *Globe and Mail*, February 14, 1986, p. A5.

2. In terms of their *present* degree of political involvement, a survey of 395 American CEOs in 1980 indicated the following:

   - apolitical   2%
   - company spokesperson   21
   - public communicator (take their own views to the public)   26
   - political activist (endorse candidates, raise funds, campaign)   40
   - full-time politicians (willing to become elected or appointed official)   6
   - not classified   5

   (Moore 1980, 48)

3. More generally, see Green (1985, chap. 2), and the brief by Cadillac Fairview Corp. on the federal Green Paper on the regulation of financial institutions (Toronto: August 1985).

4. I would not, however, go as far as Fleck and Litvak (1984, 6), who argue that "it is in the best interest of all concerned that greater interaction take place between business, labour, consumers and government. Greater cooperation is necessary between all parties to develop effective policies to achieve national priorities." On this point, see also Thorburn (1985), who notes that many submissions to the Macdonald Commission recommended more consultation between business groups and government.

5. I do not agree with Professor McCallum, who argues that "business is going to find that efforts to stem this government tide will be largely in vain and the strategy, therefore, should be one of figuring how best to 'go with the flow' " (1983, 15). Later in this article, McCallum refers to the words of the former longtime Speaker of the U.S. House of Representatives Sam Rayburn: "To get along, go along." McCallum argues that "in this battle, business isn't only outgunned, they're outmanned, outmanoeuvred and outflanked as well" (1984, 20). He goes on to suggest that business "must accelerate its efforts to look more like government. That means ever larger, but hopefully more effective and efficient, bureaucracies and a greater emphasis on the kind of consensus-style management that governments thrive on."

6. *Canadian Business*, January 1983, p. 10.

7. Gillies (1981) and Gollner (1983) appear to fall into this category. Other useful contributions to the field in book form include Fleck and Litvak (1984); Murray (1985); and Baetz and Thain (1985). Very useful articles on business-government relations in Canada in the past few years include Bartha (1982, 1985b); Blair (1984); Bliss (1982b); Bon (1981); Hardy (1982); Johnson (1983); Litvak (1979, 1981, 1982, 1983); MacLaren (1976); McMenemy (1982); Murray and McMillan (1984); McMillan and Murray (1983); Owen (1976); Partridge (1982); Thain (1970a, 1970b, 1979a, 1979b, 1980, 1981); Thain and Baetz (1979, 1982); and Traves (1985).

8. Edward Littlejohn, vice-president of public affairs for Pfizer Inc., reminds us that public affairs (or business-government relations) is not the only important element of business management:

> I spend my days in the practice of public affairs. . . . It becomes easy to believe that the business of business is not business but public affairs. A visit, however, to the company cafeteria quickly dispels that notion. Sitting among colleagues from the controller's division, marketing divisions, personnel staff, research scientists, and corporate planners, I find that scarcely a thought is given to the ideas and issues on which public affairs enthusiasts often assert the profits and prospects of the company ultimately depend. My colleagues, rather, act on the presupposition that sales, profits, market shares, new products, return on investment, and so on, are the primary elements in their success and the company's success, including the public affairs division. And they are right. (1980, 175)

9. On the concept of governing instruments, see Trebilcock et al. (1982). The extent to which a number of them is used in Canada is described in chapter 3.

10. See Biggs et al. (1983), Budd et al. (1983), Chin et al. (1982), Cook et al. (1982), Guthrie et al. (1984), Karpat (1982), Park et al. (1983), Smith et al. (1984), Campbell et al. (1985), Frank et al. (1985), Gendreau et al. (1984), Abbott et al. (1984), Hamdi et al. (1983), and Jackson (1983).

11. I have, however, participated in the preparation of two cases that deal with business-government relations in B.C. See Stanbury, Smart, and Vertinsky (1983) and Jessen, Smart, Stanbury, and Vertinsky (1983).

12. This should not be construed as a simplistic plea to cut back government activity a great deal everywhere. What is required is a scalpel, not an ax wielded by an enraged libertarian. More generally, see Stanbury (1980, 1984b); Stanbury and Thain (1984); Stanbury and Thompson (1982a); and ECC (1979), which I drafted on behalf of the council.

13. Quoted in *Maclean's*, December 21, 1981, p. 38.

14. It is not too strong to say that the bulk of government intervention is motivated by the desire to alter the distribution of income. See, for example, Stanbury and Lermer (1984) and Lermer and Stanbury (1985). The cornucopia of government programs, however, creates a large number of "crosscurrents," so the net result — as measured by the distribution of income by household or by family — has been fairly stable over time (see Osberg 1981).

15. The distinctions are developed in more detail in chapter 5.

16. As quoted in Jacoby (1975, 176).

17. By voluntary I mean that they are noncoercive, although it is acknowledged that "we all have to eat"; hence most market participants have to trade to continue to function.

18. Obviously, cases of pure monopoly or monopsony can involve substantial disparities in market power. However, without government-made barriers to entry, most positions of market power which are fully exploited are eventually undermined by competition (often induced by technological change). More generally, see Green 1985.

19. Governments also have considerable powers of suasion, i.e., the ability to influence behaviour without resort to legal coercion. See Stanbury and Fulton (1984) and chapter 3.

20. They can also get caught in what my friend Richard Schultz of McGill University calls "the vise (vice?) of federalism." See chaper 4.

2

A Framework for Analyzing Business-Government Relations in Canada

This chapter provides a general framework in which to analyze business-government relations in Canada. The framework notes the two-way nature of the relationship, although the bulk of this book focuses on the various techniques that firms, trade associations, or other interest groups can use to try to influence the decisions and behaviour of government.

1.0 OVERVIEW

A framework or "model" that can assist in analyzing business-government relations in Canada is outlined in Figure 2-1. Three levels of aggregation are identified. The highest or systemic level consists of the set of social, political, and economic variables that are largely exogenous to each firm or business interest group (i.e., beyond its control). Nevertheless, these factors directly and indirectly influence the behaviour of both business and governments.[1] For example, the choice of *targets* of lobbying efforts in Canada is strongly influenced by the fact that the system of government we enjoy (the Westminster model) establishes a policy-formulation process in which the leading actors are cabinet ministers and senior bureaucrats. In comparison, under the American congressional model of government, the most important targets of lobbying efforts are committee and subcommittee chairpersons and their advisors in both the House of Representatives and the Senate.

The second level of aggregation consists of two sets of variables that operate at the level of the individual organization, that is, the firm or business interest group, and the government. One set is exogenous (i.e., outside the power of the group to influence) and the other is endogenous (i.e., within the power of the group to influence, although the degree of influence will vary substantially across these variables).

The lowest level of aggregation consists of the strategies and tactics used by the business interest group (or firm) and the government in seeking to influence each other. While the main targets within a gov-

---

Note: An earlier version of this chapter was published in Baetz and Thain (1985, chap. 1).

ernment in Canada are senior bureaucrats and cabinet ministers, groups may seek to influence these targets indirectly by trying to influence the allies and "enemies" of those persons. In addition, firms and interest groups may seek to shape public opinion through the use of the media (see chapter 11) and by paid advocacy advertising (see chapter 12). On their side, governments have a wide variety of governing instruments with which to influence firms and individuals in the private sector (see chapter 3). In addition, they can also influence the business groups by controlling information and access to the policy-formulation process, and by assisting other groups that are working against business groups.

The interaction of business and governments produces the outcomes that can be thought of as the set of responses of one party to the actions of the other, given the context in which both sides function. In particular, I focus on changes in public policy (legislation and administrative behaviour) or the changes in the activities of firms in response to government actions that often take the form of intervention in market processes.

Having sketched the framework, I now describe in more detail the variables in each of the "boxes" in Figure 2-1.

2.0 SOCIAL, ECONOMIC, AND POLITICAL FACTORS

I can only touch upon what appear to be the most important *givens* in the social, economic, and political context in which business and government interact with each other in Canada. These factors are defined at the societal or systemic level. They change very slowly, and from the perspective of both interest groups and governments, they are beyond their control; hence they are taken as given. The significance of a number of these factors for business-government relations is outlined in Figures 2-2 and 2-3.

2.1 Characteristics of the Political System

Some of the more important characteristics of the political system that indirectly shape business-government relations include the following:
- Type of government (e.g., Westminster model [cabinet government] vs. congressional type with separation of powers)
- Political structure (federalism vs. unitary state)
- Allocation of jurisdiction among levels of government (power of the provinces relative to the federal government)
- Degree of intergovernmental conflict*
- Intensity of competition among political parties*
- Availability of information about the policy-making process and its outcomes*
- Degree of political stability*
- Rules governing the financing of political parties and candidates*

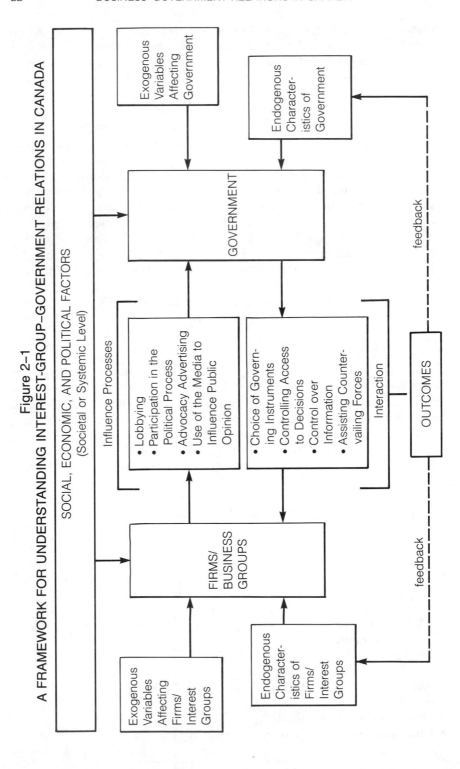

Figure 2–1
A FRAMEWORK FOR UNDERSTANDING INTEREST-GROUP–GOVERNMENT RELATIONS IN CANADA

Figure 2–2

POLITICAL AND SOCIAL FACTORS AND THEIR SIGNIFICANCE FOR BUSINESS-GOVERNMENT RELATIONS IN CANADA

Key Characteristics	Significance for Business-Government Relations
Political:	
• Type of gov't.: Westminster model (cabinet government)	• Cabinet has a monopoly on the supply of legislation; hence it and the senior bureaucrats (policy advisors) are the key targets of lobbying. High degree of secrecy. Bargaining with interest groups occurs largely in the prelegislation phase. Timing elections is up to the prime minister subject to a 5-year maximum. Committees and MPS are generally not important targets of lobbying. Governments are, however, using more advisory bodies and other forms of consultation with organized interests.
• Federalism	• The Canadian variant gives very important powers to the provinces; therefore, it is crucial to determine which gov't. has the primary responsibility. Plenty of federal-provincial conflict, which can both adversely affect interest groups or be exploited by them. Federalism is also tied up with linguistic/religious/cultural and regional conflicts—affects bus.-gov't. relations both ways, but generally complicates finding a modus vivendi for *both* sides. Business gets caught in federal-provincial battles and can be a pawn.
• Political financing laws	• Since 1974, both parties and candidates have been less dependent upon corporate contributions, which can be made without limit directly to parties and candidates. Yet today about one-half of revenues of both major parties comes from corporations, and each spent about $6.3 million in the 1984 general elections, but this figure excludes expenditure by candidates.
Social:	
• Corporatist values	• Canada is not a corporatist society, but strong corporatist values exist that shape the public policies process. These values stress the primacy of group over individual interests and an organic view of society in which the common good transcends individual interests. Groups are functional parts of a social organism in which there is "a place for everyone," and "everyone is in their place." Conflicts are to be resolved by mutual accommodation (using suasion and bargaining) among institutionalized interest groups. The state, while delegating some responsibilities to such groups, has a primary role in identifying the national interest and in harmonizing diverse group interests. Membership within groups may be based more on one's position in society and less on purely voluntary choice. Leadership of groups tends to be "strong," with decisions in some cases ratified by members.

Figure 2–2 (continued)

Key Characteristics	Significance for Business-Government Relations
Social:	
• Redistribution ethic	• Hardin (1974) argues that Canadians "have a genius for redistribution." Most strongly pushed by the NDP, only slightly less so by the Liberals, and expressed in terms of "compassion" by the Conservatives, there is a widespread feeling that the economically disadvantaged must be provided for in virtually every policy. Distributive consequences of policies are given far more weight than efficiency gains — even when they impose significant efficiency losses on the economy. The redistributive ethic takes many forms: helping low-income regions — often at great cost per job created; using direct regulation to achieve "social" objectives via cross-subsidization, e.g., in telecommunications; using cultural regulation to help domestic producers and achieve cultural objectives; location of government facilities; and the use of marketing boards to tax consumers to help farmers. The result has been the growth of elaborate and costly universal programs to deal with health care, income security, and education.
• Obsession with national unity and maintenance of a unique cultural identity	• Because Canada is an almost completely unnatural economic entity (economic forces flow largely north-south while legal jurisdiction is east-west), and because of the English-French (about 28% of the population) split, national governments have had to engage in brokerage politics designed to overcome the centrifugal forces operating on the country. In modern times this had meant (1) a policy of official and practical bilingualism/biculturalism, (2) enormous benefits conferred on the people of Quebec "to keep them in Confederation" (this is reinforced by the fact that both major parties stress the importance of strong representation from Quebec), (3) massive intervention into "cultural markets" (subsidies, tax expenditures, regulation, and crown enterprises) in an effort to increase the supply of indigenous cultural outputs and to differentiate them from the rest of the world. Moreover, a vast array of federal programs is justified in the name of "nation building," "keeping the country together," and "maintaining the federal presence" in the face of aggressive province-building. Such federal activity resembles a form of "serial potlatching," as the distribution of federal largess in one region or city creates irresistible demands — in the name of equity — for similar treatment of all regions or cities.

- Political/bureaucratic morality (implicit and explicit "rules of the game")

While the variables marked with an asterisk (*) are exogenous to business and other interest groups, they are subject to some degree of influence by a government and more so by all governments if they act in a coordinated fashion. In the short run, however, these factors are givens from the perspective of a government.

Business's capacity to influence government must begin with an understanding of the type of government we have in Canada. The Westminster model, or cabinet government, can be described in outline fashion as follows:

- The party with a majority of the lower house (Commons) forms a government after a general election in which all adults have a single, nontransferable vote.
- The leader of the majority party becomes prime minister and chooses his or her cabinet. These ministers form the core of the political executive.
- The majority party continues to govern so long as it "maintains the confidence of the legislature," that is, can sustain a majority on votes of confidence. The election date is chosen by the prime minister subject to the statutory limit (five years).
- Cabinet has a complete monopoly over the supply of new legislation (statutes, regulations, orders) that has a serious prospect of enactment. (Private members' bills are possible but only very rarely command the support of the House.)
- Party discipline is strong — backbenchers are expected to support the party's (leader's) position. Intraparty disputes are largely kept secret and reserved for discussion in caucus.
- The prime minister has enormous personal powers: to appoint and dismiss ministers and parliamentary secretaries and to strongly influence a vast array of order-in-council appointments; to largely control the committee process by means of appointments and determination of budgets/staff; to largely determine the cabinet agenda, etc.
- There is, in theory, a chain of responsibility (and accountability) extending from the people to Parliament in popular elections, then to the government and to the individual minister, and then to public servants who administer the legally mandated programs and policies. (In practice, the chain has loose links and it is hard to hold individuals accountable, although ultimately the voters can elect other representatives.)
- The public service functions anonymously. Senior members provide advice on policy issues and administer the programs/policies enacted by Parliament or adopted by the government. The public service is

based on the merit principle and except for order-in-council appointments does not change when governments come and go.
• In practice, the process of policy formulation is conducted largely in
  secret within the executive. While competition among ministers/
  departments/agencies can be strong, the public has little access to
  this vital arena; astute lobbyists do, however. (The public and particularly interest groups are demanding a more open system of policy
  making.)

In the longer run, the government of the day can change some of the
rules of the game. For example, in 1974 the statutes dealing with the
financing of political parties and candidates were altered greatly (see
chapter 10). While the tradition of secrecy in the Westminster model of
government is strong, some changes were made by the federal Liberals
in 1982 when the Access to Information Act was passed. The degree of
intergovernmental conflict — in which business interests are sometimes
pawns — is the result of the interaction of both the federal and provincial
governments, although it is possible for one side or the other "to pick a
fight." Virtually all provincial governments find it is good politics to
be strongly critical of the federal government while at the same time
seeking more and more economic benefits from the federal treasury.
The provinces maintain continuous pressure to enlarge their jurisdiction
so as to be able to reflect and respond to regional interests — frequently
at the expense of a national economic union.

In the long run, even the basic characteristics of the political system
(those without an asterisk in the list above) are subject to change by the
political process. One has only to think of the Constitution Act of 1982
and its Charter of Rights and Freedoms.

2.2 Characteristics of Social Values in Canada

The origins or bases of values are hard to identify; yet they shape both
the political and economic systems. Doern and Phidd (1983, 35) argue
that public policy is an amalgam of ideas, structures, and processes. Ideas
are the broad normative content of policy, and they form the basis for
the existence of key institutions (federalism, cabinet government, interest groups, the electoral system, political parties, and the mass media).
They suggest that the dominant ideas or enduring concerns relate to
efficiency, individual freedom, equity, stability, redistribution, national unity and identity, and regional sensitivity.

With respect to specific ideas, Doern and Phidd state that "there has
always existed in Canada an ambivalence about the idea of efficiency
inherent in capitalism. The numerous rough edges of Canadian capitalism have always been moderated by an inclination to use the state"
(1983, 25). In their view, individualism "implies a belief in the social
value of self-interest and self-development. An entrenched Charter of

Rights and Freedoms suggests in formal terms a belief that the purpose of the state is to serve the individual and not vice versa." A close reading of the charter, however, indicates that there are — unlike the U.S. Constitution — no virtually absolute rights that inhere in the individual (see Beck & Bernier 1983). Section 1, for example, "guarantees the rights and freedoms . . . subject only to such reasonable limits prescribed by law as can be demonstrably justified in a free and democratic society." Put bluntly, the War Measures Act is still on the books and may be invoked at the pleasure of a majority government. Moreover, Canadians' respect for individual rights has been and continues to be overridden — with virtually no debate — when there is a conflict between economic security and individual responsibility. Very few Canadians apparently connect the loss of individual responsibility and the loss of individual freedom with government actions designed to provide greater economic security — at least for some.

Doern and Phidd (1983, 55, n. 4) argue that "stability of income (and of other desired conditions)" is a dominant value. Such an idea "places a high value on predictability and reliability, the opposite of change." They continue, "It can take the form of a general appeal for order and continuity in social relations such as in the call for law and order and continuity, energy security, strong defence forces or the right to live and work in one's home region, near family and friends" (1983, 56). This value is exemplified in a host of public policies that are designed to protect many groups' economic status quo. The purpose of many industrial subsidies is to preserve obsolete and inefficient plants or even whole industries (e.g., textiles, shoes, and clothing in Quebec) so as to keep jobs and incomes in locations where they have been long established. Virtually the entire coastal fishing industry is a welfare case in which the public resources supplied to the industry directly and indirectly exceed the gross value of the catch. The policy is a tribute (of sorts) to this value, as well as to most Canadians' ignorance of just how much the complicated web of policies actually costs. Nor is government anxious to disclose the costs.

Regional diversity and sensitivity to regional interests are the converse of national unity. According to Doern and Phidd, "It is an idea rooted in a spatial or territorial view of policy whether the region is defined as a province, the North or the Gaspé" (1983, 56). On the other hand, it may be that a substantial variation in regional perspectives and autonomy for provincial governments is a necessary condition for "keeping the country together." Doern and Phidd continue, "The idea of regionalism pervades Canadian politics and affects the very definition, as well as the administrative delivery, of many public policies" (1983, 56). In the past decade, the vigorous efforts of "province building" have contributed to the turbulence of federal-provincial relations and to the Conservatives' view of the nation as a "community of communities."

Generalizations about Canadian values are hazardous, but I try below to identify some that seem to be important in shaping business-government relations. Those seeking to influence government must be sensitive to the widely shared, but often unspoken, values of their society. Only infrequently and for short periods can actions taken by interest groups or by governments violate characteristic values. Such values include the following:

- redistribution/"sharing" ethic;
- concern with national unity and the maintenance of a unique cultural identity in the face of cultural and linguistic duality;
- corporatist values (including elite accommodation);
- "pragmatic" approach to government intervention, which has resulted in a large volume of government activity relative to the size of the economy; and
- pluralist values (unions, farmers, regionalism, small business).

The significance of the first three values for business-government relations is discussed in Figure 2-2.

2.3 Characteristics of the Economic System

Some of the important characteristics of Canada's economic system[2] that influence business-government relations include the following:

- dependency on foreign trade — see Figure 2-3;
- barriers to trade: external and internal;
- degree of concentration (industry and macro); market power of producers and strength of antitrust legislation — see Figure 2-3;
- degree of labour organization and market power of unions — see Figure 2-3;
- degree of foreign ownership/control — see Figure 2-3;
- industrial structure (importance of resource industries vs. manufacturing and services);
- rate of economic growth (obviously the federal government may have some influence over the growth rate, but it is apparently less today than in the 1960s and early 1970s);
- level of income per capita;
- regional concentration of economic activity; and
- nature, extent, and scope of government intervention: taxes, expenditures, regulation, government enterprises, loans/guarantees, mixed enterprises, suasion, chosen instruments, "tax expenditures" — see chapter 3. (The level of government activity is obviously also a political decision reflecting basic values as well as the nature of the economy.)

One does not have to be an economic determinist to argue that economic factors strongly shape the relationship between business interests and governments. At any moment in time, the nature and size of the stock of government intervention is the base from which business and government interact with respect to efforts by either side to alter the

Figure 2–3
ECONOMIC FACTORS AND THEIR SIGNIFICANCE FOR BUSINESS-GOVERNMENT RELATIONS IN CANADA

Key Characteristics	Significance for Business-Government Relations
• Concentration (macro and at the industry level)	• Substantial market power in individual industries; fewer key decision makers to influence and be influenced by government; growing integration of the financial and "real" sectors of the economy
• Foreign ownership	• Creates splits between nationalists and other business people; government regulation produces foreign reactions which inhibit Canadian trade; focuses nationalists' desire for government intervention
• Export dependency (and corresponding level of imports)	• Creates conflict between exporters ("price takers") and protected domestic industries; results in efforts by provincial governments to create internal barriers to trade (business reaction to them is sometimes positive and sometimes negative)
• High level of gov't. intervention	• Both a consequence and a factor influencing bus.-gov't. relations; creates both dependency and an opportunity for more political-administrative decision-making
• Slow economic growth, low productivity, falling world rank in GNP per capita	• Increasingly a "zero-sum society"; more conflict among interest groups; more demands for government intervention — some by business interests
• High degree of labour-mgt. conflict	• Reduces output; results in more gov't. intervention as both sides and third parties seek the state's help; can result in reduced rate of investment; reputation as an unreliable supplier in international trade
• Weak antitrust legislation	• Permits firms to act with the recognition of their interdependence in the marketplace; allows unnecessary mergers, thereby increasing concentration; reduces pressure to be efficient; creates demands for direct regulation by those adversely affected

amount or type of intervention at the margin. Periods of slow or no economic growth, particularly if unemployment and inflation are also high (together they are referred to as the *discomfort index*), usually result in greater demands for more government activity. These demands come from a variety of interests (the unemployed, particularly depressed communities/regions) and include calls for assistance from firms in difficulty. One thinks of the Maislin trucking firm, Massey Ferguson, Consolidated Computer, Dome Petroleum, the fish processors in Newfoundland and Nova Scotia, and a number of financial institutions in Western Canada (see Trebilcock et al. 1986).

The high degree of foreign ownership and control of Canadian firms (479 of the 1000 largest nonfinancial enterprises in 1980 were foreign controlled)[3] has made foreign ownership a "hot" policy issue from time to time. For example, there has been conflict over the Foreign Investment Review Agency (FIRA) both within Canada and between Canada and the United States (see Clarkson 1982). The Mulroney government replaced FIRA with the Investment Canada Act and declared Canada was "open for business." While tariff barriers have been coming down, nontariff barriers have been increasing. Both have been the source of conflict within the business community and between business and governments.[4]

3.0 FIRMS AND BUSINESS INTEREST GROUPS

Moving to the level of the firm or business interest-group variables (see Figure 2-1), we can identify both exogenous variables and endogenous characteristics of interest groups.

3.1 Exogenous Variables Affecting Firms/Business Interest Groups

At the level of the firm or interest group (as opposed to that of society or the system as a whole), we find a number of variables that affect the activities of business interest groups, but which are largely beyond their control, particularly in the short run. These variables include the following:[5]

- nature of the relationship among (potential) members of the business interest group, that is, competitors, suppliers/customers;
- extent, intensity, and scope of government intervention in the field (industry, sector, profession). This includes all types, from taxes to regulation to subsidies to tax expenditures that have a differential effect on the particular firm, industry, or sector.
- degree of dependency upon government actions (subsidies, loans, purchases, regulation) in determining the success or failure of members of the group;
- characteristics of members: individuals versus organization; entrepreneurs versus employees; professional values; and
- public perception of the group: devoted to narrow, private interest versus broadly based "public interest" orientation (this variable can be affected by actions of the group itself to some extent).

The nature of the relationship among actual (and potential) members of the interest group depends on the definition of the "boundaries" of the group itself. While this is a matter within the collective control of the membership, once that decision is made, the basis of the members' relationship to one another is largely determined. There are several types of business or trade associations (see Litvak 1982 and chapter 9). Some are multi-industry and even cut across sectors (e.g., the Canadian Chamber of Commerce), others cover a fairly broad sector (e.g., Canadian Manufacturers' Association [CMA]), others focus on a specific industry (e.g., Canadian Carpet Institute), while others focus on a subset of firms in an industry (e.g., the association of *public* real estate developers). The scope of the activities of the group and its approach to government relations will be shaped by the fact, for example, that either all members are direct rivals, or only some are rivals while others relate to each other as suppliers (either of inputs or final products) to customers, or the members of the group may not even be in the same industry (e.g., the Business Council on National Issues [BCNI]).

It should be noted that the extent of government intervention in a particular industry (or sector) is both the cause and effect of business efforts to influence government activity. Firms (and other interest groups) often seek various forms of government intervention: for example, tariffs, regulation that restricts competition, subsidies that lower costs, or procurement contracts that increase sales (see Baggaley 1981). Hence, the existing stock of government intervention reflects, in part, the previous lobbying efforts of firms in the industry. On the other hand, the present level of intervention may be the focus of the firms' efforts to reduce such government activity. For example, the firms may be trying to (1) get rid of minimum wage legislation, (2) eliminate pollution-control regulations that are particularly expensive to comply with, or (3) get the federal government to lower tariffs on machinery used in their production process.

The importance of the government relations function will be roughly proportionate to the dependency of the firm or members of the interest group on actions by government. Not surprisingly, Bell Canada, whose prices (tariffs) are directly regulated by the Canadian Radio-television and Telecommunications Commission (CRTC), has a large "regulatory affairs" unit. Its primary task is to handle the "care and feeding" of the CRTC and to keep top management well informed about policy developments within the federal and provincial departments of communications. See the case "Bell Canada's Corporate Re-Organization" in Baetz and Thain (1985).

3.2 Endogenous Characteristics of Firms/Business Interest Groups

The variables listed below shape the structure, governance, and activities of business interest groups. They are within the power of the members of the group to change over time, although in the very short run most will be taken as givens. The variables relate to the group itself and not to its choice of strategies or techniques employed in seeking to influence a government. These are *organizational* variables rather than activity variables. They do, however, as Figure 2-1 indicates, influence lobbying strategies and techniques. Moreover, interest groups will alter these characteristics (i.e., redefine themselves) in light of the outcomes of their interaction with governments.

The endogenous characteristics of firms and business interest groups include the following:

- size of the firm's or interest group's budget and the fraction devoted to government relations activities;
- size, role, and power of the staff relative to the (elected) executive;
- size of the business group's membership (both in absolute terms and relative to potential membership);
- internal political structure of the interest group: democratic versus autocratic voting rules;
- internal techniques used to represent the interests of individual members (committees, task forces, etc.);
- costs of membership (economic and noneconomic);
- scope of the organization: local, regional, national; horizontal versus vertical; single product versus broad, "generic" group (Carpet Manufacturers Institute vs. Canadian Chamber of Commerce);
- level of expenditure on the government relations practitioners;
- scope of the organization's activities besides lobbying: for example, training, collection of statistics, publication of a trade magazine. The goods are individual, divisible, and excludable and are used to encourage membership by overcoming the free-rider effect.
- degree of internal cohesion; and
- nature of the benefits sought from lobbying: income or wealth for the firm or interest-group members versus political ideals, the achievement of which provide no pecuniary benefits for members.

Activities designed to influence governments cost money. Some trade associations in Canada operate with an annual budget of over $6 million (e.g., CFIB), but only one-quarter of national trade associations in 1981 had a total budget exceeding $1 million.[6] The government relations component of trade associations' budgets is usually only a quarter of the total. On the other hand, Gulf Canada spent an average of $2 million per year on institutional and advocacy advertisments from 1981 to 1984.[7]

The internal structure of the business group (system of representation, voting rules, power of the executive, and the role of the full-time staff members) can have a great impact on the strategies and techniques of government relations the group employs (see chapter 9). Large associations are often subject to control by an oligarchy of members or by their professional staff. The staff can be caught between their own expertise as to what actions constitute the best long-run strategy and the demands of the more hot-headed members to "do something now" to "show those bastards in government that we mean business." This occurred in the Independent Petroleum Association of Canada shortly after the National Energy Program (NEP) was announced in 1980. The result was a high-profile advocacy ad specifically naming Marc Lalonde as the object of the association's spleen. The ad proved to be counterproductive (see Alm et al. 1984).

3.3 Strategies, Techniques, and Style in Influencing Government Policy

I now outline the strategic choices of firms and business interest groups in their efforts to influence public policy, the various techniques they can use, and the firm's/group's style of business-government relations.

3.3.1 Strategic Choices
The strategic choices include the following:
- the goals/objectives to be pursued;
- selecting the policy issues upon which the business interest group will seek to exert its influence (see chapter 6);
- determining the targets (individuals/organizations) of the group's influence efforts both inside and outside government (see chapter 7);
- the timing of influence efforts (see chapter 7);
- deciding on the choice of techniques (or combination of techniques) by which the interest group will seek to influence public policy (see chapter 8);
- the decision to form alliances or coalitions with other interest groups (this includes the nature of the firm's relationship to its trade associations) — see chapter 8; and
- the choice of style of the firm's business-government relations efforts.

For more detail, see chapter 5.

3.3.2 Objectives
In functional terms, firms and business interest groups have one or more of the following objectives in seeking to influence public policy:

1. To obtain new legislation (statutes or subordinate legislation) favourable to the interests of the group. This usually results in changes in one or more governing instruments (e.g., taxes, expenditures, regulation, etc.).
2. To obtain favourable interpretations of existing legislation or policy by line departments, regulatory agencies, or the cabinet. This may involve changes in budget allocations, decisions regarding the enforcement of legislation, and the interpretation of existing policies/programs.

3. To prevent undesirable changes in legislation or in interpretation of existing legislation or policy in (1) or (2).

4. To obtain longer-term changes in access to or participation in the public-policy-making process. For example, by obtaining membership on important permanent advisory committees that deal with policy proposals, the interest group's role in the process could be expanded and its influence greater in the future.

3.3.3 Issue Definition and Management

Peter Bartha (1982), an Imperial Oil executive, has developed a model that in part "seeks to explain how societal issues emerge [and] which of the issues are likely to result in government intervention." He identified four "issue types" that consist of "an identified problem or situation that affects people and which is seen as requiring some form of government involvement" (1982, 82). *Universal issues* affect large numbers of people in many walks of life in a direct and personal way; hence, the problem is seen as imminent and serious. Because the problem is seen as "obvious," it should be matched by a "simple" solution by government. *Advocacy issues* do not emerge spontaneously. But once the problem is identified and solutions are advocated by some groups, large numbers of people react favourably to some form of government action, although the public often recognizes there are both costs and benefits to government intervention. *Selective issues* are of concern to special interests delineated by certain geographic, demographic, or occupational characteristics. Bartha argues that "the problems as well as the solutions are unique and affect only — or chiefly — certain identifiable groups" (1982, 84). The costs of government action are usually diffused widely. Finally, *technical issues* "are those in which the public has no interest and is perfectly content to leave to the experts. The vast majority of the government's day-to-day regulatory activities is in this category" (1982, 84).

The importance of defining issues lies in the fact that different types of issues develop differently, and the means by which firms/associations can influence them and the targets of such efforts are different — see chapter 6.

3.3.4 How Firms/Business Groups Can Influence Government Policy

Business-government relations in Canada are conducted on a variety of fronts. Lefever et al. suggest that larger corporations have a multiple impact on public policy and that their influence falls into six general categories (1983, 5–9). Note that the first two are not thought of as being endogenous to the government relations function.

1. *Normal Operations:* Large corporations by their normal functioning create interests among a number of "stakeholders," and they may indirectly influence public policy. These stakeholders include shareholders, customers, employees, suppliers, and creditors. In some cases, top

management seeks to marshall these stakeholders in an effort to influence public policy.

2. *Product and Service Advertising:* Corporations create images of themselves by their advertising. In politics, perception is reality, and government's capacity to influence a firm depends, in part, on how the public perceives that firm, for example, the oil companies in the energy crisis, 1973 and 1979. (Categories [1] and [2] are said to be "largely nondeliberative" but may have an effect on a variety of government policies.)

3. *Issue Advertising:* Sometimes called advocacy advertising, it involves the promotion of ideas and/or particular public policies that affect or are likely to affect the corporation (see chapter 12).

4. *Lobbying:* Economic and other interest groups in Canada have not hesitated to try to influence public policy by a wide variety of means. Lobbying in Canada is ubiquitous; yet it is almost invisible. The individuals who make a profession of lobbying have been described as "the best-informed, least-understood and perhaps most influential private citizens in the country."[8] The job of lobbyists and public policy consultants is to alert companies in advance to decisions that will influence corporate planning or to exert pressure on the government in regard to existing or proposed legislation. See chapters 7, 8, and 9.

5. *Direct Political Activity:* Lefever et al. describe financial support for candidates and parties as "purchasing insurance through investment in legislators who exercise considerable influence or in candidates who have a good chance of winning. It is a matter of prudence to have friends at court, irrespective of their party affiliation" (1983, 7). In chapter 10 I note that between August 1, 1974, and December 31, 1979, corporations gave $12.2 million to the federal Liberal party, $12.7 million to the Progressive Conservatives, but only $817 000 to the New Democratic Party. These amounts represented 55, 53, and 5 percent of the parties' respective total revenue. For the 1980 general election campaign, corporations gave $3.7 million to the Liberals and $4.4 million to the Tories, and these contributions amounted to 60 percent and 58 percent of all contributions to the parties respectively.

In this category Gillies (1981) would no doubt include personal participation in the political process by business people. The effectiveness of this alternative seems rather limited.[9]

6. *Contributions to Public Policy Groups:* Such contributions include "support for organizations, movements, and individuals seeking to influence a wide range of government policies, domestic and foreign, mainly by producing and disseminating studies, ideas, facts and recommendations for academic, business, public policy and other leaders" (Lefever 1983, 18). In Canada it appears that public policy research bodies play a smaller role than they do in the United States, but their numbers have grown over the past fifteen years.

The leading public policy "think-tanks" that receive some support from business are: the Institute for Research on Public Policy (Montreal), the Fraser Institute (Vancouver), the Canadian Institute for Economic Policy (Toronto), the Canada West Foundation (Calgary), the Centre for the Study of Regulated Industries (McGill), and the Canadian Energy Research Institute (Calgary). See Collison (1980).

Of the various techniques of influencing public policy, this book gives the greatest weight to lobbying activities both by individual firms and by trade associations (chapters 7, 8, and 9), advocacy advertising (chapter 12), participation in the political process (chapter 10), and artful use of the media to influence public opinion (chapter 11). However, before any of these techniques can be used, business interest groups must identify, define, and select those issues that will be the focus of their efforts. See chapter 6.

3.3.5 Style

The attributes of the style of a firm's approach to business-government relations can be outlined as follows:

- transparency or "publicness" of lobbying activities;
- initiation of contacts/action (proactive vs. reactive approaches);
- continuity of interaction (deal with government only during crises or on a continuous basis to maintain channels of communication);
- rhetorical style (e.g., communicating through the press vs. "quiet diplomacy" behind the scenes);
- basic approach (confrontation vs. mutual accommodation); and
- outcome orientation ("winner takes all" vs. "something for everyone," i.e., "all stakeholders").

More generally, see Fulton and Stanbury (1985).

4.0 IT'S A TWO-WAY STREET: GOVERNMENT EFFORTS TO INFLUENCE BUSINESS

The term business-government relations is most often used to refer to efforts by business (firms, individuals, associations) to influence government and how government responds to business's efforts. While this approach is the focus of this study, it is desirable to describe briefly some principal ways in which governments seek to modify the behaviour of business. As emphasized in Figure 2-1, the outcomes produced by the relationship between business and government are the result of the interaction of the efforts by each "side" to influence the other's behaviour. This point is further emphasized in the public choice model of policy formulation described in chapter 4.

Before we examine the means governments employ to influence business interests, it is necessary to appreciate that, despite their size and enormous range of legitimate coercive powers (governing instruments), governments also function in the same systemic environment. They must grapple with the same social, political, and economic parameters described above — see Figure 2-1.

In addition, we can identify a set of endogenous characteristics that determine the structure and attributes of governments as organizations functioning in the larger system. Governments are also subject to a number of important exogenous variables at the organization rather than the systemic level. Both of these are outlined now.

4.1 Exogenous Variables Affecting Government

These variables include the following:
- *Size of the goverment's majority in the legislature.* Obviously, a government seeks to influence the number of seats it will obtain in the *next* election by making decisions in light of their potential effect on voters. But in the short run the number of seats the government has is fixed.
- *Regional distribution of the seats held by the government and opposition parties in the legislature.* The past is a sunk cost or benefit, and while a government will work to change its electoral endowments, the regional distribution of seats is an important given after each election.
- *Actions of other governments both domestic and foreign.* The power and proximity of the United States represent a unique problem for Canadian governments (see Clarkson 1982). At home, the federal and provincial governments have *some* influence over each other, but it is not that great — except where their respective jurisdictions are unclear.
- *Stock of existing government intervention, all instruments considered* (see chapter 3). This is difficult, but not absolutely impossible, to change at the margin, at least as Margaret Thatcher's record in the United Kingdom and the progress with deregulation in the U.S. suggest. See Stanbury and Thompson (1982a, 1982b), and Derthick and Quirk (1985).
- *Behaviour of the media.* Although governments make considerable efforts, sometimes successful, to influence the media by control over the provision of information, there are distinct limits on a government's ability to influence the media. Columnist Richard Gwyn argues that Prime Minister Mulroney is "determined to control the media, to dominate them, to exploit them." He indicates that Mulroney is following U.S. president Ronald Reagan's approach to image making, which is based on the following rules:

> In advance of every event, decide the message or story you want to come out of that event; then stage-manage the event so that that story, your story, dominates it; keep the message simple and

strong; make sure everyone involved communicates the same message; avoid debate which happens when print reporters are given interviews or at press conferences that, unlike scrums, create opportunities for follow-up questions; use television, which is soft and undemanding, on every possible occasion, and if possible use nothing but television on every occasion.[10]

- *Constitutional allocation of powers (jurisdiction) as defined in law, jurisprudence, and convention (historical practice).* As Canada's history indicates, constitutional change is a very slow process, but the Constitution Act of 1982, which includes the Charter of Rights and Freedoms, proves it can happen on a large scale.
- *Actions of the opposition parties.* In large part their activities are reactive to the initiatives of the government of the day. In some cases they can put an item on the political agenda (e.g., the opposition Conservatives were able to make the tax collection practices of Revenue Canada a significant issue in 1984).
- *Public opinion/attitudes/perceptions.* Governments make great efforts to influence public opinion, but since there are many competing influences, public opinion is largely exogenous to governments.

4.2 Endogenous Variables in the Hands of Government

These endogenous variables include the following:
- *The choice of governing instruments* (e.g., taxes, regulation, direct expenditures, "tax expenditures," mixed enterprises, crown corporations, "chosen instruments") designed to alter the behaviour of individuals/firms in the private sector (subject to constitutional limitations) (see Trebilcock et al. 1982).
- *Scale or intensity of use of governing instruments* (e.g., small expenditures or much larger ones; "loose" regulation or very restrictive regulation).
- *Sequence in determining policy priorities,* in dealing with interest groups and in the application of governing instruments.
- *Control over information* — both its collection from private sector entities and its dissemination ("knowledge is power").
- *Control over access to (participation in) the public policy decision-making process.* Government can increase a group's influence by admitting it to the inner circle of those consulted. It can also diminish a group's influence by denying it access.
- *Timing of action(s) by government.* The electoral cycle is critical here. The party in power determines the date of the election subject to a statutory maximum. The "window of opportunity" after an electoral mandate — the period in which a government can do necessary but unpopular things — is about twelve to sixteen months. If it does not

take strong actions in this period, it will be unlikely to do so later in its term. The closer it gets to the next election, the greater the need not to offend any significant group.

- *Control over the design of legislation*, for example, the use of detailed statutes (which must be enacted by the legislature) versus shorter statutes together with many substantive regulations ("enacted" by the cabinet). If the latter is adopted, a government may legislate without consulting the legislature.
- *Control over the internal functioning of the policy-making process*, that is, strong central agencies together with a requirement for extensive interdepartmental consultation versus quasi-autonomous, strong ministries bringing proposals directly to cabinet (see Gillies 1981).
- *Use of order-in-council appointments for patronage and the control of departments and agencies*. The Prime Minister's Office (PMO) controls literally several thousand such appointments, from the Supreme Court to the directors of Air Canada. This tool gives the prime minister enormous personal power, as both Pierre Trudeau and Brian Mulroney have demonstrated. See chapter 10.

4.3 The Means by Which a Government Influences Business

In general terms, governments employ three techniques in order to influence actors in the private sector.

4.3.1 Using Governing Instruments

In imposing taxes or regulation, in allocating expenditures, in conferring tax expenditures and loans/guarantees, in creating crown corporations or mixed enterprises, and in using suasion, governments influence the behaviour of firms and individuals in the private sector. For example, an excise tax can discourage consumption of the taxed commodity, regulation can control entry or the emission of pollutants, and a tax expenditure can increase the rate of return and encourage capital investment in a particular activity. In summary, the legitimate coercive powers of the state to influence a firm's behaviour are enormous, and they have been used a great deal in Canada (see chapter 3). At the same time, policies must be used to obtain and retain political support (see chapter 4).

4.3.2 Controlling Access

By determining which groups/individuals obtain direct access to the policy-making process, government is able to influence those who seek to influence it. Access can be traded off for changes in the behaviour of business groups. Government, at any one time, has in operation a number of task forces, advisory committees, commissions, and so forth designed to provide it with advice. They can be used to control access to the real decision-making circles. They may also be used to "double back" and allow the government to influence those said to be giving it advice, who, in turn, influence others in their own "communities."

4.3.3 Assisting Countervailing Forces

By financing, granting access, and supporting the policy objectives of other interest groups, such as consumers, environmentalists, trade unions, farmers, and natives/ethnics, government can create or encourage forces that "countervail" against business interests. This can be seen as part of the classical role of government as a vehicle to mediate and reconcile conflicts in society.

5.0 OUTCOMES

5.1 Characterizing the Interaction

It is all but impossible to specify in simple terms the outcomes of business-government relations in Canada. We can, however, characterize the interaction in the following terms. First, it is dynamic. The balance of power shifts among the multiple players over time. The composition of the agenda changes; both sides are subject to exogenous forces that alter their positions and hence their relationship to each other. Second, the parties deal with a wide variety of issues in a number of different policy arenas. Some business groups are winning on certain issues while other groups are losing on other issues in other arenas. Third, the process is serial. For the major players the game has an infinite number of rounds (or innings). Success or failure depends upon the period over which it is measured. Fourth, the outcomes are frequently ambiguous. What constitutes success or failure for either side is not well defined (e.g., Is additional intervention desired or despised? — It all depends).

   Finally, the parties are highly interdependent. Society requires both business and government as institutions, and it is necessary that they relate quite closely to each other. The real world, with manifest market failures, a widespread desire to redistribute income, *and* a desire to produce goods and services efficiently in a predominantly market economy, requires both extensive government activity and the recognition that profit-motivated actors operating in markets perform a valuable service. See Bower (1983).

5.2 Criteria for Assessing Outcomes

It is very difficult to describe the outcomes of business-government relations in Canada or any other country in substantive terms. However, it may be useful to see the extent to which the outcomes produced violate one or more constraints (or desiderata) that such a macro social relationship should satisfy (achieve). These are obviously normative criteria.

5.2.1 Efficiency
Business-government relations are a means to an end. For many, the most important end is an efficient and growing economy that delivers a high level of real income per capita for its citizens. At the risk of being an economic determinist, it is hard to imagine a better solvent for a wide variety of social problems than more income or wealth. My concern is that as a result of Canada's obsession with distributive and procedural questions, we have ignored the impact of our collective decisions on the level and growth of real output per capita.

5.2.2 Dynamism
The relationship between business and government must be capable of change so as to meet the challenges of shifts and swings in exogenous forces. In particular, conflicting, organized interests must not be able to create a state of social gridlock or institutional sclerosis (see Olson 1982).

5.2.3 Openness
The nature of the relationship between business and government must be well and widely understood. The process must be open to new players (emerging interests) so that change can occur without severe discontinuities.

5.2.4 Maintenance of Individual Freedom
Every act of government intervention does *not* diminish individual freedom — despite the ideas of Herbert Spencer and the freedom to starve. However, the aggregation of interests in which institutionalized groups take on a life of their own must not limit the freedom of individuals involuntarily or irreversibly. In Canada we appear to have sacrificed freedom in the name of security in an increasingly turbulent world. In the end, to paraphrase Gibbon, we may have neither. The maintenance of individual freedom would appear to require that there be a rough balance among large-scale interests, if not an atomistic dispersion of power in general. The balance of power need not be — and indeed should not be — static. It should be capable of adaption to new equilibria as power shifts. It is critical, however, that persistent dominance by any interest group, including government, be avoided if we are to aspire to a genuinely pluralist, democratic society.

5.2.5 Healthy Rivalry but the Avoidance of Costly Conflict
Graveyards may be very peaceful, but they are hardly productive. Therefore, while extreme forms of conflict are to be avoided (they are disruptive and destructive of almost all other desiderata), healthy rivalries conditioned by mutual respect for the minimal procedural rules of the game can be highly productive. Ordinary citizens should worry a great

deal if business executives, politicians, and senior bureaucrats agree that business-government relations are placid and almost entirely satisfactory. This could mean we have a smoothly functioning "cartel" or a form of corporatism in which both market forces and individual freedom have been lost in the name of harmony.[11] A healthy relationship requires at least some element of dynamic tension if it is to grow and adapt to changes in both the participants and the environment.

5.3 Broad Categories of Outcomes

In very general terms, we can identify four possible categories of outcomes for the relations between business and government.

5.3.1 Business Dominates Government

Here business controls the policy process to obtain pretty much what it wants from the state. This may range from very little intervention to a very great deal of intervention thought to be directly beneficial to business interests.

5.3.2 Government Dominates Business

Even to the point of inhibiting business's ability to produce goods and services efficiently, thereby reducing the growth potential of the economy. Government serves interests other than those of business (e.g., the "new class," labour, or a coalition of nonbusiness interests).

5.3.3 Social Gridlock

This is like an institutional sclerosis and occurs as a result of the capacity of various conflicting organized interests (business, labour, environmentalists, consumers, *and* government) to neutralize each other and create a situation in which everyone is blocked, and positive, creative forces cannot generate the growth and dynamism possible in more open societies (see Olson 1982).

5.3.4 Win Some, Lose Some

In this scenario, business interests are able to effectively influence governments for their own benefit even in the face of countervailing efforts by other interests (labour, environmentalists, values groups, etc.) on some issues at some times. At the same time, other groups are able to influence governments for their benefit even when business groups oppose their lobbying efforts. In other words, business as a broad interest group "wins some and loses some." Moreover, there is the problem that in many instances governments are subject to conflicting pressures from within the business community (see chapter 5). However, in such a situation business executives will undoubtedly voice varying degrees of unhappiness about the state of business-government relations. When they "win big," discretion requires that business interests (or indeed any other interest group) keep quiet about their success for fear of losing their access to government or of provoking rivals to counteract their influence. When they lose, they will complain of a lack of influence. Professor Jack Granatstein, a historian, remarks that "although the reality is that business is the most listened-to group in society, businessmen always seem to feel they are not consulted. It is a historical whine and we will be hearing it even if the [new Tory] government does everything [for business] it said it would during the election."[12]

There is considerable evidence to suggest that the fourth category best describes the outcome of business-government relations in Canada, but that is another story. It is one that is revealed in many of the cases in Baetz and Thain (1985) and in the following two subsections of this chapter.

5.4 Examples of Business's Success in Influencing Government Policy

In each of these examples, it was clear that business groups lobbied either to either stop proposed actions by government or to obtain some type of desired intervention.

- Continuation of a very weak competition policy; Bill C-29 (April 2, 1984) was negotiated directly with "Gang of Three": BCNI, CCC, and CMA. Bill C-91 (December 17, 1985) was negotiated with the "Gang of Five" — the previous groups plus the Grocery Products Manufacturers of Canada and the Canadian Bar Association. It is even weaker than Bill C-29.
- Delay/weakening of proposed changes in patent and trademark law during the 1970s.
- Inco's ability in the 1970s and 1980s to resist efforts of the Province of Ontario to control its emissions of sulphur dioxide, which produces acid rain.
- The CFIB's capacity to influence the federal government to create a minister of state for small business.
- The vast growth in corporate income tax expenditures (tax incentives for business), which have reduced the effective rate of corporate income tax (see chapter 3).
- The maintenance of protective direct regulation in face of some efforts to deregulate: airlines, trucking (excluding Alberta), the professions (really small business people), and marketing boards (farmers as small-business people). (However, the federal policy paper "Freedom to Move: A Framework for Transportation Reform" issued in July 1985 indicates that the government favours less regulation in transportation.)

- Specific acts of "protectionism" vis-à-vis imports:
    - "voluntary quotas" on Japanese cars negotiated in 1982 by means of suasion (see Stanbury & Fulton 1984);
    - import quotas on textiles, clothing, and footwear to protect jobs in Quebec and to a lesser extent Ontario.
- Limitations on foreign banks (but they were increased from zero to 8 percent of domestic deposit in 1980 and were later increased to 16 percent.
- Defeat of the Borrowers and Depositors Protection Act (see Stanbury & Burns 1982).
- Delay of new federal pension regulations and/or funding requirements in the early 1980s. Business argued that the present private and public pension plans are generally adequate and that economic conditions did not permit higher pension costs.

5.5 "Conspicuous Failures" by Business to Influence Government Policy

- The growth of federal and provincial barriers to trade *within* Canada (some local firms do benefit form these barriers, however).
- The vast expansion of the "transfer state" (transfers to persons, excluding interest and transfers to the provinces, exceed one-sixth of personal income). It is not clear that business has made a concerted effort to stop such transfers. The major transfers include: universality of health care, income security, and educational programs; growth of extensive "safety net" programs, such as unemployment insurance, the Canada Pension Plan (CPP), and social assistance; and medical and hospital care (about 9 percent of the GNP).
- The NEP initiated in October 1980 gave the federal government enormous control over the petroleum industry. However, subsequent actions by the Liberals altered the original initiatives somewhat and the new Tory government almost totally dismantled the NEP in 1985.
- The enormous expansion of Petro-Canada, a federal crown corporation in the oil industry, by taking over Arco Canada, Pacific Petroleums, and Petrofina between 1976 and 1981. Even under the new Tory government, Petro-Canada acquired much of the retail operations of Gulf Canada Ltd. from the Reichmann family.
- The growth of supply-management marketing boards. They now account for 25 percent of the value of agricultural products produced in Canada and amount to a government-mandated cartel. See Lermer and Stanbury (1985).
- Some bailouts (e.g., Dome and Maislin, which were opposed by certain sections of the business community). See Trebilcock et al. (1986).
- Foreign investment controls: FIRA — but its stringency waxed and waned. Note, some nationalist business people like these controls. (The

new Tory federal government reduced the stringency of controls on foreign investment with the Investment Canada Act.)

- Pro-union labour legislation: for example, that which permits non-affiliation clauses in the construction industry in B.C. and unionization with the right to strike for public service employees, who have become "wage leaders."
- Industry-specific examples:
  - compulsory licensing/generic substitution passed in 1969 (but note that recent efforts to reverse this legislation appear to be meeting with some success);
  - government automobile insurance in Manitoba, Saskatchewan, B.C., and Quebec — in some cases the provincial crown corporation has a monopoly;
  - deductibility of advertising expenditures in foreign-owned publications (*Time* and *Reader's Digest*); and
  - creation of Canagrex, a new federal crown corporation in 1983; there was conflict within the agricultural and processing sectors. However, this enterprise was subsequently abolished by the new Tory government in 1985.
- The vice (vise) of federal-provincial conflict (overlap and duplication). For example, Alberta and the federal government fought for eighteen months after the NEP was announced over the distribution of petroleum rents, while the oil companies tried to avoid being "squeezed out."

NOTES

1. When dealing with a specific issue in the short run a trade association executive or the government relations specialist working for a major firm may not appreciate the extent to which his or her choice of strategies — and lobbying style and techniques — is attributable to the fundamental parameters of the general system (social/economic/political) in which he or she operates. These factors are so deeply embedded in the environment of the firm that individuals are not really aware of the extent to which activities designed to alter public policy are influenced by them, even though they are "givens" (exogenous) from the point of view of the firm (or trade association).

2. A very useful general source is Green (1985).

3. Statistics Canada, *Annual Report of the Minister of Supply and Services Canada Under the Corporation and Labour Unions Returns Act, Part 1, Corporations, 1980* (Ottawa: January 1983), p. 130.

4. See David Stewart-Patterson, "Canadian-owned firms favored for $3.5 billion in orders," *Globe and Mail*, April 26, 1984, p. B7. The

article refers to proposed federal expenditures on the air traffic control network. The Canadian Airspace Systems Project (CASP) is exempt from the GATT rules which require equal treatment for foreign and domestic companies. Domestic firms are to be favoured in a variety of ways: accepting bids only from Canadian companies where enough competition exists; foreign multinationals may be required to invest in Canada or give their Canadian subsidiaries a world product mandate; allow bidders as much as 5% extra margin in return for higher Canadian content; and offsets such as licensed technology and subcontracting in Canada in exchange for purchases from foreign suppliers.

5. Generally, see Moe (1980), Olson (1971), and Fulton and Stanbury (1985).

6. See John Partridge (1982a), Litvak (1982), and chapter 9.

7. Letter to the author from Bob Fenner, Director of Public Affairs, Gulf Canada Limited, May 31, 1984. The precise figures were 1981, $1.9 million; 1982, $2.2 million; 1983, $2.3 million; and 1984, $1.8 million. More generally, see chapter 12.

8. Les Whittington, "Lobbying Ottawa: It can be relatively easy if you know all the rules," *Financial Times*, June 22, 1981, pp. G1, G13.

9. Gillies (1981, chap. 7, n. 26), while recognizing that backbenchers have almost no power, argues that business people ought to run for office in order to change what they see to be undesirable policies and programs. He notes that election is a prerequisite to a cabinet position, argues that political parties do have influence and that MPs influence parties, and he maintains that the reform of the legislature depends upon nonprofessional politicians (p. 114). In my view, only the first argument is persuasive, but it is flawed when examined from the perspective of a firm or a business interest group. Once a businessman, for example, is elected to office, he represents his constituency, his party, and most of all his conscience. He ought not to represent his former firm, the industry he is most familiar with, or even business in general (if that is possible). Moreover, only the most unsophisticated firms or associations — even though they had helped elect "one of their own" would expect special treatment from the new politician should he be so lucky as to make it into the cabinet. The best business as an identifiable interest (and it is riddled with internal conflicts) can hope to do is try to elect individuals (and parties) that are broadly sympathetic to a market economy, individual freedom, and the limited use of governmental powers. There are several paths by which business interests can gain and retain influence in government. Direct election is only one of them. Lobbying and the financing of political parties and candidates are

others. They appear to be more important ways of "doing the Lord's work" on behalf of business interests.

10. Vancouver *Sun*, October 2, 1984, p. A4.
11. See, for example, Craig McKie (1977); Leo Panitch (1979); and K. J. Rea and John McLeod (1976, 334–45).
12. As quoted in Ian Austen, "The Tory-Business Honeymoon," *Maclean's*, November 12, 1984, p. 49.

3

Describing Leviathan: A Governing-Instruments Approach

Dictionaries define Leviathan as "a sea monster embodying evil." In 1651 Thomas Hobbes applied this term to the sovereign state. Three and one-quarter centuries later, we use the term only when we discuss government and political processes pejoratively, and then only when our purpose is to call attention to the dangers inherent in an expanding public sector of society. (James Buchanan, 1975)

1.0 INTRODUCTION

Government is a very important actor in Canada's economic life. Its enormous size and scope means that, for many firms, it is the single most important factor in their environment. Where that is the case, a business's ability to respond effectively to the actions of government and to influence it depends, in part, on its knowledge of the size, scope, and nature of government intervention.

The need for this knowledge transcends the current state of relations between business and government. For example, business historian Michael Bliss stated that in the summer of 1981 "business confidence in the government of Canada . . . was probably at the lowest level in the 20th century. . . . A large number of businessmen believed that Canada was being ruined by a socialist government [under Pierre Trudeau]" (1982b, 48). Thirty months later, *Maclean's* magazine described the relationship between business and the Conservative government elected in September 1984 as a "honeymoon." Business's positive feelings toward the federal government were engendered by promises of expenditure cuts, the privatization of some crown corporations, the minister of finance's economic statement, the prime minister's emphasis on cooperation and consensus-building, and the new government's openness to the suggestions of individual executives and trade associations.[1]

Note: Parts of this chapter are adapted from Howard and Stanbury (1984) and from Stanbury (1985). I am indebted to Vic Murray and Jane Fulton for helpful comments on earlier drafts.

Can the honeymoon last? Bliss argues that over the past two decades "an unbridgeable gap has grown between the way leading businessmen and Canadian politicians view the world" that is independent of the passing of Pierre Trudeau and the Liberals. In his view, "In the battle for public opinion on big questions of national economic policy, business was defeated years ago . . . on the big, general questions [such as the growth and effectiveness of government and economic nationalism] . . . business has nothing effective to say" (1982b, 48, 50). Newspaper reports in the summer of 1985 indicated that business's support for the Mulroney government had softened as it became clearer the Conservatives were not moving to cut the deficit and were not capable of stimulating economic growth.[2]

This chapter examines the growth of government activity in Canada by looking beyond the usual data on government expenditures to examine the wide scope of government activities.[3] The reason for doing so is that total expenditures (or taxes) as a percent of GNP grossly understates the extent to which governments influence economic activity in the private sector. Moreover, failure to appreciate the extensive use of such governing instruments as "tax expenditures," regulation, crown corporations, loans and guarantees, equity ownership in private firms ("mixed enterprises"), and suasion, is to ignore what appears to be a substantial shift in the techniques of government intervention. With continued poor macroeconomic performance, fiscal constraints will encourage governments to substitute "less obvious" governing instruments for the traditional tax and expenditures tools.[4] In this way, intervention can continue or even expand. Sections 2 through 8 examine the scope and growth of seven governing instruments: direct expenditures, tax expenditures, regulation, crown corporations, loans and guarantees, equity ownership in private sector firms, and suasion.[5]

In section 9, some of the implications for business enterprises are discussed. In particular, I note the fundamental ambivalence business people feel toward governments that create both threats and opportunities. Business must take a strategic approach in dealing with governments in much the same way it already does with respect to other important factors in its environment.

2.0 GOVERNMENT EXPENDITURES

As Table 3-1 indicates, since the mid-1970s the expenditures of all three levels of government ("G", which includes those on hospitals and the Canada and Quebec Pension Plans) have exceeded 40 percent of GNP in current-dollar terms. In 1950 the ratio was 22.1 percent and in 1965 it was 29.9 percent.

The Economic Council of Canada (ECC) points out that "in 1952 federal, provincial, and local governments together spent $438 for each

Table 3–1
GOVERNMENT EXPENDITURES IN CANADA BY
LEVEL OF GOVERNMENT AS A PERCENTAGE OF GNP,
SELECTED YEARS 1926–83
(current dollars)

Year	Federal In	Federal Ex	Provincial In	Provincial Ex	Local In	Local Ex	Hos-pitals	CPP & QPP	Total Expen-diture	Total Exhaus-tive	Total Trans-fers
1926	6.2	5.9	3.6	3.2	6.7	6.6	na	na	15.7	9.6	6.6
1933	10.9	9.3	8.8	8.2	10.2	9.9	na	na	27.4	13.7	13.7
1939	8.6	7.2	8.3	7.8	6.6	6.5	na	na	21.4	12.7	8.7
1946	24.2	22.7	5.3	4.6	7.6	4.2	na	na	31.6	14.8	16.8
1950	12.8	11.5	6.7	5.7	4.9	4.9	na	na	22.1	13.1	9.0
1955	16.8	15.3	6.4	5.2	5.9	5.8	na	na	26.3	17.5	8.8
1960	17.6	15.0	9.2	7.3	7.4	7.3	na	na	29.7	17.7	11.0
1965	15.4	12.9	11.4	6.8	8.2	8.1	2.1	na	29.9	19.5	10.4
1970	17.8	13.8	16.5	10.2	9.5	9.4	2.8	0.2	36.4	23.1	13.3
1975	21.5	16.8	19.1	12.2	8.8	8.8	3.0	0.5	41.3	24.0	17.3
1980	20.5	16.2	20.0	13.5	8.4	8.3	2.8	0.9	41.8	22.8	19.0
1983	24.2	19.8	21.9	14.9	8.9	8.9	3.2	1.2	47.9	24.4	23.5

In = including transfers to other levels of government
Ex = excluding transfers to other levels of government
na = not available or not applicable

Source: Canadian Tax Foundation (1985, chap. 3).

man, woman, and child living in Canada. By 1983 that sum had risen to more than $7200" (1984, 13). In constant 1971 dollars, the increase was from $635 in 1952 to $2007 in 1983. While real government expenditure per capita increased by 3.2 times, real GNP per capita increased 2.02 times over that thirty-one-year period.

As large as total government spending is in Canada (47.9 percent of GNP in 1983), it is not as large as in some countries in Western Europe. For example, in 1981 the ratio of G to GNP for the U.K. was 46.4 percent; for France, 48.6 percent; for Germany, 47.5 percent while for the Netherlands, 62.5 percent (1980), and for Sweden, 64.4 percent, excluding social security payments. On the other hand, the ratio of G to GNP for the United States was 38.0 percent in 1982 and for Japan, 32.7 percent (Department of Finance 1984, 179).

In terms of constant 1971 dollars, the ratio of G to GNP in Canada increased from 26.5 percent in 1950 to 32.6 percent in 1960 to 36.9 percent in 1970 and then to 45.4 percent in 1983 (see Table 3-2). As a fraction of GNP, total government expenditures increased from 3.7 percent in 1867 to 13.2 percent in 1913 to 19.2 percent in 1926 and then to 31.3 percent in 1968 (Stanbury 1972). Bird (1970, 13) puts real government expenditure at 7 percent of GNP in 1870, which is somewhat higher than Stanbury's (1972) estimate. In any event, we can confidently assert that the *ratio* of G to GNP in Canada has increased at least seven times over a period of 116 years, that is, from 4 to 7 percent of GNP in 1867 to 45 percent of GNP in 1983.

2.1 Exhaustive Expenditures

Exhaustive expenditures are those that use up goods and services (including labour services) that would otherwise be available for private sector activities. This type of government expenditure stands in contrast to transfer expenditures (described below), which only shift the power to exert claims over resources (dollars) from one individual to another. While the government exercises its coercive power to determine who pays and who gets these transfers, it is the recipients who decide what these payments will be spent on.

Table 3-1 indicates that in current dollars exhaustive expenditures of all levels of government increased from 9.6 percent in 1926 to 14.8 percent in 1946, then fell in the early postwar years but rose to 19.5 percent by 1965. They then rose to 24.0 percent in 1975, dipped slightly, and rose to 24.4 percent in 1983.

In constant 1971 dollars, exhaustive expenditures on current goods and services rose from 15.9 percent of GNP in 1950 to 19.9 percent in 1955 and then fell to 17.3 and 17.5 percent in 1960 and 1965 respectively. The ratio rose to 20 percent in 1970, but fell thereafter, reaching 17.3 percent in 1983. Gross fixed capital formation (1971 dollars) by all levels of government in 1980 and 1982 was the same as it was in 1955, 3 percent of GNP. In 1965 the ratio was 4.3 percent. See Table 3-2.

2.2 Transfers

Transfers are unrequited payments to individuals, firms, or other levels of government that alter the distribution of money income but are not included in GNP. Government transfer payments include the following:
* Transfers to individuals (e.g., welfare payments, unemployment insurance)
* Interest on the public debt (assumed to be an unrequited payment in the National Accounts compiled by Statistics Canada)
* Subsidies and capital assistance (e.g., regional economic expansion grants to business, subsidies paid to the railroads)
* Transfers to other levels of government (e.g., contributions to finance shared-cost programs or unconditional grants). These cancel out when the expenditures of all levels of government are combined.

Transfers of all types now account for over three-quarters of federal expenditures as the following data from the 1985–86 *Estimates* indicate:[6]

- Transfers to persons   18.9%
- Subsidies and other transfers   9.0
- Transfers to crown corporations and agencies   4.5
- Interest on the public debt   24.9
- Transfers to other levels of government   19.4

                                        Total transfers   76.7%

- Exhaustive expenditures of departments and
  agencies (including National Defence, 9.2 percent)   23.3%

In current dollars, total government transfer expenditures, net of intergovernmental transfers, rose from 6.6 percent of GNP in 1926 to 23.5 percent in 1983. In 1965 such transfers were only 10.4 percent of GNP (Table 3-1).

Table 3-2 indicates that transfers to persons (excluding interest on the public debt, subsidies, capital assistance, and transfers to nonresidents) in constant 1971 dollars increased from 7.1 percent of personal income in 1950 to 12.5 percent in 1975 and 1980. This ratio fell slightly in 1981 but then rose to 14.9 percent in 1983. All transfers as a fraction of personal income increased from 11.5 percent in 1950 to 27.2 percent in 1983. Therefore, the major growing component of government expenditures has been total transfer payments.[7] In 1950 total transfers in 1971 dollars amounted to $2690 million. The comparable total for all exhaustive expenditures was $6251 million. By 1980, as Table 3-2 indicates, total real transfers were slightly larger than exhaustive expenditures.

A rough idea of the growth of specific federal transfers to persons is provided by the Canadian Tax Foundation (1985, chap. 8). The old age security (OAS) and guaranteed income supplement (GIS) payments together increased from $3934 million in 1975/76 to $11 555 million in 1984/85. Unemployment insurance benefits grew from $2521 million in 1975 to $11 386 million in 1985. These figures exclude Canada Assistance Plan (welfare) payments of $3288 million in 1983/84 and Canada Pension Plan payments of $4150 million in 1984/85.

2.3 Expenditures by Level of Government

There have been significant changes in the fiscal role of the different levels of governments. If expenditures are measured as including transfers at the level of government making them (method B), the federal government's share of the national total has fallen from 60.6 percent in 1955 to 53.5 percent in 1982. If expenditures are calculated by subtracting them from the paying government and adding them to the expenditures of the receiving government (method A), then the federal government's share fell from 58.1 percent in 1955 to 38.3 percent in 1970 and then rose to 43.7 percent in 1982. Regardless of which measure is used, the provincial share of total government expenditures in Canada has increased sharply since 1955, from about 20 to 36 percent in 1982.

Table 3-2

TOTAL GOVERNMENT EXPENDITURES IN CANADA IN CONSTANT 1971 DOLLARS,* SELECTED YEARS, 1950–83

($ millions)

Year	Current Goods & Services	Gross Fixed Capital Formation	Total Exhaustive Expenditure	Total Transfers in Current Dollars	Personal Expenditure Deflator (1971 = 100)	Total Transfers (1971 $)	Total Gov't. Expenditure (1971 $)	Gross National Product	Total Gov't. Expenditure ÷ GNP (%)	Current Expenditure ÷ GNP (%)	GFCF ÷ GNP (%)	Transfers to Persons ÷ Personal Income (%)	Total Transfers ÷ Personal Income (%)
1950	5 367	844	6 251	1 646	61.2	2 690	8 941	33 762	26.5	15.9	2.6	7.1	11.5
1955	8 736	1 308	10 044	2 513	69.5	3 616	13 600	43 891	31.1	19.0	3.0	8.1	11.8
1960	9 218	2 142	11 360	4 588	76.3	6 013	17 393	53 231	32.6	17.3	4.0	10.4	15.5
1965	12 253	3 003	15 256	5 766	81.6	7 066	22 322	69 981	31.9	17.5	4.3	8.3	14.0
1970	17 650	3 329	20 979	11 358	97.7	11 625	32 604	88 390	36.9	20.0	3.8	10.5	17.0
1975	21 399	4 127	25 526	28 554	137.3	20 797	46 323	113 005	41.0	18.9	3.7	12.5	21.0
1980	22 932	3 676	26 608	56 399	209.1	26 972	53 580	131 675	40.7	17.4	2.8	12.5	23.1
1981	23 053	3 761	26 814	65 410	233.2	28 049	54 863	136 114	40.3	16.9	2.8	11.7	22.8
1982	23 175	3 886	27 061	80 686	258.4	31 225	58 286	130 069	44.8	17.8	3.0	13.7	25.5
1983	23 239	3 999	27 238	91 155	273.6	33 317	60 555	133 995	45.2	17.3	3.0	14.9	27.2

* Except for columns 4, 5, and 6.

Source: Derived from Department of Finance, *Economic Review, April 1984* (Ottawa: Minister of Supply and Services, 1984).

Using method B, the share of total government expenditure in Canada accounted for by local governments fell from 18 percent between 1955 and 1965 to less than 12 percent since 1975. Using method A, local governments' share moved from 22.1 percent in 1955 to 26.0 percent in 1970 to 20.4 percent in 1982 (Howard & Stanbury 1984, 140). The relative size of various levels of government and the importance of intergovernmental transfers can be ascertained by examining Table 3-1.

3.0 TAX EXPENDITURES

3.1 The Concept

Tax expenditures are potential revenues the government chooses not to collect. Kesselman defines them to be "any form of incentive or relief granted via the tax system rather than via government expenditures" (1977, 161). Smith defines tax expenditures as "indirect expenditures which generally take the form of 'special' exemptions, deductions, credits, exclusions, preferential rates or deferrals" (1979, 1). Obviously, the use of the word "special" begs the question of what constitutes the normal or reference tax base. In the final analysis, there must be an element of arbitrariness in estimating the extent of tax expenditures. However, if all the major assumptions are made clear, the concept is a useful one in analyzing another less obvious means by which governments seek to influence the economic behaviour of those in the private sector: "giving by not taking."

In its latest estimates of the size of specific tax expenditures, the Department of Finance (1985, 10) emphasizes that its estimates "do not question the desirability of the goals of the tax provisions nor their effectiveness in achieving the goals." Moreover, the department continues, "it is not a list of tax loopholes or areas for tax reform. It is simply an accounting of the cost to the federal government of these tax measures."

3.2 Personal Income Tax Expenditures

There are more than a hundred tax preferences in the Canadian Income Tax Act. In Brooks's view, "whenever the government grants a tax concession or preference, for whatever purpose, it is paying a subsidy" (1981, 32). A recent federal study of *personal* income tax expenditures estimated the revenue loss from five income exclusions, sixteen deductions, five exemptions, and six tax-credit–type tax expenditures (Government of Canada 1981, 6). The benefits, that is, revenue loss to the *federal* government, amounted to $6.2, $4.0, $2.1, and $1.3 billion respectively, for a total of $13.8 billion in 1979.[8] Because many tax expenditures also automatically reduce *provincial* taxes payable, the total value of personal income tax expenditures is about 50 percent *higher* than that indicated. Federal personal income tax actually collected in 1979 amounted to $17.0 billion. Therefore, the amount of personal tax expenditures ($13.8 billion) was 81 percent of the total personal income tax received by the federal government (Government of Canada 1981, 1). The Department of Finance estimated that for 1979 if tax expenditures embodied in the personal income tax were eliminated and the tax base thereby broadened, "a general cut of 45 per cent in tax rates could have been provided and federal revenues would have remained unchanged" (Government of Canada 1981, 2).

More recent estimates of the cost of selected tax expenditures in the personal income tax can be found in Table 3-3.

The Department of Finance's analysis of federal personal income tax expenditures in 1979 indicates that, with the exception of those with incomes under $5000, these tax expenditures *increase* as a percentage of income in each income group. We should note that those with incomes over $50 000 in 1979, less than 1 percent of all tax filers, obtained the following shares of these tax expenditures: 63 percent of exempt capital gains; 87 percent of income averaging annuity contracts; 41 percent of the dividend tax credits; 45 percent of gifts to the crown; 66 percent of Multiple Unit Residential Building (MURB) investments; 77 percent of drilling fund investments; and 64 percent of film investments (Government of Canada 1981, 19).

3.3 Corporate Tax Expenditures

An estimate of federal corporate tax expenditures places the total at $6.2 billion in 1980 (Government of Canada 1980). By comparison, the federal corporate income tax collections in 1979 were $7.2 billion. Brooks, who placed the total at $6 billion in 1979, notes that such tax expenditures have more than doubled since 1976 when they were $2.4 billion (1981, 34). He also indicates that actual corporate tax revenues have declined from 29 to 13 percent of federal revenues between 1951 and 1977. Recent estimates of the revenues foregone in the corporate income tax for selected items in 1979 and 1982 are given in Table 3-3.

A consistent series on tax expenditures embedded in the corporate income tax has been compiled by Maslove (1981):

- Corporation income tax expenditures increased from $1.9 billion in 1972 to $4.7 billion in 1975 and then decreased to $4.4 billion in 1977.
- As a proportion of corporate tax revenues, corporate income tax expenditures rose from 50% in 1972 to 67% in 1974, then fell to 59% in 1976, but rose to 66% in 1977.
- As a proportion of total budgetary expenditures, corporate income tax expenditures declined from 13.8% in 1972 to 12.9% in 1973, then rose to 14.5% in 1974, but then fell to 10.4% in 1977.

Brooks argues that "there is astonishingly little evidence that these tax breaks [for corporations] are effective" (1981, 35). He notes that while

Table 3–3
RECENT ESTIMATES OF SELECTED TAX EXPENDITURES, 1979 and 1983

	$ Millions	
A: Selective Tax Measures: Personal Income Tax	1979	1983
• $1000 investment income deduction	620	835
• Tax advantage on savings in registered pension plans and RRSPS	2950	4900
• Marital exemption	1015	1385
• Child tax credit	935	1435
• Basic personal exemption	4925	8100
• Deductibility of itemized charitable donations and $100 standard deduction	360	515
• Dividend gross-up and tax credit ($1140 million in 1982)	690	785
• Nontaxation of lottery and gambling winnings	355	465
• Multiple-unit residential buildings provision	40	65
• Nontaxation of various homeowner grants	—	140
• Age exemption	215	500
B: Selective Tax Measures: Corporate Income Tax	Upper Bound 1979	Upper Bound 1982
• Excess of tax depreciation over book depreciation	2090	2215 (1981)
• Capital gains exemptions	1785	3620 (1981)
• Small-business deduction	1065	1370
• Exemption from withholding tax for interest on foreign currency deposit	570	1490
• Oil and gas industry		
• Fast write-off or development and exploration expenses, and earned depletion	765	660
• Net petroleum and gas revenue tax	—	1650
• IORT productivity well allowance	—	1240
• Natural gas and gas liquids tax revenues	—	910
C: Selective Tax Measures: Commodity Taxes	1979	1983
• Exemption of nonmanufacturing commercial uses of fuel and electricity	220	440
• Exemption of food and nonalcoholic beverages	1800	2580
• Exemption of home-heating fuels and electricity	325	590
• Exemption of clothing and footwear	525	705
• Exemption of services from the sales tax base	4590	7065

Source: Department of Finance (1985, Tables 1, 2, 3).

corporate tax incentives in manufacturing alone cost the government $2.5 billion between 1972 and 1975, the additional amount of investment generated ranged between $340 million and $846 million.

Perhaps the most extreme case of a tax expenditure run amok is that of the Scientific Research Tax Credit (SRTC), which has been described as "almost an invitation to fraud." The provision was introduced in April 1983 (effective in October) and was terminated in May 1985. However, its projected cost to the federal treasury has been estimated to be about $2.6 billion.[9] When introduced, the measure was expected to cost $100 million in lost revenue. The basic idea was that nontaxable research and development (R & D) companies would be able to immediately pass on to investors a 50 percent earned tax credit in return for financing. Some 57 percent of all SRTC transactions (about 1786) were "quick flips"; the best involved longer-term debt or equity financing. Over and above the issues of fraud and loss of tax revenues, there is the question of the efficiency of the expenditures that were actually made on R & D.[10]

4.0 REGULATION

Priest et al. define economic regulation as the "imposition of rules by a government, backed by the use of penalties, that are intended specifically to modify the economic behaviour of individuals and firms in the private sector" (1980, 5). Economic regulation is primarily aimed at altering the set of choices available to firms and individuals. The choices affected are typically in the following areas:

- Prices, for example, airline fares, minimum wages, certain agricultural products, telephone rates
- Supply, for example, broadcasting licences, occupational licensing, agricultural production quotas, pipeline certificates "of public convenience and necessity"
- Rate of return, for example, public utilities, pipelines
- Disclosure of information, for example, securities prospectuses, content labelling
- Methods of production, for example, effluent standards, worker health and safety standards
- Attributes of a product of services, for example, automobile fuel efficiency standards, safety of children's toys, quality or purity of food products, "Canadian content" requirements in broadcasting
- Conditions of service, for example, requirements to act as a common carrier or not to discriminate in hiring or selling goods and services

The areas affected by economic regulation include not only the traditional forms of "economic" or "direct" regulation, but also what has been called the "new regulation" or "social regulation." Direct regulation is industry-specific and affects price, output, rate of return, and entry or exit. Social regulation typically affects a broad range of industries, although its impact on some may be much greater than it is on others. It includes environmental regulation, consumer protection legislation, "fairness" regulation, health and safety regulation, and cultural regulation.

4.1 The Scope of Direct Regulation

Stanbury and Thompson (1980) have estimated that in Canada 29 percent of gross domestic product (GDP) at factor cost was subject to *direct* regulation in 1978. The comparable figure for the United States was 26 percent. (The figure for Canada in the early 1980s would be several percentage points higher because of the National Energy Program, while that for the U.S. would be somewhat lower because of subsequent deregulation of several industries. However, the NEP was largely dismantled in 1985.)[11] They note that in nearly every industry group either the scope or the coverage of regulation (sometimes both) is broader or more comprehensive in Canada than in the United States. While these were not dramatic differences, they were consistent. They also found that virtually all industries or activities that are subject to these controls in Canada are *also* subject to direct regulation in the U.S., and vice versa. These include transportation, energy (notably electricity and petroleum), telecommunications, broadcasting, insurance, banking, securities, and a substantial proportion of the agricultural sector, as well as a large number of licensed occupations and businesses. Moreover, Stanbury and Thompson found that the same industries tend to be subject to the same *type* of controls in both Canada and the U.S.

4.2 Regulatory Effort

Stanbury and Thompson (1980) estimated that in 1977/78 the federal government in Canada spent $678 million on the administration of regulatory programs. This amounted to only 1.6 percent of total budgetary expenditures. For the same year, U.S. federal regulatory expenditures were $4862 million or slightly less than 1.1 percent of total federal expenditures. Such expenditures, of course, are the mere "tip of the iceberg." Their economic impact may be many times greater. For example, Weidenbaum and DeFina (1978, 2) estimate that the private sector's cost of complying with federal regulation in the United States is almost twenty times the government's budgetary outlays. In my view, however, private sector compliance costs with respect to Canadian federal regulation are far below those in the U.S. because of the latter's more extensive and more stringent health and safety and environmental regulations. They could well amount to ten to fifteen times the government's budgetary outlays.

In 1977/78, regulatory employees in Canadian federal departments and agencies accounted for 5.9 percent of total federal employment (Stanbury & Thompson 1980). In the U.S. the comparable figure was 3.1

percent. Total U.S. federal employment actually fell slightly over the 1970s. During the same period, Canadian federal employment grew by 30 percent. Therefore, in terms of the "number of regulators," it seems clear that at the federal level Canada makes a considerably larger regulatory effort than does the United States.

4.3 Growth of Regulation

The same measures that have been used to indicate the scope and coverage of regulation have also been used to indicate its *growth*: pages of regulations, number of programs, important legislative initiatives, and public expenditures. The growth in the number of new federal and provincial regulatory statutes prior to 1978 is described in Table 3-4. It indicates that the average number per decade increased from under 100 prior to 1900 to over 200 per decade between 1950 and 1969 to 324 per decade in the period 1970–78. Similar patterns were found for both economic and social regulation.

Table 3–4
GROWTH OF REGULATORY STATUTES IN EXISTENCE IN 1978

Originally Enacted	Total	Primarily Economic Regulation[a]	Primarily Social Regulation[b]	Both Economic and Social[c]
Before 1900	359	120	90	149
(avg. per decade)	(<100)	(<36)	(<27)	(<45)
1900–49	684	248	242	194
(avg. per decade)	(137)	(50)	(48)	(40)
1950–69	413	120	166	127
(avg. per decade)	(207)	(60)	(83)	(64)
1970–78	292	88	119	85
(avg. per decade)	(324)	(98)	(132)	(94)
Total 1978[d]	1744	574	613	557

[a] Regulatory statutes relating to agriculture, fisheries, communications, transportation, energy, resource management, financial markets, and land use.
[b] Regulatory statutes relating to environmental protection, occupational health and safety, consumer protection, information and standards, intellectual property, health facilities, and culture and recreation.
[c] Regulatory statutes relating to business and professional licensing, liquor control, and "framework" regulations.
[d] Does not include "miscellaneous" category.
Source: Priest and Wohl (1980) and Bird and Green (1985).

Stanbury and Thompson (1980) conclude that while it is difficult to make precise comparisons using similar measures, the growth of federal regulation in Canada in the 1970s in general terms was about as great as it was in the U.S. The stock of new or re-enacted regulatory statutes increased more than did federal regulatory employment in the 1970s. Of the 140 federal economic regulatory statutes "on the books" at the end of 1978, 27 were enacted between 1970 and 1978. An additional 10 had been passed earlier but were re-enacted in the 1970s (Priest & Wohl 1980). More new federal regulatory statutes were passed between 1970 and 1978 than between 1940 and 1969. Twenty-one new regulatory statutes and 10 re-enactments were passed between 1970 and 1975. The new regulatory statutes were concentrated in a few areas: environmental protection, health and safety, and consumer protection. It should be noted that since 1978 the growth of federal regulation, excluding the NEP, slowed down a great deal.

The growth of provincial regulation in the 1970s in Canada, as measured by the volume of statutes and pages of regulations, appears similar to that of the federal government. For example, 262 of the 1608 provincial regulatory statutes on the books in 1978 were enacted between 1970 and 1978 (Priest & Wohl 1980).

Regulatory reform has been slow in coming to Canada as compared with the U.S. (Stanbury & Thompson 1982a, 1982b). However, one can identify a number of recent actions or proposals for action that did or will result in a substantially less-restrictive economic environment in airlines, railroads, trucking,[12] telecommunications,[13] foreign ownership,[14] the pricing of oil and natural gas,[15] financial institutions,[16] and brokerage fees.[17]

With respect to the recent concern with the growth of regulation in Canada,[18] Bird and Green offer the following most useful assessment:

Although most of the recent concern with the growth and cost of governmental regulatory activities has thus been directed at social and environmental legislation, it deserves emphasis, however, that such legislation — if properly drawn up — is both more justifiable and more socially beneficial than the much less criticized economic regulation, which flourished long before the recent flurry of social concerns, and which has continued to thrive, relatively unpublicized, amidst all the fuss over the costs imposed by regulation of the environment, of working conditions, and so on. Undoubtedly, private firms perceive government regulations that require them to take into account the social costs of their decisions as imposing an undesired and undesirable burden. From society's point of view, however, such external costs of private actions should be taken into account if the best possible allocation of scarce economic resources is to be achieved. Still other "modern" regulatory measures that have been much criticized may equally be justified as achieving overriding social objectives such as nondiscrimination. Indeed, some of the most deplored regulatory actions of government may, in the end, thus turn out to be not a hindrance but an essential part of a sound industrial policy in the only meaningful sense of one which makes the best possible use of the nation's resources, given national objectives. Of course, . . . the road to bad policy is often paved with good intentions, and it is quite likely that many regulations that may in principle be rationalized as internalizing external costs are in fact so drawn as to be conducive to inefficiency, not efficiency. Blanket condemnation of "social" regulation because it gives rise to economic costs, however, is as silly as a blanket condemnation of tax incentives because they result in revenue losses. In both instances, both sides of the deal — the costs and the benefits — must be taken into account before a sound judgment can be reached. This has not yet, it appears, been done in the case of social regulations. (1985, 33–34)

They continue:

What is clearer, however, is that almost all economic regulations — occupational licensing, marketing boards, import quotas, and the like — while almost invariably clothed in the sacred vestments of the "national interest" are in fact directly and explicitly intended to be economically inefficient. In effect, the usual stated, and achieved, purpose of such regulations — once cleared of the rhetoric — is to reduce the national welfare in favour of the designated select group of beneficiaries. (1985, 33–34; see also Stanbury & Lermer 1983 and Lermer & Stanbury 1985).

5.0 PUBLIC ENTERPRISES/CROWN CORPORATIONS

5.1 How Many?

While everyone knows the names of the largest federal crown corporations (FCCs), for example, Air Canada, Canadian National Railways (CNR), Atomic Energy of Canada Limited (AECL), Canadian Broadcasting Corporation (CBC), Canada Mortgage and Housing Corporation (CMHC), Petro-Canada, and the Federal Business Development Bank, not even Ottawa specialists can provide the names of *all* federal crown corporations. For example, in 1977 the Privy Council Office published a list of 366 "government-owned and controlled corporations." A revised list in January 1978 put the total at 383, and in August 1979 the list was extended to 401. In the next year, the comptroller general identified 464 FCCs, including 213 subsidiaries and subsubsidiaries and 126 "associated" corporations.

The number of federal crown corporations has increased greatly in the last two decades. Indeed, Langford and Huffman (1983) state that

58 percent of the 119 major FCCs on his list (excluding subsidiaries) were created between 1960 and 1980, while 27 percent were created between 1940 and 1960. Foster (1984b) shows that under Laurier's administration new federal crown corporations were created at the rate of one every three years. Conservative John Diefenbaker created them at a rate of one every 9 months, and Pierre Trudeau created one new crown corporation every 3.2 months — a total of 541 in his 174 months in office up to July 1983.

Vining and Botterell (1983) identified 233 provincial crown corporations (PCCs) operating in 1980. The number by province was as follows:

Newfoundland	42	Nova Scotia	10
British Columbia	36	Prince Edward Island	10
Quebec	35	New Brunswick	9
Ontario	27	Northwest Territories	2
Saskatchewan	25	Yukon	2
Alberta	20	Regional	2
Manitoba	13		

While 76 percent of all PCCs were created since 1960, less than half this proportion (33 percent) of assets were created since 1960. Since 1970 some 48 percent of PCCs were created, but since that year only 13 percent of total assets were created (Vining & Botterell 1983).

Vining and Botterell (1983, 308–17) grouped the 233 PCCs in 1980 into twenty-four "functional" categories as follows:

- Agricultural development (13)
- Banking, saving, investment (5)
- Forest development and manufacturing (13)
- Government buildings (3)
- Government computer services (4)
- Housing (18)
- Industrial development (31)
- Insurance: general and automobile (5)
- Liquor distribution (12)
- Lotteries (4)
- Marketing and brokerage facilities (18)
- Mining and development (10)
- Manufacturing (10)
- Municipal finance (5)
- Oil and gas (5)
- Power utilities (11)
- Research and development (13)
- School and hospital financing (17)
- Shipyards (2)
- Steel (3)
- Telephones and communications (8)
- Transportation facilities (7)
- Transportation services (14)
- Water supply (2)

5.2 Economic Significance

Unfortunately, we have no simple measure of the economic significance of crown corporations, such as the fraction of GNP produced by federal and provincial enterprises. Because so little is known of their activities, the auditor general was moved to describe federal crown corporations as follows: "It may be helpful in visualizing the scale of the problem to think of the whole group as an enormous iceberg, floating lazily in the foggy Atlantic; silent, majestic, awesome" (1982, 13).

Some data, however, are available to assess their economic significance. In terms of revenues in 1984, there were 16 federal and 24 provincial crown corporations among the 500 largest nonfinancial enterprises in Canada. Twenty-one crown corporations were in the top 200. In terms of assets, 20 crown corporations were among the 100 largest nonfinancial enterprises in Canada in 1984, and 55 were in the 500 largest. Among the 100 largest financial enterprises, there were 10 provincial and 5 federal crown corporations. Eleven of the 25 largest financial enterprises were crown corporations. See Table 3-5.

Kierans (1984, 23) states that in 1983 some 50 federal commercial crown corporations and their 129 subsidiaries employed more than 209 000 persons and controlled $47 billion in assets. Eighteen provincial crown corporations recorded in the *Financial Post 500* employed more than 129 000 and controlled assets of $77.5 billion. In contrast, the 50 largest industrial enterprises in the private sector employed 1 137 000 and controlled assets of $165.3 billion.

As of 1984, some 56 parent federal crown corporations had 124 wholly owned subsidiaries and investments in another 126 companies, with total assets of $77 billion. In addition there are 12 companies in which Ottawa has some equity interest. In 1973 the value of the assets of federal crown corporations was only $26 billion.[19]

The 50 commercial crown corporations had assets of $49 billion and 193 600 employees (including CNR, 63 496; Canada Post, 620 000; and Air Canada, 42 584). The 7 other federal crown corporations (including the CBC, Bank of Canada, and Canadian Wheat Board) had assets of $26.5 billion. The 50 commercial crowns accounted for only 2 percent of total employment and less than 5 percent of the assets of all nonfinancial enterprises.

Statistics Canada indicates that federal and provincial crown corporations accounted for the following percentage of profits, sales, and assets in 1981 among the largest nonfinancial corporations:[20]

	Profits (%)	Sales (%)	Assets (%)
Top 25	14.7	17.9	30.8
Top 100	15.0	13.6	27.6
Top 500	11.6	9.9	22.1
All firms	8.0	5.4	14.6

The *OECD Observer* (March 1983, 9) indicates that public enterprises accounted for 4.5 percent of employment and 16.1 percent of gross fixed investment in Canada in 1975-79/80. The comparable figures for

Table 3–5
THE RELATIVE SIZE OF THE LARGEST CROWN CORPORATIONS, 1984

(A) Nonfinancial Corporations (Ranked by Revenues)

Rank	Ranked by Revenues			Ranked by Assets		
	Provincial	Federal	Total	Provincial	Federal	Total
1–100	4	5	9	13	7	20
101–200	8	4	12	6	7	13
201–300	5	3	8	7	2	9
301–400	3	4	7	4	2	6
401–500	4	0	4	1	0	1
Total	24	16	40	35[a]	20[b]	55

(B) Financial Corporations (Ranked by Revenues)

Rank	Provincial	Federal	Total
1– 25	7	4	11
26– 50	2	1	3
51– 75	1	0	1
76–100	0	0	0
Total	10	5	15

[a] Includes 11 corporations in the top 500 in terms of assets but not revenues, 4 of which could not be classified in detail.
[b] Includes 4 corporations in the top 500 in terms of assets but not revenues, 2 of which could not be classified in detail.

Sources: Tabulation by the author using *Financial Post 500* (Summer 1985); *Canadian Business 500* (June 1985); *Report on Business Magazine 1000* (June 1985); and selected annual reports of crown corporations.

the U.S. were 1.6 and 4.9 percent, while those for the United Kingdom were 8.2 and 19.1 percent respectively.

Langford and Huffman (1983) describe 61 of the 119 federal crown corporations (excluding subsidiaries) on their list as "corporate enterprises." These firms (and their 213 subsidiaries) operate in the following sectors: communications; culture and recreation; financing insurance and business services; industrial development; manufacturing; marketing, wholesaling and trading; resource development; and transportation systems and facilities. Only 29 would be included in Statistics Canada's definition of "government business enterprises," that is, the production of economic goods and provision of services for sale to the consumer at a price intended to wholly or largely cover costs.

Langford and Huffman (1983) note that their list of 61 federal "corporate enterprises" in 1978–79 represented roughly 68 percent of the total assets of the federal government; 32 percent of total federal government employment (departments, armed forces, and federal government enterprise employment); and had revenues equal to 37 percent of federal tax and fee revenues. In terms of both assets and revenues, federal corporate enterprises in 1978–79 accounted for 12 to 13 percent of the total public and private sector activity in the eight sectors listed above.

The auditor general (1982, 51) states that the 261 federal agency, proprietary, and government corporations (the others are mixed enterprises and "other entities") at March 31, 1982, had assets of $66.8 billion. Their revenues in 1981/82 totalled $28.5 billion. Mixed enterprises and "other entities had assets of $7.5 billion and revenues of $6.1 billion." The auditor general also noted that the 261 federal agency, proprietary and government corporations had 263 225 employees in March 1982. Canada Post, which became a crown corporation on October 16, 1981, alone had 69 457 employees on March 31, 1982. By comparison, all the federal departments on the same date had 221 000 employees, while the armed forces and the Royal Canadian Mounted Police (RCMP) had another 83 000 and 18 000 respectively. In summary, federal crown corporations now employ more Canadians than do federal departments.[21]

The total assets of the 233 provincial crown corporations amounted to $62.3 billion in 1977 or 10.1 percent of all corporate assets and 26.2 percent of corporate *fixed* assets. The PCCs' assets were substantially larger than the total assets of the federal and provincial governments respectively (Vining & Botterell 1983, 319). We should note that Vining and Botterell (1983, 340) put the total assets of the provincial power utilities at $34.5 billion or 55 percent of the assets of all PCCs. As a measure of their relative importance, Vining and Botterell (1983, 326) calculated the ratio of total PCC assets to GDP for each of the provinces. The result was as follows:

Newfoundland	123%	British Columbia	32%
Manitoba	47	Alberta	25
Quebec	47	Ontario	23
Saskatchewan	33	Nova Scotia	19
New Brunswick	33	Prince Edward Island	13

Overall, it would appear that federal and provincial crown corporations operating as commercial enterprises account for about 5 percent of the GNP. In addition, as I shall note in section 7, both the federal and provincial governments have acquired both minority and majority equity interests in privately owned enterprises, thereby creating "mixed enterprises."

6.0 LOANS AND LOAN GUARANTEES

The Economic Council of Canada points out that "through its financial intermediation activities, government ranks second to the chartered banks among Canada's financial institutions" (1982a, 3). Federal and provincial agencies accounted for 18.1 percent of the assets of the major financial institutions in Canada in 1980 (ECC 1982a, 2). The value of federal and provincial loans and investments, loan guarantees, and credit insurance[22] extended to the private sector amounted to 18.5 percent of GNP in 1980. In contrast, the ratio was 4.3 percent in 1950, but 13.2 percent in 1930 and 15.6 percent in 1939 (ECC 1982a, 3).

The federal government accounted for 74 percent of all government loans and investments and 95 percent of all guarantees and credit insurance in force in March 1980 (ECC 1982a, 5). Government financial assistance in 1980 was concentrated in four sectors: business, 13.6 percent; exports, 11.1 percent; housing, 60.0 percent; and agriculture, 10.9 percent (ECC 1982a, 6). This assistance was provided through some forty-two agencies and boards, as well as through a number of ad hoc arrangements. While the federal government's aid was concentrated in the four sectors listed above, the provinces were more active in natural resources, housing, and agriculture.

Some idea of the significance of federal and provincial financial activities for specific sectors can be gained from the following. In agriculture, governments account for 30 percent of all credit outstanding and 58 percent of long-term loans. In export financing, the federal government is the major lender and the only supplier of some forms of credit insurance through the Export Development Corporation (EDC). Governments are the sixth largest supplier of residential mortgages, but they supply one-half the mortgage insurance. In business financing, government is the fourth largest institution, but accounts for only 4.3 percent of the outstanding credit (ECC 1982a, 8).

The financial activities of governments vis-à-vis the private sector accounted for a large part of the public debt for several provinces in 1980: Alberta, 57 percent; B.C., 42 percent; and Nova Scotia, 25 percent. Financial aid to the private sector accounted for 25 percent of the federal government's total debt (ECC 1982a, 8).

An excellent example of the use of loans and guarantees is Husky Oil Ltd.'s $3.2-billion expenditure on a heavy-oil upgrading plant and associated production facilities. Energy Minister Jean Chrétien emphasized that the project (which will produce 42 000 barrels a day) would not have been undertaken without government assistance. The federal government made a grant of $50 million and provided loan guarantees of up to $780 million. In addition, the provinces of Alberta and Saskatchewan each provided loan guarantees of up to $390 million. Furthermore, Husky is guaranteed the world price for the oil it produces, is exempt from the federal petroleum and gas revenue tax until the cost of

Table 3–6
RECENT MAJOR PRIVATE SECTOR "BAILOUTS" BY THE FEDERAL GOVERNMENT*

- *Maislin Industries Ltd.* — Ottawa guaranteed loans of $33.4 million in June 1982 in exchange for a $1 option on 15% of its common shares. Maislin went bankrupt less than a year later.
- *Massey-Ferguson Ltd.* — Ottawa guaranteed $125 million and the Province of Ontario guaranteed $75 million in preferred shares in February 1981. In July 1982 when Massey failed to pay the required dividend, the governments ended up with 7% and 3.6% of Massey's common shares.
- *Consolidated Computer Inc.* — The federal government's involvement began with loan guarantees in 1971. By 1976 it had extended $30 million in guarantees and had obtained 49% of the equity. In November 1982 the federal government sold the firm for $100 000 and realized total losses of about $119 million.
- *White Farm Equipment* — The federal government guaranteed $10.5 million in loans in March 1981. An additional grant of $2.5 million was made by the Enterprise Development Board. In June 1983 White went into receivership.
- *CCM Inc.* — In the late 1970s Ottawa made direct loans and loan guarantees of $22 million. The company declared bankruptcy in October 1982. Federal losses totalled $15.5 million.
- *Lake Group Inc.* — In June 1982 Ottawa authorized $13 million in loan guarantees. The fish products firm lost $22.5 million in 1983.
- *Fish Processors in Atlantic Canada* — In July 1983 Ottawa announced it would acquire at least 51% of the three fish processors in Newfoundland for about $7 million. The Province of Newfoundland holds mortgages, loan guarantees, and equity of $47 million in the three companies. In the final arrangement, the federal government obtained 60% and Newfoundland 26% of the shares of a new firm (Fishery Products International) combining seven companies. The Bank of Nova Scotia obtained 14%. In November 1984 FPI announced it needed another $100 million in capital in order to make a profit by 1990. The federal government also moved to bail out National Sea Products of Halifax and H. B. Nickerson & Sons Ltd. — the two largest fish processors in Canada. The final deal saw control of National Sea stay in the private sector. The federal government did end up with 20% ownership and about $10 million in preferred shares while the Province of Nova Scotia converted $25 million in debt into preferred shares.
- *Co-Op Implements Ltd.* — In February 1982 the federal government forgave $7.5 million in previous loans and loaned another $5.5 million as part of a $35-million refinancing also involving Prairie provincial governments and farm co-ops. The outcome depends on recovery of the farm implement business.
- *Electrohome Ltd.* — Ottawa insured loans of $15 million in 1977 in return for an option on a block of shares. The loans were repaid by 1980. Ottawa exercised the option and made $10 million.
- *Petromont Inc.* — In March 1983 Ottawa offered a loan of $25 million, to be repaid over two years, if Quebec matched the offer. Quebec did so and the first payment was approved in August 1983. Shortly after it took office, the new Conservative government increased its aid to keep the company going.

* This list excludes offers of assistance to Dome Petroleum and to Chrysler Canada that were not taken up and assistance to crown corporations such as Canadair and de Havilland, which received well over $2 billion in financial help from the federal government in the past five years.

the project has been recovered, and the two provinces provided other fiscal concessions.[23]

How large are the subsidies inherent in federal and provincial loans to the private sector? This is not easy to measure. Do we use only the "financial costs" — the difference between the lending rate and the government's borrowing rate? Do we add to this the government's costs of administering its loan programs, which can be substantial? These two elements the Economic Council calls the "cash cost" of such loans (1982a, 131). Or do we measure the subsidy based on the social opportunity cost of capital? The ECC (1982a, 133) estimated that, for one year only, 1978/79, the subsidies amounted to $196 million on a cash cost basis or $906 million on a social opportunity cost basis. On the other hand, the council estimated that loan guarantee programs produced a slight financial surplus of $8.9 million. By sector, the subsidy in federal and provincial loans to the private sector (on an opportunity cost basis) in 1978/79 was $176 million to business, $118 million to exports, $345 million to housing, and $267 million to agriculture.[24]

In the past few years the federal government (and more provincial governments) has been involved in "bailing out" private enterprises, including financial institutions, by means of loans and guarantees.[25] Some of the most notable examples are described in Table 3-6. More generally, see Trebilcock et al. (1986).

7.0 MIXED ENTERPRISES: EQUITY OWNERSHIP IN PRIVATE SECTOR FIRMS

Canadians are long familiar with crown corporations. Recently, however, we have witnessed a rise in government holdings of equity in private sector firms. Most crown corporations were "created from scratch" (e.g., Petro-Canada, Air Canada), and some were created by "nationalizing" existing firms (e.g., CNR, Canadair, B.C. Hydro, Hydro-Québec). The "equity route" has now been used in a few cases to obtain legal or de facto control of previously privately owned firms through the stock exchange.

In addition to these wholly owned enterprises, federal and, particularly, provincial governments or their agents have an equity interest in a substantial number of privately owned firms. These range from small fractions of the voting shares in the nature of a portfolio investment, to effective control through a substantial but minority interest, to more than one-half the voting shares, which provides legal control. The largest mixed enterprises in Canada are described in Table 3-7.

Elford and Stanbury's (1986) comprehensive survey of federal and provincial mixed enterprises in Canada in 1983 produced the following findings:

- There are at least 259 first-order (167 provincial and 91 federal) and 63 second-order mixed enterprises (largely subsidiaries and subsubsidiaries of the Canada Development Corporation [CDC] and Alberta Energy Company). Using a much broader definition, Boardman et al. (1983) claim there are more than 1000 mixed enterprises in Canada, but governments' influence is several steps removed for many of these firms.

- The federal government had an equity interest in 126 mixed enterprises, while the leading provincial participants were Quebec (137), Alberta (17), Ontario (14), and Saskatchewan (13).

- Some 176 of the 322 mixed enterprises consisted of portfolio investments (100 by the Province of Quebec), 28 of the shareholdings amounted to effective control in the authors' estimation, 46 were 50:50 joint ventures, and 63 shareholdings amounted to legal control. Eight could not be classified.

- In 1983, 82 of 92 federal and 68 of 167 provincial first-order mixed enterprises had revenues less than $75 million, that is, would not have been listed among the *Financial Post*'s largest 500 nonfinancial enterprises. The federal government had effective, legal, or 50:50 control of only 7 firms with sales of more than $75 million in 1983. Provincial governments had control of 15 firms in this category. See Table 3-7.

- The federal government's interest in 59 first-order mixed enterprises ranged over 17 industries, while the provinces' equity interests in 166 firms covered 31 industries.

- In 1981 government equity investments in mixed enterprises amounted to 7.5 percent of the total equity capital in Canada. About 5 percent of the assets of all nonfinancial corporations in Canada were held by mixed enterprises that were legally or effectively controlled by a government.

- Slightly more than one-half the investments in first-order (and 78 percent of second-order) mixed enterprises were classified by Elford and Stanbury as "business investments," mainly the portfolio type. Just over one-quarter were motivated by "regional development" considerations (one-fifth in the case of second-order mixed enterprises), and 15 percent were established because of "imperfect capital markets." "National development" (3 percent), "control of a key sector" (4 percent), and "bailout" (2 percent) were said to be the other reasons for the government's original investment.

- For the 35 percent of first-order mixed enterprises for which the date of the original investment could be determined, three-quarters were made in the period 1980–84, while 18 percent were made in the 1970s.

The outstanding example of the equity approach to government intervention is the Caisse de Dépôt et Placement du Québec.[26] Its primary function is to invest the funds collected by the Quebec Pension Plan and

Table 3–7
THE LARGEST MIXED ENTERPRISES IN CANADA IN RELATION TO
THE FINANCIAL POST 500, 1983

NAME	SIZE ($ millions)		RANK		GOV'T. INTEREST		CON-TROL	YR. OF ORIG. INVEST
First-Order Mixed Enterprises	Revenues	Assets	Revenues	Assets	Agency	%		
• Provigo Inc.	3891	660	16	112	Caisse	28	EC	na
• Canada Dev. Corp.	3834	7558	17	10	CDIC	48	EC	1971
• Domtar Inc.	1820	1350	47	67	Caisse/SGF	45	EC	1981
• Westcoast Transmission	1127	1719	73	55	Petro-Canada	36.7	EC	1978
• Gaz Metropolitan	647	596	115	121	Caisse	55	LC	na
• Alberta Energy Co.	462	1613	155	59	Herit. Fund	45	EC	1972
• Donohue Inc.	357	606	188a*	120a*	SGF	55	LC	1967
• CNCP Telecommunications	315	402	206a	15a	CNR	50	50:50	pre'60
• Canron	286	210	223	235	Caisse	20	EC	1983
• Sidbec-Normines Inc.**	268	646			Sidbec	50	LC	1976
• Canpotex Ltd.	239	44	269	436	Potash Corp. of Sask.	?	EC	1976
• IPSCO	192	330	310	179	cic/Steel Alta.	20.2 20.2	EC	1977
• Fishery Prods. Internat.	178	121	331	308	Fed. Gov't.	60	LC	1984
• Marine Industries Ltd.	173	132	337a	293a	SGF	65	LC	1965
• Nordair Ltd.	155	109	361	324	Air Canada	86.5	LC	1978
• Celegic Ent. (B.G. Checo Int.)	128	35	415a	450a	SGF	50	LC	na

Asbestos Corp.	96	221	463	227	Mines SNA	55	LC	1981
Churchill Falls (Labrador) Corp.	93	884	466a	98a	Nfld. & Lab. Hydro	65	LC	na
Sceptre Resources Ltd.	88	430	479	146	Caisse	27	EC	1983
Telesat Canada	88	348	480	157	Fed. Gov't.	50	LC	1969
Panarctic Oils Ltd.**	zero	358	***	172a	Petro-Canada	54	LC	1969
Petromont	na	na	in top 500	in top 500	SGF	50	50:50	na

Second-Order Mixed Enterprises

Polysar Ltd.	1336	1452	67a	63a	CDC	100	LC	1972
Petrosar	958	1000	84a	85a	Polysar	60	LC	1975
Canterra Energy Ltd.	507	3044	140a	27a	CDC	100	LC	1981
Kidd Creek Mines Ltd.	477	1348	151a	68a	CDC	100	LC	1981
Cansolex Ltd.	242	36	265	447	Canterra Energy	43	EC	na
AES Data Systems Ltd.	188	117	313a	312	CDC	78	LC	1974
Chieftain Development	68	385	***	160a	AEC	57	LC	1982
Innotech Aviation	51	33	***	454a	Innotech Invest. / Air Can.	53 / 30	LC	1973
Pacific Northern Gas	76	108	***	328a	Westcoast Trans.	45	EC	na

* Not included in F.P. 500, but ranked by the authors; 188a, for example, means between 188 and 189.
** 1981 figures used.
*** Ranked below #500.
EC = effective control; LC = legal control

Source: Compiled from the *Financial Post 500*, Summer 1984, pp. 70–109; *Globe and Mail Report on Business 1000*, June 1984.

thirteen other public agencies in the province. As of December 31, 1984, its total assets were $20.8 billion and its equity portfolio, said to be the largest in Canada, amounted to $5.4 billion.[27] Among the almost 200 companies in which the Caisse had equity holdings in 1983[28] were the following:

- 30 percent of Gaz Metropolitain Inc., Montreal, a natural gas distributor;
- 26.7 percent of Provigo Inc., Montreal, one of Canada's largest grocery wholesalers and retailers;
- 30 percent of Brascade Resources Inc., which owns 42 percent of Toronto-based Noranda Mines Ltd.;
- 15.2 percent of Domtar Inc., Montreal, the forest-products producer;
- 15 percent of Dofor Inc., which owns 30 percent of Domtar Inc.;
- 17 percent of Quebec-Telephone, filephone service outside Montreal;
- 14.1 percent of La Verendrye Management Corp., a holding company in air and land transport;
- 18 percent of Dominion Textile Inc., Montreal;
- 13 percent of Logistec Corp., Montreal, a cargo handler;
- 11.6 percent of Domco Industries Ltd., Lachine, a flooring producer;
- 19 percent of General Trust of Canada, Montreal;
- 9.6 percent of Canadian Pacific Ltd., Montreal, the nation's largest company; and
- 7.1 percent of Alcan Aluminium Ltd., Montreal, the world's second-largest aluminum maker (Elford & Stanbury 1985).

Canadian Business states that in 1982 the Caisse was the largest *single* shareholder in the seven largest banks, Canadian Pacific, Alcan Aluminum, Prenor Group, Domtar, Gaz Metropolitain, Provigo, and probably the largest shareholder in Bell Canada with 3 percent of the shares.[29] At the end of 1984 the Caisse's equity investments in 14 firms had a market value of over $100 million each. In another 17 firms, the Caisse's stake was between $50 million and $100 million.[30] Although the Caisse does not hold *de jure* control (i.e., 51 percent of the voting shares) in any company, it obviously has effective control in several (e.g., Domtar, Gaz Metropolitain). This raises the question of when the Caisse will be able to *exercise* control with its minority holdings.[31]

When the Caisse increased its interest in Canadian Pacific Ltd. to almost 10 percent, it prompted the federal government to introduce Bill S-31 in November 1980, which would have prevented any provincial government or its agent from owning more than 10 percent of the voting shares of any company engaged in interprovincial road, rail, water, or pipeline transport. This move prompted a hostile reaction from Quebec, and the government dropped the bill at the end of 1983 (see Tupper 1984).

By early 1985, eight provinces had established agencies to provide grants, guarantees, tax incentives, and equity for new and small firms.[32] Most were billed as providing venture capital.

Several points should be made about the "equity route" as a tool of intervention. First, it creates the opportunity to either benefit or hurt the private shareholders in which the government has a substantial interest. Second, unlike many other forms of intervention, its economic effects are immediately apparent as the stock market will capitalize on the change in expectations induced by the government's action. Third, and this characteristic makes the instrument less attractive to politicians, the cost of adverse changes in government policy is not only widely apparent because of changes in stock market prices, but it is also *concentrated*. More generally, see Eckel and Vining (1982, 1985).

8.0 SUASION

Perhaps the least obtrusive instrument used by government to effect its purposes is that of suasion. Suasion may also appear to be the least coercive governing instrument. Ideally, from the government's perspective, the targeted private sector actors change their behaviour in the desired direction, but the whole operation "leaves no tracks" in terms of the government having to go to the legislature for new regulations, taxes, expenditures, or crown corporations. The government doesn't even have to exercise its existing executive powers; yet its bidding gets done. The state (politicians and/or bureaucrats) seeks to alter the behaviour of firms and individuals in the private sector without resort to legitimate methods of coercion such as regulation. Suasion offers enormous opportunities for deception, reversibility, redirection, and the selective use of information; hence, from the point of view of politicians, it is an attractive governing instrument for some purposes.

Stanbury and Fulton (1984) identify six types of suasion. *Pure political leadership* involves "the use of exhortation by politicians to persuade citizens to alter their beliefs and ultimately their behaviour on the basis of emotional and/or logical appeals without any explicit or implicit inducements to do so." The second type, *suasion with inducements*, consists of exhortation by politicians or bureaucrats that is designed to produce an involuntary change in behaviour with the aid of positive or negative inducements involving the powers of government other than actions approved by the legislature. This form of suasion may be seen as immoral because of the absence of the use of legitimate coercion, that is, the exercise of constitutionally valid powers approved by the majority of the legislature.[33] *Mass suasion*, the third type, is defined by Stanbury and Fulton as "intentionally persuasive advertising or other forms of communication paid for by a government from tax revenues." Advertisements may be designed to alter behaviour directly (e.g., "Stop Smoking," "Drive at 55") or to alter perceptions about the performance of the government (e.g., "Complete energy security for Canada is this close").

The fourth type of suasion is *monitoring and information disclosure*. Here a government agency monitors the behaviour of targetted actors and "encourages the mass media to publicize the activities of those deemed to be behaving in an 'undesirable' way." Although the monitoring agency has no sanctions to, for example, control wages or prices, "the moral force of adverse public opinion is supposed to encourage compliance with the guidelines suggested by government." The most obvious example is that of the Food Prices Review Board (FPRB) described below.

Consultation leading to co-optation is the fifth type of suasion. Actual or potential opponents of government policy are drawn into the decision-making process with a view to co-opting them and "turning them into advocates or at least defenders of what the government intended to do all along." When Peter Ittinuar, the country's first Inuit MP, crossed the floor from the NDP to the Liberals in November 1982, he was described as a "tragic victim of high powered Liberal manipulation."[34] A vocal critic became silent, but found it easier to get money for projects in his riding and to get the government to act on specific problems.

Finally, the sixth type of suasion is the *discreet use of confidential information* or the use of planned "leaks." Stanbury and Fulton (1984) argue that "politicians may 'leak' confidential information to help create a climate of opinion to facilitate planned subsequent actions, or to obtain 'feedback' concerning a possible course of action without having it attributed to them." Bureaucrats may use leaks to influence other departments in battles over policy matters or to alter the behaviour of their own political master.

Examples of the use of suasion are not hard to find.[35]

- The prime minister asks firms and unions in the private sector and the provinces to "voluntarily" comply with federal guidelines for wages and prices of 6 percent this year and 5 percent next year. The PM and other ministers make it clear that firms that don't go along with the government may find the government unwilling to support their requests for loans, grants, etc. (July 1982)
- The federal minister of finance requests the chartered banks to voluntarily "reduce substantially" the volume of loans made to finance the takeover of American-owned firms in Canada. They do so promptly. (July 1981)
- The federal minister of international trade, in light of high levels of unemployment in the Canadian automobile industry, requests the government of Japan to "voluntarily" restrict its manufacturers' exports of cars to Canada. When Japan does not accede to this request, a

"slowdown" is instituted by customs officials at the cars' point of entry. (May 1982)

- The premier of B.C., shortly after hearing of Canadian Pacific Investments' (CPI) planned bid for control of MacMillan Bloedel Ltd., calls a press conference to declare that "B.C. is not for sale." CPI subsequently withdraws its bid, citing the premier's opposition as its reason for doing so. (December 1978)
- Officials of the federal Office of Industrial and Regional Benefits insist that Gulf Resources reopen the bidding on certain equipment for Arctic drilling rigs while bids from Canadian suppliers were sought. The contract was eventually awarded to a Canadian consortium at a price 20 percent above that of a Japanese supplier. (April 1982)
- The Canadian Unity Information Office launches a planned $7-million advertising campaign "to get Canadians talking about the constitution." It is so successful that only one-half the budget is spent. (Fall 1980)
- The minister of national health and welfare, in a series of speeches and press conferences, urges her provincial counterparts to end "extra billing" by doctors and not to allow hospitals to impose user charges, as these "violate the basic philosophy of medicare." (June–November 1983)
- The federal government establishes the Food Prices Review Board in May 1973 amid sharp increases in food prices. Its mandate is to monitor price movements, to inquire into the causes of particular price increases, and to issue reports. This mandate is extended in August 1973 to inquire into any increase in the price of any food that may be unwarranted and to publish a report without delay. The FPRB's work receives enormous coverage in the media.

Stanbury and Fulton (1984) conclude that suasion is "an important governing instrument," one that "is used quite extensively either in conjunction with or prior to the use of other governing instruments."

9.0 SOME IMPLICATIONS FOR BUSINESS

What are some of the implications for the business executive of a high level and broad scope of government activity in the Canadian economy? Probably the initial reaction of many senior executives will be to bemoan their fate. They perceive government as taxing them punitively and constraining their activities at every turn by means of regulation. They see crown corporations competing directly with them in some cases, and they see the operation of the "welfare state" reducing their employees' incentive to work hard. In general, they will feel that they are negotiating with or responding to governments' actions at least as much as they respond to customers, suppliers, and competitors in the marketplace.

9.1 Threats and Opportunities

Other executives, although they also appreciate the less benign aspects of "big government," see in the existing situation a variety of *opportunities* for their shareholders. They see an enormous potential market in the almost one-fifth of GNP made up of exhaustive expenditures by the three levels of government. In short, government could be a big customer resulting in big profits. Second, direct regulation, for example, can be (and has been) designed to protect producers from competition (both domestic and foreign) and permit them to jointly raise prices at the expense of their politically ineffective customers. Third, governments can be a source of capital in the form of loans, loan guarantees, and even equity investments. In addition, there is cash, either in the form of annual subsidies (disguised perhaps) or as a lump sum capital grant. Fourth, the federal government can be used to obtain good old-fashioned tariff protection or new-fashioned nontariff barriers to temper the pressures of international competition. Fifth, by lobbying, business firms, typically through industry associations, can obtain tax expenditures that "give by not taking." The effect of such measures (called "loopholes" by the critics or "tax incentives" by the beneficiaries) is to reduce the effective tax rate in respect to corporate or personal income taxes and sales taxes. These measures are analogous to paying a direct subsidy to the firms or individuals who benefit from them.

Even suasion by governments can be exploited by business firms that can simulate compliance with governments' wishes, while avoiding most of the costs of involuntarily changing their behaviour. Firms may even be able to reverse the direction and convince government to use its powers of persuasion, short of legislative action, to alter the behaviour of employees, foreign competitors, suppliers, and so forth for their benefit.

Figure 3-1 outlines the two faces of government intervention. This approach recognizes that governments *both* constrain the behaviour of profit-oriented business firms and provide them with opportunities to benefit their shareholders and their managers.

Conventionally, business managers, and entrepreneurs in particular, express a distaste for government intervention. They glorify the workings of the market. But it is often true that those with the strongest affection for the market are usually in oligopolistic industries and hence are likely to possess a certain degree of market power. At the same time, the historical record shows unambiguously that Canadian business people have widely and actively sought the benefits of many types of government intervention. The building of the CPR was directly contingent upon federal land grants, cash subsidies, loan guarantees, and a temporary grant of monopoly. The National Policy was, in part, the product of lobbying by Ontario and Quebec manufacturing interests. Trucking regulation was imposed at the behest of trucking companies in the face of allegedly "destructive" competition. Farmers sought government-mandated marketing boards when private cartels failed because of "cheating." The enormous erosion of the corporate income tax is the direct result of business lobbying for tax expenditures. Financial assistance in the form of government loans, loan guarantees, and capital grants originated from the same forces, business lobbying. David Lewis's (1972) charge, more than a decade ago, that at least some businesses had become "corporate welfare bums," while harsh, is not without some basis in fact. Where direct regulation was not the result of business pressure, it is being maintained largely at the behest of those presently regulated. For example, Air Canada and CP Air, and Bell Canada have consistently fought airline and telecommunications deregulation respectively (Stanbury & Thompson 1982a).

In general, therefore, the record seems to reveal that Canadian business people, on balance, have sought government intervention. Perhaps their "free enterprise" rhetoric is simply a reflection of practical cynicism; that is, they want to avoid the real burdens government can impose while benefiting from its actions every way they can. In other words, they are as Janus-faced about government as the rest of us.

9.2 A Conundrum for Business

In determining their position vis-à-vis the state, business people (citizens generally) face a conundrum. In the short run and without respect to any interdependencies, the structure of incentives biases one toward exploiting the potential opportunities in government intervention. Why not try to get government to provide one with cash subsidies, institute protective regulation, grant a tax incentive, or provide capital at less than market rates? The usual marginal calculus applies: continue to spend so as to acquire bounties from government until the marginal cost just equals the expected value of benefits. However, if every business pursues the same strategy, government intervention will almost surely expand. Since such intervention will almost certainly limit individual freedom (admittedly a political value) *and* reduce allocative efficiency, the nation's welfare (at least in terms of GNP per capita) will be less than if the total amount of intervention were less. The loss in efficiency will occur because government intervention in most cases has long since gone far beyond that justified on efficiency grounds, that is, actions designed to remedy various types of market failures, such as public goods, externalities, common property resources, imperfect information, and natural monopoly. For some time, the bulk of government intervention, rhetoric to the contrary, has been designed to alter the distribution of income to favour politically effective groups — usually at considerable expense to allocative efficiency (e.g., Lermer & Stanbury 1984).

Is the expansion of government generally, and in Canada in particu-

Figure 3–1
THE TWO FACES OF GOVERNMENT INTERVENTION

Governing Instrument	Negative Aspects ("Threats")	Beneficial Aspects ("Opportunities")
• Direct expenditures	• "safety net" programs may reduce employees' incentive to work hard • "collective" decision making through the political process instead of decentralized decisions through markets	• government as a major customer (20% of GNP) • may obtain subsidies, grants, and other cash transfers
• Taxes	• depends on incidence, but likely to reduce return on capital, increase input costs, and reduce incentives to work	• may obtain "loopholes" not available to competitors • may obtain tariff protection
• Regulation direct	• can increase costs and restrict entry or other forms of competition	• can benefit regulated firms by controlling competition and facilitating higher prices and returns to shareholders
• Social	• health, safety, and environmental regulation is likely to increase costs	• may be exploited in a competitive context; benefits to the public may be made more apparent than real
• Tax expenditures	• "loopholes" will probably require higher nominal tax rates, hence require increased effort to avoid them	• may sharply reduce effective tax rates; analogous to a subsidy

• Loans and loan guarantees	• may not be able to obtain some benefits as competitors	• may obtain capital below market rates (effectively a subsidy)
• Equity interests (mixed enterprises)	• may require firm to achieve social objectives that reduce profitability	• may be passive investor interested only in financial returns • gov't board members may provide "inside information" on gov't. plans/behaviour
• Crown corporations	• may be an "unfair" competitor (almost infinite financial resources and access to inside information)	• potential customer with a "deep pocket" • sell out at a more favourable price (bail out)
• Suasion	• need to alter economic behaviour involuntarily in face of positive or negative inducements from government, yet no legislative action, i.e., legitimate coercion	• may forestall more coercive, less flexible forms of action; acquiescence may be based on a future quid pro quo
• Chosen instruments*	• may not be able to obtain same benefits as competitors	• could obtain a variety of benefits such as sole source procurement by gov't., cheap loans'guarantees, R & D grants, special tax concessions, etc. • a firm may be able to "choose the government" (e.g., Dome Petroleum & Nova Corp.) and benefit greatly

* See Howard and Stanbury (1984).

lar, attributable to the existence of a fundamental institutional failure? For example, is government action a type of common property resource? (See Fort & Baden 1981.) Are we overusing government because it is a "commons"? If a government is a commons, there will be an incentive for individuals to "grab as much as they can" before others exhaust the finite resource. (Note that the total amount of government activity potentially available is not easy to define, but the easiest way to think of the issue is to think of total expenditures as a common pool of resources.)

Open access to the commons means that too much of it will be exploited or utilized too rapidly in that the potential "rent" (social gain) will *not* be maximized. Rather, entry and exploitation will continue until, at the margin, the additional benefits from capturing and selling the resource will just equal the incremental costs (including the return to capital). In the real world, however, access to government — the ability to get government to act so as to confer benefits on the demander — is not free. Moreover, it appears that the cost of access is not symmetric for all entrants, but it is not so high that many individuals (and firms) are deterred from formulating demands for more government intervention.

The paradox (or is it really a prisoner's dilemma situation?) is that rational, self-interested behaviour produces more government than a majority of individuals want when consulted on an individual basis. It is irrational for a business executive to forego an opportunity to exploit political markets and obtain some form of government bounty. Those who play the game with relatively greater effectiveness will be able to increase their incomes by means of government bounties. The remainder will be worse off than they would be with less government intervention in general. More importantly, GNP per capita will be less than it would be if government's actions were limited to efficiency-improving policies. In that sense, "we are all worse off" because of the overexpansion of the state.

There is yet another form of market failure that limits efforts by individuals or firms to prevent the expansion of the state or actually contract it. Such advocacy is a public good (in the technical sense) and hence is subject to the free-rider effect. Even those who *don't* pay for efforts to block more intervention (or to obtain deregulation) will be able to enjoy its benefits — they can't be excluded. Therefore, unless the *absolute* size of the expected benefits accruing to the individual firm through efforts to prevent more intervention exceeds the costs of the efforts, such efforts will not be forthcoming from rational, self-interested actors.

If trade associations can provide associative benefits or by-products that are divisible, individually appropriable, and, hence, able to exclude nonpayers, they may be able to overcome the public-good aspects of advocating less government intervention.[36] Therefore, more of such advocacy would be supplied. Recently, Becker (1983) has provided a model of interest-group behaviour that offers insights into the role of competition in curbing the excesses of interest-group power.

9.3 Strategic Approach to Government Intervention

The next generation of successful business executives will have to understand how governments function and what motivates politicians (particularly cabinet ministers) and senior bureaucrats. In general, they will have to approach governments in the same *strategic* fashion as they presently deal with competitors, labour unions, and customers.[37] While ideological preferences will hardly disappear, for the sake of the shareholders they will need to be governed by a tough-minded realism about the role governments will play in the economy.

Dome Petroleum and Nova Corp. are widely perceived to have been particularly successful in dealing with governments. What is clear is that these companies, far more than others in the petroleum industry, have been attuned to the energy-policy objectives of the federal government.[38] They have been able to obtain benefits for their shareholders while, for example, responding to government concerns relating to procurement from Canadian sources, exploration in the high Arctic (i.e., Beaufort Sea), cooperation with Petro-Canada, ecological consciousness, the provision of opportunities for native peoples, heavy-oil recovery and upgrading, increased utilization of natural gas through conversion from oil, exploration on Canada Lands, and exploitation of the Alberta tar sands.

One oilman is quoted as saying, "Gallagher [then chairperson of Dome] is the smartest man in Canada, he knows which side his bread is buttered on — both sides." The allusion is to the idea that he made advantageous deals with his free enterprise colleagues *and* with the "socialist" federal government. The *Financial Post* has described both Robert Blair and Jack Gallagher as "politicians par excellence." It was said they had a "sometimes uncanny ability to sense changing political winds and shift their companies' positions so as to make it seem it was they, and not the government, who changed first."[39] The article referred to Blair's skills in leading the Foothills consortium to victory over Canadian Arctic Gas, which was backed by several large multinationals.[40]

Dome's extraordinary ability to respond to federal initiatives and obtain help from Ottawa is best illustrated by its creation of Dome Canada Ltd. shortly after the NEP was announced on October 28, 1980. For a company to get the highest ratio of grants to exploration expenses incurred on Canada Lands (80 percent), 70 percent of its shares had to be owned by Canadian residents. Dome Petroleum was far from qualifying, as over half of its equity is held by Americans. Dome needed the money in a hurry to support its large-scale Beaufort Sea exploration in the summer of 1981 (Foster 1984, chap. 7).

Dome and its legal and financial advisors set to work furiously. Within about a week the Canadian-owned subsidiary idea evolved. Then a target was set to float the new company by the end of 1980. That was impossible, but the draft prospectus was ready by mid-December. In fact, Dome moved so fast it got ahead of the regulation writers in Ottawa. Dome was able to persuade the minister of finance to write a letter that was included in the prospectus stating he would use his discretion in Dome's favour when the new legislation was made law. Thus, Dome Canada raised the largest equity financing in Canadian history.

Where government is so important in the economy, it may well be necessary for large firms to form a symbiotic relationship with it. Both sides must benefit from the relationship. In fact, governments are sometimes vulnerable in that they frequently want to achieve certain political objectives that, if publicly announced, would be difficult to defend. The point for business is to recognize that financial as well as other rewards can be obtained in exchange for performing "political chores."

While the new skills to deal successfully with governments will not be sufficient to ensure a large corporation's financial success, they are very likely to be necessary ones.

NOTES

1. See Ian Austen, "The Tory-Business Honeymoon," *Maclean's*, November 12, 1984, pp. 48-49, 50-52; and *Maclean's*, November 19, 1984, pp. 12-19, 60.

2. Deborah McGregor, "Tories relationship with business turns chilly," *Financial Times*, July 1, 1985, pp. 1, 12, and editorial, p. 9. See also Hyman Solomon, " 'Critics misjudge us': Brian Mulroney blames business for being too harsh on the Tories," *Financial Post*, February 23, 1986, pp. 1-2.

3. The information on the size, scope, and growth of governments in Canada is scattered, and it cannot be meaningfully combined into a single quantitative indicator of the magnitude of intervention. Therefore, it is necessary to proceed by examining seven of the major governing instruments independently. The list is not exhaustive. For example, Myles Foster (1984a, 6-9) indicates some fourteen ways that a government can act to increase the amount of employment in a particular region. He notes that "only three of the fourteen examples . . . necessarily involve increases in cash requirements and that most of them would not be reported in any part of the Public Accounts."

4. Myles Foster illustrates how a government can employ instruments that are less visible than direct expenditures:

For example, the provision of a government loan of $10 million will be reported as an increase in government outlays and, under the PEMS system, will decrease the remaining funds available in an "envelope" by $10 million; having a Crown corporation (like the Federal Business Development Bank) provide the $10 million will require a federal government equity investment in FBDB of $1 million and the other $9 million will be borrowed by FBDB in the market, an increase of $1 million in reported government outlays (and a decrease in "envelope" reserves); to have a chartered bank lend the $10 million under one of many guaranteed loan programs will have no effect on reported outlays or "envelope" reserves — it will merely increase the government's contingent liabilities. (1984a, 9)

5. This list is not exhaustive. "Chosen instruments" are discussed in Howard and Stanbury (1984), and taxes are discussed in Pipes and Walker (1984). Moreover, Myles Foster (1984a, 5) argues that loans and guarantees are effectively two different instruments and that regulation includes at least four distinct types of instruments: licensing, tariffs, quotas, price controls, in addition to the conventional health, safety, and fairness regulations.

6. Government of Canada, *Estimates, 1985–86* (Ottawa: Minister of Supply and Services, 1985), Part I, p. 36. In current dollars, expenditures were expected to be $102.5 billion in 1985/86.

7. The major difference between total transfers (excluding intergovernmental transfers) and transfers to persons is interest on the public debt. Because of very large federal deficits and substantial provincial deficits, interest payments have become a large component of government expenditures, particularly at the federal level. See Economic Council 1984, chap. 3; Canadian Tax Foundation 1985; and Minister of Finance, *A New Direction for Canada: An Agenda for Economic Renewal* (Ottawa: November 8, 1984). "Provincial deficits expected to lower credit standings," *Globe and Mail*, July 23, 1985, p. B16. The minister of finance estimates that the federal net public debt will rise from 45% of GNP in 1984/85 to over 63% in 1990/91. In 1974/75 it was only 16.6% of GNP.

8. We should note that for 1980 the Department of Finance estimated the total of personal income tax expenditures at $23.4 billion (Government of Canada 1980). The total was calculated by Howard and Stanbury (1984), while the department emphasizes that "the revenue impact of simultaneously eliminating two tax expenditures is generally not the same as the sum of their individual revenue impacts." Five items accounted for 66% of the 1980 total: RPP/RRSPs ($2600 million), the marital exemption ($1055 million), the nontaxation of capital gains on principal residences ($3500 million), the nontaxation of imputed income on owner-occupied houses ($5000

million), and transfers of "income tax" room to the provinces concerning shared-cost programs ($275 million).

9. See Linda McQuaig, "Research credits cost $2.6 billion," *Globe and Mail*, January 29, 1986, p. A8. For earlier estimates, see "Dumped research tax credit seen by feds as $2 billion loss," Vancouver *Sun*, June 5, 1985, p. A9; Jack Danylchuk, "Tax credit scheme draws criticism," Vancouver *Sun*, June 5, 1984, p. D1; Margaret Munro and Tom Barrett, "Costly R and D tax dodge spelled razzle dazzle," Vancouver *Sun*, June 22, 1985, pp. A1–A2; Giles Gherson, "Tax credit party gives Ottawa costly hangover," *Financial Post*, July 6, 1985, p. 4; Peter Ladner, "While the getting was good," *Canadian Business*, February 1985, pp. 88–95; and "Firm seeks to unload tax credits," *Globe and Mail*, May 17, 1985, p. B4.

10. See Linda McQuaig, "Scientists are worried by research tax credit," *Globe and Mail*, June 11, 1984, p. 14.

11. For a more recent estimate, see Khemani (1986).

12. See Department of Transport, *Freedom to Move: A Framework for Transportation Reform* (Ottawa: Department of Transport, July 1985).

13. See Hudson Janisch and Y. Kurisaki, "Reform of telecommunications regulation in Japan and Canada," *Telecommunications Policy*, March 1985, pp. 31–39; and Globerman and Stanbury (1986).

14. See "Hanging Out the Welcome Sign [to Foreign Investors]," *Time*, December 24, 1984, p. 22; "Changes planned for investment bill," Vancouver *Sun*, April 16, 1985, p. C5; and Bruce Little, "New Agency strives to erase FIRA's memory," *Globe and Mail*, July 8, 1985, p. B1.

15. See Giles Gherson, "High hopes ride on energy deal," *Financial Post*, April 6, 1985, pp. 1–2; Nicholas Hunter, "Post-deregulation price war seen possible for gasoline," *Globe and Mail*, May 8, 1985, pp. B1, B10; Giles Gherson, "Tories edge toward oil deregulation," *Financial Post*, October 20, 1984, pp. 1–2; and "The burial of the NEP," *Maclean's*, April 8, 1985, pp. 11–12.

16. See Government of Canada, (Green Paper) *The Regulation of Canadian Financial Institutions* (Ottawa: Department of Finance, April 1985); and Ontario Task Force on Financial Institutions, *Interim Report* (Toronto: Queen's Printer for Ontario, December 1984).

17. See Mike Macbeth, "Getting along without the little extras" [re. discount brokers], *Canadian Business*, August 1985, pp. 27–30; and John D. Todd, *Price Competition in the Canadian Securities Industry: A Test Case of Deregulation* (Toronto: Ontario Economic Council, 1983).

18. See, for example, Economic Council (1979, 1981) and Stanbury (1980).

19. Foster (1984b) also shows that loans to, investments in, and guarantees of federal crown corporations increased from $2.033 billion
in 1950 to $11.725 billion in 1970 and then to $32.2 billion in 1980
and $41.25 billion in 1983 (in current dollars).

20. Statistics Canada, *Corporations and Labour Unions Returns Act,
Report for 1981, Part I Corporations* (Ottawa, March 1984), Cat.
no. 61-210.

21. As of December 1984, total federal employment was as follows:

	Number	%
• Civil service	224,026	38.4
• Government enterprises	135,753	23.3
• Canada Post	74,981	12.9
• Military personnel	85,151	14.6
• RCMP uniformed personnel	18,468	3.2
• Political and short-term employees	12,454	2.1
• Other	32,390	5.5

(Vancouver *Sun*, June 17, 1985, p. B12)

More generally, see Stanbury and Doern (1985).

22. Loan guarantees are for specific transactions (e.g., export contracts)
while credit insurance is available to a class of lenders (e.g., the
Canada Deposit Insurance Corporation). Loans by the federal and
provincial governments increased from $6.7 billion in 1970 to $19.1
billion in 1980 (ECC 1982, 3).

23. Paul Taylor, "Ottawa, provinces to back Husky loans," *Globe and
Mail*, June 7, 1984, p. B1. See also *Financial Post*, June 16, 1984,
p. 4.

24. The Economic Council was able to include agencies and programs
that accounted for "almost 80 percent of public loans outstanding
to the four sectors under consideration, as of March 31, 1979" (1982a,
132-33).

25. In 1984 and 1985 the federal and provincial governments moved
to prevent the failure of a number of financial institutions based in
Western Canada. See, for example, *Globe and Mail*, April 3, 1985,
p. B1; "Trouble at Western Trusts," *Maclean's*, January 28, 1985,
p. 38; "A last-minute bank rescue" (Canadian Commercial Bank),
Maclean's, April 8, 1985, pp. 30-33. More generally, see "PC bailout policy echoes that of Grits," *Globe and Mail*, April 29, 1985,
p. B1; and "The sinkers and the swimmers," *Canadian Business*,
January 1985, pp. 43-59.

Total Bank of Canada loans to troubled banks as of August 7,
1985, totalled $1.8 billion, up from $903 million in May 1985. "Before
this year, the total figure was usually under $100 million." "Bank of
Canada bailouts reach $1.8 billion," *Globe and Mail*, August 17,
1985, p. B5. Subsequently, the cost of the bailouts rose to about

$2.5 billion when the Canadian Commercial Bank and the North-land Bank failed in September 1985.

26. Howard and Stanbury (1984) also discuss the equity investments of the Alberta Energy Corp. (now 45% owned by the Province of Alberta) and the Alberta Heritage Savings Trust Fund.

27. Caisse de Dépôt, *Annual Report*, 1984. By comparison, as of June 30, 1982, the Canada Pension Plan Investment Fund had assets of $21.6 billion earning an average return of 9.92% (*Globe and Mail*, September 13, 1982, p. 6). As of March 31, 1983, the Alberta Heritage Savings Trust Fund had assets of $13 billion. As of December 31, 1983, the Caisse had total assets of $18.2 billion (*Globe and Mail*, March 23, 1984, p. B10). On December 31, 1983, the Heritage Fund had $13.5 billion in assets — including $2.0 billion in "deemed assets" in the funds capital projects division (*Globe and Mail*, March 21, 1984, p. 2).

28. The Caisse's *Annual Report* does not provide information on the fraction of shares that it holds in individual companies, only the number and their market value.

29. Quoted in David Olive, "Caisse unpopulaire," *Canadian Business*, May 1982, p. 96.

30. Tabulated by the author from the Caisse's 1984 *Annual Report*.

31. The importance of the Caisse's 30% interest in Brascade Resources, 70% of which is owned by Brascan Ltd., which now effectively controls Noranda Mines through its 42% equity holding, should not be understated. Noranda is itself an enormous enterprise that combines both operating companies and conglomerate holdings. For example, in 1981 it had sales of $3.03 billion (ranked 19th on the Financial Post 500) and assets of $5.25 billion. But these data understate Noranda's economic reach. Consider the following partial list of Noranda's holdings: 49.8% of MacMillan Bloedel Ltd., Canada's largest forest-products company and #36 on the F.P. 500; 100% of Maclaren Power and Paper; 75% of Canadian Hunter Exploration (one of Canada's largest holders of natural gas reserves); 42% of Tara Exploration; 33% of Placer Development (#227); 20% of Craigmont Mines; 51% of Brenda Mines; 50% of Wire Rope Industries; 100% of Canada Wire and Cable; 44% of Kerr-Addison Mines; 64% of Fraser Inc. (#155); 64% of Brunswick Mining (#246); and 49% of Pamour Porcupine Mines. Note that Brascan, the Caisse's partner in Brascade, is controlled by Edper Equities, which is controlled by only two men, Edward and Peter Bronfman. For more recent information on Brascan, see Richard Spence, "Edper's astounding reach," *Financial Times*, January 9, 1984, pp. 1, 18.

32. See Robert Block, "Provinces' equity programs experience boom in popularity," *Financial Post*, February 23, 1985.

33. For an example, see "Oil firms angry with Ottawa over energy grant 'strings,' " *Financial Post*, January 14, 1984, pp. 1-2.
34. "MP's 12-month trip to oblivion," *Globe and Mail*, November 21, 1983, p. 8.
35. For more details, see Stanbury and Fulton (1984).
36. See the discussion in Olson (1971) and in Coleman and Jacek (1983).
37. See, for example, Gillies (1981), McMillan and Murray (1983) and Bartha (1985b).
38. See Bregha (1981), Foster (1980), Crane (1982), Lyon (1983) and Foster (1984).
39. "The business leader as politician," *Financial Post*, December 13, 1980, p. 18.
40. See Probyn (1977), Dizard (1977), and Bregha (1981).

4

The Political Economy of Policy Making

1.0 INTRODUCTION

This chapter deals with four major issues: the nature and many forms that public policy takes (section 3); the characteristics of the federal policy-making process that are particularly relevant to interest groups concerned with influencing public policy (section 4); policy making and the public interest (section 5); and the public choice approach to understanding how public policy is made in a democracy (sections 6–8). While this book does not include a chapter on the details of the policy-making process,[1] it does examine some of those aspects of the process that are highly relevant to efforts by interest groups to influence policy — see section 4. Nor does this book examine the various normative bases (what ought to be) of public policy actions, which fall into three broad categories: (1) intervention to improve the efficiency with which resources are allocated, largely by overcoming various market failures; (2) intervention to alter the distribution of income, wealth, or consumption opportunities; and (3) intervention to create individual or collective rights. There are several reasons for this choice. First, many books in the public finance and public policy literatures address this subject.[2] Second, space limitations prevent a proper treatment of the subject. Finally, and most importantly, individuals interested in influencing public policy through interest groups would be better served by an understanding of the positive theories of public policy rather than the normative arguments for government intervention.

Therefore, in sections 6 to 8 I focus on the positive theory of public choice, which offers a more realistic and insightful explanation of the underlying forces that produce policy initiatives by governments that affect the private sector. While the discussion is conducted at a fairly high level of abstraction, readers should be able both to understand the key elements of the theory and to apply them to particular policies they are analyzing.

Note: Parts of this chapter are adapted from Stanbury and Thain (1986).

2.0 THE CONCEPT OF PUBLIC POLICY

Public policy is defined in various ways. The Policy Studies Organization defines policy as "actual and potential government programs and actions designed to cope with various social problems."[3] This is a very broad definition, and it has the disadvantage of implying that public policies are aimed only at social problems. American political scientist Robert Salisbury offers a somewhat more detailed definition: "Public policy consists in authoritative or sanctioned decisions by governmental actors. It refers to the 'substance' of what government does and is to be distinguished from the processes by which decisions are made. Policy here means the outcomes or outputs of governmental processes" (1968, 152). In the same vein, Theodore Lowi defines policy as "simply any output of any decision maker, whether it be an individual or a collectivity, a small collectivity or a large one, a government or a non-government" (1970, 317).

Mark Nadel notes that "the line between public and private policies is sharply drawn, the line between public and private organizations has not been so exact" (1975, 5). Some corporations, simply by their size (e.g., General Motors, Canadian Pacific), take on many of the characteristics of a public organization, although it is not true to say they are truly public entities. They do, however, have an impact far beyond their relationships with customers and suppliers. Nadel offers strong support for the idea that "a significant amount of public policy is made by corporations and other private governments without having to go through formal government authority" (1975, 32).

In his discussion of the definition of public policy, Nadel (1975, 33-34) notes several of the conceptual differences that bedevil the definition. First, there is the distinction between policy outputs and outcomes: "Outputs are the formally announced decisions and intended consequences of government action. Outcomes are the second order effects of policies and the overall real world effects of policies." Because many public policies and programs have a variety of goals that are seldom defined in operational terms, it is even difficult to determine their "intended consequences." Moreover, the stated goals may not be the real goals. Finally, outcomes inconsistent with intended consequences may occur, not because of an implementation failure, but because of changes in other variables entirely beyond the control of the policy maker.

Second, there is the problem of conceptualizing the output of public policies. In the case of public education, for example, is the output of the policy merely the number of dollars spent on education (which could be considered to be a measure of input), or is it the number of people achieving a certain level of education? When it comes to government programs designed to "enhance national unity" or to "strengthen the cultural fabric of Canada," how do we define and measure the output of such programs? Obviously there will be a high degree of subjectivity in doing so.

Third, public policies need to be distinguished from decisions (see Lowi 1970). While decisions are essential components of a policy, each decision is not a policy. Hartle draws the distinction by saying that a policy change can be defined "as a change in a decision-making rule (which can be explicit or implicit) and a decision made in accordance with such a rule [is] a non-policy decision" (1979, 70). The crucial attribute of the determination of a policy is the exercise of discretion by a legitimate authority as to both goals and the means to achieve them in broad terms. Decisions in this context are choices in which discretion is tightly circumscribed. However, as Hartle points out, in a formal hierarchy, there is a cascade of authority and hence "what constitutes a 'policy' depends entirely upon where the observer cuts into the inevitable hierarchy of policies. . . . A change in the coffee break rules goes unnoticed by the deputy minister and certainly the minister. It is a policy decision as seen by the clerks!" (1979, 70–71).

Fourth, there is the problem of symbolic policies[4] in which there is a designed gap between what is announced (and perhaps perceived by citizens) and the outputs and outcomes of the policy. This raises the question of whether a public policy should be defined in terms of its intended consequences, the public's *perception* of its intended consequences, or the actual consequences in terms of outcomes.

In their book, which they claim "provides the first reasonably integrated examination of public policy making in Canada," Doern and Phidd (1983, 34) argue that the public policy system is a subcomponent of the political system and that "it consists of an amalgam and interplay of ideas, numerous structures . . . , and processes." For them, the main features of public policy and the policy system involve:

- expressions of normative intent and therefore of ideas, values, and purposes;
- the exercise and structuring of power, influence, and legitimate coercion;
- process, including not only the need to deal with uncertainty but also with equally normative judgments about the legitimacy and fairness of the dynamic processes used to develop policy;
- changing or sustaining human behaviour in desired ways, in short, implementing desired behaviour; and
- a series of decisions and nondecisions.

3.0 GOVERNMENT ACTIONS THAT EMBODY PUBLIC POLICY

As we have seen, "public policy" is a broad concept. However, when many people hear it, they think of government programs stemming directly from statutes enacted by Parliament or a provincial legislature. While virtually all public policies may be traced back to their legislative foundations in the form of a statute authorizing a particular action by government, the legislative base for most public policy as it affects business (and other interest groups) on a day-to-day basis may not be apparent. In general terms, we think of public policy as various expressions of the will of a government designed to modify the behaviour of citizens that are ultimately backed up by the legitimate (constitutional) coercive powers of the state granted by a democratically elected legislature. Using this concept, I note that the "bottom line" of a firm can be affected materially by the many ways that public policy is made or expressed. These are outlined in Figure 4-1.

Public policy is most obviously embodied in new legislation or amendments to existing legislation, that is, statutes enacted by Parliament or a provincial legislature (municipal bylaws would also be included here). Certainly a widely debated new statute is the most dramatic and obvious instrument of public policy. But it is only one of many expressions of public policy. It would be a major mistake for interest groups to concentrate all or even much of their efforts in seeking to influence new legislation (including amendments). The fact is that a great deal of law (let alone policy) is *not* enacted by the legislature. The consequences of many statutes are only understandable by reference to the regulations

Figure 4–1
ACTIONS BY GOVERNMENT THAT EMBODY PUBLIC POLICY

- New statutes enacted by the legislature
- Amendments to existing legislation
- Subordinate legislation that does not require approval of the legislature, i.e., regulations, and orders-in-council that need be approved only by the cabinet or a single minister
- Formal decisions of regulatory agencies to grant a licence, alter the terms of a licence, set tariffs, or otherwise constrain private sector decisions
- Authoritative decisions of the courts (precedents)
- Cabinet appeal decisions (from the decisions of regulatory agencies)
- The exercise of discretion by line departments and regulatory agencies in day-to-day dealings with private sector firms. This involves budget allocations, application of regulations, and the interpretation of policy guidelines, internal policy manuals, or external interpretation bulletins
- Ministerial policy statements (in the legislature, in the form of press releases, or internal guidelines to bureaucrats)
- The revenue budget, i.e., changes in tax policy including tax expenditures
- The annual *Estimates*, i.e., expenditure allocations among departments and agencies
- Central agency (Treasury Board, PCO, auditor general) directives to line departments that affect that department's "clients"

passed by the cabinet (not the legislature) pursuant to the statute. As important are the operational interpretations of statutes made by senior bureaucrats who direct the administration of statutes and regulations, as well as the less frequent but important formal interpretations made by the courts.

Because the enactment of new statutes (or amendments) is so visible, uninformed students of government tend to spend too much time on this one expression of public policy and too little on the other less visible, more arcane, but nevertheless important instruments of public policy.

One of the least understood, but most important, instruments of public policy consists of new subordinate legislation (or amendments), including regulations, orders, and other statutory instruments such as orders-in-council. Subordinate legislation has the same force of law as a statute, but it is not enacted (and this is a common practice) by the legislature (see Anderson 1980). Rather, it is approved by cabinet (more precisely, the governor in council) or, in some cases, by an individual minister or even by an "independent" regulatory agency. Where broadly worded statutes are enacted, their real force and effect usually depends upon the regulations that are made pursuant to them at a later date. Orders-in-council are made by the cabinet and amount to legislation by fiat without reference to the elected legislature. When the legislature is not in session, the cabinet can effectively vote itself money to run the government by means of governor general's warrants. The point is that cabinet, by means of literally thousands of orders-in-council each year, can make law over a very wide domain without the approval of a majority of the democratically elected legislature.[5] No wonder the cabinet has been described as a periodically elected, collective kingship.

Public policy is also embedded in policy announcements by a minister — these involve "official" interpretations of existing legislation (statutes and regulations) and are designed to act as guidance for departments, agencies, and those currently or potentially affected by a government policy. For example, the federal government's air carrier policy in the 1960s and 1970s was to be found in large part in a series of press releases on ministerial statements, most of which were not even made in the House of Commons. Yet the Air Transport Committee of the Canadian Transport Commission was guided by these policy statements in making its decisions on individual cases under the Aeronautics Act, Air Carrier Regulations, and other statutes. Unfortunately, a department's policy position is often hard to determine for several reasons. First, there may be a policy vacuum on certain issues. Second, there may be conflicting statements of policy. This is not surprising given the multiplicity of policy objectives and the serial attention to different goals over time. Third, the public servant administrators may claim they are speaking "for the department," that is, in the name of the minister, although there may be no documentation available by which a firm or interest goup can verify that what is said to be the policy is, in fact, sanctioned by the minister responsible. Attempts at verification may create waves with adverse consequences for the individual or organization questioning the lower-level bureaucrat.

A related type of policy statement consists of interpretation guidelines issued by specific departments or agencies. The most famous example is the *Interpretation Bulletins* of the Department of National Revenue (DNR), which now cover at least four feet of shelf space. In effect, these state how DNR officials interpret the Income Tax Act and related statutes, until such time as (1) Parliament enacts new legislation or the cabinet passes new regulations; (2) the Tax Appeal Board alters its more authoritative interpretation of the statutes/regulations; or (3) until a regular court of appeal, ultimately the Supreme Court of Canada, states a new, authoritative interpretation of the legislation. The most sophisticated tax practitioners know there is yet another layer of "policy" in dealing with DNR. This consists of formal individual "advance rulings" and the chancier informal ruminations of senior officials of DNR when faced with new and highly imaginative "tax planning" measures brought to their attention by the tax advisors of individuals and firms. (See, for example, the ruling that saved Olympia and York some $111 million in its takeover of Gulf Canada described below.)

Public policy is also expressed in the decisions of the hundreds of regulatory boards and agencies.[6] They make decisions on thousands of individual cases, as do the regular courts of law. The regulators' task is to apply various statutes and regulations to specific cases. On doing so, agencies like the CRTC set prices (telephone rates, cable TV rates) and determine who will be allowed to enter the industry, whether a merger can take place, and whether a licence should be revoked for failure to meet the performance guidelines established by the agency. For a high fraction of regulatory agencies, their decisions may be appealed to the cabinet. Decisions pursuant to these "political appeals" are means by which the government of the day can modify public policy on a case-by-case basis without having to obtain the approval of the legislature or even announcing their new direction in the legislature. The cabinet can engage in an exercise in "discretionary accountability." See Janisch (1979) and ECC (1979).

Public policy is also made by the regular courts as they interpret statutes and regulations in tens of thousands of individual cases that wend their way through the trial court, court of appeal, and eventually the Supreme Court of Canada. (Until 1949 the highest court of appeal for Canadians was the House of Lords in Britain.) While judges often say they only interpret the law, their interpretations are authoritative until a higher court provides a new interpretation or the legislature changes the legislation. In the 1840s Chief Justice Taney of the U.S. Supreme Court stated: "It is the province of the court to expound the law, and not to make it." Yet, to paraphrase another, later justice of the court: the Constitution is what the judges of the Supreme Court say it is from time to time. At the same time, to quote Justice Cardozo writing in 1921, "a judge is not a knight-errant roaming at will in pursuit of his own ideal of beauty or of goodness." However, it must be recognized that the words of the Constitution Act of 1982, for example, are very general in many places. It is left to the courts to determine in a practical sense the meaning of those words. As a result, there has been a virtual explosion of cases requiring interpretation under the new Charter of Rights and Freedoms.

The "plain meaning" of the words is of particular significance in the Canadian context because, following the British tradition of statutory interpretation, our courts do not as a rule — in contrast to the U.S. — seek to determine the meaning intended by the legislators who passed the statute under consideration. Rather, Canadian courts focus on what the legislators actually wrote as evidence of their intent. But that does not in any way reduce the problem of discerning the meaning, for example, of section 2(b) of the Charter of Rights and Freedoms, which states that "Everyone has the following freedoms: . . . freedom of thought, belief, opinion and expression, including freedom of the press and other media of communication . . . ." The task is not made any easier by section 1, which qualifies these rights and freedoms by saying they are "subject only to such reasonable limits prescribed by law as can be demonstrably justified in a free and democratic society." So we may have come full circle. It is to be left to the courts to determine what statutory constraints on freedom of thought and freedom of the press, and so on, "can be demonstrably justified in a free and democratic society."

For most people in their day-to-day dealings with government departments, government policy is effectively embodied in the exercise of discretion by senior bureaucrats and individual ministers. Anisman (1975, 23) identified some 14 885 specific discretionary powers in the federal statutes of 1970. He defined discretionary powers as including "any decision in which the result is not predetermined by statute." He continues, "They therefore comprise decisions involving a choice whether to exercise a power, decisions concerning the manner in which a power is to be exercised and, as well, any matter involving judgment, for example, a decision as to whether a particular set of circumstances exists or has existed" (1975,2). The focus of his research was on discretionary powers explicitly conferred in statutes, and he classified them into 5938 judicial powers, 2933 administrative powers, 1298 investigative powers, and 3468 rulemaking powers. Anisman stresses that his catalogue shows only the tip of the iceberg of discretionary powers subordinate to Parliament (1975,23).

One of the hallmarks of Canada's approach to economic regulation (both direct and social), for example, is the large amount of discretion delegated by the legislature to specialized agencies, senior bureaucrats, and individual ministers. The federal Department of Fisheries, in particular, gives the minister wide scope in the granting of licences. The application of ministerial discretion is well illustrated by the following newspaper article:

Mr. Snarby [a Nova Scotia fisherman] approached the Department of Fisheries last November to obtain a charter replacement for a [repossessed] freezer trawler he was in the process of buying from the Nova Scotia Government. . . . Mr. Snarby and his partner, Steiner Engeset, . . . said they never intended to use it for fishing because it was unsuitable for their purposes. Instead, they wanted to transfer its licence to another vessel while they had a replacement built in Norway. . . . Mr. Engeset said they tried to go through the civil servants, "but they made it difficult for us. They are the ones who should be looked into. They are there to help fishermen, not to get in the way."

Under federal policy, two-year charters of fishing vessels are permitted if a licenced Canadian fishing vessel is unexpectedly removed from the fishing fleet for a period greater than four months. The policy allows a fisherman who has lost a vessel through fire or sinking to fish under a foreign-flag charter until a permanent replacement can be acquired. These short-term charter replacements are supposed to follow a number of policy guidelines set out by the Department of Fisheries. One of the guidelines says that "the charter vessel is to be of similar catching capacity" as the vessel being replaced. Since Mr. Snarby wanted to replace the 157-foot "Martin and Philip" with the 196-foot "Osprey," Fisheries officials would not approve the charter application and referred Mr. Snarby to the Minister. Though they approved the fishing licence for Mr. Snarby, they wanted him to use the "Martin and Philip."

"The department was against approving his application because it was on the very margin of the federal policy," Dr. Art May, deputy minister of Fisheries, said in an interview. "For one thing, the 'Martin and Philip' hadn't exactly been unexpectedly taken out of services, as the policy allows for; it was being sold offshore. For another, the vessels were not of similar catch capacity. We felt that, at some point, Mr. Snarby would have to come back to us for an increased enterprise allocation to economically fish the 'Osprey.' It was a decision that only the minister could make. . . . " After the meeting, Mr. Fraser [the minister] told his officials that he wanted Mr. Snarby's problem solved. He later sent a Telex to Mr. Snarby approving his charter application subject to certain conditions, one of which was that he accept the enterprise allocation of the smaller "Martin and Philip" for his larger replacement vessel, the "Osprey." Mr. Snarby agreed, though he has since approached the department to

transfer additional enterprise allocation to the "Osprey."[7] [This will
require another discretionary decision!]

Another excellent example of the exercise of discretion, in this case
by the Department of National Revenue, concerns a revaluation of a
refinery involved in Olympia and York's acquisition of control of Gulf
Canada from its American owner, Chevron Corp., and subsequent sale
to Petro-Canada.[8] The effect of the revaluation was to reduce DNR's tax
revenues by $111 million, and this amounts to a subsidy or gift to the
Reichmann family — Canada's wealthiest — of the same amount. It has
been suggested that the Reichmanns would not have acquired Gulf Canada — thus "Canadianizing" it — without this highly favourable tax ruling from the federal government. In other words, the cabinet made a
policy decision to use $111 million in public funds (revenue foregone) to
permit one of the nation's largest conglomerate enterprises to become
much larger. Subsequently, it was revealed that the benefits of tax rulings were some $500 million.[9]

On an annual basis, one of the most important and insightful indicators of a government's policies is how it raises and spends its money. At
the federal level, the government's planned expenditures are embodied
in the several volumes of the *Estimates* introduced in Parliament in the
spring of each year. In 1985/86 the federal government will spend about
$105 billion but will collect only $70 billion in taxes and other revenues.
Unless authorized by parliamentary approval of the *Estimates*, no planned
program or activity that requires the expenditure of public funds can
be carried on.[10] While approval of the *Estimates* is a formality, they do
embody a reasonably good indication of a government's priorities. For
example, the Liberals voted over $100 million annually to subsidize two
heavy-water plants in Cape Breton (in the riding of Allan MacEachen,
the deputy prime minister). In 1984/85, taxpayers paid some $130 000
for each person-year associated with the plants that produced a product
for which there was no market. The new Tory minister of finance in his
May 1985 budget ordered that the two plants be closed and the area
made a virtual tax-free zone for corporations willing to locate there.[11]

Changes in policy priorities may involve much less money. While
frequently endorsing science and technology as important factors in
Canada's economic development, the Tories cut the budget of the Science Council of Canada by one-half in 1985.[12] This illustrates a crucial
point: one should watch what a government does (e.g., the money it
spends) rather than what it says (e.g., its rhetoric).

On the revenue side, the new Tory minister of finance proposed a
number of changes in the tax system in 1985 that indicated different
values and priorities than his Liberal predecessor. For example, capital
gains to a lifetime maximum of $500 000 will be exempt from income
tax, limits on contributions to Registered Retirement Savings Plans
(RRSPs) are to be increased substantially over several years, exemptions

and deductions were partially de-indexed, a surtax on personal income was imposed, and the excise tax on gasoline was increased by two cents per litre.[13]

Doern and Phidd (1983, 103) explain that there can be "policies without resources" to support them. Resources include money (taxes and spending), personnel, time, and political will. "Many governments find it necessary to enunciate policy to express their concern about, and support for, a particular constituency or group, since this is usually preferable to expressing no public concern whatsoever." In other words, the policy consists of rhetoric and does not utilize one or more of the various governing instruments — except exhortation — to achieve a substantive change in the behaviour of individuals or groups. This takes us into the world of symbolic politics. The object is to show concern, to temporize, to husband scarce resources whose expenditure may produce little or no substantive result — but above all, to be seen to be "doing something" in response to interest-group pressures or the politician's identification of a latent concern of important groups of voters. Policies embodying traditional governing instruments, in practice, may be largely symbolic because they have not been given the resources (money, administrative power, personnel) to do more than "show the flag."[14]

4.0 UNDERSTANDING THE FEDERAL POLICY-MAKING PROCESS

Dan Fenn has correctly emphasized that "the efforts of business [to influence public policy] would be greatly enhanced if it had a clearer, more comprehensive model of the government decision-making process. It is difficult to develop a coherent strategy and a set of tactics appropriate to a given situation without a useable sense of how and why decisions get made in government" (1979, 144–45). In other words, interest groups need to learn how the policy-making process functions in practice so that they can be more effective in influencing policy outcomes. The purpose of this section, therefore, is to identify some of the important characteristics of the policy-making process at the federal level as they relate to efforts to influence public policy.

4.1 Varied and Complex

The policy-making process in Canada at both the federal and provincial level is variegated, complex, and dynamic. Van Loon makes a telling point when he says that "any description of planning processes in Ottawa has only an ephemeral value — making it incumbent on the wise reader to consult sources such as newspapers, magazines and journals for the latest grey pattern of the kaleidoscope" (1985, 432). Textbooks and articles describe the institutions and processes by which new legislation is created, but they suffer from two major failings. The first, as implied by Van Loon, is that subtle but important shifts occur fairly frequently; hence, it is hard to avoid being out of date with respect to the latest "wrinkles," and where an interest group doesn't understand the subtleties of the process as it applies to the case at hand, it is likely to be less effective in influencing policy. Second, and in my view more important, there is inadequate published material on numerous forms of policy making that do not require the approval of the legislature. As emphasized in section 3 above, there are a variety of policy actions that can have a great impact on a firm, an industry, or members of other interest groups that do not stem directly from action by the legislature (e.g., subordinate legislation; the exercise of discretion). In other words, rather than one complex process, there are at least several different complex processes that must be understood if a major business group is to succeed in influencing public policy.

4.2 Many Actors: Who Has Power?

The number of individuals and groups having some role in shaping a particular public policy can be quite large — see Figure 7-2 in chapter 7. However, in a few instances, very few people will have shaped the policy action. In the former case, an interest group has to set priorities and allocate its scarce resources so as to produce the greatest expected effect. Unfortunately, it is not always easy to determine a priori (1) who the key actors in a given situation are, (2) which actors are likely to have the greatest influence in the proposed policy, and (3) which of the more influential targets is likely to be more amenable to the appeals of the interest group. Like war, lobbying is conducted in a fog of uncertainty.

The identity and importance of different individuals and groups (e.g., committees) in the federal policy-making process can vary greatly depending upon the type of policy action that is being taken, that is, a ministerial policy statement versus a decision by a regulatory agency versus an entirely new statute. In order to influence public policy, it is necessary to identify the important targets for each of a number of different types of policy actions. This is discussed in more detail in chapter 7. Furthermore, the degree of influence or power exercised by various actors in the policy-making process is, not surprisingly, quite unequal. As lobbying is about the use of power, it is often critical to appreciate which of the relevant actors has how much power in the case at hand.

> The basic [power] centers are always there — the legislature, the chief executive, the media, other agencies, the bureaucracy, interested groups, the decision maker and his or her boss — but the amount of clout they hold or exercise varies. Those shifts are, obviously, crucial to trace if an "interested group" is to participate effectively in the policy-making process. (Fenn 1979, 152)

Moreover, the degree of influence exercised by an actor is not constant across different policy issues. For example, on a piece of new legislation which he deems is a priority, the prime minister may strongly influence the content of a bill and have it expedited through both the preparliamentary and parliamentary phases of the process. On the other hand, the prime minister may have no influence on the decision of the CRTC with respect to a rate increase proposed by Bell Canada. (The prime minister could play a role if the cabinet decides to hear an appeal from the regulatory agency's decision, although such appeals are not routine and the cabinet refuses to hear a substantial fraction of them.)

In the matter of the rancid tuna fish, which made the headlines for several days in September 1985, it was the minister of fisheries (John Fraser) who first exercised his discretion to permit the sale of about one million cans of tuna produced under Star-Kist brand in April — over the recommendations of his own inspectors. Apparently he did so out of his concern for some 400 jobs in the New Brunswick cannery and after obtaining information from another laboratory outside his department. The minister was also lobbied by Premier Hatfield of Nova Scotia and by his cabinet colleague James Kelleher, whose riding is close to the cannery. When a storm of controversy erupted following a television show that revealed the minister of fisheries' exercise of discretion, he reversed his position. However, it soon became clear that he did so because Prime Minister Mulroney personally made the decision to order the tuna from the grocers' shelves. A few days later Fraser resigned as minister of fisheries. Therefore, in this case, there were three different decision makers involved: the inspectors in the Department of Fisheries (middle-level public servants); the minister of fisheries; and the prime minister, who, in effect, reinstated the decision of the inspectors.[15]

The critical point for interest groups is to determine not only which actors are involved in the issue at hand, but also how much influence they are exercising (or trying to exercise). In Ottawa jargon, the interest groups want to know who "has the file" and is "taking the lead" in dealing with a particular policy initiative.

4.3 Targets Depend on the Type of Policy Action

A great deal of public policy, in an operational sense, is made outside the legislature, although in principle all policy must be sanctioned by a statutory mandate. The linkage between statutory authorization and policy action is often long and rather loose. By and large, under the Westminster model,[16] the legislature is a passive instrument. It does not, for example, initiate legislation, although it may well be able to require the government of the day to amend the legislative proposals it puts before it. This point is developed in more detail in chapter 7, where the importance of MPs as targets of lobbying is discussed.

Interest groups err if they focus most of their energy upon new statutes or amendments to existing ones, that is, if they focus on the activities of the legislature. Because most statutes are "frameworks" that depend for their operationality upon subordinate legislation, notably regulations, interest groups must pay close attention to the vast array of laws that are not enacted by the legislature but are authorized by the cabinet or by a minister. (In a very few cases, regulatory agencies can make new regulations that have the force of law without the approval of the governor in council, or cabinet.) However, most government policy is made in the thousands of discretionary decisions of public servants and ministers within the confines of existing broadly defined statutory mandates. In large companies, for example, it is very rare for anyone to have a continuing, comprehensive picture of the multiple working contacts between various units of the firm and various departments or agencies of government.

As emphasized by Pross, "the entire political community is almost never involved in a specific policy discussion. Specialization occurs throughout the system" (1985, 302). The subject matter of the issue and the type of policy action (e.g., new regulation vs. an increased budgetary allotment) go a long way toward defining which subunits of government and actors outside government are likely to be involved. Pross (1985, 302) argues that most policy issues are dealt with by two segments of the policy community: the relevant subgovernment (for all practical purposes the policy-making body in the field) and the related attentive public. The relevant subgovernment "processes most routine policy issues and when doing so is seldom successfully challenged by interlopers." For virtually any issue, there is a "lead agency" that has been given or has successfully sought the responsibility of moving the policy issue through the process. It will become the locus around which most (but not all) of the efforts to support or change the policy will be focused.

One of the standard strategies of an interest group (whether it be inside government or outside it) is to broaden the scope of the conflict or bargaining over policy by bringing other actors into the issue so as to alter the outcome. For example, suppose an industry association is very unhappy with a new regulation as drafted by a department's technocrats — one that would normally either be given final approval by a minister or by the cabinet in a routine fashion. The association could bring this draft regulation to the attention of other ministers, explaining why this apparently small regulatory matter is going to have a major adverse impact on their industry. These ministers might then raise tough questions when the proposed regulation is put forward for otherwise automatic approval by the cabinet. Such questions and the refusal to approve the new regulation will require the minister responsible to go back and consult with the industry association so that an acceptable compromise is reached.

4.4 Locus of Hidden Conflict and Bargaining over Policy

Much of the serious conflict and hard bargaining over public policy issues in Canada is hidden from public view. This is in contrast to the United States, where, because of the different institutional framework and responsibilities, both the conflicts over policy and the process of bargaining and accommodation are more open to public view. Registered lobby groups in the U.S. deliver briefs before public meetings of congressional committees. They also meet with individual legislators and with their staff. On the other hand, most lobbying in Canada is conducted in a much less open manner. Competition occurs inside the executive within and among various departments and central agencies. Lobbyists are, however, able to participate in this process to varying degrees. Their ability to influence policy depends on obtaining access to the very early stages of the policy-formulation process. The requirement of ministerial and cabinet responsibility over all actions of the bureaucracy has led to the practice of conducting the public's business in secret. In general, although the federal government passed an Access to Information Act in 1982, governments believe that it is best to hold discussions with interest groups behind closed doors and without publicity. Public discussions often result in embarrassing questions from opposition members and are therefore to be avoided. (In some cases, however, public debate is encouraged so that the government will be perceived as responsive to a variety of public concerns.)

In Canada, because the cabinet has a monopoly over the supply of legislation, subordinate legislation, changes in the revenue and expenditure budgets, many appointments, and the determination of the government's priorities, it becomes the focus of efforts to influence policy directly or indirectly.

The critical point is this: once a policy has obtained cabinet approval it becomes almost "cast in stone" in the sense that it is very difficult to change during subsequent stages in the policy process because of the coercive demands of collective responsibility of the cabinet and the continuous need to retain the confidence of the legislature. Charlotte Gray observes:

> The most effective point at which to influence policy is within the middle ranks of the bureaucracy, while it's evolving and malleable. The next target is the senior levels of the public service, when the deputy minister is explaining proposed legislation to his minister. Once legislation reaches cabinet, the lobbyist turns his powers of persuasion to ministers. (1983, 12)

Savoie quotes a federal cabinet minister to the effect that many policy initiatives are "cast in stone" even before they reach the desk of the sponsoring minister: "By the time something is brought to my level, the die is cast. Essentially, I have two choices: I can go along with what the department is proposing or I can refuse to sign. That is the only power I have to check the department. It is a negative power and consequently I very rarely employ it" (1983, 519–20). Moreover, the minister emphasized that control over the first draft of a cabinet document is vital if one is to truly shape the final draft; yet as a minister neither he (nor his colleagues) had been able to have access to the first draft of a cabinet document.

Real influence in policy making requires that those wishing to have influence operate "cheek-by-jowl" in the early stages of policy formulation when problems are being defined, information gathered, theories explored, and the first step is made in defining options for policy action.

One of the core doctrines of the Westminster model of government holds that the government as a whole stands or falls on each matter approved by cabinet, which has a virtual monopoly over the supply of policy initiatives that stand a high probability of having the force of law. The convention is that the government can't back down once it has committed itself to a policy action that has been approved by cabinet. In practice the government can alter its position, but elaborate rituals are necessary to give the appearance of "not losing face." For example, legislative initiatives that run into heavy fire can be left to "die on the order paper," without the government ever announcing to the world that it had made a mistake and was withdrawing its legislative initiative. Another common technique is for ministers to offer their own set of amendments to their own bill at the committee stage. Then only a very close observer may note that a good many of these incorporate suggestions (demands?) made by opposition members or by interest groups appearing before the parliamentary committee. The point is that they are officially the government's initiatives, even though their real paternity may be elsewhere.

Because of the design characteristics of our system of government, the most intense conflict and bargaining over policy occurs behind closed doors prior to the time a policy receives the approval of the cabinet or fails to gain it. These battles are fought on a number of "battlefields." First, there are the interdepartmental committees of senior bureaucrats. New policy initiatives of any significance must be vetted through the process of interdepartmental consultation, with a view to making them consistent with the multitude of existing policies and interests in government.

Policy initiatives become the bases of conflict over "turf" (i.e., the scope of different departments' policy responsiblities), over status and prestige within the bureaucracy, and over resources (budget, people, mandate). More often than not, departments take on the role of representing their "client's" interests in the discussions; for example, the Department of Agriculture puts forward the views of farmers, Labour makes sure that the interests of working people are not ignored, and bureaucrats from Industry, Trade and Commerce may speak up for a particular industry or sector to which the department has close ties and policy responsibilities. There are some voices that tend to take a government-wide perspective; for example, Department of Finance and Treasury Board officials often focus on allocative efficiency and the impact of a proposed policy on the budget as a whole. The Trudeau government sought to improve the policy-making process by creating an elaborate system of cabinet committees, through the use of interdepartmental committees of bureaucrats, and by greatly enlarging the role of central agencies (PCO, PMO, TB, FPRO, etc.). These considerable efforts were designed to rationalize, coordinate, and integrate the efforts of individual departments and agencies. While definitely changing the locus of power — and the flow of paper (the process) — it is not clear to most observers that the changes begun by Pierre Trudeau and continued by both Joe Clark and Brian Mulroney have actually made the policy-making system more rational and efficient. (See Kirby 1985, Neville 1985, and Van Loon 1985.)

Even Michael Pitfield, who headed the public service under Trudeau, has said that "there's no absolute truth in public policy. All we can say for sure is what duly elected representatives decide and take responsibility for." After a decade of helping to remould the process, it appears that one of its architects has reverted to a normative view of the system characterized as pluralist politics in which varied interests (presumably including bureaucratic interests) compete to shape public policy. Pitfield emphasizes that governments must enact policies, created from consensus and full of imperfections, and they must operate within the constitutional rules of a pluralistic, representative democracy. "You can't by a mathematical formula arrive at truth. It's arrived at by debate and juxtaposition of a large number of variables. Therefore, it's very important in the decision-making process at the top that the major variables have their spokesmen."[17]

Second, battles over public policy are fought in the various cabinet committees. Every policy initiative of substance must typically pass through two cabinet committees before it reaches the cabinet as a whole, by which time the issue may be resolved and the recommended course of action for cabinet is quite clear. Policy initiatives first go to the relevant "subject matter" committee of cabinet. For every cabinet committee of ministers, there is a parallel "mirror" committee of deputy ministers from the same department, who normally meet the week before their ministers are to deal with a specific issue. "Ostensibly, the mirror groups produce an analysis of every departmental memo to cabinet, hammer out interdepartmental rivalries and prepare a brief 'assessment report' on options. Officials insist that the assessments are unswervingly neutral, but some ministers are not so sure." Some contend that the system filters out options and limits the scope for ministerial decision making (Lewis 1982, 26–27).

After a policy initiative has been approved by a committee (and this process may take more than one cycle; i.e., it may be sent back for more analysis and redrafting), it must still go to the very powerful Cabinet Committee on Priorities and Planning (P&P). In many cases, the way P&P deals with the issue will determine how the entire cabinet will deal with it. The subject matter committee of cabinet will see individual ministers pitted against each other as rivals for all the resources that affect the rise or fall of ministers as influential politicians: budget, policy turf (jurisdiction), public visibility of being associated with winning policies, and power within the cabinet itself. Van Loon points out the inherent conflict for ministers between their role as head of a specific department and their membership in the collectivity of the cabinet, that is, the government:

> Ministers, after all, thrive on individual recognition, and collective responsibility may sit less happily on the shoulders of the most powerful among them than the visibility and control over resources which has hitherto come from heading important departments. Too, the departments themselves are large and powerful institutions with their own clienteles and considerable ability to frustrate any planning system should they choose to do so. (1985, 432)

Ministers come to such cabinet committees briefed by their public servants to advance the interests of their department and its clients. They want to have their own initiatives (often the work of the senior public servants in their departments) become the policy of the government (i.e., gain cabinet approval). The arguments ministers use around the cabinet committee table are often supplied by the interest groups that support or oppose the initiative or issue under consideration, as the following example illustrates:

> The Pharmaceutical Manufacturers Association of Canada, for example, has not stopped at the department of consumer and corporate affairs in its lobbying against the department's new patent policy proposals. Department sources indicate some of the toughest criticisms have come from the departments of finance, health and welfare, industry, trade and commerce and the ministry for science and technology. The other departments' positions have been presented through an interdepartmental committee working on refinement of the policy. A spokesman for the pharmaceutical association confirmed the organization has been working closely with all four departments. (Harrison 1978b)

Third, conflict and bargaining over proposed policies occurs in intradepartmental committees. Within a department that acts or wishes to act as a lead agency on a policy initiative, policy making is coordinated by a number of individuals, each with specialized knowledge through an intradepartmental committee. It may be chaired by the deputy minister or by an assistant deputy minister, who, in turn, reports to the deputy minister. The fact is that policy making is generally a collaborative effort. Even where one individual is given the responsibility for drafting the necessary cabinet documents (i.e., memorandum to cabinet and its related discussion paper), they will usually be read and commented on by scores of individuals both inside the department and in other departments via the interdepartmental consultative process. In a somewhat different form, proposed policy initiatives are often circulated among influential groups in the private sector and among those provinces where the federal-provincial aspect may be important.

The point is that departments are not perfectly coordinated entities in which there is complete agreement on policy issues. Intradepartmental debates can be vociferous, and conflicts of interest can be endemic. Even when an initiative has the imprimatur of the minister, interest groups opposed to the policy may ally themselves with dissident elements within the department and thereby gain valuable information about how that policy initiative is developing inside the government more generally. Recall the adage that "the enemy of my enemy is my friend."

The points for interest groups are clear: (1) it is crucial to get involved in the policy-formulation process early, before the policy is cast in stone; and (2) at the early stages interest groups have to participate through proxies — while they can meet with bureaucrats and ministers, they cannot be at the table when issues that concern them are dealt with by interdepartmental committees of bureaucrats and by cabinet committees. Interest groups, however, by providing credible information and ideas can influence the nature and content of these internal debates within government. For more detail, see chapters 7, 8, and 9.

4.5 Dynamics of Policy Making

It is hard to overemphasize the dynamics of the policy-making process. The system — hence outcomes — changes over fairly short periods of time. This is due to a variety of factors: changes in personnel, changes in political priorities, perceived changes in public opinion, and exogenous events.

Changes in personnel both inside government and outside include the turnover associated with a change of party in power, cabinet shuffles, and changes in the senior officials of a department or agency. Changes in political leadership, most notably a change of government, bring with them new ideas, new values, and new policy priorities. For example, shortly after the new Mulroney government came to power in September 1984, it announced the extinction of FIRA and the creation of Investment Canada with a view to stimulating foreign investment in Canada. A year later, the government announced it was planning to spend $10 million on domestic and international advertising over the next two years to promote foreign investment in Canada.[18] Similarly, the new minister of national revenue, Perrin Beatty, made some noticeable changes in that department, one of which was to no longer require taxpayers to pay any assessment for back taxes to the government *before* they could file an appeal of the assessment.

Changes in political priorities result in changes in government policy. Public opinion polls, the public and private reaction of interest groups, the happenings in the daily Question Period, and the stories given priority by the media all influence what issues get on the agenda for political action and the ranking of individual items. (There is a joke to the effect that no one in Ottawa knows if it's business as usual each day until the top people have read the *Globe and Mail* in the morning.)

An example of shifting priorities occurred in 1982 shortly after Marc Lalonde took over the Finance portfolio from Allan MacEachen. In light of the enormous hostility generated in the business community by the NEP and the last MacEachen budget, which threatened to close many lucrative tax loopholes (tax expenditures), Lalonde decided the government had to become much more solicitous of business interests. The Liberal party needed to get back in business's good graces. Sitting before the cabinet was the fourth draft bill since 1977 embodying the Stage II amendments to the Combines Investigation Act.[19] The amendments were to follow the Stage I amendments enacted in December 1975, and address such matters as mergers, monopoly, joint monopolization, and the relationship between regulated conduct and competition legislation (see Stanbury & Reschenthaler 1981).

Lalonde was able to persuade his cabinet colleagues that the introduction of such new legislation would — at that time — further erode the business community's confidence in the Liberal government. Therefore, the minister from the Department of Consumer and Corporate Affairs (DCCA) was told to hold the bill in abeyance and to engage in another round of consultation with business interests on the issues in the bill. This was done, but when the minister returned with the bill, only very slightly modified, to cabinet, he was told that competition-policy reforms were being put on hold. There were other more important priorities. Upon hearing that news, the policy secretariat that had developed the bill within DCCA disbanded and sent its files to storage. It was only after the appointment of a new minister in 1983 that senior bureaucrats began secret discussions with the representatives of a committee formed by what was jokingly called "The Gang of Three": BCNI, CMA and CCC. Negotiations resulted in a new bill, Bill C-29, which was given First Reading on April 2, 1984 (see Stanbury 1985b). However, the Liberals were voted out of office in September before the bill could even get to Second Reading and be referred to a committee for study. The new Tory government introduced a new bill, C-91, on December 17, 1985. See Stanbury (1986).

It should be noted that "official" shifts in priorities are announced less frequently than actual changes in priorities. To the cognescenti, shifts are identified by fairly subtle changes in official language. For example, when Prime Minister Mulroney began to speak of freer trade or trade enhancement or "security of access" rather than free trade, he was not merely proliferating synonyms. Stewart MacLeod refers to such terms as part of a more general phenomenon: "those shifting sands of speech, those descriptive detours that, when deftly applied, leave the listener with no firm foothold on the original commitments, serious doubts about the revised ones and, in some cases, uncertainty about whether they ever existed in the first place."[20] Moreover, familiar terms — even emotional code words — become reinterpreted. For example, full employment in the late 1960s was defined in operational terms as about 4 percent unemployment. The Macdonald Commission in 1985 suggested that it will be a lengthy and difficult process to reduce unemployment below 6.5 to 8.0 percent.[21]

Perceived changes in public opinion also can result in changes in the set of policy initiatives a government puts forward. If politicians believe that public opinion indicates a reasonable and intensely held consensus on particular issues, then avenues for some policy actions are opened up and others are closed, temporarily at least. Divided public opinion favours the status quo, since any action will displease about half the voting public. (More generally, see chapter 11.)

Because timing is of critical importance in politics, it is also an important factor in policy formulation. For example, newly elected governments with a substantial or large majority have a twelve- to sixteen-month "honeymoon" period after assuming office in which to take strong action that may not be popular in the short run, but necessary for the general welfare.[22] Subject to the statutory maximum of five years, a government can choose the date of the next election. The few months prior to a planned election day are believed to be critical in the shaping of a victory at the polls. Put crudely, there is an oestrus cycle in politics: politicians' behaviour changes when they "come into heat," that is, when an election approaches. Their willingness to placate almost every interest group increases greatly, particularly if they view them as marginal voters. Therefore, an interest group may want to accelerate government action by taking advantage of the honeymoon period (i.e., where it is asking for some action that will be unpopular, but beneficial to the economy in the longer run). Conversely, if a government does not favour what a group wants mid-way through its term, the group may wish to delay its initiative until the government is less able to resist, namely, in the months leading up to an election.

Events that are exogenous to both the government and an interest group can turn the best-laid plans into a shambles. Indeed, one of the least attractive features of the job of a cabinet minister is the propensity for being "blind-sided" by events entirely beyond his or her control. The minister goes to bed with a carefully planned set of proposed actions based on extensive negotiations and wakes up to newspaper headlines about events that will completely disrupt those plans.

It appears that the collapse of the Canadian Commercial Bank in September 1985 was totally unexpected, except perhaps by a very few insiders who became aware after the bailout in March that the loan portfolio was greatly overvalued. In any event, its collapse created a political crisis for the Mulroney government that rudely pushed aside — at least temporarily — virtually all other policy initiatives and threatened to change a number of these. The most notable is the set of policy proposals in the federal government's Green Paper published in April 1985, *The Regulation of Financial Institutions*. It appears that some parts of the Green Paper dealing with protecting depositors and the protection of the solvency of financial institutions will be rushed into legislation by a government under severe pressure; yet other parts of the policy package may be delayed indefinitely or be altered very greatly in light of new priorities.

> When Barbara McDougall, Minister of State for Finance, launched her drive last spring to overhaul Canada's outdated financial sector legislation, her green paper laid out a well-ordered plan of action. However, two bank failures have caused Mrs. McDougall to re-examine her reform package and reorder its priorities. Suddenly, two issues — tighter regulation and deposit insurance — are receiving immediate attention, while the rest of the reform package is largely ignored. Many observers believe this is a sign that the broad overhaul of financial sector laws envisaged only last spring is already beginning to falter. "I can't help but think that the green paper proposals will be put on the back burner," said one investment dealer. One Ottawa consultant who has been following the green paper was blunter: "It's a dead fish." The two issues now on the fast track were the only things that made Mrs. McDougall's policy politically attractive, he said. A less-obvious blow to Mrs. McDougall's plan may have been the departure during the summer of former deputy finance minister Marshall Cohen. He was regarded by many as the man who provided the intellectual leadership for the policy changes, while his successor, Stanley Hartt, will not push the issues as hard.[23]

4.6 Federalism

An understanding of federalism is critical to the understanding of lobbying and policy making in Canada. In general see Cairns (1977, 1985), Schultz (1979, 1980), Schultz and Alexandaroff (1985), Simeon (1962, 1979, 1982, 1985), Smiley (1964, 1970, 1971, 1980) and Economic Council (1982b). In fact, the 1867 Confederation was itself the product of competing interests. The "deal" united two dominant linguistic groups and several diverse regional economies over a sparsely and unevenly populated territory of vast proportions.

Although the allocation of powers was formally enumerated in the British North America Act of 1867 and again in the Constitution Act of 1982, the actual division of powers evolved over time in less formal ways (see Hogg 1985). These include such varied instruments as interpretation by the courts, federal-provincial agreements such as those involving the income tax and unemployment insurance, informal arrangements in particular areas, pressure by the provinces, and federal "incursions" into what the provinces believe is their jurisdiction. One of the important effects of Canada's complex system of federal-provincial relations is the elaborate set of fiscal transfers between the two levels of government. In 1985/86, for example, one-quarter of federal expenditures consist of transfers to the provinces in the form of unconditional grants and payments for shared-cost programs. In addition, the federal government increases the fiscal resources of the provinces by sharing certain sources of tax revenues. One of the primary purposes of fiscal federalism has been to redistribute resources so that the citizens in less fortunate provinces are able to enjoy a level of government services equal to the national average. (See chapter 3 and ECC 1982b).

The ongoing reinterpretation of federal and provincial authority has led to the evolution of a vast "industry" in federal-provincial relations, the diplomacy of which is more voluminous, complex, and costly than Canada's external relations. One manifestation of this industry has been an increase in federal-provincial agreements, notably those by first ministers that bypass both federal and provincial legislatures. Smiley (1970) has described this tendency as "executive federalism."

Obviously, an ever more institutionalized system of federal-provincial relations, superimposed upon two constitutionally recognized levels of government that share rather imprecisely allocated areas of authority, will affect relations between business and government. For example, lobbyists will have a more difficult time identifying which government has the power to give them what they want. In addition, the entire policy-making process will be lengthened as a logical outcome of the increased number of actors. As a practical matter, groups will need more, if not double, the resources to operate at two rather than one level of government. It is even more difficult to decide whether on balance interest groups are more able to influence policy in a federal than in a unitary state.

Schultz (1977) has aptly characterized Canadian interest groups as being caught in the vise of federalism and that federalism is a double-edged sword for such groups. On the one hand, "the 'multiple-crack' thesis contends that federal systems are particularly valued by interest groups because the existence of two levels of government provides groups with multiple access points to pursue their objectives" (Schultz, 1977,

375). On the other hand, Schultz qualifies this "multiple-crack" thesis by pointing out that groups do not have complete freedom in choosing the level of government with which to ally themselves:

> When a group endorses one level of government it may find itself the object of attention as the other level seeks its support. Perhaps even more significant for group fortunes is the fact that the group may find itself subject to abuse from the rejected government. (1977, 394)

Interest groups, then, may become pawns in intergovernmental conflict. Thorburn further develops Schultz's characterization of the vise of federalism by noting that interest groups must be diplomatic with all levels of government:

> Sometimes the accusation is made that interest groups attempt to play governments off, one against another. This is an easy accusation to make and a difficult one to demonstrate. In fact, it is dangerous for interest groups to engage in such behaviour openly, because governments can always retaliate against those who declare themselves their enemies. The real situation is one in which groups do not declare themselves as the allies of any one government. This, in turn, means they will try to maintain civil relations with any and all governments, and the nature of the relationship in any particular case will depend on the particular circumstances uniting it with the respective government. (1985, 117)

In the Canadian context, many interest groups must necessarily become involved in intergovernmental relations. Thorburn has divided the mechanisms for this involvement into the categories of informal and formal. The first, the informal mechanisms,

> are irregular, spontaneous and ill-defined involvement often based on networks of personal contacts . . . . Both institutionalized and issue-oriented groups have difficulty determining and rationalizing the place of interest groups in a process where provincial governments make legitimate demands for greater provincial autonomy and control over their spending and the federal government seeks to establish itself as the legitimate voice of the national interest. (1985, 77)

The formal mechanisms can be subdivided into a further two categories. First, there are those that allow groups to participate at one level of government, for example, the Joint Senate-House Committee on the Constitution in 1981 and the Breau Task Force on fiscal federalism in 1981. Second are those mechanisms that involve joint discussions between provincial governments and interest groups. Thorburn (1985) notes that these mechanisms are of limited use to interest groups for the simple reason that they are ad hoc. Groups may only participate in such debates at the pleasure of the government, and the government is not compelled to follow their advice unless they reflect a strong public sentiment. Groups are often placed in the position of having to react to government policy rather than participating in its formulation. Thorburn puts the case strongly by stating that groups "can only respond when government provides an opportunity, so they are usually really accomplices rather than countervailing forces in the policy-making process" (1985, 78).

Federalism requires that national interest groups establish organizations that are parallel to governmental structures. The relationship between interests and federalism is interactive rather than static, but some general tendencies have been identified:

> The asymmetry of the Canadian interest group structure, as it relates to the different levels of government, is twofold. As indicated above there are substantial interests traditionally linked to the federal government, such as transportation and finance, and there are dominant Central Canadian interests located in Ontario which are "naturally" closer to the levers of power in Ottawa than are the resource-based industries and interests in the peripheral areas. At the same time, however, substantial economic interests are closely linked to provincial governments such as the energy-related industries in Alberta, and the entire complex of socioeconomic province-building in Quebec. (Thorburn 1985, 119)

Although the distribution of authority between the two levels of government is constantly evolving, one aspect of Canadian federalism, the propensity for elite accommodation, has remained a pervasive influence in policy making. Thorburn (1985, 121-23) has listed five consequences of this tradition in Canadian federalism. First, caught between disparate economic and cultural demands, governments will tend toward inaction and deadlock. Second, elites will adopt the "knee-jerk" reaction of always favouring incremental change or maintaining the status quo as solutions to problems. Third, in his view, there will be a waste of governmental resources due to the overexpansion of government activity. Fourth, government will have to make hard choices in order to accommodate the competing demands of older, institutionalized interests and the newer, issue-oriented groups. Finally, amidst the competition between interests and countervailing pressures the government actors will be afforded greater autonomy through confusion. This is what Cairns (1979) called "the other crisis of Canadian federalism."

A preoccupation with federal-provincial relations has the effect of removing issues that do not have regional bases of support from the political agenda. If the price of Canadian unity is federalism, then that price is born by those interests that seek to remedy problems that cut across regional differences.

5.0 FROM PROBLEMS TO POLICY ACTIONS

The development of public policy actions can be divided into two components: idea generation and promulgation; and implementation of ideas into operational policy. A very great deal of policy stems from the perception of a "problem"; that is, most policy is remedial — it is designed to solve problems and to redress wrongs.

It appears that policy initiatives originate from three principal sources:

- new or more specialized knowledge that identifies "problems" that were not perceived before;
- somebody (from an individual to a large group) is hurt (suffers a decline from his or her current/accustomed position) in terms of income, wealth, status, or a loss of "rights," and he or she wishes redress; and
- someone identifies an opportunity to advance his or her own interests (economic, ideological, moral, etc.) by means of government action.

One of the hallmarks of a wealthy and highly developed society is the relatively large fraction of resources that is devoted to "problem finding" activities of various sorts. The spread of higher education, and with it the expansion of research of all kinds, has the effect of generating a large supply of "problems" that are perceived at least by some people as deserving government action. This has little to do with ideology and much more to do with specialization. When people study a narrow domain of human knowledge deeply (and in the process create more knowledge) over a period of years, they will usually become convinced of the importance of what they are doing. They will, naturally, see and understand things that other people with less specialized knowledge or other types of specialized knowledge do not. They are also wont to see problems that others do not and often feel an obligation to share their insights with a wider audience. The advance of technology itself can have the effect of revealing problems we never knew existed. For example, the most sophisticated gas spectrometers can measure substances in concentrations of one part per billion. We now know the world is laced in varying concentrations of literally hundreds of toxic substances. A policy problem occurs because our ability to identify these substances has been associated with statistically sophisticated epidemiological studies that connect toxic substances with morbidity and mortality. People have been dying for millions of years — what is different is that we now have a better idea why they died and how their deaths from certain causes could have been delayed or prevented.

More generally, even a casual observation indicates that modern government and research and educational institutions employ a large number of people whose activities effectively generate problems. Some of these become the basis for actors inside or outside government to seek to initiate a policy action. Moreover, the 1960s and 1970s might be described as "the age of policy analysis," as governments created specialized units in almost every department or agency to do program evaluation, policy planning, and policy analysis. At the same time, the incentive systems within the public service changed to give greater rewards to the architects of new policies than to the administrators of well-established programs. Not surprisingly, more problems were identified and more policy actions were proposed to "solve" them.

A great number of public policy actions occur in response to persons and groups hurt by the vicissitudes of life. Research indicates that people feel losses more acutely than they do the failure to obtain a potential gain (i.e., an opportunity lost). Being hurt may consist of a decline in income, wealth, or status, or a loss of various "rights" that the individual believes he or she enjoys. The loss of accustomed position may be attributable to a wide variety of factors such as:

- exogenous events, that is, acts of God (bad weather, earthquakes, etc.);
- the process of competition in which someone gets hurt economically;
- technological change, which may, for example, eliminate the demand for certain products or services or reduce the value of earlier investments; and
- negative externalities — a form of "market failure" in which some of the costs of certain economic activities fall onto persons not directly involved in their production and sale; for example, fish stocks are depleted by pulp mill wastes dumped into rivers.

Not surprisingly, people hurt by the exigencies of life seek redress from government — they seek to socialize risks while individuating benefits for themselves. For example, the volume of Japanese cars imported and sold in Canada is a public policy issue largely because unionized Canadian autoworkers are unwilling to suffer higher unemployment and lower incomes than they had been accustomed to. Their inability (as well as that of their employers) to be competitive in the world automobile industry led them to seek policy actions from the federal government (principally "voluntary" quotas)[24] so as to restore their previously rather favoured position. In effect, Bob White (head of the new Canadian autoworkers union) and his co-workers together with their employers were able to convert their problem into a public policy problem that was "solved" by shifting the problem onto all car buyers in Canada. As a result of the action of the federal government, buyers of new cars have had to pay an additional $1500 to $2000 for their vehicles — and this applies to both Japanese vehicles and all those that are reasonably close substitutes.

Public policy actions also arise when groups or individuals perceive there is an opportunity to advance their own (private) interests by means of government action. This case is distinguished from the previous one in that those who seek to initiate a policy action are not responding to having been hurt by the vicissitudes of life.[25] Rather, they are exploiting what they see as an opportunity to "use the state for fun and profit." To use the jargon of the public choice writers, they are engaging in rent-seeking behaviour (Hartle 1984, 1985). Instead of operating in economic markets to increase their fortune, a large number of individuals and groups use their resources to influence government in ways that will benefit them economically, ideologically, or in other ways. It is necessary for rent seekers to redefine what they see as an opportunity as a "problem" worthy of government action. For example, middle-income Canadians not wishing to pay for their own day-care services argue that, without universal day care, poor mothers cannot enter the labour force and hence are being discriminated against. They also argue that wholly government-financed day care is a "right" that should be available to all citizens with children.

It should be appreciated that rent seekers include politicians who try to gain or retain office (for the array of personal benefits) by proposing a vector of public policy actions that they hope will generate the requisite electoral support. A realistic view of the political process requires that we include politicians within the orbit of those persons in the policy process who act according to their self-interest as they define it. Those politicians who appear to be selling an ideology presumably derive psychological satisfaction (if not wealth or a position of power) from doing so — more satisfaction than they would from advocating another set of policies, which might even have sufficient appeal to gain their party enough seats to form a government.

For interest groups seeking to block or initiate a policy action, it is most useful, therefore, to identify the nature of the problem (or opportunity) that lies behind the action under consideration. Identifying the problem is essential to identifying the key targets for lobbying activity, namely, those persons who could "push" the proposed action or those in a position to block, delay, or derail it. See chapter 7.

6.0 POLICY MAKING AND THE PUBLIC INTEREST

There are few more evocative phrases associated with the making of public policy than "the public interest." Following Cassinelli (1962, 45), it is frequently argued that "the public interest is a standard of goodness by which political acts can be judged." Going further, he argues that it is "the highest ethical standard applicable to political affairs." Yet it is a phrase that puzzles philosophers, generates much debate among political scientists, and has been declared to be a snare, a trap, and a delusion — of no operational consequence in terms of the actual basis of policy making. J. E. Hodgetts (1981, 218) has said that the concept of the public interest is "slippery, mercurial and possessed of the qualities of the chameleon." He also notes that "it is akin to the Holy Grail, in that its relevance for political life may reside in the pursuit and anticipation rather than in the actual grasping or attainment of the reality it is supposed to represent."

6.1 Public versus Private Interests

Schattschneider (1960, 23) argues that the distinction between public and private interests is "a thoroughly respectable one; it is one of the oldest known to political theory." The public interest "refers to general or common interests shared by all or by substantially all members of the community." He makes a telling point when he argues that "presumably no community exists unless there is some kind of community of interests, just as there is no nation without some notion of national interests." He continues: "The reality of the common interest is suggested by demonstrated capacity of the community to survive. There must be something that holds people together."

In contrast to the common interests are the special interests — those shared by only a few people or a fraction of the community. Schattschneider emphasizes that special interests exclude others and may be adverse to them (1960, 24). He draws a careful distinction between interest groups that seek exclusive benefits (i.e., only for their members) and those that seek nonexclusive benefits (i.e., essentially available to all) (1960, 26–28). The second distinction is between organized groups and unorganized groups with a definable interest, even large ones. As Mancur Olson (1965) has emphasized, there are sound technical reasons why this is the case.

6.2 Unrepresented Interests

Olson (1965) explains why it is that rational, self-interested individuals will not necessarily act to achieve their common or group interests. They will not do so where the achievement of a common goal creates a public good in the technical sense. The essential characteristics of such goods are (1) their external economies in consumption and jointness in supply (once they are created, they are available for all, and consumption by one individual does not reduce the amount available for others), and (2) the fact that they are subject to the free-rider effect (i.e., it is impossible or inefficient to exclude anyone from enjoying the benefit of such goods, even if they have contributed nothing to their creation). Therefore, large numbers of people will remain unorganized unless

- the absolute benefits to a few individuals exceed the costs of creating the common good, so they will proceed despite the existence of free riders;
- the free riders can be corralled; that is, the group can coerce its members (potential beneficiaries) into paying the cost of organizing and representing their common interest;
- lobbying for common interests can be financed as a "by-product" of

the sale of individuated, excludable goods and services to members; or

- a political entrepreneur can overcome the communications and trans-actions costs so as to persuade the members of the large, unorganized interest group to vote for him or her in exchange for representation of their interests in the governmental process.

The critical point is that in the real world with its imperfect political markets (analogous to what economists call "market failure" in eco-nomic markets) the domain of interests represented by organized groups is a modest subset of all important interests in society. By and large, producer interests are well organized and represented in the bargaining processes of a pluralist democracy. However, most other interests remain latent, or if they are formally organized, they are seldom politically effec-tive. The fact that so many interests are subject to the free-rider effect (e.g., "values" groups of all kinds — see Figure 8-1 in chapter 8) is a tribute to behaviour that is not economically rational. It seems that partic-ipation in values groups provides other rewards (e.g., affiliation needs, the opportunity to publicly express one's opinion) that outweigh the costs of participation. See Hardin (1982).

6.3 Widespread Use of the Concept of the Public Interest

While the public interest is all but impossible to define in a way that makes it an operational guide to government policy making, the term is (or its similes are) frequently used by all actors in the process. Interest groups seek to justify their claims on government (in reality, on other groups and individuals) in terms of the public interest. Government agen-cies make decisions and justify them as being in the public interest. For example, on August 28, 1985, the CRTC rejected CNCP Telecommuni-cations' application to compete against Bell Canada and BC Tel in the supply of long-distance voice telephone service, saying that such com-petition "would not be in the public interest." Yet, as one commentator argued, "the CRTC could just as well have said it would not be in Bell's interest."[26] He noted that a recent poll indicated that 70 percent of con-sumers want competition (although the Consumers' Association of Can-ada opposed it, saying the result would be much higher monthly rates for local service), and he argued that "the consumer stands to be the loser with a decision that represents the worst of two worlds: rejection of competition, but the possibility of some form of rate restructuring."

Even in particular decision contexts, the phrase "the public interest" is very seldom defined and when it is, only through other enigmatic short phrases. For example: illegal mergers under the Combines Inves-tigation Act are defined as those that involve "acquisition of control of a business . . . whereby competition . . . is or is likely to be lessened to the detriment or against the interest of the public, whether consumers, producers, or others." In telecommunications regulation, the statutes refer to the obligation of the regulator to set "just and reasonable rates" and to establish tariffs "without undue discrimination." The Aeronautics Act uses as its criterion in respect to decisions on route licences the phrase "present and future public convenience and necessity." The Foreign Investment Review Act established the criterion that foreign investments had to be "of significant benefit to Canada" if they were to be approved.

The National Energy Program, introduced in October 1980, contained three objectives that implicitly defined the government's concept of the public interest. The policy was to be the "basis for Canadians to seize control of their own energy future through security of supply and ultimate independence from the world oil market." It "must offer . . . all Canadians the real opportunity to participate in . . . the petroleum industry, and to share in the benefits of industry expansion"; and the policy "must establish a petroleum pricing and revenue-sharing regime that recognizes the requirements of fairness to all Canadians no matter where they live."

In 1884, the Adulteration of Foods Act was justified by federal cabinet ministers on the grounds that it was "in the interest of public honesty, in the interest of the protection to health, in the interest of the life of our children."

The point is that the nebulous concept of the public interest is sufficiently elastic to accommodate a wide variety of potentially conflicting objectives or to rationalize decisions made on a great variety of other grounds.

Without a rudimentary understanding of the concept of the public interest, lobbyists are likely to be less effective. They must, however, focus on the strategic use of the term in seeking to persuade policy makers to do what they want (see chapter 9). It will now be useful to examine the attempts to define "the public interest" and to try to understand why the phrase has such a strong appeal.

6.4 The Perceived Moral Inferiority of Private Interests[27]

A critical element in the psychological environment of business-government relations is the moral value (usually implicit) that is placed by the majority of citizens on the activities of each of the parties.[28] The activities of business enterprises are based on the pursuit of material wealth — a manifestly private interest — and such an objective is seen by many to have a lower moral value than the activities of governments. The latter are deemed — without much reflection or analysis — to be acting "in the public interest." Hence, in their dealings with both politicians (notably the cabinet) and senior bureaucrats, firms and trade associations operate from "behind the moral eight ball." They have an inherent disadvantage in their efforts to influence public policy.

In a free enterprise system, the central motivating force of business people is the lure of profits. They are to be maximized subject to the legal and moral interest and private interest in the following analytical dichotomy:

Connotations of Private Interests	*Connotations of the Public Interest*
• selfishness	• "other regarding" — even altruistic
• benefiting the few	• benefiting many
• narrow in scope	• wide in scope
• pecuniary	• social; political
• special/elite	• broadly based; all of the people
• identifiable; represented	• unrepresented; "silent majority"
• short term; immediate	• long term; future generation

As will be described in the next section, the public interest has the distinct connotation of serving ends that are larger and more significant than that of increasing the income/wealth of particular individuals. And, as the experience of the Spanish Inquisition showed, people can be "licensed" by society to undertake extreme acts in the name of a goal that is larger than the individual and is perceived as being beyond mere self-interest. In short, there is a widely held belief — obviously not shared by the public choice theorists — that politicians and senior bureaucrats are virtually always acting in the public interest. They — unlike business people — are not moved almost entirely by their own interests. Rather, they are intent upon the public weal or the welfare of society as a whole — or so it is believed.[29]

Private interests are seen by many as inherently narrow and selfish, designed to benefit the few usually at the expense of the many. Canadians find it all but impossible to believe that self-seeking behaviour in a competitive environment will in any sense maximize society's welfare — even in economic terms. In short, they reject the efficacy of the invisible hand of Adam Smith. Moreover, private interests are perceived as myopic, concentrating on short-term or immediate gains for a small number of identifiable individuals. In contrast, our concept of the public interest has the connotation of a long-term perspective including even the interests of future generations — who, of course, cannot be directly represented in present decision making. While the public interest is broadly based, private interests are, by definition, "special" interests. It is argued that they do not reflect the full range of social and political considerations that ought to be taken into account via some form of collective decision making.

Lord Keynes reflected on the morally ambivalent status of pecuniary self-interest as follows:

Most religions and most philosophies deprecate, to say the least of it, a way of life mainly influenced by considerations of personal money profit. On the other hand, most men today reject ascetic notions and do not doubt the real advantages of wealth. Moreover, it seems obvious to them that one cannot do without the money-motive, and that, apart from certain admitted abuses, it does its job well. In the result the average man averts his attention from the problem, and has no clear idea what he really thinks and feels about the whole confounded matter. (1932, 320)

The great economist Joseph Schumpeter also remarked on the relatively low social status of those involved in business. He noted their inability — unlike a military commander or politician — to elicit the loyalty of a people:

> There is surely no trace of any mystic glamour about him [the industrialist and merchant] which is what counts in the ruling of men. The stock exchange is a poor substitute for the Holy Grail. We have seen that the industrialist and merchant, as far as they are entrepreneurs, also fill a function of leadership. But economic leadership of this type does not readily expand, like the medieval lord's military leadership, into the leadership of nations. On the contrary, the ledger and the cost calculation absorb and confine. . . . A genius in the business office may be, and often is, utterly unable outside of it to say boo to a goose — both in the drawing room and on the platform. (1949, 137–38)

Joan Robinson, a famous neo-Marxist economist, has argued that "it is precisely the pursuit of profit which destroys the prestige of the businessman. While wealth can buy all forms of respect, it never finds them freely given" (1983, 24). As a result, there is the strong, but unarticulated, premise that politicians and bureaucrats operate on higher moral ground than do the leaders of business enterprises. Business goals are not just different or necessarily more limited than those of politicians and bureaucrats, they are seen — albeit implicitly — as morally inferior. In short, they do not have the same degree of legitimacy and hence are forced to operate defensively. This feeling is reinforced in a society like Canada's that tends to favour the interests of the collectivity over those of the individual.

6.5 Attempts to Define the Public Interest

There are many different concepts or definitions of the public interest. These are usually vague, highly general, and abstract. Virtually all are impossible to transform into criteria for decision making in a range of specific situations. It is a long and high leap from the general definitions of the public interest to criteria for decision making in a particular situation. Operational definitions of the public interest that can in fact be used as criteria for public decision making are dynamic. They change with the political context and with the problem or policy context.

Some efforts have been made to group the many definitions of the public interest into a handful of categories — see, for example, Cochran (1974) and Stanbury (1979).

Category #1:

Definitions in this category hold that the public interest results from the aggregation, weighing, and balancing of a number of special interests. It includes the following examples:

- The public interest is "determined and established" through the free competition of interest groups. "The necessary composing and compromising of their differences is the practical test of what constitutes the public interest" (Binkley & Moos 1950, 7).
- The public interest "must necessarily represent a working compromise and be subject to continuous definition, as the need arises, in the process of achieving an often delicate balance among conflicting interests" (Boudreau 1950, 371).
- The public interest is the "policy resulting from the sum total of all interests in the community — possibly all of them actually private interests — which are balanced for the common good" (Marks et al. 1972, 51).
- "The interest of the community then is, what? — The sum of the interests of the several members who compose it" (Bentham 1823, 126).

These definitions appear to stem from the pluralist ideal of political competition among groups. This ideal assumes there will be representation of all interests (many groups), reasonable parity of power, and diffusion of both public and private power, that political market failures are unimportant, and that the balancing of competing interests results in the ideal for society as a whole. These definitions implicitly assume a modest role for government. It is to be limited to restoring/maintaining the equilibrium among the competing groups and to maintaining the rules of the game that are "fair" to all. In this approach, the collective interest is the "sum" of individual/group interests where the weights are such as to maintain an equilibrium. The equilibrium, however, is not defined. At the very least, it must suppose that agreement on the process and/or outcomes is sufficiently widespread for the game to continue.

Category #2:

Here the public interest is defined as the common or universal interests of all or almost all members of the political unit. The following definitions would appear to fall into this category:

- "The public interest . . . is the common interest. That which results in satisfying those wants which all members of a community share constitutes the public interest. [It is] the interest that is unanimously shared with no reluctant losers" (Hartle 1979, 4).

- "To say an action is in the public interest is to judge it consistent with a political situation that is beneficial to everyone, if not immediately at least in the long run, and whether or not everyone realizes it" (Cassinelli 1962, 46).
- "What the public requires as its own good, what is specifically the good of all without distinction, is a sum total of general conditions under the protection of which the legitimate activities of everyone within the public may be exercised and developed comfortably" (Dabin 1944, 355).
- "A decision is said to serve special interests if it furthers the ends of some part of the public at the expense of the ends of the larger public. It is said to be in the public interest if it serves the ends of the whole public rather than those of some sector of the public" (Banfield 1955, 322).
- "Something is a public interest, if, and only if, it is an interest of anyone who is a member of the public; that is, if and only if it is essential for the protection, and even for the improvement, of anyone's welfare or well-being, where the means for protecting or improving this interest are out of the hands of most of the members of the public and is likely to be achieved only if the public takes a hand" (Benditt 1973, 301).

An obvious question to ask is, how large is this domain of common interests that is said to represent the public interest? The widely shared desire for security of person and property, national defence, and the prevention of communicable diseases seems fairly obvious, although reasonable persons can disagree about the amount of resources that should be devoted to them and exactly how these objectives should be achieved.

What exactly are the interests that every member of the community has in common? Do the following qualify?

- Maintaining the constitutive rules of a democracy
- Fundamental political rights (free speech, periodic elections, freedom of religion)
- Anything for which there is unanimous (majority?) agreement
- Economic efficiency
- Redistribution to avoid destitution (or only for the deserving poor)

Anthony Downs suggests in his definition of the public interest as the common interest that this is "closely related to the minimal consensus necessary for the operation of a democratic society. This consists of an implicit agreement among the preponderance of the people concerning two main areas: the basic rules of conduct and decision-making that should be followed in the society; and general principles regarding the fundamental social policies that the government ought to carry out" (1962, 5). These ideas, regrettably, don't take us very far, since there is bound to be conflict over "the basic rules of conduct and decision-making," not to mention the "fundamental social policies that the government ought to carry out." In the case of the latter, one has only to think of the debate over the Macdonald Commission's (1985) recommendation concerning a universal minimum income. With respect to the former, the wise student of government knows that "bloodless procedures" can be critically important in shaping the outcomes of governmental processes. Hence, there will be conflict over the basic rules of decision making.

What we have in common may be a function of the size/composition of the political unit: local, provincial, national, international, global. This category of definitions of the public interest suggests a number of questions. Must a policy action be beneficial to everyone? What about trade-offs, which are required by all policies? How do we make interpersonal comparisons of utility? What weights are to be applied? Does the intensity of interest matter or only the number of people who hold some interest in common to some degree? Can these definitions help policy makers deal with the common case where both allocative efficiency and the distribution of income are affected?

Hodgetts (1981, 218) argues that today it is impossible to define the public interest in terms of a moral absolute, or as a "mystical formula of a general will as propounded by Rousseau." Instead, the concept must be defined in terms of "a search for consensus — the hard core of accepted values and traditions that holds a community together, enabling it to pursue common objectives with the expectation of securing sufficient collective agreement to ensure a stable political regime." This expression is quintessentially Canadian in its emphasis on "a stable political regime." Canada is a nation founded on the principles of "peace, order and good government," in sharp contrast to those of the United States: "life, liberty and the pursuit of happiness."

Category #3:
The public interest is defined here as an ideal usually based on some absolute standard of values with respect to (1) outcomes (ends), or (2) processes (means). In some cases this standard of values is independent of the preferences of individuals. The following definitions, based on the idealist perspective, focus on the outcomes or substantive ends of public policy:

- "The public interest is never merely the sum of all private interests nor the sum remaining after cancelling out their various pluses and minuses. It is not wholly separate from private interests, and it derives from citizens with many private interests; but it is something distinctive that arises within, among, apart from, and above private interests, focusing in government some of the most elevated aspiration and deepest devotion of which human beings are capable" (Appleby 1952, 35).

- "I suggest, that the public interest may be presumed to be what men would choose if they saw clearly, thought rationally, acted disinterestedly and benevolently" (Lippman 1955, 42).
- "The public interest is ultimately identified with the achievement of a society based upon or pervaded by intelligent goodwill" (Griffith 1962, 19).
- "All measures which promote, serve, and benefit the human desire for affirmative and constructive participation in the enterprise of civilization must be deemed to be in the public interest because they increase the good of all as intelligently conceived" (Bodenheimer 1962, 213).

The following definitions define the public interest in terms of an ideal *process* of decision making:

- "The public interest in a problem is limited to this. that there shall be rules, which means that the rules which prevail shall be enforced, and the unreasonable rules shall be changed according to a settled rule. . . . The public is interested in law, not in the laws; in the method of the law, not in substance; in the sanctity of contract, not in particular contract; in understanding based on custom, not in this custom or that. It is concerned in these things to the end that men in their active affairs shall find a modus vivendi; its interest is in the workable rule which will define and predict the behaviour of men so that they can make their adjustments" (Lippman 1925, 104, 105).
- "Decisions that are the product of a process of full consideration are most likely to be decisions in the public interest. . . . people accept democratic decision making processes because these provide the maximum opportunity for diverse interests to seek to influence governmental decisions at all levels" (Schubert 1960, 204, 205).
- "The primary determination of the public interest for public servants is by the action of his political and hierarchic superiors, acting through the conventional channels, by legislation, and court decisions where applicable." In areas where the public servant has discretion, he must consider the consequences to those immediately affected by the proposed action, but he must remember there are others unorganized and unrepresented and "as far as he can perceive the consequences to them, he must be their representative" (Monypenny 1953, 441).

With respect to the ideal-outcome concept of the public interest, do these outcomes relate solely to individuals or do they also relate to collectively consumed goods and services? Does who gets what matter?

With respect to the process-oriented concept of the public interest, we must ask if it is widely acceptable to divorce outcomes from the process by which public decisions are reached. Do "fair" processes always produce "fair" or even acceptable outcomes? How does this perspective on the public interest deal with the interdependence of means and ends found in all human decision making? Is the ideal process one in which everyone participates? Are there not certain inherent biases in well-known democratic processes, including majority rule?

Category #4:

In this category we find what Cochran (1974) calls the "abolitionist" theories, which argue that the public interest concept is empty, there are only the private interests of individuals or groups. For example, the strongest proponent of the group theory of politics, Arthur Bentley, specifically denied there is a public interest, since "there are always some parts of the nation to be found arrayed against other parts." In his view, "The opinion activity that reflects one group, however large it may be, always reflects the activity of that group as directed against the activity of some other group" (Bentley 1908, 220, 240).

For the "abolitionists," the public interest concept is incapable of yielding measurable data about the process of public decision making. Therefore, it has nothing to contribute to the scientific study of politics. There are no universal ethical norms; hence there are no truly common interests. According to Bentley (1908), "There are no political phenomena except group phenomena. Society is nothing other than the complex of groups that compose it." When we examine government decisions, we find they are based on competition among interest groups.

Cochran argues that

> the dominance of the politics of interest [where politics is understood in terms of autonomous individuals and groups who enter the political arena to advance their own interests] makes impossible within contemporary political science any credible notion of a public interest or a common good. There can be no public interest because there is no public or community other than the aggregation of individual and special interest groups which they form. There is no common good because there is nothing which is good for the community as a whole; there are only goods or interests pursued by individuals or groups. (1974, 328)

Cochran challenges the abolitionist theories in a number of ways. His most trenchant observation is that interest-group conflicts can only be resolved by applying a standard that transcends the conflict among the groups. What is this standard and how do we arrive at it? If, as Bentley and other group theorists suggest, politics is merely a Hobbesian struggle of conflicting interests, why does it not end up as "might makes right"? Cochran (1974, 335) argues that an interest must be a justified claim, not merely a want or desire. He also notes that interests are reconciled only when groups feel that justice has been done, not merely by getting what they want. Cochran concludes that "political society is not characterized by the struggle of interest forces alone, but rather by a complex mix of searches for justice and attempts by groups and individuals to advance their own desires" (1974, 337).

6.6 Strategic Use of the Concept of the Public Interest

The concept of the public interest is worth noting not only because of the intellectual challenge in formulating a theoretically and operationally satisfying definition, but also because it plays an important role in public policy. As we have seen, it is used both as a criteria for decision making and as a justification for policy actions already taken. In addition, the concept of the public interest is of considerable significance in the efforts of interest groups to influence public policy. In general terms, it is necessary for business groups and other interest groups to convince the targets of their lobbying efforts that the advancement of their private interests is either in the public interest or is at least not inconsistent with it. How this is done is discussed in chapter 9.

7.0 POSITIVE THEORY AND POLICY FORMULATION

7.1 Modelling Public Policy Formulation

There are many approaches to the study of public policy making. There is a trade-off in the analysis between simplicity and clarity (i.e., using a few, well-defined variables) and comprehensiveness. While more comprehensive treatments introduce more variables into the discussion, they tend to rely more heavily on description than on analysis, that is, the formulation and/or testing of refutable hypotheses.

Invariably, therefore, writers on public policy must choose which variables to deal with and what emphasis to place on each of these. It should be recognized that the first step (which variable on which to focus) may be a pre-analytic act; that is, it may be based as much on intuition as on previous analytical work.

Different models or approaches emphasize different variables.[30] They also place different emphasis on normative and positive types of analysis. Various positive approaches to understanding public policy formulation stress the following themes (clusters of variables):

- the history and the evolution of institutions;
- the behaviour of interest groups;
- the role of ideology (values/ideas);
- the personalities of important actors in the political system;
- marginal-voter politics; and
- the constitutionally determined structure of government and policy processes.

In this chapter I have chosen for several reasons to emphasize the public choice approach to understanding how public policies are formed. First, it gives great weight to two elements that appear to be of major significance in policy making: the activities of interest groups, and the motivation of politicians to get elected and stay in power through the practice of marginal-voter politics. The public choice approach integrates these two elements into what appears to be a more realistic (some would say cynical) analytical framework. As this book is largely about the behaviour of businesses and trade associations acting as interest groups, it seems reasonable to focus on an approach to policy formulation that gives greater weight to the role of interest groups in shaping public policy than, for example, to the formal institutions and processes associated with public policy making.

Second, the public choice approach, while not denying that constitutionally determined institutions, structures, and processes matter and that history also shapes all of these elements, argues that these aspects of the policy system can be taken as the framework in which interest groups and politicians interact to make policy. The public choice approach applies both to Canada and the U.S. despite the fact that the very structure of governmental institutions and allocation of powers in the two countries are quite different. Canada's system of government places enormous power in the cabinet to initiate legislation and to shape policy through the executive.[31] In the U.S. congressional system, the power to initiate legislation and to enact it is more diffused among individual legislators, notably committee chairpersons. On the other hand, the power of Canada's provinces is much greater than that of the states in the U.S. Moreover, the constitutional division of labour is less clear-cut in Canada than in the U.S. The widespread use of concurrent jurisdiction means that the need for federal-provincial diplomacy is a persistent constraint on a federal government with a large majority in Parliament. Despite these differences, two critical factors are the same: politicians wish to attain and retain power, and to do so they must offer policies that command the support of sufficient voters to form a government; and interest groups wish to influence public policy to achieve their own objectives.

Third, the public choice approach focuses on outcomes — specifically, who gets what. It is based on one of the strongest propositions concerning individual behaviour, namely self-interest. However, the approach does not rule out the idea that for some the process is as important as the substantive policy outcomes.[32] The analyst using the public choice perspective would try to understand who benefits and who loses in terms of the choice of particular processes. At the highest level of abstraction, the choice of a constitution or of a set of rules generally determining how other rules may be made, can be analyzed not as an exercise in finding a consensus among differing concepts of the public interest, but as an exchange process between interest groups and politicians.

In the same vein, the public choice approach does not ignore ideology.[33] Rather, ideology is seen, not as an end in itself,[34] but as a means by which political actors (voters and politicians) economize on information and reduce the cost of information processing. Moreover, it is hard to find a successful politician whose ideology would lead to decisions much different from those predicted on the basis of his or her electoral self-interest.

7.2 The Public Choice Approach

The term *public choice* refers to the processes by which public collectivities (e.g., governments, individual bureaus) make decisions. The term is in contradistinction to the process by which *individuals* or private economic units (firms) make decisions, presumably to maximize their welfare.

In general terms, positive theories in the public choice approach have the following characteristics:

- They recognize that decisions by a government to intervene in the market economy are *political*, rather than technical, decisions.
- They assume that the various actors involved in these political decisions (voters, politicians, bureaucrats, interest groups) behave in a rational, self-interested fashion. Each is "looking out for number one," but their behaviour is influenced and constrained by other actors as well as by the rules of the game. As Hartle notes, "The public choice approach emphasizes the incentives under which the principal actors play their parts in each of the unique public decision-making games" (1984, 79).
- They take into account, in varying degrees, a number of the characteristics of the "real world" (e.g., imperfect knowledge, costly information, variations in stakes, legal constraints) that shape the functioning of democratic political processes.
- These theories often make use of analogies of processes in economic markets.

Breton points out an interesting bias that existed (and still exists to some extent) in the literature on the role of government: "Some half a century ago, governments were usually conceived — at least in the Anglo-American literature, although not in the Continental, and especially not in the Italian literature — as institutions dedicated to the single-minded pursuit of the public good — that is, politicians were assumed to be motivated not by self-interest, but by a desire to improve the position of the governed" (1976, 13–14). He suggests that the idea may have evolved from the much earlier belief that authority is of divine origin. While normative theories of government actions abound (Stanbury 1984b), such naive views of government as an institution have increasingly been replaced by more realistic perceptions, such as those associated with the public choice literature (Mueller 1979).

Samuels indicates that one of the strengths of public choice theory is that it provides a more realistic formulation of the governmental process. For example, many public choice theorists would agree with the statement that "government is a mechanism through which individuals act collectively to improve their private utility. Government is a vehicle through which is promoted the self interest of whomever can get into a position to control it" (1978, 57).

Samuels also notes that "the conduct of positive public choice theory is fraught with opportunities for the intrusion of subtle normative premises" (1978, 64). He points out that there is an important difference between describing certain more or less objective features of how collective decisions are made and "judging those features to be adequate, inadequate, or excessive; effective or ineffective; and/or successful or a failure" (1978, 58). "More" or "less" is *not* the same type of statement as "too much" or "too little."

It is recognized, however, that behind the political calculus may well lie substantive problems attributable to various types of market failures. These are impediments to the functioning of markets that prevent them from achieving allocative efficiency, that is, optimal price and output — a point at which it is not possible to rearrange inputs or outputs so as to make one person better off without *also* reducing the economic welfare of at least one other person in society. Market failures include natural monopolies, externalities, imperfect information, destructive competition, public goods (in a technical sense), and common property resources. (See Stanbury 1984b, chap. 2.)

At the same time, we must not lose sight of the fact that politics is a battle over who gets what. In other words, most of the participants in public policy making are interested in altering the distribution of income rather than improving the efficiency of resource allocation. The structure of incentives in a democratic political system does not favour allocative efficiency.

8.0 THE PUBLIC CHOICE APPROACH IN MORE DETAIL

Downs offers an "economic theory of democracy" that "explains how the governors are led to act by their own selfish motives" (1957, 136). It is a forerunner of what is now called the public choice approach to positive theories of government action. I use Downs's model as the centrepiece of my analysis in this chapter and enrich it with the insights of others.

8.1 Definitions and Axioms

The definitions employed in Downs's model are the following:

- Government is a social agent with the legitimate power to coerce all other actors in society, i.e., individuals, firms, unions, etc.

- A democracy is a political system in which there is competition among political parties for control of the executive. The party (or coalition) with a majority of seats forms the government. Losers don't prevent winners from taking office, nor do winners prevent losers from contesting future elections. Each sane, law abiding citizen has one [nontransferable] vote in each election.

Downs then formulates the following axioms:

- Parties are coalitions of individuals who seek office to enjoy the income, prestige and power that go with holding power.
- The winning party has complete control over the government's actions until the next election. (In short, there is no implementation problem in the form of bureaucratic foot-dragging.)
- Government's economic powers are unlimited — in other words there are no constitutional constraints on the power of the government over economic matters, presumably including private property.
- The incumbent party has unlimited power, but it can't restrict the political freedom of opposition parties, unless they seek to overthrow the government by force. (The first statement is a very strong assumption that is unnecessary for the positive theory of government policy.)
- Each agent (politician, voter, interest group, etc.) behaves rationally, i.e., proceeds toward its goals with the minimum use of scarce resources and acts only where the marginal benefit exceeds the marginal cost. (1957, 137)

8.2 The Role of Policies/Government Action

The central hypothesis is that "political parties in a democracy formulate policy strictly as a means of gaining votes" (Downs 1957, 37). Politicians do not seek office to implement an ideology embodied in certain policies or to serve a particular interest group. "Rather, they formulate policies and serve interest groups in order to gain [or retain] office." This is not to say that ideology plays no role. In fact, "lack of information creates a demand for ideologies in the electorate" (Downs 1957, 142).[35]

8.3 The Role of Politicians

Politicians, like the other actors in the model, are assumed to act in a rational, self-interested fashion. They wish to be elected because the holding of office is assumed to maximize their welfare in terms of income, power, and prestige of being in office.[36] Hobbes, a shrewd and still relevant observer of human nature, put it this way: "The business of the World consisteth in nothing else but a perpetual contention for Honour, Riches and Authority." In Hartle's view, it is the "proximate objective" of politicians "to be elected (or re-elected) as a member of a government in power and to obtain positions of ever-increasing power in that government" (1984, 66). Breton observes, however, that, "as in the rest of us, self-interest in politicians is not inconsistent with a degree of altruism" (1976, 14).

Politicians, in this model, are entrepreneurs "selling policies for votes instead of products for money." Bennett and Di Lorenzo put the matter a little differently, but the point is the same: "Politician(s) use the machinery of government to bestow favors on special-interest groups that, in turn, provide votes and campaign contributions for the next election battle" (1983, 4).

The politician's life, however, is frequently not an easy one.[37] Certainly it is fraught with a variety of risks: defeat at the polls; the failure to obtain a position of real power, that is, a cabinet post; the possible loss of reputation while being in cabinet; enormous stresses on family life; and the uncertainty of a patronage appointment when out of office.[38] Cabinet ministers, aided by polls and the analytical capability of numbers of public servants, have the difficult job of identifying those policies that will attract or retain political support. Despite its great power, the cabinet must necessarily deal with a number of other interests that can constrain its behaviour: the bureaucracy, the courts, other levels of government, and public opinion, particularly as represented in the media — hence the very important role for politicians in building a consensus or at least ameliorating the inevitable conflicts in public policy formulation. As Hartle notes: "Most of us seem to ignore or denigrate the politician's role as a consensus builder. No politician would prefer a painful compromise over a decision supported unanimously. . . . Many of the rituals that attend the political/legal process can be thought of as serving the function of helping to legitimize the outcome — an outcome which may be distasteful to the losers" (1979, 35).

Most politicians don't get into the cabinet and many don't even sit on the government side. They never experience the power and prestige of being at the centre of the political process. The resources and scope of action for individual backbenchers are limited, although in recent years there have been a number of proposals to enlarge the role of the "ordinary member."[39] These seem doomed to failure, as the reforms would reduce the power and prerogatives of the cabinet, which, with the prime minister, is the apex of power.

When I say that politicians "sell" policies in exchange for votes, the reader should not draw a pejorative conclusion. The essence of democratic governments is that they move by persuasion and that they respond — albeit imperfectly and with a lag — to the desires of the people. The legitimate use of coercion by the state is based largely on the governors' exercise of power with the consent of the governed and on their accountability for the exercise of that power. To "sell" policies is to persuade people, and persuasion is easiest and least coercive when what is being offered is, in fact, desired by those to whom it is offered. Hence, in a democracy, public policies — in broad terms — must reflect the desires of the electorate. Abraham Lincoln put it this way: "Public sentiment is everything. With public sentiment nothing can fail. Without it nothing can succeed."

Public sentiment, however, is not entirely exogenous to politicians or to others: it can be influenced to some degree on some issues. Hartle argues that "without the efforts of some politicians to nudge the system toward a slightly different and unpopular course, from time to time, the ability of a nation to adapt to changing circumstances would undoubtedly be less than it is" (1979, 35). So the effective and ambitious politician is not an entirely passive interpreter of polls who then "gives the people what they say they want." There is scope for leadership:

> Political leadership does not usually entail that the outstanding politician personally discover a new theory or a new concept or a new policy or a new constraint, or foresee emerging trends hidden to others. Rather, it means that the rare politician is able to discern in the discoveries of a few others an insight "just slightly ahead of its time," and through a mixture of persuasion and demonstration bring it to bear on policy decisions before it has been widely recognized by voters. (Hartle 1979, 35)

8.4 The Role of Political Parties

The imperatives of political competition in a democracy imply that "the government always acts so as to maximize the number of votes it will receive" (Downs 1957, 137). Where the electoral system uses geographic constituencies, this translates into seat maximization. And within each constituency (or riding), it is the interests of the *marginal* or uncommitted voter that must be most closely attended to.[40] Hartle puts it this way: "Parties, leaders and candidates increase their likelihood of success (obtaining the largest number of seats) by seeking to appeal to the uncommitted voters in marginal constituencies. . . . At the extremes, rewarding the faithful is unnecessary and rewarding staunch opponents is futile"[41] (1984, 67).

Trebilcock and Hartle indicate how marginal ridings and marginal votes "can be identified operationally, albeit crudely." They continue:

> Marginal ridings are those where the party affiliation of the MP elected in the riding differs from that of his or her predecessor x or more times in the previous y elections. Once these ridings have been

identified (a simple matter except when redistribution of votes has taken place), a scientific survey is carried out in each of them. The survey has two purposes:

1. To identify the voters who switched party affilitaion in one or more previous elections.
2. To determine their characteristics (e.g., age, sex, occupation, marital status, income, ethnic origin, and so on).

These are the marginal voters. The next obvious step is to ascertain, again through surveys, the policy issues to which they attach the most importance. From there it is a relatively short step to the production of an election platform that is most likely to attract their support. (1982, 35)

This statement merits two comments. First, marginal ridings may also be defined as those in the previous election that were won/lost by the party in power by only a small fraction of the total votes cast, perhaps 5 or 10 percent. In other words, if a small number of voters switched parties, the riding could be won by another party. Of course, more complex measures of the marginality of ridings have been developed.

Second, and more importantly, I would challenge the idea that it is fairly easy — as Trebilcock and Hartle suggest — to design an election platform once a party understands which issues are most salient for marginal or swing voters.[42] The problem lies in a fact emphasized by Hartle in an earlier book, namely, "full-line forcing" (1979, 68). Each political party offers a full line of policies in which specific policies may be added or deleted as the party tries to find the best package. As Hartle remarks, "Local party candidates can be thought of as retailers of the full line of policies offered by one of the few competing suppliers [parties]" (1979, 68). The problem is that the mix or line of policies that maximizes the party's overall chances (i.e., retaining its "committed" support and attracting marginal voters in sufficient number) may not maximize the party's chances of electing a member in certain swing ridings. Hence, local candidates will try to reshape the platform to increase their own electoral chances.

More generally, it is necessary to ascertain the importance of issues or policy programs[43] in determining the outcome of election campaigns. It is usually argued that in Canadian general elections the quality of individual candidates and the exact nature of a party's policies are not very important. The perceived characteristics of the leader, the condition of the economy, and the ability of the party to communicate an attractive image in the media, particularly television, are much more important factors in electoral success. A confidential memo, based on extensive research and prepared by a longtime senior advisor to the Liberal party, indicates that the following four factors largely explain the voting behaviour of electors:

1. The activity and strength imagery of party leaders is the fundamental motivating factor behind voting behaviour. Also of great importance in influencing voter behaviour is the degree to which each leader is perceived as understanding and wishing to work for the average voter rather than for him- or herself or a special group. This is called "sensitivity to and real interest in the voter," or more simply, rapport.

   "With few exceptions, voting behaviour is influenced to a much greater extent by the party leaders than by the parties, the candidates representing the parties in each electoral district, or by the party platforms in specific terms." "Imagery of strength of the leaders invariably is associated with imagery of activity in politics, and either strength or activity imagery may be the prime causative agent affecting voting behaviour." Charisma in politics means the leader is perceived as understanding and being keenly interested in helping the average person/voter. Since the voters have neither the time nor ability to understand the welter of issues the government of the day must deal with, they focus their choice upon the party leader who is expected to act in their best interest and whom they can respect as a person and a leader.

2. The second most important factor is the electors' concepts of human beings relative to their environment. Research has identified two broad philosophies. One, the political "right," sees the character and behaviour of individuals, except for maturation, as largely immutable beyond one's genetic inheritance and childhood upbringing. Those in this group see little value in government intervention to improve the lot of the disadvantaged, and they believe that with the incentives of substantial personal reward the more capable will naturally rise to the top. The other philosophy (the political "left") sees the individual's behaviour as largely determined by environmental forces. People are capable of change and government is capable of modifying the social and economic environment to permit individuals to change in beneficial ways. The object of political research is to identify the number of voters subscribing to these basic philosophical positions and their various mixtures. It has been argued by successful political analysts that factors 1 and 2 together can predict which party a person will vote for 80 percent of the time. Specific platform planks (policies) usually have little influence on voting behaviour except as they affect factors 1 and 2.

3. The social-political-economic climate prevalent at any particular time and place influences voting behaviour. If a sense of general well-being does not prevail (at election time), there is a greater tendency for electors to "take a chance on the leader of a party not in power." This factor is analogous to the concept of retrospective voting (see Fiorina 1981).

4. Voting behaviour is influenced by the proportions of all electors who

have a sense of loyalty to particular parties or persons, and the strength of any such loyalty. Political research can identify the number and characteristics of those voters who remain loyal to the same party and those who have changed their preferences. It can also identify the reasons for these shifts in preference and the relative intensity of party preferences. The so-called undecided vote is usually greatly overestimated in most polls. Most people in this category are simply offering a polite refusal to give their preference or voting intention.

8.5 Marginal-Voter Politics in Practice

Escott Reid's account of the operation of the Saskatchewan Liberal machine prior to 1929 is still highly relevant today. He noted that "the preliminary work of the constituency organization was to divide the voters into those who were strong Conservatives, those who were strong Liberals and those who were doubtful" (1979, 21). He explains the significance of this tripartite classification as getting "the greatest results out of the efforts of the party workers, both between elections and on polling day. The workers . . . had four objects in view in their work which went on continuously between elections: the doubtfuls must be persuaded to Liberalism, the Liberals must be kept in line, the Conservatives must be weakened, and the path of Liberal supporters to the polls must be made as easy as possible" (1979, 23). In particular, party workers focused their attention on "key men" who were "doubtfuls" or already in the Liberal camp. They were key men because they might influence the vote of a dozen or more ordinary voters.

A more modern version of this process is described by Clive Cocking in his book on the 1979 federal general election campaign. He describes the focus of the parties' campaign efforts as follows:

> What all this sound and fury ultimately comes down to is a battle for the hearts and minds of the coin-flipping, hatpin-wielding set: the "undecided voters" in the catch-all phrase of pollsters; the "low interest transient voters" in the (slightly) more precise language of political scientists. The hatpin element represents about 15 percent of the total electorate and, in a country where the total swing in the vote is rarely above five percent, the party which wins most of their votes is likely on its way to forming a government. They're the main target of television-oriented campaigns. (1980, 182)

Who are these "swing voters"?

> The group is comprised of newly eligible voters, people who are not very interested or knowledgeable about politics and individuals whose voting is irregular. "They're the people who are supposed to be most easily influenced by TV" [according to Fred Fletcher, a political scientist specializing in the role of the media in politics]. (Cocking 1980, 183)

What is the relationship between media use, interest in politics, and strength of party affiliation? According to Professor Fletcher,

> there is . . . about 40 percent of Canadian voters who have a rock solid party affiliation and who are well-informed, heavy users of all news media; there is another approximately 25 percent who are fairly consistent in their voting patterns and reasonably knowledgeable. The bulk of the floating vote is comprised of two groups: about 10 percent of the electorate who have high political interest but are flexible in their voting and then the approximately 15 percent low interest transient voters — the hatpin people. They're most susceptible to the televised political gospel, not only because it's what they're inclined to see, but also because they're primarily motivated by "matters of style or personal qualities of leaders rather than issues." (Cocking 1980, 183)

But the parties cannot ignore their dyed-in-the-wool supporters.

> Parties must also be concerned with retaining and activating their own base of support. "There are these highly interested and informed people," said Dr. Fletcher, "who have a party affiliation, but who could be turned off if they didn't think the party was articulating the issues that they agree with." (Cocking 1980, 184)

In a democracy this responsiveness of political parties to changes in the perceptions of voters or to more accurate information concerning their preferences is "customarily greeted with derision by political observers, who take [it] as evidence of cynical opportunism or worse" (Hartle 1984, 9). But both political survival and democratic responsiveness dictate that "when voter perceptions change in response to a real or an illusory change in circumstances, an 'unthinkable' policy option can become not only 'possible' but, finally, 'inevitable' " (Hartle 1984, 7). Such changes can be construed as "evidence of the effectiveness of interparty competition for voter support — the foundation of responsible and representative government in the face of changing circumstances and perception" (Hartle 1984, 9).

But even doing the Lord's work costs money — a point much emphasized by television evangelists. Yet until recently too little attention has been given to the connection between financing political parties and policy formulation. As Breton points out, "Practically all political theory is formulated in terms of mechanisms for the representation of the preferences of people. The election of representatives, and the orderly succession of one government by another are assumed to operate costlessly. . . . [Hence] the cost of democracy . . . had to be borne privately by individuals who entered politics" (1976, 15). Since this was not an efficient solution, political parties were created and they absorb a substantial fraction of the costs not borne by the state (taxpayers).

But how do political parties obtain the wherewithal to bear these costs?

In Breton's view, they obtain it by trading with the private sector. "The trading process can be caricatured as follows: 'if you will donate some money to our party, we will provide you in exchange with a tariff which will allow you to reap monopoly rents of such and such magnitude, or we will allow you to form a professional or trade association that will have the power to set standards, to define the terms of licences, to set the rates that can be charged for services rendered, and so on!' " (Breton 1976, 16). In other words, political parties obtain campaign contributions from interest groups in exchange for promises of favourable policies when they gain or retain power. However, as will be shown in section 10 below, the political exchange process is rather more complicated in reality.

It is critical to appreciate in discussing the motivation of voters, politicians, and parties that while a social function (the supply of public policies) is being performed by harnessing private motives (pay, power, prestige of office), we cannot assume a priori that this behaviour is socially optimal in the sense that collective welfare is maximized.

8.6 A World of Imperfect Knowledge and Costly Information

Downs makes the important observation that, in a world of perfect knowledge and costless information, "the government gives the preferences of each citizen exactly the same weight as those of every other citizen" (1957, 139). Moreover, there is no role for interest groups in such a world, as each voter not only knows his or her preferences well, but also is perfectly informed about the likely consequences of every policy in place or proposed by the government or opposition parties. In other words, no citizen can influence another's vote. In the "real" world, however, things are quite different.

The positive theory of government action will now be examined under the more interesting and realistic assumptions of imperfect knowledge (uncertainty) and costly information. Imperfect knowledge means that voters are unsure about their preferences, about the effects of past, current, and future government policies on their own utility income. It means that parties are uncertain about voters' preferences and about which policies are best able to satisfy them. Because information to dispel (or reduce) uncertainty/ignorance is costly, political parties must obtain the resources to acquire such information.

Hartle's (1984) analysis of policies resulting from rent-seeking behaviour of politicians, bureaucrats, pressure groups, and journalists is squarely in the public choice approach to collective decision making. It differs little from Downs's formulation of the problem almost three decades earlier. Hartle defines rent seeking as "an investment of real resources [time, money, expertise] by individuals or interest groups in obtaining favourable (or avoiding unfavourable) government decisions. These decisions involve the *redistribution* of income/wealth rather than the *creation* of income/wealth" (1984, 34).

Rent seeking occurs in a variety of ways and in a number of forms. It consists of

- expenditures on lobbying to secure favourable legislation or prevent unfavourable legislation — including subordinate legislation created by the cabinet, a minister or a regulatory agency;
- expenditures on efforts to seek favourable (prevent unfavourable) interpretations of the discretionary provisions of existing legislation, policy and programs. The "targets" of such activities include politicians, bureaucrats, regulators and the courts.
- efforts by politicians, bureaucrats, and others seeking elected or appointed office in the expectation of receiving the pay, power or prestige associated with such offices. (Hartle 1984, 36)

In a world of imperfect knowledge (uncertainty), the arts of persuasion become important. Voters and parties need information to help them achieve their objectives. However, those in a position to finance the acquisition of information are also self-interested. Therefore, imperfect knowledge makes the governing party "susceptible to bribery" in the sense that it is willing to "sell policies" in exchange for the resources to persuade voters to elect them. (Opposition parties sell the promise of what they would do if they attain power.) This form of persuasion takes the form of "free" information to voters to help them make up their minds about the best party to support. Downs points out: "Essentially, inequality of political influence is a necessary result of imperfect information, given an unequal distribution of wealth and income in society. When knowledge is imperfect, effective political action requires the use of economic resources to meet the cost of information" (1957, 141).

8.7 The Role of Voters

The assumption of rational self-interested behaviour applies also to voters. They are assumed to vote according to expected changes in their utility incomes (i.e., self-defined welfare) from government activity and the alternatives offered by the opposition parties. Hartle states that the interests of individuals "can be thought of as a bundle of rights to such diverse things as: real and personal property; personal health and reputation; skills; tenure of offices and employment; entitlements to public and private transfer payments; and tax liabilities (a negative right); and access to transportation, communications, legal and other systems" (1984, 64). This bundle of rights, less obligations, he calls the individual's Comprehensive Net Worth. "Political activities [informed voting and lobbying] can be thought of as investments made in the expectation of, in the first instance, maintaining existing right holdings and, in the second instance,

expanding those rights" (Hartle 1984, 65). In estimating his or her utility income from public policies (hence, which party to support), the
voter, according to Downs, will engage in what has subsequently been
called "restrospective voting" (see Fiorina 1981); that is, "the primary
factor influencing his [or her] estimate of each party's future performance is not its campaign promises about the future but its performance
during the period just ending."

Downs (1957, 149) points out that "men are more likely to exert direct
influence on government policy formation in their roles as producers
than in their roles as consumers." The absolute size of their single stake
dictates this conclusion. Governments do not attend much to people's
interest as consumers "because consumers rationally seek to acquire only
that information which provides a return larger than its cost." Ignorance is rational in the sense of being economically efficient. The same is
true for voters. Downs notes that "for most voters in most elections
the incentive to become well informed — a costly process — is practically
nonexistent" (1957, 146). Hence, "the startling conclusion [is] that it is
irrational for most citizens to acquire political information for the purpose of voting." The problem is that such information is costly (ignoring
the substantial amount of "free" information available, including the
biased/selective information provided by political parties and interest
groups), and the expected benefit is trivial in that a single vote almost
never swings an election. Thus, "the rational course of action for most
citizens is to remain politically uninformed" (Downs 1957, 147).

It is the existence of rational ignorance and bounded rationality on
the part of voters (i.e., there are limitations on the ability of individuals
to acquire, process, and respond to information) that "creates possibilities for the provision of subsidized, selective information by groups of
voters [including interest groups] to other groups of voters, by groups of
voters to political parties and by political parties to groups of voters"
(Trebilcock & Hartle 1982, 38). In particular, interest groups representing individuals with relatively concentrated stakes in issues (i.e., where
the stake is sufficiently large in absolute terms that it overcomes communication and organization costs and also constitutes a substantial proportion of the individual's income/wealth) will tend to find it beneficial
to provide information to more numerous but dispersed groups of voters
who each may have only a small stake in the issue. It is also likely that
groups of individuals most constrained by bounded rationality will be
the target of parties and interest groups seeking to influence their voting behaviour.

8.8 The Role of Lobbying

Those most willing to provide the resources that politicians need to operate
in a world of imperfect knowledge and costly information are those with
the biggest stake in the system, that is, those with the largest amounts of

Figure 4-2
MODEL OF EXCHANGE PROCESSES IN A
POSITIVE THEORY OF GOVERNMENT ACTION

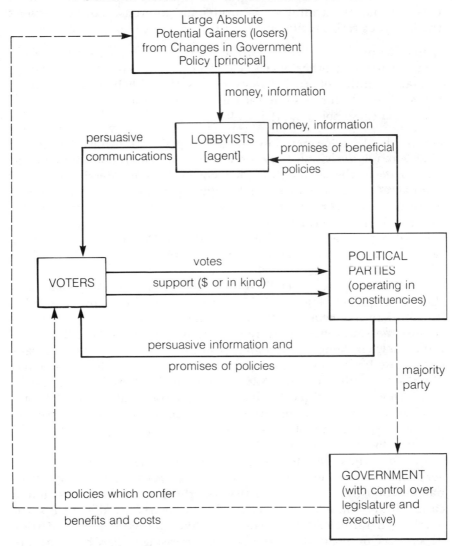

wealth or income susceptible to change as a result of public policy. We should expect that any inequalities in the distribution of income or wealth at the "beginning of the game" would continue or increase as a result of the political exchange process (sketched in Figure 4-2) in a world of imperfect knowledge and costly information.[44]

A principal-agent relationship is created. Those who (largely by reason of the *existing* distribution of income and wealth) have the most to lose or gain by a change in public policy will employ lobbyists (specialists in influencing government/political parties) and arm them with tangible resources and a clear knowledge of the types of policies that are likely to be beneficial or harmful to the principals' interests. Downs describes the lobbyist's task as follows:

> In order to be an effective lobbyist, a citizen must persuade the governing party that the policies he wants either are already desired by a large number of other citizens or are sufficiently beneficial to the rest of the electorate so that it will, at worst, not resent the enactment of these policies. (1957, 148)

Downs's model appears to envisage two types of lobbying: that by citizens with relatively small stakes on their own behalf; and that by large stakeholders either acting through agents or dealing directly with political parties. In the latter case, stakeholders exchange their political help (e.g., campaign contributions, specialized [costly] and valuable information) for policy favours, a "transaction eminently rational for both themselves and the government." Moreover, as Downs points out, "such favor buyers need not even pose as representatives for the people"[45] (1957, 141).

Lobbying requires specialized knowledge of particular policies and their consequences for groups of voters. The level of knowledge is far greater than that required by the rational voter to vote. Lobbying also requires persuasiveness. Both require money, as the data in Table 4-1 indicate. Even though *campaign* expenditures by both parties and candidates are limited by law, the three main parties and their candidates spent $24.8 million in 1979, $26.1 million in 1980, and $42 million in 1984. However, as Table 4-1 indicates, a substantial fraction of total campaign outlays was reimbursed by the federal government under the Election Expenses Act of 1974: 41 percent in 1979, 42 percent in 1980, but only 36 percent in 1984.

However, these data on campaign expenditures do not include the very considerable and growing expenditures by the parties outside campaign periods. For example, in 1984 the three main parties (excluding candidates) spent $38.8 million of which only $17.4 million was spent on the general election campaign. In other words, the main parties' dependence on political contributions is increasing as they become more institutionalized in their activities between elections. Boyer concludes that "Canada's political parties at all levels have an unquenchable thirst for funds" (1983, 1). (More generally, see chapter 10.)

Despite the "democratization" of political party financing stemming from the Election Expenses Act, corporations accounted for over one-half the revenues of the federal Liberals and Conservatives in the 1979 and 1980 general election campaigns. In 1984, including the election campaign, the Tories raised $11.0 million from corporations and $10.1

Table 4–1

EXPENDITURES ON FEDERAL GENERAL ELECTION CAMPAIGNS, 1979–84

($ thousands)

Expenditures by		1979	1980	1984
• Parties	Conservative	3 845	4 407	6 389
	Liberal	3 913	3 846	6 293
	NDP	2 190	3 086	4 731
	Total	9 948	11 339	17 413
• Candidates	Conservative	6 016	5 680	10 726
	Liberal	6 186	6 074	9 447
	NDP	2 665	2 987	4 479
	Total	14 867	14 741	24 652
Reimbursement from federal government to				
• Parties	Conservative	794	977	1 438
	Liberal	718	910	1 416
	NDP	496	677	1 064
	Total	2 008	2 564	3 918
• Candidates	Conservative	2 868	2 871	5 117
	Liberal	3 594	3 656	4 081
	NDP	1 671	1 886	1 917
	Total	8 133	8 393	11 115

Source: *Report of the Chief Electoral Officer Respecting Election Expenses, 1979, 1980, 1984* (Ottawa: Chief Electoral Officer).

million from individuals. The Liberals raised $5.3 million from corporations and $5.2 million from individuals. Large corporate contributions — those over $10 000 — generated $4.32 million for the Tories in 1984 (n = 198) and $2.37 million for the Liberals (n = 113). It should be noted, however, that while the two main parties still rely quite heavily on large contributions from corporations, interest groups including trade associations do not give much money to the federal Liberals or the Conservatives. See chapter 10.

The lobbyist's living depends on providing valuable services to his or her principal. Essentially, he or she is an intermediary in an exchange between the large potential gainers or losers (in absolute terms) from policy actions and political parties. In return for some combination of money, political support, and information, political parties offer the promise of policies favourable to large stakeholders.[46]

Lobbyists seek to influence the party in power in a variety of ways, but in functional terms there are three categories:

- The provision of information about voter preferences, particularly the likely political consequences of future policies and the responses to existing policies.
- Financial contributions (or resources in kind) to permit the party to acquire costly information in a world of imperfect knowledge and to pay for efforts to persuade voters to support the party.
- The mounting of publicity campaigns designed to convince large numbers of voters to support (or not support) candidates, a party, or a particular policy.

Hartle lists the following as "the most important determinants of the formation and maintenance of an organized lobby group":

- the *average* value of the issue at stake to the individuals who have a common interest;
- the number and geographic dispersion of these individuals;
- the ability of the organization to provide some [individually appropriable] benefit, over and above the pursuit of the common interest through lobbying, as an added inducement to membership; and
- the ability of the organization to minimize the number of "free riders" — who share in the benefits provided by the organization but would not contribute their share of the costs if they could be avoided. (1984, 69–70)

It is critical to appreciate that, despite the enthusiasm of the pluralists, many important interests fail to find representation in the political process. This is true even though the aggregate value of the economic stakes involved are many times that of interests that are able to lobby effectively. These economic stakes can also be much larger than the total costs of lobbying on behalf of the interests that don't get represented. The problem is that the benefits of such representation are a public good in the technical sense (Olson 1965). In a competitive environment, such goods will be undersupplied. They will only be supplied if the benefit to an individual or a small group of individuals able to overcome the free-rider problem is greater than the cost of providing the good, that is, paying the cost of the lobbying effort.

Where the benefits of collective action are widely diffused and small relative to the Comprehensive Net Worth of the individual (to use Hartle's phrase), the interest will remain latent unless (1) members of the group can be coerced into paying dues to finance the lobbying or other representational activities, or (2) group membership and financial support are necessary to obtain some other noncollective benefit. This latter approach Olson (1965, 132) calls the "by-product" theory of large pressure groups. See also Lowi (1969, 36).

9.0 THE PUBLIC CHOICE APPROACH RESTATED

To ensure that the public choice approach to a positive theory of government intervention is not lost in the detail, its central elements can be summarized as follows:

1. All actors (voters, politicians, stakeholders, lobbyists) act in a rational,[47] self-interested fashion; that is, they seek their objectives at the least cost and only act where the additional benefits outweigh the additional costs. They do this in both the economic and political arenas.

2. Politicians seek office for the income, prestige, and power that are attributable to the holding of office. Other actors maximize their utility incomes broadly defined.

3. Political parties formulate policies strictly as means of obtaining political support (votes) so as to gain or retain office. Politicians are political entrepreneurs "selling" (exchanging) policies for votes rather than products for money.

4. Political competition results in efforts by parties to maximize the number of votes they receive. In a representative democracy based on geographic constituencies, parties shape their policy proposals to appeal to marginal voters (uncommitted) in marginal ridings.

5. In a world characterized by imperfect knowledge (uncertainty) and costly information, lobbying activities take on considerable importance. In particular, interest groups (those with absolutely large stakes of wealth or income susceptible to alteration by government policy and able to overcome the transaction and information costs of organization) provide the resources for political parties to acquire information and to finance efforts to persuade voters to support them on election day. (Note that in a world of perfect knowledge lobbyists would not exist because no citizen would be capable of influencing the vote of another, as each has full knowledge of his or her own preferences and of the consequences for him or her of all policies in place or being proposed by all parties.)

6. Imperfect knowledge and costly information make the governing party "susceptible to bribery." Resources are needed to acquire knowledge of voters' preferences (over and above that which can be obtained by party representatives) and to persuade voters that the party's policies are good for them. "One way to get such resources is to sell policy favors to those who can pay for them [large stakeholders], either by campaign contributions, favorable editorial policies, or direct influence over other voters. . . . They merely exchange their political help for policy favors, a transaction eminently reasonable for both themselves and the government" (Downs 1957, 141).

   Therefore, the resulting inequality of political influence is a necessary result of imperfect knowledge, costly information, and the prior unequal distribution of income and wealth. "Lobbying in a democracy is a highly rational response to the lack of perfect information, as is government submission to the demands of lobbyists" (Downs 1957, 141).

7. Public policies (government actions) are formulated to generate one or both of the following types of political support: votes and financial support with which to acquire information to persuade voters. As Trebilcock et al. (1982) emphasize, governments seek to sell their policies by means of subsidized, selective, persuasive information. In general, governments will adopt those policies that will be most effective in getting the support of marginal or uncommitted voters.

8. The name of the game for the party in power is to woo uncommitted voters while not alienating committed supporters. Two general techniques achieve this objective. First, the party can impose costs on committed opponents (preferably, but not necessarily, in a disguised fashion) while conferring benefits on the uncommitted voters. This is constrained by the effectiveness of the counterpromises of other parties. Second, the party can try to spread the costs of its policies that benefit uncommitted voters so widely that no individual finds it worthwhile to invest in political action to avoid these costs.

Following Trebilcock et al. (1982), we can draw the following conclusions:

- It is in the interests of the party in power to choose policies that confine benefits to marginal voters and confine costs to inframarginal voters.
- Policies should be chosen so as to provide benefits in a concentrated form so that their visibility is enhanced and to impose costs in dispersed form so that their visibility is lessened. However, as benefits become more clearly visible, the smaller the number of voters on which a party can realize a political return.
- The perceived benefits of a policy can be made to appear greater than the real benefits through the strategic use of subsidized, selective information, often of a symbolic nature. A similar approach may be taken when the dispersion of costs does not fully obscure their existence from marginal voters who bear them.
- The more widely dispersed the group of marginal voters sought to be benefited by a chosen policy, the less real the benefits need be. Widely dispersed interest groups and voters who possess inferior information-processing capabilities are particularly vulnerable to the substitution of symbolism for substance in the choice of policies.

9. The core of the positive theory of government action lies in the idea that particular policies have no meaning to political parties except as vehicles to obtain political support. Parties compete to identify and shape policies that appeal to voters in order to gain or retain office.

10.0 WHAT IS EXCHANGED IN POLITICAL MARKETS?

The public choice approach to a positive theory of government intervention argues that, in part, policies are "sold" by political parties in exchange for financial and other resources. Breton (1976) comes closest to Downs in his theory of regulation. Breton argues that political parties exchange promises of favourable regulation (or other forms of intervention) for campaign contributions. It is noteworthy that Downs's model does not rule out what we usually think of as bribes. His directness and simplicity is admirable, but probably an affront to the tender-minded. In the real world there are some legal and institutional constraints on the straightforward exchange of money for political favours.[48] In addition, some indirection and euphemisms are required in light of the considerable idealism of many voters.

Regarding what is actually exchanged in political markets in the Canadian context, several facts are salient. First, the overt exchange of policy favours for campaign contributions is widely condemned as undesirable or even immoral behaviour.[49] Second, an elected official who accepts money for actions by the government beneficial to the person paying the money may be violating the Criminal Code. Boyer summarizes the Canadian law on political contributions by saying that they "should be invested with a spirit of altruism. When they originate with a corrupt interest the Code is offended" (1983, 52).[50]

Third, contributions to political parties and candidates by individual donors, by agreement between the two major parties at the federal level, don't exceed $50 000 (Stevenson 1982, 31).[51] Moreover, there are legal limits on campaign spending and advertising activity, and there is a requirement to disclose the names of persons contributing more than $100 in cash or kind to any party or candidate. Moreover, there are a number of direct and indirect subsidies for political expenditures. See chapter 10.

All of this indicates that policies are not simply "sold" for campaign contributions. A richer explanation is required. What then is the medium of exchange between interest groups and political parties? First, interest groups may spend their own money directly on campaigns to support candidates, parties, and policies (in lieu of that by parties) following an agreement by the party to take the actions requested by the interest group.[52]

Second, the interest group can engage in reciprocal cooperation with the party in power in which it agrees to go along with the party on policy A (which it would otherwise oppose) in exchange for the party implementing policy B (which the group favours).[53] Where trust is well developed, the exchange may not be contemporaneous. If a *high* degree of trust exists, the governing party may agree to implement a policy desired by the interest group on the understanding that the group will "owe the party one" at an unspecified time in the future. Or the converse may occur: the interest group agrees not to protest a particular government action now, receives "a marker," and expects to cash it in in the future when it really needs a favour.

The norm of reciprocity is both strong and universal. Cicero remarked that "there is no duty more indispensable than that of returning a kindness — all men distrust one forgetful of a benefit." Alvin Gouldner (1961, 171), after an extensive survey of the sociological and anthropological literature, concluded that "contrary to some cultural relativists, it can be hypothesized that a norm of reciprocity is universal." He held it to be "no less universal and important an element of culture than the incest taboo, although similarly its concrete formulations may vary with time and place."

Lobbyists can persuade politicians to act in ways that advance their clients' interests by making extensive use of the norm of reciprocity. This point is addressed in some detail in chapter 8.

Third, possibly the most valuable resource the interest group has to offer the politician/party is *information*, the exchange of which is subject neither to campaign-financing legislation nor to moral strictures. The information most valuable to politicians consists of the following:

- Knowledge of the preferences of voters, particularly uncommitted voters — in the first instance it is critical for the politician/party to be able to identify which voters are strongly inframarginal (positive and negative) and those that are marginal or uncommitted, that is, subject to persuasion by the right mix of policies, promises, and communications.
- Knowledge of the likely political reactions of voters to both existing policies ("We have run it up the flag pole, is anyone saluting?") and potential policies that the party might propose.
- Knowledge of the most efficient and effective ways to influence uncommitted voters, by means of both substantive policy actions and intentionally persuasive communications.[54]

In accepting information from interest groups, political parties/politicians appreciate the fact that what they receive is not so much likely to be wrong or untruthful, but rather selective in terms of the facts presented and in terms of the interpretation placed upon those facts. An interest group that lied or engaged in misrepresentation would soon lose its credibility with those it is seeking to influence. Virtually all writers on the politics of interest groups emphasize the critical importance of the credibility of interest-group representatives. See chapter 8.

Politics (and public policy) is a serial game of an almost infinite number of innings. Success on future rounds depends, in part, on one's behaviour in previous encounters. Moreover, a record of credibility makes it easier for a lobbyist to make his or her case, as is occasionally necessary, without the assistance of well-documented analysis. Politicians are willing to rely solely on a lobbyist's word — provided that his or her representations have been credible in the past. In other words, the ability to stretch a point at time t, and not suffer recriminations, is a function of one's truthfulness at times t-1, t-2, and so on.

The fourth possible medium of exchange between interest groups and political parties relates to the capacity of the former to shape public opinion and to help define the limited number of issues that make up the visible, public policy agenda. While politicians in power use large amounts of taxpayers' money on public opinion polling (and those in opposition use smaller amounts of their own funds to do the same thing), broadly based public opinion is shaped (which is not to say determined) by the actions of a much smaller number of influentials. The media, especially television and newspapers, are particularly important here (see the discussion in chapter 11). Hartle puts it this way:

> Voter perceptions . . . are the reality of public policy decision making. Those perceptions are greatly affected by the news coverage and its interpretation by the mass media and in particular newspapers and television. [But] news reporting . . . is inherently a highly selective activity. . . . By giving prominence to a news item that, superficially at least, seems readily understandable, concerning an event that affects the interests of many individuals and is consistent with their prior beliefs (favourable or unfavourable prejudices) the mass media, particularly newspapers, can largely determine the agenda for public policy debate. (1984, 71–72)

Columnist and press critic Ben Bagdikian has written that the syndicated columnist is "the voice of the government subsconscious, viceroy of political kings, imperious controller of public emotion, (and) proctor of public servants." This is undoubtedly an exaggeration, but contains a hard kernel of truth.

But what influences the media? First of all, the media are influenced by the fact they are (with the exception of the CBC) profit-seeking enterprises in the business of selling readers/viewers/listeners to advertisers. The objective is to obtain the largest potential audience, subject to certain demographic considerations — advertisers are seldom interested in low-income consumers. This means supplying items that are of interest to the audience — particularly those that are seen to affect their interests. Second, individual media enterprises are heavily influenced by their competitors — particularly those that are held to be leaders in their field. The term *pack journalism* is not without force. Third, political journalists are influenced by the suppliers of grist for their mill because of the constraints under which they function (frequent deadlines, desire for novelty, reporters' lack of specialized knowledge). Hence, the information provided by and the opinions of representatives of "important interests" (large numbers of people, large absolute economic stakes, or heart-tugging human-interest situations) are able to influence what journalists write or say. These will have greater influence if they are easily available, personable and colourful, to the point, and can be packaged to suit the constraints within which the media operate.

Therefore, to the extent that interest groups can put issues on the public policy agenda (which has a fairly high degree of turnover), sustain them there, or shape them, they will have a potent medium of exchange in seeking policy favours from politicians and political parties.

This discussion, therefore, makes it clear that the exchange process in political markets is more subtle and complicated than Downs (1957) suggests. The contribution of the public choice theorists, however, is enormous. By applying the calculus of economic and other incentives to basic ideas of rational, self-interested behaviour, they have moved us beyond the naive "public interest" conceptualizations of how political markets work.

NOTES

1. Some of the most useful volumes on the policy-making process in Canada, particularly at the federal level, are the following: Doern and Phidd (1983); Van Loon and Whittington (1981); Dwividi (1982); Hartle (1979); Pross (1975); Smiley (1980); Wilson (1981); Campbell and Szablowski (1979); Doern (1978, 1981); French (1980); Good (1980); Hartle (1978, 1982); Hockin (1980); Jackson and Atkinson (1980); Van Loon (1985); Doern and Aucoin (1979); Phidd and Doern (1978); Campbell (1983); Clarke et al. (1980); Schultz et al. (1979); Whittington and Williams (1985); Simeon (1979); Privy Council Office (1981); and Kernaghan (1985a).
2. See, for example, Alt and Chrystal (1983), Auld and Miller (1982), and Stanbury (1984b).
3. See *Policy Studies Journal* 1 (Autumn 1972).
4. See Edelman (1964), for example, and the discussion in Stanbury and Thain (1984, chap. 4).
5. An excellent visible example of this phenomenon concerns the funding of grade 11 Roman Catholic high schools in Ontario. In September 1985 the government of Ontario, by means of a change in regulations, allocated $34 million in "interim" financing to cover costs until January 1986. Columnist Orland French (*Globe and Mail*, September 17, 1985, p. 7) described the action as flouting democracy because a legislative committee was still holding hearings on Bill 30, which, if enacted, would provide authority to fund more grades in the Catholic high schools. Moreover, the constitutionality of the bill has yet to be determined. As French remarked, the minister of education's action "means . . . that the public can jaw away all it wants, and the judges can deliberate to their hearts' content,

but Roman Catholic separate school funding is going ahead regardless. With the stroke of a pen, Cabinet has somewhat legalized extended funding without resorting to legislation or the courts." (More generally, see "RC boards given $34 million," *Globe and Mail*, September 17, 1985, pp. 1–2.)

6. In Canada a large fraction of economic activity is subject to direct regulation. See Doern (1978), Stanbury (1980), ECC (1979, 1981), and Stanbury and Thompson (1980).

7. Michael Harris, "Tory-owned consulting firm shows clout in Fisheries switch," *Globe and Mail*, June 27, 1985, p. 8.

8. See Christopher Waddell, "Petrocan deal to cost millions in lost taxes," *Globe and Mail*, August 11, 1985, pp. B1, B5.

> As part of the original $2.8-billion purchase by Olympia & York Ltd. of Toronto of the 60.2 per cent interest in Gulf Canada held by Chevron Corp., the Edmonton refinery was included in a partnership of Gulf Canada Ltd. and Norcen Energy Resources Ltd. created to hold certain Gulf Canada exploration properties. At the dissolution of the partnership, Petrocan will buy the Edmonton refinery from Gulf Canada. Under the partnership arrangement, Revenue Canada has allowed Gulf Canada to revalue the Edmonton refinery to a level of $268.9 million, eliminating all the accumulated depreciation without paying any tax on it. The difference between the $275-million selling price of the refinery to Petrocan and the net book value thus becomes $6.1-million rather than $247.6-million, making the tax bill $2.8-million at a 46 per cent rate, rather than $113.9-million, producing a $111-million loss of tax revenue. Revenue Canada officials would not comment on any rulings related to the case. Neither would they offer any general description of how assets can be revalued in such a fashion, arguing that any comments could threaten the confidentiality of individual taxpayers.

See also "Who paid for Gulf?" *Globe and Mail*, August 20, 1985, p. 6.

9. According to a story in the *Globe and Mail* (October 22, 1985, pp. B1, B17), "newly formed Gulf Canada Enterprises Ltd. will save about $500 million in federal and provincial taxes over five years as a result of the proposed reorganization of its predecessor, Gulf Canada Ltd. Another $50 million to $90 million in taxes could be saved after five years, the Toronto-based companies said." Paul Reichmann, a principal in Olympia & York, which controls Gulf Canada Enterprises, stated that "the tax rulings, which have not involved any special government concessions, confirm the application of existing laws to the facts of the proposed transactions." He said it was a totally

wrong understanding to think of the tax savings as concessions by the federal government. The *Globe* continued, "As to the notorious Gulf tax ruling, it 'is simply an interpretation of law,' Mr. Reichmann said. 'It is nothing given.' " The tax rulings were merely answers to questions arising out of the complexity of the Income Tax Act. See Dianne Maley and Bruce Little, "Gulf Canada's reorganization to save $500 million in taxes," *Globe and Mail*, October 22, 1985, pp. B1, B17; "A sweetheart tax ruling," *Maclean's*, October 14, 1985, p. 69; and Christopher Waddell, "Gulf avoided $1 billion in taxes, Turner says," *Globe and Mail*, October 2, 1985, pp. A1–A2.

10. There are two exceptions: (1) when expenditures exceed those authorized in the *Estimates*, Parliament votes additional money through the *Supplementary Estimates* during the fiscal year; and (2) when Parliament is not in session, the cabinet can obtain additional spending by means of governor general's warrants.

11. See "Federal tax haven to ease cost cutting for Cape Bretoners," *Globe and Mail*, May 24, 1985, p. 13; and "Atlantic assessing impact of cuts," *Financial Post*, June 1, 1985, p. 8.

12. See "Funding cuts for Science Council," *Financial Post*, June 1, 1985, p. 8; and "Science Council cuts condemned by Smith," *Globe and Mail*, August 19, 1985, p. 3.

13. See the various stories in the *Financial Post*, June 1, 1985, pp. 3–9; and *Globe and Mail*, May 24, 1985, pp. 10–13.

14. For a discussion of the ways this may be done, see Stanbury and Thain (1984).

15. See the stories in the *Globe and Mail*, September 24, 1984, pp. 1, 2, 4, 6.

16. The main characteristics of the Westminster model can be found in chapter 2.

17. Judy Steed, "Power and the process man," *Globe and Mail*, September 24, 1985, p. 10.

18. "Ottawa plans ad campaign for [foreign] investment," *Globe and Mail*, September 26, 1985, p. B2.

19. This example is described in much more detail in Stanbury 1985b.

20. Stewart MacLeod, "The shifting sands of speech," *Maclean's*, September 9, 1985, p. 60.

21. Royal Commission on the Economic Union and Development Prospects for Canada (1985, 390).

22. See, for example, "Mulroney at a crossroads," *Maclean's*, September 2, 1985, pp. 8–9.

23. Bruce Little, "Bank failures put McDougall plan on hold," *Globe and Mail*, September 19, 1985, p. B1.

24. See Stanbury and Fulton (1984).

25. One lobbyist emphasizes that the real test of a lobbyist's skill is his or her ability to "persuade the government to make a positive deci-

sion, whether legislative or discretionary, in favour of one's client, even when it is rather clear that it is not necessarily in the interests of the broad general public, and may be opposed by certain other not inconsiderable specialized interests. This is the real test for the lobbyist's skill and power" (Roman 1978, 215).

26. Lawrence Surtees, *Globe and Mail*, September 6, 1985, p. B16.

27. This subsection is taken largely from Stanbury (1985e).

28. For example, almost all public policies require trade-offs among the interests of various groups in society. Yet the general definitions of "the public interest" provide no guidance as to who should "win" or "lose." Are the poor (how defined?) always deserving? Should we always favour the interests of farmers at the expense of consumers?

29. It is neither unfair nor incorrect to describe those models of public policy making based on positive or normative views of the public interest as naive. What is remarkable is that, despite the rise and spread of the more realistic public choice model of policy making (see section 8), so many believe that people do seek the public interest, that the concept has any operational utility, and that they expect interest-group representatives to act in ways consistent with the public interest or at least use the rhetoric of the public interest.

30. Doern and Phidd (1983, chap. 6), for example, identify four major models and four other approaches to understanding the process by which public policies are formulated: the rational actor model; disjointed incrementalism model; public choice model; and the class analysis model. The four approaches discussed are Lowi's typology, Allison's three models, Vickers's concept of a policy maker's "appreciative system and of policy as governing relations," and comparative studies of policy outputs.

31. Van Loon points out, "In Canadian parliamentary government [the choice among policy alternatives] is centred squarely in the Cabinet for it is the prime minister and the Cabinet who must determine which of society's demands are to be satisfied; and it is they who are accountable to Parliament and eventually to the electorate for their decisions" (1985, 412).

32. Doern and Phidd state, "It is a fact of Canadian democratic political life that policy processes are as much valued and are the object of as much dispute as are the substantive purposes and outcomes of policy" (1983, 36).

33. For a useful discussion of ideology in Canadian politics, see Christian and Campbell (1983). See also Neville and Gibbins (1984).

34. Navarro (1984) offers an analysis of policy formulation in the U.S. that emphasizes the roles of ideology and of interest groups. In his view, ideology ("a set of beliefs and values about how the world should be") is "synonymous with the individual's conception of what would serve the public interest. The actions taken in the policy arena

to fulfill that vision of the world may likewise be equated with altruistic or public-interested behaviour" (1984, 8–9). It seems to me, however, that an individual's ideology could be entirely self-interested.

35. Under conditions of imperfect knowledge and costly information, not to mention the proclivities of political parties to propose hundreds of policies (see Simpson 1980), "many a voter finds party ideologies useful because they remove the necessity of relating every issue to his own conception of 'the good society.' Ideologies help him to focus attention on the differences between parties" (Downs 1957, 141). Ideology is used as a form of shorthand by parties to summarize their complex bundle of policies and thereby make it easier for voters to make choices. Downs points out that "once a party has placed its ideology 'on the market,' it cannot suddenly abandon or radically alter that ideology without convincing voters that it is unreliable" (1957, 142). Hence, parties' ideological stances must be differentiable but also "fuzzy" to easily permit adaptation to new concerns of voters.

36. Canadians probably underrate the costs and value placed on the consumption perquisites received by cabinet ministers. For example, in their first six months in office, thirty-nine Tory cabinet ministers spent about $3 million to decorate and furnish their offices. See Jamie Lamb, "When times get tough they call in the decorators," Vancouver *Sun*, August 19, 1985, p. A4. However, this is a small part of the nontaxable benefits conferred on cabinet ministers (and to a much lesser degree, MPs). See Stevie Cameron, "Parliament Hill a perk paradise," Vancouver *Sun*, August 19, 1985, p. D12. For example, ministers may use govenment jet aircraft if they would be delayed more than ten minutes using a scheduled carrier. Prime Minister Mulroney has called government jets "sacred instruments of travel." Ministers receive unlimited free first-class travel on Air Canada, CP Air and VIA Rail, a car and driver plus a tax-free $2000 car allowance, and virtually unlimited nonaccountable travel and hospitality expenses. A former cabinet minister is quoted as saying, "I could have asked for a $10,000 [cash] advance for a trip and put it on my mortgage and no one would have known the difference." In 1984/85 Premier Richard Hatfield's expense account exceeded $365 000.

37. Journalist and author Walter Stewart (1981) describes politicians as "weird birds, patient enough to weave together compromises, open enough to absorb a lot of good and bad advice, conscientious enough to perform the hundreds of chores that make up the bulk of their work, smart enough to sound agreeable to a lot of disagreeable onlookers and honest enough to withstand the kind of scrutiny few businessmen and fewer journalists could survive."

38. See Sandra Gwyn, "Yesterday's princes — the bleak future for unem-

ployed cabinet ministers," *Saturday Night* 95, no. 1 (January/
February 1980): 18–23.

39. See, for example, Gillies (1984), Thomas (1983), and McGrath
(1985).

40. Nozick (1974, 274–75) applied the marginal-voter calculus to
explain why (1) many government programs most greatly benefit
the middle class, and (2) the least well-off 51% ratio of the voters
vote for redistributive policies that would greatly improve their position at the expense of the other 49%:

> The fact will seem puzzling until one notices that the bottom
> 51 percent is not the only possible (continuous) voting major-
> ity; there is also, for example, the top 51 percent. Which of
> these two majorities will form depends on how the middle 2
> percent votes. It will be in the interests of the top 49 percent to
> support and devise programs to gain the middle 2 percent as
> allies. It is cheaper for the top 49 percent to buy the support of
> the middle 2 percent than to be (partially) expropriated by
> the bottom 51 percent. The bottom 49 percent cannot offer
> more than the top 49 percent can to the middle 2 percent in
> order to gain them as allies. For what the bottom 49 percent
> offers the middle 2 percent will come (after the policies are
> instituted) from the top 49 percent; and in addition the bot-
> tom 49 percent also will take something for themselves from
> the top 49 percent. The top 49 percent always can save by offer-
> ing the middle 2 percent slightly more than the bottom group
> would, for that way they avoid *also* having to pay to the remain-
> der of the possible coalition of the bottom 51 percent, namely
> the bottom 49 percent. The top group will be able always to
> buy the support of the swing middle 2 percent to combat mea-
> sures which would more seriously violate its rights.

Nozick continues,

> Of course, speaking of the middle 2 percent is much too pre-
> cise; people do not know precisely in what percentile they fall,
> and policies are not easily geared to target upon 2 percent some-
> where in the middle. One therefore would expect that a middle
> group *considerably* larger than 2 percent will be a beneficiary
> of a voting coalition from the top. (1974, 275)

41. Politics, however, is a dynamic process, a fact reflected in the aphor-
ism that "politics makes strange bedfellows." Therefore, governing parties often appear to, inefficiently, provide substantial rewards
for their strongest supporters (e.g., Quebec in the case of the federal Liberal party prior to their defeat in the 1984 election) and
also to sprinkle some largesse on what appears to be stony ground

(e.g., Western Canada). They do so because unanticipated exogenous forces may cause a shift in political fortunes, and a party does not want to be seen as crassly practising the dictums of marginal-voter politics. To extend Yogi Berra's dictum, "It ain't over 'till its over, and in politics it's never over." Yesterday's opposition supporters may be tomorrow's uncommitted voters and therefore potential supporters. Gratuitous political insults (the failure to provide *any* "goodies" for inframarginal voters) make it harder for such changes to occur.

42. I note that there are both practical and legislative constraints on the "targeting" of governing instruments. For example: family allowances cannot be paid only to mothers who are uncommitted voters or to those who live in "swing" ridings. A national highway system means the road must be built through the ridings of both types of inframarginal supporters. There can be, on the other hand, considerable discretion in the location of defence establishments. For example: the pension administration unit of the Department of Veterans Affairs was moved from Ottawa to Prince Edward Island. The new F-18 fighter planes were placed at Cold Lake, Alberta, in July 1984, whereas their predecessors were based at Comox on Vancouver Island.

43. In practical terms, a political insider whose identity cannot be revealed defines an issue as "any problem or interest which has the potential to influence voting behaviour in an upcoming election." A problem or item of interest is not an effective issue (i.e., a vote getter) unless a significant proportion of voters, with a reasonable level of intensity, feel that (1) the problem is subject to improvement by the level of government concerned; and (2) voters believe that one party (leader) can handle the problem better or faster than other parties (leaders).

44. Another consequence of imperfect knowledge and costly information is the transformation of democratic into representative government. Representatives (usually based on geographic constituencies) are needed to ascertain the preferences of voters and to persuade voters to re-elect the party in power. Members (and candidates) become agents for parties in trying to sell the party's bundle of policies.

45. In adopting the policy proposed (and "purchased") by the interest group, a political party has a practical problem in the real world. Popular sentiment requires that where such policies are made public (and not all policies important to interest groups are), they be presented in terms of "the public interest." Stanbury and Lermer state: "Obviously, naked self interest must be clothed with more socially acceptable rationalizations. For example, farmers asking for a supply management scheme are not merely trying to raise their

incomes, they are 'preserving the family farm,' maintaining the rural way of life, and asking only to 'recover their costs' " (1983, 381).

46. Perhaps the most naked example of this type of exchange is the $632 500 in campaign contributions by dairy farmers to Richard Nixon made shortly after dairy support prices were raised by $300 million per year. See Greenwald (1977, 3–9). The Watergate prosecutor found a letter from a dairy lobby saying a campaign contribution of $2 million could be had if import quotas on certain dairy products were imposed. Two weeks later Nixon did so and also raised the support price for milk. See Navarro (1984, 118–19). For examples of political corruption in Canada, see chapter 10 and Malvern (1985).

47. Rationality is taken to mean that people consistently seek to maximize a well-ordered set of preferences and that they alter their behaviour in response to changes in incentives in a way consistent with such maximization. Bounded rationality is based on the premise that individuals can neither hold all the information necessary to analyze complex decisions nor possess the mental capacity to process such information within the time allowed for most decisions. Therefore, argues Simon (1955), people engage in approximate optimization and they "satisfice"; that is, they accept the first conveniently available solution that achieves their aspiration level.

48. Recently the City of Vancouver agreed to waive a major violation of its zoning laws in exchange for a payment to the City of $500 000 by a property developer. The latter had built two more luxury townhouses in a development than had been approved in his building permit. The payment, based on the estimated profit on the two units of $400 000 plus a punitive exaction, was in lieu of an order to tear down the two units. Despite the fact that (1) the money went to the City, not to any politician or party, (2) the selling of the "indulgence" was an efficient solution, and (3) the money was paid after the event in lieu of an apparently *less* costly alternative, there was an intense controversy in the city. The deal made the headlines. See "City buyoffs called unlikely," Vancouver *Sun*, August 20, 1984, p. A9.

49. Section 110 of the Criminal Code creates several indictable offences regarding frauds upon the government. Section 110(1)(a) makes it an offence to directly or indirectly give or offer, or agree to give or offer, to an official "a loan, reward, advantage or benefit of any kind as consideration for cooperation, assistance, exercise of influence with or any act or mission" in connection with the transaction of business with the government or any matter of business relating to the government whether or not the official is able to cooperate etc. Boyer (1983, 52) points out that the word "official" has been interpreted in the case law to include MPs and cabinet ministers. The

most notorious case of bribery of a minister occurred in B.C. regarding forest licences — see *R. v. Sommers* (no. 3) (1958) 26 W.W.R. 244 (no. 4) (1958) 26 W.W.R. 246. More generally, see chapter 10.

50. Section 110(1)(e) is a similar section in respect to "a minister of the government or an official." Section 110(2) makes it an offence for government contractors or would-be contractors to make political contributions in order to obtain or retain a contract with the government. This applies to both federal and provincial parties and elections.

   Section 108 of the Criminal Code provides that an MP or member of a provincial legislature who corruptly accepts or obtains money or valuable consideration for him/herself or another person in respect of anything done or omitted, or to be done or omitted by him or her, in his or her official capacity, is guilty of an indictable offence and liable for imprisonment for up to fourteen years (Boyer 1983, 52).

51. After the federal election of September 4, 1984, it was revealed that the largest single contribution to any political party was for over $453 000. It was made by a widow to the NDP. See Robert Sheppard, "Unsung heroine of barren lands," *Globe and Mail*, September 4, 1984, p. 7. In 1984 the Progressive Conservatives received contributions of $150 000 from Candor Investments, $100 250 from Denison Mines, and $100 000 from Roman Corp. — the last two companies are controlled by Stephen B. Roman. See chapter 10.

52. I note, however, that on October 25, 1983, Parliament unanimously enacted, in forty minutes, legislation (Bill C-169) to very sharply restrict political advertising by third parties during federal election campaigns. The National Citizens' Coalition has obtained a trial court decision ruling that these amendments to the Elections Act violates the Canadian Charter of Rights and Freedoms in the new Constitution. See *Globe and Mail*, June 27, 1984, pp. 1–2; *Maclean's*, July 9, 1984, p. 40; and *Financial Post*, July 21, 1984, p. 28. The federal government has announced it will not appeal the case. More generally, see Aubrey Golden, "Pandora's box opened on election spending," *Globe and Mail*, July 17, 1984, p. 7. See three large ads by the National Citizens' Coalition, *Globe and Mail*, July 19, 1984, p. 9; August 16, 1984, p. 9; and August 30, 1984, p. 9. More generally, see chapter 10.

53. It should be obvious that there is a potential for deception, bluffing, and other forms of strategic behaviour. For example, a group could launch a vigorous campaign against an existing policy, toward which it really was indifferent, to create a "bargaining chip" to be exchanged for an action on a policy it really cared about.

54. Advertising agencies frequently provide free services at a subsidized rate to parties during election campaigns in the hope of receiving lucrative contracts for advertising by government departments and agencies. See Whittaker (1977, chap. 5), and Stanbury et al. (1983, 148–51).

5

The Government
Relations Function

1.0 INTRODUCTION

In this chapter I make the transition from chapters 3 and 4, which focused on understanding certain aspects of the size, scope, and growth of government and the political economy of policy making, to an analysis of the ways in which firms may seek to influence government. This requires an examination of the government relations function. Then in chapters 6 through 12, a number of the more important techniques used by business firms to influence public policy for their benefit are discussed.

This chapter begins with a brief discussion of the growth of the public affairs/business-government relations function in Canadian business enterprises. Section 3 describes the range of activities conducted by such public affairs/business-government units. Section 4 complements section 3, as it examines some evidence on the degree of political involvement by Canadian firms as indicated by a survey conducted in 1977 and 1980. Political involvement is broadly construed — it ranges from face-to-face lobbying of politicians and bureaucrats to encouraging employees to become more involved in politics.

Section 5 examines some recent empirical evidence on the perceptions of bureaucrats and business managers concerning the influence of business interests on government. Section 6 expands on a point noted in chapter 1, namely, that "business" does not speak with a single voice in dealing with government. Rather, it is often riven with conflict based, not on differences in personalities, but on the fact that firms in different industries, of different sizes, and of different ownership have different economic interests when it comes to specific government policies.

Finally, section 7 discusses in general terms the central strategic considerations associated with the government relations function of a business enterprise. The emphasis is on the strategic choices that must be made if the firm is to be effective in influencing public policy.

2.0 THE GROWTH OF THE GOVERNMENT RELATIONS/PUBLIC AFFAIRS FUNCTION

Andrew Gollner's (1983) study of the public affairs function in major Canadian businesses fills a significant gap in our knowledge of business-government relations in Canada. He sent questionnaires in 1982 to 384 firms listed in the *Financial Post 500* and received replies from 142 (37 percent) of which 60 percent (n = 85) were in the 100 largest nonfinancial enterprises in Canada (Gollner 1983, 18, n. 22).

In his view, the growth of the public affairs function is attributable to (1) "gradual emergence of the megacorporation" and the increasing concentration of economic activity; (2) the expansion of the service sector in industrially advanced economies; and (3) the decline of productivity growth (1983, 34–38). Gollner states: "The concentrated economic sector requires a substantial degree of public affairs capability from its corporate members. . . . The freely competitive market system needs comparatively less public affairs involvement from its corporate constituents" (1983, 36).

Despite the enormous size and scope of government activity in Canada, Litvak observes that "only a few Canadian firms have established a government relations unit, separate and distinct from the other external affairs units. In some such cases, this governmental relations unit is the company's Ottawa representative" (1981, 50).

Where they do exist, government relations units "in most large . . . firms [are] either in the 'public affairs' or legal departments." But identifiable public affairs departments are by no means universal even among the largest firms in Canada. Gollner found that 68.3 percent of his total sample of 142 had established a "distinctive public affairs department, unit or equivalent" (1983, 106). The fraction for firms in the top 100 (n = 85) was 79.0 percent.

Moreover, such public affairs units tend to be of fairly recent origin, as Table 5-1 indicates. For the full sample (n = 97), Gollner (1983) found that 59 percent of the firms had created their public affairs department within the last decade. For firms in the top 100 nonfinancial corporations, the fraction was 43 percent. At the other end of the distribution, Gollner found that 42 percent of his sample in the top 100 established their public affairs department prior to 1960. For the whole sample, the comparable percentage was 27 percent.

Post et al. (1983, 136) provide data on the growth of the public affairs function from a 1981 survey of U.S. corporations with about 400 respondents. They found that the period in which the public affairs function was created was as follows:

before 1950	8.9%
1950–59	10.3
1960–69	22.1
1970–74	27.7
1975–79	31.0

Forty-four percent of the firms spent less than $500 000 on their public affairs operations in 1980/81, while 35 percent spent more than $1 million. Seventy-one percent had ten or fewer full-time professional staff

Table 5–1

DATE OF ORIGIN OF CORPORATE PUBLIC AFFAIRS DEPARTMENTS IN CANADA

Date of Establishment	Full Sample (%)	Firms in the Top 100 (%)
Before 1950	11.6	22
1951–60	15.8	20
1961–70	16.8	15
1971–75	17.9	15
1976–82	37.9	28
	n = 97	n = 67

Source: Gollner (1983, Tables 2.1, 2.4, 5.1).

members, while 11 percent had twenty-six or more (Post et al. 1983).

Reich (1981, 87) indicates that 50 to 60 percent of firms with sales under $1 million in the U.S. have a government relations unit, while between 80 and 90 percent of those with more than $1 billion in sales have such a unit. The larger the firm the more likely it is to have personnel both in Washington and at headquarters. For example, firms with sales of over $10 billion had an average of thirteen people in Washington and nine at headquarters.

Gillies's survey of eighty Canadian CEOs and/or corporate directors in mid-1980 found that

fewer than 10 per cent of the corporations have a senior officer with full-time responsibilities for business-government relations. Approximately 25 per cent of the firms assign the bulk of the work in the area, particularly staff work in terms of preparation of speeches, submissions to committees, briefs to Royal Commissions, and so on, to their public relations departments. . . . In the rest of the firms, it is considered part of the responsibilities of the corporate affairs group, a group that also includes, in many cases, public relations. In general, government corporate affairs are handled on an almost ad hoc basis with most activity being in response to some public initiative. (1981, 34)

Gillies notes from his survey that few companies maintain full-time employees in Ottawa (except for regulated firms). They prefer to use trade associations or public affairs firms as listening posts.

What forces were thought to be responsible for the creation of public affairs departments in Canadian corporations? Gollner (1983) found that the two most significant were the "growth of government intervention" and "the increasing socio-political complexity of the business

Table 5–2

THE RANKING OF FORCES RESPONSIBLE FOR THE CREATION OF PUBLIC AFFAIRS DEPARTMENTS IN CANADIAN CORPORATIONS, 1982

(n = 142)
(Scale: 1 = Highly significant; 5 = Insignificant)

Forces	Score
1. Growth of government intervention	
2. The increasing socio-political complexity of the business environment	1.9
3. The impact of external issues on profits	
4. Personal interest of the CEO	2.3
5. Growing awareness of social-ethical responsibilities	
6. The growth of media scrutiny	2.6+
7. The decline of business credibility	
8. The increasing assertiveness of consumer advocacy groups	
9. Demonstration effect from U.S. corporations	3.7
10. A particularly significant event	
11 The increasing power of organized labour	4.0

Source: Gollner (1983, Table 2.3).

environment" — see Table 5-2. Of little or no significance — at least as perceived by his sample of public affairs executives — were "the increasing assertiveness of consumer advocacy groups," the "demonstration effect from U.S. corporations," "a particularly significant event," such as a crisis or policy failure, and "the increasing power of organized labour."

The eighty CEOs and/or corporate directors interviewed by Gillies were directors of over 400 Canadian corporations, many of which were among the largest in the nation (Gillies 1981, 143–44). In their view, the reasons for the deterioration of business's relations with the federal government during the 1970s can be grouped into two categories: the failure of business to have sufficient impact in the determination of the public interest; and the failure of government to operate effectively. Four reasons were given for business's lack of impact on the policy-making process: "an inability to communicate effectively; an ineffective consultative process; a lack of understanding on the part of business of the political process; and a lack of ability to communicate the position of business on various issues to the public" (Gillies 1981, 30). Presumably the growth of public affairs/government relations units in major corporations is partly due to these perceptions.

The evolution of the public affairs function in Canadian corporations, as seen by Gollner, is described in Figure 5-1.

Figure 5–1

THE EVOLUTION OF THE PUBLIC AFFAIRS FUNCTION

From	*To*
• Public affairs function enjoys only a limited degree of internal legitimacy. Senior management does not fully understand its uses, and is skeptical about its effectiveness, although it is tolerated. Public affairs officers are engaged in excessive internal proselytizing at the expense of external/internal action programming.	• The function has the full support of senior management and is perceived to be a legitimate element of the corporate arsenal. This acceptance produces a decline in proselytizing and an increase in the use of diverse and analytically sophisticated external/internal action programs.
• Public affairs officers pursue contacts and relations with external groups or individuals on an irregular basis, surrounded by secrecy and based on personality, style, and informal connection.	• Officers liaise with external groups on a systematic, open, and institutionalized basis. The interaction is grounded on objective analysis, mutual interest, and formalized procedures.
• The public affairs program is basically reactive to external challenges and is seen as crisis management. It is a fire-fighting approach to socio-political events.	• The program is essentially that of relationship management, whereby interaction and interpenetration with key external or internal groups is the rule. The program is one step ahead of issues, rather than behind them. It serves as management's "eyes and ears" into its socio-political environment, helping to narrow the divergence between corporate and environmental change.
• Public affairs is a line position. The unit is the only source and executor of the corporation's socio-political action plan.	• Public affairs is a staff position. The public affairs officer is a catalyst, facilitator and cajoler, of socio-political involvement, wherever needed throughout the organization.
• Public affairs is a centralized function with little room for participation in the process by local or middle-level managers.	• Public affairs is diffused so that in addition to its central staff, local and middle-level operating managers are active participants in the development and delivery of public affairs programs.
• Public affairs is an "add-on" dimension to strategic planning. It is peripheral to the central decision-making, planning, and asset management function.	• Public affairs is institutionalized and closely tied to strategic and planning processes.

Figure 5–1 (continued)

From	To
• The information sources and the analytical tools of public affairs are eclectic and largely qualitative.	• The information sources are focused and are based on systematic environmental scanning, social audit, issues management, and planning techniques that use quantitative measures wherever possible.

Source: Gollner (1983, 155–56).

3.0 ACTIVITIES IN THE GOVERNMENT RELATIONS/PUBLIC AFFAIRS FUNCTION

What are the most important activities of public affairs units in Canadian corporations? Gollner found that — in the perception of those engaged in such activities — the most important activities were "alerting governments to possible impacts of various legislative scenarios upon the company," "systematically anticipating legislative and regulatory trends," and "projecting a favourable image to rule-makers." See Table 5-2. The first of these is complementary to often-expressed desires of policy makers (cabinet ministers and senior bureaucrats) to fully appreciate the impact of existing government programs and to anticipate the consequences of policies in the formulation stage (Stanbury 1978). With respect to the second activity, Litvak remarks:

> The key responsibility of the government relations executives is monitoring, analyzing and communicating government related activity. Lobbying, including telling the company's story to legislators, bureaucrats and regulatory officials, has become a secondary although still important function. Anticipation of government action enabling a timely response is the key function. (1981, 50)

Litvak's point is reiterated by the ranking of activity 7 in Table 5-3 — "Working to reduce the level of government regulation in the company's economic sector."

The Institute for Political Involvement (IPI) identifies the following components in what it calls the "system" of business-government relations:

- representation/communications:
  - through business associations
  - directly to a ministry
  - through consulting firms
  - via bipartite or multi-partite consulations

Table 5–3
PERCEIVED SIGNIFICANCE OF GOVERNMENT RELATIONS ACTIVITIES BY CANADIAN CORPORATIONS, 1982

(n = 142)
(Scale 1 = highly significant; 5 = insignificant)

1. Alerting governments to possible impacts of various legislative scenarios upon the company	2.0
2. Systematically anticipating legislative and regulatory trends	2.2
3. Projecting favourable image to rule makers	
4. Keeping governments advised on a regular and systematic basis about the company's special needs	2.4
5. Working to create a more favourable political climate for free enterprise in general	2.8
6. Scanning existing and future governmental legislation for provisions that would increase the company's business opportunities	
7. Working to reduce the level of government regulation in the company's economic sector	2.9
8. Developing and proposing new alternatives for improving business-government relations within the company's sector of the economy	
9. Voluntarily advising governments on how to improve the quality of regulation	3.0

Source: Gollner (1983, Table 5.3).

- financial/marketplace activities by government:
  - Crown corporations
  - loans/guarantees
  - subsidies
  - trade policy
- interchange/education:
  - executive interchange
  - Niagara Institute and IRPP [Institute for Research on Public Policy] seminars
- policy research:
  - IRPP, the Fraser Institute
  - business associations research, i.e., CFIB, BCNI
- obtaining public support for business' positions:
  - public opinion
  - advocacy advertising
- political involvement by business:
  - personal participation
  - campaign contributions
  - running for office.
  (1978, 3–4)

Steiner et al. indicate that the public affairs function in a corporation includes the following responsibilities:

- monitor the social and political environment to identify forces which may have a potential significant impact on company operations;
- coordinate the analysis of environmental forces throughout the company;
- identify the forces in the environment which are most likely to have the most important impact on the company and transmit that information to top management and other staff;
- help top management in the selection of those public policy issues on which the company will concentrate attention;
- prepare appropriate analyses of public policy issues which top management chooses to address;
- contribute to and participate in the injection of social and political projections in the strategic planning process;
- develop communications programs aimed at various company publics of the enterprise and framed within policies of the company;
- develop programs to advance the interests of the company in the political processes of federal, state and local governments;
- develop programs by means of which the company may respond appropriately to the interests of the people in the communities in which it does business. (1981, 16)

For a similar list, see Post et al. (1983).

Public affairs is a broad function within the corporation and includes activities unrelated or only peripherally related to how the firm deals with governments. This becomes apparent when we examine Table 5-4. In my view the three top-ranking activities found by Gollner's survey to be those in which the public affairs department played a leading role, do not involve government relations. Moreover, government relations may not even be the most important activity for the public affairs department. In Table 5-4 we note that for only one-half the sample did the public affairs department play a leading role in relations with provincial or federal governments. For over 40 percent of the sample the public affairs department played only a supporting role. Moreover, in only 38 percent of the sample did the public affairs unit play a leading role in "developing corporate responses and strategies toward changing external issues." In 58 percent of the firms it played a "supportive role." What is really remarkable about these public affairs units is that in less than a majority of firms (43 percent) did the unit have the lead responsibility for "conducting in-house research on social and political trends and issues." We note, however, that some 16 percent of the sample did not perform this activity *anywhere* in the company.

Table 5–4

RANKING OF ACTIVITIES IN WHICH PUBLIC AFFAIRS DEPARTMENTS IN CANADIAN CORPORATIONS PLAY A LEADING OR SUPPORTING ROLE, 1982

(n = 142)

Activity	Percentage of Responding Departments with Leading Role	Percentage of Responding Departments with Supportive Role
1. Communications with the media	87	13
2. Communications with the public	83	17
3. Corporate donations	63	24
4. Monitoring and anticipating social-political changes	57	39
5. Communications with employees	56	35
6. Development of programs to increase public affairs skills of line managers	54	25
7. Provincial government relations	53	41
8. Federal government relations	50	44
9. Measurement of corporate social impact	44	31
10. Conducting in-house research on social and political trends and issues[3]	43	27
11. Communications with financial stakeholders	39	37
12. Developing corporate responses and strategies toward changing external issues	38	58
13. Involvement in local community affairs	35	56
14. Implementing corporate responses and strategies toward changing external issues	32	58
15. Advocacy advertising[1]	31	19
16. Municipal government relations	24	54
17. Product advertising	16	33
18. Development of corporate strategic plans	7	77
19. International government relations[2]	7	31

[1] No such activity at company 40%.
[2] No such activity at company 33%.
[3] No such activity at company 16%.

Source: Gollner (1983, Tables 5.6, 5.7).

Table 5–5
THE MAJOR MECHANISMS USED BY CANADIAN CORPORATIONS IN THE MANAGEMENT OF FEDERAL GOVERNMENT RELATIONS, 1982
(n = 142)

Mechanisms	Percentage Who Use It
Trade association(s)	95
Frequent visits to Ottawa by senior executives	95
The Ottawa office	34
Government relations consultants situated in Ottawa	50
Plant visit by members of Parliament	68
Speakers bureaus	52
Advocacy advertising	43

Source: Gollner (1983, 118).

Gollner (1983) found that the firms in his sample, in dealing with the federal government, used a variety of "mechanisms." Almost all (95 percent) participated in trade associations and had their executives make "frequent visits to Ottawa." See Table 5-5. Gollner (1983, 118-19) argues that membership in trade associations can be of great importance to the corporation from a public affairs standpoint. First of all, associations can serve as important sources of research and information about socio-political issues relevant to their members. Such research services could significantly reduce the financial burden upon individual corporations otherwise compelled to conduct their own, and often duplicative, socio-political analyses. Effective relations with business associations also provide the corporation with a "loudspeaker." Through its associations, the corporation can rally support for its socio-political strategies and inject these strategies into the public policy process with greatly enhanced power or credibility. The old adage that there is strength in numbers is nowhere more relevant than here. For many corporations, a full public affairs management program is both humanly and financially out of reach. The establishment of public affairs services by the firm's trade association can significantly enhance the effectiveness of members.

On the other hand, only 34 percent of the 142 firms in the sample maintained an Ottawa office. Litvak (1982) found that 45 percent of his sample (n = 101) of national trade associations had an Ottawa office in 1981 and only one-third had their headquarters in the nation's capital. Gollner found that one-half the firms made use of government relations consultants situated in Ottawa. Litvak (1982) found that just over one-half of national trade associations made use of outside services such as law firms, consultants, or public relations advisors.

Over two-thirds of Gollner's sample invited MPs to visit their plants. While this is a nice gesture, the efficacy of lobbying MPs is usually thought to be low. See chapter 7. On the other side of the ledger, just over one-half of the public affairs departments sought to spread their company's message by operating a "speakers' bureau" staffed by corporate executives.

Only 43 percent of Gollner's sample made any use of advocacy advertising. (Note the number *not* using this technique does not jibe between Table 5-5, 57 percent, and Table 5-4, 40 percent.) This approach to influencing governments is discussed in more detail in chapter 12.

The leading public affairs and government relations units are now actively involved in *issues management*, defined as "the process by which the corporation can identify, evaluate and respond to those social and political issues which may impact [sic] upon it" (Johnson 1983, 22). Such issues *cannot* actually be managed, rather they can be *influenced* to some degree. More generally, see chapter 6.

Gollner (1983) provides some insights into the tools that are currently being used or likely to be adopted by Canadian firms to grapple with socio-political issues. See Table 5-6. While only one-eighth of the companies surveyed use a full-time issues manager, 70 percent have their decision makers' attention drawn to public issues on an ad hoc basis. Over three-fifths engage in an institutionalized and systematic scanning of public issues relevant to the sector or the firm. In over one-half the firms, line and staff officers actively participate in corporate issues programs. However, in only one-quarter of the companies is a quantitative assessment of the economic impact of public issues integrated in the corporate planning process.

4.0 DEGREE OF POLITICAL INVOLVEMENT

In 1977 the Institute for Political Involvement (1978) conducted a major survey of over 2000 firms in Canada with more than 100 employees and obtained 703 replies suitable for analysis.[1] The focus of the survey was to measure the degree of involvement of corporations in politics and government policy making.

The survey identified various measures of involvement with the federal government. Just over one-half the firms had communications with political leaders (53.2 percent) and with civil servants (55.3 percent). Unfortunately, the published version of the study does not indicate the frequency of such communications, that is, weekly or just annually. Forty-two percent of the companies in the sample had made representations to government departments, boards, or commissions. By size of firm, the study found that 55.8 percent of large firms (over 500 employees) made such representations as compared with 28.2 percent for firms with

Table 5–6
THE RANKING OF ENVIRONMENTAL ANALYSIS, ISSUES-MANAGE-MENT, AND RESEARCH MECHANISMS CURRENTLY USED OR BEING CONSIDERED FOR USE BY CANADIAN CORPORATIONS, 1982

(n = 142)

Issues-Management Mechanisms	Percentage of Respondents Currently Using	Percentage of Respondents Not Using but Considering*
1. Ad hoc attention of decision makers to the business implications of public issues	70	20
2. Institutionalized and systematic scanning of public issues that are relevant to business sector	63	22
3. Institutionalized and systematic scanning of public issues that are relevant to the company	61	27
4. Institutionalized and systematic scanning of major short-term strategic issues (major impact 1–5 years)	57	29
5. Active participation of relevant line and staff officers in corporate issues programs	56	29
6. Identification and analysis of corporate response alternatives to public issues	55	30
7. Informal corporate planning guidance from issue impact analysis	51	31
8. Quantitative assessment of economic and financial impact of public issues on company	47	34
9. Institutionalized and systematic scanning of major long-term emerging issues (5–15 year impact frame)	32	45
10. Formal integration of quantitative issues analysis into corporate planning process	25	45
11. Using institutionalized, inter-departmental issues committees	17	32
12. Use of full-time issues manager(s)	12	29
13. Location of issues management and corporate planning function in one body	8	31

* The balance are not using these techniques and see no need for them.

Source: Gollner (1983, Tables 6.1, 6.2).

less than 500 employees. Eighty-five percent of the firms had made representations to the federal government through a business or trade association. On the other hand, only 4.9 percent of the firms had been involved in the Executive Interchange or Career Assignment Plans under which managers from the private sector take jobs in government and vice versa.[2] Overall, less than 3 percent of the over 700 companies in the sample had not initiated any type of involvement with the federal government.

The IPI (1978) survey found that 33.1 percent and 6.7 percent of the firms surveyed stated they had a "moderate" or "high" degree of involvement in the political process at the federal level. The comparable figures for the provincial level were 30.2 and 9.4 percent respectively, while the figures for the municipal level were 22.6 and 4.1 percent respectively. By level of government, the fraction of firms reporting no involvement in the political process ranged from 16.5 percent at the federal level, 14.8 percent at the provincial level, to 27.5 percent at the municipal level.

Political involvement can take the form of contributions to political parties and candidates. The IPI survey found that

- 35 percent of the companies had received a request for a nonfinancial contribution to a party, while 87 percent had received requests for financial contributions;
- 52.8 percent of the firms made nonfinancial contributions to political parties (56.0 percent to candidates) depending on the party and/or the nature of the request; and
- 51.9 percent of the firms made financial contributions to certain political parties (46.2 percent to candidates).

The perceived need for some form of political response to the growing role of government in business by level of government is described in Table 5-7.

Table 5–7
NEED FOR A RESPONSE BY BUSINESS TO INCREASED
GOVERNMENT ROLE, 1977
(n = 703)

Level of Government	None (%)	Minimal (%)	Moderate in a Few Selected Areas (of the Firm) (%)	Critical in a Number of Areas (of the Firm) (%)	High and Pervasive throughout the Firm (%)
Federal	9.0	14.5	27.7	38.0	8.1
Provincial	9.2	15.5	30.4	36.0	6.0
Municipal	18.8	32.3	25.3	12.8	3.4

Source: Institute for Political Involvement (1978, 10).

The IPI survey found that a majority of firms believe business can influence electoral outcomes: 37.6 percent believe business can have a "moderate" effect on election outcomes; 35.6 percent believe it can have a "considerable" effect; and 6.5 percent believe it can have a "very considerable" effect. Only 2.3 percent believe business can have no effect or "little" effect on election outcomes. Moreover, 55.2 percent of the firms believe there would be "some improvement" and 38.5 percent believe there would be a "profound improvement" if business people sought and attained elected office in Canada.

Thirty-four percent of the firms indicated a "moderate" willingness to allocate greater resources for political participation at the federal level, while 12.4 percent indicated a "considerable" and 1.8 percent indicated a "high" willingness for such allocation. Only 19.8 percent of the firms indicated they had no willingness to allocate greater resources for this purpose. In general, larger firms were more willing to allocate more resources for political involvement than smaller ones.

Companies are in a position to influence the political activities of their employees. The IPI (1978) survey found that

- 85 percent of the firms said they encourage employees to vote on election day;
- 28 percent said they encouraged employees to participate in politics beyond merely voting;
- 74 percent said they would grant employees leaves of absence to run for public office, but only 17 percent would grant leave without pay;
- 59 percent would grant a leave of absence if an employee is elected to office, and 44 percent would guarantee the same level of salary when the employee returns;
- 3 percent provide basic information on Canadian politics, and 11 percent distribute information about political issues related to the company's business;
- 36 percent would allow political candidates to meet employees on company premises — the overwhelming preference is for a nonpartisan, all-candidate approach; and
- 89 percent do not encourage their employees to contribute to federal political parties — even though generous tax credits have been available since 1974.

Gillies (1981, 39) found that 90 percent of the eighty CEOs/directors he surveyed in mid-1980 believed that business people should publicly try to influence political decisions, but most believed they should do so as individuals rather than as leaders of corporations. For example, 70 percent said they would be willing to testify on legislation not directly concerned with their firm or industry, but most would do so as individuals, not as CEOs.

What actions do CEOs favour as part of an active role in politics? Gillies (1981, 41–43) found that

- slightly more than one-half believe that corporations should not endorse positions before and/or during elections, and almost all believe that if it is to be done it should be done, prior to the campaign;
- there is almost unanimity that if someone wants to stand for elected office he or she should be granted leave to do so and also be granted leave to serve (this is much higher than the IPI [1978] survey);
- there is strong support for companies to have a well-developed political education program, but it must be done in a nonpartisan fashion; and
- almost 60 percent believe that advocacy advertising is a poor way of influencing public opinion; 42 percent of CEOs in large publicly held companies think their firm should use advocacy advertising, but with caution.

5.0 PERCEIVED INFLUENCE OF BUSINESS ON GOVERNMENT

5.1 Conflicting Views

There are sharply conflicting views regarding the ability of business interests to influence the behaviour of government in Canada. Most business people writing or speaking on the subject stress how little influence they have and point to a host of government actions inimical to business interests that were inspired by the desire to garner votes or placate other lobby groups, such as environmentalists, consumers, or particular regional interests. In general, business portrays itself as ineffectual in influencing government.

On the other hand, writers from a Marxist perspective or those who stress the process of elite accommodation in Canada see business interests as highly influential in their dealings with government. Detailed case studies of lobbying and policy formulation note that business interests win some and lose some. Those who attempt to understand the totality of government activity note that, regardless of the rhetoric, a considerable amount of government intervention has the effect of benefiting business firms, for example, tariffs, quotas (both of which also benefit labour), a host of tax expenditures, billions in direct cash subsidies in the name of economic development, protective regulation such as control over entry (however, most social regulation does impose costs on business), and loans and loan guarantees that subsidize a private firm's cost of capital.

There is, however, little systematic empirical evidence on how business people perceive government and their own effectiveness in influencing it and, conversely, how public sector executives perceive business and its influence on government.

5.2 Recent Empirical Evidence

In 1982 Islam and Ahmed (1984) conducted a survey of both business and government, obtaining data from 132 business executives and 183 government executives. These executives came from a reasonable cross-section of industries and government functions, although the defence and foreign affairs areas in government were underrepresented. In both groups, just over 60 percent of the samples were assessed as coming from middle-class backgrounds and "on the whole, . . . academic training [did] not reveal a highly significant difference between the two groups" (1984, 92). However, not surprisingly, business executives scored significantly higher on business administration as an academic discipline than did the government executives. The executives were rated on six personality traits (excellence, acquisitiveness, status with peers, achievement via independence, status with experts, and competition), but the only statistically significant difference was on the acquisitiveness trait, with business respondents being relatively more money-oriented.

Some 49 percent of business executives did not have any experience in the public sector, but only 27 percent of government executives had no work experience in the private sector. "On the average, the business respondents had spent ten years in their present organizations and two years in the government sector while their government sector counterparts had spent seven years in their present departments and three years in the business sector" (1984, 93). The authors note that "these findings question the popular stereotype of the isolated bureaucrats with no knowledge and experience in other sectors." Rather interestingly, more government executives (70 percent vs. 54 percent) said their organizations had a specific government-business relations function. However, in business this function tends to be performed by upper-echelon executives, while in government it is performed at the middle and upper-middle level.

Islam and Ahmed (1984, 94–95) indicate that "personal contact tended to be the method used by the majority of [the] respondents both in business and government in carrying out the government-business relations function." They continue:

> The second most important medium used by the business sector was trade associations (27 percent of respondents used them). Only 13 percent of the respondents in the business sector acted through consultants. The respondents in the government sector indicated that 61 percent of them acted directly in the performance of this function while 26 percent acted through other members of the department and 10 percent through other departments.

5.3 Actual Contact, Desired Contact, and Perceived Influence

The amount of contact both types of executives have had with persons in the other sector and also the *desired* level of contact with representatives of the "other side" is reported in Table 5-8. Several points should

Table 5–8
INTERPERSONAL CONTACT
(average scores on a 7-point scale)

	Perceived/ Actual Contact	Desired Contact
Business Executives (n = 132) Personal Contact With		
• Federal civil servants	4.3	4.4
• Federal politicians	2.7	4.1
• Provincial civil servants	3.0	4.1
• Provincial politicians	2.4	3.8
• Municipal civil servants	2.8	3.5
• Municipal politicians	2.3	3.3
Federal Government Executives (n = 183) Personal Contact With		
• Top business executives	3.9	4.7
• Middle business managers	4.4	4.6
• Small-business people	3.5	4.4
• Heads of business associations	3.3	4.4
• Officials of business associations	3.3	4.0
• Business consultants	3.6	3.9

Source: Islam and Ahmed (1984, 95).

be noted. First, business executives have more contact with federal public servants than with either provincial or municipal public servants. Second, they have more contact with bureaucrats at all three levels than with politicians. Third, in all cases, the desired level of contact with politicians and bureaucrats is greater than the present actual level of contact, although the difference is very small with respect to federal public servants.

From the perspective of government managers, they have the most contact with middle-level business managers followed by top business executives and by other categories such as heads and officials of trade associations and consultants. See Table 5-8.

In all cases, the desired level of contact with executives in the private sector was higher than the current level, although the difference was least for the group they presently are in contact with most frequently.

Using a 7-point scale, Islam and Ahmed (1984, 97) found that government managers consistently rated business's influence over the federal government, civil servants, and MPs more highly than did private sector managers. See Table 5-9. In other words, business executives see business interests as less potent in dealing with the federal government than do their counterparts in government. Even allowing for the subjective nature of the responses, the differences are both noticeable and

Table 5-9
PERCEIVED LEVEL OF BUSINESS INFLUENCE OVER GOVERNMENT
(average scores on a 7-point scale)

	Business Executives	Federal Government Executives
• Influence of business people over federal government	3.4	4.9
• Influence of association over federal government	3.7	4.8
• Influence of business people over federal government due to mass media	3.3	4.3
• Influence of business people over civil servants	2.9	3.9
• Influence of business people over MPs	3.6	5.1
• Influence over respondent's organization by the other sector	3.8	3.8
• Level of pressure on respondent by other sector	3.5	3.8

Source: Islam and Ahmed (1984, 97).

consistent across five categories. Where senior business executives are making public statements with which they will be personally identified, strategic considerations may dictate a posture of modesty regarding business influence on government. However, this potential bias should be eliminated when an executive's responses are anonymous and pooled with many others.

On the other hand, data in Table 5-9 indicate that, with respect to their own organization, executives in both sectors perceived the same level of influence by the other sector. Government respondents — as one might expect — perceived a slightly higher level of pressure on themselves by the private sector than vice versa. In fact, one would have expected the difference to be greater, as business usually takes the initiative in business-government relations. The opposite is the case when a government is using suasion (see Stanbury and Fulton 1984).

In addition to these differences in perceived levels of influence of business on government, we should note that executives in both sectors rate business influence over civil servants as being less than that with respect to MPs, or the federal government generally. In light of the literature on lobbying, which states that backbench MPs — even on the government side — are unimportant targets for lobbyists (see chapter 7), it is surprising that federal government executives rate business influence over MPs so highly, for example, 5.1 versus 3.9 for civil servants and 4.9 for the federal government as a whole. Perhaps federal managers believe that business is effective in influencing MPs, but realize that MPs usually have little impact on the shaping of public policy.[3]

On the other hand, as Islam and Ahmed emphasize, "in spite of the acceptably high level of personal contact with the civil servants (4.3), business managers felt that their influence over civil servants was rather low (2.9). But the reverse was the case for federal MPs: low contact but a higher perceived level of influence" (1984, 98).

Islam and Ahmed conclude that the difference in business and government executives' perceptions of level of influence exercised by business "signals the presence of conflict and discord in business-government relations" (1984, 100). At the same time, they argue that their research indicates that "business-government relations are neither entirely conflictual nor are they completely cooperative" (1984, 101).

5.4 The Desire for Consultation and Consensus

Whalen (1961, 7), like many Canadians, assumes that despite the obvious differences in the worlds of profit and vote maximization and the diversity within them, business-government relations "ought to be directed towards a single end: the devising of procedures and standards of accommodation consistent with the public interest." He notes that the "vast majority of Canadians have long rejected laissez-faire in practical public affairs, and have required co-operation between business and government in a dominantly empirical pragmatic atmosphere."[4] No wonder Robert Presthus (1973, 1974) was able to describe public policy making in Canada as a process of "elite accommodation."

The yearning for cooperation and consultation makes it clear that many Canadian business people favour corporatist arrangements. The president of the Toronto Board of Trade, for example, has called for "better consultative arrangements among the major economic and social forces — business, labor and government — that will encourage them to work together, harnessing the energies of these partners toward mutually advantageous objectives. [Moreover], if such a partnership can be forged . . . the country's economic problems and social tensions would be greatly eased."[5]

Developer Robert Campeau — a rags-to-riches entrepreneur — has proposed that an elected council of business leaders from a broader business association "would provide effective representation at senior government levels with respect to productivity, taxation, foreign investment, exports, etc." Moreover, this group would seek greater cooperation with labour to take the initiative in stabilizing the economy and controlling inflation.[6]

It is hardly surprising that a political scientist should emphasize the need for mutual accommodation among the elites. Whalen, for example, states, "In a democratic environment, if the representatives of business and government know the rules and play the game accordingly, the accommodations necessary for political stability and social growth can be achieved" (1961, 15). However, the desire for consensus and cooperation between business and government seems extraordinarily strong in senior Canadian business leaders. For example, Peter Gordon, CEO of the Steel Company of Canada, has argued that "it is in the national interest for government and business to get closer together to solve the problems at hand," such as inflation, recession, unemployment, and "the very critical energy problem of the future." He called for joint ventures such as Panarctic Oils Ltd. and Syncrude, "which combine the ability of industry to get things done in the most efficient way with the responsibility of the government to uphold the legitimate public interest" (1975, 7).

It is common to hear a very highly regarded business leader state that "what we need is a consensus on what constitutes the public interest, and how much legislation is necessary and desirable to enforce it" (Gordon 1975, 7). On the other hand, Gordon emphasizes that, in his view, "the most unethical thing you can do in the business world is not to make a profit." He continues, "Business must be prepared to articulate its legitimate interests which are compatible with the public interest, or private enterprise will lose by default" (1975, 7).

Grant Reuber (1978, 3), then an academic and now vice-chairperson of the Bank of Montreal, points out that additional effort by governments to promote improved consultation and consensus is a form of government intervention — even though it can be called "government by ear-stroking" (alluding to the third method of getting a donkey to move — the other two being a carrot and a stick). He finds it hard to identify the market failure that produces an inadequate (inefficient) level of consultation.[7]

Moreover, Reuber (1978, 5) provides several reasons why consensus among the important economic interest groups in Canada is elusive:[8]

- Policy issues have become technically more complex.[9]
- Private decision making (e.g., business and trade unions) remains highly decentralized.
- The scope and complexity of intergovernment relations are increasing.

Reuber argues, furthermore, that "the notion of the 'public interest' which consensus-building exercises are presumably intended to identify and promote, has . . . largely become something of a chameleon." (See Stanbury 1979.) He continues: "In reality, consultation and consensus-building exercises provide yet another avenue for the promotion of self-interest [by the already powerful interest groups] via the invisible hand of politics [the rules and incentives embedded in the process]" (1978, 6).

Consultative processes in practice invariably bring the *interested* publics in contact with government (and each other), but they do little to involve the general public (see also Pross 1985). Perhaps this is inevitable. After all, government activity is not the stuff of immediate concern in the everyday life of average people.[10]

Reuber (1978, 10) notes that improved consultation may not result in greater consensus. And even if there is consensus among leaders, can they "deliver" the concurrence of their followers? (See, Swimmer 1984.)

6.0 CONFLICTS WITHIN THE BUSINESS COMMUNITY

Many times in this book I refer to "business" as if it is a monolithic entity. There are, however, a number of disagreements or conflicts among different segments of the business community that relate to public policy. These disagreements mean that business does not speak with one voice and governments receive conflicting advice. In this section of the chapter, I will describe some of these conflicts.

6.1 Interregional Rivalry

As illustrated in Table 5-10, different industries tend to be concentrated in certain provinces or regions in Canada. The Atlantic provinces, for example, accounted for 60.3 percent of the Canadian fisheries' output in 1981, while Ontario accounted for 50.1 percent of Canadian manufacturing. Governments within each province or region tend to support its major industries. The effects of this tendency are exaggerated by the important role of the provinces in Canadian federalism. The high concentration of industries in provinces or regions pits one business sector (backed

Table 5–10
PERCENTAGE OF CANADIAN GROSS DOMESTIC PRODUCT
BY PROVINCE OR REGION FOR SELECTED INDUSTRY GROUPS,
1981

Industry Group	Atlantic	Quebec	Ontario	Manitoba	Saskat- chewan	Alberta	British Columbia
Agriculture	3.0	12.9	25.1	8.9	24.2	20.9	5.0
Forestry	7.7	19.2	17.5	0.8	1.7	2.6	47.8
Fishing	60.3	5.6	3.7	2.1	0.4	0.1	27.6
Mines (including oil)*	4.3	6.1	13.4	2.3	7.7	56.6	8.6
Total Mfg. Ind.	3.9	27.5	50.1	2.8	1.1	5.4	9.1
Knitting	*	60.2	30.8	*	—	*	*
Clothing	0.3	58.8	27.6	7.2	0.6	2.3	3.2
Wood	3.8	23.5	17.9	1.7	1.2	7.2	44.5
Total GDP**	5.4	23.1	36.5	3.5	4.4	15.6	11.0

* 1.3 to Territories.
** 0.4 to Territories.

Source: Statistics Canada, *Provincial Gross Domestic Product by Industry 1981* (Ottawa: Minister of Supply and Services, 1983), pp. 42–49.

by a province or region) against another sector (also backed by a province or region) and is a major source of conflict within the business community in Canada. Policies that favour one industry/region (e.g., protectionism for Central Canada's manufacturing) impose costs on others (the resource-based industries in Western Canada).

6.2 Free Trade versus Protectionism

Closely connected with conflicts brought about by interregional rivalry are conflicts that originate between those industries favouring free trade and those favouring protectionism. Manufacturing is highly concentrated in Central Canada, with Ontario and Quebec accounting for over three-quarters of Canadian manufacturing (see Table 5-10). Canadian manufacturers have traditionally favoured protectionist policies. While tariffs have been reduced, nontariff barriers have become far more important. On the other hand, the industries concentrated in Western Canada, such as forestry (B.C.), petroleum (Alberta), and agriculture (Saskatchewan), are export-oriented. These industries have traditionally favoured a policy of freer trade for Canada, recognizing that liberalization is a reciprocal proposition. As a result, there have been conflicts and disagreements between the business people of Central Canada and those of Western Canada, again each group backed by its respective provincial governments. This conflict is well illustrated by the recent debate in Canada over free or freer trade with the United States.[11] These industrial differences in support for free trade underline who wins and loses by the present tariff structure. A study by the Canada West Foundation of the costs and benefits of tariffs on imports in 1983 shows the effect by province:[12]

- Ontario   + $494 million
- Quebec   +   80
- Alberta   −   167
- Atlantic Prov.   −   138

- B.C.   − $119 million
- Saskatchewan   −   80
- Manitoba   −   39

6.3 Trading Enterprises versus Firms with a Domestic Focus

A survey of 397 of Canada's largest firms found a number of attitudinal differences between companies involved in domestic markets only and those involved in both domestic and international markets (Trebuss 1981, 23–24). Two of these differences are as follows: firms operating only in the domestic market assign a higher influence to the growth rate of the Canadian economy than do the other firms; and companies involved in both domestic and international markets assign a higher degree of influence to the value of the Canadian dollar than do the other firms.

Since government programs that concentrate on domestic growth rates and government actions that influence the value of the Canadian dollar do not necessarily coincide, there is potential for conflict between businesses that favour one program over another.

6.4 Foreign versus Domestic Ownership

Trebuss (1981, 23) found attitudinal differences between Canadian-owned and foreign-controlled firms. These were statistical differences in attitudes toward wage, salary and benefit costs; legislation regarding competition policy; and Canadian economic nationalism. Again, attitudinal differences may contribute to conflicts within the business community over government policies and priorities.

Bliss (1982a, 55) argues that Canadians are addicted to economic-nationalism. "A major reason why Canadian business had trouble resisting economic nationalism is the fact that many Canadian business leaders are employees of branch operations. . . . Many of the spokesmen for foreign-controlled operations decided . . . to practice 'good corporate citizenship' and be silent." On the other hand, there is a small but vocal group of Canadian business people who believe passionately in economic nationalism and some have profited handsomely from it (Bliss 1982a, 52). Thomas says:

> Today the most clamorous Canadianism comes from businessmen. And profit — as much as patriotism — is their motive. . . . To U.S. critics, Canadian flag-wavers are merely exploiting patriotism for profit. Says Alan Buckley of . . . The Conference Board: 'The maple leaf is really just a fig leaf to hide anti-competitive business strategies.' The most nationalistic Canadian businessmen, Buckley points out, are those who compete directly with foreigners for domestic markets. (1981, 54)

The internal conflict within the Canadian business establishment is illustrated by what *Maclean's* has called "the country's least familiar but most powerful business lobby": the Business Council on National Issues. BCNI is described as "a select club of 150 chief executives of multinational corporations, the big banks and some Canadian-owned businesses [in which] the Canadian firms are allied in interest and ideology with the foreign-owned giants" (Thomas 1981, 56). BCNI has made it clear that it opposes the federal government's various efforts to foster Canadianization (e.g., the NEP, FIRA).

6.5 Interfirm Competition

We have noted in chapter 3 that the typical industrial structure in Canada is that of a moderate to highly concentrated oligopoly. (See Green 1985.) In other words, firms recognize their interdependence and perceive themselves more as head-to-head rivals than do firms in an atomistic industry unaffected by the actions of any single firm.

There is general agreement, however, among business people in Canada that more stringent competition legislation is not required.[13] As Stanbury states: "Anti-combines policy in Canada finds almost no support among businessmen. This is different from the situation in the United States" (1977, 45). There is little internal conflict among members of the business community over the competition policy to be pursued by government. In respect to Bill C-29 introduced in April 1984, but not enacted before the general election of September 1984, three of the largest business associations (CMA, CCC, BCNI) supported these proposed amendments to the Combines Investigation Act. However, they were directly involved in negotiating the words of the bill.[14]

6.6 The Voice of Business?

The voice of business may well be a "tower of babble," for, as a *Financial Post* editorial in 1976 noted, "there are dozens upon dozens of business associations stoutly defending viewpoints that at times clash sharply." The president of the Toronto Board of Trade, A. R. Murrich, observed: "The diversity of view which the *Post* and others observe is accurate because business in our society is a kaleidoscope, as diverse in its problems and aspirations as the country itself. Furthermore, it is the nature of business in a market economy to be competitive, not collaborative." Murrich argued, however, that business does subscribe to "a single theology . . . free enterprise, the backbone of our business society; the carrier of economic advancement to all Canadians." In his view, free enterprise provides individuals and groups with "responsibility, motivation, participation, satisfaction, incentive, reward, status and above all — purpose."[15]

7.0 STRATEGIC CONSIDERATIONS IN BUSINESS-GOVERNMENT RELATIONS

7.1 The Need for a Strategy

Just as firms must develop a competitive strategy in which to integrate the traditional functional areas of their business (marketing, finance, production, personnel/industrial relations, etc.), they must learn to think in strategic terms in their dealings with government. Indeed, for interest groups in general, the centre of their existence is their strategy for influencing government policy to the greatest advantage.

There are numerous parallels between the development of a strategy for a firm's government relations activities and the much broader issue of a competitive strategy. For example, Porter states that "developing a competitive strategy is developing a broad formula for how a business is going to compete, what its goals should be, and what policies will be needed to carry out those goals"(1980, p. xvi). He identifies four key factors that jointly determine the limits of what a company can achieve: the company's strengths and weaknesses relative to competitors; the personal values of the key people who conceive and implement the strategy; the set of threats and opportunities (economic and technical) associated with the industry (or industries) in which the firm operates; and society's expectations embodied in public policy, social values, and evolving mores (1980, p. xviii).

In the case of a government relations strategy, the critical internal variables are (1) the values, beliefs, and assumptions of the senior people responsible for the function within the organization — this will have a major impact on the choice of goals or objectives of the firm in its dealings with government; and (2) the capabilities of the firm in dealing with government: What skills and "tools" does it have? What are its weaknesses and can they be remedied?

In developing its government relations strategy, the firm must deal with the following important exogenous variables or parameters: the nature of governmental institutions and the policy-making process; the behaviour of both parallel and rival interest groups; societal values and mores; and the role of the communications media.

7.2 Broad Approaches to Government Relations

Before I identify the important choices a firm must make in developing a strategy to deal with governments, it will be useful to consider several broad approaches to government relations proposed by others.

In a preliminary report on Canadian CEOs' perceptions of the role of social and political factors in their strategic decision making, Blair (1985, 19) indicates that forty-three of the fifty-six respondents said that socio-political factors will have a significant impact on their corporate strategies in the future. Some CEOs noted that with the change of government at the federal level in 1984, some of the actions of the federal government could have a positive impact on their enterprises. However, the strategic significance of public policy initiatives in general varies markedly across industries.

The CEOs identified three main approaches to dealing with socio-political issues:

- increasing their own organization's resources for identifying, monitoring, and analyzing these issues and trends (e.g., issues management in the planning or public affairs units);
- "working within industry associations to ensure that a coordinated, active and unified position is presented to government on specific policy issues" along with maintaining personal contacts with politicians and bureaucrats; and
- "contributing to and participating directly in the development of public policies, particularly those designed to enhance the competitiveness

of Canadian industry" — this includes making the best use of various consultative mechanisms (Blair 1985, 19).

Blair (1985, 20) points out that independent of which approach a company adopts, the CEOs clearly recognize that their firms must continually monitor and assess changes in the external environment; respond quickly to change by participating in the formation of public policy and by modifying their corporation's strategy; and ensure that the firm's approach to strategic decision making is flexible.

Murray Weidenbaum identifies "three basic patterns of reaction to government controls over industry":

Passive. Some corporate managements simply react to each new or expanded federal control. They may criticize the development or they may attempt to postpone its effects through litigation and administrative appeals. But, sooner or later, they gear their firm's operations to meet the new government requirements.

Anticipatory. Other corporate managements rely on their planning capability to estimate in advance likely changes in federal controls over business. Thus, for example, prior to congressional passage of restrictions on the use of private land, they will reorient their construction projects to minimize the likelihood of subsequently running afoul of new federal regulations. They also voluntarily may take socially responsible actions to make the initiation of more government controls less likely. . . . As corporate managers become more sensitive to evolving social demands, they will consider response to at least some of the public's expectations as being a normal aspect of conducting business. To the extent that this development occurs voluntarily, businesses themselves will be providing an important constraint on the degree of political pressure that social action interests can effectively exert against them.

Active. Still other business executives attempt to head off or shape the character of federal intervention by playing a more active role in the development and enactment of such legislation. Thus, some companies are strengthening the division of their Washington offices that deal with pending legislation, or are setting up such operations if they do not exist. Trade associations that are active on Capitol Hill are being supported more strongly. Despite the growing restrictions on political contributions and practices, many businessmen and businesswomen — as individuals — attempt to exercise leverage on government decision-making by participating more actively in the political process [by running for office, by working in campaigns, by in-house publications/communications programs on political issues, and by providing analytical information to government on the impact of proposed legislation]. (1977, 167–68)

Professor James Gillies (1981, chap. 4) identifes the following categories of strategies Canadian businesses have used since World War II
in dealing with government:

- *Mutual Accommodation:* Under this approach, business and government engage in mutual planning and establish a social contract. In
  general, governments formulate the goals and strategies for the economy and business has a major role in implementing them. This
  approach assumes there is a shared belief in both the goals "the system" should seek and the way they should be pursued. It also requires
  that the leaders of both sides have a great deal of knowledge and understanding of how the other functions.

- *The Issue-by-Issue Approach:* This is the strategy most frequently used
  by firms. "It means that business reacts to individual initiatives of the
  government as those initiatives are introduced" (Gillies 1981, 48). Those
  issues that are perceived to be inimical to the firm's/industry's interests are opposed. Those that are beneficial are supported. This approach requires an early warning system that alerts managers about
  actions planned by government, and the ability on the part of the
  firm to marshall reasons justifying its opposition to the government's
  plans where the proposed action is perceived as detrimental to the
  firm's interests. As Gillies notes: "An underlying assumption of the
  strategy is that policy flows in government from the bottom up. In
  many cases this is indeed true, but with respect to significant issues it
  often is not [e.g., energy policy in the Clark government of 1979-80]"
  (1981, 49).

- *The Political Strategy: Direct Action:* This approach is based on the
  idea that if new economic power is administered by public decisions
  coming out of the political bargaining arena, then business must enter
  the arena and exert its power in the bargaining process to influence
  public policy. The direct version of this approach requires that more
  business people become involved in the political process and seek election with a view to attaining a position of some power, for example,
  in the cabinet. Even as MPs, business people can be effective in speaking
  out for the free enterprise system as a whole.

- *The Political Strategy: Indirect Action:* This approach involves mobilizing support for (or against) policies that the firm supports (or does
  not support). The techniques include lobbying politicians and bureaucrats, marshalling public opinion via public relations campaigns,
  advocacy advertising and letter-writing campaigns, the strategic use
  of political contributions, the formation of alliances with other interest groups, and the strategic use of the media to amplify and target
  one's persuasive efforts. As Gillies emphasizes, to be successful, business must develop creditable political positions that reflect the public
  interest so as to mobilize a constituency (1981, 56).

It is clear that Gillies prefers the political strategies, and while he hopes that the direct involvement by business people in politics will increase, he appreciates that, as a practical matter, the indirect approach is the one to adopt. He says, "The need for . . . an organized, coordinated, pro-active [government relations] division within the company — as opposed to a reactive *ad hoc* capacity to respond to external changes and pressures — is self evident" (1981, 60).

7.3 Strategic Choices in Seeking to Influence Government Policy

These basic approaches or broad strategies of dealing with governments can be better understood if we factor them into a number of separate but related strategic choices. I suggest that the central strategic choices concern the following:

- the goals/objectives to be pursued;
- the relatively small number of policy issues that will be the focus of the firm's efforts designed to influence government policy;
- the "targets" (individuals/organizations) of the firm's efforts to influence public policy, whether they are inside government or outside it;
- the timing of the firm's activities designed to influence public policy;
- the choice of techniques or means by which the firm will carry out its plan to influence public policy;
- the decision to form alliances or coalitions with other interest groups, including the relationship of the firm to the trade associations of which it is a member;
- the personnel who will design the strategy and implement it; and
- the general style the firm adopts in its dealings with governments.

7.3.1 Goals/Objectives
Considered very broadly, a firm might adopt one of the following as the goal of its government relations activities:

- minimize the cost of inevitable government intervention to the firm;
- maintain the "free enterprise system" (market economy);
- obtain the maximum economic benefits from government (tariff protection, quotas, subsidies, financing, procurement opportunities);
- participate in the policy-making process of a pluralist democracy as one of many stakeholders; or
- attempt to repeal big, intrusive government and the "welfare state."

At a more practical level I suggest that the objectives of the firm's efforts in dealing with government are the following:

- to secure favourable (prevent unfavourable) legislation/subordinate legislation;

- to secure favourable (prevent unfavourable) interpretations of the discretionary provisions of existing legislation, policy, and programs; and
- to secure longer-term changes in access to or participation in the process by which public policy is made with a view to increasing the group's influence over policy in the future.

7.3.2 Issues

Limitations on resources (dollars, executive time) require that a company be selective concerning the issues that become the focus of its government relations activities. The term *issues* is used here to refer to the subject matter that is or is likely to be the object of some type of action by a government. Issues management — the subject of chapter 6 — is a process by which a company seeks to be effective in the shaping and resolution of public policy issues that are having or are likely to have a significant impact on its performance. This process involves, among other things, the following activities:

- The scanning of the environment to identify issues that could potentially be important to the firm, and the subsequent monitoring of those issues
- The classification of issues and the publics influencing them or being influenced by them
- The identification of the source(s) of policy issues that stem from social, economic, and political forces
- Plotting and understanding the life cycle of policy issues so as to facilitate effective action to protect the firm's interests
- Assessment of current and emerging issues and forecasting their likely development
- Analysis of issues and their ranking in importance to the firm, taking into account timing, potential impact on the firm, and likelihood of various consequences for the firm
- The development of strategies to deal with both emerging and existing issues (see chapter 6 for more detail)

The critical point to appreciate is that issues management necessarily functions in a world of considerable uncertainty. Second, there are almost always more issues of interest to the firm than it has resources to deal with — even applying the usual marginal calculus. Third, in practical terms, a firm can only mount and operate a small number of major efforts to influence government at one time or even in the course of a year. Often difficult choices must be made under uncertainty. Hence, the firm should establish an issues-management capability with considerable flexibility so that it can adapt to new information about the public policy issues within its purview.

7.3.3 Targets

Targets refer to those individuals, groups, or organizations that the firm seeks to influence in the policy-making process. Some of these targets are inside government (e.g., cabinet ministers, public servants who are policy advisors, MPs, and senators) and some are outside (e.g., the media, other interest groups, the "attentive" portion of the general public). The choice of targets is related to several other strategic variables: the timing of efforts to influence policy; the choice of vehicles and techniques; the nature of the issue; and the amount of resources available for the government relations function.

Targets may be approached directly (e.g., face-to-face lobbying) or indirectly (e.g., by using advocacy advertising to alter public opinion, which in turn persuades the cabinet to alter a proposed or existing policy in the direction desired by the firm). The details concerning the choice of targets are discussed in chapter 7.

7.3.4 Timing

As in most strategic behaviour, timing is often of the essence in seeking to influence public policy. In general, interest groups in Canada want to begin their representations as early as possible in the policy-making process when the situation is more fluid and the government of the day (through action by the cabinet) has not publicly committed itself to a particular course of action. Obviously, the timing of representations is influenced by the nature of the process under which the particular policy action occurs and the stage the issue has reached. As emphasized in chapter 4, a great variety of government actions embody public policy that may have a significant effect on a firm (or other interest group). Therefore, it is necessary to identify the timing of the various steps in the process associated with each of these actions.

The timing of representations or other efforts to influence policy have to take into account decisions concerning targets as well as those concerning vehicles and techniques of influence. In general, the firm has to decide when it will initiate action and when it will follow up, since it is often more effective to make inputs at several different points (and at several targets) in the policy process. Obviously, the timing of particular actions depends on what has happened in earlier phases. Even if a firm has had little success in influencing a policy in the form of new legislation before cabinet made its decision, it should appreciate that it may not be too late to have an impact on the policy, although the likelihood of obtaining the desired change is smaller. For example, businesses may be able to influence the actual implementation of new legislation, as line bureaucrats and regulators exercise discretion in translating the legislation into programs and scores of microdecisions. If it is too late to change the law itself, it is not too late to persuade those who administer it to exercise their discretion in a way that is more beneficial or less costly to the firm (interest group). Generally, see chapter 7.

7.3.5 Techniques

This term refers to the various means that firms or other interest groups have at their disposal in trying to influence public policy. The list provided in Figure 5-2 suggests that interest groups have a wider range of techniques to influence governments than is usually encompassed by even a broad definition of lobbying. While not all of these techniques are discussed in detail in this book, separate chapters are devoted to direct lobbying (chapters 7, 8, and 9), shaping public opinion by using the media (chapter 11), advocacy advertising (chapter 12), and political contributions (chapter 10).

Figure 5–2
CLASSIFICATION OF THE TECHNIQUES USED BY INTEREST GROUPS TO INFLUENCE PUBLIC POLICY

1. **Direct Lobbying**
(a) Personal Communications, Presentations, and Contact
— face-to-face formal and informal meetings (e.g., entertainment)
— formal presentations/briefs
— letters
— telephone calls
— this form of lobbying may be conducted by individual firms or through a trade association

2. **Indirect Lobbying**
(a) Direct or "Pressure Mail"
— individual initiated
— third-party initiated, i.e., by interest groups
(b) Public Relations Campaigns
— speeches, articles, newspaper coverage (media campaign)
— personal criticism of lobbying targets
— protest marches, meetings, "rent-a-crowd" tactics
— advocacy advertising
(c) Legal Approaches
— testing the constitutionality of legislation in the courts
— appeals to the courts and/or cabinet from decisions of administrative tribunals

3. **"Dollar Lobbying"**
(a) Campaign Contributions to Parties and Candidates
— cash
— benefits in kind/support services
(b) Illegal/Questionable Payments
— direct bribery (illegal)
— indirect inducements — delayed employment opportunities, speaking fees, gifts, access to profit-making ventures

Figure 5–2 (continued)

---

4. **Questionable Practices**
(a) Deception, Distortion, Lying
   — obfuscation of the real issues; throwing up smokescreens
   — selectivity in provision of facts/information
   — fear mongering/Chicken Little approach
   — mudslinging/personal attacks on targets/opponents
(b) Inundation, Delay
   — phony lawsuits to create pressure and delay
   — provisions of overwhelming amounts of paper in a form that is time consuming/costly to analyze
   — playing "procedural chess" to exhaust an opponent's resources
(c) Co-optation
   — win over or neutralize targets/opponents by very attractive job offers or other benefits
   — retain and pay high fees to experts who might be used by the other side

5. **Coalition Building**
(a) Coordination of Lobbying Efforts with Other Interest Groups
(b) Legislative Logrolling, i.e., exchanging support/opposition with respect to item A for support/opposition with respect to item B

Source: Adapted from Navarro (1984, 92).

1. *Direct Lobbying:* The focus here is on face-to-face contact with those persons believed to be influential in shaping public policy. These contacts may be made in both public and private forums. The vehicles employed include personal meetings (both formal and informal), the presentation of briefs, telephone calls, and letters. It is usually argued that the ideal is one-on-one contact with key decision makers: "When lobbyists prepare their cases well and argue them effectively, such direct communication is most persuasive" (Navarro 1984, 92).

The survey of senior executives and/or directors by Gillies (1981, 35) found that slightly over one-half of the eighty CEOs in his sample believe that direct, personal dialogue with a minister or senior public servant is the most effective method of influencing public policy. Twenty percent believe that business can be most effective by working closely with such organizations as BCNI, the C. D. Howe Research Institute, or trade associations. A similar percentage believe they can be most influential by speaking out on issues in an objective, nonpartisan manner. Ten percent endorse direct political action as the most effective method of influencing federal policy.

Mark Green (1981, 9), long associated with consumer advocate Ralph Nader, argues that corporations in the United States have generally adopted three lobbying techniques:

- the Chicken Little approach in which executives predict that great evil will befall business or indeed the nation if a particular legislative proposal is enacted;
- the "jingle of cash" approach in which business provides campaign contributions to those politicians who initiate and support legislation favourable to business interests; or
- the lobbying-by-inundation approach in which business interests use plenty of resources to document and disseminate their position to a variety of audiences including legislators.

However, more publicly oriented and less direct techniques of influencing public policy appear to be becoming more important. The targets and timing of lobbying activities are discussed in chapter 7, while lobbying techniques and vehicles are discussed in chapters 8 and 9.

2. *Shaping Public Opinion:* Publicity is vital to any form of individual or organizational protest. But since the public has become more familiar with "media events," activists need new tactics to ensure that their message finds its target. King suggests that "the next stage for special-interest groups has been to publicize selected results of opinion research: that is, to use a more direct method of establishing their own ideas as the majority view" (1981, 90). Not only does such research interest the media, but it has special relevance for politicians, who are widely believed to be greatly concerned with losing votes. Moreover, the results of polls may have a bandwagon effect on the general public. The use of polls in lobbying is discussed in more detail in chapter 8.

Public opinion may be influenced by such activities as public relations campaigns, advocacy advertising, and support for public policy research bodies. (We note that public opinion concerning a major business enterprise depends a great deal on its ordinary commercial activities, i.e., its relations with customers, employees, competitors, and suppliers.)

Public relations campaigns that make artful use of the media can be used either to increase or to decrease the visibility of an issue with a view to making it easier for decision makers to move in the direction desired by the interest group. Grefe draws the following distinction between public relations and public affairs: "Public relations seeks to explain that which *is*, in the best available light. Public affairs seeks to formulate or shape events *prior to* their occurrence" (1981, 17).

Volker Stoltz (1983, 29–30) has defined "conflict PR" as the mobilization of public opinion or the prevention of the mobilization of public opinion. It is based on Lincoln's observation that "nothing can fail which is supported by public sentiment" and the reverse proposition. The objective is to participate in "the process of opinion formation and attempt to control this process with regard to one's own particular interest."

It should be recognized that even if business is well organized and vocal on a specific issue, it may not be able to move a government if public opinion is or is believed to be adverse.

A high-level official in the Mulroney administration says government is far more inclined to give business what it wants if it perceives that there is no strong opposition. "When all the ducks are lined up pointing in the same direction, it's easy to get action," he says. That explains why business gets its way more readily on some issues such as tax policy or competition laws, where the public shows little interest. But business can find it harder to woo governments when there are strong competing lobbies or when public opinion points in the opposite direction.[16]

Stoltz (1983, 30) argues that "the company which believes that the ability to act is threatened only by politicians and governments is making a big mistake. The threat comes . . . from public opinion, which can also make it impossible for politicians to carry out a certain policy." He formulates what he describes as a "venturous hypothesis," namely, that "the opinion held by the majority about a certain subject is completely irrelevant as long as this opinion is not organized." The "pressure of public opinion," therefore, is that opinion which is organized and claims to speak for the majority even though it may, in fact, be the view of a minority.[17]

To change government policy, interest groups sometimes seek to alter public opinion and to raise the visibility of an issue on which they seek government action. If they are successful, it is easier for politicians (and bureaucrats) to accede to their requests. Consider the following example:

To step up the pressure on Finance Minister Marc Lalonde to rescind the proposal to tax after 1983 the housing and travel benefits allowed mining employees in the Far North, the territorial chambers of commerce are taking their protest across the country. A key thrust of the campaign will be to increase "media awareness" of the issue by briefing journalists, in both official languages, including the parliamentary press gallery, about the "detrimental impact" of removing the allowances.

To reach the general public, the chambers plan advocacy advertising to "ensure as broad a range of the public as possible understands the implications of this issue." Also planned are public speaking tours by mining industry experts, efforts to encourage the public to express their views directly to Mr. Lalonde and their members of Parliament, and meetings with MPs of all parties "to ensure they understand the consequences of the Government's proposal." . . . To finance the campaign, which he estimated would cost above $100,000, Mr. Wilson said the chambers would seek support from private mining companies, labour unions, local governments, business groups, and citizens' associations.[18]

Advocacy advertising is the use of paid advertising designed to sell ideas rather than products. While far from a universal technique of influencing public policy, it is growing in importance. See chapter 12 for a discussion of its use.

Financial support for public policy research bodies is clearly a longer-term, indirect approach to influencing public opinion. While the role of ideas is often disparaged in politics and policy making, research bodies, through the work they support, can shape the policy agenda in several ways: by defining "problems" that could or should be addressed by government, and by generating alternative approaches to those problems — including the idea that government intervention is more likely to make things worse in some sense.

The major public research bodies in Canada are the Institute for Research on Public Policy, the C. D. Howe Research Institute, the Canadian Institute for Economic Policy, and the Fraser Institute. The Fraser Institute was created in 1974 entirely with financing from the business community. (More than one-half of IRPP's endowment was provided by the federal and some provincial governments.) It is modelled after the U.K. Institute of Economic Affairs. By the end of 1983, the institute, located in Vancouver, had produced thirty-six books that had sold some 105 000 copies. However, as Tafler points out,

> they are only the tip of an iceberg of media penetration. Aside from interviews and speeches, Mr. Walker [director of the institute] and Walter Block, the Fraser's senior economist, write about 60 [?] columns and articles a month, many of which appear in community newspapers. Mr. Walker is also published regularly in The Province, the Financial Post, Citibusiness and Equity Magazine, and gives a daily commentary on a Vancouver radio show. Mr. Walker's firm grasp of McLuhan's media massage has greatly expanded the Fraser's influence on public opinions. If the opinions that are influenced are those of premiers and cabinet ministers, so much the better. It's called "the idea business" or replacing the wrong ideas with the right ideas. (1983)

One reporter has identified what he believes to be fairly clear links between some of the ideas in books published by the Fraser Institute and legislative actions by the Social Credit government in British Columbia:

> In 1977, the Fraser Institute published a volume of essays based on a series of lectures delivered by U.S. supply-side economist Milton Friedman in England the year before. Mr. Friedman was discussing methods of turning over public assets to the private sector. Instead

of auctioning off a government-owned corporation, Mr. Friedman suggested "giving every citizen in the country a share of it." Two years later, Mr. Friedman's idea was followed almost to the letter by Premier Bennett, who created the B.C. Resources Investment Corp., from resource company assets acquired five years before by the NDP Government. Mr. Bennett offered five free shares to every B.C. resident in his successful bid to gain re-election in 1979.

In 1980, Fraser published a book called *Unions and the Public Interest*, written by economics professor Sandra Christensen, which focused on government strategies in dealing with public-sector unions. Much of Mr. Bennett's 1983 restraint legislation, designed to permit the Government to fire public employees and gain control over their conditions of employment, is outlined in a section of Miss Christensen's book entitled Work Force Adjustments. "Public employment can be cut directly when public employees become too expensive, either by automating their functions or contracting them out to companies in the private sector," Miss Christensen wrote. "When advantageous, the public employer should be free to accomplish this cut in public employment by layoffs, rather than by having to rely on attrition alone."[19]

3. *Alliances/Coalitions:* Politics, it is said, makes strange bedfellows. Interest-group representation is political activity par excellence, so it is not surprising that firms have to make strategic decisions concerning the formation of alliances or coalitions in their efforts to influence public policy. Two basic decisions can be identified. The first concerns the individual firm's relationship with the trade or industry associations of which it is a member. Most firms belong to such associations, and large firms operating in several industries may belong to several product-specific, industry, sectoral or activity-specific associations. In addition, the largest firms (e.g., those in the *Financial Post* top 200) are likely to be important members of such umbrella associations as BCNI and the CCC. Therefore, the firm has to decide what will be the division of labour on a particular issue between the trade association and itself. As noted earlier, even firms in the same industry may have significant differences of opinion on specific policy issues. If such conflict "splits" an association, it will often take a highly equivocal position or none at all on the issue. As a result, firms for whom the issue is deemed to be important may proceed independently (or in alliance with other like-minded firms or groups). Even where the firm's position and that of its trade association are the same, the firm may choose to leave the matter entirely to the association's efforts, or it may wish to reinforce the association's efforts by parallel or complimentary actions of its own. See chapter 8.

The second type of decision relates to the creation of ad hoc coalitions of firms and/or other interest groups. It is becoming more common for business groups to establish informal coalitions to lobby on particular issues, as the following example illustrates:

> Borrowers will have to pay a new insurance fee and bankers will have to assume more of the risk for bad loans under the Small Businesses Loans Act as a result of changes to a Government bill announced yesterday. . . . Small business groups [notably CFIB] and the Canadian Bankers' Association joined forces to persuade the Government to shift the fee to the borrowers. They argued that, "if the banks had to pay the fee, it would kill the program." . . . When the amending bill was introduced two months ago, it brought in a 1 per cent fee — to be paid by the banks — to compensate the federal Government for some of its losses. It also reduced the guarantee.[20]

The corporation exists in a complex web of transactions (which are not entirely pecuniary) with employees, customers, suppliers, and creditors. It is becoming more common for managers to broaden the base of their efforts, to influence government by mobilizing members of what has been called its "natural constituency." Grefe argues, for example, that

> the blue collar worker with whom management should seek an alliance will eventually see that he has more in common with the management of the company than with the management of the union. There will still be disputes, but when the issues are vital to the survival of the company, it will have a solid cadre of defenders if union and white collar employees have been approached in the proper way. (1981, 66)

While lobbying alliances or coalitions are becoming more common, there are trade-offs that have to be made in creating them. This point is discussed in more detail in chapter 8.

4. *Dollar Lobbying:* This term is used by Navarro (1984) to refer to political contributions to candidates and parties in cash or in kind. While bribery is a criminal offence, it is widely believed that political contributions help firms and other interest groups gain access to top political decision makers. Access, of course, is the first step in persuasion. Moreover, political contributions are a highly tangible "token of esteem" that may become the basis for an implicit obligation for politicians to reciprocate by being more sympathetic to the briefs, letters, and oral communications from the contributor (see chapter 10).

5. *Legal Approaches:* While Canadians do not have the reputation of being litigious (as do Americans), they may make greater use of the courts in the future as a method of influencing public policy. The principal reason is that the Constitution Act of 1982 with its Charter of Rights

and Freedoms effectively gives to the courts a great deal more power over the interpretation of legislation. Presently, interest groups (including firms) use the courts to appeal decisions of administrative tribunals on a fairly limited basis. For example, appeals from federal administrative tribunals, under section 28 of the Federal Court Act, may be made on three grounds: that the tribunal, commission, board or agency "(a) failed to observe a principle of natural justice or otherwise acted beyond or refused to exercise its jurisdiction; (b) erred in law in making its decision or order . . . ; or (c) based its decision on an erroneous finding of fact that it made in a perverse or capricious manner or without regard for the material before it."

However, with the new charter, a much broader set of arguments concerning the constitutionality of legislation is opened up in cases before the courts. It should be noted that this technique of influencing public policy generally comes late in the day — usually after legislation (including new regulations) has been enacted. For example, the National Citizens' Coalition successfully challenged a 1983 amendment to the Federal Elections Act that would have completely prohibited advertising expenditures by interest groups during election campaigns. The court held that the amendment violated the freedom of speech provisions in the charter. See chapter 10.

More recently, the National Citizens' Coalition has financed a case brought by community college teacher Mervyn Lavigne that "has struck fear into Canada's labor movement."[21] Lavigne (and NCC) "oppose any use of compulsory union dues to support the New Democratic Party and such causes as the peace movement and widely available abortions." He is arguing that the part of the dues he pays to the Ontario Public Service Employees Union under the Rand formula violates his rights to freedom of association and freedom of speech under the 1982 Charter of Rights and Freedoms. Lavigne is also challenging an Ontario law that makes it illegal for college teachers to be paid if they cross a picket line, as he did during a strike in 1984.

According to Dennis McDermott, then president of the Canadian Labour Congress, if Lavigne wins his case on using union dues for political contributions, "the obvious effect would be to render the labor movement absolutely impotent." He accused the NCC of wanting to reduce the unions "to nothing." The NCC expects that it will cost $500 000 to take Lavigne's case all the way to the Supreme Court of Canada. As the case went to trial, the NCC stated it had spent about $300 000, of which $100 000 went to legal fees. In order to help finance the case, the NCC used advocacy ads to solicit contributions. For example, the one in the *Globe and Mail* on August 27, 1985 (p. 3), used the following headline, "Should unions force Canadians through compulsory union dues to finance political parties and causes?"

Another example is the effort by a multinational drug manufacturer to have the 1969 compulsory licensing provisions in the Patent Act declared unconstitutional.[22] In this case, the issue was taken to court some years after multinational pharmaceutical firms began lobbying to have the law changed.

Another negative feature of resorting to the courts is that legal challenges are costly. The National Citizens' Coalition spent some $200 000 on the Elections Act case, and it ended at the trial court level; that is, the NCC did not have to fight it at the provincial court of appeal and on to the Supreme Court of Canada. Moreover, an appeal to the courts is largely a negative instrument. It can rule a piece of legislation unconstitutional, but it can't (directly) result in new legislation, new programs, or policies.

One might include in the category of "legal approaches" appeals to the cabinet over decisions of regulatory agencies. It is quite common — as noted in chapter 4 — for the decision of "independent" regulatory agencies to be subject to appeal by unhappy parties to the cabinet. For example, under section 64(1) of the National Transportation Act, the cabinet may at any time, at its own discretion, by petition from a party of interest or upon its own motion, vary or rescind any order, decision, or regulation of the Canadian Transport Commission. These "political appeals" have been the subject of much criticism by scholars and less influential interest groups (see Janisch 1979 and ECC 1979), but generally have been supported by large firms and trade associations on the grounds that they make regulatory bodies more accountable to the political leadership. On this point MacCrimmon and Stanbury argue that cabinet appeals mean accountability to politically effective business interests, not to the public. Such appeals tend to "open the door to the crassest form of political pressure . . . and the most opportunistic form of decision making by the Cabinet" (1978, 103).

7.3.6 Vehicles
Vehicles are the specific modes of communication used by an interest group in the various techniques designed to influence public policy. As Figure 5-3 indicates, the list of such methods of communication is quite lengthy, although when most people think of efforts by interest groups to influence government, they think of lobbying. And when they think of lobbying, they think of the following vehicles:

- informal discussions (meetings and telephone calls) with politicians and bureaucrats;
- formal presentations (briefs and testimony) before a legislative committee or to a minister; and
- mass campaigns, that is, multiname petitions, rallies, protest demonstrations.

Figure 5–3
THE RELATIONSHIP BETWEEN THE TECHNIQUES
AND VEHICLES OF INFLUENCING
PUBLIC POLICY

Vehicles	Techniques				
	Direct Lobbying	Shaping Public Opinion	"Dollar" Lobbying	Marshalling Stake-holders (forming coalitions)	Legal Approaches
• Briefs (written presentations)	* * *	*		A	* * *
• Letters					
— individual	* *		A	*	
— mass campaign	*	P		* *	
• Meetings					
— private forums	* *		A		
— public forums	* *			* *	
• Telephone calls	* * *		A	*	
• Plant visits by bureaucrats or politicians	*			A	
• Entertainment	* *		A		
• Speakers bureau		*		*	
• Protest demonstrations/ rallies	*	* *		*	
• Mass petitions	*	*		* *	
• Use of media					
— institutional advertising		*			
— advocacy advertising		* * *		*	
— public relations		* *		* *	P
• Cash payments (and services in kind)			* * *		

P = possible vehicle depending upon the circumstances
A = ancillary activity to other vehicles

* The number of asterisks indicates the typical importance of vehicle.

While this picture of lobbying in the narrow sense is a reasonably good one, direct lobbying is only one of a number of techniques to influence public policy. In general, indirect approaches have become more important in the area of government relations. By indirect I mean that (1) the proximate target of activity is not an individual or group that directly influences policy (e.g., a minister, the cabinet, a regulatory agency, a top bureaucratic policy advisor), and/or (2) the act of influence is not directly connected to the issue at hand. For example, efforts to shape public opinion (at least the opinions of the attentive public) through the use of mass and specialized media with vehicles such as advocacy advertising and public relations are designed to influence the general climate so that policy makers are able to do what the interest group wants or are unable to take some action opposed by the interest group. In other words, the objective is to influence policy makers indirectly by influencing public opinion. The proximate target is public opinion, but the ultimate target is the individuals who directly shape policy.

While briefs and meetings in public forums are usually focused on a specific issue (or a set of related issues), success in influencing governments by major interest groups with a large stake in the system usually requires the use of vehicles that are not directly related to specific problems. For example, institutional advertising, public relations, and campaign contributions are designed to create a positive image and to show the firm's (group's) support for the political process. When a company maintains a speakers bureau it is "telling its story" in general terms to service groups, high school students, and various other organizations. By encouraging politicians and bureaucrats to visit its plants and other facilities, the firm is trying to make these policy makers familiar with the company's activities and its personnel. The object is to build a personal relationship and create linkages that may be useful in the future. Similarly, telephone calls to various participants on a regular basis to "shoot the breeze" are another way of keeping in touch, exchanging information informally, and literally maintaining the lines of communication in one's network. The general objective is keep the channels of potential influence in good running order so as to identify and resolve problems before they become crises. As importantly, the objective of these "maintenance" activities is to increase the group's effectiveness in dealing with specific issues in a crisis situation or when the group has an intense interest in a particular issue. As farmers say: If you want a big harvest in the fall, you have to prepare the ground properly in the early spring and plant quality seed.

Persons knowledgeable about business-government relations, particularly practitioners, emphasize the importance of maintaining a continuous relationship with current and potential policy makers rather than simply responding to crises as they arise ("firefighting"). Unfortunately, too few firms and associations follow this advice, often because they find it hard to get the necessary resources except when a crisis is apparent to

everyone. A strategic approach to government relations focuses on longer-
term considerations. It recognizes that for firms significantly affected
by the actions of government, the "game" has many "innings" and success or failure cannot be measured by the outcome on a single issue. Moreover, interest groups of all types recognize that by forming coalitions
they often can be more effective in promoting or inhibiting policy actions
affecting them. Consultants, in particular, appreciate that they can't
work miracles in a specific case if the firm or association has not already
established channels of communication and its credibility with those
persons it seeks to influence. That requires regular contact to maintain
rapport and to stay abreast of the subtle shifts in government policy.

7.3.7 Personnel

Effective interest-group behaviour is largely a matter of people. While
other inputs can be important in using particular techniques (e.g., major
advocacy advertising campaigns can cost in the millions of dollars), the
most critical resource consists of people. They are important in at least
three ways. First, the development of an effective strategy to influence
public policy requires a creative and knowledgeable individual or small
group of individuals. In short, strategy is made by people. Second, many
of the most important influence techniques are carried out by people on
an individual basis. The classic method of lobbying, namely, face-to-
face contact in which the lobbyist seeks to persuade another individual,
is as heavily dependent upon the interpersonal skills of the lobbyist as
on the substance of the message. People are the medium by which the
message is carried whether it be in an informal meeting, a telephone
call, a chat over drinks and dinner, the formal presentation of a brief,
or testimony before a legislative committee or task force. In some cases,
a firm, trade association, or other interest group becomes characterized
by the behaviour and personal style of one individual. The heads of
major trade associations, while acting as spokespeople for the association, can over time, with plenty of media exposure and contacts with
top policy makers, become the embodiment of that association. This
has been the case for Tom d'Aquino of BCNI, Sam Hughes when he
headed the CCC, Robert MacIntosh of the Canadian Bankers' Association, Patrick Lavelle, formerly of the Automotive Parts Manufacturers'
Association, and David Kirk of the Canadian Federation of Agriculture.

The longtime president and CEO of Canadian Tire, Dean Muncaster, used what was described as a modest, unstructured approach to
government relations. According to one account, Muncaster

> doesn't visit politicians and civil servants on a regular basis. And he
> is very selective about the issues he raises, choosing only those of
> importance to Canadian Tire. He co-ordinates the monitoring of
> issues and government lobbying himself. . . . What Muncaster has is
> credibility. He goes to Ottawa just three or four times a year, but

finds that, "when we have something to say, we tend to be listened to," specifically because he arranges meetings only to discuss a serious issue, one whose effects he can describe in basic bread-and-butter terms. Because such meetings deal with issues of primary importance to the company, it is logical, he says, that the firm's senior executive handle the arrangements directly. When appropriate, as in the sales tax issue, Muncaster recruits his network of dealers, prominent businessmen in their communities, to directly lobby their members of parliament. For broader issues, Muncaster relies on the trade associations.[23]

The third way in which people are important in lobbying is as voters. Interest groups able (or perceived by politicians to be able) to influence the voting behaviour of a substantial number of voters constitute a force to be reckoned with for politicians. Three variables are relevant in this context: (1) the absolute number of voters whose choice can/will be influenced by how a government responds to the interest group's pressure; (2) the distribution of such voters (i.e., are they concentrated in a few ridings or are they strategically distributed in meaningful blocs in marginal ridings?); and (3) the intensity of the voters' preference with respect to this issue (the most dangerous situation for politicians occurs where the issue is "all important," i.e., it creates a single-issue voter).

The firm seeking to influence public policy often has a variety of people to draw upon in designing and carrying out its strategy:

- staff specialists within the firm's government relations or public affairs unit;
- the firm's top management;
- outside consultants
  - general public affairs/government relations firms,
  - lawyers (to handle appeals to the courts and to assist with the drafting of regulations),
  - media specialists (PR, advertising),
  - technical-issue specialists, such as academics (e.g., scientists studying acid rain, toxic chemicals); and
- ad hoc coalitions
  - staff specialists,
  - representatives of members of the coalition, usually executives.

7.3.8 Criteria for the Use of Specific Techniques and Vehicles
To begin with, the choice of techniques and vehicles obviously depends upon the target of the lobbyist's efforts and the timing of the input in the policy process. Second, the "medium" or vehicle must be capable of carrying the message. For example, while an informal conversation can effectively convey the lobbyist's tone in respect to certain tax legislation, a formal brief is needed to spell out in detail the objections to the proposed legislation.

Third, the method of communication must be consistent with the values and expectations of the message's target. As Jackson and Atkinson state:

> Some organizations have employed tactics which violate accepted norms. For example, the government cancelled Local Initiative Projects for groups which publicly demonstrated to have their grants extended. The norms of mutual accommodation exclude the type of ultimatum conveyed by demonstrations. In Canada the standard practice is negotiation of individual group claims, a rule which is violated at a group's peril. Thus, the legislative system demonstrates a certain rigidity in interest group relations. (1977, 41)

Causey et al. emphasize the nature of the "Canadian style" of government–interest-group interaction:

> If the American way of getting things done is one of dramatic overstatement, the ideal Canadian way of making arrangements (between governments and business) has been one of elegant understatement, the politics of keeping things pleasant, dull and controlled. Influence comes from very private meetings with very important people. Public displays of power and verbal abuse are vulgar and should be avoided. (1976, 89)

Jerry McAfee, chairperson of Gulf Oil and former chairperson of its Canadian subsidiary, has spoken nostalgically of the style of lobbying and access enjoyed by large firms in Canada:

> Canada has things in small enough doses that you can get your arms around it. You can deal on a personal basis with some of the prominent government people — both federal and provincial. . . . In the U.S. "there is a greater antipathy from government toward business," McAfee says. "There's a greater reluctance for government people to have direct contact with decision makers in industry, particularly in the oil industry. We are daily directed by all sorts of bureaucrats in Washington. . . but their contact with us is on a very arms-length — and many times hostile — basis. We ought to be on the same side in solving our energy problems. We can't afford the luxury of this type of war.[24]

Fourth, lobbyists need to recognize the utility of both formal and informal contacts. J. E. Anderson states that "consultation between civil servants and pressure group officials is often informal rather than formal or institutionalized" (1977, 293). He points out that even the rules of the game are cloaked in secrecy, a state of affairs with advantages to the pressure groups, the civil servants involved, and the government (1977, 302). Blunn describes the informal contacts between lobbyists and civil servants:

While constantly defending their line of work as honorable, lobbyists do admit that the kind of relationships they have with people in
government can make a difference in how their message is received.
And the best way to get to know civil servants is casually, over a
drink or a meal at Ottawa's elite Rideau Club, or even better, the
fairway at the Royal Ottawa Golf Club. (1978)

John Bulloch, president of the CFIB, was also creator of the Canadian
Council on Fair Taxation, which lobbied for changes in the tax reform
legislation of 1969. He describes the vehicles of communication between
interest groups and the government:

I begin to see how the system is stacked in favour of those who own
all the lawyers, I found out that the big corporations, without being
conspirational, control the knowledge factory in this country. All
the positions that government takes are the results of conversations,
the chinwags, that go on between the experts who are owned by the
major corporations and the trade unions, and the experts who work
for government. It's a mandarin-to-mandarin process.[25]

Formal briefs (and letters) to ministers and to House and Senate committees can constitute an important means of communication on some
issues. In some cases, the number of formal briefs can be enormous.
With respect to the 1971 White Paper on Taxation, the House of Commons Committee on Finance, Trade and Economic Affairs received 520
briefs (Campbell 1978, 15). The Senate Banking and Commerce Committee received 343 briefs on the same issue. Between 1969, when the
Economic Council's *Interim Report on Competition Policy* was published, to mid-1977, when the Stage II amendments were analyzed by
the House and Senate committees, a total of 522 briefs were submitted
on the various proposals to reform Canadian competition policy (Stanbury 1978). Consider also the response to the *Working Paper on Patent
Law Revision* issued in June of 1976:

The patent law revision — technical and complex — has made few
headlines. . . . But it has been the source of a spirited response by
many companies, large and small. In the six months since the original patent-law working paper was released, they have flooded
Ottawa with briefs and letters, almost 100% of them opposed to all
or parts of the new proposals.
    The response has astounded many officials here. At last count,
236 briefs and letters had been received at Consumer and Corporate Affairs, with copies often sent also to the Finance Department
and Industry, Trade and Commerce, to cabinet ministers and MPs.
    "I can't recall ever seeing so much paper go over my desk con-
cerning a single issue, not even counting the competition policy
review a few years ago," says one senior official.[26]

The proposed Borrowers and Depositors Protection Act, also sponsored by Consumer and Corporate Affairs, attracted a considerable number of briefs. Again, they were mainly adverse. Given their financial and political weight (they included the chartered banks, sales finance companies, trust companies, the provinces, and even the Consumers' Association of Canada), it is not surprising that the bill did not get reintroduced in the session of Parliament beginning in the fall of 1977.[27]

In many instances, formal briefs simply reinforce the private conversations between lobbyists and ministers, key civil servants, and other influentials. They may simply be a form of "window dressing" that legitimizes outcomes negotiated in private.

Fifth, lobbyists need to recognize that ambiguity concerning who is representing whom may be a double-edged sword. It may increase effectiveness in some circumstances, but it may also generate distrust, public criticism, and the threat of regulation. It is precisely the opaque character of the communications between lobbyists and their ministerial and civil service targets that prompted the former Conservative House leader Walter Baker to introduce a bill to regulate lobbying in Canada. Baker wanted "as much lobbying as possible to be carried [on] out in the open 'so people can see who is trying to influence what.' "[28] The same point is made in a *Business Week* editorial: "The problem (in reforming U.S. lobbying legislation) is to distinguish honest lobbying from covert pressure tactics."[29] It is hard to imagine how regulations can ensure that both the interests of every lobbyist and the techniques they use can be made transparent to the public.

Sixth, in some cases, where the stakes are large, the interest group's resources are great, and there is plenty of competitive lobbying, all of the vehicles for putting pressure on the government may be used. One such case was that of the *Time* and *Reader's Digest* efforts to retain their special tax status in Canada. Litvak and Maule summarize the vehicles used as follows:

> In defending their corporate interests, Time and Reader's Digest were able to manoeuvre within the two North American political units. The parent companies petitioned for assistance from their home government in Washington; at the same time their Canadian subsidiaries worked at mobilizing support locally. Thus, they enjoyed advantages and were able to muster resources unavailable to competing Canadian publishers. They exploited policy-input channels fully and launched an extensive campaign that employed simultaneously an array of pressuring techniques. At times their methods seemed more appropriate to a congressional form of government than to Canada's parliamentary system. Besides soliciting aid from the U.S. government, Time and Reader's Digest presented oral and written submissions to the Royal Commission on Publica-

tions, attempted to influence Canadian public opinion in their favour through their Canadian editions, mobilized the support of employee associations dependent on their operations, mailed written presentations to each member of Parliament and personally contacted a number of members of Parliament and cabinet ministers, and eventually inspired the creation of a trade organization that gave Canada's major publishers an interest in the status quo. (1975, 619–20)

7.3.9 Style

Interest groups that seek to influence public policy on an ongoing basis usually develop an identifiable style or general approach to such activities. While lobbying styles are not as easily specified as those for furniture or women's clothing, and while no well-accepted categories yet exist for such activities, important differences can be seen in business organizations' efforts to influence public policy. For example, does the firm generally take a confrontational stance in dealing with government, or does it generally seek mutual accommodation by means of low-key bargaining and persuasion? (See, for example, Fulton & Stanbury 1985.) What is the firm's outcome orientation? Does it characterize most situations as zero-sum, winner-take-all "games" or does the firm try to find solutions that ensure that most or all participants end up with something?

Does the firm (interest group) generally eschew certain techniques of influencing government as a matter of principle? For example, does it stay far away from questionable payments, public personal attacks on lobbying targets, and the kind of "questionable practices" listed in Figure 5-2?

Does the organization operate largely in a reactive, crisis mode, that is, make a major effort to influence government only when it is evident that large stakes are involved in specific situations? Or does the organization emphasize the continuity and pervasiveness of its contacts with various targets in an effort to detect and solve problems before they reach crisis proportions? Does the interest group keep its fences in good repair even though there is no apparent immediate need to do so? Does it stress the continuity of its relationship with government at several levels rather than short bursts of intense effort focused largely on people at the top?

Lobbying style is also shaped by the organization's willingness to be persistent in trying to achieve its objectives in dealing with government. Staying power, the ability to accept defeats and learn from them and to return to the field to advance one's cause with vigour, is not a characteristic of all interest groups. Some operate like a "flash in the pan." They are able to obtain and focus their resources on government only for a short period. Whether they succeed or fail on a particular issue, they melt away like the snow in spring.

NOTES

1. There were 379 firms with under 500 employees and 323 with more than 500 employees (IPI, 1978, 6).
2. For a more recent study of these programs, see Bon and Hart (1983).
3. On the role of MPs in each party's caucus, see Rivington (1983), McCormick (1983), and Gold (1983). More generally, see chapter 7.
4. At the same time, however, Whalen (1961) identifies two bases for conflict between business and government in Canada: business's canons of conventional wisdom and its quest for simplicity that promotes the view that the national economy will perform best when government's role is minimized. Business fails to distinguish the essential nature of public (vote maximization) and private (profit maximization) transactions. "The intangibles of business are as nothing compared with the intangibles of democratic politics." Governments stand or fall in their ability to please a "revolving majority" on a complex *set* of policies.
5. Board of Trade, *Journal*, December 1976, p. 10.
6. Ibid., p. 12.
7. Historian Michael Bliss points out that, "contrary to the beliefs [and rhetoric] of some businessmen, Ottawa does consult regularly, sometimes exhaustively, with special-interest business groups. Sometimes their views are dismissed as predictable pleas for special treatment. Other times, they have vitally important effects on public policy-making. . . . Ottawa listens fairly well, on specialized, often industry-specific, issues [the NEP being a conspicuous exception as a special case]" (1982b, 50).
8. Gillies (1981, 32–33) gives five reasons why conflict between business and government increased in the 1970s:
   - business people have difficulty in making their case to the bureaucracy;
   - business is seen as a vested interest, hence its representations lack credibility;
   - business executives do not understand sufficiently the political process and the pressures under which politicians operate;
   - business executives do not have a sufficient understanding of how decisions are made in the public sector and where power lies in the process; and
   - the ineffectiveness of government in dealing with the problems it tackles.
9. Reuber (1978, 10) also identifies a number of weaknesses in the present system of policy analyses:
   - excessive secrecy among both government and private sector groups;
   - "weak and inadequate staff, particularly among private sector

groups . . . as a result, much of what is done is little more than repetitious, self-serving propaganda";
- lack of an adequate professional forum for reviewing and assessing research results; and
- a relatively weak system for communicating analytical findings to opinion leaders and the public generally, i.e., a low standard of journalism on economic affairs in Canada.

10. A national Gallup poll of 1049 Canadian adults in August 1983 found that 18% had "no interest" in the activities of Parliament, 46% said they had "little" interest, while 27% said they had "quite a lot" of interest, and 9% said they had a "great deal" of interest. As for who or what body they thought was most important in making major government decisions, the results were as follows:

- the cabinet   33%
- Parliament   29
- prime minister   19
- senior civil servants   8
- don't know   11

Asked how they thought MPs should vote in the House of Commons, those polled replied as follows:

- as their constituents would vote   50%
- use their own judgment   38
- as their party required   8

Asked what they thought MPs should consider their first duty, the responses were as follows:

- looking after the needs of the constituents   62%
- serving as a watchdog on government
  activities and spending   18
- passing laws   7
- party loyalty   6.5

Some 13% of those polled said they "regularly" or "very often" watch the televised proceedings of the House of Commons — largely clips from Question Period. See Jeff Sallot, "Poll suggests House [of Commons] is irrelevant to majority of Canadian public," *Globe and Mail*, September 10, 1983, pp. 1–2.

11. See, for example, "Ontario black sheep on free trade issue," Vancouver *Sun*, August 23, 1985, p. A10; Robert Collison, "The move toward free trade," *Maclean's*, December 10, 1984, pp. 46–50; Martin Cohn, "Free trade would turn us into 'bloody Americans' top labour official fears," *Toronto Star*, June 28, 1985, p. A1; Don McGillivray, "Nobody here but enhanced traders," Vancouver *Sun*, July 23, 1985, p. B3; Michael Salter, "The rising barriers to trade," *Maclean's*, July 1, 1985, pp. 46–47; David Crane, "Free trade could tighten U.S. grip on our economy," *Toronto Star*, June 10, 1985,

pp. A1, A15; David Crane, "Trade pact with the U.S. alone is risky," *Toronto Star*, June 11, 1985, pp. A1, A12; Barry Critchley, "The great free trade debate," *Financial Post*, December 8, 1984, p. 17; Rod Nutt, "Free trade with U.S. backed," Vancouver *Sun*, January 7, 1985, p. B8; Giles Gherson, "Tug of war over regional trade with U.S.," *Financial Post*, March 16, 1985, p. 9; and Angus Reid, "Business sees few drawbacks in a U.S. free-trade pact," *Report on Business Magazine*, March 1985, p. 120.

12. As cited in Rod Nutt, "Free trade with U.S. backed," Vancouver *Sun*, January 7, 1985, p. B8.

13. See Stanbury (1977, 1985c); Rowley and Stanbury (1978), and Stanbury and Reschenthaler (1981).

14. See Stanbury (1985a, 1985b).

15. (Toronto) Board of Trade, *Journal*, Christmas 1976, p. 9.

16. McQuaig (1985, 72).

17. Don Jamieson, when he was leader of the Liberal party in Newfoundland, commented on the proliferation of government regulations, many of which were implemented as a result of the actions of a vocal minority. "The problem for governments is that the vocal groups can give the impression of a public demand that doesn't always exist, or exists only to the extent that the vocal groups create the impression. I wanted to get across the point that government — before getting involved in the regulatory field — should consider all points of view. I don't believe for the most part there has been enough aggressive counter-attack against some of the criticisms of this business [advertising] that have led to regulations."

18. *Globe and Mail*, August 30, 1983, p. A15.

19. Ibid., December 10, 1983, p. 8.

20. Ibid., March 21, 1985, p. B7.

21. Lorne Slotnick, "Charter Challenge on the use of dues worries unions," *Globe and Mail*, December 18, 1985, p. A1. More generally, see "Getting even cited in labor case," *Globe and Mail*, January 24, 1986, p. B9; "A court challenge for organized labor," *Maclean's*, February 10, 1986, p. 58; and "Colin Brown targets the Tories," *Sunday Star*, February 2, 1986, p. H4.

22. See "Act cuts drug cost, Federal Court says," *Globe and Mail*, November 20, 1985, p. A9.

23. *Financial Times*, July 12, 1982, p. 11. In mid-1985 Dean Muncaster was replaced as CEO of Canadian Tire.

24. *Toronto Star*, "Yes, Ottawa, Jerry Likes You," July 16, 1977, p. A-7.

25. Quoted in Alexander Ross, "How to Join the March to the New Politics," *Quest*, February 1977, p. 47.

26. Stephen Duncan "Patent furor spurs rights rewrite," *Financial Post*, January 29, 1977, p. 11. "So far, the only support for patent revision has come from the Economic Council of Canada and Consumer

& Corporate Affairs [CCA]," says one senior government official. "Most Canadians — including a lot of companies — don't realize the impact on their everyday cost of living, or on the cost of doing business, of a patent system that confers benefits in excess of those required to stimulate invention and innovation.

"There are many specific objections to the proposed law (in fact many of the briefs run 70 to 80 pages). But essentially, the debate is over monopoly rights and what the costs and benefits are of extending those rights.

"CCA and the Economic Council's recent report on intellectual property argue that the existing system is costing the Canadian public (both corporate and private consumers) too much. But the proposed law's numerous critics argue CCA would swing the pendulum too far, that the new law's provisions would so reduce the value of patents in Canada that the result would be less research and innovation."

Melvin Sher ("Ottawa heeds protests over patent law," *Canadian Business*, July 1977, p. 25) quotes the assistant deputy minister for intellectual property as saying of the more than 250 briefs and letters, "There was everything from letters saying we heard there's a new Patent Law and we don't like it, to well thought out, well reasoned briefs expressing legitimate concerns."

27. The bill, given First Reading on October 26, 1976, as C-16, was the subject of extensive hearings before the Commons Health, Welfare and Social Affairs Committee (a rather surprising choice). An Ottawa *Citizen* story (June 27, 1977, p. 25) said:

> Easy passage might have been expected for the bill. It has not turned out to be so — for a bill with such generally laudable objectives as a uniform and high disclosure in consumer credit transactions and the suppression of loan-sharking. Instead, the Standing Committee on Health, Welfare and Social Affairs of the House of Commons has been met with a steady flow of largely critical briefs. Nor have the criticisms been restricted to the credit industry. Several provincial governments have also expressed serious misgivings — on constitutional as well as other grounds — and likewise the Consumers' Association of Canada. As a result the government has found itself on the defensive, forced to prepare numerous amendments to accommodate some of the criticisms.

Although it was mentioned in the fall Speech from the Throne, Conservative MP and finance critic Sinclair Stevens is quoted as saying, "I wouldn't give it a snowball's chance in hell of getting through" ("Conservatives to renew fight against federal consumer bill," Montreal *Gazette*, October 13, 1977, p. 5). See also Winnipeg

Free Press, October 13, 1977, p. 8. For one editorial in support of the anti-loansharking aspects of the proposed act, see the *Toronto Star*, July 5, 1977, p. B4. Lawyer/academic Jacob S. Ziegel appraised the bill in an article in the *Financial Times of Canada*, June 20, 1977, p. 8. More recently (March 18, 1978, p. 4), in an article entitled "It's pragmatism all the way to the election," Stephen Duncan of the *Financial Post* argues that the new pragmatism in Ottawa "has spelled an end, temporarily, to the proposed Competition Act and the Borrowers and Depositors Protection Act. The tone and objectives of both bills antagonized and worried large parts of the corporate sector, on the other side, there is little apparent support for the bills among consumers."

28. Duncan, *supra*, note 26, p. 3.
29. *Business Week*, May 26, 1976, p. 110. *Business Week* (May 23, 1977, p. 31) reports: "Business may soon find that it is doing a lot of its Washington lobbying in a fish bowl. A recent U.S. Court of Appeals decision holds that once a government agency asks for public comment on a rule proposal, its officials should refrain from discussing the proposal privately with interested parties. If such discussions do take place, full memoranda on what was said must be put in the public record."

The magazine quotes the judgment as saying, "The public record must reflect what representations were made to an agency so that relevant information supporting or refuting those representations may be brought to the attention of the reviewing courts by persons participating in agency proceedings."

6

Issues Management

1.0 INTRODUCTION

Peter Bartha notes that "during the last decade, which was characterized by frequent confrontations between private and public sectors, many
of Canada's larger corporations came to learn that socio-political pressures — expressed through legislative and regulatory measures — can
severely affect profitability, the conditions of doing business, and even
organizational survival" (1985b, 203). Andrew Gollner suggests that there
has been a "crowding in of external issues on traditional management
domains" (1984b, 29). A Conference Board survey in 1976 found that 57
percent of the CEOs polled spent up to a quarter of their time on external relations and that 39 percent spent up to half of their time on this
activity (McGrath 1976, 49). These proportions have increased since
then (see chapter 11). The demands of consumers, environmentalists,
various types of "rights" organizations, and other interest groups have
been translated into an unprecedented amount of government intervention.

Social, economic, and political forces impinge upon the welfare of
individuals, groups, and organizations. Those adversely affected or seeing
an opportunity to advance their interests articulate demands for action
by government. Some of these demands, particularly when they are taken
up by the more politically effective interest groups, create issues on the
public policy agenda. Some of these issues, in turn, result in government actions that produce favourable or unfavourable consequences
for business organizations. Hence, firms and trade associations, even
when passive, are affected by external issues operating through the political process. This chapter is devoted to the concept of issues management, which is the first stage in increasing the competence of business in
dealing with government.

In the past, business organizations usually adopted a reactive posture
in dealing with governments. Social, economic, and political forces that
impinged on business were monitored, and active efforts to influence
policy were deferred until government was on the verge of implementing its policy. In general, little effort was made to influence the forces
that produced demands for government action.

Note: This chapter is co-authored with Norm Couttie, who received his M.B.A. from
the University of British Columbia in May 1985.

Today, simply monitoring the environment at the "forces stage" and attempting to influence government once action has been demanded, is insufficient, as these three writers suggest:

- The company which believes that the ability to act is threatened only by politicians and governments is making a big mistake. The threat comes . . . from public opinion, which can make it impossible for politicians to carry out a certain policy. (Stoltz 1983, 30)
- Too often business and industry have ignored issues until it is only possible to reduce the negative consequences of proposed legislation. As a result, critics charge that business is always against new legislation. In fact, business and industry frequently are "creative," since an issue may have developed for months, even years, with little or no business input prior to the legislative stage. (Nolan 1985, 73)
- Without a proper business response, societal expectations of today become the political issues of tomorrow, legislated requirements the next day, and litigated penalties the day after that. At each stage there is a diminution of business freedom to manoeuvre and operate. (Brown 1979, 12)

Issues that at first appear narrow and insignificant can quickly be blown up into major causes by interest groups and politicians. With respect to the United States, Grefe observes:

Today, elections are often decided by one single-issue constituency, and the elected politician, who wishes to be re-elected, is even more of a lightning rod for discord among his electorate. Failure to promote the minority's views may make the incumbent a victim of the challenge by an opponent who senses the frustration of a group large and determined enough to tip the balance. (1981, 27)

Issues that at first appear to have nothing at all to do with a particular business may still be used by special interests to create extreme pressures on the political system. In his book *Rules for Radicals*, Saul Alinsky writes:

In a complex, interrelated, urban society, it becomes increasingly difficult to single out who is to blame for any particular evil. There is a constant, and somewhat legitimate, passing of the buck. . . . One of the criteria in picking your target is the target's vulnerability — where do you have the power to start? Furthermore, any target can always say, "Why do you center on me when there are others to blame as well?" . . . disregard these arguments and, for the moment, all the others to blame. Then, as you zero in on your target and carry out your attack, all of the "others" come out of the woodwork

very soon. They become visible by their support of the target. . . .
All issues *must* be polarized if action is to follow. (1971, 130)

Thus, a particular business or industry need not have been the "cause"
of an issue — or even have any ability to help resolve it — in order to be
the focus of interest-group demands. It only needs to be vulnerable —
and what business is not vulnerable in *some* way?

In order to respond effectively to these increasing pressures, business
organizations have expanded their monitoring activities to identify those
issues that are likely to generate demands for government action that in
turn will impinge on the organizations.[1] Ideally, in addition to trying to
influence governments directly, business organizations should attempt
to influence the *process* by which issues[2] are converted into effective
demands for political action.

1.1 Definition

Arrington and Sawaya describe issues management as "a process to organize a company's expertise to enable it to participate effectively in
the shaping and resolution of public issues that critically impinge upon
its operations" (1984, 148). It involves the process of reconciling the
conflicting interests of business organizations with those of other organizations and interest groups, including governments.

The use of the word *manage*, as in "manage a business," in the phrase
issues management is rather sanguine. The word *handling*, as in "handling a circus lion," might be more appropriate. With great care and
attention, and without getting too close, you may be able to get it to do
your bidding — but don't turn your back to it.

It should be emphasized that a company's concern with a public policy issue is not merely akin to an individual's concern as a citizen. Rather
"its focus must be on actual, business concerns; a company's effective
participation in public policy making is simply never unrelated to bottom-
line consequences" (Arrington & Sawaya 1984, 148).

Arrington and Sawaya (1984, 149–51) suggest that there are three
concurrent activities in the process of issues management:

- *Foresight:* the identification, monitoring, analysis, and ranking of issues
  in terms of their likely impact on the firm
- *Policy Development:* "the reconciliation of conflicting internal interests on public policy issues of strategic importance in order to make a
  coherent external advocacy"
- *Advocacy:* the action side of issues management in which the strategy
  is implemented using one or more of a variety of techniques — lobbying, coordination of positions with trade associations, building a grass-
  roots constituency, forming alliances with other interest groups, public information campaigns, and advocacy or issue advertising

2.0 ISSUES AND PUBLICS

In order that the characteristics, causes, and effects of issues be better understood, some attempt must be made to classify them and identify the "publics" for which they are most relevant.

2.1 Issue Classification

Many classification systems are possible. The important thing is that the system not overlook major aspects of the environment. Brown (1981, 5) describes Sears' (the largest retailer in the U.S.) classification system as follows:

- *Demographics* — population, employment, income, spending, housing
- *Values/Lifestyles* — work, leisure, entitlement, mobility, shopping habits
- *Resources* — energy, minerals, chemicals, agriculture, water, strategic depletion, land
- *Technology* — R & D expenditures, alternate energy, plastics, electronics, transport, manufacturing techniques, production development
- *Public Attitudes* — consumer confidence, attitudes toward issues, interest groups, consumerism
- *Government* — operations, regulations/agencies, legislation, employment, environment, credit, privacy, products, communications, services, health care, taxes
- *International* — world demographics, resources, trade, developing nations, technology transfer, economic indicators
- *Economics* — GNP, inflation, interest rates, unemployment, productivity, wages, benefits, profits and cash flow, capital formation

Bartha (1982) groups individual issues into "issue types" or "categories of issues which have different characteristics and which follow different paths in the policy development process." The following is a very brief summary of his four issue types:

- *Universal Issues:* These issues affect most people and have a personal impact upon them or are comprehensible to them without the intervention of "experts." The public generally believes that the government should do something to rectify the situation (e.g., the energy crisis, inflation, unemployment, capital punishment, and abortion).
- *Advocacy Issues:* These issues affect large numbers of people. They are introduced and promoted by advocacy or interest groups that claim to represent broad public interests (e.g., environmental, consumer, and various "rights" groups).
- *Selective Issues:* These issues affect smaller, identifiable groups of people and are of concern to only these groups. The general public, though perhaps not interested in them, does have the power to veto govern-

ment action if it is aroused and focused (e.g., day care, import/export quotas, and gay rights).

- *Technical Issues:* The public has little interest in these issues and is willing to leave their resolution to the experts because the resolution is not perceived to affect them in any way. This perception is often erroneous as exemplified by such issues as product standards, public utility regulation, and various tax expenditures given to business.

It is important to appreciate that issues are dynamic. Over time, an advocacy issue may broaden into a universal issue or it may narrow to a selective issue. Usually one interest group is trying to increase the importance of an issue while another group is trying to dampen it. See Bartha (1982).

A rather different approach to identifying the various types of issues is taken by Frank Corrado. He emphasizes the role of time and the "distance" between an issue and the business organization:

1. *Current Issues:* These are issues already being considered or acted on by government bodies. . . . At this stage companies can only react to an issue, though sometimes changes in public and legislative perception of such issues can be effected either by companies or by external events in the society.
2. *Emerging Issues:* These issues will probably be acted upon in the near future but have not yet been formulated or "hardened." This is an evolutionary stage and a good point in which to influence policy. Emerging issues have also been divided into three subcategories:
    a. *Operational.* Dealing with regulatory issues such as product labelling, pollution, and safety
    b. *Corporate.* Involving issues such as plant-closing legislation, corporate disclosure, takeover laws, minimum wage
    c. *Societal.* Broad issues such as inflation, national healthcare, and defense.
3. *Societal Issues:* Changes involving human attitudes and behaviour fall into this category, and these issues are difficult to deal with. They include demographic changes in family size, household formation patterns, reproductive rates, values, and lifestyle preferences. (Corrado 1984, 51–52).

2.2 Key Publics

As noted, Bartha's (1982) framework also identifies *key publics* or "segments of the public which play distinct roles in identifying issues and in generating, advocating or opposing, deciding and implementing policy actions."[3] The following is a very brief summary of his five key publics:

- *The General Public:* In a pluralist democracy, the general public (voters) can often only express its preferences for policies, rather than its will. Policies, in turn, are available only in "packages" associated with political parties. Consequently, in the short run, government actions may not represent the desires of the public. However, in the long term, the overall direction of the policies tends to be more in keeping with the public's expectations, particularly in this age of heavy reliance on public opinion polls.

- *The Media:* The media act as recorders of events, gatekeepers/filters, and "amplifiers" of the information that passes through them, and advocates of positions on the issues. The media can tell people what issues to think about (agenda setting), but are less successful in influencing their opinions. McGrath describes the importance of the media to business as follows:

  > Through selection, interpretation, and transmission, they determine what others will hear or see. Management believes it must make a definite effort to influence or win over the media because the media have become the most important direct source on which the public relies for opinions. The media — and particularly the electronic media — have so much power over the perception of business credibility that many feel the media must be considered a separate public. (1976, 4)

- *The Interest Groups:* These groups act to promote the interests of their members by seeking to influence public policy. They are the activists of society and often define issues that can have broad public implications (see Alinsky 1971). Access to the media is a key requirement for the success of most interest groups. Armstrong states: "Some consider these groups creatures of the media. All can agree that they could not have prospered and thrived as they have without substantial media exposure" (1981, 763). As noted in chapter 5, "business" consists of quite a number of specific, sometimes conflicting, interest groups. The range of interest groups is enormous; see Figure 8-1 in chapter 8.

- *Political Leaders:* Except for cabinet ministers, members of Parliament generally do not exercise significant power in policy making. In some cases, the caucus of the party in power can be influential. Some opposition members can be "fed" questions to raise in the legislature. Parliamentary committees, because they come late in the policy-making process, usually have a modest impact, but in some cases they provide an important point of access for interest groups. Bartha also includes in this category the official and unofficial advisors of politicians.

- *Public Service:* Surrounding every cabinet minister is a coterie of civil servants who both offer advice at the policy-formulation stage and are responsible for administering the programs approved by the legislature. In Canada, senior public servants often exercise considerable influence on policy making, although their role and influence vary somewhat, depending upon the style of leadership exercised by the political executive. One of the principal reasons why senior public servants have influence on policy making is their specialized knowledge of problem areas and of the machinery of government itself. While the theory of public administration holds that public servants are politically neutral, there is no doubt that individual policy advisors do have preferences for how things should be done and this fact shapes their advice. It should be appreciated that "the bureaucracy" is not a homogeneous entity. Rather, there are important conflicting interests often institutionalized in the organizational structure of government itself (e.g., while the Department of Agriculture tends to advance the interests of farmers, the Department of Consumer and Corporate Affairs worries about the welfare of consumers).

2.3 Sources of Public Policy Issues

How are issues brought onto the public policy agenda? What is the process by which they are defined and recognized? What follows is an extension of the discussion in chapter 4. Four elements play critical roles:[4]

- *Public Opinion:* Namely, those opinions held by individuals that governments find it prudent to heed. There are, however, many "special publics" within the "general public." Public opinion differs in the salience of policy issues and the intensity with which it is held. Moreover, public opinion changes over time, as the monthly Gallup polls indicate.
- *Interest or Pressure Groups:* Groups of like-minded individuals who try to advance their interests (pecuniary or otherwise) by influencing public policy. They can help define problems, focus public attention on them, and propose solutions. Their ability to do so effectively depends upon their size, resources, degree of cohesion and persistence, and their ability to identify themselves with what is perceived to be in the interest of other groups, particularly politicians in the governing party. The activities of such groups are described in much more detail in chapters 7–9.
- *Leadership:* Namely, that leadership exercised by key individuals and groups who because of their own characteristics or association with an issue are able to "make their mark" with respect to that issue. The role of broader, structural forces is also important, but leadership can be crucial in determining the timing of public policy initiatives. Littlejohn notes that

> Bertrand de Jouvenel asserts that political science should focus its attention on the initiator, on the promoter. He argues that the

critical process in the relationship between the state and the individual is the rallying of individuals at the call of some person. Such a rallying of individuals builds up into a cumulative power in the simple and immediate sense of the word. This is the basic political phenomenon, he says. And in a vigorous society there will not be one leader, one person, who rallies such energies, but many. (1980, 180–81)

A superb example of an individual who made a difference through personal leadership is Judge Emily Murphy, who initiated the litigation that saw the Judicial Committee of the Privy Council declare that women were "persons" and could not be excluded from holding public office. See Kome (1985, chap. 2).

• *Technical Expertise:* The ability to understand the causes and characteristics of public policy issues and the methods of dealing with them. Such expertise can be enormously valuable in recognizing the domains over which government action could or could not be effective. Technical expertise usually has more sway in the development and implementation of solutions after problems have been identified and a political coalition formed that supports government action.

Cobb and Elder (in Nolan 1985, 73) suggest four ways in which public issues are created. First, groups develop an issue in order to change a policy perceived as unfavourable to their interests (recall chapter 4). For example, when the multinational pharmaceutical companies felt that the domestic "generic" drug manufacturers had been given an unfair advantage due to patent law changes in 1969, they mounted an aggressive campaign to have the legislation rescinded. This stimulus for the development of public issues often comes from organized interest groups, although a group may come into existence to push a specific issue.

Second, a politician may develop an issue in order to advance his or her campaign for office. Politicians can be thought of as political entrepreneurs in the business of obtaining votes in exchange for the promise of policy actions (chapter 4). At times it seems as if *any* issue, no matter how obscure, can find an adopted home in some politician's platform. How far the issue develops depends on its merits, on the ability of the politician to publicize it, and on whether it attracts the attention of voters.

Third, an important source of issues is the unanticipated event. An issue that has been dormant for years may be propelled into national prominence by a single unforeseen occurrence. Until a train derailment in Mississauga, Ontario, the Canadian public never really considered the manner in which dangerous chemicals were transported across the country. While legislation on the transportation of dangerous goods existed, the crisis stimulated rapid enactment of new legislation that had been on the back burner for some time.

Fourth, issues may also be generated by individuals or groups that seem to be motivated solely by what they think is in the public interest.[5] In other words, they have no pecuniary interest in the issue itself. A great many groups claim this motivation — although analysis usually uncovers more self-serving reasons. (This brings to mind a wag's definition of an environmentalist: a person who built his cabin last year and now wants to prevent others from doing the same in order to preserve the unspoiled wilderness.) However, "Ralph Naders," who appear to be sincere in their beliefs, do exist and they can be a formidable force in the development of some issues.[6] The absence of a pecuniary interest in an issue, however, does not mean that its advocates do not obtain a great deal of utility from securing government action that advances their cause.

2.4 Life Cycle of Issues

Nolan (1981, 15) argues that there are three identifiable phases in the emergence of issues that affect business:

1. *The Latent Phase:* In this stage, the issue is recognized by relatively few people. In some cases, if caught early enough, it may be handled by the private actions of the parties involved. An example is the response of large corporations to demands that they include more women on their boards of directors. As soon as this issue surfaced, several corporations actively sought out women for these positions and before long the steam went out of this issue — at least temporarily — and activists turned their attention to more promising areas.

2. *The Opinion Development Phase:* By this time, the issue has come under scrutiny in the media and this stimulates public debate. During this stage the issue may be resolved by voluntary cooperative action. The motion picture industry, by agreeing with other interest groups to develop a content-rating system, may have forestalled legislation that would have restricted their operations much more severely than their own "code" does now. It is at this stage that government may use suasion to alter business's behaviour without resort to formal governing instruments (see Stanbury & Fulton 1984).

3. *The Institutional Action Phase:* In this stage, governments and the courts get involved with the issue. By this time, it is usually too late for the private sector to exert significant influence.

A more detailed, seven-step model of the development of public issues is offered by Frank Corrado:

1. *The Problem:* There is a general public feeling of dissatisfaction, a sense of frustration, and recognition that a problem exists, but there is yet no name for it.

2. *The Label:* A group, usually an interest group, grabs the issue and labels it, e.g., "redlining," "productivity," "occupational health."[7]

3. *Crystallization:* Attitudes begin to form, the media becomes involved, the reason for the problem becomes apparent.
4. *Answers and Solutions:* As the issue is pushed by the interest groups and fanned by the media, all kinds of solutions begin to emerge.[8] A business organization must be involved no later than this stage [if it is to have a chance to shape the development of the issue].
5. *Legislation:* Reacting to public outcry, political leadership begins to introduce legislation and hold hearings. The bandwagon is rolling. The company can only try to affect the course of events at this stage; it is not in control. Legislators become the brokers of the issue, bending in directions that reflect their constituencies and pressures.
6. *Implementation:* Judicial review and regulation results in implementation of the solutions and interpretations of the legislation. Court action is possible here.
7. *New Problems Emerge:* Previously nonexistent or unnoticed problems arise after the cycle is completed, and start the cycle again in a new context. Overregulation and reindustrialization are examples where the issue becomes turned around. (1984, 51)

Corrado (1984, 52) also offers a visual representation of the issue cycle, developed by the Continental Illinois National Bank (see Figure 6-1).

Anthony Downs argues that in the U.S. "public attention rarely remains sharply focused upon any one domestic issue for very long — even if it involves a continuing problem of crucial importance to society" (1972, 38). This means that public attention may not be focused on a particular problem/issue long enough for government to be able to enact new legislation or to alter significantly its programs within existing legislation. Therefore, business organizations may be able to wait out the initial rush of interest-group enthusiasm in the expectation that only a fraction of "hot issues" will produce government actions adverse to them. What Downs calls the "issue-attention cycle" also implies that business organizations — by understanding the dynamics of the cycle — may be able to influence the process itself and defeat legislative or program changes counter to their interest. They may also be able to define and advance issues for their own benefit.

Downs argues that "public perception of most 'crises' in American domestic life does not reflect changes in real conditions as much as it reflects the operation of a systematic cycle of heightening public interest and then increasing boredom with major issues" (1972, 39). The issue-attention cycle, he says, is rooted "both in the nature of certain domestic problems and in the way major communications media interact with the public." Downs states that the issue-attention cycle has five stages:

Figure 6–1
THE ISSUE LIFE CYCLE

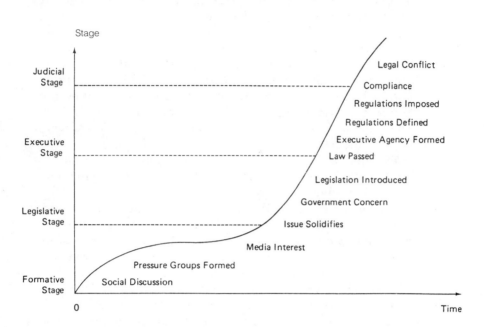

Source: Corrado (1984, 52).

1. *The pre-problem stage.* This prevails when some highly undesirable social condition exists but has not yet captured much
   public attention, even though some experts or interest groups
   may already be alarmed by it. Usually, objective conditions
   regarding the problem are far worse during the pre-problem
   stage than they are by the time the public becomes interested in
   it. For example, this was true of racism, poverty, and malnutri-
   tion in the United States.
2. *Alarmed discovery and euphoric enthusiasm.* As a result of some
   dramatic series of events (like the ghetto riots in 1965 to 1967),
   or for other reasons, the public suddenly becomes both aware of
   and alarmed about the evils of a particular problem. This
   alarmed discovery is invariably accompanied by euphoric enthusiasm about society's ability to "solve this problem" or "do something effective" within a relatively short time. The combination
   of alarm and confidence results in part from the strong public
   pressure in America for political leaders to claim that every problem can be "solved.". . .

3. *Realizing the cost of significant progress.* The third stage consists of a gradually spreading realization that the cost of "solving" the problem is very high indeed. Really doing so would not
only take a great deal of money but would also require major
sacrifices by large groups in the population. The public thus
begins to realize that part of the problem results from arrangements that are providing significant benefits to someone — often
to millions. . . . In certain cases, technological progress can eliminate some of the undesirable results of a problem without causing any major restructuring of society or any loss of present
benefits by others (except for higher money costs). . . .

4. *Gradual decline of intense public interest.* The previous stage
becomes almost imperceptibly transformed into the fourth stage:
a gradual decline in the intensity of public interest in the problem. As more and more people realize how difficult, and how
costly to themselves, a solution to the problem would be, three
reactions set in. Some people just get discouraged. Others feel
positively threatened by thinking about the problem; so they sup-
press such thoughts. Still others become bored by the issue. . . .
And by this time, some other issue is usually entering Stage Two;
so it exerts a more novel and thus more powerful claim upon
public attention.

5. *The post-problem stage.* In the final stage, an issue that has
been replaced at the centre of public concern moves into a pro-
longed limbo — a twilight realm of lesser attention or spasmodic
recurrences of interest. However, the issue now has a different
relation to public attention than that which prevailed in the "pre-
problem" stage. For one thing, during the time that interest was
sharply focused on this problem, new institutions, programs,
and policies may have been created to help solve it. These entities almost always persist and often have some impact even after
public attention has shifted elsewhere. (1972, 39-41)

Downs points out that when interest in an issue declines, it may not
be pushed off the public policy agenda forever. The issue "may sporadi-
cally recapture public interest; or important aspects of it may become
attached to some other problem that subsequently dominates centre
stage" (1972, 41).

3.0 ISSUES-MANAGEMENT MODEL

In order to respond effectively to developing issues, business organizations must have both a systematic means of identifying those issues that
will be important to it and a strategy for dealing with them. Figure 6-2
describes the major components of an issues-management system.

Figure 6–2
OUTLINE OF THE ISSUES-MANAGEMENT PROCESS

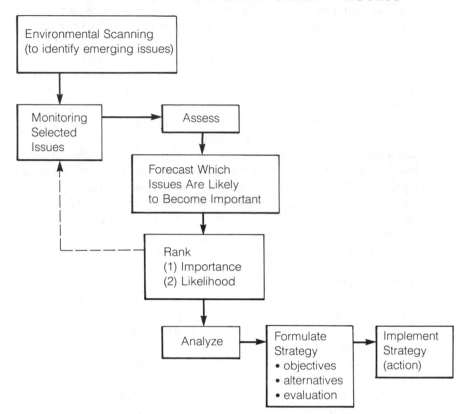

The environment should be scanned continuously to detect the early stages of developing issues. Issues must then be assessed to determine their likely importance for the firm. A thorough analysis must be carried out on all the key issues so that a strategic response can be formulated. Implementation of the strategy typically relies heavily on communication with other actors in the environment. The evaluation function is an attempt to measure the effectiveness of the strategy in modifying the environment.

The following sections will describe each of these functions in greater detail.

3.1 Scanning/Monitoring

In the context of this issues-management model, *scanning* is defined as a survey of as wide an area as possible so as to detect the weak signals of new trends or concerns that may later develop into significant public issues with considerable impact on the business organization. *Monitoring* is a more systematic and regular tracking of a predetermined trend or issue, with the intention of following its development and learning as much as possible about it.

3.1.1 Scanning

Since the purpose of scanning is to generate advance warnings of emerging trends, it must be a very wide-ranging process in the case of a large, diversified firm — almost all communications media could be included. The process can be simplified somewhat by the identification of "high yield" sources that appear to be regularly in the vanguard of new trends and ideas. Brown states, "Scanning, in the sense of looking over hastily, is precisely what should be done . . . and not careful study, given the huge volume of literature that contains useful information about trends and issues" (1981, 18).

Items that appear to have the potential for significant impact on the business should be considered for more systematic monitoring. Also, even after high-yield sources have been located, the full range of sources should be periodically scanned in order to pick up newly developed sources or ones that have improved their coverage of the desired material.

It is obvious from the above discussion that only the very largest corporations (or trade associations) can afford to perform the scanning function in-house. To maximize their return on this expenditure, several approaches have been tried. One of the more interesting ones is the Trend Analysis Program (TAP) of the American Council of Life Insurance (Brown 1981, 11). Each of the over 100 volunteers regularly scans several publications, focusing on one of four subject areas (science and technology, social sciences, business and economics, and politics and government), and abstracts any article that meets two critera: (1) it involves an event or idea that is indicative of either a trend or a discontinuity in the environment; and (2) it contains implications for the long-range concerns of society and the life insurance business. The abstracts are analyzed periodically by a committee that tries to detect developing trends that would not be apparent from reading any of the abstracts alone, and to determine the speed at which the trend is growing or shrinking.

Smaller companies may find it more appropriate to use outside specialists to perform the scanning function. Trade and professional associations often monitor issues and legislation that affect their members. Contact with interest groups can be an effective means of keeping up to date with the issues that will be promoted as well as giving the business a chance to present its concerns in an informal manner. Commercial "futurists" range from econometricians to pollsters to "seers" who speculate on the distant future. Bartha (1984a) mentions several Canadian sources for these last types of scanning activity.[9]

Figure 6–3
FRAMEWORK FOR INFORMATION GATHERING

Source: "Who"	Monitoring Database: "What"	Research Techniques: "How"
1. Public • General • Key segments	• Opinions • Attitudes • Knowledge level • Expectations	• Surveys • Special studies
2. Media • Print • Electronic	• News • Editorials • Features • Coverage/Position	• Content analysis • Contact program • Editorial briefings
3. Thought Leaders • Organizations • Academics • Activists	• Position statements • Publications • Conferences • Activities	• Literature search • Surveys • Contact program
4. Government • Politicians • Civil servants • Advisors	• Policy statements • Background studies • Legislation	• Legislative review • Issue analysis • Contact program

Source: Adapted from Bartha (1984a).

3.1.2 Monitoring

Issues and trends that are likely to have a significant effect on the firm or industry should be followed more carefully and additional sources of information should be developed. Figure 6-3 identifies the sources of issues that are most often monitored (and scanned) by corporations, the outputs that are monitored, and the techniques used to locate this information.

Bartha emphasizes that "selectivity is essential; a well-designed monitoring system will pick up only those signals that are likely to have significant consequences for the company and that — based on careful analysis — require some action: adapting internal conditions to the outside world, seeking to influence the external environment or both" (1984b, 26).

Bartha notes also that "there are many media scanning services which provide customized reports on the coverage given to a particular company and/or issue in the print and electronic media" (1984b, 27). Obviously, as well as monitoring the mass media and the specialized media in its own industry, a business should monitor the specialized media of other publics that have the potential to generate adverse effects upon the firm. This may often be the leading indicator of the issues that will become more important in the future.

The largest and most obvious source of issues is the general public. Its attitudes can best be monitored by surveys and polls, although these can be costly. However, as Corrado observes:

> The general public usually does not initiate issues. Their greatest strengths are passive — passive acceptance, as in pollution controls, or passive rejection, as with Prohibition or seat belts. [Rather] pressure groups are the initiators and activators in issue formation. A small group can be as effective as a large group, depending on its ability to form coalitions, interest the media in its cause, and get support from political bodies. (1984, 53)

Corrado goes on to describe the role of the media as a mirror — albeit an imperfect one — of developments that could become policy issues: "The role of the media is not to create issues but rather to spotlight them — building them up or letting them die, depending on editors' perceptions as to general public interest or sympathy. Many experts recommend close monitoring of the media to determine whether involvement in an issue is warranted" (1984, 53).

Although there is a bewildering variety of print publications and electronic broadcasts, the media must be scanned and monitored on a regular basis. This can be done through media content analysis, a process in which a value is placed on an issue according to the amount of media coverage it receives. Another effective method is to have a media relations program, using frequent contacts with members of the media industry both to keep informed of their interests and to provide an opportunity for conveying business's views on issues.

Thought or opinion leaders, particularly the leaders of interest groups or organizations that frequently originate issues by adopting advocacy positions, should also be monitored. These sources are usually tracked by monitoring appropriate publications, although more direct methods can also be effective (e.g., obtaining copies of speeches, statements before legislative or regulatory bodies, or materials sent to the groups' members).

Another important source of information on existing or emerging issues is the various levels of government, not just because they originate new legislation in response to the demands of the public, media, and interest groups (the scanning/monitoring system should already have identified these issues), but because governments often initiate legislative and regulatory changes on their own, without any apparent stimulus from other publics. Such changes may not receive much publicity, but they may have a more direct impact on a firm than any of the other issues. Governments also finance and publish the largest volume of research and analysis on policy issues or potential policy issues.

Two other monitoring approaches are worth mentioning — "leading sources" and internal issues reviews. Grefe (1981, 28) describes Graham Molitor's grouping of "leading sources":

- *Leading Events:* In the case of a broad umbrella issue such as consumerism, a leading event might be the first demand by a small vocal group for breakfast cereal manufacturers to lower the amount of sugar in their products.
- *Leading Personalities:* Certain advocates and celebrities are often among the first to climb on any new issue bandwagon.
- *Leading Organizations:* Certain organizations also have a history of getting involved in the earlier phases of issue development.
- *Leading Publications:* Issues are often reported in the fringe or underground media long before they gain the attention of the major newspapers.
- *Leading Political Jurisdictions:* Certain countries (Sweden), states (California, Massachusetts, Oregon, Minnesota, Wisconsin, and Illinois), and cities (New York City, Boston) often seem to legislatively address issues well before they gain credence elsewhere.

Finally, an internal issues review should be a part of any issues-monitoring process. This simply entails tapping into the current knowledge and experience of the members of the organization. Brown suggests that this approach enables the company to

> keep tabs on internal trends; bring to light forthcoming decisions the company will have to make which can alter the equilibrium between the company and its environment; and gain information from, and the opinions and insights of, those whose regular responsibilities require them to pay continuing heed to one or another of the company's external environments . . . and who understand the implications of trends and issues in these environments for the company. (1981, 20)

The review could be a survey of the opinions of the managers or employees, or it could be made a part of the divisional corporate planning process — the important thing is that these discussions be held regularly so that those involved develop a habit of noticing and informally tracking trends and issues in the course of performing their regular duties. An informal network of employees (a kind of mini–trend analysis program) could be a valuable addition to the internal issues review process — employees read, view, and participate in a vast array of both work and leisure activities on their own — these may be the source of future issues and trends. A considerable stock of data and facts exists on issues and trends, but it must be carefully assessed before it can be transformed into *information* that can be used effectively by a business organization.

The problem is more often how to organize and interpret the signals, rather than finding and recording them.

4.0 ASSESSMENT OF ISSUES

Activities that assess/forecast/rank issues overlap the scanning/ monitoring functions because it is only by intelligently analyzing the raw information that one can give some direction to the data-gathering process. As there is just too much information being generated for any one organization to handle, this pre-analysis is intended to guide the monitoring effort in focusing on those sources that have the most impact on the company or are especially efficient providers of appropriate information. Corrado notes:

> Once issues are identified, they need to be classified and categorized. Robert Moore of the Conference Board has suggested a list of questions that can help this process:
> • To what extent is the emerging issue due to internal as opposed to external factors?
> • From a detached, analytical viewpoint, what is the content of the issue? Its inherent characteristics?
> • Is it a current issue or an emerging issue?
> • What degree of impact is it likely to have on the company? Is it going to be a public-policy issue or a strategic issue, one affecting financial well-being?
> • Will the issue affect the entire world or just a few corporations within an industry? (1984, 54)

Before any analysis can be made, the organization must attempt to distill the real events underlying the "facts" accumulated by the scanning and monitoring phases. As an example of the approach that could be taken, we will consider only one of many sources in detail: the news media.

4.1 The News Media as a Source of Information

The various types of media can provide a firm or trade organization with information about the government, the general public, interest groups, and other businesses. They can serve as a window on the current environment outside the firm as well as an indicator of developing trends. If the view through this window is analyzed accurately, both threats and opportunities may be foreseen early enough to allow appropriate action to be taken. The way to effective media monitoring is to distill information from a confusing mixture of news stories, each with varied subjects, issues, and purposes.

In order to generate this information, one must understand the players and their strategies as well as the media themselves, their methods, and their constraints (see chapter 11).

4.1.1 Categories of News Stories

At first glance, the content of the news media appears to be a convoluted mass of issues and characters, but closer examination reveals a pattern. The characters are usually the same five "publics" described earlier, and the "stories" about them tend to fall into two broad categories. The first includes stories that *report*, more or less factually, the behaviour of a particular public. In this case, the public is the subject of the news story and the reporting is largely out of its control. It may or may not desire the publicity.

The second broad category are stories that *transmit* information from one public to others. In this case, the transmitting public is attempting to use the media as a channel to send information to another public. The method used will depend upon whom it is attempting to reach, what type of issue is involved, and what it is trying to say. The distinction between these two categories is not always clear, since often the very reporting of the actions of one public serves to transmit information to another. The reverse is also possible, with sometimes damaging results — the transmitter loses control of the intended situation and becomes reported news.

While it may appear that most news stories are of the "report" variety, the news event is often actually being manipulated in order to transmit information. Thus, the first step in analyzing media content is to determine whether a given story is a reported situation or an attempt by one public to communicate with another.

From the point of view of a business, the "transmit" category can be further broken down into four subcategories. One public can attempt to transmit information to another public (but not business, in this case), or it may attempt to send disinformation to another public. Alternatively, one public may attempt to transmit information to a particular business public, or it may try to disinform in the same manner.

- *Pure Reported News:* Reported news relates the facts, as interpreted by the media, in those situations in which the events are largely out of the control of the subjects. A story on a train derailment, for example, may contain significant information for several publics. However, the subject of this news event is not expected to have deliberately caused it for the purpose of transmitting its views on such matters to any other public.

   The first step in analyzing any reported news is to "de-filter" it — in other words, attempt to remove the effects of the media's methods, constraints, and biases in order to expose the underlying information (see section 4.1.2 below). This information should then be analyzed

to determine the underlying causes of the event and the possible repercussions that it may have vis-à-vis the business.

Reported information is a good indicator of developing trends
because, except for the filtering done by the media, it is a reasonably
unbiased reflection of what is actually happening in the environment.
On the other hand, the various types of transmitted news events,
because they are manipulated, tend to express the intentions or desires
of the public rather than what may actually be occurring.

- *Transmitted Information: Public to Public:* Transmitted information
  includes press releases, planned events, leaks, etc., that are intended
  to convey information from one public to another. When the government indicates that it considers the deficit to be a high priority item
  on its agenda, it transmits to all the other publics the information
  that government largesse will be reduced in the future. When parents
  stage a protest concerning education cutbacks, they are attempting
  to transmit information to the government through the media. When
  the government leaks proposed changes to its health-care plan, it is
  attempting to send information via the media. This is a form of suasion (see Stanbury & Fulton 1984).

  The first step in understanding transmitted news is again to remove
  the filtering effects of the media in an attempt to reveal the underlying message. This step must also take into account whether the transmitter understood that the media would modify its message and so
  adjusted the message accordingly, and if so, by how much. The next
  step is to try to discern which publics the transmitter was attempting
  to reach and what it was trying to say to them.

- *Transmitted Disinformation: Public to Public:* Transmitted disinformation includes press releases, planned events, leaks, etc., that are
  intended to obscure actual (or reported) events. When the government makes an extensive effort to repatriate the Constitution (which
  is within its capabilities) to cover its dismal economic performance
  (which appears to be outside its capabilities), it is attempting to disseminate disinformation via the media (see Stanbury et al. 1983 and
  Stanbury & Fulton 1984). When a local, left-of-centre alderman claims,
  in a televised council meeting, that large corporations are holding
  vast amounts of the public's money as deferred taxes, in order to shift
  the blame for lack of social program funding onto business, he
  is attempting the same thing. When the Defence Department
  announces the date of cruise missile tests and then postpones the
  tests due to "inclement weather," thereby disrupting the plans of
  protesters who have organized a demonstration in a remote area
  of the countryside, it is effectively transmitting disinformation via the
  media.

A recent wrinkle is the creation of "research events" or self-serving
statistics or polls. (We note that the results of a public opinion poll

can be influenced by carefully framing the questions.)[10] King describes them as follows:

> As the "media events" become more familiar and as, under pressure to provide drama for the editors, they become ever more bizarre, their effect seems gradually to be diminishing. They are increasingly being seen for what they are — merely a dramatic way of presenting the arguments of a self-interested group, in the hope of establishing those arguments as the majority view.
>
> The next stage for special-interest groups has been to publicize *selected* results of opinion research: that is, to use a more direct method of establishing their own ideas as the majority view. Quite clearly opinion research gives a much more convincing backing to arguments than a "media event" — though it may sometimes lack the drama needed to capture the attention of editors and readers. . . . Activists believe that . . . politicians are likely to be uncomfortable if their policies are opposed by a large majority of their constituents. . . . As a result, there is a growing tendency for special-interest groups to fight out their social and political battles via publicized opinion research. (1981, 90)[11]

Again, the first step in understanding the underlying message is to de-filter the media effects. Next the message should be analyzed to determine its obvious, surface meaning and then what disinformation is attempting to accomplish or hide.

- *Transmitted Information: Public to Business:* Transmitted information aimed at the firm includes press releases, planned events, leaks, etc., that are intended to be noticed by the firm directly. Government announcements of new investment incentives or publishing of the results of food price surveys are examples of attempts to transmit information through the media to business. When a union stages a demonstration at one firm to protest the hiring of nonunion labour, it is attempting to transmit information to other firms not directly involved in that particular dispute. When a consumer group publicizes the faults of a particular product, it is endeavouring to influence business as a whole through the media. As always, an attempt must be made to remove the media effects in order to discern the underlying message.

- *Transmitted Disinformation: Public to Business:* Transmitted disinformation aimed at a firm includes press releases, planned events, leaks, etc., intended to *obscure* actual events. When a union claims that management incompetence is resulting in higher costs and loss of competitiveness, it may be attempting to cover deterioration in productivity caused by union practices. When the government lauds the performance of a profitable crown corporation, it may be glossing over the fact that the same business, in private hands, may have been even more profitable.

As before, the first step in analyzing such "news" is to de-filter the media effects. Next, the message should be analyzed for its surface message and for the information or event that it is intended to hide. Consideration should also be given as to why the disinformation method was used in this case and whether the firm should let on that it has seen through the ruse.

In summary, the media should be studied by business in the same way that a CIA analyst would study an issue of *Pravda*. Look for the hidden messages and symbolic meanings as well as the more obvious ones — they may be the most important.

4.1.2 Media as a Filter

The media filter the true news in two significant ways: by the stories that they choose to cover and by the manner in which they report them. The result is that the news consumed by the general public is both distorted and biased.

The media select the stories that they will cover, to a large degree, on the basis of their perceptions of what they believe their audience wants (see chapter 11). Thus, bad/conflict news and unusual news tend to receive a disproportionate amount of coverage. This process introduces distortion because certain types of issues get amplified by extensive coverage while others are suppressed by lack of coverage. Then, in moulding the news to fit their particular format (newspaper, TV, etc.), the media introduce additional distortion and bias.

Add to this varying degrees of unconscious bias (as well as varying degrees of conscious bias) due to the background and education of the journalists, and the reported news may end up bearing little resemblance to the actual event.

4.2 Assessing Issues

Once the underlying facts have been exposed as well as is possible, a preliminary analysis of the issue should be made. What kind and type of issue is it? Which publics does it affect? What is the source of the issue? Is it possible to derive any cause/effect relationships?

An attempt should be made to estimate the current stage of the issue's "life cycle" and whether it will have a short- or long-term effect on the environment. Just because it seems that an issue will be short-lived does not mean that it cannot have a lasting effect — after all, income tax was originally just a temporary wartime measure, hardly worth commenting on, or so some important interest groups believed at the time.

5.0 FORECASTING

The next stage in the preliminary analysis of an issue is to try to get some idea of what it is leading up to. How fast is it developing? Where is it going? Is there time to react?

It is especially important to develop a feel for its probability of occurrence and the time of its impact upon the organization, as well as, of course, its possible effects. Cross-impacts on other publics should also be considered, as the effects of issues are rarely as isolated as they may at first seem.

An estimate should be made of the likely behaviour or response of the other publics and of their abilities to influence the development of the issue. Their method of solving their problem could create side-effects for other interest groups.

Corrado argues that the methods for identifying issues are similar to those used in technological forecasting:

- *Intuitive forecasting.* Expert opinion, Delphi studies, or structured polling
- *Trend extrapolation.* Plotting change in variables
- *Normative forecasting.* Looking at established goals and outlining efforts to achieve them
- *Monitoring events.* Environmental scanning
- *Cross-impact analysis.* Studying the interaction of issues with each other and with other events
- *Scenario building and modeling.* Exploring implications of alternative actions and events. (1984, 51–52)

These methods can be grouped into two general categories: expert opinion methods or mathematical methods. Expert opinion methods range from asking one person for his or her views on the future of the issue to generating opinions from groups of "experts" using a Delphi approach. Mathematical methods go from simple extrapolation of existing trends or data to probabalistic methods that attempt to inject more realism by taking into account the compounding effects of events on each other.

6.0 RANKING

Given the large number of public policy issues that may have an adverse effect on a business organization, and given a firm's inherently limited resources, some method must be used to decide which issues are the more important. The critical questions to be answered are the following:

1. How likely is the public policy issue to produce a response by government that will have an impact on the firm?

2. How large an impact (positive and/or negative) will the government's response to the policy issue have on the firm?
3. At what stage is the issue now? What is the likely time-path of the development of the issue; that is, will it become high on the legislature's agenda in six weeks, six months, or in three or four years?
4. What capabilities does the firm have to (a) influence the process by which the issue develops, and (b) influence government policy responses to the pressure of interest groups and/or public opinion? How much will these actions cost? How likely is the firm to be successful?

A probability/impact matrix can be used to subjectively rank the issues — see Figure 6-4. "The high-probability/high-impact issues appear in the top left hand corner of the matrix. These are the issues which could have the greatest strategic importance to the corporation and on which the corporation might be able to initiate some form of action" (Johnson 1983, 25).

Figure 6–4
PROBABILITY/IMPACT MATRIX FOR POLICY ISSUES

		Probability of Occurrence		
		High	*Medium*	*Low*
Severity of	*High*	Cell #1	Cell #2	Cell #3
(Adverse)	*Med-*	Cell #4	Cell #5	Cell #6
Impact on the Organization	*Low*	Cell #7	Cell #8	Cell #9

Obviously, the business organization must pay the most attention to those issues that fall into cell #1 in the matrix in Figure 6-4. Conversely, for the time being at least, the organization can give a low priority to issues in cells 6, 8, and 9. The importance of issues in the other cells will depend upon the organization's degree of risk aversion. For example, issues in cell #3 may be deemed more important than those in cell #7.

Brown suggests a more precise method: "By assigning weights to importance, and probability of occurrence to individual issues, and taking the products of these weights, one can arrive at a simple ranking of issues" (1981, 14). While still subjective, this method may be useful in assigning priorities among the high-probability/high-impact issues generated by the matrix method.

In any event, the value of trying to place issues in Figure 6-4 lies not in the precision achieved, but in the process itself. The matrix simply forces individuals to ask tough questions and to inquire more deeply about issues that may adversely affect their organization.

It must be emphasized that engaging in this process should not be a one-time thing for each issue. Public policy issues are dynamic, rising and falling in importance over time — and they may rise again. A classification at a point in time is like a snapshot in a world that functions like a continuous, episodic motion picture. Recall the discussion in Downs's issue-attention cycle above. Therefore, there is a need to add a third dimension to the matrix in Figure 6-4, namely, time. Even if an issue has a high salience for an organization and is highly likely to occur, it is still crucial to determine when this issue will reach its zenith. Obviously, the strategy of dealing with an issue likely to peak in six months is different than one for an issue that will peak in six years.

Another aspect that should be considered when ranking the issues is whether the company has any *ability* to influence the issue. A strategy designed to influence the course of development of an issue may be more complex than one whose purpose is solely to respond to external forces.

A decision should now be made as to which "indicators" would best provide the information that will be required as the issue develops. It may now be possible to narrow the focus of the monitoring effort on certain issues, with very little loss of effectiveness. It may be necessary also to increase the monitoring activity on certain issues when the ranking procedure indicates a shift in their importance to the company. This feedback to the monitoring process is crucial in preventing the dissipation of effort on too wide a spectrum of issues.

In summary, there are two keys to an effective scan/monitor/assess/forecast/rank process. It must be very systematic in order to identify pertinent issues — a random sampling method would let too many slip by. And it must have a simple and efficient means of "sorting the wheat from the chaff" — it is impossible to keep track of everything that might have an impact on the company.

7.0 ANALYSIS

The previous elements of the issues-management model should locate those issues of significant importance to the company and provide a stream of information on their development. Before any strategy can be considered, a more detailed analysis of these issues must be conducted.

Two approaches are commonly used to analyze issues. A task force may be organized to study an issue and determine its effects on the company. The same method may be used to decide on a strategy and to implement it. The second approach is to have a public affairs or government relations unit as a coordinator in getting the functional departments to analyze and respond to the issues. The important thing is that an overall view be maintained in addition to the detailed analysis of the issue.

Brown (1981, 21) describes an "issues main frame," used by a consulting firm to give a complete picture of the characteristics of social and political issues, as follows:

- *Who Started the Ball Rolling? (Historical View):* Why; how; when; what was to be gained; what were their methods/funding/momentum; what were their proposals/points of compromise; what were the results? Wissema observes: "At first glance there seem to be sudden changes . . . but accurate analysis of such sudden changes teaches us that it is our limited perception and combinative powers that cause the change to seem sudden" (1981, 30).
- *Who Is Now Involved? (Contemporary View):* Why; how; when did they jump in; what is to be gained; what are their methods/ funding/momentum; what are their proposals/points of compromise; what are the results?
- *Who Will Get Involved? (Future View):* Why; how; when will they jump in; what is to be gained; what will be their methods/ funding/momentum; what will be their proposals/points of compromise; what will be the results?
- *What Are the Implications:* What alternatives do we have; what if we take no action; what cost-effectiveness could our alternative actions have?

It is also important to try to isolate the forces that are helping to create the issue from the issue itself. Is there anything that might speed up its development process or slow it down? Wissema observes: "Changes, then, occur gradually. A change begins when all the necessary conditions are fulfilled. This seems trivial, but leads to an operational question: what conditions must be fulfilled before the change process we are studying can start?" (1981, 30).

Issues can be thought of as puzzles: Are there any pieces of the puzzle that are about to fall into place? This could signal an abrupt change in the speed of the issue's development.

This analysis exercise will shed light on the nature of the issue, its possible effects on the organization, its expected time and point of impact, the character of the groups promoting it, and the possible means of influencing it.

8.0 FORMULATING STRATEGY

A strategy may be usefully thought of as an "ends-means-conditions" relationship, in which the ends are the goals of the firm, the means are the methods used to achieve these goals, and the conditions are the range of circumstances over which the ends-means combination will be pursued (MacCrimmon 1983). Thus, the first step in formulating an issues-management strategy is to decide how the firm would ideally like the issue to be resolved. "Some issues call for a corporate action, others for the expression of a position, others simply call for continued attention" (Armstrong 1981, 764). An assessment of the methods available for exerting influence on the issue will usually indicate that the ideal goal is unreachable, so the goal must be revised downward until it reaches a realistic level. After the goal has been reconciled with the available means, conditions should be attached so that the strategy will not continue to be pursued after circumstances have rendered either the goals or means inoperative.

The refinement of the conditions component of the strategy naturally leads to the question, What do we do if the strategy *does* become inoperative? The answer is that there must be contingency plans. Every strategy should have alternate, fall-back plans sketched out for all conceivable disruptions to its execution. This serves two purposes: it helps to illuminate internal inconsistencies in the reasoning behind the main strategy (and may suggest even better strategies or some means of making the original one more flexible); and it provides a reasonable starting point for action if the disruption to the original strategy does not allow enough time to formulate a new one. Obviously, it is preferable to reassess the entire situation upon a change in strategy, if time allows.

It is important that the issues-management strategy be integrated with the overall corporate strategy (see Fleming 1980). Issues are only one aspect of the environmental conditions that provide the threats and opportunities the corporate strategy will be based on.

In order to be viable, the strategy should try to realistically reconcile the company's internal interests with the public policy aspects of society the issues are reflecting. There is no point in pushing for a six-day work week when "society" is contemplating one only four-and-a-half-days long.

Gram and Crawford (1981, 31–33) suggest that there are five general approaches that a company can take when confronted by an issue:

1. *Pre-emption:* The company can "anticipate what is going to be demanded and respond before the demand is made." This approach bypasses the issue-resolution process entirely and allows the firm to choose a solution as close to its optimum as it thinks it can get away with. It entails the risk that the response will either not be satisfactory, perhaps eliciting more ambitious demands, or be more than the opposition wanted in the first place.

2. *Co-optation:* The company can

> endeavour to blunt the demands and constraints of self-interest and stakeholder groups by having them participate with the firm in solving the social issue, winning over the leadership of the group, or confusing the group's leadership in various ways. The process of

co-optation may, and sometimes does, include illegal means such as bribery, threats and/or intimidation. It may also include the approaches by which the social interest group is won over by facts, the openness of management, and the opportunity to participate in making decisions.

This approach relies on management's ability to convince the group's leadership that the firm's position is justified or that lesser measures are acceptable. There is always a risk that the group will reject this approach and move on to more radical measures.

3. *Interpenetration:* "This process is similar to co-optation but without the negative connotations. It involves real sharing of leadership and joint programs, typically in those areas where the goals or methods are not clearly defined." For instance, in a joint effort to clean up a river, how do the parties decide what level of impurities is clean enough? In order for there to be a joint effort, there must be a joint commitment. This implies that the interest group considers the company to be a responsible and suitable partner. The risk is that an unsuccessful partnership would probably result in mudslinging and even greater difficulties in finding common ground.

4. *Conflict:* The company may decide, for any of a variety of reasons, that it will oppose the social demand: it does not have the resources or technology to give in to the demand; it may not feel it is the appropriate body to negotiate or resolve the demand; it may feel that others should be included in the bargaining process; it may believe that the issue should be decided by the courts or by some process other than the firm and the interest group reaching a decision; or it may merely disagree with the goals of the interest group.

> Conflict technique is perhaps best described as calculated risk. Management may utilize conflict either as a means of resisting the imposition of impossible and non-negotiable demands, or as a tactic to persuade the opposition that it is serious and will only trade concessions for concessions.

5. *Destruction:* "The management of the firm may decide that the social issue itself or the demands or tactics used by the interest group are neither acceptable nor negotiable, and that they are not supported by the general sentiments of society. In this case, management may actively undertake actions to neutralize, overload, exhaust and destroy the interest organization." The firm may go public, either through the courts or the media, to expose the unreasonableness of the group's demands or tactics. A lengthy legal battle can also be used to exhaust the group's manpower, finances and member commitment.

Delaying tactics may serve another purpose. Recall that in what Downs (1972) calls the "issue-attention cycle" some prominent issues simply fade away through lack of interest by the general public or through being supplanted by newer, more interesting issues.

The tactic of delay brings into play another important phenomenon: differences in the resources of various interest groups to keep a policy issue moving toward the kind of government action its proponents desire. Obviously, large trade associations are in a different position to maintain or to fight an issue than a small volunteer organization, all other things being equal. Delay tests both the psychological and financial staying power of an interest group.

9.0 IMPLEMENTATION

Once strategy options have been generated and evaluated, and a final strategy decided upon, it must be implemented. The remainder of this book is largely devoted to the problem of implementation. Critical to effective implementation is top management's full support for the government relations unit. McGrath puts it this way: "It is generally agreed that the impetus for a corporation's externally oriented efforts must come from the chief executive officer; in those instances where the CEO is sensitive to the importance of this area, the mandate will be passed down through the entire organization" (1976, 49).

Since so much of the activity surrounding an issue is usually outside of a business's control, implementation can be the most difficult aspect of the entire issues-management process. As noted in chapters 1 and 5, "there is general agreement within the business community that business does not control a voting bloc, as do organized labour, farmers and ethnic groups. But executives know that legislators do respond to the sentiments expressed by their constituents" (McGrath 1977, 12).

Thus, the key to influencing issues is to convince constituents (or voters) that the company's position is a reasonable one. A good way to start this process is to communicate with (and mobilize, if possible) the natural constituencies of the business — its shareholders, employees, and retirees (see Grefe 1981). These groups have a vested interest in the company, its activities, and its success. This does not mean that they can be manipulated, but it does mean that they will usually at least listen to the company's point of view. Additional constituencies that may be receptive are the firm's suppliers, customers, and competitors.

Many methods can be used to try to communicate the company's viewpoint to its constituencies, opponents and supporters, and to the government.

- *Lobbying:* The most direct method is to go straight to the government, its regulatory agencies, or its civil servants. The main advantage of this approach is that the company can communicate directly with those who will be framing and/or enforcing the legislation. The major disadvantage is that, as illustrated earlier, by the time an issue

gets to this stage, there may be so many prior commitments, pressures, and involved parties that there is no room left for anyone to
manoeuvre. It can also be costly, but there may be no more effective
method of influencing government.

Lobbying includes establishing contacts with interest groups — even
those that oppose the company. This serves two purposes. It helps the
company keep informed of interest groups' concerns, and it allows it
to communicate its views in an informal manner. An indirect form of
interest-group representation includes speeches by high-level executives, and speech reprints are another method of communicating the
corporation's position to other publics. Public-speaking programs that
encourage lower-level personnel to speak at community-level functions and schools can also be used. This can be an effective method if
the publics to be reached are small, but is less useful in reaching wider
audiences. Ontario Hydro, for example, advertises its "Speakers
Bureau" in the *Globe and Mail*. Lobbying is discussed in some detail
in chapters 7, 8, and 9.

- *Trade Associations:* These organizations may use the media, advertising, and personal appearances, as well as lobbying, to attempt to communicate their message to the various publics and to the government.
  Advantages of this method are that it may be more economical than
  individual action and it provides a more united front to the other
  publics. The disadvantage is that the messages being communicated
  may not be representative of a particular company's view. The lowest-
  common-denominator principle may be in effect. The role of trade
  associations is discussed more fully in chapter 8.

- *The Media:* Press releases, planned events, media contacts, and leaks
  can all be used to transmit information to the media and thence to
  various publics. The main advantage to this method is that it is inexpensive. The big disadvantage is that the company loses control over
  the information and the uses to which it may be put. The information-
  provision approach includes "public service" publications, such as
  newsletters distributed to customers and local communities, and more
  specialized documents, such as submissions to government commissions. Its uses obviously range from generating "goodwill" to ammunition in life-and-death struggles. The cost/benefit equation also
  varies accordingly. The media as communication channels in business-government relations are analyzed in chapter 11.

- *Advertising:* This method ranges from institutional ads to full-fledged
  advocacy campaigns intended to change public opinion. The proper-
  ties of advertising are the reverse of those in using the media — the
  company has full control over the context of the message, but the
  advertising vehicle can be very costly. Advocacy or issue advertising is
  considered in more detail in chapter 12.

- *Special Projects:* These include sponsoring community-level sports events, clubs, charities, and special historical events, and can be seen as purely PR projects or as unique opportunities to advance noncommercial messages to the public.[12]

10.0 EVALUATION

While it may be fairly easy to judge the effectiveness of a public relations department in fast-breaking events, it is much more difficult to measure the efficiency of an issues-management department in modifying the perceptions and opinions of the general public. McGrath states:

> As is the case with many other staff functions whose impact on corporate profits is not immediately evident, external relations does not readily lend itself to measurement. This general difficulty is compounded in the case of external relations by the multitude of influences outside of management's sphere of control that can and do affect the issues and publics that the corporate relations programs are aimed at. (1976, 64)

While it is almost impossible to quantify the results of an issues-management program, there are methods that can be used to gain a subjective feel for its effectiveness. McGrath (1976, 64) describes some of these:

1. *Evaluation on the basis of previously defined objectives or results.* Goals such as "improved business credibility" or "a positive corporate image" can be measured by informal feedback or formal opinion surveys. Positive movements in these attitudes may be difficult to measure, but negative ones are commonly quite pronounced.
2. *Evaluation on the basis of activities.* Is proposed legislation that will affect the company fair or punitive, drafted intelligently or out of ignorance? It is not a question of whether or not the laws are enacted — it is whether the legislators receive enough input from business to permit a balanced judgment.
3. *Subjective opinion of CEO.* The quality of the feedback that the CEO gets from his or her peers, friends, stockholders, employees, government officials, and the public can be used to judge the quality of the issues-management process. "One CEO admitted that he determines the success (or the failure) of his company's external relations program by the variations in his blood pressure!" (McGrath 1976, 68).

Some argue that it is not efficient to try to measure the effectiveness of an organization's issues-management process. Since it cannot be measured properly, why bother? There are so many factors that interact in the passage of a specific piece of legislation, how can one say that the activities of one's issues-management program caused it to develop as it did? Many CEOs question whether there is any need to measure such efforts at all — it is simply a job that must be done in order to function in the world today. This seems to be the counsel of despair.

NOTES

1. It should be emphasized that such actions by government may contain threats or opportunities or both. For example, stringent water and air pollution control regulations add to the costs of manufacturing pulp and paper, but they also create a market for emission control devices. Tariffs may raise the cost of certain inputs, but they may also create barriers to foreign competition. Recall the discussion in chapter 3.

2. The following definition of an "issue" has been proposed by Brown: "An issue is a condition or pressure, either internal or external to an organization, that, if it continues, will have a significant effect on the functioning of the organization or its future interests. . . . this definition implies that sooner or later an organization has to make a decision about each issue that confronts it" (1979, 1). Saul Alinsky argues: "The rise of the adjective 'controversial' to qualify the word 'issue' is a meaningless redundancy. There can be no such thing as a 'noncontroversial' issue. . . . issues only arise when there is disagreement or controversy" (1971, 117).

3. In general, it is useful to distinguish between "the general public" and "opinion leaders" or "doers." The latter are relatively few in number, more sophisticated than the average citizen, and vastly more influential directly and indirectly with government, interest groups, and others.

4. As adapted from Preston and Post (1975, 76–79).

5. This is a notoriously difficult — some would say various — concept. Because it is so evocative, for strategic reasons most groups claim that what they want is "in the public interest," and not merely of benefit to their members. Recall chapter 4 and see also chapter 9.

6. See Allan Fotheringham, "Recognizing the Raider's Legacy," *Maclean's*, December 2, 1985, p. 80.

7. Saul Alinsky (1971) argues that the role of the organizer (read activist) is to convert someone's plight into a problem and then into an issue. This is done by fanning resentments, showing the prospect for change, and indicating to those with the problem that there is a proven means to effect change that will benefit them. Issues, he emphasizes, must be specific, of immediate concern to the group's members, and their solution must be realizable. Alinsky also argues that an organization needs multiple issues to sustain itself and broaden its appeal. In his view, single-issue organizations have less

staying power. He also argues that activist organizations need action rather than simply rhetoric — it is their oxygen.

8. Saul Alinsky (1971) notes that "the price of a successful attack is a constructive alternative."

9. Bartha (1984b, 26) lists the following information sources in Canada:

Public Opinion Surveys	— "Decima Quarterly" by Decima Research
	— "Goldfarb Report ' by Goldfarb Consultants
	— regular Gallup polls
	— Centre de Recherche sur l'Opinion Publique
Media Analysis	— "Canadian Trend Report" by Trans-Canada Social Policy Research Group
	— "Political Alerts" by Deacon Hodgson Inc. various media-scanning or clipping services
Interest Groups	— "Connectives" by Pat Delbridge Associates
	— "Opinion Leader Research Project" by Hay Associates
Government	— Institute for Political Involvement
	— Institute for Research on Public Policy
	— C. D. Howe Research Institute
	— Niagara Institute
	— The Fraser Institute
	— government relations firms and "think-tanks"

10. The use and abuse of public opinion polls has been noted by an American senior executive:

> Part-time data gatherers hurry into our office; they reassure us that they will not take too much of our time. They then rush through a whole mass of questions, taking our temperature on each. They do so whether or not we understand the question, know about the subject or care about it, or are going to do anything about it — or whether, indeed, we believe the question is properly phrased as to the information to be elicited. Nothing disturbs a pollster more than a question about a question, such as how will you interpret this answer or that answer.

The fact is, such surveys raise more questions than they answer. More important, they put the cart before the horse. The dominant theory of politics in business schools and in public relations departments seems to be that public opinion rules. Our representatives ascertain what the public or their constituents think and then vote their wishes. Now no one would deny that, in some way or other, on some issues, something called public opinion has some influence. But anyone with the slightest acquaintance with politics knows how inadequate such a theory is. We are not governed like a town meeting, and to plan on that assumption will be to make bad plans. Public opinion on many of the most difficult and complex yet most important issues does not exist. In any case, it does not govern. What then does? Possibly, to a large degree, it is power and influence. (Littlejohn 1980, 179–80)

11. King's (1981, 91) review of the use of polls by interest groups in the U.K. indicates that: (1) they are greatly oversimplifying what are complex issues, making use of the media's demand for the dramatic — hence, we now have "research events"; (2) they rely for the effect on numbers rather than depth, and they are usually a matter of yes/no answers to "belief statements." King (1981, 91) suggests there are two potential dangers for opinion research. First, "a fair amount of dubious research may be published." Second, "many of the research events will contain figures that are directly opposed to each other." In his view, "the reality is that we all have, on most topics, complex sets of ideas and feelings and opinions and they are not even necessarily mutually compatible." It cannot be properly represented by a simple opinion poll.

12. More generally, see "Corporate Communications: The Battle for Hearts and Minds," *Saturday Review*, September 29, 1979, pp. 16–31.

7

Lobbying Targets
and Timing

1.0 INTRODUCTION

Lobbying involves a variety of activities designed to influence public policy in ways desired by the individual or group making the representations. Lobbying efforts are directed toward decision makers and those who have the ear of decision makers (advisors); these efforts are also directed at shaping public opinion, which in turn influences policy makers, particularly politicians. This chapter is concerned with two strategic choices: the targets of a group's lobbying efforts, and the timing of those efforts during the course of the policy-making process.

One of the major differences between the Canadian and American lobbying processes relates to the importance of various targets of lobbying groups. The type of institutional structure of government in Canada (the Westminster model) influences the types of targets of lobbying efforts to a considerable extent. Gillies and Pigott explain the general strategy for lobbying in Canada with respect to targets, timing, and the importance of repetitiveness:

> It is well known that the process by which organizations put forth their views tends to bypass Parliament. Skilled lobbyists always begin well down in the system so that they will always have a place to which they can appeal if they lose in their first efforts. Thus when legislation is being prepared the first efforts of interest groups are directed at the department involved, their goal being to exclude from the all-important memorandum to cabinet recommendations which would adversely affect their interests. They generally recognize that once a position has been taken in that document, it can be changed only with difficulty. If, however, a special interest group does fail in its first efforts, it may meet with senior members of the department; perhaps the deputy minister and then even the minister. If these efforts are unsuccessful and legislation is proposed to which it is opposed, the group may then decide to lobby members of Parliament and eventually appear at the hearings on the bill before a committee of the House of Commons. Parliament, in other words, is the last line of defence. (1982, 256)

This chapter is organized in the following way. Section 2 assesses the general strategic factors in determining which individuals or groups should be the targets of lobbying efforts. The potential number of targets can be quite large when an interest group needs to focus its efforts on actors both inside and outside the government. Sections 3 to 9 examine in more detail the following potential targets of lobbying activities: the bureaucracy, cabinet ministers, the parapolitical bureaucracy or "exempt" staff, members of Parliament, House of Commons committees, the Senate, and the media. (The discussion here of the media as a target of lobbying activity is very brief, as chapter 11 deals with the role of the media in business-government relations in detail.) Section 10 deals with the timing of lobbying efforts. While most analyses focus on the legislative process, some effort is made to look at the timing of representations in a number of other types of policy actions.

2.0 IDENTIFYING THE TARGETS

2.1 Strategic Factors

At whom should lobbying be directed? Which individuals or entities constitute the potential targets at which interest-group representations are directed? See Figure 7-1. First, one must identify the actors who are likely to participate in the policy process under analysis. One cannot use the same list (even in generic terms) for every possible policy action. While each situation is not unique, it is necessary to appreciate that the identity of targets (and their importance) is largely a function of the type of policy action under consideration. For example, a new bill dealing with airline regulation in general will have a different target list than an airline route application filed with the Air Transport Committee of the Canadian Transport Commission. More generally, see Figure 7-2. Lyon points out that when Jack Gallagher was chairperson of Dome Petroleum, he "approached lobbying as methodically as a life insurance salesman zeroing in on potential clients: he drew up a list of 'prospects' — ministers and senior mandarins he must buttonhole — and he tracked them down relentlessly, using his famous charm to soothe any irritation they might feel at his persistence" (1983, 53). See chapter 9.

Second, one must determine who are the *important* actors — those that can determine choices or significantly influence them. Who has how much power or influence? What type of power do these individuals have? Do they have the power to initiate a policy action? Do they have the power to delay, derail, or block a policy action (i.e., negative power)?

Third, one must determine if the interest-group representatives have *access* to the important actors. As Jackson and Atkinson point out: "Access to decision-makers at important stages becomes a necessary condition of success. The existence of an access point is not a guarantee of influ-

Figure 7–1
RELATING LOBBYING TARGETS TO POLICY ACTIONS

Policy Actions	Important Lobbying Targets
• New statute or amendment of an existing one	Middle- to senior-level bureaucrats acting as policy advisors in the department sponsoring the legislation; minister responsible and his or her political ("exempt") staff; bureaucrats and ministers of other departments likely to be "allies" or "enemies" of the sponsoring department; media to try to shape media opinion and/or public opinion; Commons committees studying the legislation; Senate committees or individual senators who are in favour of or oppose the bill (really a delaying tactic to force minister to amend the bill); if enacted, lobby bureaucrats writing the regulations (possibly try to gain support of provincial government as early as possible).
• Subordinate legislation (orders, regulations, etc.)	Bureaucrats in the department responsible for drafting the regulations; minister and his or her political staff in the department responsible; ministers of other departments who are "allies" or "enemies" of the responsible department; PCO officials handling the matter before being approved by cabinet; possible use of a media blitz after regulations are published for notice and comment.
• Exercise of discretion pursuant to authority delegated within existing legislation	
— cabinet as a whole	Cabinet ministers and political staff of departments identified as "allies" and "enemies"; PCO officials; PMO to influence PM; media to create positive or negative opinion as desired by the interest group; bureaucrats in departments identified as "allies" and "enemies"; MPS, government caucus; possibly opposition MPS to raise questions in the Commons.
— an individual minister	Minister responsible; his or her political staff; policy advisory bureaucrats in the relevant department; media (as above); MPS, government caucus; possibly the PMO and opposition MPS to raise questions in the Commons.
— senior bureaucrat	The bureaucrat responsible; other more senior bureaucrats, e.g., ADM or DM; minister and political staff of the department; possibly the media, but could backfire.
— regulatory agency	If an administrative decision, lobby relevant professional staff (bureaucrats); try to get commissioners to overrule staff decisions.

Figure 7-1 (continued)

Policy Actions	Important Lobbying Targets
• Ministerial policy statements (guide to interpretation of existing legislation)	Bureaucratic policy advisors who probably drafted the statement; minister and his or her political staff; outside advisors if they appear to have much of a role; possibly the PMO to get PM involved—likely only on major political issues; media in some cases depending on the nature of the issue; possibly MPs in government caucus.
• Decisions of regulatory/ administrative agencies (both substantive and procedural)	Appeal format decision of agency to the courts or to cabinet —then lobby cabinet; lobby the department with primary responsibility for the area, e.g., Department of Communications in cases of the CRTC; may try to get province(s) involved lobbying individual ministers or PMO, PCO for cabinet as a whole (e.g., CTC award of Toronto-Halifax route to CP Air reversed and given to EPA); may use media to alter climate of opinion and influence cabinet.
• Changes in the revenue budget, i.e., taxes and tax expenditures	Department of Finance; senior bureaucratic policy advisors; minister and his or her political staff; try to gain allies among the taxation specialists (lawyers, accountants, economists) who shape the specialized climate of opinion in which Department of Finance operates; target individual ministers who may pressure minister of finance; possibly target top PCO and PMO officials; possibly get help from government caucus; media may be useful in some cases — particularly trying to shoot down proposals in the budget.
• Annual department *Estimates* (expenditure program)	Middle to senior bureaucrats in department whose budget will be affected; minister and political staff of that department; Treasury Board and Department of Finance officials who try to control spending and make it more efficient; bureaucrats and ministers in other departments who may be "allies" or "enemies"; possibly try to get provincial governments to pressure federal government via FPRO, PCO, PMO.

ence, but without access almost nothing else is possible" (1974, 33). In general, access points consist of institutionalized mechanisms for obtaining input from those outside government (e.g., parliamentary committees, advisory task forces, etc.) and, potentially, each actor inside government who has some role in shaping a policy initiative. Therefore, the list of access points includes the following:

• advisory committees (regular or ad hoc) — these may be used at various stages but most often at the problem-identification and early stages

Figure 7-2
POTENTIAL TARGETS OF LOBBYING ACTIVITIES

1. **Targets inside Government**
  (a) Departmental bureaucrats
      — in the department initiating the policy action
      — deputy minister (possibly more than one associate deputy minister)
      — assistant deputy minister(s)
      — director(s) general   ⎫ focus on people in specialized "policy
      — directors   ⎬ units" or those in this case who are
      — senior policy analyst   ⎭ directly involved in the initiative
      — in other departments, particularly those sitting on the interdepartmental
        committees dealing with the policy initiative; try to identify potential "allies"
        and "enemies" of the initiating department
  (b) Minister of the initiating department
  (c) Political or exempt staff in the minister's office
  (d) Other cabinet ministers; try to identify potential "allies" and "enemies" of
      the minister of the initiating/leading department
  (e) Bureaucrats (advisors) in key central agencies: PCO; Treasury Board; FPRO;
      Dept. of Finance; PMO
  (f) Members of Parliament
      — government MPS
        — parliamentary secretaries to ministers
        — members of key committees, particularly the chairperson
        — ordinary backbenchers
      — opposition MPS
        — critics/shadow ministers
        — committee members
        — backbenchers
  (g) Administrative/regulatory agencies
      — commissioners
      — professional staff: legal counsel; analysts; administrators; researchers
  (h) Senate
      — members of key committees, particularly the chairperson
      — other senators

2. **Targets outside Government**
  (a) Media
      — political columnists, e.g., Richard Gwyn, Jeffrey Simpson, Douglas Fisher,
        George Bain
      — news service reporters, notably Canadian Press
      — network electronic news — particularly television
      — reporters for major dailies specializing in politics and business
      — reporters/writers for specialized periodicals, e.g., *Financial Post*, *Financial
        Times*, *Canadian Business*, *Executive*, *Report on Business Magazine*,
        and a host of trade or industry-specific magazines
      — reporters/writers for major mass-market weeklies: *Maclean's*

Figure 7–2 (continued)

(b) Other Interest Groups
- potential allies or members of a coalition
- competitors or rivals offering a conflicting point of view
- "neutral" groups who are either not involved in this issue or who are advancing a position that doesn't affect that of our interest group

(c) External policy advisors to government departments (bureaucrats; the minister directly)
- academics
- lawyers
- advisory committees set up by or formally acknowledged by government

(d) Political parties
- party in power
- opposition parties

(e) Provincial/Local governments
(f) Foreign governments

---

of policy formulation, but can also be used at the implementation stage to smooth the administration of a policy;

- the minister for the department responsible for that area of public policy;
- the minister's political or exempt staff;
- the bureaucracy
  - department/agency responsibility
  - central agencies (TB, PCO, FPRO)
  - other departments/agencies participating in interdepartmental committees;
- parliamentary committees;
- individual MPs (government and opposition);
- informal consultative efforts launched by individual ministers or departments; and
- feedback to department in response to formal public notice and comment periods on new regulations posted in the *Canada Gazette*.

Fourth, the interest group must determine what are the *objectives and interests* of those with the power to shape the policy initiative the group is interested in. What sort of appeals are likely to be successful with each target? In short, how can those with influence be influenced? Gray notes:

Bureaucrats and politicians, lobbyists soon learn, respond to different pressures. Bureaucrats want to develop a statement that won't embarrass their superiors and may enhance their own careers. They can be won with technical data and good analysis. Elected representatives, on the other hand, are always looking for votes. They want to be seen by colleagues and constituents as bringing out useful, popular policies. They dread negative press and are made nervous by mailbags of angry letters. (1983, 12)

Fifth, the interest group must ask what the possibilities are for forming alliances/coalitions (see chapter 8).

2.2 Who Initiates/Pushes a Policy Action?

Policy changes that affect the members of an interest group do not occur by some form of "spontaneous combustion." Every change has to have a sponsor or advocate — someone (or some group) that wants to change the status quo (see chapter 4). The status quo usually has an enormous mass, thus great intertia — meaning that considerable energy or force must be applied to effect a change. That energy will only be applied if some individual or group wants a change to occur sufficiently to expend the energy to try to "move the mountain." The point for the interest group in targeting its lobbying efforts is twofold. First, if it prefers things as they are, its prime target must be the principal initiator of the proposed policy action. In this case, the interest group is playing a negative or blocking role, and its objective is to stop the proposed action before it is implemented. Therefore, the group must find out as early as possible who the "pusher" is — before that individual or group has time to find allies and develop its own momentum for change. Finding the real driving force (conceptually and operationally) for some policy initiatives may not be easy, particularly if it resides deep in the bowels of the bureaucracy. As I note in section 7, bureaucrats may be able to have their way on some policy issues even when their minister wishes to do something else.

The list of potential initiators of policy action is a long one and it includes the following:

- Bureaucrats at several levels in departments/agencies
  - political analysts/policy secretariats,
  - program administrators,
  - special policy development units.
- "Clients" of a department or agency.
- Interest groups who are not regular "clients" of a particular department or agency.
- Party personnel: organizers, researchers, "bagmen," etc.
- Individual ministers (and their political [or "exempt"] staff).
- Individual MPs.
- Party caucus or various subcaucuses (e.g., Quebec caucus, Western caucus, etc.).
- Ad hoc policy advisory bodies (e.g., royal commissions, task forces, special inquiries).

2.3 Potential Targets

For analytical convenience, I have divided the targets into two broad
categories: those inside the parliamentary/bureaucratic system[1] and those
usually defined to be outside it. See Figure 7-2. Interest groups have to
lobby members of both of these systems.

In general, the targets defined to be outside the legislative/bureaucratic
(i.e., government) process are indirect or intermediate targets. The objective of interest groups in influencing these targets is to have them in
turn influence actors inside government. An interest group may be able
to use public relations and "media events" to alter the climate of media
and public opinion and thereby influence politicians and bureaucrats
— see chapter 11. For example, for many years of debate (1971-78) over
competition policy, business interests made their case to the newspaper
and trade press media sufficiently well that they were able to obtain
widespread sympathetic coverage and extensive editorial support for their
opposition to the proposed legislation (Stanbury 1977).

Traditionally, one thinks of specific interest groups external to government lobbying MPs, cabinet ministers, and civil servants to support
or block a proposed policy action, but probably just as much lobbying
takes place within the parliamentary/legislative process among the
formal actors themselves (MPs, etc.). In addition to the purely internal
lobbying, internal participants lobby potentially influential groups
outside the government to gain allies and build support for (or block)
the initiatives taken by insiders.[2] Figure 7-3 illustrates the possible combinations of the directions of lobbying activity.

Interest groups also use indirect approaches to lobby within the set of
targets inside government. For example, in their effort to abolish or
limit compulsory patent licensing legislation enacted in 1969, the Phar-

Figure 7-3
TARGETS AND THE DIRECTION OF LOBBYING ACTIVITY

Location of the Target Group	Location of Initiating Actor(s)	
	Inside the Government	Outside the Government
Inside the Government	e.g., a cabinet minister lobbies his or her cabinet colleagues to gain support for legislation he or she wishes to pass	e.g., an interest group such as the CMA submits a brief to a parliamentary committee or meets with the minister sponsoring new legislation
Outside the Government	e.g., a federal department seeks support of interest group (e.g., farmers) in advancing a new price support program	e.g., an interest group seeks a coalition with other group(s) to advance or block certain legislation

maceutical Manufacturers Association of Canada (PMAC) lobbied MPs to pressure the minister and made use of a former minister. Harrison explains that PMAC

> persuaded one MP, whom it has not identified, to speak directly to the consumer and corporate affairs minister on its behalf. A second, Martin O'Connell, a former cabinet minister, wrote a lengthy paper — "Most of which," according to the industry spokesman, "is supported by the drug manufacturers." The paper was presented to the minister. (1978a)

Lobbying circles are quite small in Ottawa and interconnected. For example, after PMAC had been able to pressure the federal government to reopen consideration of its compulsory licensing legislation in 1982, the minister of consumer and corporate affairs appointed Martin O'Connell as a special advisor on the problem. A few weeks earlier, O'Connell had been a consultant to PMAC.

Lobbying can involve enormous amounts of detail work to orchestrate one's case. Sometimes many contacts must be made and both direct and "round about" approaches used. Hayes (1983) provides an excellent case study involving the work of Gordon Floyd, president of Public Affairs Management of Toronto, to illustrate these points. Floyd was retained by Roadway Expressway, an American trucking firm, who wanted to acquire Harkema Express, a small trucking line located in Brampton. Similar acquisitions had been turned down by the cabinet under the Foreign Investment Review Act.

> Floyd's first step was a thorough researching of FIRA's predisposition and identification of all likely opponents and supporters. He lobbied local, provincial and federal members of parliament and asked them to make representations to FIRA. He directed the same campaign at Herb Gray, federal Minister of Industry, Trade and Commerce, by enlisting provincial Ministry of Transport and Industry, Trade and Commerce officials, local MPs, the Ontario caucus of the Liberal Party, and especially Ross Milne, president of the federal Liberal Party's Ontario branch and a man likely to run in the Brampton riding in the future. Floyd also approached the opposition critics for assurance that they supported the idea and would not be likely to roast Gray afterward. . . .
>
> Floyd's strategy was successful. Roadway Expressway's purchase was approved last November — 14 months later — and four business days after the decision, the U.S. lifted its moratorium on [the granting of licences to] Canadian truckers. (Hayes 1983)

3.0 BUREAUCRATS AS LOBBYING TARGETS

In Canada, senior bureaucrats are usually important targets because the Canadian variant of the Westminster model of government is based on a strong executive — effectively the cabinet and senior policy advisors, largely bureaucrats. Key public policy decisions are *not* shaped (as they often are in the U.S.) by interest groups bargaining with the members of the many specialized congressional committees. Writing about John Bulloch, president of the CFIB, Brimelow observes: "He has to deal mainly with civil servants, he notes wryly, whereas his U.S. counterparts lobby legislators. 'We're more relevant than the opposition and I don't like it' " (1977, 51).

3.1 Who Has Power?

Presthus (1974c, 255) provides some more general empirical support for the proposition that Canadian interest-group representatives focus their efforts on bureaucracy, while their American counterparts expend their energy on individual legislators. He asked almost 1000 directors of interest groups, "Which three of the following elements in the political system receive the greatest amount of attention from you and your association?" In terms of the proportion of respondents ranking each target first, he obtained the following results:

Target of Interest Group	*U.S.*	*Canada*
Bureaucracy	21%	40%
Legislators	41	20
Legislative committees	19	7
Cabinet	4	19
Executive assistants	3	5
Judiciary	3	3
Other	9	6
	100	100
n =	604	393

These results should not be surprising, given the different political structures of the two countries. The Canadian version of cabinet government, characterized by the discipline of party-line voting, has resulted in the reduced influence of backbenchers. McGillivray quotes a lobbyist as saying, "Power of the individual member of Parliament or senator is just about zero" (1970, 164). Presthus (1974b, 46) states, "Backbenchers are largely excluded from policy determination." He quotes a federal MP, "If they lobby, they lobby the Cabinet and deputy ministers. They know we have no power." A Quebec deputy is quoted as saying, "An ordinary member can't do enough to make it worthwhile for a lobbyist to see him. It occurs at a higher level" (Presthus, 1974c, 248). Van Loon and Whittington summarize the view that the cabinet and the civil service are where the real decision-making power resides:

Modern government in Canada concentrates the bulk of power in the cabinet and the bureaucracy. Parliament, therefore, is not likely to provide interest groups with a successful arena. As one experi-

enced lobbyist said, "When I see members of Parliament being lobbied, it's a sure sign to me that the lobby lost its fight in the civil
service and the cabinet." He might have added that while the group
lobbying MP's may occasionally win some temporary victory, its
chances of success in the longer run are slight unless they can convince some cabinet ministers as well. Most interest groups and their
agents in Ottawa acknowledge this fact, yet it is surprising how
much effort occasionally goes into a pressure campaign when legislation is before Parliament. (1970, 293)

A more recent survey by Litvak (1983, 38) of 143 national trade associations in Canada with an annual budget of at least $100 000 found
that "senior civil servants are by far the most frequently contacted government members, followed by junior middle-level civil servants and
the Cabinet." An experienced government relations consultant, Bill Lee,
insists that "85 percent of all government decisions are taken by officials"
(quoted in Whittington 1981, p. G1). If this is the case — and one would
want to distinguish among the *types* of decisions being made — then the
lobbyist must focus his or her efforts on those who actually make (or
strongly contribute to) the decisions in question. Lee continues:

> In many cases, the minister's not the guy he should be talking to. If
> the businessman can talk to a public servant and convince him that
> what the government has in mind is detrimental to the public interest
> — that it may cost jobs or trade opportunities, for example — the
> public servant likely will not do it. (Quoted in Whittington 1981,
> p. G13)

3.2 Mandarin Power

The cabinet in Canada has a monopoly over the supply of legislative
initiatives that are likely to be enacted. In turn, the cabinet is supported
by a cadre of "permanent" officials (both in line departments and central agencies) who provide policy advice and administer the programs
legally mandated by the government and the legislature. Political scientist Hugh Whalen (1961) puts the matter this way: "Notwithstanding
our elaborate mythology on such subjects as parliamentary supremacy,
ministerial responsibility and the rule of law, it is now clear that officials
design and execute policy because of their technical skills, and because
of the wider discretion that accompanies the growth of governmental
functions." Vis-à-vis where the power lies, Ottawa and Washington are
quite different capitals. In Washington, the experienced lobbyist will
devote much of his or her effort to courting individual legislators, especially the chairpersons of committees and subcommittees that initiate
and in many cases decide the fate of legislation. The situation is quite
different in Ottawa.[3]

Robert Lewis, writing in *Maclean's* in May 1982, emphasized — and exaggerated — the power of the "mandarins" or senior public servants in Ottawa:

> It is the age of mandarin power in Ottawa. Parliament, with only ringing exceptions, has become a rubber stamp, with little real control over the public purse. Government regulations, drafted by bureaucrats, customarily pass in secret on the distracted nod of ministers at the rate of more than 3000 per year. The tourists throng the corridors of power this spring to catch a glimpse of Question Period, but the real decisions are made out back in the mandarin grove. (1982, 20)

But Lewis is not alone in his assessment. He quotes the former leader of the Conservative party, Robert Stanfield, as saying, "More and more matters are being decided by and implemented by the bureaucracy." Mitchell Sharp, both a former deputy minister and a Liberal minister, is quoted as saying that in most cases senior public servants "have a greater influence upon the course of events than have ministers, particularly the less competent ministers." Speaking as a former prime minister and as leader of the opposition, Joe Clark stated that "the appointed government decides more than the elected government does" (Lewis 1982, 20).

The reason that Parliament has little or no control over the public purse is not due to the machinations of senior bureaucrats. It is due to the institutional design of the Canadian variant of the Westminster model of government. The real battles over public money go on behind closed doors among scores of departments and agencies in the months leading up to the tabling of the annual *Estimates*, that is, planned budgetary expenditures. These battles are fought among bureaucrats and among ministers. "Spending" departments, such as Health and Welfare, Defence, Transport and others, go "head to head" with those departments and agencies that try to control expenditures, notably the Treasury Board and the Department of Finance. Individual spending ministers fight with each other in what is perceived largely as a constant-sum game: if Department A gets more, Departments B, C, etc., get less. If Parliament has no control over the *Estimates* (other than to vote its approval as presented), it is precisely because the cabinet wants it that way. The fact is that no cabinet wants to reduce its own power, and one of the critical forms of power in any government is the power to allocate resources — and the critical resource is money. With enough of it, most other resources can be purchased.

The power of middle- to senior-level bureaucrats stems from several sources. First, they often have more specialized and comprehensive information on public policy than do outsiders. Hence, they are often seen as authoritative on what is currently considered to be both possible and advisable. Second, ministers, in practice, have little control over the career progress of the permanent public servants in their department. They frequently are not able to pick their own deputy minister. That is done by the Committee of Senior Officials in the PCO in conjunction with the prime minister. Third, under the Trudeau government the rate of turnover of both ministers and deputy ministers increased greatly over previous decades (see Royal Commission on Financial Management and Accountability 1979). Therefore, longer-serving, lower-level officials supplied the continuity and had greater staying power in advancing policy initiatives.

Fourth, senior bureaucrats — if they have a mind to do so — have ways of circumventing the wishes and policy directions of their ministers. In Washington, they use the phrase "bureaucratic repeal" to refer to situations where professional public servants refuse to enforce legislation they feel is undesirable (e.g., the Robinson Patman Act). More generally, bureaucrats can get their way by such activities as providing incomplete information, "rigging" the set of policy options they provide, by collusion with other senior bureaucrats to "pre-cook" the full range of advice received by different ministers, playing one minister off against another, or manipulating the time available for decisions. In the bureaucratic farce *Don't Despair, Fonctionnaire* by Chris Burke, one of the more experienced public servants advises a junior: "Our job is to keep those politicians happy — so that we can get on with running the country."

Fifth, departmental officials who develop policy initiatives have power because of their greater command over resources than most other potential initiators of policy. They have bigger budgets, larger numbers of staff, and greater access to other sources of information (in theory the entire government apparatus, but in practice this is sharply limited by rivalries among departments and agencies).

> A typical government department in Ottawa has rather large policy planning, policy coordination, and policy and program evaluation units. Headed by an assistant deputy minister and directors general, these units are "plugged" into the system in Ottawa or into central agencies and other policy units in other departments. (Savoie 1983, 518)

Sixth, departmental bureaucrats can often have greater influence than ministers in shaping public policy because ministers are overloaded — they are required to play too many roles. They are MPs who have to look after their constituency; they are also the administrative head of a government department that may allocate billions of dollars. Ministers often have special political responsibilities for a particular regional or sectional interest in the government. They are members of that critical collectivity, the cabinet, which means they are inundated with thousands of pages of documents concerning other departments. As head of a department and member of cabinet, an individual minister must be a front-line advocate and defender of the government in the Commons, before committees, and in a variety of public forums. Robert Lewis observes they are "weighed down by three-inch-thick briefing books that they don't have time to read, [they] flit between caucus, question [period], committees and contituency [matters]" (1982, 21). In summary, the many roles a minister is called upon to play divides his or her time and attention, making it easier for specialists who concentrate on a narrow domain to have a great deal of influence in making public policy.

3.3 Dealing with the Bureaucracy

A senior civil servant, as quoted in an article in the *Financial Post*, described the locus for influencing government in Canada in the fol lowing way:

> People who really want to guide and influence government policy are wasting their time dealing with members of parliament, senators and, usually, even ministers. If you want results — rather than just the satisfaction of talking to the prominent   you deal with us, and at various levels. . . . To produce results you need to see the key planners, who may be way down in the system, and you see them early enough to push for changes in policy before it is politically embarrassing to make them. (Baxter 1977, 206)

It is apparent that Canadian interest groups recognize the importance of the bureaucracy in the formulation of policy, and lobby accordingly. As Litvak points out: "One indication of the influence of the civil service is that by far the largest number of Cabinet documents [about 600 per year] are written within the bureaucracy. For this reason alone, it is crucial for business interest groups to maintain open and strong ties with the civil service" (1983, 47).

In dealing with the bureaucracy, however, lobbyists need to appreciate that it is a formal hierarchy and it is necessary to enter at the appropriate level and move through the chain of authority rather than try to use political clout to overcome the resistance of lower-level officials. As one writer remarks, "One of the most common mistakes businessmen make is that they take their case directly to the ministerial level rather than start at the administrative level [of the public service] — where the legwork gets done. It's rather like doing business with a company. . . . You transact your business with management before you go to the president."[4] Companies seeking financial assistance from government often make the mistake of trying to use political clout either to expedite the process or to increase their chances of success. However, "that process can shut as many doors as it can open . . . if you try to circumvent the bureaucratic process, civil servants will close ranks against you," noted a management consultant very familiar with the scores of industrial assistance programs in Ottawa.[5]

The time for resort to political clout is *after* you have gone through the front door, followed all the rules, filed all the required documents, met with the appropriate program administrators, and still feel that you have been hard done by. Ministers are not in the business of trying to do the work they delegate to technical specialists in the bureaucracy. They are, however, in the business of exercising discretion on policy matters in areas where well-defined rules do not exist or as a "court of appeal" in the application of rules and procedures by the bureaucracy.

Moreover, the one-shot or crisis approach is less effective over the long haul than are efforts to develop "an ongoing rapport with bureaucrats and elected officials [so as to] stay abreast of subtle shifts in policy."[6] However, ongoing relationships can be disrupted by shifts in personnel within the bureaucracy. Charlotte Gray describes the response of sophisticated lobbyists as follows:

> In the 1970s cabinet ministers as well as mandarins were being shunted among government departments at dizzying speed. The perception soon developed that only second-rank bureaucrats — assistant deputy ministers, directors general, directors — had a grip on the issues. They had hands-on experience, they'd developed policy, and they held the reins of power. They were the people lobby groups had to cozy up to. Obviously, their former colleagues were the ideal bridge-builders. They spoke the same language, understood each other. (1983, 12)

This point is also emphasized by Jim Bennett, a lobbyist for CFIB and a former special assistant to two federal Liberal ministers: "You start down in the bureaucracy. With an analysis that bespeaks his years in Ottawa, Mr. Bennett describes the goal as starting '. . . at the level of director or director-general' where policies have their birth."[7]

This point is strongly emphasized by Andrew Roman, general counsel of the Public Interest Advocacy Centre. He notes that the deputy minister and assistant deputy ministers

> rely, for most of their initiatives, on employees with a myriad of classifications who might be considered the privates or corporals. Such a person might characteristically be under thirty years old, a few years out of university, and a generalist with five years' experience spread across two or three departments of government, but with no specialized knowledge in any particular field. In preparing any policy, such a person would survey some of the literature, do a bit of thinking and talking around the office, bounce his ideas off a

few of the affected groups, and prepare a draft Cabinet document. Even with this hasty and somewhat superficial basis for policy formulation the originator of the "cab doc" would have a great advantage over anyone above him in the departmental hierarchy. He would now be the department's authority on the subject, and for reasons of organizational solidarity, his superiors would feel compelled to defend his views against "outsiders" once the "cab doc" has gone up the ladder. It is absolutely crucial for those who wish to influence the governmental process on an on-going basis to identify the policymaking privates and corporals and to present their ideas and needs to them at an early stage. Then, the effective lobbyist will maintain contact with the project as it goes up through the department, making sure that he talks to every rung on the ladder. If you forget to talk to someone, he or she may be offended, and may influence the policy to your detriment. (1978, 214–15)

4.0 CABINET MINISTERS AS TARGETS

4.1. Cabinet: Roles and Functions

While the prime minister has been aptly described as being at the apex of power in a parliamentary democracy, it is the prime minister together with his or her cabinet that form the government of the day. The centre of power and the political authority of the executive is the cabinet. It has been described as a "periodically elected, collective kingship." Some indication of the importance of the cabinet in shaping public policy is the following partial list of its functions:

- The cabinet supplies (introduces) new legislation (and amendments to existing statutes) to the legislature.
- The cabinet supplies and enacts subordinate legislation (orders-in-council, regulations, etc.).
- The cabinet establishes the government's broad priorities in terms of policies, people, legislation, and resources.
- The cabinet makes several thousand order-in-council appointments.
- The cabinet acts as an appeal body regarding certain decisions by some regulatory agencies (e.g., the federal cabinet at its discretion may hear appeals on airline route awards made by the CTC).

Individually and collectively, the cabinet is responsible to the legislature for the administration of the full range of activities of the government; that is, ministers individually are heads of their departments and supervise the work of the "permanent" civil servants who carry out the details of implementing the programs and policies approved by the legislature or cabinet. Individually, ministers also have considerable discretion in dealing with matters within their own department.

4.2 Evolution of Cabinet

Van Loon (1985, 414) notes that "over the past fifteen years the Cabinet has evolved from a single decision-making body to a series of committees which possess considerable autonomy within their own spheres of activity." He points out that the work of the full cabinet is "now delegated to a major central coordinating committee (Priorities and Planning) and to a series of sectoral or 'policy' committees." He states (1985, 415) that "the Treasury Board and the closely related Government Operations Committee act as *de facto* boards of management for government, the Legislation and House Planning Committee manages all aspects of the government's legislative program, and the Government Communications Committee attempts to coordinate dissemination of information about government programs."

The Priorities and Planning Committee is of special importance. It is the "inner cabinet" and membership is highly prized by ministers. Van Loon (1985, 417) indicates that it performs four major roles: (1) it allocates budgets to the standing (policy area) committees — these are the envelopes in the new envelope budgeting system; (2) it reviews all the decisions of other committees, although this usually amounts to ratification; (3) it "deals directly with big or important issues or those that cut across the lines of responsibility of other committees"; and (4) "it has some funds and program responsibilities of its own, such as equalization payments to the provinces."

4.3 Cabinet Support Systems

Van Loon notes that

> since the late 1960s the role of the PCO has evolved from that of an agency almost entirely concerned with moving paper to Cabinet, through an attempt to coordinate all aspects of government policy, to a position of arbiter of much of the machinery and process in government and as briefer of the prime minister on the activities of the government. These latter tasks are now combined with the functions of providing major logistical support for the Cabinet. (1985, 420)

For example, the PCO provides secretariats (four to eight officials) for each cabinet committee. There are also units in the PCO dealing with the machinery of government and for senior personnel. While the PMO by definition focuses on political and partisan considerations, the PCO members are politically neutral career civil servants who provide policy and technical advice to whichever party forms the government.

Figure 7-4 describes the extensive network of advisory agencies supporting the work of the cabinet.

Figure 7–4
EXECUTIVE SUPPORT AGENCIES FOR PRIORITY DETERMINATION

Partisan Political Advisors	• Prime Minister's Office (PMO) • Individual Ministerial Staffs
Process and Procedure Advisors	• Privy Council Office (PCO) • Federal-Provincial Relations Office (FPRO)
Policy Design and Integration Advisors	• Ministries of State for Economic and Social Development • Department of Finance • Department of Finance • Federal-Provincial Relations Office (FPRO) • Treasury Board
Financial Advisors	• Department of Finance • Treasury Board Secretariat • Ministries of State for Economic and Social Development
Ad Hoc Advisors	• Royal Commissions, Task Forces, Parliamentary Advisory Committees

Source: Van Loon (1985, 419).

4.4 The Changing Role of Individual Ministers

Power in the federal government appears to be concentrated in the cabinet, but in fact it is quite widely dispersed, argues Hugh Faulkner (1982), formerly a minister in the Trudeau government. Individual ministers need the support of their cabinet colleagues, the caucus, and public opinion. Moreover, successful implementation requires the active support of the bureaucracy. Certain structural and procedural changes have operated to disperse power in Ottawa: new ministries have been created; the new policy and expenditures management system (budget envelopes) has increased collegial interdependency (see Van Loon 1985); central agencies have become more important, that is, PMO, PCO, TB (Campbell & Szablowski 1979); the number of advisory and regulatory bodies with inputs to policy have increased; and in some cases (e.g., the Quebec caucus of the Liberals), MPs have created a greater role for themselves (Faulkner 1982, 243–44; see also Gillies 1981 on this point).

It appears that Prime Minister Mulroney has sought to increase the influence of the PMO in Ottawa policy making. He increased its total annual operating cost from $4.35 million under Trudeau to $6.7 million. The total staff complement increased from 90 under Trudeau to 114. The number of policy advisors has increased from 3 under Trudeau to 13. The PMO has taken over some of the functions previously performed in the PCO. The PMO has also sought greater control over the communications function and political appointments: "Under Mulroney the PMO has taken on the task of reviewing all major press statements by cabinet ministers before they can be released as well as clearing all important patronage appointments and senior hirings by cabinet ministers."[8]

Michael Kirby, who has held senior positions in both the PMO and PCO under Trudeau, says that changes in the size and roles of the PMO under Mulroney amount to a shift of power into the prime minister's hands and those of his closest advisors: "To the extent that you control putting the right people in place and control what the government says, you have an enormous impact that spreads your power very wide. That would appear to contradict the image of decentralized power that is being cultivated by this government."[9]

Bill Neville, chairperson of Public Affairs International and a former chief of staff for Joe Clark when he was prime minister in 1979–80, describes how in the early months of the new Conservative government the prime minister and his ministers sought to gain and exercise firm political control over the federal government:

> The prime minister is firmly in control of this government, especially in strategic terms, and will continue to be involved directly and decisively in charting its overall course and resolving the major issues before it. The Planning and Priorities Committee is his prime vehicle for doing just that. More questionable at this early stage is who will exercise significant influence over the deliberations of that committee, other than the prime minister himself and the 14 ministers who sit on it with him. . . . Restoration of ministerial stature and authority certainly is one of the political goals of the Mulroney government. In addition to changes in the cabinet committee structure, the prime minister has taken other initiatives towards this objective. While other issues, including the election of 211 MPs, unquestionably influenced the size and shape of his cabinet, the prime minister was attracted to a 40-member ministry as one way to divide the government into more politically manageable units. Moves to increase the size and seniority of ministers' personal staffs also were designed to give cabinet members more resources to help them control directional issues within their own offices and less within the public service bureaucracy. Finally, the emphasis placed on individual ministers as focal points for much of the consultative process was a further effort to signal an enhanced role for them within the system. (1985, 14)

4.5 A Symbiotic Relationship

The relationship between interest groups and cabinet ministers is symbiotic. Faulkner (1982) argues that the politician is often an interest

group's most important ally in obtaining a change in policy or new legislation, and on the other hand, interest groups provide information
and political support. Yet many groups perceive the relationship as
adversarial rather than cooperative, but that may change as groups
become more sophisticated about how to influence public policy.

"The best way to influence the executive is to influence the advice the
executive receives" (Faulkner 1982, 242), for ministers are overextended
and have to rely on the advice of officials (see MacDonald 1980). Contact with the bureaucracy is multifaceted, diffuse, and often confidential. Groups must recognize that "most civil servants are professionally
disposed to push or recommend a policy that is likely to achieve political
support both at the cabinet level and within the civil service" (Faulkner
1982, 242).

4.6 The Importance of Cabinet Ministers as Targets

In section 3 I have noted that senior bureaucrats can and often do exercise a great deal of power in the formulation of public policy in Canada.
It would be wrong, however, for the reader to conclude that they routinely dominate the process and, in particular, routinely exercise more
power (or have more influence) than their minister or the cabinet collectively. The importance of bureaucrats in the process varies greatly
depending on the policy or program, the department or agency involved,
the ability of both bureaucrats and ministers, and particularly their minister's view of the proper role of bureaucrats in the policy process. It should
be clear that where ministers are determined to dominate the policy-
making process, they can do so provided they are sufficiently energetic
and can obtain high-quality advice from sources independent of the
departmental and central agency bureaucracies. Yet ministers who wish to
have a major role in policy formulation will be more successful if they
try to avoid an adversarial relationship with their senior officials. If they
treat them as the neutral professionals they are supposed to be, but at
the same time ask tough questions based on their own analyses and the
advice of independent advisors, they are more likely to create allies and
supporters rather than potential "enemies."

For lobbyists, ministers are important targets for several reasons. First,
they are the apex of power regarding most policy and administrative
matters in their departments and can exercise a great deal of discretion
(they can overrule their public servants, although not always with the
best results for themselves as the "tainted tuna affair" in September 1985
indicated).[10] Second, without a minister's signature departmental initiatives cannot be put forward for consideration by cabinet. This constitutes a negative form of power and has distinct limits. However, a minister
can use it to influence his or her own officials and to put forward his or
her own policy initiatives.

Third, in a country that provides its executives with great discretionary power, often used to facilitate administrative convenience, cabinet ministers provide an important counterweight because they are more concerned with the political aspects of policy making. They keep considerations of popular support, responsiveness to various interests, and what is acceptable to public opinion at the forefront. Walter Stewart, writing in praise of politicians, notes that they are "weird birds, patient enough to weave together compromises, open enough to absorb a lot of good and bad advice, conscientious enough to perform hundreds of chores that make up the bulk of their work, smart enough to sound agreeable to a lot of disagreeable onlookers and honest enough to withstand the kind of scrutiny few businessmen and fewer journalists could survive" (1981, 67). In his view, complex and interventionist government is here to stay, and to make it more responsive we must increase our awareness and participation in politics. The greatest virtue of politicians — unlike the bureaucrats, pollsters, and lobbyists — according to Stewart, is that they are within reach of the ballot box. Cabinet ministers, individually and jointly, provide the political authority for policy making. They are the primary target for political arguments over the value judgments of who ought to get what.

Fourth, cabinet ministers are important targets if the object of the interest group is to obtain changes in a bill that has been given First Reading. The best way to get changes is to persuade the minister — usually at the stage of committee hearings — that he or she should propose amendments to his or her own bill. Admittedly, it is usually difficult to get changes when a policy has reached that stage, but it may be worth the effort. For example, several industry groups were able to obtain beneficial amendments to the bill incorporating the Stage I amendments to the Combines Investigation Act during committee hearings in 1975. The minister of consumer and corporate affairs' set of amendments reflected the pressure exerted by certain franchisors (e.g., Canadian Tire), soft-drink bottlers, the real estate industry, securities dealers, and newspaper publishers. See Stanbury (1977, 182–84).

Fifth, cabinet ministers have control over various modes of access to the most senior people in their department, both political and bureaucratic. It is they who decide to set up permanent or ad hoc advisory committees of outsiders and who shall be appointed to them. Such committees provide an institutionalized method of access to the policy-making process for the representatives of interest groups appointed to them. Ministers also consult informally with interest groups by using their own exempt staff, by appointing an ad hoc outside advisor, or by personal contact. For example, the Conservative minister of consumer and corporate affairs, Michel Côté, during the preparation of proposed amendments to the Combines Investigation Act (which later became Bill C-91), engaged Bill McKeowen, a Tory lawyer and former senior official in the

Bureau of Competition Policy, as his "personal emissary" to discuss amendments to competition policy legislation with business associations (BCNI, CMA, CCC, etc.), individual senior executives, and prominent lawyers. The minister also appointed a special advisory committee composed of representatives of consumer groups, the media, the legal community, and interested citizens. However, it had much less influence than business interests.

5.0 PARAPOLITICAL BUREAUCRACY/EXEMPT STAFF

Blair Williams (1980, 215) defines the parapolitical bureaucracy as "those individuals who are employed in the public sector paid from the public purse, but who perform tasks largely for partisan purposes." These individuals are "hired specifically to assist elected officials in their role as politicians as opposed to their roles as policy-makers, legislators or administrators." Individuals in the parapolitical bureaucracy fall into four principal categories:

- assistants to MPs (each MP has a budget to hire several people to help run his or her office);
- the party caucus research bureaus (since 1968 each party has had a budget allotment to hire research personnel to support MPs in their work);
- the Prime Minister's Office; and
- the "exempt staff" of cabinet ministers.

Individual cabinet ministers traditionally have had the right to choose the members of their office staff who are paid out of a specified budget of public funds. Ministerial aides are usually referred to as "exempt staff," as their hiring and firing is not subject to the rules and regulations of the Public Service Commission. Typically, each federal minister employs at least one-half-dozen special assistants, administrative assistants, executive assistants, or special advisors. This is in addition to the secretarial/administrative/clerical staff, which is about twice as large.

The new Mulroney government, reflecting both the growth of ministerial staffs since the late 1960s and the Conservatives' desire to exert political control over the bureaucracy, created a new senior position in each minister's office: the chief of staff or *chef de cabinet*. Among the wags and cynics in Ottawa, this person is described as "the political commissar." But this function is hardly a new one. Tilley quotes a former minister as saying that ministerial aides "have to look at everything from a political perspective as opposed to primarily a departmental or civil service perspective. . . . Otherwise, there wouldn't be any real purpose to having a personal staff. You could rely on the public service to be your staff" (1977, 413).

Exempt staff are usually young and ambitious, and many have often worked for the party or individual candidates. As Williams puts it, "In general, ministers' offices are made up of young, upwardly mobile, relatively well-educated individuals who regard their stint in Ottawa as a valuable stepping stone on their way to a more permanent career" (1980, 221). That career may be in politics, in the permanent bureaucracy, or in business (including government relations positions or consulting).

While frequently said to be well educated, exempt staff often have no training or experience directly relevant to the policy issues they and their minister must deal with. However, their youth, level of education, and most of all their closeness to power often mean they have only a modest interest in or respect for the old hands in the regular bureaucracy. The loyalty of exempt staff is primarily to their minister personally and secondarily to their party. Their stock rises and falls with their minister, although it is not unknown for an experienced aide to move from one minister's office to another, or to have more experience in running a minister's office than a newly appointed minister.

Savoie (1983, 514) notes that ten of the twenty ministerial assistants he interviewed "had either no other work experience or had worked in another minister's office or in a member of Parliament's office before joining the minister's office they were with at the time of the survey." He also found that of the twenty surveyed, two had two university degrees, eleven had one degree, and seven had no university degree. These two facts led Savoie to question the competence of ministerial staff. He also noted that on the basis of their education and experience these ministerial aides would, if they were in the public service, have been at the relatively junior and middle levels and it is unlikely that they would have been in any policy, planning, or research units. The characteristics of ministerial aides may be explained by three factors: the low level of pay for the positions; the low degree of job security afforded by such positions; and the poor prospects for advancement within the units in which they presently work.

Williams (1980, 222) states that the activities of exempt staff can be grouped into four categories: planning, organization, and administration of the office itself; liaison (with the minister's constituency, the party, the department, MPs/caucus, other ministers); public relations (i.e., ensuring that the minister has a favourable profile in the media); and research (not so much original research as making effective use of existing materials to support the wide range of activities of a minister).

Tilley reports that ministerial aides emphasized the following two points about their roles:

> First, they felt it was their job to keep their minister aware of all potential and continuing problems and issues within his department and constituency and to bring these to his attention before they got out of hand. Second, they believed they were public relations persons for their minister, that they should keep his image

before the public and try to insure that the image presented was as favourable as possible. In addition, the respondents saw their function as one of handling routine inquiries and questions and generally administering the office in order to allow the minister to make the best use of his time for matters that were indeed important. Closely related to this duty was that of obtaining and preparing material in concise form for the minister. (1977, 413)

In addition, because each minister has an aide in charge of his or her constituency and the political affairs of his or her region, this individual can be a useful point of contact for interest groups where their problem directly affects either of these domains.

The role of an individual ministerial aide varies greatly, as Bill Lee, a former executive assistant, has pointed out:

The Ministerial Executive Assistant can be anything from an extremely powerful, policy-influencing, unelected official to a glorified, overpaid baggage-handler. . . . His actual place in this spectrum depends upon many things: the breadth of responsibility and authority the Minister wishes to have him assume; the background and capabilities of the aide; plus such other associated matters as the nature of the Department, the attitude of co-operation or intransigence of the Deputy Minister and other senior civil servants; and the ability and capacity for work of other ministerial staff members. (Quoted in Lenoski 1977, 169)

Lenoski (1977, 167) describes ministerial aides as "middlemen" who are "the functional dividing line between politics and administration." He continues, "Their chief preoccupation is to serve, and in the process to further, each minister's aims and interests according to his specific departmental responsibilities combined with his general political duties inside and outside the Cabinet as determined by regional and other representational factors."

Savoie (1983, 518) states that, on the basis of his interviews with ministerial aides, they "have no appreciable influence on shaping government policies and programs." However, "in some isolated instances, ministerial assistants were able to stop or delay initiatives before they were brought to cabinet committee." They did this by pointing out what they saw as problems to their minister. Savoie does state that ministerial aides do influence the timing of announcements of policy actions so as to maximize their political advantage. In a similar vein, Lenoski argues that while a minister's exempt staff may have "only a peripheral impact on policy development, they can, however, exert a substantially controlling influence in the process of making policy" (1977, 168). The degree to which they are able to do so depends on their own capabilities, their minister's support, and the cooperation of the civil service.

A completely different view of the role of ministers' exempt staff is provided by Andrew Roman, a former executive assistant to a minister:

> Let me share with you the innermost secret of lobbying, by letting you in on a little known fact I discovered a few years ago: The Government of Canada is secretly being run by persons earning no more than $20,000 a year. Anyone who has worked for a minister can tell you that it is a rare minister who runs his department, or even knows what is going on in it. He spends a great deal of his time attending Cabinet meetings and handling onerous political responsibilities for his region of the country, his constituency and the party. The Cabinet minister has become an institution, whose time is planned on flow charts by his staff, whose correspondence is written for him, and whose information is carefully filtered and selected by those around him. Given these facts, not only might you have to wait several weeks to get an appointment with a minister, the chances are you will be given no more than fifteen minutes to half an hour, following which audience, the matter will be turned over to his staff for follow-up and decision. While the minister undoubtedly has a veto, he really cannot do much more than prevent others from doing something he considers foolish, since he does not himself have the time to move levers to get things done the way he might want them done. (1978, 214)

While Williams emphasizes that the parapolitical bureaucracy focuses on partisan politics rather than on politicians' roles as legislators, policy makers, or administrators, it is all but impossible to separate — particularly in a minister's office — politics from policy making. What roles do a minister's exempt staff play that bear upon policy making? First, they exercise some control over access to the minister. Second, some exempt staff are privy to intradepartmental papers and cabinet documents. One of their primary tasks is to analyze such material for its political repercussions for their minister, both as an individual MP and as a member of cabinet. Third, they act as the eyes, ears, and arms of the minister in dealing with (1) his or her constituency and (2) the public servants in the department. Tilley reports the comments of a deputy minister on the role of exempt staff in this regard as follows:

> A most obvious reason, I think, is that particularly in our system, ministers are extraordinarily tied-up. You have the minister in Parliament, . . . he can't be reached or contacted. He sits in cabinet, he can't be reached or contacted by his deputy minister or by his department. He sits in caucus, he can't be contacted. He has his constituency to worry about, he can't be contacted. The nature of his responsibilities in the Parliamentary system are so overwhelming and so arduous that it is often the case that ministers get a chance

to focus only rarely on administrative responsibilities in terms of their portfolio. . . . So in many, many ways I think the only way that one can dialogue with a minister, get his response, find out what he thinks, is through a member of his personal staff who is with him all the time or is closely available to him in his outer office or on the plane. (1977, 413)

Savoie (1983, 512–13) notes that "in more recent years, ministers' staff, notably executive assistants, have had to deal with lobbyists. Executive assistants report, however, that they sense they are frequently the last resort of lobbyists. That is, experienced lobbyists in Ottawa have established channels of communication with senior departmental officials." He continues:

When it is clear that the department is coming forward with a recommendation or in some instances a decision that runs counter to the position of a lobbyist's client the executive assistant can become the access point to the minister. Executive assistants reveal, however, that such instances are much less frequent than what one would imagine. They suggest that lobbyists tend to turn more to central agency officials to challenge a departmental position than to ministers' offices.

This finding is surprising, but it may reflect the period when Savoie did his interviews (apparently between 1980 and 1982), which may have been marked by the peak in the importance of senior departmental and central agency bureaucrats in shaping government policy. See, for example, Gillies (1981), Kirby (1978), Campbell (1985), Lewis (1982), and Van Loon (1985). It seems clear that even within the Liberal party there was a reaction against the decline in political control/influence in the making of public policy. Certainly the Mulroney government, as noted, has made noticeable efforts to increase the role of ministers, and particularly of the prime minister, in the formulation of policy.

Williams correctly emphasizes the use of publicly paid employees for wholly partisan purposes: "Ministerial aides can rightly be regarded as a phalanx of highly motivated, well-informed, organizationally competent individuals who can perform valuable services on behalf of the governing party during and between elections" (1980, 225).

6.0 MPs AS THE TARGETS OF LOBBYING

6.1 How Important Are MPs?

The conventional wisdom is that MPs and parliamentary committees, with very few exceptions, are not important targets of lobbying efforts. For example, when he was prime minister, Pierre Trudeau described backbench MPs as "nobodies" when they were a few yards off Parliament Hill. While putting it crudely, Trudeau was expressing a home truth in terms of the role of MPs in formulating public policy. The concentration of the power over policy making in the cabinet, its committees, and in those who give advice behind closed doors means that MPs serve different roles, as George Bain points out: "This leaves the backbenchers as tokens to be counted, first, to see which side has more and thus gets to form the government, and subsequently to provide figures for vote tallies in *Hansard*. They do not legislate so much as they ratify, and they examine only what is allowed them to examine."[11]

From time to time, individual MPs acknowledge publicly that they have a very modest role in the shaping of public policy. For example, in the recent *Report of the Special Committee on Reform of the House of Commons*, new Conservative MP Barbara Sparrow (Calgary South) is quoted as saying:

> I am absolutely amazed at how little input private members have into the formulation of legislation, policies and/or regulations. It appears to me that most of the time we are told what a minister will be announcing in 48 hours and we do not have access, any means to study or contribute or change the finished product. But members must go to their constituencies to explain and support the decision of the government. Sometimes this is extremely difficult. (McGrath 1985, 1)

As the *Report* makes clear, MPs on both sides of the House want to change this situation. They want a larger role in the sun. However, it would be surprising to learn that the current holders of power (the prime minister and the cabinet) have any interest in voluntarily reducing their ability to produce intended results, which is the core of the concept of power. Bain explains the significance of institutional changes that would give MPs a greater role in the policy and legislative system:

> Giving MPs more say means giving them more independence, and more power to initiate; which means both more interference from the Opposition and less party discipline; which means weakening the hold that governments have on power (at least in times when the balance in the House is closer than it is now); which means perhaps accepting that governments should serve for a fixed term and be relieved of the risk of being defeated on votes of non-confidence in the House; which means a fundamental departure from the idea of responsible government.[12]

Bain notes that "most MPs are good people. They are conscientious and work hard. They are driven, most of them, by an irrational urge to Do Something for the country. They often make substantial personal sacrifices to be MPs."[13] Unfortunately, apart from their legislative ("I always voted at my party's call"), watchdog ("The duty of the opposition is to oppose"), and constituents' ombudsman (helping out the little people caught in the toils of the system) roles, they play a very small part in the formulation of public policy. Occasionally, the cabinet may take the political advice of their backbenchers, "although even there the MPs increasingly are supplanted by the quasi-scientific head counters of the polling organizations as sources of advice on what the country can or cannot be made to swallow without gagging." Bain continues, "For ideas about policy and legislation, the real stuff of government, the cabinet relies on the bureaucrats."[14]

How do lobbyists see MPs as targets of their efforts? Litvak (1982, 39) reports only 6 percent of his sample of 101 national trade associations (NTAs) rank interaction with government MPs as "very important" in terms of their contacts with government. The figure for "appearances before Parliamentary committees" is 21 percent. Jim Gillies, a former MP, later senior advisor to Joe Clark, and now an academic, has described testimony before committees as "useless." In contrast, "interaction with senior-level civil servants" was rated as "very important" by 75 percent of NTAs and interaction with cabinet ministers was rated as "very important" by 50 percent. Gillies and Pigott go so far as to argue that lobbyists may have more impact on *opposition* MPs than on the government:

> Government policy is normally developed by the cabinet with the aid of the public service; ministers have their departmental specialists and rely on them. Government backbenchers must follow cabinet's lead. The opposition parties on the other hand have small research staffs and therefore anyone bringing information about the consequences of legislation to the MP who has the responsibility of following it for his part is usually welcomed warmly. The well-informed leader of a special interest group, therefore, can have an impact on the formulations of policy by opposition parties. (1982, 257)

What they ignore, however, is the fact that a majority government, in principle, has the power to enact almost whatever it wants — regardless of the opposition. It is, however, constrained by the Constitution, adverse public opinion (as reflected by and amplified in the media), and the amount of time until the next election.

Since power tends to seek power, interest groups devote their efforts to the cabinet and the key figures in the bureaucracy. If this is true, why do legislators in the figures given above slightly outrank the cabinet as the prime target of the interest groups' activities? Presthus attributes this to the growing importance of committees in the Canadian legislative process. Of particular importance are certain members of committees, for example, the chairperson.[15] More important, says Presthus, is the apparent division of labour between the cabinet and backbenchers. The former concentrates on substantive policy issues, while the latter deals with the demands of the constituents. Since "a high proportion of Canadians feel considerable diffidence[16] in approaching federal (and, by inference, provincial) officials," they use interest-group representatives to intercede on their behalf (Presthus 1974c, 248). Apparently for some groups, or for some issues, backbenchers constitute the preferred point of access. There are some other reasons for talking to backbenchers, despite their alleged lack of importance in the policy process: (1) a significant number of lobbyists may simply not ''nderstand the system and not realize that backbenchers have little influence; and (2) lobbying backbenchers may be seen to be an investment in the future. Jackson and Atkinson remark:

> Lobbying both the individual legislator and the committee system represent long-term interest group investment. In majority governments and even in minority situations, individual legislators are unable to alter dramatically the course of public policy. Throughout the legislative system responsibility and control of legislation rests in the hands of the government. The Canadian Parliament, as we have already suggested, does not make laws, it passes them. (1974, 37–38)

Alternatively, one can point out that some backbenchers obviously become cabinet ministers in time. A little gentle courting in the past is probably remembered when the MP is elevated to the cabinet. In any event, an interest group would be unwise to openly snub backbenchers, even if they possess limited influence. Ignoring MPs ignores the potential influence of the party caucus. Jackson and Atkinson state:

> Before a bill is introduced in the House an outline of the new policy direction is given to the government caucus. At the weekly meetings which follow, caucus members are given opportunities to express the sentiments and grievances of interest groups. Even when the bill has been introduced for first reading in the House, caucus continues to debate the bill and sometimes prevents the moving of second reading. (1974, 36)

Jackson and Atkinson also point out:

> Members may also become good public relations agents for various interests. Although most members do not acknowledge much interest group influence in their own elections, there are strong possibilities for group activity in those constituencies where group interests are concentrated. But the major reason for constant group pressure on the backbench may be the belief that a changed opinion there may force an alteration in cabinet's position. (1974, 37)

Backbenchers themselves provide similar reasons why lobbyists try to influence individual members. Presthus's (1974c, 249–50) data indicate the majority of members (in the sample) believe that lobbyists think, however wrongly, that if they can persuade a sufficient number of backbenchers to support a given policy, they may be able, in caucus, to change the mind of the relevant minister.

6.2 MPs May Be More Important Than You Think

But is the locus of power shifting? Dann (1980) suggests that in the case of revisions to the Bank Act (completed in 1980) the "old-boy network" continued to be important, but that the committee reviewing the legislation became *more* important than previously. He notes that the hearings on the Bank Act preceding the December 1980 amendments resulted in the House Committee on Finance, Trade and Economic Affairs championing the suggested changes proposed by cattlemen, auto dealers, trust companies, and consumer groups (Dann 1980, 4). In this case, lobbying a parliamentary committee was effective for some groups.

While the main targets of lobbying continue to be the senior public servants and cabinet ministers, lobbyists are "foolish not to lobby MPs. It's not good to antagonize [them]. [They] become very involved in the really controversial issues" (an MP quoted in Dann 1980, 3). MPs appear to be having more influence, not only on committees but through caucus, the party, and their research bureau. Lobbying MPs is useful to counter the efforts of those inside the government, that is, the executive. If backbench MPs are not *seen* to be important participants in the process, they will *not* be important contributors.

MPs are generally receptive to interest-group representations. They want to appreciate the different views on policy questions. They want information on the potential effects of a change in policy/legislation.

A backbencher can often compensate for not having the immediate clout of a minister by being able to devote more attention to your problem. And although a government member can probably get a minister's ear more quickly, opposition members frequently have more flexibility to pursue a matter because they don't have to worry about embarrassing the government. Says [Walter] McLean [then a Conservative MP in opposition]: "No doors in this country are closed to me. When I want to speak to the deputy minister, he sees me."[17]

Lobbying MPs is a way of keeping in touch — and it can't hurt. It is useful to brief the party caucuses on major issues. Individual members are becoming more specialized and gaining expertise/influence on particular matters, e.g., Harvey André on oil and gas, Ged Baldwin (now retired) on freedom of information, Stanley Knowles (now retired) on poverty and pensions, and David MacDonald (now retired) on development and human rights. Some opposition members become their party's spokespersons on these issues in the House. Unlike many interest groups, the Canadian Federation of Independent Business makes a greater effort to enlist the support of ordinary MPs: "Although they try to get to the bureaucracy first, Federation [staff] members are probably unique among lobbyists in the amount of time and effort spent in trying to pressure politicians. They worry not only about ministers but also about backbenchers, and opposition backbenchers at that."[18]

Lobbying MPs complements but is not a substitute for efforts made *earlier* in the process (i.e., policy formulation, interdepartmental and central agency review, pre-drafting stage with ministers). Not only must lobbyists "get in early," they must focus on key bureaucrats and on the key ministers. However, access is one thing, effectiveness is another. The first is a necessary, but not sufficient, condition. The *quality* of the representations is very important. There should be public presentations *and* private meetings with the "movers and shakers."

MPs can, on occasion, play a valuable role as a *broker* between interest groups and the political/policy process.[19] They provide inside knowledge of how the system works, where the issue stands, who the key people are, and how to make more effective representations. MPs can: provide access ("a window on the Rideau"); provide a political perspective (while the bureaucracy provides the administrative perspective); and help identify targets and vehicles and determine timing of representations. But interest groups must appreciate that by the time MPs become directly involved (in the House and in committees), it is already late in the day.

MPs may have other uses for business interest groups, as the following quotation indicates:

- *Local information*: Politicians are often valuable sources of local commercial intelligence. That's because they are usually on the receiving end of a flood of complaints, requests, suggestions, rumors and gossip that should enable them to divine how their riding is doing economically. . . .

- *Government information*: MPs should be able to help you gain access to commercial information that government agencies have collected. Sometimes they can even persuade a bureaucrat to provide a vital piece of information that would not otherwise be available. Equally important, your MP should be able to guide you to a civil servant who has studied your industry or market and who may be prepared to offer informal advice. . . .

- *Financial assistance*: Drawing on the past experience of other constituents, your MP or MLA should be able to guide you through the bewildering maze of economic grants and incentives offered by the federal and provincial governments to the program best suited to your needs. He or she may also be able to tell you how to tailor your application to make it more likely to succeed.

- *Expediting matters*: A call or letter from your elected representative can often galvanize the civil service into action. It may still not move quickly, but at least it will move. And if your request is poised on the edge of some sheer procedural cliff, an MP or MLA can sometimes tip the balance in the right direction.[20]

6.3 Lobbying MPs

It is critical to develop succinct, clear arguments for MPs. They are busy and often harried in their efforts to play their many roles. It is helpful to tie your group's interest to specific constituencies. Remember MPs don't get elected at large, but on a riding-by-riding basis.

Some MPs are more important on particular issues than others (e.g., shadow cabinet members in the opposition). Some are more articulate and get more media coverage.

Opposition MPs can be fed material for Question Period when the House is in session. However, one must consider the possibility of setting loose an untethered cannon on a rolling deck ("With friends like this, who needs enemies?").

Some national interest groups have used the "buddy system" under which they assign a member of their group to handle the liaison between the group and each MP. The group member lives in the constituency of the MP with whom he or she is "paired." This approach has been used by the Canadian Construction Association and by the B.C. Medical Association for B.C. MLAs (see Fulton & Stanbury 1985).

When lobbying an MP, it is sometimes useful to send copies of the brief or letter to the local media in the MP's riding, reinforcing the constituency element in the group's representations.

MPs have only a very small personal staff. As in the case of lobbying a minister's executive assistant because the minister is overloaded, it now pays to try to sell the man or woman who does research and/or handles certain issues for the individual MP.

MPs have stressed the valuable contribution interest groups can make in educating MPs on specific issues. They want more information. Hard facts, presented in a reasonably neutral way, can be highly persuasive. See chapter 9, section 2.2.

7.0 HOUSE OF COMMONS COMMITTEES AS TARGETS OF LOBBYING

Interest groups should be aware that there are three types of committees:
- committees conducting inquiries: special committees and task forces;

- committees (standing or special) reviewing legislation; and
- committees studying departmental estimates (i.e., next year's expenditures).

Who testifies before parliamentary committees? Usually the decision is made jointly by the chairperson, clerk of the committee, and special advisor to the committee. However, anyone can request to be heard and send a brief. There is a problem in ensuring adequate representation from "public interest" groups (financing, free riders, expertise).

7.1 Role/Importance of Committees

The limited role of the entire committee system in Canada's Parliament must be appreciated by those proposing to make committees a target of their lobbying efforts. R. M. MacIntosh, now head of the Canadian Bankers' Association, has referred to the "farcical procedure of parliamentary committees . . . most representations are merely on-the-record prepared positions. Nobody is listening. Nobody expects a change to arise out of an appearance before a committee. . . . We get up in front of committees and make pompous statements. No one expects you to be examined on them. If you were, you would be shot down" (quoted in Dodge 1978, 15). Alfred Powis, the CEO of Noranda Mines, has said, "Parliament doesn't mean a thing except as a debating forum . . . parliamentarians . . . as far as I can see . . . are just there to vote" (quoted in Dodge 1978, 17). John Bulloch, head of the CFIB, has put it this way: "We have become probably one of the most effective lobby, pressure or political action groups . . . [and we have learned] that success is achieved by staying away from parliamentary committees and politicians and going directly to voters, key civil servants and cabinet ministers" (quoted in Dodge 1978, 18).

There are, however, important institutional reasons why parliamentary committees generally have little sway in formulating public policy. They are highly partisan in nature in most cases; thus, party discipline is maintained. There is a lack of professional support staff on an ongoing basis, although since 1982 standing committees can initiate hearings on their own initiative. Senate committees are often business lobbies from within. (They can, on occasion, undertake a serious study of important problems, e.g., poverty, and free trade with the U.S.) Committees lack financial resources (e.g., they seldom finance witnesses' travel, independent research, etc.). Members have only short tenure on committees. They depend on the PMO/House leader for their appointment. Members, because of the structure of incentives, fail to develop expertise in an area as congressmen do in the U.S. Line departments provide support only for government members. Most important, committees can obtain amendments to legislation only by "selling" the minister sponsoring it. That requires the approval of cabinet.

It should be noted that as a result of the *Report of the Special Committee on Reform of the House of Commons* in 1985 a number of potentially important changes have been made in the structure and activities of parliamentary committees. Only time will tell what their impact will be.

7.2 Criticisms of Committee Hearings

Criticisms of the private sector (twenty-five interviews) concerning the hearings on the Bank Act were as follows:

22 — MPs lack depth of knowledge,
18 — Poor questions — no agenda,
15 — Lack of research help and comprehensive briefing,
11 — lack of dialogue and feedback, and
9 — Lateness, poor attendance, substitution of MPs. (Dann 1980, 5)

The nine MPs interviewed by Dann gave the following main criticisms of the committee process:

9 — Lack of research help and comprehensive briefing,
8 — Committee needs alternative advice,
8 — Constraints on time and number of witnesses,
6 — MPs lack depth of knowledge,
5 — Partisanship, and
5 — Lateness, poor attendance, substitution of MPs. (1980, 5)

When the press is present, MPs may "grandstand" in an effort to obtain favourable coverage. Second, very broad terms of reference may not result in a well-focused debate/analysis and the final report may not be sufficiently pragmatic to be a blueprint for changes in policy or legislation.

Witnesses before such committees may not have the benefit of being questioned by well-prepared MPs. There are few incentives for MPs to work hard on their committee assignments. W. O. Twaits, the former chairperson of Imperial Oil, has said:

> The committee system as it exists today is probably one of the most degrading performances I have ever participated in. . . . There is no continuous attendance, people come and go out of the room and Members obviously aren't familiar with the subjects. We arrive with a presentation that has involved a great deal of work and preparation and nobody knows what we are talking about.[21]

R.M. MacIntosh, president of the Canadian Bankers' Association, has remarked:

> The format is unsuitable to achieving the purposes because the chairman has no more authority than that of a glorified time-keeper. He has little authority to intervene to keep committee Members

relevant and he has no control over the discussions because the Members are each allotted 10-minute intervals, the result of which is a mechanical transfer of time from one Member to another. Therefore, you can't possibly keep focused on a given issue until you are finished with it. The next Member will revert to some other clause or section. It's very repetitive and wasteful of time and, on top of that, committee Members have never been well served by staff.[22]

In general, on business issues the members of Senate committees are more knowledgeable, less harried, and more sympathetic to business witnesses. Senate committees can also be more independent of the government. However, in most cases, the Senate's direct impact on most legislation is small. On certain issues such as those affecting business, its indirect impact can be much greater — see section 8 below.

Most writers on lobbying in Canada downplay the importance of government MPs and the Senate as targets of interest-group pressure:

By and large, always with a few exceptions, the government member of Parliament has little or no impact on policy formation. It is developed in the central agencies and the departments, approved by the cabinet, introduced into Parliament, and supported by the members; and to the extent a government member does not support the party position, as stated in the policy, his or her future in politics is jeopardized.

The same is true to an even greater degree of the operations of the Senate. While all legislation must be passed by the Senate, and occasionally the upper house holds hearings on a particular piece of legislation, the influence of the Senate in shaping legislation is even less than that of the House of Commons. As a matter of form, many special interest groups appear before Senate committees and lobby senators, but such action is normally only of cosmetic value. (Gillies & Pigott 1982, 259-60)

I have challenged this conclusion regarding the efficacy of the Senate, particularly as it relates to business-related legislation, in section 8 below.

What do MPs on parliamentary committees want? Committee members want to know how a piece of legislation will work in practice. Therefore, lobbyists should stress the "nitty gritty" realities that can impair the effectiveness of the most well-intentioned bill. In other words, eschew rhetoric and remember the words of Sergeant Friday in the television show "Dragnet": "The facts ma'am, just the facts." The potential impact of legislation is best driven home by having someone testify who is/will be directly affected. Committees want hard data and verifiable information that is directly relevant to the terms of reference and can be used in preparing the committee's report to the House.

In the case of committees reviewing legislation at the Second Read-

ing stage, witnesses must focus on (1) getting amendments the government can accept, or (2) seeking to delay the proposed legislation. The
basic principle of the bill cannot be altered, but amendments can alter
its effects rather significantly. While committees can only recommend
amendments, if their report is unanimous it can sway the relevant minister and cabinet.

In the case of parliamentary committees conducting an *inquiry*, the
government is seeking *advice*, not simply approval of its proposed legislation. The field is much more open, but the importance of facts and
analysis is still great. Unless there is a hidden agenda, the government
doesn't have a predetermined position. Even senior bureaucrats can speak
more freely as individual experts rather than as representatives of their
departments upholding their minister's announced position. The general atmosphere is far less partisan or confrontational. Instead, the
members and those testifying are more problem/issue-oriented. Inquiry
committees need both analytical/factual input and political input. The
latter is often based more on feelings, perceptions, values, and beliefs
than on objective factual information. That does not make it less important.

Interest-group representations to committees can be expensive: expert
advice/analysis; travel to Ottawa; and time foregone on other business.
At the same time, the benefits are both uncertain and hard to measure.

7.3 Improving Committees

How can the operations of committees be improved? The size of most
committees should be reduced, and substitutions should be sharply cur-
tailed or eliminated. Committees need their own professional staff to
assist members and to relate to witnesses on some of the technical issues.
There is need for formal feedback from the government on committee
reports (excluding committees reviewing legislation in which it is built
in).

It should be emphasized that improving and strengthening the role
of committees inevitably involves the executive *sharing* its powers with
other bodies. The hallmark of the Canadian legislative system is the
cabinet's monopoly over the initiation of legislation and over the policy-
formulation process (see Thompson & Stanbury 1979). Those with power,
whether in the public or the private sector, are reluctant to give it up.
More generally, see McGrath (1985), Gillies (1984), and Thomas (1983).

8.0 THE SENATE'S ROLE IN BUSINESS-GOVERNMENT RELATIONS

Canada, like the United States, has a bicameral system of government.
The two chambers of the Canadian Parliament are the House of Commons and the Senate. Unlike members of the House of Commons, who

are elected for terms up to five years, senators are appointed by the prime minister and may hold office until they are 75 (before June 1965 they were appointed for life).

In certain cases, the Senate can play an important role, notably in regard to specialized financial and/or economic legislation. The Senate committees often provide a congenial forum for the representation of business and economic interests. By holding hearings on competition policy prior to the House committee in respect to Bill C-227 (later named C-7 and C-2) in 1974 and 1975, and again in respect to Bill C-13 in early 1978, the effect was to build up a climate of opinion adverse to the proposed legislation. By holding hearings at the same time as the House committee, the Senate committee provided opponents of the legislation with a second forum to put forward their views to the government. See Stanbury (1977, 1985c).

8.1 The Traditional Viewpoint

Traditionally, many political scientists have held the view that the Senate plays only a minor role in the Canadian political system. Cairns, one of the most astute observers of Canadian government, reflects the general opinion of political scientists when he states that "various features of [the Senate's] composition assured it a distinctly secondary role, reducing it almost to the status of spectator of the political battles fought out by the cabinet and the Commons" (1981, 8). Van Loon and Whittington put the point this way:

> The House of Commons . . . functions virtually exclusively as the effective legislative branch of the Canadian political system, while the Senate . . . plays a relatively insignificant role. While it is likely that the Senate was always intended to be a minor partner in the business of passing legislation, its legislative role was once seen as more significant than it has become today. (1981, 656)

McMenemy, however, suggests that some scholarly studies of the Canadian Senate exhibit an unrealistic disregard for the substance of power:

> When senators are discussed, scholars stress their role as superannuated party supporters. Such jejune analyses usually avoid or minimize the intensive and influential activities of nearly a quarter of the senators (Trudeau nominated senators who continue to be active key Liberal party officials). These activities relate particularly to the scrutiny of proposed legislation affecting (large) corporate organization, practices and activities, and political party organization and fund raising.[23] (1977, 454, 461)

The fact that the Senate is not a democratically elected body, it is argued, has diminished its stature vis-à-vis the House of Commons. This erosion has been exacerbated by the partisan nature of Senate appointments (Albinsky 1973, 469). Van Loon and Whittington comment:

[A] weakness of the Senate has been the tendency to offer Senate positions largely to people whose useful political lives have terminated. As a reward for many years of faithful service to the party, an old politician is "retired" by being put in the Senate. Because of this tendency, the image of the Senate is that of an "old folks' home" for tired and retired party faithfuls, an image which severely restricts the prestige of the upper house. (1981)

8.2 The Senate as a Lobby for Business

Two political scientists, Colin Campbell and John McMenemy, argue that the traditional view of the Senate ignores the substance of power exercised by it in certain cases. Shifting scholarly attention on the Senate from structure to process, Campbell (1978) found that the Senate almost exclusively represents the interests of key sectors of the business community. McMenemy argues that the Red Chamber not only functions as an "internal business lobby," but also serves as a "publicly financed and prestigious repository for *active* party organizers and fund raisers" (1982, 547). (This point is illustrated in chapter 10.)

Campbell (1978, 11) describes the Senate as "the lobby from within" and emphasizes that "senators' lobbying activities are paid for by the people of Canada and not by the business firms and groups whose interests they advance." Campbell describes Senate lobbying and legislative activity as "business review." It typically operates as follows:

First senators hear grievances from the business community members who feel that civil servants and Cabinet Ministers have ignored them. Then, senators astutely wield their corporate reputations through the powerful Banking Committee to persuade the department in charge of a bill that certain "technical" changes must be made within it. If the department's Minister finds the case convincing, he will arrange for the government to sponsor amendments which would accommodate the senator's concerns. Cumulatively, "technical" changes often water down such bills, and this result is the aim of lobbying from within. With the help of senators, in other words, business has been able to get its main points across to the government. (Campbell 1978, 69–70)

The focal point of "the lobby from within" is the Senate's Committee on Banking, Trade and Commerce. Senator Salter A. Hayden, chairperson of the committee for over thirty years, was reputed to be "the most influential single member in the Upper House" (Stevens 1976, 6). A major factor in the committee's role as the champion of the business community in the legislative process has been the freedom of senators to espouse the cause of special interests, unencumbered by conflict-of-interest legislation. McMenemy (1982, 542) points out that "there is no federal law requiring parliamentarians to disclose, let alone restrict, directorates, property and financial holdings and legal or other activities which might be construed as lobbying." Senators are bound by a rule under which they are not allowed to vote on any question in which they have "any pecuniary interest whatsoever, not held in common with the rest of the Canadian subjects of the Crown." This latter restriction is mute, however, since "senators may define 'pecuniary interest' in a very narrow way; but in any case, voting in the Senate or in a committee is not the most effective way to influence a legislative issue."

In writing about conflicts of interest in the Senate, I outlined in an earlier study the different roles Senator Salter A. Hayden played in connection with Atlantic Sugar and the sugar-refining industry:

> [Senator Hayden] was . . . for many years, a vice-president and a director of Atlantic Sugar Refineries Co. Ltd. . . . In November 1958 and February 1959 Hayden appeared as counsel with two other members of his Toronto law firm for Acadia-Atlantic Sugar Refineries and its associated companies in hearings on the Director of Investigation and Research's Statement of Evidence before the Restrictive Trade Practices Commission. The RTPC concluded "that the practices engaged in by the three eastern refiners . . . have limited competition in the eastern sugar refining industry to the detriment of the public. . . ." Senator Hayden's efforts on behalf of Atlantic Sugar [occurred] while he was both chairman of the Senate Committee which reviews combines legislation, and an officer and director of the sugar refinery. (Stanbury 1977, 145–49)

In 1964 the Committee on Banking, Trade and Commerce attracted public attention in its deliberations on three bills to incorporate mortgage companies and three bills to create banks. According to McMenemy,

> four directors of established banks were members of the Committee, including . . . Senator Salter Hayden, then a director and shareholder of the Bank of Nova Scotia. The committee readily passed the three bills to incorporate mortgage companies despite reservations on one bill and serious objections to another by the federal superintendent of insurance. The Bank of Nova Scotia was associated with the companies whose incorporation legislation troubled the superintendent. . . . The senator's critical consideration of the three proposed bank incorporations also drew public attention because of their private interests in established financial institutions. (1982, 542–43)

McMenemy concludes that while there is evidence to believe that senators have "become sensitized to the question of personal conflicts of interest," nevertheless the Senate has been able to quash proposals for conflict-of-interest legislation that might impede the freedom of senators to represent special interests (1978, 548).

Campbell (1978) outlines two methods used by senators to influence the outcome of the legislative process in favour of business. The first involves drafting "technical" improvements to proposed legislation. Campbell states that senators, after listening to the views of corporate interests, astutely "wield their corporate regulations through the powerful banking committee" to persuade the minister responsible for the proposed legislation that "certain 'technical' changes must be made within it" (1978, 69). Commenting on this pattern of lobbying, one senator noted: "I go to the Minister in charge and show him what I think should be changed in the bill and ask for his cooperation; then I go over to the Commons and start lobbying among the MPs, pointing out, of course, that I have been to see the Minister and that I have his blessing" (quoted in Campbell 1978, 71).

Ministers sponsoring the legislation often put forward amendments to accommodate the senators' concerns. Commenting on this type of influence, Campbell states that "cumulatively 'technical' changes often water down" proposed legislation (1978, 69–70). The power of the Committee on Banking, Trade and Commerce to influence the legislative process in this manner is illustrated by the committee's success in obtaining amendments to a government bankruptcy bill. According to the *Financial Post*, "Of 140 proposed changes to Consumer and Corporate Affairs' bankruptcy bill — some major ones. . . — 109 were accepted outright and 19 in part."[24] In another example, Senator Hayden's committee pressed the government for 27 amendments to the Canada Business Corporations Act. The government had asked the House to accept the amendments in one motion on short notice. The minister responsible for the legislation commented: "The Senate Committee . . . acted objectively, fairly and reasonably, arguing clearly and forcefully for each proposed amendment. I felt it impossible not to be responsible to these suggestions" (quoted in McMenemy 1982, 544).

Campbell (1978, 15–16) cites another example of the subtle power wielded by the Senate Committee on Banking, Trade and Commerce. The government introduced an Income Tax Reform Bill in 1971, and the Banking Committee immediately began studying the legislation. However, as the government was anxious to pass the legislation before the end of 1971 so that the tax measures could apply the following year, it did not incorporate any of the amendments suggested by the committee. The Senate approved the legislation without the amendments:

> The press charged the Senate with "rubber-stamping." . . . The media, apparently, were not paying close attention to events in the Banking Committee. . . . Indeed, by April 1973, a new Minister

of Finance, John Turner, appeared before the Banking Committee with a package of amendments which responded to all of the key recommendations of the committee. Parliament enacted all of those retroactively to January 1, 1972. (Campbell 1978, 16)

Secondly, as "key intermediaries" between business and government, senators influence the legislative process by providing business leaders with access to key government decision-makers. A number of senators, especially those who sit on the Banking Committee and also hold multiple corporate directorships,[25] are well connected with both business and government elites. As Campbell states, senators are able to "provide for fellow members of the business elite a preferential access to legislative decision makers, and thus to the process of decision making itself; they also teach their business associates how to live with government intervention in the marketplace" (1978, 32). Campbell sees the intermediary role of the Senate as a stabilizing influence on Canada's liberal democracy. But he also claims that "the business community is the only segment of Canadian society which benefits to any significant degree from senators' ability to maintain jointly offices in private and public sectors" (1978, 33). He argues that, in fact, some senators can be considered part and parcel of the (big) business lobby, and goes on to state:

> The reader must keep in mind the fact that senators' lobbying activities are paid for by the people of Canada and not by the business firms and groups whose interests they advance. . . . The system provides extreme accommodation, of course, by paying the salaries of business lobbyists, giving them full membership in the community of legislators, and protecting them from public review of their tenure. (Campbell 1978, 11)

As McMenemy (1982) has noted, however, the Senate also serves to provide a public subsidy to political parties by paying the salaries of party presidents, organizers, fund raisers, and other functionaries who are appointed to the Senate. One of the best-known examples of this practice is Keith "The Rainmaker" Davey. Davey was the national organizer of the Liberal party between 1961 and 1965 (see McCall-Newman 1982, 411). He continued his labours on behalf of the party after his appointment to the Senate in 1966, serving as co-chairperson of the National Campaign Committee in both the 1974 and 1979 elections. McMenemy lists over a dozen other active Liberal party organizers and fund raisers appointed to the Senate, as well as several Conservative party appointments, including Lowell Murray after he had organized Joe Clark's 1979 election victory.[26]

Another way in which the Senate or a Senate committee can wield more influence in the policy process is through delay:

Business efforts aimed at slowing down progress of the legislation through the parliamentary machinery can be reinforced by the dynamics of the legislation process itself. The minister is faced with a fight for House time, with opposition threats to filibuster (often to achieve victories in other areas) and the emotional drain of committee hearings in both the House and the Senate. Toward the end of each session the inter-ministerial manoeuvering for time becomes fierce. In almost all these circumstances compromise to get the bill through, particularly in view of the total amount of time taken by the legislation in its earlier form, becomes increasingly attractive. As the total time in process lengthens, the ability to maintain intellectual and emotional commitment is reduced. After the "pressure cooker" atmosphere and exhaustion have taken their toll, the ardent advocates of reform may not recognize what has been wrought by compromise. (Stanbury 1977, 178)

9.0 THE MEDIA

It should be obvious that interest groups can, in some cases, "leverage" their positions and expand their influence by skillful use of the media. The pressure of daily deadlines (in the case of radio or television, hourly deadlines) can often be used to advantage by sophisticated interest groups. Pratt describes the problem well: "Too often reporters and commentators rely heavily on press handouts from the corporations and governments for their information. That it is a difficult, tiresome, expensive nuisance to generate alternative information, particularly on highly technical issues is true, but it is a lame excuse for not trying harder" (1976, 18).

One of Canada's most respected journalists, Robert Fulford, has pointed out that the generalist still dominates newspaper reporting:

Most reporting, on TV or in the papers, is done by men and women who appear innocent of serious knowledge in the fields they describe. You have a sense, as you listen to them or read them, that all they know of the subject is what they heard from the last expert they met. In the Press Gallery in Ottawa there are about 175 reporters, but I don't believe there is one of them who could be called an expert on, say foreign policy. There isn't a single man or woman who could speak with independent authority on defence, on welfare policy, or on constitutional law. A politician or civil servant speaking to a reporter usually — not always, but usually — expects to encounter profound ignorance of whatever subject is on the agenda. After a while he comes both to fear that ignorance and to depend on it. (1977, 4)

He should have also pointed out that such ignorance can be a most useful condition for the PR men of the interest groups who provide the "handouts" that are often repeated verbatim in news stories.

The purpose of this very brief introduction is to whet readers' interest and to refer them to chapter 11, which discusses the role of the media in business-government relations more generally.

10.0 TIMING

We begin with the essential question: When in the policy/legislative process can an interest group make an input? While practically it is difficult to separate the question of timing from those of targets and vehicles (mode of delivery), it is desirable to try to do so for analytical purposes. Obviously, the variables are quite interdependent in many circumstances.

The effective interest group must have a good understanding of the various steps in the public policy formation process. In particular, it must recognize that much of the activity in the preparliamentary and postparliamentary stages is invisible to outsiders. Yet it is vital to begin making inputs as early as possible.

The relationship of targets, timing, and points of access to the policy making process is captured in the following quotation:

> Where then should we expect to find the influence exerters? The answer is that they are out looking for "intervention ports," which may be found almost anywhere in Ottawa. Mr. Gander [public affairs officer for the Canadian Construction Association] here employs a trade term meaning channel of access. Why port is to be preferred to channel is not altogether clear. The essential point is that either leads to someone or some group in the legislative process, whose understanding and assistance may be of value in the important work of killing bills. Intervention ports occur at various levels, starting with the bureaucracy. If a bill moves unscathed to cabinet committees, it is necessary to move in at that point, contacting ministers or setting one against another. (Warn Eugene Whelan [then minister of agriculture] that Warren Allmand [then minister of consumer and corporate affairs] is up to no good.) Failing success at these stages, the resourceful lobbyist will concentrate in turn on caucus, House committees or, in last resort, on the Senate. Mr. Gander's statistics are, perhaps, even more impressive than his imagery. The construction people, we learn, have a 500-member liaison committee; two being paired with each MP. Is this over-kill or is a spare deemed essential to ensure that no parliamentarian goes unaccompanied to the washroom? By Mr. Gander's reckoning, the number of lobbying organizations in Ottawa is approximately 350. How, it may be wondered, does anything survive? A partial answer may be that some MPs are impervious to factual infor-

mation, "quiet persuasion," "careful coaching" and discerning inti-
mations of impending political disasters. It may also be that far too
many lobbyists are disorganized amateurs in comparison with the
ubiquitous construction men.[27]

Because the matter of timing depends on the type of policy action
under consideration, I have arranged the discussion in terms of a number of major policy actions that embody government policy.

10.1 New Statutes or Amendments to Existing Legislation

The process by which new statutes or amendments to existing ones are
created can be divided into three stages, each of which has a number of
recognizable steps.

1. *The Preparliamentary Phase:* The preparliamentary stage is primarily
concerned with issue identification, the drafting of policy papers for
submission to cabinet (and its committees), and the testing of the general thrust of the policy proposals with key interest groups. In general,
we can identify the following steps in the preparliamentary phase:

- perceiving the need for change (including the opportunity for purely
  partisan political gains);
- development of policy/ideas/concept (maybe external to the government, political or bureaucratic sides);
- writing a policy paper for internal circulation in PMO, PCO, or one of
  the functional departments;
- "trial balloons" in the media, circulation to outside experts (political
  and technical), and provincial governments;
- interdepartmental circulation of policy paper and consultation;
- checking with key interest groups; and
- preparation of a cabinet document specifying the proposed policy in
  considerable detail, submitted to cabinet by a minister.

2. *The Parliamentary Phase:* This phase can be divided into the cabinet process and the legislative process.

(a) *The Cabinet Process:*

- Consideration of policy in a subject-matter committee and decision or recommendation (the original proposal may be modified).
- Cabinet confirmation of committee decision (the decision or certain details may be modified).
- The responsible minister issues drafting instructions for legislation to Department of Justice.
- A draft bill is prepared by Department of Justice and approved
  by responsible minister.
- Consideration of the draft bill by Cabinet Committee on Legislation and House Planning.

- Cabinet confirmation of committee decision and prime minister's signature.

(b) *The Legislative Process:*

- First Reading in either Senate or House of Commons (reading of title and brief explanation of bill; all money bills must be introduced in House of Commons, most bills begin in Commons).
- Second Reading in same House of Parliament (debate and vote on principle of bill).
- Consideration by the appropriate parliamentary committee (clause-by-clause examination of bill).
- Parliament, report stage, and vote on any amendments prepared by committee.
- Parliament, Third Reading, and vote.
- Introduction of bill into other House of Parliament (usually Senate) and repetition of the process.
- The governor general in the presence of Senate and House of Commons assents to bill and signs it into law.

The output of the cabinet process is a draft bill, the output of the legislative process is a new statute or amendments to an existing statute. From the point of view of the interest group, the legislative process of the parliamentary stage is easier to follow, as the official steps are conducted in public and recorded in easily available documents. Also, changes in the policy may be detected, even if the reasons for them are not discernible.

3. *The Postparliamentary Phase:* This phase includes the following:

- Writing of regulations by the department (or agency) charged with the administration of the legislation (see subsection 10.3 below).
- Administration and enforcement of the legislation and regulations.
- Judicial (and quasi-judicial) interpretation of legislation.

10.2 Lessons for the Timing of Interest-Group Representations

Because it is the most visible phase of the public policy process, it is often assumed that interest-group representations will be focused on the parliamentary phase. A wise (and effective) lobbyist knows better. Although much lobbying is reactive, the truly compleat lobbyist seeks to plant the seed of his or her own ideas (beneficial to the interest group he or she represents) very early in the policy process. Baxter quotes "a highly successful lobbyist for some years now":

> First of all you have to keep a good lookout on what is going on, on how the government is thinking. That means knowing, and keeping in with, cabinet ministers and some senior civil servants. But that is only part of the craft.

Really, most new ideas begin deep in the civil service machine. The man in charge of some special office . . . writes a memo suggesting a new policy on this or that. It works its way slowly up and up. At that stage civil servants are delighted, just delighted, to talk quietly to people like us, people representing this or that corporation or industry directly involved. That is the time to slip in good ideas. Later it oozes up to the politicians and becomes policy. By the time it is a government bill it takes the very devil to change it. Then you have real trouble. (1977, 207)

Put very simply, get your oar in early, but do so with a modicum of taste. Blunn (1978) quotes an Ottawa lobbyist: "The quickest way to push your way out of influential Ottawa circles is to push your way around." But there is a conundrum here. How do you know that a policy proposal of interest is brewing before it becomes public knowledge? Answer: through the critical resource of access.

Access is usually thought of as the ability to gain entry to key decision makers to make a representation. Real access is knowing *very early* what issues are under review that are potentially important to an interest group.

The second principle of effective lobbying activity is to recognize there are, as indicated above, quite a number of stages at which lobbying can be done. Failure to achieve the desired result early in the process should not be taken as a signal to withdraw from the field.

Rule three is persistence: (almost always) never give up. The passage of a law does not necessarily mean it will have the effects its advocates anticipate. There is "many a slip between cup and lip" in the implementation or postparliamentary phase (see Pressman & Wildavsky 1975; Bardach 1977). The regulations accompanying new legislation are often very important in determining the actual impact of the words of the statute. Although it is perhaps more difficult to "get at" the drafters of the regulations, lobbyists offering expertise and evidencing a desire to be helpful can become involved in the process of creating regulations (see subsection 10.3). Even beyond this stage, there is the possibility of pushing for "bureaucratic repeal" of legislation or regulations. Lobbyists can seek to pressure the civil servants responsible for administering and/or enforcing the legislation to fail to do so. At the very least, they can seek to have civil servants restrain their enthusiasm for carrying out their legislative mandate. Such efforts by lobbyists do not often involve corruption. The fact is that much legislation puts a generous amount of discretion in the hands of its civil servant administrators. For example, in the case of competition policy, few restraints of trade will be taken to court if few investigations are initiated, few convictions will be obtained if few charges are laid, and few real remedies will be obtained if the crown fails to make strong representations in respect to possible penalties/remedies provided for in the act.

10.3 Subordinate Legislation

Eric Hehner (1985, 342) notes that "it became the norm [in Canada] for a statute to delegate authority to make regulations to achieve objectives which have been expressed in very general terms." He continues: "If regulations extend only to details of mechanical procedures, no real discretionary powers are delegated. However, where the statutory provisions are only a skeleton and it is left to regulations to say 'what, where, when, why, how and who,' then we have created meaningful discretionary powers and should examine the mechanisms available to review the exercise of these powers." This is frequently the case in Canada.

Three bodies have the power to make law without reference to the legislature in the form of subordinate legislation, notably regulations:

- *The governor in council, that is, the cabinet as a whole.* This may take the form of orders-in-council regulations and other more arcane types of subordinate legislation.
- *An individual minister, that is, without reference to the cabinet for approval.* Note in most cases it is a minister who initiates the writing of regulations under legislation which his or her department administers.
- *A statutory regulatory agency.* In some cases, the agency can make and "pass" regulations without referring them to the cabinet for approval; more frequently the agency drafts the regulations and submits them to the cabinet for approval. (Note, in the case of the provinces, a number of private bodies, notably self-regulating occupational groups, have the power to create regulations having the force of law without the approval of the cabinet — see ECC 1981, chap. 10.)

Let us examine the sequence of steps involved in the most common method of creating regulations — those initiated by a federal department and authorized by the cabinet (governor in council):

1. *Statutory Authority*: A statute must have been enacted that provides that the governor in council may make regulations to carry out the purposes of the act. Hehner explains that "under the *Consumer Packaging and Labelling Act*, 1981, full power to exempt goods from the application of the act is delegated to the governor-in-council. The labelling requirements that are to apply to goods are to be prescribed by regulations. Thus, in passing the act, Parliament prohibited the sale or import of goods not packaged in compliance with regulations that had not yet been made and were therefore unknown to Parliament" (1985, 343).

2. *Drafting*: The actual drafting of regulations is done by middle-level officials in the department that will administer them, together with drafting specialists in the Department of Justice. It is at this stage that interest groups should make the greatest effort to influence the words being put on paper. However, it is often hard to detect that regulations are

being drafted. Only the closest liaison will be sufficient to gather this type of intelligence if the department does not plan to consult with potentially affected interests.

3. *Consultation*: While it is becoming more common to consult such interests informally and formally, departmental officials usually wish to do so only after they have a complete draft. This requires close collaboration with the Department of Justice and occasionally with specialists within the PCO. Informal consultation can be done in a number of ways: sending copies of the draft regulations to those individuals, firms, and associations likely to be interested in them and requesting their comments; formation of a special consultative committee to advise the department (deputy minister and minister); and referring the draft regulations to an existing advisory committee for discussion and comment. In some cases, "consultation" only occurs if a significant interest group is able to learn that regulations are being drafted and is able to convince the deputy minister or minister that it should have a chance to read and comment on the draft regulations. See, for example, Brown-John (1985).

Departments are sometimes required to publish draft regulations in the *Canada Gazette* some period before they are to become law for a "notice and comment" period. This is the case, for example, under the Socio-Economic Impact Analysis requirements of the Treasury Board that came into effect in 1978 (see Anderson 1980). Some departments — even though not required to do so — make it a practice to publish their draft regulations in the *Gazette* or to distribute them widely prior to the date they are to come into effect so as to give notice to those likely to be affected. The notice period is used by interest groups to lobby for changes in the regulations before they become law. Many groups claim that too few departments use a notice period and that the period is too short to prepare a proper response. The Economic Council (1979, 73) apparently agrees, for it recommended that "for major new regulations, early consultation be encouraged, systems be instituted to ensure that advance notice is given of the proposed regulations, and that systems also be established to ensure that costs and benefits of major new regulations are evaluated." The council continued, "Early consultation should take place during the 'problem identification' stage when a government is attempting to discover if a problem exists and whether intervention is necessary."

The council's (1979, 83) recommendation that the federal and provincial governments establish an annual "regulatory calendar" to consolidate advance notice of new regulations was adopted May 1983. In Canada, major regulatory departments, including Agriculture, Communications, Consumer and Corporate Affairs, Energy, Mines and Resources, Environment, Fisheries and Oceans, Health and Welfare, Indian Affairs and Northern Development, Labour, and Transport, are to publish early notice of potential changes in their regulatory activities in the form of a regulatory agenda twice per year. In addition, the major federal regulatory agencies in Canada, such as the CTC, CRTC, NEB, and AECB, publish their own regulatory agendas. The agendas, pursuant to Treasury Board requirements, include the following information: short statement of the problem requiring regulatory action; brief description of the action contemplated; legal authority for the action; person to be contacted for more information; and schedule of evaluation of regulatory programs. (In the U.S. a regulatory agenda is published twice per year. The *Unified Agenda of Federal Regulations* of April 1985, published in the *Federal Register*, April 29, 1985, was 1145 pages long and has been described as a "comprehensive overview of pending Federal regulatory activities.")

4. *PCO/Cabinet*: After regulations have been drafted and perhaps revised on the basis of consultation, they are sent to the Privy Council Office to be reviewed to ensure that they are in the proper form. After this is done, they are submitted to the cabinet for approval. It should be appreciated that approving regulations, with very few exceptions, is viewed as mechanistic, routine business devoid of any political significance by ministers — except perhaps by the minister of the department putting them forward for approval. In fact, regulations enacted by the governor in council are usually only cursorily examined by a handful of ministers on behalf of the cabinet as a whole. See Anderson (1980). The point is that once draft regulations have reached the PCO and are being readied for cabinet approval, they are "cast in reinforced concrete." Moreover, interest groups will probably find it difficult to gain access to the officials in the PCO responsible for checking draft regulations and preparing them for cabinet approval. In fact, in many cases the first time an interest group hears about new regulations is when they are printed in the *Canada Gazette*, after they have been approved (made into law) by the cabinet. Since the *Gazette* is a highly technical periodical, the average citizen affected by the hundreds of new regulations each year will not become aware of them until they have been implemented for some time. For example, the regulation passed by the Ontario cabinet in September 1985 that provided $34 million in additional funding for Catholic high schools will "show up" in the form of higher local property taxes (about 6 percent), but it is unlikely that taxpayers will be aware why their taxes increased.

5. *Joint Committee on Statutory Instruments*: Under the Statutory Instruments Act of 1972, certain regulations and other statutory instruments, after they are enacted, are referred to what is now the Standing Joint Committee on Regulations and Other Statutory Instruments (see Hehner 1985, 347). The committee's job is to review and scrutinize the subordinate legislation referred to it. It has published a series of analytical reports that have been highly critical of the statutory instruments it has reviewed

and of the sponsoring departments and the Department of Justice for their lack of cooperation by withholding information (see Hehner 1985, 348–49). The committee has repeatedly pointed out that regulations are badly drafted and may be unconstitutional. "The deliberate ignoring of the Standing Joint Committee is the ultimate in contempt" (Hehner 1985, 349).

Therefore, while the Standing Joint Committee may constitute a potential ally for interest groups that have been hurt by new and possibly unconstitutional regulations, it is obvious the committee has no power to change the present situation, which gives the cabinet enormous power to make law without resort to the legislature. The cabinet of a majority government even has the power to decide, when drafting new legislation, how much power it will give itself to subsequently create new regulations with the force of law.

6. *The Courts*: Once new regulations are law, interest groups can look to the courts as the target of their efforts to alter government policy (see Kernaghan 1985h). As emphasized in chapter 5, this method of altering policy is often slow, expensive, and uncertain. However, it is not unknown for the federal government to provide grants to some disadvantaged groups to launch legal actions to challenge the constitutionality of new statutes and/or regulations. For example, in September 1985 the federal government announced that it would provide some $9 million over two years to groups representing handicapped persons, women's groups, native people, and others to use the 1982 Charter of Rights and Freedoms to challenge federal and provincial legislation.

10.4 Changing Public Expenditures

In 1985/86 the federal government will spend about $105 billion. If an interest group is able, at the margin, to shift 0.01 percent of these expenditures to its own benefit, it will receive $10.5 million. If the group can shift one-tenth of 1 percent to its own benefit, its members stand to gain some $105 million. The process by which the annual *Estimates* are determined is described in Figure 7-5.

The process merits several comments. First, the process is quite well defined with respect to the actors involved and the timing of its various stages. Second, the process, while lengthy, is characterized by regularity; that is, there is a publicly known, fixed timetable. Third, virtually all of the activity takes place inside government, and there is little systematic effort to consult actors outside government. Therefore, interest groups have to find or make their own points of access.

Fourth, once the *Estimates* have been tabled in the House of Commons, the die is cast — except for the subsequent Supplementary Estimates. It is virtually unknown for the legislature to alter the government's spending plans as stated in the published *Estimates*. However, even though the *Estimates* may indicate, for example, that the Department of Transport proposes to spend $50 million over the next two years to renovate and enlarge the terminal at the Ottawa airport, they do not indicate who will get the contract for the design or for the construction. In the same vein, the new Tory minister of international trade discovered that the Export Development Corporation spent some $1 million on legal fees. Subsequently, a personal friend of the prime minister from college days, Sam Wakim, became a partner in the Ottawa office of a Toronto law firm and began receiving legal work for EDC amounting to some $200 000 per year in fees.[28] In other words, interest groups have to lobby departments and ministers to get desired expenditures into the *Estimates* in principle; then they have to work to ensure that the "right" people actually get the intended benefits.

10.5 The Revenue Budget

One of government's unique coercive powers is the power to tax and conversely to provide tax expenditures. Although at the federal level total revenues are only about 70 percent of expenditures — the balance is the deficit — they nevertheless constitute an enormously important expression of public policy. In his report on fiscal year 1983/84 the auditor general pointed out that tax expenditures (or revenues deliberately foregone in the interests of some policy objective by means of exemptions, tax credits, and special rates) amount to an additional $30 to $50 for

Figure 7–5
THE WORKING OF THE FEDERAL POLICY AND EXPENDITURE MANAGEMENT SYSTEM

In general terms the system works in the following way, with the annual cycle beginning each September, over a year and a half before the start of the fiscal year in April. (See Chart: Policy and Expenditure Planning Cycle.) Note that the system is described below as it operated under the Trudeau government. The system is quite similar under the Mulroney government but is being simplified.

1. **Envelope Setting** *(Late Summer/Early Fall)*
        The dollar value for each envelope is decided upon each year by the Cabinet Committee on Priorities and Planning in the context of establishing the fiscal plan and the general directions for each policy sector on the basis of:
   • a fiscal plan submitted by the minister of finance assessing the economic environment, projected revenues and expenditures, and the financial requirements of the government;
   • a presentation from the minister of finance, in consultation with the president of the Treasury Board, on the overall expenditure level and the appropriate levels for each envelope; and
   • policy sector reports from each committee chairman outlining the strategy for his sector.

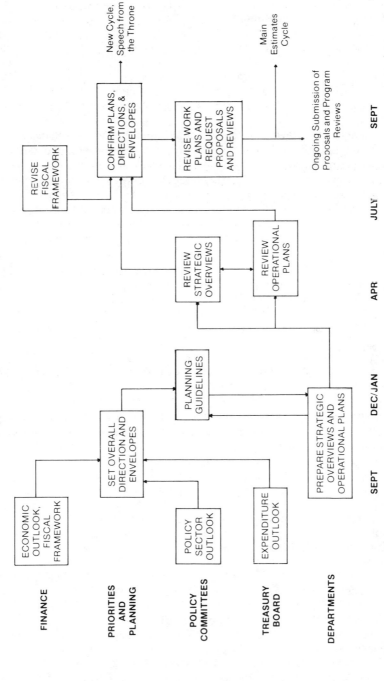

Figure 7-5 (continued)
Policy and Expenditure Planning Cycle

Source: Privy Council Office (1985) as reproduced in Kenneth Kernaghan, *Public Adminstration in Canada: Selected Readings*, 5th ed. (Toronto: Methuen, 1985), p. 200.

Figure 7-5 (continued)

2. **Directions for Policy Sectors** (Early Winter)
   Each policy committee of cabinet is assigned the responsibility for managing its envelopes. On the basis of its policy and program objectives, the committee provides the necessary direction to departments and agencies in preparing their strategic overviews. This includes the overall direction for the department and the identification of reviews and lower-priority programs within the sector as the means to generate funds for program expansion and new initiatives.

3. **Strategic Overviews and Operational Plans** (Spring/Early Summer)
   On the basis of committee directions and planning guidelines, departments and agencies prepare and submit strategic overviews and operations plans to the policy committees and the Treasury Board for review. The Treasury Board carries out a review of the operational plans to determine the costs of carrying out those policies and programs that have to that point been approved by the committees. With this up-to-date costing, and within the context of the multiyear envelope ceilings, policy committees decide upon the policy proposals and program reviews to be undertaken.

4. **Priorities and Planning** (Late Summer/Early Fall)
   The Cabinet Committee on Priorities and Planning considers any revisions to the fiscal plan in light of a revised economic outlook and considers committee strategic work plans, including policy proposals and program reviews.

5. **Ongoing Process** (Throughout the Year)
   On the basis of the decisions by Priorities and Planning, policy committees revise their strategic work plans, and on this basis departments and agencies prepare proposals (new initiatives and reviews) for consideration by the policy committees in the context of the policy sector priorities and envelope levels.
   In order to assist policy committees in their planning, the resource envelopes are established on a five-year basis and are updated annually in order to maintain a continuing five-year perspective.
   Bearing in mind the likelihood that economic assumptions will change, the system is intended to allow progressively tighter planning for any particular fiscal year through a five-year period.
   In 1981 the first limits were defined and established for fiscal year 1985/86 in light of the current economic assessment, the proposed tax structure, the anticipated fiscal stance of the government, and other variables such as expenditure trends.
   In 1982 the overall target for 1985/86 was revised and redefined in light of the latest assessments of economic prospects and other variables.
   In 1983, after further updating of the targets for 1985/86 had been done, along with the preparation of strategic work plans for the policy sectors and the government as a whole, strategic decisions were taken on programs to be undertaken and detailed work on these programs was begun.
   In 1984 final planning decisions were taken for 1985/86, again within the context of the latest assessments of the economy, expenditure trends, and so forth.

Figure 7-5 (continued)

With the beginning of the 1985/86 fiscal year, program changes will be introduced and the government's overall program will be managed and evaluated. The information developed in this process will in turn feed into planning for future years. At this point, initial limits will be established for 1989/90.

The Main Estimates Cycle noted on the right side of the chart extends the expenditure budget process to the following April. Departments and agencies present their Main Estimates (proposed expenditures for the upcoming year) to Treasury Board by the end of October. Treasury Board reviews and approves these in November and December. Finally, in February, the Main Estimates are tabled in Parliament and the legislative phase of the budgetary process begins.

Source: Privy Council Office (1985, 199–202).

every $100 of direct expenditures. He described them as "a huge hidden budget in the financial affairs of Canada" (p. I-23). Moreover, "programs fuelled by tax expenditures have expanded, their real costs unquantified, their total effect a mystery" (p. I-24). It is precisely these characteristics of tax expenditures that make them so attractive to interest groups, particularly business interests.

Revenue budgets that incorporate significant changes in tax legislation do not appear with the same frequency and consistency as do the expenditure *Estimates*. The following is a list of the past eleven revenue budgets, their date, and the finance minister involved:

- February 1986 (Wilson)
- May 1985 (Wilson)
- November 1984 (economic statement by the new minister of finance, Michael Wilson)
- February 1984 (Lalonde)
- April 1983 (Lalonde) — called a budget to benefit business
- June 1982 (MacEachen) — included the 6-and-5 plan regarding wages and prices
- November 1981 (MacEachen) — very controversial effort to reduce some tax expenditures
- October 1980 (MacEachen) — included the National Energy Program
- December 1979 (Crosbie) — some of the provisions of this budget, notably the increased taxes on gasoline, led to the defeat of the Conservatives under Joe Clark
- November 1978 (Chrétien) — a pre-election budget including the child tax credit
- May 1976 (Macdonald)

Goode (1980, p. ix) notes that "while taxation is a central function of government we know little about how tax policies are actually formulated." He shows that in Canada "tax policy-making is an inside and private affair. Its central participants operate within a tightly-knit community of shared perception about what is a tax issue, how it should be conceptualized, what alternatives and consequences are to be considered, and how decisions are to be taken." He goes on to point out that few outsiders are involved in the process, although insiders do try to anticipate the reactions and interests of the many outside of the small circle of advisors and decision makers in the Department of Finance. These people constitute the core of "the tax community," but it also includes a small number of specialists (lawyers, accountants, and sometimes academics) who devote their professional energies to the subject of taxation.

Goode (1980, 3) defines the tax community as including the following persons:

- Minister of finance,
- Deputy minister of finance,
- Five assistant deputy ministers, including those for tax policy, fiscal policy,
- A few directors in the tax policy and fiscal policy branches, and
- Slightly over two dozen tax policy officers.

Slightly further from the core but part of the tax community are the following:

- Prime minister,
- A few ministers in the "inner cabinet,"
- Minister of finance's parliamentary secretary,[29]
- Minister of state for finance, and
- Officials in the legal services branch of the Department of Finance.

The "attentive actors" are outsiders in the formulation of tax policy. Goode (1980, 4) lists the following as being in this group:

- Special-interest groups — usually but not always business groups,
- Provincial governments — premiers and ministers of finance and of intergovernmental relations,
- Spending cabinet ministers in the federal government and their departments,
- Minister of national revenue and his or her officials,
- The party caucus,
- Other MPs, and
- Foreign governments, particularly the U.S.

"Attentive actors are advocates for their constituencies' interests. Behind each attentive actor is a constituency, but each constituency is inattentive to taxation" (Goode 1980, 4). Goode states that "tax professionals, composed primarily of lawyers and accountants, rarely influence tax policies but have considerable effect on technical provisions. They are the tax community's 'practical conscience' on technical matters and provide a partial bridge between the way the tax system is actually applied and the way the tax community considers technical changes" (1980, p. xv).

Goode (1980, p. xiii) makes it clear that the members of the tax community shape tax policy in light of the "political climate" (what the tax public — including those who pay the bill — will accept). Sometimes they "guess wrong" as the reaction of the "attentive public" to the last MacEachen budget in November 1981 made clear. The moderate- to high-income beneficiaries and potential beneficiaries of a host of tax expenditures "screamed blue murder" when they saw that some of their favourite vehicles for tax avoidance were to be eliminated or made less attractive.

The targets of lobbyists interested in tax policy are few: the tax policy officer dealing with the particular area, the assistant deputy minister for tax policy, the deputy minister, and ultimately the minister of finance. The timing of representations is much more problematic, at least as compared with the expenditure budget (*Estimates*), as we have seen. In some cases, the minister of finance announces some months in advance when he or she will be "bringing down a budget." In the past few years, more efforts have been made to consult — primarily the business community — in the course of preparing the budget. This is the exception rather than the rule, however. Moreover, it is argued by senior officials in the Department of Finance that such consultation cannot involve the same frank exchange of information and alternatives because of the possibility that private sector actors would be able to profit from such inside knowledge. Certainly this has been the rationale for the obsessive secrecy associated with the budget. For example, in most instances, the revenue budget is not taken to cabinet and in some cases the prime minister has only limited knowledge of its contents during its preparation (Hartle 1982).

Interest groups concerned with influencing tax policy over the longer run should not worry much about "getting their oar in" at exactly the right time before a particular budget. Rather, they should appreciate that analysis and evaluation of alternative policies is going on almost continuously inside the Department of Finance. Besides, budgets are very seldom more than twelve months apart. Major tax changes — resulting from the efforts of interest groups — do not occur rapidly. It takes time to prepare analyses, to gain access, and to convince officials who, in turn, must "sell" the idea to the finance minister.

"Throughout the year and especially prior to the spring budget the Finance Minister is swamped by voluminous briefs from tax interest groups" (Goode 1980, 105). In addition, the minister holds many meetings with such groups at which he or she sits and listens, careful not to indicate support or hostility to one group's positions or another's. The minister's officials may need to consult with industry officials and tax consultants after a budget has announced a change in taxes. Such consultations focus not on the policy issue, but on how to implement it in a practicable way. See Goode (1980, 111).

Attentive actors constitute a source of uncertainty and embarrassment for the insiders in the tax community. The point is that the greater the potential embarrassment (read political noise) a group can cause, the greater its ability to be consulted about changes in taxes and tax expenditures. Where uncertainty about reactions is less, the more likely the Department of Finance will rely on its ability to anticipate consequences and adjust policy or implementation accordingly (Goode 1980, chap. 5).

Goode (1980, 122–23) states that "the morning following the budget speech the government is already preparing for its next budget and its accompanying tax changes. Departments are examining their requests for monies for the forthcoming fiscal year and the Finance Department is updating its revenue estimates and undertaking tax analysis which was pushed aside in the race to meet the budget deadline." He notes that the minister submits his or her proposals for the fiscal framework (expected revenues, target expenditures, estimated deficit) to the Cabinet Committee on Priorities and Planning. According to Goode, "Throughout the entire year, and in particular in the last few months before the budget [a moving target as we have seen], the Finance Minister and his Department receive voluminous suggestions for tax changes from the public, spending Ministers, Members of Parliament, and Senators." Moreover, the tax administrators of DNR always have a set of technical amendments waiting for each budget.

The preparation for the revenue budget must be distinguished from ad hoc "rulings" or authoritative interpretations of existing tax legislation. In routine cases, these are handled by the DNR. Only where the stakes are very large will the Department of Finance get involved. For example, when the Reichmann family acquired control (60 percent) of Gulf Canada, they obtained a confidential tax ruling permitting the transfer of many of the assets into a partnership between Gulf and Norcen Energy, thus allowing the partnership to increase the value of its assets from depreciated book value to market value, so they can be depreciated again when the partnership is dissolved. Higher depreciation means that taxable income is reduced. One oil industry analyst estimated the size of the tax savings at $1.65 billion. Another said it would amount to between $100 million and $130 million per year for ten years.[30]

Obviously, when this much revenue is at stake, the minister of finance is involved and in this particular case it appears that the minister of energy, mines and resources (Pat Carney) acted as an advocate for the

Reichmanns, claiming the deal would both "Canadianize" Gulf and permit Petro-Canada to acquire much of Gulf Canada's retail network together with refineries to supply it.[31]

10.6 Regulatory Agencies

Government regulation is pervasive in Canada (see Stanbury & Thompson 1980). Despite some recent moves to liberalize or eliminate some regulations, this type of government intervention remains of great importance to business interests and to Canadians generally. The Economic Council (1979, 10) estimated that roughly one-third of all federal and provincial statutes are regulatory, that is, designed primarily to alter the economic behaviour of individuals and firms in the private sector.

Much regulation is administered and enforced by quasi-independent, statutory regulatory agencies (SRAs). (The rest is administered within units of line departments of government. SRAs such as the CRTC, CTC, and NEB are "structural heretics.") They usually perform a number of functions: adjudicative, legislative, research, advisory, and administrative (ECC 1979, 56).

From the perspective of interest groups seeking to influence public policy made by SRAs, the timing of inputs is a much simpler matter than it is for most other types of policy actions. The reason is that the major policy outputs of SRAs are preceded by formal public hearings or by notice of a pending decision to those likely to have a direct interest. For example, before the CRTC makes a decision on an increase in telephone rates by Bell Canada or BC Tel, the following will occur:

- The telephone company will file with the CRTC its application for a rate increase. This is a public document and hence available to potential intervenors (supporters or opponents of the application).
- The CRTC will announce and widely publicize a notice of hearing — hence potential intervenors will be alerted.
- Prior to the beginning of the hearings, the applicant will be required to file a copy of its evidence. It actually contains an *outline* of the case that will be developed in much more detail, but it is most useful to potential intervenors in preparing their position and getting ready for cross-examination. In addition, intervenors, prior to the hearing, may submit written interrogatories to the applicant. These can elicit much valuable information for interest groups seeking to influence the ultimate decision.
- The CRTC will hold public hearings on the telephone company's application for a rate increase. At these hearings, intervenors who are given standing by the CRTC are entitled to argue for or against the application and to cross-examine the witnesses produced by the applicant. At the same time, the witnesses offered by intervenors may be cross-examined by the applicant's legal counsel.

- Subsequent to the hearing, the CRTC issues its decision together with reasons. This is a public document.
- The applicant and intervenors may appeal the decision to the courts on matters of law and procedure (natural justice) and to the federal cabinet on the grounds of public policy. (See Janisch 1979.)

In the case of major policy hearings by a regulatory agency, the timing of each step is well defined and publicly announced in advance:

- Announcement of the hearing.
- Prehearing conference of interested parties and the staff of the agency to discuss the details of the terms of reference and the structure of the hearings.
- Hearings — perhaps in several cities to facilitate public inputs.
- Announcement of the proposed change in policy by the agency.

Note that this does not end the matter for interest groups. They can continue the battle by making representations to the department that also has policy responsibilities in the area.

There is one area in which the timing of representations to an SRA is much more difficult to determine. That is the matter of *ex parte* contacts by regulated firms and others with the senior professional staff and commissioners of the agency. Many of these "one-sided" contacts involve purely mechanical matters associated with the administration of the agency's responsibilities. There is a danger, however, that such contacts can cumulatively give those making them, usually the regulated firms, substantially greater influence with the agency than that enjoyed by potential competitors, consumer groups, and others. The problem for the latter is that they may never know about such *ex parte* contacts — even after they have occurred.

NOTES

1. This refers to the federal department which is or may be likely to initiate and sponsor a policy change, e.g., new legislation, new regulations, or new spending/taxing plans.
2. John Fisher makes the interesting argument that business interests should support the Consumers' Association of Canada, not as an ally, but as a defence against more extensive government regulation: "The business community needs a strong, well researched and organized consumer movement . . . if they don't do the job that's needed, then government certainly will and there are lots of votes in this motherhood area" (*Marketing*, July 4, 1977, p. 17).
3. "Lobbyists in Ottawa present briefs to Commons committees and a few groups such as the Canadian Chamber of Commerce and the Canadian Labour Congress make presentations to the full cabinet.

But the real stuff of lobbying in Ottawa is done in private, in Ministerial offices, at Rockcliffe soirées over cocktails in a quiet bar and especially in the corridors of bureaucracy where policies are first born and where their essential shape is set" (Jo Rush, *Globe and Mail*, October 25, 1980, p. 11).

4. Sandy Fife, "How to go about getting that assistance," *Financial Times*, August 8, 1983, p. 14.
5. Ibid.
6. *Financial Post*, July 28, 1984, p. 19.
7. *Globe and Mail*, October 25, 1980.
8. Michael Rose, "A quiet exercise of power in the PMO," *Maclean's*, April 8, 1985, p. 14.
9. Ibid. See also Bruce Little, "New Solitudes in the Capital," *Report on Business Magazine*, December 1985, pp. 32-38.
10. See, for example, "A Fishy Can of Worms," *Maclean's*, September 30, 1985, pp. 12-13; and Michael Harris, "Fraser resigns post, says action proper," *Globe and Mail*, September 24, 1985, pp. 1-2, 4, 6. But see Hugh Winsor, "Firing of tuna-tainted mandarin holds a chilling message," *Globe and Mail*, December 30, 1985, p. A2.
11. George Bain, "Hill Seat Blues: Why MPs are Nobodies," *Quest*, March 1984, p. 58. See also Charlotte Montgomery, "Bleak picture painted of government back bench," *Globe and Mail*, November 25, 1985, p. A4.
12. George Bain, "Why Canada's Loyal Opposition Should Be Disloyal to Itself," *Report on Business Magazine*, March 1985, p. 19.
13. Ibid., p. 18.
14. Ibid. But see Harvey Enchin, "Tory caucus scuppers broadcasting law amendments," *Globe and Mail*, December 28, 1985, p. B1.
15. Salter Hayden, chairperson of the Standing Senate Committee on Banking, Trade and Commerce for over 30 years, provides an outstanding example. See Philip Teasdale, "Senators with clout expert group hard at it despite all the sniping," *Financial Post*, April 2, 1977, p. 7; and Stanbury (1977, 145-49). On the role of senators as lobbyists or quasi-lobbyists, see John McMenemy (1977) and Richard Cleroux, "Competition act study raises conflict issue," *Globe and Mail*, February 12, 1975.
16. Surely this diffidence does not apply to the corporate, legal, and media elite (see Clement 1975 and Newman 1975).
17. Larry Smith, "Ethical ways of using politicians for profit," *Canadian Business*, February 1981, p. 129.
18. John Gray, "The lobby is spartan, but it works," *Globe and Mail*, October 25, 1980, p. 11.
19. See *Parliamentary Government*, Autumn 1980, pp. 13-15.
20. Larry Smith, op. cit.
21. Quoted in *Parliamentary Government*, Autumn 1982, p. 7.

22. Ibid.

23. Despite the recent Green Paper, *Members of Parliament and Conflict of Interest* (1973), "there is no federal law requiring parliament to disclose, let alone restrict directorates, property and financial holdings, and legal or other activities which might be construed as lobbying" (McMenemy 1977, 455). In August 1985 Prime Minister Mulroney promised new conflict-of-interest regulations — see chapter 9.

24. Linda Sandler, "Cardinals and cucumber sandwiches," *Financial Post*, November 18, 1978, p. 1.

25. McMenemy states: "An examination of public records by the Canadian Press showed that eight of the 22 members of the Senate's committee on banking held 130 company directorships. These 22 senators accounted for 75 per cent of reported directorships of the then 93 senators. The committee members were executives or directors of businesses in banking, investment and insurance, mining, real estate development, and manufacturing and retailing of pulp and paper products, aircraft parts, feed products, clothing, and soft drinks" (1982).

26. See William Johnson, "The Tories' eminence grise," *Globe and Mail*, December 18, 1982, p. 5.

27. *Financial Post*, January 20, 1979.

28. See Vancouver *Sun*, September 11, 1985, pp. 1–2; and Jeffrey Simpson, *Globe and Mail*, September 12, 1985, p. 6.

29. This person is an addition by the author.

30. See Warren Caragata, "Deal costs feds $1 billion," Vancouver *Sun*, September 26, 1985, p. D7. Also see note 9 in chapter 4.

31. See "PetroCan may be Gulf deal winner," *Financial Post*, June 29, 1985, pp. 1–2; "Dealing for an oil giant," *Maclean's*, August 12, 1985, pp. 24–26; "Black, Gulf near complex deal," *Globe and Mail*, August 3, 1985, p. B11; "Gulf will be core for resource grant," *Financial Post*, August 10, 1985, pp. 1–2; "The riddle of the Gulf deal," *Maclean's*, July 29, 1985, pp. 32–33; "Petro-Canada takeover stunning," Vancouver *Sun*, August 19, 1985, p. B8; "100 service stations, 4 refineries in deal," Vancouver *Sun*, August 13, 1985, p. B1; "Gulf dealings end in Tory coup," *Financial Post*, August 17, 1985, p. 13; "Gulf deal policy Carney says," *Globe and Mail*, August 22, 1985, p. 5; and "Carney denies Gulf deal broke election promise," Vancouver *Sun*, August 22, 1985, p. B7.

8

Lobbying Techniques and Vehicles: Part 1

*Writing authoritatively about lobbying is as difficult as writing authori-
tatively about the practice of espionage. Anyone who has any relevant
current information is likely not to be writing about it but practising it,
yet will not tell you how, or with what success. (Roman 1978, 209)*

1.0 INTRODUCTION

Lobbying is one of the most widely used methods of influencing the
behaviour of government. Indeed, in a democracy where elections only
occur once every three to five years and where voters are able to choose
among candidates representing a small number of parties offering a
"full line" of policies, lobbying is essential if public policy is to be even
reasonably responsive to the changing desires of citizens. This chapter
and chapter 9 provide a considerable amount of practical advice for
interest groups wanting to influence public policy. While the material is
divided into two chapters for reasons of length, the chapters should be
read as one integrated piece.

Section 2 of chapter 8 describes the nature of lobbying in general
terms and notes the wide range of interest groups that may at some time
engage in lobbying. Section 3 addresses one of the central ideas in successful lobbying — reciprocity. In section 4 a number of lobbying techniques are discussed: suggestions for sizing up negotiating situations;
paralleling public opinion; lobbying as a competitive process; the use of
public opinion polls; forming coalitions or coordinating lobbying efforts;
and the role of trade associations.

A summary of chapter 9 forms the introduction to that chapter.

2.0 THE NATURE OF LOBBYING

Lobbying in Canada is ubiquitous; yet it occupies an uncomfortable
position in our political life. The individuals who make a profession of
lobbying have been described as "the best-informed, least-understood
and perhaps most influential private citizens in the country" (Whittington
1981, p. G1). Collectively, lobbyists in Canada might be called a "fourth
level of government." (In the U.S., the term "fourth branch of government" is used.)

The scope of lobbying in Canada is hard to document, as Andrew Roman (1978) has emphasized. However, Whittington suggests there are some 300 professional and trade associations in Ottawa "employing 2,000 people and spending $100 million-plus a year getting their messages across to ministers, MPs and bureaucrats" (1981, p. G1). Harrison (1979a) noted that in 1958 the Ottawa telephone book recorded 119 listings under "associations" while in 1978 the total was 511, and that for "more than one-half of them . . . [their] main role is to lobby the federal government." The job of lobbyists and public policy consultants in his view is to "alert companies in advance to decisions that will influence corporate planning or to press the government for changes in existing or proposed legislation."

What is a lobbyist? In the most general terms, a lobbyist is any person who seeks to influence public policy. Hence, the term could be applied to the senior citizen who writes a letter urging his or her MP to fight the proposal to de-index the old age pension, to a former deputy minister retained by a large trade association to advise it on how to persuade the cabinet to increase subsidies and tax expenditures to that industry. It also includes the head of the Canadian Federation of Agriculture who meets with politicians urging them to change a regulation raising the subsidy on industrial milk that now costs the federal treasury more than $300 million annually.[1] Therefore, lobbyists may be paid professionals representing a firm or other interest group or they may be "amateurs" representing only themselves or a volunteer group.

Fred Moonen, vice-president of government relations for MacMillan Bloedel, Canada's largest forest-products company, describes his role as a lobbyist as "creative loitering." By this he means that he haunts the corridors of the legislative building in Victoria waiting to catch cabinet ministers and backbenchers (including those in the opposition) for a few minutes' discussion about legislation or administrative policy (Comparelli 1983).

Lobbyists may be seeking to advance the pecuniary interests of an individual, a firm, an industry, or a group. This is what people mean when they think of "special interests" seeking some economic advantage from government, despite the fact that such entreaties are almost always couched in rhetoric that claims the public interest will be served by government acting in the way the lobbyist wants.

While direct (and indirect) economic interests motivate the majority of lobbying efforts, there are plenty of interest groups seeking actions by government that do not confer an economic benefit on their members. These groups are seeking some type of collective, nonpecuniary, nonexclusive benefit that usually represents some "value" they hold dear. The aims of such "values" groups range widely (see Figure 8-1) and include:

- the prevention of abortions or, conversely, the right of women to have a great deal of personal control over reproduction;

- the advancement of individual civil rights by protecting such fundamental rights as freedom of speech;
- the protection of wildlife and the environment generally (although,
  in some cases, members of a particular group may benefit directly
  from successful lobbying, e.g., preventing logging in a wilderness area
  in which they have a cabin or enjoy recreation); and
- ideological or religious objectives that they seek to embody in legislation (e.g., right-to-work legislation, regulations closing businesses on
  Sunday).

Because such groups seek a collective benefit (although the number
of the beneficiaries may vary greatly), they often claim they are not self-
interested but are acting "in the public interest". (See, for example, the
discussion in Kernaghan 1985e, 310.) We should not forget, however,
that people can and do gain utility from government actions that embody
their values as well as those actions that improve their income or wealth.
In other words, it is hard to escape from the fact that all interest-group
lobbying is designed to improve the welfare, broadly defined, of the
members of the interest group. Moreover, the proponents of "values"
objectives rather than pecuniary objectives are seldom sensitive to the
idea that what they believe to be "good for everyone" is seen by some
other persons as making them worse off. Religious fundamentalists are
the most obtuse to this idea.[2] More generally, see Malvern (1985).

There is widespread confusion between "private" and "public" interests. This is well illustrated by the remarks of a Liberal MP during the
debate in 1983 on a private member's bill to require the registration of
paid lobbyists. Gary F. McCauley, the Liberal member for Moncton,
argued that any bill requiring the registration of lobbyists should distinguish between "special interest advocates" and "public interest" lobbyists. He offered the following quotation to explain what he meant by
the latter:

> Public or citizens' interest groups can and should be distinguished
> from special interest groups. Public interest groups have no finan-
> cial or other vested interest in the causes they support — They want
> a better society and so challenge politicians, bureaucrats, business-
> men and others to take into account in their decision making aspects
> of the public interest that might otherwise be overlooked or not
> given proper weight. (Bon 1981)[3]

He then went on to provide an example of a public interest lobby that
had met that morning with the Atlantic-area government caucus:

> We had before us representatives of the International Union of the
> Marine and Shipbuilding Workers of Canada, Local 3, Saint John,
> New Brunswick. They presented to us in a forceful and passionate
> way their beliefs regarding the shipbuilding industry, not only on

Figure 8–1

ILLUSTRATIVE CLASSIFICATION OF INTEREST GROUPS IN CANADA

1.0 BUSINESS GROUPS

1.1 Umbrella/Conglomerate Associations

Business Council on National Issues
Canadian Chamber of Commerce
Canadian Federation of Independent Business
(also size specific)
British Columbia Business Council

1.2 Sectoral Associations

Canadian Manufacturers' Association
Council of Forest Industries of British Columbia
Canadian Credit Institute
Grocery Products Manufacturers of Canada

Canadian Real Estate Association
Retail Council of Canada
Fisheries Council of Canada
Retail Merchants Association of Canada

1.3 Activity-Specific Associations

Canadian Direct Marketing Association
Canadian Export Association
Canadian Importers Association
Canadian Industrial Traffic League
Packaging Association of Canada

1.4 Industry-Specific Associations

Canadian Bankers' Association
Canadian Broadcasters Association
Canadian Pulp and Paper Association
Canadian Drug Manufacturers Association

Canadian Food Processors Association
Canadian Gas Association
Insurance Bureau of Canada
Canadian Institute of Mining and Metallurgy

Mining Association of Canada
Independent Petroleum Association of Canada
Canadian Petroleum Association
Council of Printing Industries of Canada
Canadian Ship Building and Ship Repairing
    Association
Canadian Textile Institute
Housing and Urban Development Association
    of Canada
Urban Development Institute of Canada

Canadian Jewellers Association
Association of Canadian Distillers
Investment Dealers Association of Canada
Canadian Toy Importers Association
Canadian Association of Motion Picture
    Producers
Canadian Daily Newspaper Publishers Association
Canadian Paper Box Manufacturers Association
Canadian Federation of Independent Petroleum
    Marketers
Pipeline Contractors Association of Canada
Soap and Detergent Association of Canada
Canadian Soft Drink Association
Canadian Steel Industry Research Association
Canadian Association of Movers

Pharmaceutical Manufacturers Association
    of Canada
Aerospace Industries of Canada
Bakery Council of Canada
Canadian Chemical Producers Association
Canadian Construction Association
Canadian Association of Data Processing
    Services Organization
Canadian Electrical Association
Canadian Trucking Association

1.5 Product-Specific Associations

Canadian Shipbuilders Association
Automotive Parts Manufacturing Association of Canada
Motor Vehicle Manufacturers Association
Canadian Booksellers Association
Brewers Association of Canada
Canadian Retail Building Supply Council
Canadian Portland Cement Association
Federation of Automobile Dealers Association of Canada
Coal Association of Canada
Canadian Machine Builders Association
Canadian Electrical Distributors Association
Canadian National Millers Association
Canadian Shoe Retailers Association
Shoe Manufacturers Association
Canadian Council of Furniture Manufacturers
Canadian Life and Health Insurance Association

Figure 8–1 (continued)

2.0 LABOUR GROUPS

Canadian Labour Congress
Various local/regional labour councils,
  e.g., Calgary Labour Council and
  provincial federations of labour
Confédération des syndicats nationaux
Confederation of Canadian Unions
AFL-CIO (Building and Construction Trades
  Department)
Hundreds of individual trade unions, e.g.,
  Food and Service Workers of Canada,
  United Steelworkers of America

3.0 AGRICULTURE-RELATED GROUPS

Canadian Federation of Agriculture
Dairy Bureau of Canada (includes processors)
Dairy Farmers of Canada
National Dairy Council of Canada
Canadian Egg Producers Council
Canada Grains Council
Canadian Meat Council (includes processors)
Canadian Pork Council (includes processors)
National Farmers Union
Canadian Broiler Council
Saskatchewan Wheat Pool
Prairie Canola Growers Council
Ontario Federation of Agriculture
B.C. Pork Producers Association

4.0 PROFESSIONAL ASSOCIATIONS

Society of Management Accountants of Canada
Canadian Institute of Chartered Accountants
Certified General Accountants' Association
Canadian Bar Association
Canadian Dental Association
Canadian Medical Association
Association of Consulting Engineers of Canada
Canadian Marine Pilots Association
Canadian Institute of Actuaries
Canadian Professional Golfers Association
Canadian Council of Professional Engineers
Canadian Society of Petroleum Geologists
Interior Designers of Canada
Canadian Council of Financial Analysts
Canadian Nurses Association
Canadian Actors Equity Association
Canadian Police Association
Canadian Association of University Teachers

5.0 GOVERNMENTAL BODIES

Federation of Canadian Municipalities
Association of Municipalities of Ontario
Union of B.C. Municipalities
Provincial-Municipal Council, Inc.

6.0 UNIVERSITIES AND RESEARCH ORGANIZATIONS

Canadian Association for Dental Research
Canadian Energy Research Institute
Canadian Institute for Advanced Research
Federation of Engineering and Scientific Associations
Royal Society of Canada

Association of Atlantic Universities
Association of Universities and Colleges
of Canada
Canadian Association of Graduate Schools
Institute for Research on Public Policy
The Fraser Institute

7.0 "VALUES" ORGANIZATIONS

7.1 Environmental Groups

Federation of Associations on the
Canadian Environment
Friends of the Earth
Greenpeace
Air Pollution Control Association

Energy Probe Research Foundation
Joint Air Pollution Control Association
Canadian Wildlife Federation
Sierra Club

7.2 Reproduction-Related Groups

Coalition for the Protection of Human Life
Birthright (various local groups)
Serena (various local groups)
Planned Parenthood Federation of Canada
Canadian Abortion Rights Action League

Figure 8–1 (continued)

7.3 Health/Handicap Groups

Canadian Hearing Society
Canadian Heart Foundation
Canadian Council on Smoking and Health
Canadian Mental Health Association
Canadian Public Health Association
Action League for Physically Handicapped
    Adults
Canadian Rehabilitation Council for the
    Disabled
Canadian National Institute for the Blind
Council for Exceptional Children
Canadian Institute for Child Health
Canadian Association for Health, Physical
    Education and Recreation

7.4 Ideological/Nationalist Groups

Council for Canadian Unity
National Citizens' Coalition
Revolutionary Workers' League
Libertarian Party of Canada
Socialist Party of Canada
Coalition Canada
Canadians for Canada
Canadians for One Canada

7.5 Religious and Ethnic Groups

Canadian Zionist Federation
Canadian Jewish Congress
Native Council of Canada
Inuit, Tapirisat of Canada
National Indian Brotherhood
National Association of Japanese Canadians
Ukrainian Canadian Committee
Ukrainian National Federation of Canada, Inc.
Clans and Scottish Societies of Canada
Fédération des francophones hors Québec

7.6 Women's Groups

National Action Committee on the Status of Women
Women for Political Action
Voice of Women (various provincial bodies)
Federation of Junior Leagues of Canada
Soroptomist International of the Americas, Inc.
Elizabeth Fry Society (provincial and local
    chapters)

IODE National Chapter of Canada
Canadian Association of Women Executives
Federated Women's Institutes of Canada
Society for Canadian Women in Science
    and Technology

7.7 Other

Canadian Civil Liberties Association
Canadian Council of War Veterans Association
Canadian Library Association
Canadian Federation of Humane Societies
National Anti-Poverty Association

Source: The categories and the classification of individual groups was done by the author, while the names of the groups were obtained
    from Brian Land, ed., *Directory of Associations in Canada Fifth Edition, 1984* (Toronto: Micromedia, 1984).

the East Coast of Canada but on the West Coast and wherever that industry is situated in this great country. They did a fantastic job presenting their case. We were very impressed by the quality of their arguments. I do not think any of us who heard them would be of the opinion that they were a special interest advocacy group about which we have to be concerned, that they were the kind of people who had to be registered, noted and so on.[4]

This is a truly charming example of naiveté in this regard and illustrates the practice of private pecuniary interests wrapping themselves in the flag of the public interest. Why are the members of a shipbuilding union so passionately concerned about the shipbuilding industry? Could it be that their incomes are directly affected by its fortunes? Surely a passionate concern about one's own income is a private interest — an obviously pecuniary interest at that.

Kernaghan (1985g, 309), following Pross (1975), states that "a broad and useful distinction can be made between *institutional* groups and *issue-oriented* groups."[5] The former are "characterized by organizational continuity and cohesion. They are highly knowledgeable about the policy-making process and about how to get access to public officials; their membership is stable; they have concrete and immediate operational objectives but their ultimate aims are sufficiently broad that they can bargain with government over achieving particular concessions; and their long-run credibility with government decision makers is more important than any single issue or objective."

In contrast, according to Kernaghan, issue-oriented groups "tend to be poorly organized; they have little knowledge of government and of how to contact public officials; there is constant turn-over in their membership; they have trouble developing and sticking to short-run goals; and they are not usually concerned about their long-run credibility with public officials" (1985g, 309). An example of an issue-oriented group is the "Dandelions," a group representing the unemployed in Alberta. According to press reports, "In five months, the Dandelions have grown into a potent pressure group for government to speed recovery from a stubborn economic slump [10.6 percent unemployment]."[6] Its members are predominantly unemployed, middle-aged, skilled workers who previously would not have been seen demonstrating on the steps of the legislature, although the group is nonpartisan. The group is said to have 3000 adherents, but there are no membership lists or fees. As the leader of the NDP remarked: "They're not behaving in the normal Alberta way of accepting things. They are fighting back, and they've brought the issue of unemployment front and centre."[7] The group is credited with pressuring the Lougheed government to create fifteen make-work capital projects ranging from reforestation to sewage repair.

In a pluralist democracy, government functions largely by persuasion, despite the enormous powers that reside in the cabinet (recall chapter 4). There are many visions of what we call the public interest, and a large number of individuals and groups seek to use the power of the state to bring about their vision of what constitutes the good society or, more commonly, to advance their own private interests. One of the primary functions of the political system is to find ways of accommodating conflicting interests, perhaps even finding a consensus. It would be naive, however, to suggest (as some advocates of pluralism do) that competitive interest-group behaviour produces socially ideal outcomes. Gillies sets out the argument for why it is legitimate for business to take an active role in a pluralist democracy:

> It follows that, under such a system of government, it is not only a right, but a requirement, that business have an input in the establishment of public policy. Businessmen, of course, should not expect to determine the public interest — it must be determined through the political process — and they should not expect that the end result of the interplay and accommodation among groups with different goals will be policies that have no other purpose than to enable business to maximize profits. But businessmen should have, as an important group in society, an effective input into the process through which the decisions under which they operate are made. (1981, 7)

While lobbying in one of its many forms is a pervasive activity, the very work has negative connotations for many people. As Herb Perry, executive director of the Institution of Association Executives (the trade association for the senior personnel who run trade associations and other formal groups), points out: "There is sometimes an impression that lobbying is dirty or immoral. [Yet] every time a voter phones a school trustee he's lobbying. When the Society for Crippled Children asks for larger doorways on washrooms, it's lobbying."[8]

Lobbying has also been described as "the world's second-oldest profession." But like the world's oldest profession, it is not a respected one: "Very few parents want their children to grow up to be lobbyists." Lobbying by government affairs professionals in Ottawa is "sort of like adultery . . . it's not the sort of thing successful ones will talk about," says Andrew Roman of the Public Interest Advocacy Centre (as quoted in Hayes 1983).

The term *lobbying* most often refers to the activities of organized interest groups designed to influence public policy in some way. Yet the ubiquity of lobbying is illustrated by the fact that, within government, ministers lobby one another and provincial governments frequently lobby the federal government. Both types of lobbying are illustrated in the following news story:

Gerald Merrithew, Canada's Minister of State for Forestry, says he will press federal Employment Minister Flora MacDonald to devote a large chunk of her $1-billion in job-creation money to forest renewal. "If we're going to try to create some short-term jobs, let's do it in forests," Mr. Merrithew told reporters after a meeting of federal, provincial and territorial forestry ministers in Toronto yesterday. The ministers unanimously supported a resolution from Newfoundland to lobby the federal Government for funds to enable all the provinces to copy a successful forestry job-creation scheme in Newfoundland.[9]

The process of resolving conflicts among competing interests through political bargaining does not imply that government is passive. Indeed, it commonly issues invitations to interest groups to lobby it. This often takes the form of task forces, commissions of inquiry, and various other mechanisms for consultation with organized interests or what is called the "attentive publics." Consider the following two examples:

Federal Minister of Regional Industrial Expansion Sinclair Stevens has asked the members of the 1982 auto industry task force for advice on policy for the sector. . . . The task force group [consists of] representatives of the Automotive Parts Manufacturers Association of Canada, the Big Three auto makers and the United Auto Workers union. . . . Among the questions to be considered are the current validity of the two-year-old task force recommendation for minimum domestic content in all vehicles sold in Canada, the need for continued restraints on imports of Japanese cars and the possibility that changes are required to the Canada-U.S. auto pact.[10]

In August 1985 Trade Minister James Kelleher announced plans to set up a private sector advisory committee on trade matters that will be composed of representatives of business, labour, and other groups. Between twenty and thirty people will be appointed. According to the newspaper stories, the committee is being modelled after a U.S. group in operation for a decade that reports to the Special Trade Representative. The proposed committee is expected to become a permanent body with about twenty subcommittees representing different industry sectors. "Members of the committee will be asked to state the needs of Canadian industry in any trade talks with the United States and during GATT [General Agreements on Tariffs and Trade] negotiations so that Canadian negotiators stay plugged in to companies that might be affected."[11]

In January 1986 the federal government named the thirty-eight members of the International Trade Advisory Committee (ITAC) that will report to the minister for international trade (James Kelleher) and is "intended to give him a sense of private-sector sentiments as the Government moves ahead with key trade talks." While the committee and

its chairperson were announced in the fall of 1985, "the delay in naming the members was disagreement between Mr. [Walter] Light [its
chairperson] and Mr. Kelleher over the sort of people who should be on
the committee. In the end it was the Government that made the choices,
and the result appears to be a political masterpiece." Ontario has fourteen members, while Quebec has eleven, but all provinces are represented. Francophones make up eight of the thirty-nine members. Only
one union leader, James McCambly, head of the 220 000-member Canadian Federation of Labour, agreed to join the committee. Also on the
committee is the president of the Consumers' Association of Canada
and a "handful of academics." In addition, there will be a range of subcommittees known as sectoral Advisory Groups on International Trade.
According to a government statement, the ITAC will "provide a two-way
flow of information and advice between Government and business, labor
and other groups."[12]
  While the many advisory committees that are attached to government departments and agencies provide a useful, legitimate, and institutionalized point of access for organized interests (e.g., business and
unions), important but unorganized interests (consumers, taxpayers) are
not at the same table. However, some people argue that it is the role of
public servant advisors and politicians to speak for the unorganized.

3.0 RECIPROCITY AND THE ART OF LOBBYING

3.1 Lobbying as an Exchange Process

In chapter 4 it was noted that the norm of reciprocity is a strong one in
almost all societies. Indeed, a wide range of individual and group
behaviour can be fairly characterized as some type — often implicit — of
exchange process. The employment relationship is easily seen as an
exchange process, although it is naive to believe that all that is involved
is the exchange of money for work. Both sides of the transaction, particularly in the case of professionals and more senior personnel, are complex and subtle, as such words associated with the employment
relationship — loyalty, integrity, understanding, and personal growth —
imply. Certainly, at the core of most personal relationships (e.g., marriage) is an exchange process, although we don't like to think of love,
kindness, and esteem as items of exchange.
  At first glance, lobbying and other techniques designed to influence
the behaviour of government appear to be unilateral in character. The
firm or other interest group is using resources in an effort to persuade
policy makers to alter their behaviour. If the group succeeds, its targets
do not do what they originally intended to do. It appears that through
the application of pressure or other forms of persuasion the interest group
has acted unilaterally to produce an involuntary change in the policy
maker's behaviour.

While successful lobbying is sometimes a unilateral (one-way) process, more commonly (as emphasized in chapter 4) it is a two-way or exchange process. Lobbyists are likely to be more successful more often if they start out with the recognition that lobbying is a process of exchange. If they want something from government (a cabinet member, a senior civil servant, etc.), they should begin by thinking of what they can offer in exchange.

Effective lobbyists make use of the norm of reciprocity by thinking of what it is they or their organization can offer the target of their lobbying to induce the policy maker to give them what they want (or at least half a loaf). This often requires that lobbyists go beyond the simple exchanges posited by the public choice approach to policy making (i.e., policies are exchanged for votes or for campaign contributions). It may also require that the interest group go beyond the broader process of exchange outlined in section 10 of chapter 4.

To engage in the effective use of reciprocity in the context of lobbying, the interest group has to begin by determining two things:

• What is it that the interest group wants from the various individuals and groups that are believed to have an impact on government policy?
• What is it that the interest group has that it can offer to the targets of its lobbying efforts in exchange for what it wants from them?

3.2 Power and Reciprocity

Pfeffer (1981, chap. 4) argues that the power of individuals in an organizational context comes from the importance of what they do in the organization (the dependence of others on them) and their skill in doing it — including their skill in convincing others of the importance of their skill. The relationship of power to dependence is as follows: "Power derives from having something that someone else wants or needs and being in control of the performance or resource so that there are few alternative sources, or no alternative sources, for obtaining what is desired" (Pfeffer 1981, 99). But power is based on *net* dependence of one individual or organization on another. It stems from the ability to provide resources (in a controlled fashion) that facilitate the attainment of other people's objectives. Resources include such disparate items as money, prestige, legitimacy, expertise, the ability to deal with uncertainty, and the ability to offer rewards and levy sanctions. The heart of power is the ability to exercise discretion over these resources, that is, who gets them, in what amount, and on what terms.

Power can also stem from the ability to affect some part of the decision process by, for example, controlling the premises used in making decisions, the set of alternatives considered, and the information about the alternatives that is disseminated to other participants.

3.3 Denying Approval and Legitimacy

With this advice in mind, the critical question to answer is this: What resource(s) does the interest group have that the target of its lobbying effort is dependent upon, that is, strongly desires? Specifically, what is it that those who have power in governments (cabinet ministers, as well as senior bureaucrats, who can exercise considerable discretion) want? In the first place, the "governors" in a democracy want approval for their actions (or at least acquiescence). See Partridge (1971). In the second place, they want their actions to be seen as legitimate. Interest groups are capable of denying the governors approval of their actions or proposed actions. They may do this vigorously but quietly in the context of advisory committees, personal letters, telephone calls, and meetings with key decision makers. They can also indicate their disapproval to other active participants in the policy system. Note that informing others who are part of the same system is a step between keeping one's advice confidential and "going public" (e.g., seeking media publicity for the group's position).[13] Since policy making is a serial game, nattering and gossiping about a decision by respected players can influence the climate of opinion regarding subsequent issues. Harsh criticism of government actors that is made known to other groups can harm the reputation of those actors. (Indeed, in some primitive societies, gossip is a powerful method of social control.) At a personal level, most people care a great deal about what others think of them. Criticism of government decisions is often taken as personal criticism by those who had a significant role in the decision. Because the desire for approval is strong, well-reasoned criticism of a particular decision may well make it easier for the interest group to get its way in future encounters with the targets of their criticism.

The withholding of approval can take the strong form of highly visible public criticism. In Canada, this is not a course of action to be undertaken lightly by well-established players for several reasons. First, the culture of policy making in this country is more one of quiet elite accommodation behind closed doors (or at least in forums that have a quite restricted list of familiar participants) than it is of harsh public exchanges or "bargaining in the media" (see Presthus 1974c). When a group "goes public with a bang," it is violating widely accepted ideas of how groups should participate in the policy process (see Kernaghan 1985e and Faulkner 1982). Such action is usually taken as a last resort after other less public and confrontational representations have been made. Alternatively, harsh public criticism of senior players in the government is a sign of an inexperienced interest group that doesn't understand the cultural nuances of the process. (Of course, some groups routinely engage in strong public criticism of policy makers and stage "media events" to publicize their cause, e.g., the anti-sealing campaign by Greenpeace.)

Second, interest-group leaders hesitate to criticize targets in government in the mass media because they know that their message can easily be distorted. This may occur, not so much because the media is biased, but because it must necessarily be selective and what makes a good news story (see chapter 11) is often at odds with reasoned discourse. In addition, once one seeks media coverage, it is hard to control the volume or amplitude of what is communicated. The criticism may come across as either too muted (it may even be ignored by the media) or far too loud.

Third, under the Westminster model of government, public servants who are publicly criticized cannot answer back.[14] Indeed, since they are supposed to be anonymous, it is deemed to be unfair and unsportsman-like to attack them in public. In fact, doing so may require their minis-ter (who is publicly and politically responsible for their behaviour) to defend them. That may escalate the conflict to the disadvantage of the interest group.

It should be recognized, however, that for cabinet ministers the threat by a reputable interest group to "go public in a big way" is seldom taken lightly. Most ministers prefer to be perceived as being in control of events — they cherish the ideal of smoothly functioning competence. They don't want to appear to be "event driven." Public conflicts are seen by tidy-minded and consensus-seeking Canadians (the majority) as both unseemly and a sign of poor political management. Moreover, public criticism — if it is prominent in the mass media — requires the politician to respond, if only to deny the validity of the criticism. In addition, reporters, sensing the possibility of a good story, may take the issue away from the interest group, change its direction, or amplify it out of proportion. The mass media view politics as a form of legal "blood sport." Many reporters tend to operate on the assumption that the cut and thrust of the daily Question Period exemplifies the entire political process.[15]

In general, therefore, ministers are not anxious to have major, usu-ally placid, interest groups vigorously criticizing them in the media. Some-times, however, ministers apply the dictum that the quality of a person is measured by the number and character of his or her enemies. They may relish public criticism from some groups in certain situations, as it gives them an opportunity to appeal to a larger or politically more impor-tant constituency. For example, when he was minister of agriculture under Pierre Trudeau, Eugene Whelan frequently made political hay out of the public criticisms of supply-management marketing boards advanced by academics, consumer groups, or food processors.

Denying legitimacy to major policy-making actors in the government is much harder to accomplish than it is to offer trenchant criticism and thereby deny approval of policy makers' actions. In general, it is hard to convince others (notably other major players in the policy system and public opinion) that decisions taken by cabinet ministers with the advice of senior public servants lack legitimacy where they follow the standard, legally prescribed procedures. The crux of the argument must turn on the distinction between "convention" and "law" along the lines described by the Supreme Court of Canada in its decision on the federal government's reference regarding the process of amending the Constitution.[16] The interest group must argue that while legally the government has the authority to do what it proposes to do (or has done), either the way that it has gone about its decision violated the usual method of doing things or the substance of the decision was widely different from the usual or customary way of dealing with the issue. To undermine the legitimacy of the decision, the group could argue that not every important interest group was consulted, insufficient time was given for consultation, the government failed to appreciate or be sensitive to the interests of large numbers of people who have a "right" to be treated better by the decision, or the process of consultation was "a farce" in that some groups had access to key people while others had to be content with written briefs.

The interest group's objective is to convince others (including the government itself) that a "fair and reasonable" decision could not and was not arrived at because the process of decision making was "unfair." It was not in accord with contemporary thinking about what constitutes proper decision making in a pluralist democracy. If a group is able to gain considerable support for its view that the process (or outcome) was not legitimate, it can put enormous pressure on a government because of the norm in a democracy that governors should only govern with the consent of the governed. This consent is far more than a matter of narrow legal authority, as the case of Prohibition in the U.S. so clearly indicated. Therefore, by denying the legitimacy of the process, the interest group seeks to put pressure on decision makers to accede to its demands in the future. Put the other way, the interest group can offer policy makers tacit legitimacy for their actions by not challenging them publicly or even within the relevant "policy community." The obverse of the coin is that the group will try to deny legitimacy in various ways as discussed above.

3.4 Weaving a Delicate Web

What else can the lobbyist provide to a minister so as to evoke reciprocity — other than the traditional media of exchange (information, campaign contributions, and efforts to obtain helpful media coverage)? The lobbyist can offer empathy for the overburdened minister who must function in several roles: head of a department, MP, member of cabinet, representative of a regional/ethnic/sectoral interest. The workload is very heavy, the time pressures are great, and the risks of making politically embarrassing mistakes are fairly high. Ministers are aware that theirs is a high-wire act without a net. The often intense partisanship of the House of Commons and the "glare of the omnipresent media" mean that someone who is personally sympathetic and supportive of the minister's efforts is likely to be appreciated. Besides, "understanding" is one of the most subtle forms of flattery. Politicians, it is safe to say, usually have large egos, but they are also racked by feelings of insecurity. Therefore, lobbyists who can gain access, preferably in informal settings, are in a strong position to spin a subtle web of tacit obligation with a minister by friendship and understanding, by appreciating the man or woman, not simply the person who fills the formal position.

A most useful way to create in others an implicit need to reciprocate is to provide help when and where it is most needed. The most valued friend is the one who pitches in without reproach to solve a problem on a no-questions-asked basis. Effective lobbyists, therefore, set out to make themselves helpful, to solve problems — in many cases quite small problems — for the people they seek to influence. For example, the minister is giving a speech to an industry group and his or her staff has forgotten to have plenty of copies run off for the press and members of the audience. The head of the association (and its chief lobbyist) can move quickly to have the association's staff do the job on a moment's notice to save the minister embarrassment. This is a small thing, but a sense of obligation may be built up from doing a lot of small favours. The point is that lobbyists try to build up a bank account of goodwill that can be drawn upon on behalf of the interest group they represent. There is no need to overtly "call in one's markers."[17] Only a totally insensitive ingrate fails to appreciate that he or she has been the beneficiary of "kindnesses" from others. The name of the game is not to try to establish a "contractual" exchange of favours on a tit-for-tat basis, but to establish a framework or climate in which lobbyists' efforts at persuading a minister (or senior bureaucrat who can be plied with valuable information) to do (or not do) something have the greatest chance of success on an ongoing basis. They want to be sure of being heard when others are not, and heard sympathetically — by someone who wants to help them, even though it may be difficult for a minister to do so.[18]

Lobbyists are likely to be more effective if those they seek to influence like them as individuals (e.g., they are well-spoken, have a sense of humour, are well informed and highly credible, are able to be empathetic, and are well-mannered). The less attractive the group's case or reputation, the greater the need to have an envoy who outshines his or her client in these regards. The messenger can, by his or her personal characteristics and behaviour, obtain a fair hearing for a message that may be unpalatable. There is no question that in both lobbying and the courtroom a client's arguments can be made more (or less) persuasive by his or her choice of advocate.

3.5 Reciprocity and the Integration of Interests: An Example

In August 1985 the federal Conservative caucus whip, Chuck Cook, joined the board of Seastar Resource Corp., a "fledgling aquaculture company." Immediately after the announcement, the company's stock shot up substantially on the Vancouver Stock Exchange. The president of Seastar, Frank Ceconi, was Cook's campaign manager in the 1984 federal election. The company's secretary put it this way: "Frank worked hard during (Cook's) campaign and now it's time for Chuck to work damn hard for us." While Seastar isn't looking for "any special deals" from the federal government, "we certainly expect (Cook) to act as a sounding board for the entire aquaculture industry." Cook will not be paid for being a director, but he is a shareholder in Seastar. Cook stated that "not being in Cabinet, there's no reason why I shouldn't sit on the board. You have to be very careful that you don't get yourself into a conflict situation." However, Cook is writing a brief on aquaculture to the federal government, but this "is not a conflict situation that I can see," said Cook. "We're not really looking at any government contracts at all." Other people familiar with the rapidly growing industry say that it has problems, and it is likely that some of the firms will be asking for government help.[19] Less than two weeks later, Cook resigned from the board of Seastar, expressing concern about perceptions of conflicts of interest.[20]

This example illustrates a melange of motives and interests. By joining the board of Seastar, Cook is reciprocating his former campaign manager's efforts on his behalf and is looking after his own investment. And by helping the industry (by providing information about developments within the federal government and by acting as a sounding board for industry concerns), Cook can claim that he is not acting in a self-interested fashion. Rather, he is advancing a regional or constituency interest in the name of high technology, new jobs, and local economic development. There is obviously a remarkable integration of interests in this situation.

4.0 LOBBYING TECHNIQUES

In this section I discuss a number of lobbying techniques. Six are analyzed in this chapter and eight more are dealt with in chapter 9.

4.1 Sizing Up Negotiating Situations

Howard Raiffa (1982, chap. 1) provides a check list of important characteristics of conflict situations that are to be resolved by negotiation and persuasion. With a little imagination these can be adapted and applied to efforts by interest groups to lobby government.

- Are there more than two parties?
  - Are the identities of all the parties known?
  - Multiple parties raise the question of coalitions and coopera-tive strategies.
  - Is the number of parties likely to change during the process?
- Are the parties monolithic?
  - Is there internal conflict in government (e.g., different departments have different positions) and/or in rival groups seeking to influ-ence government?
- Is the game repetitive?
  - Once-and-for-all negotiations can make short-run behaviour/ strategies rational, but these would be quite inappropriate if the protagonists are involved in a serial or multi-inning game.
  - In repetitive situations, reputation counts. How you behave today affects how you will be seen in the future.
  - Even if the game is serial, the issues and circumstances of future encounters may be uncertain.
- Are there linkage effects?
  - One negotiation (issue) may be linked to another; hence there are externalities to be taken into account.
  - Astute negotiators (lobbyists) have to think in terms of "packages," although all of the items/issues may not be well defined or even contemporaneous.
- Is there more than one issue?
  - Is there one dominant issue for both sides or are there several inter-related ones?
  - Which issues are more or less important? Beware of bluffing in this context.
  - How are individual groups likely to resolve trade-offs among issues (objectives)?
  - Are there issues on which cooperation is easier and others that are more clearly "I win, you lose"?
- Is an agreement required?
  - What is the possible set of outcomes? Is partial or limited agree-ment possible? Can things be left the way they are? Are there exog-enous forces that could take it out of the hands of both parties?
  - What are the consequences of nonagreement? (Temporarily? Permanently?)
- Is ratification required?
  - Do the negotiators have to go back to their principals for approval?
  - How much influence does the spokesperson (agent) have with his or her principals?
  - The need for ratification can be a double-edged sword; it can be used strategically.

- Are threats possible?
  - What sanctions (negative or positive) can the various parties impose on others?
  - Are the threats fixed or variable?
  - How is the other side likely to respond to threats (inducements)?
- Are the contracts binding?
  - How can the parties be sure the other side will live up to the deal? In lobbying, there may be no external authority to enforce the understanding reached.
  - Changing exogenous conditions may require changes in the terms of the agreement. What mechanisms are available to modify the original arrangement?
- Are the negotiations private or public?
  - It is hard to gain concessions in public when an interest group has "backed itself into a corner" by taking a strong public stance on some point (but this move is also a tactical one).
  - When negotiations are private, public statements or leaks, if artfully used, can be useful, but there are risks too.
  - Negotiations conducted in public often encourage posturing aimed more at one's own side rather than being effective with lobbying targets.
- What are the group norms?
  - What expectations does each group have about each other and about the process of relating to each other?
  - Can government and interest groups behave as "cooperative antagonists" (i.e., they have conflicting interests but desire to reach a "solution" by a cooperative process)? Alternatively, are they "strident antagonists" or "fully cooperative partners"?
- Is third-party intervention possible?
  - What role would outsiders play? Would they impose a settlement or merely offer assistance in the negotiations?
  - In the case of lobbying, negotiations may be conducted at a middle level of the hierarchy; then if agreement can't be reached, the problem can be "bucked upstairs" to the "statesmen" who take a wider and longer view of the issues and the process itself.

4.2 Paralleling Public Opinion

It is often critical for an interest group to align itself with public opinion, if not with that nebulous but powerful idea, the public interest. Bill Neville, formerly chief of staff for Joe Clark and now chairperson of Public Affairs International, put it this way, "When a general objective has widespread public support [e.g., Canadianization under the NEP] associating yourself with that objective, then trying to alter how it is eventually expressed as public policy . . . is the key to successful lobbying" (quoted in Hayes 1983). A variant on this proposition is, "Never stonewall a government when the odds are stacked against you."

After the first OPEC oil crisis in 1973 shocked the Canadian public, and Marc Lalonde, then Minister of Energy, Mines and Resources, stated clearly his intentions to intrude upon virtually every significant industry activity as well as the laws of supply and demand, the oil industry refused to play ball. Negotiations between the oil barons and the bureaucrats stalled and were frequently stalemated, the customary presentation of private sector interests, information exchange, and orderly bargaining process was short-circuited. In essence, the industry broke unwritten Lobbying Rule Number One: never stonewall a government when the odds are stacked against you. When the NEP was finally introduced in October, 1980, its effect was dramatic — even tragic from the oil industry's point of view. A senior official of the Canadian Petroleum Association recalls: "We just didn't believe it was going to happen." (Hayes 1983)

Public opinion, as noted in chapter 5, operates in two ways in the process of public policy formation. First, if an interest group is on the side of public opinion (or at least not in conflict with it), it will be much easier for the group to convince the government to go along with its wishes. Second, where public opinion is strongly held and opposed to the position advanced by an interest group, the group will find it all but impossible to convince a government to act as the group wishes, even if the group is usually considered to be powerful. The party in power is likely to lose more political support by acceding to rather than rejecting the group's demands.

For quite a number of issues that are important to a single firm, an industry, or members of another interest group, there is no public opinion at all. This may be because of the low visibility of the issue or the low priority the public puts upon it. However, because of imperfect and costly information, rational ignorance, and the free-rider effect, the public may either not appreciate that an issue could have a substantial impact on their wallets or be unable (or unwilling) to organize against the group seeking action from government.

4.2.1 Strategies for Dealing with Public Opinion
There are several strategies open to an interest group for dealing with public opinion in the lobbying context:

1. The group can lobby only when public opinion is supportive of or neutral toward its objectives. Obviously, this may limit the group's lobbying efforts. But it is important to appreciate that public opinion on a particular issue often changes over time. For example, it appears that Canadians' attitudes toward foreign investment swing back and forth

partly in response to economic conditions (slow growth, high unemployment). Public opinion may change in time as people become more familiar with an issue, and interest groups can help to alter public opinion by public relations efforts, advocacy advertising, and other forms of persuasion.

2. The interest group can seek to define or redefine its issues in a way that reduces their visibility and makes them seen as "technical" issues (Bartha's terminology) that can best be resolved by specialists within the group and government, since they do not appear to be relevant to a significant body of public opinion as an "advocacy" or "universal" issue would be (see chapter 6). This will require the group to change its rhetoric, to appear to show the proper sensitivity to public opinion, and to convince other groups and the government that it is dealing with another matter.

3. The interest group can embrace the position seen as consistent with public opinion, notably by agreeing openly with the noble goals or objectives held by public opinion on the issue. The group, however, may use this as a smokescreen to pursue its own interests that are, in fact, inconsistent with public opinion. Alternatively, the interest group may try to argue that its position, perhaps rephrased, actually is perfectly consistent with the noble objectives inherent in the position favoured by public opinion. In both cases, the objective of the group is to quiet opposition to its position by altering how the group is perceived. People frequently judge an individual or group by its intentions or objectives rather than its substantive actions ("His heart is in the right place"). This strategy, therefore, involves changing the rhetoric to parallel public opinion while "burrowing from within" to achieve the group's true objectives. Example: there is no question that public opinion strongly supported the National Energy Program introduced in October 1980.[21] The public still generally embraces its objectives: increased Canadian ownership of the petroleum industry; the achievement of energy security; and a made-in-Canada pricing regime for oil that is fair to all Canadians. The opponents of the NEP figured out that strategically they had to embrace these "motherhood" objectives while suggesting to the federal government that not all of the many means it had chosen to achieve them would produce the desired results. Debate, therefore, was shifted from a set of "universal" issues in a world still rocking from the OPEC oil crunches to much more specialized or "technical" issues of how best to achieve the objectives "everyone" agreed upon.

The best way to actually change widely and deeply held public policy objectives is to argue cogently that a particular method or program that is part of the general policy will, in the complex world of reality, turn out to be counterproductive to the government's (and the public's) objectives; that is, "You can't get to here from there using this particular road." However, lobbyists point out, after assuring the government they accept the faith (agree with the general objectives), that if it will just change these few details it will be able to get from here to there — and the members of their group will not be hurt.

4. An interest group can eschew direct bottom-line considerations that appear to and do benefit its members in economic terms in favour of a much broader perspective on policy issues. The group modestly claims that its views are put forward, along with those of other groups, in order to help to determine the public interest. In other words, it appears to embrace the pluralist ideal of a wide variety of interest groups offering sometimes competitive concepts of the public interest in the process of policy formulation. It is believed that what emerges from the trading off and compromising of interests through the intermediation of government is the public interest.

4.2.2 The Approach of BCNI

The Business Council on National Issues is made up of 155 CEOs of some of Canada's largest corporations. These firms had more than $650 billion in assets, generated over $250 billion in revenues, and employed more than 1.5 million Canadians in 1985. Forty-three of the top 100 nonfinancial enterprises in Canada are members of BCNI. In addition, the CEOs of 13 of the 100 largest financial enterprises are members.

Tom d'Aquino, president of BCNI, argues that BCNI is not a typical lobbying group:

> There's absolutely nothing wrong with being a lobbyist. . . . It's just that I prefer to think that, since the council was founded in 1976, we've demonstrated that we're above bottom-line preoccupations. Our members are all chief executive officers of large companies who are invited to join because they can rise beyond day-to-day concerns and contribute to national issues. We are, I like to think, the board of directors of last resort, exercising our responsibility to help determine the public interest. (Quoted in Gray 1983, 11)

BCNI emphasizes that its focus is on national issues, not on the concerns of specific forums or industries. Its approach is nonpartisan, research-based, and uses both public and private advocacy. It is unique in requiring the personal participation of CEOs, a substantial fraction of whom are members of one of the organization's several task forces in operation at any one time. A recent article on BCNI expands on the group's approach to influencing public policy in Ottawa. According to d'Aquino,

> "We've tried very hard to get away from the idea of a group of power brokers working behind closed doors." A lawyer and an aide to Pierre Trudeau when he was prime minister, d'Aquino instead

tries to carve out a statesmanlike image for the BCNI. He speaks of it as a creator of "new frontiers" and a "harbinger of what is to come." He talks about its "missionary activity" and sounds almost like a social activist when he says such things as: "Business just can't drop nitric acid into the environment. There's a responsibility to society as a whole." . . . D'Aquino says the stands his organization takes "are motivated by genuinely lofty ideas." From the old days of narrow self-interest, he suggests, "business must cross the Rubicon to broader issues." ". . . [F]ar from being a special-interest lobby, the BCNI is more like a senior advisory council to government, a roundtable of wise and selfless men." (McQuaig 1985, 68)

There is no question that BCNI believes that its work "is to help build a strong national and international economy, progressive social policies, healthy political institutions, and a more secure Canada in a peaceful world" (BCNI 1986, 6). By taking a broad perspective, the council feels that its approach "represented a break from the more limited, traditional perspective from which the business community had often contributed to public affairs in the past" (BCNI 1986, 6). The council makes a great effort to achieve consensus among its members, and it seeks to balance contending interests in its public documents. Some of the major initiatives of BCNI in its first decade include the following: parliamentary reform, including revamping the role of committees and the Senate; a joint initiative with the CLC to establish the Canadian Labour Market and Productivity Centre; a national campaign to bring about voluntary restraint on wage and price increases; efforts to reduce the conflict over energy policy between the producing and consuming provinces; a study of youth unemployment; advocacy of a trade enhancement agreement; participation in the Quadrangular Forum in Tokyo in April 1986; a major study of Canada's defence policy; extensive efforts to introduce new competition policy legislation, including preparation of a draft bill; a detailed study of ways of reducing the federal deficit; and a review of Canada's social policies.

When we recall Adam Smith's words ("I have never known much good done by those who affected to trade for the public good"), we must ask how such an approach is beneficial to the firms that pay BCNI's not inconsiderable bills. I suggest that the benefits of BCNI's approach are as follows:

1. It probably helps to create a general climate of public and government opinion favourable to business. As discussed in chapter 4, there is a widespread perception in Canada that private interests are morally inferior to the public interest. Moreover, capitalism as it is practised — as opposed to the descriptions of its romantic proponents like George Gilder — has a dark face. The fact that these "market failures" are structural imperfections in the system rather than in the actors is lost on the critics of a competitive market economy (see Stanbury 1985c). By not

appearing to be obsessed with increasing the wealth of their shareholders, senior business executives demonstrate that they appreciate that there is more to life than the cold-hearted, relentless pursuit of economic advantage, and also that they understand the complexity of making public policy in a democracy where equity is usually more prized than efficiency.

2. BCNI's approach not only helps to establish trust and credibility for itself but probably creates a type of "halo effect" for other business interests. It is fair to say that business's reputation with the Trudeau government was not as favourable as it would have liked. It is hard to overemphasize the importance of trust and credibility in the lobbying process. Such an asset is hard to create and easy to dissipate. An interest group with credibility can use it to facilitate future favourable action by government on specific issues when they are raised by the member firms of BCNI.

3. BCNI's efforts could be construed as being designed to establish that organization's legitimacy as a group to be reckoned with in the councils of federal policy making. One way to gain legitimacy is to pay one's dues by sacrificing immediate benefits and investing one's resources in activities that benefit other actors in the policy-making community. Moreover, a group's legitimacy is enhanced if it appears committed to "the system" regardless of the outcome of particular issues.

4.2.3 BCNI and the Pensions Issue

In his budget of May 1985 the minister of finance, Michael Wilson, announced that Old Age Security payments ($276 per month) to all persons over age 65, previously fully indexed to the Consumer Price Index, would be partially de-indexed in order to reduce the huge federal deficit. Effective January 1, 1986, only increases in the CPI over 3 percent per year would be indexed. The proposal met with a very angry response from pensioners, opposition parties, and other groups.[22] According to the *Globe and Mail* and *Maclean's*, "spokesmen for three of the country's major business lobby groups — the Canadian Chamber of Commerce, the Business Council on National Issues, and the Canadian Organization of Small Business — say pensions for the elderly should be fully protected from inflation and that the Government can find the money to reduce its deficit elsewhere."[23] Mulroney's promise that social programs were a "sacred trust" became a political nightmare, and the government was forced to reverse itself and restore full indexation in just five weeks. According to Jeffrey Simpson, the retreat was "complete and humiliating," as it showed the conflict between Mulroney's "all-things-to-all-people campaign rhetoric [and] the Government's proposed course of action."[24] Simpson argued that Mulroney was furious at the business organizations' support for the pensioners in view of the many benefits the budget bestowed on business. Simpson said that the government's extension of the corporate income surtax, implemented when it reversed itself on partial de-indexation in order to generate revenue to offset higher expenditures, was attributable to Mulroney's anger.

Hyman Solomon of the *Financial Post* stated that Mulroney "exploded" when told of articles in the press reporting the views of the major business associations. "He felt simply that he had been betrayed by those who had urged him to attack the deficit and create a new climate for business — both of which are primary goals of the budget. It took some time for him to calm down, and the heat of his anger was felt by several business organization officials."[25] According to *Maclean's*, "The business leaders' defence of the pensioners clearly angered the government." Both the head of the 6000-member Canadian Organization of Small Business (rival to the 73 000-member CFIB) and Tom d'Aquino of BCNI received angry calls from leading government figures. D'Aquino explained: "We do not oppose partial deindexing. We think it is fine so long as the GIS [Guaranteed Income Supplement] is increased so that support for the elderly poor is not eroded."[26]

The minister of finance said that reversing the partial indexation increased expenditures by $245 million in 1986/87. The "deficit-reduction" 5 percent surtax on large corporations was extended from twelve to eighteen months to match the term of the surtax on high-income individuals and would generate $200 million in 1986. In addition, the excise tax on gasoline and other motive fuels was raised by another one cent per litre effective January 1, 1987, to yield another $450 million annually.[27]

The media reports gave the clear impression that BCNI and other business groups had undermined the new Tory government's efforts to reduce the deficit. Some of the criticism of the Mulroney government's policy on de-indexation took or appeared to take the form of criticism of Mulroney's political acumen.[28] Politicians can be insulted when they receive political advice from business people. They pride themselves on their ability to feel the pulse and understand the grass-roots sentiments. By criticizing the prime minister, the minister of finance, and indeed the whole government, the business associations were seen by the Tory leadership as "kicking a man when he is down."

It also appeared that the heads of the business associations violated two of the unwritten rules of lobbying: try to avoid embarrassing the government by criticizing it publicly in the media; and don't take a strong stance on an issue that is obviously not of vital interest to your group's members. In short, the associations were no doubt seen by the top Tories as "meddlers" who exacerbated a sensitive issue that was hardly of great relevance to the interests they purport to represent.

Media reports suggested that the heads of the associations failed to appreciate the symbolic importance of the government having to back down on this issue. The prime minister was clearly in a delicate position: he was trying to cut back expenditures on social programs that he had trumpeted as a "sacred trust." By holding firm against obviously self-interested pressure groups like the 400 000-member National Pensioners and Senior Citizens Organization, the government would find it easier to refuse to budge when approached by other groups unhappy with budget cuts or tax increases.[29]

In the case of BCNI at least, the government's wrath was misdirected. Its position on de-indexing was badly misinterpreted in the media and by some members of the government and its advisors. The problem arose when Tom d'Aquino, in response to a reporter's question, said that BCNI stood by its earlier position. However, its earlier position was misconstrued to suggest that BCNI opposed de-indexation when, in fact, it favoured it.

In its paper "The Federal Deficit: Some Options for Expenditure Reduction," dated August 2, 1984, and which had been seen both by Brian Mulroney and by Michael Wilson, BCNI identified several sets of expenditure reductions ranging from $5 billion to $10 billion annually. The council recognized that the cuts it proposed would "affect many Canadians who are beneficiaries of public largesse — among them many of the member companies of the Business Council." However, BCNI argued that "the poor and the disadvantaged must not in any way be victimized as we return collectively to a position of fiscal integrity" (p. ii). When discussing the social affairs envelope, the council suggested that greater selectivity be used in income transfer programs and that, "as a start, consideration be given to de-indexing the universal OAS and enriching the income tested Guaranteed Income Supplement (GIS)." The council pointed out that OAS, GIS, and the spouse's allowance were estimated to cost $11.3 billion in 1983/84 (p. iii). These themes were repeated in BCNI's "Perspective in the Mulroney Government's Agenda for Economic Renewal" dated April 1985 (pp. vii, 3, 47).

According to d'Aquino, BCNI "simply adopted a position fully consistent with our long standing policy in favour of de-indexation, coupled with offsetting measures to protect the elderly poor" (by increasing the GIS, then a maximum of $329 per month). He continued, "We are not prepared to accept responsibility for the fact that the reports in question down-played or ignored our support for de-indexing and the budget as a whole."[30] BCNI could be criticized, however, for failing to be sufficiently sensitive to the way the issue was reported in the media and the effect such reports were having on the government. According to officials in the Department of Finance, there was a breakdown in communications during the pressure-filled days in June 1985 that should be blamed on both sides. They believe that while business leaders were consistent on the whole, they were probably naive about the politics of the situation.

But as to the politics of de-indexation, it was the government that made a major error in judgment and then lashed out at certain business groups who, in effect, pointed out its error. In this case, BCNI's advice in its August 1984 document (de-index the OAS while at the same time enriching the GIS for the elderly poor) was probably also good politics.

4.3 Lobbying as a Competitive Process

Lobbying is often a competitive process in which different groups are in conflict over what each is urging government to do or not do. These conflicts stem largely from the differential impact of alternative policy actions on the income or wealth of members of various organized interest groups. Conflicting claims may be couched in the rhetoric of the public interest or in ideological terms. However, the best way to predict a group's position on an economic issue (as opposed to a nonpecuniary or "values" issue) is to determine whether its members believe they are likely to be economically better or worse off because of a particular proposal. Even on a values issue, such as environmental protection, narrow self-interest often lurks just beneath the surface: In the case of Canadian nationalism, it is hard to avoid the conclusion that the strongest proponents of policies in the name of such nationalism also stand to gain in economic terms from such policies: while wrapping themselves in the flag they are also filling their pockets (see Thomas 1981).

The point is that an individual firm, or even a product-specific trade association engaged in lobbying on a specific issue, is likely to face competing groups of two general types. The first might be described as business's "natural enemies," such as environmental groups, consumer groups, and labour unions. On most but certainly not all issues, business can expect these groups to be opposed to its position. The second type of competing group comes from within the business community broadly defined. As noted in chapter 5, the potential or actual cleavages in business interests are many:

- competitors in the same industry;
- size (e.g., big business may be able to deal with many government programs more easily and cheaply than small firms);
- foreign versus domestic ownership;
- different industries/regions;
- tariff/quota-protected industries versus those not so protected;
- potential entrants/competitors versus existing firms; and
- export market-oriented versus firms that rely solely on the domestic market.

Over and above these factors, which can produce conflicts based on differing economic interests, there are the "softer" variables that also influence the stance of an enterprise: philosophy, attitudes, education, and the experience of its top executives.

4.3.1 Example No. 1

This first example deals with import protection for the Canadian foot-wear industry and falls into the first category of conflicting interests. However, in addition to the consumers-versus-manufacturers conflict, domestic manufacturers are in conflict with businesses that retail shoes and those that import them.

> Canadian footwear manufacturers, claiming at anti-dumping tri-bunal hearings in Ottawa this week they are still being kicked around by imports, found a formidable array of foes lined up ready to scuff the shine off their arguments [in favour of five more years of pro-tection from imports]. Ranged against the industry are such groups as the Retail Council of Canada, the Canadian Importers Associa-tion, the Consumers' Association of Canada, and representatives of exporters from Brazil and Europe. The opposition's main theme is that the industry has had plenty of time to get its act together, time bought at the expense of Canadian consumers, importers, and retailers. . . . This time the impact of quotas on importers, whole-salers, and retailers, as well as the effect on prices paid by the Cana-dian consumer, will be considered.[31]

4.3.2 Example No. 2

A somewhat simpler case of intraindustry conflict took the form of lob-bying by five mining companies (Kidd Creek, Nanisivik, Brunswick, Westmin, and Pine Point) against proposed federal government assis-tance to the Cyprus Anvil mine in the Yukon. The companies met with the minister of finance and sent a letter to the prime minister arguing that money spent on reopening the Cyprus Anvil mine (to be acquired from Dome Petroleum by Curragh Resources) would exacerbate the excess-supply/low-prices problem of the other lead-zinc mines in Can-ada. A representative of the companies said they were not concerned about subsidies or using government money to create jobs, only with the timing of government assistance: "They're just going to make a difficult situation more difficult."[32]

4.3.3 Financing the Opposition

Firms in regulated industries may have to help finance certain inter-venors opposed to their rate increases in hearings before certain regu-latory tribunals, notably the CRTC.

> The Consumers' Association of Canada (CAC) will fight Bell Cana-da's proposed rate hikes — with money from the company's own coffers. Bell Canada was ordered Tuesday to pay $22,492 to the association by the Canadian Radio-Television and Telecommuni-cations Commission (CRTC), the regulatory body which oversees

increases to monopolies like Bell. . . . The award — along with others totalling $61,735 to the National Anti-Poverty Organization, the Inuit Tapirisat, the Wa-Wa-Ta Native Communications Society and Action Bell Canada — will be used to pay a financial expert from the University of Toronto to argue the Association's case. "Anyone can apply for costs (to contest increases) if they fall under certain categories," added [CAC lawyer Hank] Intven. "But you have to represent a group or class of subscribers who stand to gain or lose from the outcome of the proposed hikes." While Bell officials say they don't like having to pay for opponents to argue against proposed rate hikes, they know they have to obey the CRTC ruling.[33]

Several points should be noted. First, only a very few agencies make cost awards to intervenors. Second, the regulatory agency itself (rather than the firms) may pay such cost awards. Third, cost awards are not guaranteed but are at the discretion of the agency after it has seen the quality of the performance of the interest group. Fourth, no interest group is able to finance its lobbying efforts solely from cost awards. More generally, see Kane (1980, chap. 6).

4.3.4 Example No. 3
The case of intense conflict both within the industry and with "outsiders" is well illustrated by the efforts of Daly Gordon Securities to transfer all of its nonregulated securities business — private placements, dealings between institutions, offshore offerings, etc. — to a new company that would be partially foreign owned (40 percent of the shares but 90 percent of the votes).[34] The move prompted the Ontario Securities Commission (OSC) to hold a "generic" hearing into the regulation of ownership of investment dealers (i.e., how much equity capital — foreign or otherwise — should investment dealers be able to use?). Therefore, it addressed the question of whether other domestic financial institutions, such as banks or trust companies, could own more than 10 percent of an underwriter/investment dealer.[35]

Some forty briefs were submitted to the OSC, and there were clear differences within the underwriting/investment dealer industry. Obviously Daly Gordon favoured both "outside ownership" of dealers and foreign ownership. Since the early 1970s, nonresidents can own up to 25 percent of an investment dealer (only 10 percent by a single nonresident). Nonindustry investors (banks, insurance companies) can only own up to 10 percent of a dealer.

However, most of the dealers lined up with the position of the Securities Industry Capital Markets Committee comprised of the Investment Dealers Association and a number of the stock exchanges, such as the Toronto Stock Exchange. It wanted stringent controls on both owner-

ship and dealer registration to restrict the growth of the private placement market.

One of the nation's largest investment dealers, McLeod Young Weir
(MYW), did not agree with the position of the Securities Industry Capital Markets Committee. According to Austin Taylor, chairperson of MYW,
the industry brief was "disappointing, self-serving to the securities industry, anti-competitive, and definitely not in the interest of either the development of the Canadian capital market or consumers. It is a classic case
of ostrichism." Taylor admitted that his industry had "used regulation
of the securities industry to our advantage, rather than to that of the
consumer, by building protective measures around the industry to the
virtual exclusion of competition."[36] In particular, MYW proposed that
the limit on foreign ownership be set at 40 percent and that other financial institutions, including nonresidents, be allowed to own up to
40 percent but no one financial institution could own more than
10 percent.[37]

The corporate finance committee of the Financial Executive Institute of Canada (FEIC), which represents capital users, proposed even
higher limits on foreign ownership and that by other financial intermediaries (49 percent). In support of its position the FEIC presented the
results of a survey of corporations that use the capital market.[38]

Not surprisingly, the association representing over 500 North American (largely U.S.) securities firms thought that the Canadian capital
market could benefit from vigorous competition from non-Canadian
firms.[39] The Canadian Bankers' Association supported the regulatory
status quo, but not all of its members agreed with its position.[40]

After the OSC recommended to the Ontario government that the ownership rules be liberalized (up to 30 percent by nonresidents, financial
and commercial investors, and up to 49 percent uncertain ownership
combinations), the Securities Industry Capital Markets Committee sent
a fifteen-page letter to the premier denouncing the proposals. They
would, according to the committee, allow too much concentration of
economic power in the Canadian financial system and would permit
foreign brokers to dominate the securities industry.[41]

4.3.5 Example No. 4
Changes in public policy can generate protracted competitive lobbying battles. Ontario's Environmental Protection Act seeks to control
litter, encourage recycling, and control the use of cans by the soft-drink
industry. However, along with refillable glass bottles, the only type of
can permitted for use in the province is one made of tin-plated steel.
This gives steel makers Dofasco and Stelco a monopoly on the supply of
cans (estimated sales of over $50 million annually — some 60 percent of
the soft-drink container market), much to the dismay of the makers of
aluminum cans (Alcan Aluminum) and nonrefillable plastic bottles. The
Globe and Mail formulated the choices facing the minister of the envi-

ronment as follows: "How much of Ontario's lucrative soda-pop market should go to cans and how much to bottles? Should non-returnable aluminum and plastic be legalized? Should shoppers pay a deposit on every container? Should the Government get into large-scale recycling? Will jobs be lost or created?"[42]

Alcan's approach was to present the Environment Ministry with a recycling project for aluminum cans and other reusable materials, such as glass bottles and newspapers. Such a project should be compelling for the government in a province where most automobile licence plates bear the logo: "Keep It Beautiful." The steel makers, based in Hamilton, told Ontario cabinet ministers that the tin can industry directly supported some 600 jobs in Ontario and a $75-million investment. Alcan, the steel executives emphasized, was the subsidiary of a Quebec-based company.

To defend its position, the steel industry went further. Noting the appeal of Alcan's litter-management efforts, Dofasco and Stelco developed their own recycling project, and the two-member Tinplate Council with its $150 000 annual budget was born. Unlike Alcan, which hired outside consultants, the steel companies' efforts were entirely in-house. The steel makers have to contend with the fact that "more than 50,000 tonnes of steel pop cans go into Ontario's overcrowded garbage dumps each year [costing] municipal tax payers about $1.5 million each year."[43]

While steel executives went on the road, speaking to service clubs in a number of smaller cities, Alcan focused its efforts on Queen's Park (the legislature): "Government officials say steel has been less visible at Queen's Park than aluminum. 'I could count the contacts I've had with them (steel) on one or two hands,' said Mr. Tory [a senior advisor to the premier]. 'The contact I've had with Alcan and the bottlers has been many more times than that.' "[44]

But Alcan also sought allies. As the minister of the environment himself pointed out:

> Interestingly enough you have people who are competitors in the (soft drink) business coming together and saying: "Look, we can put in a multi-faceted recycling program and we feel it will work." So in that particular instance, you have glass and paper and plastics supporting aluminum, even though plastics would fight tooth and nail (against Alcan) to get their share of the market if a new plastic container was allowed.[45]

Alcan's efforts were said to have cost about $1 million versus about $150 000 by the Tinplate Council. The battle must have been evenly joined because fourteen months later the next minister still had not changed the legislation.

In the interim, four militant bottlers, seeking approval for a two-litre, nonrefillable plastic bottle, had defied the government and used the new containers. In their view, political posturing was costing jobs.[46] Soft-drink bottlers, who are anxious to use plastic bottles, didn't want to return to a situation like that in Saskatchewan where the government banned cans and 99 percent of sales are in returnable, refillable glass bottles. According to the executive director of the forty-five–member Ontario Soft Drink Association, "The consumer just won't buy it." In the words of an independent bottler, "That would be like Volkswagen moving back to the Beetle." The bottlers proposed that each household be provided with a special plastic box for all glass, steel, plastic, and newspapers to be collected at the curb once a week. This proposal is supported by the nonprofit Recycling Council and by Pollution Probe. This system would cost about $25 million to set up, one-half of which would be paid by governments.

On the other hand, the Federation of Ontario Naturalists didn't believe it would be effective. They favoured higher deposits on all soft drink containers. The Retail Council of Canada "[doesn't] want dirty soft-drink containers in their store" taking up valuable space and requiring labour to sort out.[47]

With these conflicting interests both within the industry and outside it, it is not surprising that the Ontario government stalled on the issue for several years. However, in September 1985 the Ontario minister of the environment announced that aluminum cans can be used in 1987.[48] In addition, new regulations will require that 40 percent of soft-drink containers be refillable bottles with the remainder divided among plastic bottles and steel and aluminum cans. Therefore, bottlers will now be able to use plastic two- and three-litre bottles and ten-ounce nonreturnable bottles wrapped in a plastic shield.

A spokesperson for Alcan called the decision "unfair" and "not logical." Both the Bottlers Association and the steel makers approve of the new policy. A representative of Stelco said the minister's decision "will assure steel's position in the market [and] give us the time frame to be competitive."[49] Hence, no jobs will be lost as a result of the entry of aluminum cans into the Ontario soft-drink market.

4.4 Using Public Opinion Polls

One of the distinctive characteristics of the period since World War II has been the growth in the use of public opinion polls of all types. They are used extensively in the marketing of goods and services, by political parties and individual candidates to assess their electoral chances and formulate strategy, and by governments to aid in the policy-formulation process. (Some say that most of such polling is for narrow partisan purposes to benefit the party in power, which gains valuable information at the taxpayers' expense.) In recent years interest groups, including individual corporations, have begun to use public opinion polls to help them in their efforts to influence public policy.

Scientific polls can be useful to interest groups in several ways. First, they can help to identify emerging issues and how the public perceives them. Is a problem or concern likely to become a policy issue? Is an issue of national scope or confined to one province or region? How intensely do people feel about the issue — might it alter their voting behaviour? In general, this type of information will be used in developing strategies to deal with issues as they relate to government policy and the group's role in influencing policy. Consider the following example relating to the Canadian Gas Association:

> The gas industry should be fighting for federal deregulation with a multi-million dollar issues advertising and lobbying campaign, says Jerry Goodis, chairman of Commonwealth Systems Inc., a Toronto-based marketing communications firm. In an address to the annual meeting of the Canadian Gas Association in Ottawa, Mr. Goodis advised the industry to focus on a theme of "natural gas; unnatural taxation" in order to create a consumer political constituency for the next federal election. Advertising, he said, could be used to show the public that a dramatic reduction in the cost of home heating could mean more winter vacations or extra money for other money-saving gas appliances. Mr. Goodis made the comments in relation to the results of a poll announced at the meeting, which showed dramatically different sides of public opinion on gas heating. Conducted by Goldfarb Consultants of Toronto, the study showed that 64 per cent of Canadians believe gas is the least expensive fuel choice after oil and electricity, 56 per cent think it is the best value for the money and 55 per cent regard it as the most efficient fuel. On the other hand, the same survey showed that Canadians believe natural gas is less safe, that it is taxed at the same level as electricity and oil, that it pollutes the air, and that supplies of natural gas are fast running out.[50]

Second, polls may be used to show the government that the position espoused by the interest-group leadership represents the views of all or at least most of the group's members. For example, the targets of lobbying efforts in government often ask lobbyists, "Whom do you represent?" Greg Kane, formerly counsel for the Consumers' Association of Canada, notes: "One approach which regulated companies (and . . . the regulators themselves) traditionally take in attempting to question the 'representativeness' of consumer groups is to begin with questions concerning the number of members in the organization, its internal structure, and finally the number of members who actually agreed with the position put forward by the group in the particular hearing" (1980, 17).

This problem is relevant to trade associations with a large number of members. The way that the 73 000-member[51] Canadian Federation of Independent Business deals with this problem is of particular interest:

Nine times a year the federation polls its members on issues of the moment. There may be up to 20,000 ballots returned, and those individual ballots are sent to the MPs from whose constituency they are submitted, along with a tabulation of the total.

As an example of the efficiency of the polling system, Mr. Bennett cited a recent survey on the Government employment tax-credit system. To the surprise and dismay of Employment and Immigration Minister Lloyd Axworthy, half of the small businessmen who replied wanted the scheme scrapped.

So rather than rely on officials who had devised the employment tax-credit scheme in the first place, Mr. Axworthy went to the federation and asked it to conduct another poll in order to refine the results. Eager to please and to preach, the CFIB agreed.

That sample survey of 2,000 CFIB members produced 900 replies and more detailed explanation of why small businessmen regarded the tax credit as either useless for most of them or a swindle for others.[52]

It is the official policy of CFIB that "staff members cannot speak definitively on an issue unless they have polling facts to back themselves up." According to senior CFIB personnel, typically, 20 to 25 percent of the members vote on the questions included in the association's *Mandate* publication. It is published nine times per year (four pages), combining a newsletter/information bulletin describing the activities of CFIB and a national survey reply form dealing with several questions accompanied by a brief statement of the issue and brief pro and con arguments. The national summary of votes on the questions posed in mid-1985 was as follows:[53]

Question/Issue	For (%)	Against (%)	Undecided (%)
(1) Are you for or against reducing interprovincial barriers to trade?	80	10	10
(2) Are you for or against introducing competition in in long-distance telephone services?	72	19	9
(3) Are you for or against a tax-assisted educational savings plan?	48	43	9
(4) Are you for or against the establishment of tax incentives for exporting firms?	47	37	16

An example of how the questions are posed is taken from the July 1985 *Mandate*:

Are you for or against experience rating for workers' compensation? Boards in several provinces are investigating the feasibility of applying experience rating to workers' compensation premiums for individual firms. One plan under consideration would base premiums on the expected eventual cost of a year's accidents plus a charge for indirect costs, adjusted for the firm's safety record. Further refunds and surcharges would respond to the firm's safety and rehabilitation efforts.

Arguments for experience rating for workers' compensation: It would promote occupational health and safety, and rehabilitation of injured workers. A small firm would still be protected against the full impact should it have a poor accident experience.

Arguments against experience rating for workers' compensation: Such a plan compromises "collective liability" in which all firms in an industry share the cost of claims. Small firms with good safety records will receive only a limited rebate.

FOR _____   AGAINST _____   UNDECIDED _____

The August issue reported that 56 percent of the replies were for experience rating, 27 percent were against, and 17 percent were undecided.

The third way in which public opinion polling data may be useful is where an interest group seeks to convince government that not only do its members strongly support its position but also there is widespread public support.[54] Sometimes, however, the results are more equivocal than the group would like, as the 888-member Canadian Association of Japanese Automobile Dealers found in 1984 with respect to "voluntary" quotas on Japanese cars:

A randomly selected cross-country telephone poll of 1,063 male and female heads of households resulted in 14 per cent of the respondents saying restrictions should be removed, 35 per cent stating they should be relaxed, 32 per cent indicating they should be continued and 13 per cent replying that import restrictions should be made harsher. The remaining 6 per cent either did not know or would not answer. . . . Eighty-five per cent believe that "auto competition from Japan is beneficial because it forces North American manufacturers to moderate prices and improve quality." . . . The responses, obtained during an Oct. 22 to Nov. 8 survey period, are similar to those from a poll the group conducted in February. "There has been movement from last year to this year in our favor," said Robert Attrell, Ontario vice-president of CAJAD and a Toyota dealer in Brampton, Ont. "It's not a lot, but there has been some."

The group plans to take the survey results to Ottawa for a meeting with the Conservative Government at which it will seek an end to quotas on Japanese car imports when the formal agreement with Japan comes up for renewal on April 1.[55]

In the throes of the third year of zero salary increases and after a succession of large cuts in university budgets in British Columbia, the Confederation of University Faculty Associations of B.C. commissioned a poll of over 500 people age 19 and over in the Lower Mainland area of the province. Sixty-seven percent of those polled said the quality of university education was threatened by cutbacks, and more than 70 percent said they disagreed with government funding cutbacks to universities. The president of the UBC Faculty Association is quoted as saying, "The Faculty felt that the public wasn't on our side and they realize now there is indeed a lot of support. I think faculty spirits (at UBC, SFU and the University of Victoria) will be buoyed by the poll."[56] The president of the Simon Fraser University Faculty Association said he expected the provincial government to look at the results of the poll "with some concern. The poll results give us encouragement that there is a chance that the policy of the present government will be altered."

Stephen King (1981), a man with a great deal of experience with public opinion research, emphasizes that public opinion research can be misused by interest groups in their effort to influence governments and to influence public opinion itself by means of public opinion polls. He points out that the release of polling results can greatly enhance a media event. The logic of using polling results is as follows:

> Activists believe that the only thing that ultimately motivates politicians is their fear of losing votes; or, to take a more charitable view, that politicians are likely to be uncomfortable if their policies are opposed by a large majority of their constituents. There is also the possibility of some form of bandwagon effect . . . it is hard to believe that people are not to some extent conditioned by what they believe the rest of the public thinks. (King 1981, 96)

Frequently, public opinion research that is conducted for strategic reasons and conveyed to the public greatly oversimplifies what are usually fairly complex issues. The result can be what King calls "research events": "They are often subject to secondary and tertiary reporting, which is likely to remove any remaining qualifications and warnings that might have been built into the original reports" (1981, 97).

Second, King points out, research events based on public opinion surveys "rely for their effect on numbers rather than depth. . . . They are usually yes/no answers to 'belief statements' that are not necessarily framed in the words the respondent would normally use" (1981, 97). The phenomenon of "garbage in, garbage out" applies to public opinion research in that the way you frame and/or phrase the question can greatly influence the responses obtained. This is well illustrated by surveys dealing with the public's attitude toward government activity. There will be dramatic differences in the percentage favouring an expansion of a *particular* program depending on whether the question specifies that the individual's taxes will rise as a result of the greater expenditures.[57]

The fact is that a fair amount of dubious research is put forward by interest groups in an effort to shape public policy. They seek to obtain the "right" answers to a few plausible questions that support their predetermined positions. This means that targets or "consumers" of such data have to become more sophisticated about the design, conduct, and analysis of opinion surveys. As King (1981) points out, it is not too difficult to find contradictory results on apparently similar issues/questions. It seems likely that we will see more and more media contests and published "research events" as interest groups compete with each other and expand the scope of the techniques they use to try to shape public policy.

4.5 Forming Coalitions/Coordinating Lobbying Efforts

There is an old maxim of warfare and politics that there is strength in numbers. There is evidence that ad hoc lobbying coalitions are becoming more important. Norman Aspin, president of the Canadian Nuclear Association, has said that "coalitions of associations are the order of the day."[58] Some are very loose arrangements among groups that are moving in the same direction and keep each other informed so that each can improve its effectiveness while acting independently. Other alliances take the form of a more formal — albeit ad hoc — coalition in which lobbying and other persuasive activities are closely coordinated.

The strength-in-numbers maxim in the context of lobbying has several facets. First, a coalition, particularly one that is well organized, may represent a sizeable number of votes directly or indirectly. For example, when corporations wanting protectionist measures (e.g., domestic automobile manufacturers) are able to form an alliance with the union representing their employees, the number of votes that may be affected is greatly enlarged. Second, coalitions can also alter the distribution of potential votes so as to make the issue much more salient to politicians. Norman Aspin advises that at a delegation meeting a politician should be "geographically and politically distributed. . . . Don't talk to half a dozen guys from Toronto or you will go down the tubes before you even speak."[59]

The greatest potential impact on the party in power would occur if a coalition is able to involve substantial numbers of voters in several marginal ridings held by the party in power and where the voters in the coalition feel intensely about the issue. This is more likely to happen where a coalition incorporates groups that have a different geographic base; instead of threatening the political future of one or two legislators, failure to resolve the issue might have an impact on a dozen ridings.

Third, ad hoc coalitions of groups that are perceived as strange bedfellows (i.e., those normally in conflict with each other) are likely to have a greater impact on both public opinion and on politicians precisely because the alliance appears to be so unnatural. In other words, unusual coalitions/alliances provide a measure of the seriousness of the problem. Only if people are significantly affected are they likely to get organized and make common cause with their traditional "enemies."

Fourth, lobbying coalitions/alliances, by incorporating groups with widely differing interests, can give the appearance of "representing everybody." Therefore, it is easier for them to argue that what they want from government is "in the public interest." The fact, as Olson (1965) reminds us, that there are for sound reasons many interests that are not organized or only ineffectively organized (e.g., consumers, taxpayers) seldom detracts from this perception. Hence, if the federal government were faced with a coalition lobbying for equal pay for work of equal value comprised of the CCC, CMA, BCNI, the Canadian Federation of Labour, the National Action Committee on the Status of Women, and the Canadian Civil Liberties Association, they would find it easy to go along with what the coalition proposed as being "in the public interest."

Efforts to form broadly based coalitions may even be undertaken by individual MPs who see their own fate tied to that of a particular industry. Consider the following example:

> Shipyard operators, trade unions and members of Parliament from shipbuilding ridings have stepped up the pressure on the federal Government to deliver on its pre-election promises of support for the marine construction and repair industry. . . . The meeting was organized by Montreal MP Edouard Desrosiers.[60]

The loose coalition even included provincial governments, who seldom resist the opportunity to obtain funds from Ottawa to help their local economies:

> Efforts by the shipbuilding industry — supported by the governments of New Brunswick, Newfoundland, Quebec and Ontario — to gain Ottawa's attention come at a time of crisis in the industry. Commercial business has all but disappeared, leaving shipyards clawing for a place in the narrow field of federal shipbuilding orders.[61]

Lobbying coalitions are often encouraged by a present or pending crisis. And in a country with a notoriously high longer-term unemployment rate, the loss of jobs provides a strong call to arms. In this case, "days before the meeting in Ottawa, a leading shipping industry consultant said half of Canada's shipyards might have to close or diversify if the domestic industry is to survive after 1990."[62]

Fifth, lobbying coalitions are an antidote to the frequent problem of competitive lobbying by various groups on a specific issue (recall subsection 4.3 above). Competitive lobbying means that Ottawa or a provincial government receives conflicting advice about what it should do or not do. Cognitive dissonance results from a cacophony and the government may find the status quo more attractive as it strikes a balance among the competing claimants. Tidy-mindedness, and the desire for consensus rather than conflict, is strong among Canadians — including politicians and bureaucrats. Hence, various broadly based interests (business, environmentalists, women, native people) are frequently urged to "get their act together" and speak with one voice so that government may be more responsive. "The Goverment is not unresponsive to business, but the Canadian business community is fragmented and does not speak with a single voice, [according to] Toronto lawyer Robert Kaplan. . . . Mr. Kaplan, a former Liberal member of Parliament for Don Valley, said if business spoke with one voice 'there would be a response.' "[63]

In Quebec the Conseil du Patronat and in British Columbia the Employers Council of B.C. (now the B.C. Business Council) were set up with the avowed purpose of giving business a unified structure speaking with a common voice. It is argued that one unified voice will be more effective in gaining benefits from government and in providing feedback to government on its initiatives.

The desire to create a unified front and thereby be more successful in dealing with government has become an issue in the rapidly growing software industry in Canada. With some 2200 vendors, the industry is fragmented in terms of production. Moreover, there is no national organization to lobby on the industry's behalf, although there are regional groups.

> After abandoning its efforts to form a national organization last fall, the Canadian Advanced Technology Association is trying once again to arouse interest. This time, however, CATA will not collaborate with other regional organizations. "We couldn't reach agreement," said executive director Robert Long. "There are a lot of regional issues that have to be addressed," countered Robert Bruce, chairman of the Toronto-based Software Developers Association. For instance, at SDA's monthly meetings, the topics range from dealing with retail sales tax changes in Ontario or with the City of Toronto's proposed incubator strategy for entrepreneurial ventures. . . . The newness of the industry has a lot to do with that fragmentation. Nevertheless, Mr. Long of CATA argues, there is a need for a national body to deal strategically with national and international interests.[64]

Often a specific policy issue stimulates the creation of a lobbying coalition. For example, a flurry of studies and government reports on the aging of Canada's population and the need for new policy initatives concerning pensions resulted in the Business Committee on Pension Policy. Members of the committee include the BCNI, CCC, CFIB, CMA, the Canadian Life and Health Insurance Association, and the Canadian Bankers' Association.

The committee undertook its own study of the cost impact of various pension reform proposals and presented these to the federal and provincial governments. In March 1983 the committee lobbied the Manitoba government to delay changes until the cost implications were studied more thoroughly. It emphasized that, in poor economic conditions, "heavy additional costs [could result in] adverse consequences for employees and employers in Manitoba."[65]

The pressure of rising workers' compensation premiums and the lack of success on previous issues in which it used confrontational tactics on an individual basis (e.g., ringing the legislature with large dump trucks), prompted the 900-member Ontario Trucking Association (OTA) to become a prime mover in the eighteen-member Employer's Council on Workers' Compensation of Ontario (ECWC). The OTA expanded the membership of the ECWC and convinced umbrella associations of both large and small firms (CMA, CFIB) to pool their resources.

Set up in 1983, the Employer's Council on Workers' Compensation of Ontario grew as the province's employers became convinced extraordinary measures were necessary to curb the growth in workers' compensation costs. The new association spearheaded this joint effort because there was duplication of private-sector efforts. OTA was convinced too many voices calling on the government to take differing actions merely confused the government, in some cases allowing it to get off the hook entirely. . . . Banding together under the roof of the CMA, truckers, foresters, contractors, shoe manufacturers, hospitals, miners, retailers, recyclers and other major trade assocations were flanked by the small business lobby. Meeting frequently, the group began to build consensus. . . .

Lobbying hard, the ECWC began the long drive to develop the high level of trust and respect any organization or individual must earn when it negotiates with politicians and civil servants. Slowly and carefully building credibility, the ECWC and the key players in the WCB and Ministry of Labour began the sharing of views, essential to developing effective public policy. Politicians and civil servants learned that ECWC leaders could, and did, speak for most of Ontario's employers. Several testing skirmishes quickly established that chief executives were eager to back the fledgling coalition when they were called upon for support. . . .

The coalition's co-operative effort broke new ground in Ontario and underscores the benefits of joint-lobbying ventures. The ECWC's ultimate aim is to work directly with injured workers to find mutual ways to solve employer and employee battles, by focusing on mutual need to improve Ontario's competitive position in the marketplace.[66]

One of the most interesting and successful ad hoc lobbying coalitions of sixteen business and consumer groups was created in response to Canada Post's attempt to define and enshrine its monopoly over the delivery of letters. Members of the coalition included the Consumers' Association of Canada, the TSE, CMA, and the Conseil du Patronat du Québec. The coalition was organized by Norman Stewart, a staff lawyer for General Motors, who wrote a paper for the CMA on the issue. Its evolution and tactics are described in the following *Financial Times* story:

> [The coalition] held its first meeting in early October 1982. The worried participants exchanged what information they had on the regulatory process and discussed the definition's impact on the users of Canada Post and its competitors' services. At a second meeting, on Oct. 18, the lobbyists agreed on their goal: "to gain time and support for 'constructive dialogue' between users and Canada Post before the new regulations were approved." They agreed to concentrate on trying to change a few key points of the proposals: to narrow the post office's broad definition of a "letter," to ease its suggested restrictions on the bulking of mail, and to provide more freedom for the use of private couriers. . . . The committee considered hiring a professional lobbyist to carry its message to Ottawa, but decided against it, because of both the expense and the possible damage to the group's image. (Fife 1983, 17)

In allocating the work to be done, the coalition's members drew upon their different knowledge and skills in lobbying:

> Having already demonstrated his ability to muster support, Stewart was put in charge of taking their concerns to the public via the media. Jim Bennett, then director of national affairs for the Canadian Federation of Independent Business, was to take the case to the bureaucrats and politicians in Ottawa. Bennett . . . had spent 10 years working for the federal government — two of them in a minister's office — and had valuable contacts and savvy. Other committee members acted as liaisons with the organizations in the ad hoc group, which were consistently encouraged to continue their own efforts to change the definition. The Toronto Stock Exchange, for instance, asked individuals associated with it to write to Canada Post and [André] Ouellet [the minister responsible for Canada Post] about their concerns. (Fife 1983, 17)

As in many lobbying campaigns, skill in using the media is important for several reasons: to gain more support; to raise the political visibility of the issue; and to put pressure on the government to respond to the lobby group.

> Stewart's media campaign, meanwhile, was intended to generate new support for the lobby among small companies and independent businessmen. His approach to publicity was unsophisticated but effective. He quickly put together an information package on the lobby, and gave it to the Toronto papers, along with the reasons he felt it was newsworthy. "Then the story was picked up by Canada AM (a CTV public affairs program), and after that it mushroomed," he says. (Fife 1983, 17)

The media coverage did generate the interest of other organizations in the group's efforts. At the same time, Jim Bennett, of the CFIB, urged the group to work closely with the bureaucrats in the Post Office and in several departments likely to be concerned about the economic effects of the proposed change (Treasury Board; Finance; Industry, Trade and Commerce). The political pressure on the Liberal government increased. In late November Canada Post announced it was working on amendments to the definition to be considered by the cabinet. The ad hoc coalition was not satisfied with Canada Post's approach of "let's push this thing through and then amend it." The group applied more pressure on the government, including communications with Liberal MPs. On November 23 the cabinet announced that it had rejected Canada Post's definition. The crown corporation "was directed to amend its proposal and resubmit it for regulatory approval within a few months' time. Consultations began in earnest" (Fife 1983, 17). The ad hoc coalition reduced its media efforts and focused on negotiations with Canada Post. The result was a new definition published in the *Canada Gazette* in February 1983. A lawyer for Canada Post praised the consultative process that resulted from the efforts of the ad hoc coalition: "It's useful when a bunch of essentially different groups get together to debate common interests and discard what's unimportant. It saved us time to meet with these organizations on an umbrella basis" (Fife 1983, 17).

4.6 The Role of Trade Associations

Most large and a substantial fraction of small firms (perhaps 25 percent) are members of at least one trade association. While lobbying is only one of the activities trade associations engage in, it is that facet of their operations that will be the focus of this subsection. One of the important issues for a large firm to consider in developing its lobbying strategy on a policy issue is the role of the trade association(s) of which it is a member. It is not a foregone conclusion that in every case the firm and its association(s) will be taking highly similar approaches.

4.6.1 Types and Number of Trade Associations

Trade associations can be defined as nonprofit, voluntary associations of business firms designed to deal with common problems, which often involves making representations to governments. There are several types of associations: horizontal (i.e., includes competitors or potential competitors); vertical (i.e., includes firms in a customer-supplier relationship, such as manufacturers, wholesalers, retailers); and "conglomerate" (i.e., includes individuals, firms, institutions, and other associations sharing some interest in common, but not necessarily being in the same industry or vertically related). Recall Figure 8-1 above.

The scope of the many trade associations in Canada varies greatly:

- Sector-specific: Canadian Manufacturers' Association,
- Industry-specific: Grocery Products Manufacturers of Canada,
- Product-specific: Canadian Carpet Institute,
- Activity-specific: Canadian Exporters Association, and
- Size-specific: Canadian Federation of Independent Business (Litvak 1982).

In addition, there are the associations that are very broadly based, for example, CCC and BCNI. The latter is patterned on the Business Roundtable in the United States (Archbold 1977).

Stevens (1980, 29) estimated that in May 1980 there were some 300 trade and professional associations operating in Ottawa. They employed over 2000 people and spent over $122 million per year. Applying the general rate of inflation, this means that these associations are probably spending over $200 million in 1985. There is no lobbyist registration legislation at the federal level, although the Mulroney government announced in August 1985 it would bring in such legislation. See chapter 9.

Litvak (1982, 35) indicates there were 700 national trade associations (NTA) in Canada in 1981 as compared with 3200 in the U.S. His research found there were 143 NTAs in Canada with an annual budget exceeding $100 000 in 1981. One-quarter of the sample (101 of the 143 eligible) had fewer than 50 members and over one-half had less than 50 members. A few associations have more than 1000 members (e.g., CFIB had over 73 000 in 1985), but some, reflecting the concentrated nature of the industry, have only a few. For example, the Association of Canadian Distillers has 12 and the Motor Vehicle Manufacturers Association has 9.

Sixty-four percent (60 of 95) of the NTAs had an annual budget of less than $600 000 in 1981, while 26 percent had a budget of more than $1 million.

Coleman and Jacek (1983, 262–63) identified some 15 associations in the food-processing sector in Canada:

    4 — slaughtering and processing of meat
    4 — manufacturing of dairy products

    2 — processing of fruits and vegetables
    3 — intersectoral associations

Their budgets (in 1980) ranged from $4000 to $900 000, and they had from one to eighteen full-time staff.

Coleman and Jacek (1983, 278) identify four distinct types of activities of trade associations in the food industry: public policy formation, policy implementation, commercial, and selective benefit/membership activities. In their view, "To consider business interest associations as simply 'pressure' or 'lobby' groups, is to ignore some important roles these groups come to play in the policy process."

4.6.2 Relations with Government

One-third of the NTAs (31 of 93) in Litvak's (1982) sample are in almost *daily* contact with government and another third are in frequent contact. Contacts are often initiated by government — to obtain industry input for policy formulation or to obtain technical information. Saumier (1983) notes that governments in Canada have created lobby groups. Wilson argues that "in seeking to create more general support of public policies, the Canadian bureaucracy, with the full acquiescence of the government, has enlarged the scope of conflict by fostering and encouraging interest groups, particularly over the last three or four decades" (1981, 387). An outstanding example is that of farm interest groups (see Hannam 1953, Dawson 1960, and Dawson 1975). In the case of business groups, the federal government has been helpful by facilitating access through the extensive use of consultative committees. See Aucoin (1971).

About 60 percent of the NTAs said that coalitions between business associations or with other groups are becoming increasingly important. The heads of 21 major NTAs meet every six weeks in Ottawa to discuss public policy issues. Ten of these are headquartered in Ottawa and 10 are based in Toronto.

Litvak (1982, 36) provides the following data on the major activities of his sample of 101 national trade associations:

— government relations	90%*
— industry/market inform.	60
— public relations	54
— product/service stds.	38
— inter-industry relations	36
— industry promotion	36
— interest group relations	29

(* % reported as being amongst the association's top 4 activities)

Note that "government relations" was ranked by 55 of the 101 NTAs as their most important activity. Over 80 percent of the respondents feel that such activity will be the main one performed by NTAs in the next few years.

Sixty percent of the respondent NTAs described their relations with government as cooperative in varying degrees, while 28 percent described them as adversarial in varying degrees. The overall split between the NTAs' federal/provincial activities was 60/40. Forty-five percent of the NTAs active in government relations had an Ottawa office, although only one-third of the sample had their headquarters in Ottawa. Over one-half those in the sample spend less than $200 000 annually on government relations. The fraction of their total budget spent on this activity ranged from 0.5 to 90 percent. The NTAs' budgets are increased by services in kind provided by members (i.e., committees, preparation of briefs, providing information). Only 16 NTAs of the 101 in the sample had a "special government relations staff person" (Litvak 1982, 38).

In 1981 just over one-half had used outside services to support the work of the NTA in government relations — typically law or public relations firms. Expenditures ranged from 2 to 60 percent of the total government relations budget.

Only 10 percent of NTAs reported they use paid advertising to support their government relations activities. Contrast this figure to the fact that the federal government is by a factor of at least two the largest national advertiser in Canada. It spent about $65 million in 1982/83 (Stanbury et al. 1983). Subsequently, such expenditures declined.

4.6.3 Targets

Who are the targets of the NTAs' contacts with government? Litvak (1982, 39) reports that NTAs ranked the following categories as "very important":

- interaction with senior-level civil servants   75%
- interaction with Cabinet ministers   50
- favorable media coverage   36
- public opinion   35
- participation on joint bus.-gov't committees   32
- support of other trade associations   28
- interaction with junior/mid-level civil servants   22
- contact with the Prime Minister's Office   22
- appearances before Parliamentary committees   21
- support of special interest groups   18
- union support   12
- interaction with Government MPs   6
- interaction with Opposition MPs   4

4.6.4 Staff

Of 89 respondents (permanent heads of the NTAs), 37 had a salary between $50 000 and $75 000, while 13 were in the $75 000 to $100 000 range. Ten earned over $100 000 per year. Twenty-six had a masters or Ph.D. degree or an LL.B. Twenty-two had previously worked for government. Most had business or association work experience. Harrison

(1978b) notes that Canadian trade associations frequently employ former public servants to head their professional staffs. In recent years, the
following associations have been headed by former deputy or assistant
deputy ministers in the federal government: Canadian Association of
Broadcasters, Grocery Product Manufacturers of Canada, Dominion
Maritime Association, Pharmaceutical Manufacturers Association of
Canada, Air Industries Association, Canadian Export Association, and
the Canadian Construction Association.

Association presidents and consultants and lawyers operate openly —
they are not really "hidden persuaders." The latter should refer to legislators and members of the press gallery who engage in lobbying under
the guise of their official positions.

4.6.5 Effectiveness

NTA members rate their association's effectiveness in influencing government in terms of policy outcomes or results. Two-thirds of NTA executives rated their association as only "moderately effective" in influencing
government while 16 percent said it was "not effective."

4.6.6 Internal Problems

Trade associations have to cope with a number of internal problems:
developing a consensus on issues (this takes time and a prompt response
can be very important); potential splits between the permanent staff
members and the association executive/membership; annual turnover
of elected head of the NTA; short-term/instant-results perspective versus a long-run view in an area of intangibles; the maintenance of support of the membership; and ability to attract the top people from
member companies.

The professional staff seek stability and predictability in the NTAs
relations with government. Senior public servants and politicians have
a similar interest. This acts as a moderating force on business-government
relations. Litvak (1982, 42) suggests that NTAs could become more successful in the future by taking a marketing orientation to their lobbying
activities.

Association executives are often, like foremen in a manufacturing
plant, the "men in the middle." They are caught in a vise between some
of their members, who want vigorous rhetoric and action, and their
targets in government, who are often better influenced by a more conciliatory, low-key approach.

> Part of the Stan Roberts Dilemma at the [Canadian Chamber of
> Commerce] for example is that he was accused by some members
> of not going hard enough on the government over the budget. "I
> was under criticism for not speaking out strongly enough on that
> one," he recalls.
>
> At the Business Council, composed of 140 chief executives, pres-
> ident Thomas D'Aquino has been urged by at least one member to

take a harder line. In yet another revealing example of how associations are forced to juggle internal politics, the Prospectors and Developers Association came out publicly swinging at the recent mineral strategy paper released by Mines Minister Judy Erola after having praised her privately for consulting it closely through the paper's formation. When confronted by an angry Erola after all the negative headlines, the PDA's somewhat sheepish response was that it simply couldn't be seen by its members to be agreeing with the government. (McGregor 1982b, 2)

How well do the various trade and business associations represent the views of the thousands of individuals they claim to represent? Signs of internal conflicts in some organizations have surfaced occasionally. Writing in the *Financial Times*, Deborah McGregor noted:

A recent example is the sudden resignation of Stanley Roberts, 53-year-old president of the Canadian Chamber of Commerce. The chamber is the country's largest business group, with 140,000 members. The events leading to the Roberts resignation make one of the more dramatic examples of how divided and unsure some business groups have become about how to present the business position so it will be heeded by government.

In the weeks before the resignation, Roberts, Chamber president for just over a year, had been locked in an internal wrangle with his board of directors. The problem: his high profile and strongly political style. Roberts was making six to eight speeches a week. He spent most working days on the road. A lifelong Liberal, he had become disenchanted with the current regime in Ottawa. He pulled no punches in criticizing the policies and orientation of the federal government on behalf of the Chamber.

Roberts' 42-member board was decidedly uncomfortable with the controversy and publicity. But that wasn't all. Roberts' outspoken political style was judged by many on the board to be generating an ominous side-effect. They said doors in Ottawa were slowly closing to the Chamber. Sources say Prime Minister Trudeau's top advisers were rapidly cooling. They saw a political enemy masquerading as a business spokesman. Roberts does not acknowledge this, although he concedes there were some "intense" meetings with his board of directors over his unwillingness to be a "stay-at-home administrator."

For the Chamber, a group that has prided itself on excellent government contacts and on carrying a broad business view to government, the Roberts resignation resolved the immediate problem but left the chamber facing some tough soul searching on future approaches to government relations. (1982b)

The discussion of lobbying techniques is continued in chapter 9.

NOTES

1. "Dairy farmers demand action," Vancouver *Sun*, August 9, 1985, p. C8.
2. Evans points out that "the Moral Majority in the U.S. is a dramatic example of a group with very complex utility function interactions, who allege that their welfare is affected by all sorts of activities by others which have no discernible direct impact on them, and who argue that the state . . . should respond to their preferences with regulations to control such behaviour" (1982, 465).
3. House of Commons, *Debates*, January 19, 1983, p. 22015.
4. Ibid.
5. Fulton and Stanbury (1985) draw the distinction between output- and process-oriented interest groups.
6. Andrew Nikiforuk, "An unemployed lobby," *Maclean's*, July 15, 1985, p. 10.
7. Ibid.
8. *Globe and Mail*, March 23, 1983, p. 11.
9. Ibid., January 17, 1985.
10. Ibid., February 22, 1985, p. B3.
11. Ibid., August 30, 1985. See also "Preparing a free-trade strategy," *Maclean's*, September 30, 1985, pp. 16–17.
12. David Stewart-Patterson, "38 named to trade advisory group," *Globe and Mail*, January 10, 1986, p. B12. See also Lorne Slotnick, "CLC rejects federal invitation to join trade advisory group," *Globe and Mail*, October 11, 1985, p. 1.
13. See the very useful discussion of confrontational versus cooperative tactics by interest groups in McGregor (1982).
14. Recall the outline of the Westminster model in chapter 2. On this point, see Kernaghan (1985f).
15. In September 1985 the Mulroney government had to cope with three major contretemps that illustrate this point very well: the failure of the Canadian Commercial Bank, the "tainted tuna affair," and the resignation of Communications Minister Marcel Masse while under RCMP investigation into possible irregularities in his campaign spending. See *Maclean's*, October 7, 1985, pp. 10–24. He was later cleared.
16. See (1981) 1 S.C.R. 753 and (1981) 125 D.L.R. (3d) 1.
17. It is important not to leave one's markers outstanding for too long a period for at least two reasons. One, the memory of beneficiaries grows dim. Two, the individuals who owe the favours may be moved to other positions where they may be unable to reciprocate.
18. See chapter 10 on the role of campaign contributions in this regard.
19. See Brian Power, "Fish farm stock up as MP joins board," Vancouver *Sun*, August 31, 1985, p. A13.
20. "MP quits post on firm's board," Vancouver *Sun*, September 10, 1985, p. A4.

21. In the smoke and mirrors game that is policy making, we note that the federal government's key objective in the NEP was not stated. It was to prevent Alberta from getting "too much" revenue from rising petroleum prices and to generate enormous revenues for itself. Hence the federal government would not lose power to Alberta and would be able to play Santa Claus with yet more politically popular social programs and to pay for the vast array already in place.

22. See Gifford (1985); *Maclean's*, June 17, 1985, pp. 8–10; Jamie Lamb, "Tory fur is flying over de-indexing," Vancouver *Sun*, June 14, 1985, p. A4; Marc Clark, "Pointing the index finger," *Maclean's*, June 24, 1985, pp. 40–41; Charlotte Montgomery, "PM faces politician's nightmare over Canadian pension furor," *Globe and Mail*, June 20, 1985, p. 8; and Deborah McGregor, "Tories relationship with business turns chilly. Retreat on pension issue carries a stiff political and economic price tag," *Financial Times*, July 1, 1985, pp. 1, 12.

23. "Business joins outcry over old-age security," *Globe and Mail*, June 12, 1985, p. 8. See also *Maclean's*, June 24, 1985, pp. 40–41.

24. *Globe and Mail*, June 28, 1985, p. 6.

25. *Financial Post*, June 29, 1985, p. 4. See the same source for a story on the views of senior executives.

26. *Maclean's*, June 24, 1985, p. 41. D'Aquino states he never received any such telephone calls.

27. For a digest of the minister of finance's statement, see *Toronto Star*, June 28, 1985, p. A19.

28. See the reports of interviews with business executives in the *Financial Post*, June 29, 1985, p. 4.

29. It is interesting that no comparable lobby was mounted against the government's proposal to de-index family allowances.

30. Letter from Tom d'Aquino to Ronald Stewart, MP, August 23, 1985, p. 2.

31. *Financial Post*, December 1, 1984, p. 27.

32. "Zinc rivals lobby Ottawa to not help Anvil," *Globe and Mail*, September 26, 1985, p. B25. See also "Board sends Anvil issue to Ottawa," *Globe and Mail*, October 1, 1985, p. B23.

33. Montreal *Gazette*, February 21, 1980, p. 5.

34. *Financial Post*, April 7, 1984, p. 1.

35. Ibid., November 17, 1984, p. 27.

36. Ibid., October 22, 1984, p. 7.

37. Ibid., December 8, 1984, p. 4.

38. Ibid., December 1, 1984, p. 25; *Globe and Mail*, November 27, 1984, p. B5.

39. *Financial Post*, December 8, 1984, p. 4.

40. *Globe and Mail*, November 30, 1984, p. B6.

41. Ibid., May 17, 1985, p. B13.

42. Ibid., August 16, 1985, p. 1.

43. Ibid.

44. Ibid., January 21, 1984, p. B1.

45. Ibid.

46. Ibid., March 16, 1985; see also *Globe and Mail*, November 3, 1984, p. B6.

47. Ibid., August 16, 1985, p. 3.

48. See Ibid., September 21, 1985, p. B9. "The Government also launched a municipal roadside recycling program at a cost of $2.8-million a year, and formed a recycling council of industry, Government and environmental representatives to oversee the program."

49. Ibid.

50. "Gas lobbying urged," *Globe and Mail*, May 30, 1984, p. B6.

51. This figure is from a story in the Vancouver *Sun*, August 29, 1985, p. B6.

52. John Gray, "The lobby is spartan, but it works," *Globe and Mail*, October 25, 1980, p. 11.

53. CFIB, *Mandate*, no. 117, July 1985.

54. See "Shoe-makers' survey of public finds support for border curbs," *Globe and Mail*, October 9, 1985, p. D9. But see also Donn Downey, "Petrocan's gas station buy unpopular, Gallop poll finds," *Globe and Mail*, October 23, 1985, p. A3.

55. *Globe and Mail*, November 23, 1984, p. B4.

56. "Poll slams university cutbacks," Vancouver *Sun*, September 16, 1985, p. A15.

57. See the study cited by R. M. Clark in Conkin, ed., *Pensions Today and Tomorrow* (Toronto: Ontario Economic Council, 1984), pp. 266–72. More generally, see Patrick Martin, "The delicate art of polling," *Globe and Mail*, September 1, 1985, p. 10; and "Here's how pollsters pump the answers," Vancouver *Sun*, September 13, 1985, p. B3.

58. *Globe and Mail*, March 10, 1983, p. B9. See also Duncan Cameron, "Labor's new blueprint: forge links to other groups," *Globe and Mail*, January 29, 1986, p. A7.

59. *Globe and Mail*, March 10, 1983, p. B9.

60. Ibid., January 28, 1985.

61. Ibid.

62. Ibid.

63. Ibid., March 15, 1985, p. B2.

64. Ibid., April 19, 1985.

65. Ibid., March 31, 1985, p. B10.

66. Susan Gibson, "New route planned for lobbying tactics," *Financial Post*, April 6, 1985, p. S6.

9

Lobbying Techniques and Vehicles: Part 2

1.0 INTRODUCTION

This chapter continues the discussion of lobbying techniques and vehicles begun in chapter 8. Section 2 discusses the following lobbying techniques: the role of consultants; information and the lobbying process; informal approaches in lobbying; the dynamics of the policy issues and their impact on lobbying; suggestions for dealing with regulatory/administrative agencies; and confrontation or conciliation — the choice of approaches.

Section 3 discusses the characteristics of an effective lobbyist. Section 4 provides a case study of lobbying techniques and style, that of Dome Petroleum under the direction of its former chairperson, Jack Gallagher. In section 5 I further explore the strategic use of the concept of the public interest in lobbying situations. This is the second half of the analysis of the concept of the public interest begun in section 6 of chapter 4. Finally, in section 6 I discuss the proposals for regulating lobbying in Canada.

2.0 LOBBYING TECHNIQUES CONTINUED

2.1 The Role of Consultants

The use of public affairs consultants is becoming more common. They are often described as professional lobbyists. What services do they usually provide?

> When a client solicits the services of a lobbyist, he is usually paying for technical advice and guidance through the bureaucratic labyrinth. A lobbyist may also open a door into a cabinet minister's or senior bureaucrat's office, but it is the client himself who engages in face-to-face meetings and other acts of direct diplomacy. Most lobbyists insist a firm's reputation would be shattered if it routinely made sales pitches on the many, often conflicting, interests in Ottawa. Bill Lee, who with Bill Neville formed Executive Consultants Ltd. in 1968, says: "We provide a strategy. We tell our clients who to see, what to say, and how to say it."[1]

More generally, see Figure 9-1 for a portrait of the largest government relations consulting firm in Ottawa.

Recently, the activities of Frank Moores, former premier of Newfoundland and now part owner of Government Consultants International (GCI) and Alta Nova Associates, have caused some controversy. One competitor has said that Moores "is changing the whole nature of the game and giving us all a bad name."[2] Moores was a director of Air Canada when he was also a consultant to both Nordair and Wardair. He and the co-owner of GCI, Gerry Doucet, whose brother is a senior advisor in the

Figure 9–1
PUBLIC AFFAIRS INTERNATIONAL: PORTRAIT OF A GOVERNMENT RELATIONS CONSULTING FIRM

PAI has been an astonishing success story. For fees running from $3000 to more than $10 000 a month, the company tells more than 50 corporate clients what it thinks they need to know about the political and bureaucratic workings of Ottawa. Besides its own staff of 30, PAI makes use of links with Decima Research of Toronto, the Tories' polling firm, and Government Research Corp. of Washington, which watches the U.S. scene with special attention to Canadian-U.S. relations. "Our job is first and foremost about information," says Neville. "We want to be sure our clients are clear about what government is doing and why. Our client needs to know who are the key decision-makers, what kind of information might be helpful to him, and how the client can best make representations to government."

Some of that information is culled from public sources by PAI staff with the specialized knowledge and background to make sense out of the torrent of paper spewing from Ottawa's vast bureaucracy. The company's hottest property, though, is its network of personal contacts with bureaucrats and their political masters. At the centre of that network is Neville* himself, the consulting architect for the initial Mulroney power structure and a continuing confidant of the Prime Minister. Neville speaks regularly with Mulroney, and occasionally does work for the Prime Minister, such as giving advice on drafts of speeches or on personnel changes in the civil service.

Each month, PAI sends clients a summary of information about pending decisions and personnel changes in key government departments. Each week, a PAI staff member tries to be in contact with each client by telephone. And every three months Neville and other PAI officials sit down with clients individually for a detailed briefing about forthcoming government decisions or policies.

Occasionally, PAI puts together a major briefing paper on an important policy issue. What PAI will not do, insists Neville, is lobby — or, to use the Ottawa euphemism, do "representational work." The company's "whole approach and relationship," he says, "is based on the notion that we're going to be around for a while, that we don't depend upon which party is in power. We're here because clients believe we have a continuing, solid source of intelligence and advice."

PAI now dwarfs its rivals. Its staff of 30, working from offices in Ottawa, Halifax, Toronto (just opening), Regina, Calgary, Victoria and Washington, is more than four times the size of that of any competitor. PAI employees offer an impressive blend of political and administrative experience, although Neville concedes that PAI remains

Figure 9–1 (continued)

weak in analyzing developments in Quebec and in providing services in French. Many PAI staffers have worked for Liberal or Conservative Ministers, although only one (Sidney Handleman, a former Ontario cabinet minister) was ever a politician.

The two firms** combined to produce *The Decima Quarterly*, an expensive compendium of public opinion attitudes sold to corporations and governments. (The publication had only two subscribers when it began; it now boasts more than 50, including some of the country's largest corporations.) Decima, PAI's sister firm, is on the cutting edge of public opinion research in North America. Its numbers, along with Gregg's analysis of them, are poured into *The Decima Quarterly*, and into Gregg's work for corporate clients — and incidentally pepper Gregg's many public speeches and appearances in the mass media.

Neville and Gregg say they do not automatically tell those from whom they get information who that information will be passed to. "I've always operated on the basis that if they ask who my client is I'll tell them. Some ask, some don't," says Neville. Still, word gets around a small city that's as dependent on politics as Ottawa, and government officials do come in time to know some of PAI client base. After all, most of PAI's staff members specialize in one or two departments. For example, Brian Mersereau, a 14-year-veteran of the Supply and Services Department, keeps tabs on his former department for PAI clients interested in securing Government contracts. Tom Burns, a former federal trade official, is PAI's trade expert.

Neville sees similarities between how PAI operatives work and how good political journalists ply their trade: both make use of a mass of written material from and about government, but rely even more heavily on personal contacts over lunch and on the telephone. "We've got a different agenda than the newspapers," Neville says. "We're writing about information that's important to our clients . . . and there's also the fact that Government people talk to me more easily than to newspapers."

The key to the success of government-watching firms is their ability to predict what's coming. Bill Lee of Executive Consultants Ltd., for example, recalls telling a group of clients the broad outlines of the Liberal Administration's National Energy Program several months before the policy appeared in a budget speech. Neville, too, says PAI's major selling point is its ability to tell clients what to expect. "One of the things we sell is the need for corporations and associations to be proactive, to be involved before decisions are taken."

That means PAI staff members spend most of their time trying to determine from public officials what policies are being developed and what options the Cabinet will be considering. PAI will then tell its clients who to see in a Government department or the Cabinet, and will help prepare material for the client's lobbying campaign.

While that stops short of what other politically connected companies offer, PAI clients who want to change Government thinking evidently do not mind going into battle on their own. Knowledge can indeed be power, and if a corporation is going to lay siege to Ottawa's bureaucratic fortress it could do worse than buy its advice from someone who has had a hand in the citadel's design.

---

* Bill Neville, chairman of PAI.
** PAI and Decima Research.

Source: Simpson (1985).

PMO, have been earning substantial fees by setting up meetings for their clients with cabinet ministers.[3]

More importantly, Moores, who describes lobbying as his profession of which he is proud, is accused of "running an escort service." In the words of a competitor, Moores "packs the client's bag, carries it through the right door, and then makes his case for him. Frankly, he's marketing his connections, and if it doesn't stop, this whole profession is going to be under a cloud."[4] Moores called that description "completely unfair and untrue." He says his firms do not practice face-to-face advocacy on behalf of the twenty or so clients of GCI. Yet it is a fact that Moores's partner did attend a meeting he arranged with the minister of fisheries with his client Ulf Snarby, who was making an unusual application to transfer a fishing licence.[5] The minister was not aware that Snarby was being charged a fee of $2000 plus $500 per month for a year by GCI for the meeting and related services.[6] Subsequently, both the prime minister and the minister of fisheries, John Fraser, stated in the Commons that no one has to pay a fee to a consultant to obtain a meeting with any minister. Mulroney said "payments are not appropriate or necessary," and Fraser said no influence was used on him to approve the licence transfer.[7] It should be noted that according to Snarby the fee covered several days of meetings with public servants and that "the meeting was arranged after the deputy minister of fisheries and the assistant deputy kept stonewalling, saying the minister wouldn't see me."[8] Time was of the essence in Snarby's case, and GCI was able to arrange the meeting with the minister in a few days.

Moores subsequently issued a statement saying there is no conflict of interest involved in being on Air Canada's board and having his firms work for Nordair and Wardair so long as he personally did not service those accounts.[9] He also defended the right of lobbyists such as GCI to have direct access to elected officials, their staff, opposition MPs, and bureaucrats, where they are furthering the legitimate interests of their clients. Moores said he supported a "properly constituted regulatory framework . . . for government relations people, or lobbyists. . . . [It] would also help to recognize the important role such lobbyists play, and will continue to play, in our country."[10] (See section 6 below.)

In early August 1985, Moores resigned as a consultant to Wardair and Nordair after discussing the potential conflict of interest with Claude Taylor, the chairperson of Air Canada. Then in early September Moores resigned his seat on the board of directors of Air Canada.[11]

Consultants may be retained on an ad hoc basis to deal with a specific problem. They may be retained on an ongoing basis so that their assistance can be sought regularly. Or consultants can, in effect, substitute for the firm or trade association in the performance of one or more of its government relations activities.

The larger public affairs consulting firms monitor social, economic, and political issues relevant to their clients or potential clients. As I emphasized in chapter 6, lobbying is likely to be more successful if conducted early in the policy-making process. Therefore, public affairs consultants try to identify, as early as possible, the issues that are likely to be subject to some form of policy action by government. While consultants will develop strategy and prepare briefs for clients, they seldom make presentations directly to public officials. Many strongly believe that senior executives of the firms involved are likely to be more effective. By maintaining close contact with public servants, politicians, and regulators, consultants are able to indicate whom their clients should contact and what arguments are likely to be more effective. Both formal and informal contacts are used. Such contacts are based very heavily upon the exchange of information that is valuable to all participants. See section 2.2 below.

Skilled, specialized professional help can be quite expensive, and hence beyond the reach of some interest groups. Those with large stakes in an issue may still find it worthwhile.

> Fees, [the president of Public Affairs Management Inc.] explains, vary greatly. On a project basis, a clearly-defined brief alone would run $2,500 ("for a short, simple one") up to $15,000. An onerous, time-consuming assignment, like helping a firm lobby for a legislative amendment or other significant change that might take a year, would average $60–75,000. Clearly the marginally funded public interest group would have to rely on some very creative lobbying — perhaps buttressed by divine intervention — to compete in this league.[12]

2.2 Information and the Lobbying Process

2.2.1 The Information Market

Information is the coin of the realm of lobbying. It is the commodity that is most frequently traded between lobbyists and their targets, among lobbyists who are either allied or competing with each other, and between all participants and the media. Indeed, as I emphasized in chapter 4, lobbying can only exist in a world of imperfect knowledge and costly information. If everyone in the policy arena knew everything there was to know, there would be no need for lobbying at all.

Interest groups need to gather intelligence about the current and prospective activities of government in order to determine how they are likely to be affected and to shape their lobbying strategies. The government of the day wants to know the likely response of a wide range of actors to various initiatives it might take. Media outlets compete by trying to "scoop" each other with information not yet available to competitors. Government relations consultants may be able to solicit business by telling a potential client about what could be a problem looming on the horizon in the form of a prospective policy action. (Of course, the implied solution is to hire the consultant to deal with the matter.) Bureaucrats responsible for advising ministers know that one of the best ways to build a good reputation is to be able to perceive, categorize, and head-off potential problems for government. They take seriously Holiday Inn's slogan: "The best surprise is no surprise at all." This requires more information than that possessed by others or the same information before others have it. In short, information is a valuable resource — in many instances "information is power." See Figure 9-1.

The critical fact is that in lobbying one has to have information in order to get more information. Money and other resources are not a perfect substitute for information, although with large amounts of money one can acquire valuable information (even if we rule out bribery). And some of that information can be traded for other information. It is precisely because some information is proprietary that participants in the lobbying game insist on exchanging information for information, not for cash or other fungible resources.

The exchange of information in the context of lobbying is unlike a conventional market in many ways. First, the price of the goods being exchanged is not clearly marked and is often impossible to determine ex ante and may not even be clear ex post. Second, some exchanges may appear to be unconditional (i.e., unilateral flows) because they are not contemporaneous. Information of value to a recipient may only be "paid for" some time later with information given to the original initiator of the exchange. In other words, credit is extended in information markets, although those who regularly fail to pay their debts will find it hard to function in the future with the same players.

Third, certain purveyors of information develop reputations for being "good sources" (i.e., plenty of high-quality information) and these are likely to be persons who make the most exchanges. Fourth, in some cases, the same information may be exchanged for "full value" with several players without necessarily reducing its value. Other types of information become essentially valueless the moment they are passed on. Fifth, the players have imperfect information about the volume, balance of trade among various participants, and the quality of information supplied by those in the same market. This is a greater problem in information than in regular markets due to the nonsimultaneity of exchanges, the nonhomogeneity of the product, and the nature of the commodity itself.

2.2.2 Lobbyists as a Source of Information

Perhaps the strongest functionalist argument for the legitimacy of interest groups is that they provide valuable information to other actors in the policy-making process. This information is of two broad types:

- assessments of the impact or potential impact of an action or proposed action by government (e.g., who wins and more importantly who loses[13] from a policy action); and

- the likely political response of the members of the interest group (and of a possible wider constituency with which the group is familiar) to various possible actions by government.

Jim Bennett, of the CFIB, emphasizes the role of lobbyists as sources of information valuable to both bureaucrats and politicians:

> Lobbyists also represent another kind of knowledge that makes them welcome in the offices of bureaucrats and politicians alike. They are regarded as a source of information that governments find difficult if not impossible to discover easily. That special access to information may be technical or it may flow from the very nature of the membership of groups like the CFIB. The federation specializes in information gathered as the voice of small business.[14]

Decision makers need to know about the potential outcomes of the policy alternatives arrayed before them if they are to make the best choice. No one sitting in Ottawa or in any of the provincial capitals can predict with great accuracy how a policy action will affect those remote from the centre. Interest groups can provide accurate and valuable information or expertise not available even to politicians and the bureaucracy. Donald Macdonald, speaking as a federal cabinet minister, has commented on this point as follows:

> In the process of preparing legislation and also in considering general policy changes, the government requires as much information as possible about the areas to be affected and the possible implications of any proposed changes. . . . What is of the greatest value is for the Minister to be apprised of the impact of the legislation from the particular viewpoint of the group concerned. Legislation must of necessity speak generally, but there may be special cases which persons in a particular industry or group might recognize more easily than can someone in government, surveying industry or the community generally. (As cited in Anderson 1977, 297)

In many cases, it is necessary — in the jargon of the advertising trade — "to run it up the flagpole and see who salutes," or who howls in disgust. While the information supplied by special interests may be selective and biased, it may still prevent policy makers from implementing policies that are extremely unpopular or have counterproductive outcomes.

There is empirical support for the view that the provision of "information" is key to the functional aspects of interest-group activities. Presthus (1971, 448) found that 40 percent of his sample of federal MPs ranked "providing information on pending legislation" as a "very important" or "fairly important" function of interest groups; 39 percent gave the same ranking to "helping me represent all community interests"; and 28 percent ranked "giving me attitudes of my constituents" as a "very" or "fairly important" function performed by interest-group representatives. Obviously, the latter two functions deal with attitudinal information and political support rather than technical information about proposed legislation.

2.2.3 Political Feedback

The feelings of voters are important, and it is one of the functions of interest groups to aggregate and articulate the values of voters between elections. It should be emphasized that voters only infrequently get to directly reward and punish politicians on election day. The "voice" option, to use Albert Hirschman's term, between elections takes the form of lobbying. In other words, when people can't change their elected representatives to obtain policies more closely aligned with their preferences, they urge legislators to alter existing or proposed policies. This is done by persuasion through the technique of lobbying.

Obviously, politicians care a great deal about how important groups of voters are likely to perceive a policy action. (I must emphasize that in politics, perception is reality.) If 90 percent of 20 000 owners of small businesses replying to a CFIB questionnaire vote thumbs down on a piece of proposed legislation thought by the federal government to benefit small business, politicians may wish to rethink the issue. It's not just the numbers of those who favour or oppose a particular measure that counts with politicians, they are also interested in the intensity of preferences. In particular, they want to know if there is a sizeable group of individuals who are prepared to make the issue highly visible in the media (thereby possibly influencing others) and/or switch voting allegiance.

2.2.4 Information for Bureaucrats

Analytical information is relatively more important to some of the lobbyists' targets than to others. Politicians are more interested in political arguments, facts, and analyses. Their bureaucratic advisors are more interested in analyses that would help them assess how well a policy achieves or is likely to achieve its substantive (as opposed to symbolic) goals:[15] that is, Will this industrial incentive grant create jobs? How many? Where? What type? What will be the budgetary cost per job? Will competitors of subsidized firms complain? While politicians provide plenty of evidence that allocative efficiency is a low priority for them, many senior bureaucrats are genuinely concerned that public programs promote this objective. Or they try to minimize the misallocation of resources caused by public programs designed to achieve other objectives, notably the redistribution of income. (More generally, recall chapter 7.)

Bureaucrats who have to administer the policies and programs approved by legislators also care a great deal about their practicality or workability in implementation. Bureaucrats need analytical information to assess the administrative problems associated with a policy. Since it is the bureaucrats who have to live with programs long after the excitement of their creation, they have a vested interest in this side of a government program. Interest groups may be able to identify potential pitfalls so as to avoid a "bureaucratic nightmare."

> Sometimes the government, by its sheer size or drafting ineptitude, may propose a law which would inadvertently cripple or injure an industry and it is important for the lobbyist to communicate these problems. However, such gross errors, once communicated, are easily corrected or exemptions provided, and do not require inordinate lobbying skills. (Roman 1978, 215)

Thoughtful advice from interest groups whose members will be directly affected by a policy change can be very valuable to bureaucrats, since many public programs fail because of problems in implementation rather than basic design. Public servants are often open to alternative techniques of implementing a program provided its fundamental purposes are achieved. (In fact, only cabinet ministers can negotiate on the purposes.) Pareto improvements are nearly always welcome, that is, those that make some people better off, but make no one worse off. For example, interest groups may be able to provide information on ways to reduce their members' compliance costs while in no way increasing costs borne by taxpayers or reducing the effectiveness of the program.

Moreover, by avoiding administrative "snafus," bureaucrats may save their ministers from public embarrassment and themselves from "Excedrin" headaches. The point is that middle and senior public servants take pride in their professionalism. While they may privately disagree with the objectives and substance of a particular program, they know it is their job to make it work as well as possible within the spirit intended by their political masters.

Senior bureaucrats also play an important role in providing policy analysis and advice to cabinet ministers. Their influence in this process is often proportionate to the information they are able to bring to bear on policy issues. This point is developed in the following quotation from an article on lobbying in the *Financial Times*:

> Several experts interviewed agreed that knowledge is power to an ambitious civil servant. Experienced lobbyists seek to tap such people for their knowledge of the system, its programs and administrations. In turn, they feed them tidbits to help them enhance their own power base. The tactic, though, shouldn't overshadow the bureaucracy's ongoing need for reliable, useful economic information. "When I was in government," recalls Ernest Steele, a longtime civil servant who rose to be secretary to the treasury board before becoming president of the Canadian Association of Broadcasters,

"what I needed most was accurate information and good constructive advice directed at the national interest. I especially welcomed
innovative and practical thoughts on how to achieve goals at lower
costs, with less direct government intervention." (H. Black 1982, 9)

2.2.5 Hard Facts Please

An analytical approach to lobbying can identify those claims made by
the group that can be justified to an objective third party. Lobbying is
the art of persuasion. Claims or demands by one group on the state —
hence on other citizens — must be justified. Changes in public policy
must be rationalized. Since the rationalist paradigm does dominate the
system, it is necessary to provide reasons why a change should be made.
These reasons, however, may be either logical or emotional.

Lobbyists in Canada often neglect to develop the facts important to
government (e.g., documentation of the adverse consequences of government actions) and to provide an analytical basis for their position.
McGregor observes:

A point of weakness, one acknowledged by many of the groups, is
the lack of sophistication in briefs they routinely submit to the government on specific policies. An increasing number of groups are
hiring economic consulting firms to prepare technically convincing briefs.

The need for a business group to do its homework thoroughly on
an issue is stressed by the Business Council [on National Issues']
D'Aquino: "Fundamental to the quiet and reasonable approach is
the need to do incredibly thorough homework, equal to that done
by the officials themselves. To not do your homework is to go in
with one hand tied behind your back." (1982b, 2)

The fact is that the amount and quality of analytical work prepared by
most interest groups are low. Most briefs contain undocumented generalizations about the actual or potential impact of an existing or proposed policy. They may clearly convey the opinion or feelings of the
members of the group, but there is seldom any analysis to support those
conclusions. Bill Lee, an experienced government relations consultant,
provides the following advice: "Use hard, defensible facts, and remember the government has lots of people ready to uncover specious arguments. Your believability and impact also will be improved through
credible research, reasoned analysis, logical conclusions, acceptable alternatives, public interest awareness, political sensitivity, and your own confidence and credibility" (quoted in H. Black 1982, 9).

In many cases, the greatest potential contribution of interest groups
to a reasoned debate is ignored — namely, the provision of microdata
(e.g., company by company) on the effects or likely effects of a policy.
For example, following the First Ministers' Conference in February 1978

the federal government requested the Economic Council of Canada to prepare an extensive study of the scope and impact of government regulation in the economy (ECC 1979). Soon many business people and trade association officials were heard complaining loudly about the costly burdens of various types of regulation without, however, actually trying to estimate the costs of the major regulatory initiatives to which they were subject. This stands in sharp contrast to a number of such studies in the United States. When officials of the ECC approached individual companies and trade associations to gain their cooperation in undertaking studies of the costs of regulation, very few were willing to help. As director of research for the regulation reference at the time, I made it clear that analysts and technocrats within the government were unlikely to take seriously claims that business was bearing heavy regulatory burdens if firms and associations were unwilling to assist in the admittedly difficult task of actually counting the costs.

While politicians may take the intuition of senior executives as gospel truth, their bureaucratic advisors function within a different paradigm. The stronger the statement, the better the analysis should be to back it up. It is not enough, for example, to say that a policy change will "cost a lot of jobs." Both politicians and bureaucrats want to know how many jobs, of what type, and where they are located. In a nation suffering high levels of unemployment, jobs are a critical theme, as the following newspaper story illustrates.

> The Canadian Toy Manufacturers Association wants the Government to review federal sales tax legislation that has resulted in the loss of 2,000 jobs in the toy and packaging industries. The crux of the problem is that sales tax paid on an imported product as it passes through customs is considerably less than the 10 percent paid by Canadian manufacturers at the retail level. . . .
>
> The consequence of this current sales tax system has been the loss of jobs so "we are now asking the federal government to rectify these inequities" and recreate those jobs, Mr. Irwin [chairperson of the CMTA] said. . . . "The biggest mandate of the Mulroney government is to create jobs," said Mr. Irwin. "If you want to create jobs, you don't create a sales tax system that benefits imports."[16]

The Toy Manufacturers have taken a major step in documenting or supporting their argument for a change in policy. However, the wise minister will ask his deputy to check out *how* the association obtained its estimate of 2000 jobs lost. It is critical for the Toy Manufacturers to be able to show government officials that their figures are based on a reasonable method of calculation. Perfection and the latest scientific methodology is not required but the association will lose credibility if it (1) knowingly exaggerated the figures to make their point, or (2) failed to use a reasonable method under the circumstances (i.e., in light of the time and resources available and in light of the emphasis to be placed on the specific statistics).

Unfortunately, many interest groups adopt the Chicken Little (or "the sky is falling") approach in dealing with government: they greatly exaggerate the adverse consequences of an existing or proposed policy (see Roman 1978, 209). Moreover, they fail to appreciate that many policies are like the Curate's egg: parts are bad, but others are quite good. It is not intellectually honest for an interest group to focus only on the adverse consequences of a policy. To do so only undermines their credibility.

2.2.6 Modelling the Impact of Government Policies

The most valuable information to both politicians and bureaucrats relates to the broad consequences of existing and proposed government actions. Ideally, they would like to know the change in utility for every individual as a result of each public policy action. Politicians would then want to know how to translate that into likely changes in voting behaviour. Bureaucrats, to fulfill their analytical role, would like to know how these changes in each person's utility translate into changes in behaviour in terms of the substantive goals of various policies. An increase of one cent per litre in the excise tax on gasoline will generate how much revenue in the long run and the short run? How much will consumption be affected in the long run and the short run? If the federal government "caps" its contributions to medicare, what will be the effect on the health of the nation? Or more narrowly, will the average income of doctors be changed and by how much?

Obviously, interest groups cannot begin to achieve this ideal, but it should be kept in mind when providing information to government in an attempt to influence public policy. The importance of government activity for many industries means that the corresponding trade associations should try to build a formal model designed to assess the impact of major policy changes on the industry. The federal government has several, large-scale macroeconomic models (e.g., in the Department of Finance, Economic Council, Bank of Canada) that it can use to test possible changes in monetary or fiscal policy. However, there is a paucity of even crude industry or sectoral models capable of simulating the likely effects of macro- or microeconomic policy changes. The firms in a specific industry (or their stakeholders) have the largest incentive in developing such a model, if only as a defensive measure to try to prevent government actions that needlessly hurt the industry.

In some ways, government in Canada is like a friendly but myopic elephant. Because it is large, awkward, and doesn't see too well, its movements can inadvertently wreak havoc on those nearby. Governments generally take seriously the admonition "do no harm." Therefore, if an industry association (or other interest group) can demonstrate in a fairly sophisticated way that some policy action will indeed inflict substantial pain on that industry (group), it stands a much better chance of alter-ing the proposed policy. It should be emphasized that "pain" in this context will be more clearly perceived if it is measured in terms of jobs lost, output foregone (particularly exports), and a drop in tax revenues rather than in terms of a decline in net profits and dividends — particu-larly if the shareholders are all wealthy foreigners.

Actually, several different "models" may be necessary in some cases because an econometric model may not be able to incorporate some important aspects of government intervention. The point is that the indus-try needs to be able to identify the size of the impact of changes in major policy variables on a number of "performance" variables. In general terms, this process would have three main steps. First, identify which specific programs/policies within each of the major governing instru-ments appear to have a major impact on the economic health of the industry. Of particular importance are those measures that apply to this industry and not to others or appear to be particularly impor-tant to this industry. For example, the shipbuilding industry is heavily dependent on certain targeted subsidies and concessionary financing terms provided to buyers. This means that in building the model for the first time, analysts must scan all the governing instruments and within each of these instruments they must sort through scores of specific programs/policies to determine their application to this industry. For example, monetary policy is one of general application, but its signifi-cance for different industries varies enormously (e.g., the housebuilding industry is acutely sensitive to changes in mortgage rates).

Second, the analyst must identify those dimensions of industry (and firm) performance that appear to be important to various stakeholders — employers, suppliers, shareholders, customers — and also that are likely to be important to goverment. Employees and trade unions as well as politicians care deeply about jobs, particularly the loss of jobs. They also care about the level of pay and security associated with the job. Shareholders obviously care about profits, dividends, and the cost competitiveness of their firm. Governments care about export earnings, new capital investment (a proxy for innovation and future growth), and tax revenues.

Third, and this is the most difficult part of the task, the analyst must study the cause and effect relationship between the set of public policy variables and the set of performance variables. It is not enough to know, for example, that if pollution control regulations are tightened in a partic-ular way, a company's costs will increase. Rather, if a trade association is going to have a reasonable chance of altering an existing or proposed policy, it will need such information as the following:

- the increase in both operating and capital costs associated with com-plying with the policy on a company-by-company basis (some firms may be hit harder than others);

- the effect of those cost increases on prices, outputs, employment, and competitiveness of the firms; and
- a comparison of the total costs of compliance with the expected benefits of a more stringent pollution control regulation.

Facts alone seldom determine the outcome in the political arena. However, it is clear that a very large part of government intervention has taken place without much in the way of factual information about the likely consequences of such action. By trying to model the impact of major policies on their industry, a trade association can help to improve the policy-making process by providing facts regarding the important consequences of political choices. Business, however, should not expect that only those policy actions where the expected economic benefits to society exceed the social costs will be adopted, even where all the key decision makers have full information. In many cases, nonefficiency objectives, particularly the desire to redistribute income, will dominate. However, more hard, factual information on the likely consequences of public choices is most unlikely to make business interests as a group worse off.

2.3 Informal Approaches

Lobbying in Ottawa is both a formal process (e.g., presenting briefs, testifying before committees) and an *informal* one. Jackson provides two examples of how the latter approach works:

> A senior foreign diplomat wished to influence a foreign policy decision in Canada. He managed to do precisely that by first persuading a member of the Opposition to ask a question in Parliament, and then actually providing the answer himself at the request of his friends in the department of external affairs who were asked to brief the minister. Thus he both asked and answered his own question in the House of Commons.
>
> In another case, a representative of a powerful trade association took a cabinet minister to lunch at a first class restaurant in order to ask him for a favor. The executive wanted to be called as the chief witness before the standing committee of the House of Commons that was investigating the details of a particular bill. He was called. (1982)

Consultant Bill Lee explains the need for lobbyists to get "plugged into" the informal network: "It's very insular here in Ottawa. People play squash together, have dinner together, and their sons and daughters marry each other" (quoted in Hayes 1983).

2.4 Dynamics of Issues and Lobbying

Lobbying and interest-group power is not static. Whittington describes briefly how the powerful Canadian Bankers' Association "found themselves badly outmanoeuvered" in the fight over the new Bank Act in 1980:[17]

> Feeling threatened by the early proposals for Bank Act changes forwarded by the federal finance department, the near-banks, such as trust companies, leasing companies, credit unions and caisse populaires, left no stone unturned in a furious lobbying effort that led to extensive alterations before the legislation was finally approved.
>
> The banks' competitors applied relentless pressure on federal MPs, both at the grass-roots levels and in innumerable interviews in Ottawa, and sought help from provincial governments in getting certain aspects of the proposed legislation altered. What the banks, through their organization, the Canadian Bankers' Association, seemed not to realize was that lobbying had become much more complicated since the previous Bank Act changes way back in 1967. (1981, p. G13)

Not only does the balance of advantage in lobbying battles shift because of unexpected behaviour of a participant (including rival interest groups), but it can also be shifted by forces entirely beyond the control of any of the key actors. For example, the major chartered banks in 1981 were under severe public attack on several related fronts. They were said to be causing inflation or at least to be major beneficiaries of it. Their profits were described by some critics as "obscene" as middle-class Canadians felt the burden of rising double-digit mortgage rates. The opposition parties were able to obtain an investigation by a parliamentary committee. However, while the work of the committee was under way (during the period March through July 1982), the definition of the problem changed as more evidence became available that both many large borrowers and the banks had overextended themselves.[18] The most obvious example was Dome Petroleum, whose massive indebtedness forced the federal government to intervene to save the banks at great cost to Dome's shareholders and almost none to those of the banks that had lent Dome billions (see Foster 1984).

Because the situation changed so drastically in less than a year, Richard Gwyn (1982) noted that the bankers ("our fiscal father confessors," to quote Peter Newman) were able to get a favourable report in late July 1982 from the House of Commons Standing Committee on Finance, Trade and Economic Affairs, which had set out originally to examine their allegedly "exorbitant profits." The report ended up focusing on maintaining confidence and security in the banking system in the face of overexpansion. For example, it recommended that the level of insurance for individual depositors be raised from $20 000 to $60 000. The committee, Gwyn said, "in character, has gone down on its knees before the banks." In particular, the committee said "nothing about the imprudence of the banks in lending so much money last year that if some large customers like Dome [Petroleum] go down a couple of their banks, while they won't themselves go down, will go wobbly." Moreover, nothing was said "about the way the banks have transferred all the financial risks from themselves to ordinary Canadians" by shortening the terms of loans and requiring floating rates. In short, in Gwyn's view, the report was "a whiteout. A worshipful silence."

The point is that a report that fully exposed the vulnerability of the largest banks, which was attributable to their own poor management decisions, might have caused fear and panic in the entire financial system. This could then have had disastrous consequences for the entire "real" economy.

Now, the latest debacle concerning the attempted bailout in March 1985 and then collapse of the Canadian Commercial Bank (CCB) and Northland Bank in September 1985 may well alter the nature of the lobbying battle over the Green Paper *The Regulation of Canadian Financial Institutions*, introduced in April 1985. If the Green Paper's proposals were implemented, trust and insurance companies, investment dealers, and other nonbank financial firms would be allowed to enter into new markets. In particular, trust companies would be able to compete against banks in the important business of commercial lending. On the other hand, it was expected to be 1990 — the next scheduled revision of the Bank Act — before the banks would be permitted to extend their activities to the turf of other "pillars" of the financial sector (e.g., offering trust services, selling mutual funds, annuities, and insurance).

The banks' strategy had been to delay new legislation based on the Green Paper until 1990.[19] Conversely, the other financial institutions generally wanted any new legislation quickly so that they could get a head start before facing the new competition from the big banks with their great resources.

The collapse of the CCB and Northland Bank has put great pressure on the federal government to bring in new, tougher regulations immediately to reassure the public. Newspaper accounts suggest that some of the items likely to be plucked from the Green Paper amount to closing the barn door after the horse has bolted. But "once those sections are taken out of the green paper, the heart and soul are gone." In other words, the government is unlikely to proceed with the other measures that would generally increase competition among financial institutions because it can be argued that it is new entrants that have got into trouble. This development will greatly please the banks, who will be able to wax eloquent about the dangers of overly aggressive new competitors, not only risking their shareholders' money, but also that of their depositors — forcing the government to guarantee all deposits, not only those below $60 000 covered by the Canada Deposit Insurance Corporation.

2.5 Dealing with Regulatory/Administrative Agencies

A great deal of public policy is created and administered by quasi-independent administrative or regulatory agencies (see ECC 1979). One of the theories underlying the use of such agencies to deal with government regulation — rather than conventional line departments — is that in this format it is easier to reduce the "political" content of public decision making and substitute a greater degree of rational, technical expertise. For some of its advocates, the role of the specialized "independent" regulatory agency was to take regulation out of politics. In the case of direct or economic regulation, for example, the regulator is called upon to decide such things as:

- who should be allowed to enter the industry;
- the relative prices of various industry outputs;
- the allowable rate of return on capital employed by the firms in the industry;
- the appropriateness of the firms' capital expenditure programs; and
- whether mergers should be permitted.

Therefore, it is hard to see how regulators can avoid fundamental political decisions. After all, politics, according to one of the most widely cited definitions, is about who gets what and how they get it.

In any event, persuading a regulatory agency to act in ways that benefit one's interest group is a specialized form of lobbying. By definition, certain techniques designed to influence public policy are ruled out, for example, political contributions to registered parties and candidates (although they might be helpful when one appeals the decision of a regulatory agency to the cabinet). Similarly, there is only a very limited value in making one's case in the media to generate public support or rally a regulated firm's "natural constituency" when the target is a regulatory agency. In the same vein, advocacy advertising is seldom used. Indeed, to do so when an issue is before the agency may be construed as being in bad taste or even as analogous to being in "contempt of court."[20]

In general, persuasion is confined to formal briefs and testimony under oath before the regulatory agency's commissioners or members. Informal, *ex parte* (one-sided) contacts, particularly with the professional staff of the agency, do occur. They can be valuable, but the astute representatives of interest groups appearing before regulatory agencies have to be sensitive to what is and is not appropriate in this regard. For example, some Ottawa insiders were slightly shocked when, during the course of hearings on pay-television licences, one of the applicants hosted a cocktail party for CRTC commissioners, CRTC staff, and various representatives of other applicants. Almost all the commissioners attended and during the course of the event were seen in conversation with employees of their host.

Three distinctive features of interest-group representation before regulatory agencies should be noted. First, in formal hearings before the agency, it is common for the parties to use experts. The name of the game here is to find apparently disinterested persons of high professional reputation (i.e., widely regarded as experts) and have them pour forth their wisdom on some aspects of the matters at hand with the expectation that what they say will strongly confirm (or at least not contradict) the group's official position. The group does not try to bribe or persuade the experts to ensure that their testimony is consistent with the "party line." Rather, two completely legal and honourable strategies are employed. The first — which requires a plenitude of pecuniary resources — is to retain as many experts as possible; then have each prepare a draft statement. Then the interest group puts on the witness stand only those experts who quite independently are ready to say what is consistent with the group's position. Those whose statements are not used have been neutralized. They cannot testify for other parties, as they have already accepted money from a party of interest. The second strategy is to be selective in what the experts are called to testify about. There is a danger here, however, in that under cross-examination the group's experts may be led into areas where their statements may damage the group's case.

Second, the briefs, interrogatories, and testimony before regulatory agencies are given under oath. Obviously this limits a group's scope in some cases, not so much because in ordinary oral and written communications in a lobbying context people lie, but rather because what they say very seldom becomes part of a formal public record that can be easily obtained and studied. Language and argumentation are likely to be less precise or more ambiguous when no public record is made. The combination of being on the public record and under oath requires that interest groups and their witnesses — if they are to be persuasive — speak more coherently and consistently than if these two constraints were not present. Moreover, these two constraints, notably the former, mean that some arguments or appeals that might be effective in a regular lobbying situation simply cannot be used.

The third distinctive feature of regulatory hearings is the right of cross-examination. In principle, any party of interest can cross-examine at length every witness presented by every other party. (This helps to explain why lawyers and papermakers think formal regulatory proceedings are the cat's pyjamas.) This means that the evidence and arguments advanced by any interest group will be subject to a type of "trial by combat." Opponents are expected to try to identify the errors in one's logic, facts, and analyses so that the regulators can discern "the truth." The theory is that the truth will emerge with stark clarity as a result of this process. While that may be the case in criminal trials — although many doubt it — what happens is that the adversary procedure in regulatory matters strongly favours the status quo. This is so because in their obsession with determining with certainty what is true and what is not, lawyers (and those over whom they have influence) find it easy to understand the truth of what is already in place or has actually happened. However, they always have grave doubts about the future precisely because no one can say for sure *exactly* what will occur (and lawyers do require witnesses under hostile cross-examination to be exact). Since the truth must be a matter of certainty — even though a regulatory proceeding does not properly require proof beyond a reasonable doubt — the truth must necessarily be found in the comfort of the status quo rather than in the admittedly uncertain prospects of change. Since such change often will hurt an existing interest, it is often rejected because the prospective hurt is seen as certain while the prospective benefits to those not at the table are nebulous.

But the practice of cross-examination does have certain virtues. It prevents the use of hit-and-run tactics in lobbying whereby a group advances certain arguments in the expectation that neither a competitive group nor its target will be able to disprove those arguments. Cross-examination, therefore, can remove from serious consideration phony "facts," specious arguments, and errors in logic. The prospect of cross-examination tends to discipline all the parties appearing before a regulatory agency, thereby reducing emotionalism and purely political appeals. It should be noted, however, that where a disadvantaged group makes its case largely in normative and emotional terms, they create a problem for economic interests, since it is easy for even gentle cross-examination to be construed as an attack on the "sacred" principles that have been advanced.

Finally, I note that in large-scale regulatory hearings involving such giants as Bell Canada, the giants may be little affected by cross-examination from small intervenors. The giant may be able to create such a voluminous public record that without comparable resources to analyze that record, the right of cross-examination may be devoid of significance. Lawyers cross-examining the giant's experts need their own experts to fully appreciate the testimony of the first set of experts. Moreover, it is not sufficient to "rattle" the testimony of the giant's experts; one has to offer a superior counter-paradigm. That is very difficult, but at all times the onus of proof rests on those seeking to alter the conventional wisdom embodied in the status quo.

Figure 9-2 provides a host of tips on how an interest group can convince an administrative agency to exercise its discretion in a way that is beneficial (or less costly) to that group.

2.6 Confrontation or Conciliation?

Does a confrontational style work in influencing government policy in Canada? Or are compromise and conciliation more consonant with Cana-

Figure 9–2
HOW TO CONVINCE AN AGENCY

Principle	Usage
Limits of legal materials	First: explain why your policy is sound Second: explain why the law compels it or at least would allow such an interpretation
Do not ask the impossible	Do not ask the agency to break the law or clearly violate well-specified government policy in order to satisfy your needs
Policy analysis	Know the limitations of your analysis as well as its strengths Never convert a marginal probability into a certainty and thereafter treat it as "true" Do not use jargon for effect only Useful to determine the impact on distribution of wealth Cost-benefit analysis should not consist of you getting the benefit while others get the cost Be careful about unsupported claim — "the consumer always pays"
Uncertainty	Policy decisions are never final Winning on a dubious argument is debatable — there are long memories Issues shift — the agenda changes Possible to promote incremental or experimental shifts — help to make experiments work or face a leap backwards How you lose is important; remember there will be more appearances before the agency
Know thyself	Have direct contact with someone high enough in the organization to make decisions affecting the options and uncertainties involved
Know when principles do not apply	If it is known that the agency is not going to budge, it's probably OK to take an intransigent position and try to reverse the agency in the courts
Concentrate on the agency's problem, not your own	Show how the policy will damage interests of the agency Evaluate secondary issues that are crucial to the agency Identify issues where the agency can eliminate your problems without compromising its goals

Figure 9–2 (continued)

Principle	Usage
Bureaucratic Process	
Focus	The right material for the level
Format	Use an executive summary, synthesis, appendices — detailed technical issues
Intra-agency conflicts	It may be worthwhile to translate arguments in terms of agency's thrust (provide alternative views)
Oral presentations	Bureaucrats move through paper Opportunity to gain information Put significant points on paper Be scrupulously accurate but diplomatic Use French where appropriate at the federal level
The hierarchy	Decreasing time and attention as issue moves up Reluctance to overrule lower-level decisions
Specificity	The more specific your point the better your chances of success
Knowing the decision maker's starting point	Understand the context in which the agency is working The agency may have been given a contradictory or impossible task — understand its problems
Political environment	One may be unloved and therefore find other groups and compromise to obtain a broader base Policy by consensus — how much of the agency's original position will be given up to get you in the tent

Source: Adapted from de Long (1982).

dian values? The MacEachen budget of November 12, 1981, was not immediately unpopular. Indeed, many editorial writers praised it for trying to reduce the revenue drain through tax expenditures. Even the initial comments by business representatives on budget night gave it faint praise. However, as people studied the budget, it became unpopular and produced a storm of protest from some groups and individual firms. McGregor (1982b, 2) reports that in March 1982 Dominion Life Assurance undertook a highly confrontational tactic in response to that budget. The company sent letters to some 7000 mortgage-holders urging them to oppose a supposed government intention to impose a tax on homeowners. McGregor states that

MacEachen quickly and firmly denied he ha[d] any intention of imposing such a tax or that it has ever been considered. He accused the company of being "mischievous," trying to frighten and confuse people as a way of gaining support for a narrow change the life insurers want to achieve in the government's proposed taxing of accrued income on life insurance policies. (1982b, 2)

How do the targets in government feel about a confrontational style? Then minister of finance Allan MacEachen, the target of much aggressive lobbying, is quoted as saying, "I am impressed by logic, argumentation, the strength of the argument, rather than by hastily arranged coalitions, press conferences and rhetoric." Politicians, like all other human beings, do not react well to hostile criticism, particularly when it is conducted in the full glare of the media. McGregor quotes John Evans, the former parliamentary secretary to the minister of finance, as saying:

"Do you listen to people when they scream at you? Absolutely not," . . . He has been meeting with several business groups on budget issues in recent months. Evans gives high points to the broad-based business groups such as the Business Council on National Issues and the Canadian Manufacturers' Association for what he calls a "more balanced approach. They don't drag it down into the mud with far overblown statements designed to inflame public opinion," he says. (1982b, 2)

The conciliatory approach is advocated by many Canadian lobbyists, but it may not please some members of interest groups:

Jean-Jacques Gagnon, a vice-president with Alcan Aluminum Ltd. and chairman of the CMA, who also sits on the policy committee of the BCNI, believes a quiet, consistent offering of views to government is more useful than public fanfare and emotional appeal. Yet, endorsement from politicians is not considered entirely a boon by the rank and file of many business groups. The "reasonable" approach praised by the politicians appears too soft to many of the groups' members. (McGregor 1982b, 2)

The Employers Council of B.C. (now the B.C. Business Council), founded in 1966, represents over 100 major corporations and more than two dozen bargaining associations. The council favours

conciliation rather than confrontation [which] pervades the Council's dealings with government, both federal and provincial. What [William] Hamilton [then president and chief executive of ECBC] calls a "non-pushy atmosphere" prevails. Many contacts are informal, such as an exchange of ideas over lunch with a new Cabinet member. The Council also prepares several formal briefs each year to Ottawa and Victoria. It maintains a full-time government services manager in the provincial capital (John Nixon), who serves as a "facilitator" rather than a lobbyist. If you have a problem with government, Nixon will tell you who to see, but he will not make the appointment for you. The Council makes representations only on behalf of its members as a whole; it does not advocate for individual companies. . . .

Hamilton's approach to public affairs has more than one dimension. The Council does not simply convey business opinion to government. It also attempts to inject into that opinion an understanding of the public interest.[21]

2.6.1 CFIB and the November 1981 Budget: A Case Study[22]

Two months before budget night, November 12, the Canadian Federation of Independent Business (then representing 63 000 firms) submitted a prebudget brief to the minister of finance recommending cuts in the corporate income tax, increases in the small-business deduction limits, a tightening of unemployment insurance regulations, extension of the low-interest Small Business Development Bond program, an increase in the RRSP tax-deductible contributions, and reductions in federal spending to reduce the deficit. The headline in the association's newsletter was, "Ottawa told: shape up." It was a portent of things to come.[23]

CFIB's confrontational approach to the budget began with their media interviews the night the budget was tabled in the House of Commons. While other business representatives were approving of or neutral to the budget, John Bulloch, founder and president of CFIB and its chief spokesperson, described it as "a bag of snakes."[24] He also described it as "misguided, incompetent, arbitrary, insular, dogmatic, hasty and tyrannical," and as "a cancerous abortion."[25] Bulloch was particularly angry because the budget, in his view, was a "tax grab" disguised as "tax reform." On November 15, another senior official of CFIB, Jim Bennett, sent a telegram to Finance Minister MacEachen recommending that he delay the budget's implementation until a parliamentary committee had held public hearings and issued a report.[26] Two days later, CFIB's tax advisory committee advised Bulloch to begin an "all-out confrontation" over the budget. This group, composed of tax practitioners, felt the budget was so flawed that it must be totally withdrawn. Since governments traditionally fall over lack of confidence in a budget, this task was highly improbable. CFIB strategists decided to completely risk their credibility in a direct frontal attack on the budget, and if necessary, on the minister. The CFIB board of governors authorized a special appropriation of $250 000 to be spent on the campaign — later described as a war.

On November 19 during Question Period, MacEachen stated that he would be willing at a later date to answer Bulloch's allegations about the impact of the budget on small business. One week later, John Bulloch spoke to the Chartered Accountants Association of Western Ontario. It was part of CFIB's campaign strategy for its representatives to give speeches in vulnerable (marginal) Liberal ridings. Jim Bennett sent a CFIB report highlighting the ten most harmful budget proposals to all federal cabinet ministers, including Don Johnston, president of the Treasury Board.

On December 2, CFIB placed a full-page ad in the *Globe and Mail* giving "ten reasons why open hearings should be held on the Federal Budget before going any further." It was designed to show senior bureaucrats that CFIB was reasonable and constructive, and to alert the "educated/influential" public to the budget's flaws.

Two days later MacEachen made a statement rebutting CFIB's claims regarding the budget. However, he also indicated that he might make amendments to the budget in the weeks ahead. Special meetings of the Liberal caucus on the budget took place where backbenchers were alleged to pressure him for changes. During this time, CFIB had been communicating extensively with officials in MacEachen's department, opposition members, Liberal backbenchers, and senators.

On December 8, CFIB ran its second, and more controversial, full-page ad on the budget in twenty-three major dailies. Using a photograph of a pair of hands moving three shells on a tabletop, the ad's headline stated: "The MacEachen budget is not what it seems to be. It is a sly, devious document that nearly fooled us all." The ad claimed that "the unanimous conclusion of the best tax experts in the country is — disaster. A disaster for small business, farmers, working Canadians, professionals and the unemployed. In short, the whole economy. . . . your Member of Parliament probably does not understand what this budget will do to his constituents." CFIB recommended that the budget not be enacted until after hearings before the House of Commons Standing Committee on Finance, Trade and Economic Affairs. The object of the ad was to force the minister to make major rather than minor amendments to his budget. It was also designed to get journalists to focus on the budget. The ad also asked those persons who took issue with the budget to write CFIB expressing their concerns. The ad was provocative by design, since the CFIB wanted to get the general public aroused. This would in turn create pressure beyond that brought forward by the business community, which was now beginning to mobilize. CFIB delivered several thousand responses, in both official languages, to MacEachen's office.

On December 9, a coalition of twenty-three major associations held a joint press conference and issued a press release calling for major changes in the budget. CFIB was the key organizer of the coalition. CFIB staff members contacted over eighty associations to get them to voice their concern. Most had to hold board or committee meetings to get approval to join the coalition. Many could not arrange their meetings in time for the press conference. Eventually, over fifty associations joined the coalition.

On December 10, Bulloch agreed to a personal meeting with Mac-Eachen and his former parliamentary secretary, John Evans. It became a media event after the fact:

Following [the] meeting in Ottawa . . . Bulloch met with the media and described the session as stormy, saying that it became a yelling match as each side accused the other of incompetence. Nonsense, says Ottawa member of Parliament John Evans, who also attended the meeting. There was no shouting, claims Evans, and Bulloch refused to detail specific complaints, preferring instead to talk about the political impact. Says Evans: "He has destroyed his effectiveness as a force for small business."[27]

Patricia Johnston, then vice-president of CFIB, is quoted as saying: "They [government officials] prepared a press release before the meeting and released it afterward. That set up insularity between us and the government. After that, they offered to have us meet with the officials who drafted the original material, but we declined because we knew what reception we would receive."

Part of CFIB's "fight-back" approach to the November 1981 budget was its 113-page *Federal Budget: Report No. 2*. It was distributed widely and sent to all MPs. It prompted analyses by the Small Business Secretariat of the Department of Industry, Trade and Commerce and the Department of Finance, but these were not sent to CFIB for comment or rebuttal. Other techniques were described in the *Financial Post* as follows:

CFIB lobbyists and members "looked at every conceivable angle and talked to every politician under the sun," Johnston says. Efforts included encouraging questions in the House of Commons, educating journalists about small-business issues, sending *Report No. 2* to accounting firms, and encouraging members to "put the heat on local MPs where they have to get re-elected — and we're going to make sure they don't have a long, lazy summer this year [1982], either."[28]

On December 18, 1981, the minister of finance announced twelve revisions to his budget, but they did little for small business. More importantly, MacEachen released "Budget 1981: What It Means for Small Business,"[29] using a list of small businesses apparently obtained from the Department of National Revenue. This action provoked a strong reaction from John Bulloch, who called it part of a "massive and deceitful propaganda machine" which, he said, is run by a "frightening, self-serving bureaucracy using the Big Lie technique."[30] Bulloch called the distribution of 200 000 brochures an abuse of public money for partisan purposes. "Eminent Ottawa tax lawyer Arthur Drache argues that the brochure [was] rife with 'half-truths and distortions.' "[31]

In 1982 CFIB continued to battle in the media over MacEachen's budget. Members were encouraged to keep the heat on, through letters, phone calls, or personal visits to their MPs. CFIB continued to lobby federal and provincial governments to reverse some of the provisions of the MacEachen budget. The provincial governments were in themselves an effective "voice" to the federal government.

On June 28, 1982, MacEachen brought in a new mini-budget. It featured the 6-and-5 program of wage and price controls (see Swimmer 1984) and a few more modest concessions in response to CFIB's complaints concerning the November 1981 budget.

In November 1982 CFIB published in its *Mandate* an evaluation of its efforts to change the 1981 budget. On eleven items, CFIB scored four as A or A +, four as B − to B + and three as C, C +, or F. Describing its efforts to change the budget as a "war," CFIB concluded that at least $0.5 billion of the proposed taxes were reversed. CFIB described its efforts in highly confrontational terms:

> The story can now be told: our credibility was under attack because we were implacable foes; we refused to make behind the scenes deals which would have sacrificed one group of members for the sake of another. Some said the Federation had lost contact with its members, others said we were hysterical and still others treated us as outcasts, yet they all eventually agreed we were right. Our war against the budget was the toughest test the Federation has ever faced, even more severe than the 1970 battle against the Benson White Paper [on taxation] which was instrumental in the development of our organization.[32]

CFIB's response to the November 1981 budget was highly confrontational for the following reasons:

- CFIB's chief spokesperson repeatedly used very strongly pejorative language ("a cancerous abortion") in the media to describe the budget.
- CFIB made very extensive use of the media to get its views across, although it also prepared and distributed widely a lengthy technical analysis of the budget. However, the politicians, bureaucrats, and the public were most aware of the colourful and highly negative adjectives used by John Bulloch in the media.
- CFIB's second major ad describing the MacEachen budget as "a sly, devious document" amounted to a direct personal insult to the minister of finance and deputy prime minister, who was also a close political friend of the prime minister. The minister's integrity was called into question in the most public possible way. Such an ad may have given CFIB visibility, but by being so extreme it almost certainly caused the minister's officials to rally around him, the Liberal caucus to publicly defend the budget, and the minister to be determined not to give in to CFIB's demands. In short, the ad probably soured CFIB's generally good relations with the federal government. In the view of a senior

official of CFIB, "the Minister was defending his officials (plus John Evans and Michael Pitfield) since they designed the package. I have it from competent sources that MacEachen did not even look at most of the measures before he tabled the budget. Many Liberal backbenchers, Ministerial aides, and some Senators privately encouraged the Federation to keep the pressure on the budget."

• The widely reported conflict as to what transpired during Bulloch's meeting with MacEachen (after the controversial ad) appears to have been the result of Bulloch's effort to gain more media attention. Again CFIB's chief spokesperson appeared to be acting and speaking intemperately. However, according to a senior official of the association,

> CFIB fully realized there would be some rallying around Mr. MacEachen, and that relations with the Finance Department would suffer. To not realize that would have been naive, to say the least. The objective by now was not to have the legislation changed through low-key quiet lobbying. That approach failed the night the budget came out, as it was in direct conflict with everything presented to Mr. MacEachen in our pre-budget submission weeks before. Obviously, no government or its elected officials like to be openly challenged or attacked, but at times this is the only option left if one believes their cause is correct, and if the end justifies the means. CFIB believed it was better to have responsible legislation for the good of the economy and the nation as a whole, than friendly relations with Mr. MacEachen.

CFIB genuinely felt the budget was hostile to small business and wrong for the country as a whole. The careful technical analysis of the budget's provisions was a very good idea, as was distributing it widely. Obtaining media coverage for the critique was also a good idea, but the use of extreme language was not — it got the "target's back up." However, it also attracted public attention to business tax issues, something that is normally difficult to do. The second ad was, frankly, a disaster in terms of actually having influence with those able to change the provisions in the budget (or not in it). It violated the most fundamental values of almost all the key players in the policy-making system. According to CFIB's Bennett, the federation recognized in advance the potential humiliation and loss of credibility CFIB would face if it did not turn public opinion against the budget. For this reason its approach was much tougher than any federation lobbying campaign before or since.

Did CFIB's confrontational style increase or decrease its effectiveness in dealing with the MacEachen budget? What were the longer-run effects of the way CFIB responded to the November 1981 budget? Did CFIB win the battle but lose the war? Were CFIB's actions aimed more at solidifying the support of its own members than at changing some of the provisions of the budget? These questions are very difficult to answer.

By personally challenging many of the key players in the policy-making system, the CFIB forfeited the chance for quiet compromise. CFIB staff claim they were offered a quiet deal on "one or two of the worst measures," but declined, since so many different measures hurt various sectors of their membership.

In their own view CFIB officials are convinced that their confrontational style in this case was successful. As evidence of its effectiveness they argue that it

- convinced over 50 other associations to join the coalition,
- caused thousands of Canadians to write us, and untold more to write and/or phone their MPs,
- led to dozens of withdrawals and amendments to budget measures both by MacEachen and by Lalonde, his successor,
- led to the removal of both the Minister and Deputy Minister of Finance,
- resulted in the term "MacEachen budget" becoming archetypal or generic for a badly-conceived budget,
- ruined the leadership ambitions MacEachen was alleged to have before the 1981 budget, and
- encouraged other, usually cautious groups (like Dominion Life) to come out swinging 4 months after the budget.

The federation felt and still feels that the end justified the means. "It is not our usual approach to be so confrontational, but we felt we had no choice: MacEachen's advisors had sold him a bill of goods, and there was no discrete way to get him to change his mind. Although it is unfortunate that the fight became personalized we were privately encouraged by members of the Liberal caucus all through the episode," according to Jim Bennett.

CFIB officials state that their analysis of the results of the confrontation over the budget reveals the following:

1. Public opinion was changed about the budget. The fact that 22 other associations, including some that are pretty cautious, publicly joined CFIB in denouncing the budget, shows that the initial acceptance on the part of many business spokespeople of MacEachen's description of "fairness and equity" was reversed.
2. Most of the budget measures were eventually modified or abandoned. Whether as many changes would have been made as quickly without CFIB's public attack is pure conjecture, but there is strong reason to suggest our efforts made a difference.
3. John Bulloch lost some personal access in the short term. "John was deliberately not invited to a couple of state dinners, but

other CFIB staff were. It was the only feeble weapon certain members of former Prime Minister Trudeau's staff had of showing their displeasure at our approach," according to Bennett. He added that one of the first business leaders Mr. Lalonde met with after taking over from Mr. MacEachen was John Bulloch.

CFIB states that it has continued to be involved in extensive public consultation with both of Allan MacEachen's successors, Marc Lalonde and Michael Wilson, before their subsequent budgets. Finally, to show that the loss of access was indeed short term, CFIB indicates that John Bulloch has been personally consulted by both of Pierre Trudeau's successors, John Turner and Brian Mulroney, the latter inviting Bulloch to join the organizing committee for the 1985 National Economic Summit. Furthermore, many CFIB proposals were accepted and incorporated in the May 1985 federal budget.

2.7 Dealing with Those Directly Affected

One way of making it easier for government to approve of your initiatives with respect to public policy is to do your homework with the individuals and groups likely to be directly affected by the proposed action. Consider the following example:

More and more at Imperial [Oil], people in management are accepting the idea that virtually no major policy can be adopted without taking into account the views of people affected by it outside the company, not just in government but in the communities and public-interest groups. This is especially true for Esso Resources, the subsidiary of Imperial that is active in the North. "Building mutual understanding and consensus is without doubt one of the most important aspects of our northern activity," says Jack Underhill, manager of Esso Resources' external affairs department in Calgary. "And we've learned that what is essential in our relationship with government is also necessary in our relationship with public-interest groups in the North, continuous consultation and cooperation. So, with the participation of northerners, we're trying to design projects that, as much as possible, serve not just our corporate requirements but the legitimate aspirations of northern residents for meaningful jobs and business opportunities." Underhill is adamant that the dialogue is not mere window dressing but a genuine attempt at mutual accommodation. "There are many examples of practical benefits," he says. "One of the most significant is the creation of Shehtah Drilling Limited, a company jointly owned by Esso Resources and corporations operated by Métis and Déné natives. And the idea for it came directly out of our consultation with northerners." Esso Resources people also consult regularly with the environmen-

tal group known as CARC (Canadian Arctic Resources Committee), an organization based in Ottawa. "We meet with them from
time to time to discuss some of our general concepts of northern
development," says Underhill, "which include issues such as the
timing, scale and benefits of projects." The executive director of
CARC, Peter Burnet, agrees that the communication is genuine and
useful. "It helps both parties," he says, "to overcome a tendency to
stereotype and oversimplify. It permits us to get to know one another
and to become more familiar with the other's perception of issues
and options. I know we, as a northern resource policy group, certainly obtain a much better understanding of the economic and
technical aspects of northern projects through these discussions."
(Kruk 1984, 6)

2.8 Countering Stereotypes

Business organizations may find it useful to publish their own analyses
to counter stereotypes and what they feel is misinformation. In the first
example below, a report by the Canadian Bankers' Association (CBA),
showing that nine families control stock worth 46 percent of the value of
the most important companies on the Toronto Stock Exchange, was done
to "debunk" the "myth" that the banks are increasing their control of
the financial system. Helen Sinclair, CBA's director of public relations,
is quoted as saying:

> We were getting concerned by the arguments raised by some mem-
> bers of the financial community that changes happening in the
> financial sector would cause the banks to dominate the financial
> system. . . . Underlying the whole thesis was the innuendo that the
> levels of concentration were increasing, which was contrary to fact.
> They are decreasing. And the arguments being levied were being
> levied in large part by some of these very large conglomerates which
> in fact really rival the banks in size.[33]

The CBA was able to obtain some media coverage for its report, which
was distributed quite widely.[34]

The second example concerns the Canadian sugar industry:

> The chairman of the Canadian Sugar Industry Institute says it has
> published a study of the industry "to a large extent" to counter
> misinformation resulting from publicity that followed a charge that
> three major sugar companies conspired to unduly lessen competition.
> The convictions for breach of the Combines Investigation Act were
> subsequently quashed in 1980 by the Supreme Court of Canada,
> which ruled the Crown could not establish that competition had
> been "unduly" lessened.[35]

But the original convictions left the general perception that the industry produces something that is not good for people, W. C. Brown told a press conference. Another "general perception" is that the sugar industry makes a "horrendous" profit by fixing prices in a back room, he added.

However, a study by an independent authority may not provide concurring evidence for information that is not flattering to the firms or associations involved. W. C. Brown stated that

> included in the institute's study is a review that confirms profit figures made public by the Food Prices Review Board for 1967 to 1972. Based on book value of invested capital, the industry's return before taxes was 29.5 per cent. The study by the accountancy firm of Deloitte Haskins and Sells of Toronto indicates, however, that if replacement value were used instead of book value, the figure for the same period would be 9 per cent.[36]

3.0 CHARACTERISTICS OF AN EFFECTIVE LOBBYIST

Much of lobbying involves negotiation and persuasion, and face to face contact is a major mode of interaction. Individual differences in reputations for judgment, brightness, and ability can have an impact in political processes. In addition, articulateness can increase the individual's interpersonal effectiveness considerably. An individual's effectiveness in the business of negotiation and persuasion is also affected by his or her knowledge of the (initial) distribution of power in specific situations, that is, a clear-eyed realization of how decisions actually get made as opposed to the official version.

Pfeffer points out that "there have been relatively few studies of influence strategies . . . [and] even fewer have examined the effectiveness of the strategies employed and the role of personal skills in the process" (1981, 133). He reports some of the results of a study by Allen et al. (1979) concerning the perceived effectiveness of the personal characteristics of effective political actors. In that study the following percentages of the respondents mentioned the characteristic listed:

• articulate	29.9%	• aggressive	16.1%
• sensitive	29.9	• ambitious	16.1
• socially adept	19.5	• devious	16.1
• competent	17.2	• "organization man"	12.6
• popular	17.2	• highly intelligent	11.5
• extroverted	16.1	• logical	10.3
• self-confident	16.1		

Tommy Shoyama, a former federal deputy minister of finance and previously a senior public servant in Saskatchewan, describes the characteristics of a good lobbyist as follows:

> The characteristics of a good lobbyist are one who is well informed, a good communicator, and not overly strident and aggressive, one who is not seen as beating the drum for a particular cause. The person with documentary information to back up his cause is far more effective than one who pounds you on the back and says you're a wonderful fellow. (As quoted in Sawatsky 1983)

Clare Westcott, former executive assistant to Ontario's former premier William Davis, has sought to debunk some of the mystique associated with effective lobbying:

> Many who see themselves as lobbyists create and advance the view that there is some mystique, some intense area of expertise that is required to ensure smooth and effective relationships with government.
>
> In the 30 years that I have been in one way or another associated with [the legislature in Ontario], it has intrigued me to see so many that maintain substantial and meaningful ongoing relationships with their banks and their bank managers because that relationship is so fundamental to their ongoing activity and survival. Yet they keep almost no consistent relationship with the government that often regulates or controls the circumstances within which they operate.
>
> There is no better lobbyist than the individual citizen, corporate executive, union leader or association president — himself or herself — who maintains a relationship with the government that is ongoing, well informed, frank and consistent.[37]

Andrew Roman, a lobbyist for what are often called public interest groups, puts it this way:

> What makes one lobbyist effective and another ineffective? In addition to general intelligence and the all-important social skills, I would suggest discretion and good contacts. The lobbyists are so discreet, so secretive that you have probably never heard of them. Indeed, some lobbyists I know who depend for their success on close relationships with a small group of public service mandarins would probably sue me if I even suggested that they were lobbyists, as any publicity of their activities could damage their credibility. This small elite denies the label "lobbyist" because they do not themselves make presentations to government officials. They gather information from the bureaucracy as to what sorts of things they would like to see in a presentation, then write the script for the clients, who deliver the presentation themselves.
>
> The second important attribute is the ability to develop and maintain close contacts, both with the political party in power and with the bureaucracy, and of course, with the industry who is the client.

The Ottawa lobbyist has to know who in government actually does what, and who really runs or decides what, and where. It is not enough to know titles and names, as in many cases large departments will have a small number of key individuals, not necessarily at the top, who, because of length of tenure, personal skills, or contacts of their own are the principle influence in the making of a particular decision. (1978, 212)

Sawatsky explains that it is important to have personal contacts and that information is the medium of exchange in lobbying:

Lobbying requires personal contacts. A new lobbyist to Ottawa specializing in petroleum will go to lunch with people in the department of energy, mines and resources and become a familiar face, then do the same in the department of the environment, the department of Indian and northern affairs and any other organization with an interest in his field.

Inevitably he will pick up an amazing amount of information about the goings-on inside government and begin trading his information with public servants. Lobbyists endear themselves simply by giving the public servant a wealth of information about the industry they represent. The public servant uses this knowledge to enhance his position with his boss and his peers. (1983)

It is widely agreed that credibility is the most important asset any lobbyist has. This involves providing government "with relatively unbiased information as a quid pro quo for the privilege of being taken seriously when [the lobbyist] tries to nudge the system in his direction" (Hayes 1983). Although it is hard to do so, lobbyists should try to separate their information provision and advocacy roles. "Information should be balanced and accurate, but when you are asked to comment on a matter of policy, it is possible to exercise your bias" (Hayes 1983).

David Kirk, head of the Canadian Federation of Agriculture, has been called the "dean of the Ottawa lobbyists." He came to Ottawa in 1953. According to Charlotte Gray:

Kirk soon learned the timeless principles of lobbying. First, establish credibility. The key assets are an understanding of issues, reliable information, persistence, and workable policy proposals that harmonize with government goals. Most important, a lobbyist must be able to deliver. When Kirk said that he had the solid support of the farmers, successive agriculture ministers knew he wasn't exaggerating. (1983, 12)

Besides the provision of reliable information, two other elements contribute to the credibility of lobbyists. First, to be credible, lobbyists have to be able to indicate to others, particularly the targets of their efforts, that they have a substantial understanding of the policy issues they are addressing. This includes an understanding of the problems (or opportunities) as seen by the government (politicians and bureaucrats). Empathy for the government's position is not, however, the same as agreeing with its position. Lobbyists lack credibility with government officials where they evince little appreciation of the goals and options facing both politicians and bureaucrats. These points come through clearly in the comments of Jim Bennett of the CFIB:

> As a model of what lobbying should be all about, he recalls his days as a ministerial adviser. One regular visitor to the office was a man who had been a public servant and who was working for a clothing association: "He came in with information, very, very good information. He knew people in the department that I didn't know."
>
> The secret of the man's success was that he understood the obligations of the Government, the interests of his clients, and where they were compatible. He could solve his own problems without causing any embarrassment to either the politicians or the bureaucrats: "A good lobbyist will combine knowledge of the law and policy with a knowledge of political realities."
>
> It's at the level of the politician that political realities become more real. A bureaucrat may not be impressed, says Mr. Bennett, that a CFIB survey says that 85 per cent of Canada's small-business interests want to keep indexing of income tax but that's the kind of intelligence that interests a politician. With officials, there is a different pitch: "With them it's straight knowledge. . . . And you have to show them you've done your homework. . . . The games are different with them."[38]

Second, in a bargaining context, which lobbying frequently becomes, credibility is also a matter of having the authority to "cut a deal." This means that the interest-group representative has sufficient authority to bind the members of his or her group to any deal he or she makes, or that he or she is sufficiently respected within his or her own constituency that the group can be persuaded to go along with the understanding he or she has reached with the government. In the lobbying context, agreements are not reduced to an elaborate written contract, there are no formal mechanisms existing to enforce the understandings worked out orally and followed by a handshake, and the lobbyist has no formal authority to ensure all the members of his or her group will abide by the deal. In this context, credibility is based on a representative being able to follow through on the agreement.

Wise lobbyists don't brag, at least in public, about their achievements. Visible power or influence becomes a target and, moreover, may inhibit relations with the wide spectrum of people an effective lobbyist must be able to deal with. "Don McGillivray, economic columnist for Southam

News, likens a successful lobby to the perfect crime. He says if it is conducted properly no one knows it has taken place" (Sawatsky 1983).

Patience and persistence are the hallmarks of a successful lobbyist. Pat Hrushowy, a B.C. lobbyist, states:

> I think the people I've seen that have been successful and are still here have been patient people, people with a sense of humor. I guess tied in with that sense of humor is some kind of sense of perspective.
>
> The government moves at its own pace and sometimes to its own unique logic, and you have to accept that. You can't bend that, you can't change it. It just is.
>
> You gotta be tenacious and never give up. . . . "When everybody's folded their tents and the show's over, you try another time. And it's usually the time it works." (Quoted in Comparelli 1983)

Fred Moonen, for many years the only full-time government relations specialist dealing directly with the B.C. legislature, stresses " 'patience and humility' and the ability to get along with people are necessary qualities. 'Patience is a virtue, and integrity is vital,' he says. The lobbyists to whom officials give information are discreet and able to maintain a confidence. 'You don't tell tales out of school.' " (Comparelli 1983).

4.0 LOBBYING TECHNIQUES AND STYLE: THE EXAMPLE OF DOME PETROLEUM

The following extended example illustrates many aspects of lobbying techniques and style. It also illustrates the two-way interaction between business and government. Lyon points out that Dome Petroleum recognized that "real influence . . . is exercised . . . not in strident confrontation [that produces a twenty-second clip on the evening news] but, as Dome does so well, quietly, persistently, persuasively, and professionally" (1983, 52). In particular, Dome's political style was Jack Gallagher's style.

Dome's case was presented by Gallagher personally. Bureaucrats and politicians knew they were talking to the chairperson and CEO. Simply because he handled government relations, the issue on the table must be important. Moreover, because of his position at the top of the corporate hierarchy, government people could get answers quickly and authoritatively. In short, Gallagher could deliver both in terms of making an agreement and ensuring that information he had agreed to provide to the government would indeed be provided.

Gallagher attached a high priority to Dome's relationship with governments. While some have argued that Dome Petroleum was a "chosen instrument" of the federal government, I would argue that Dome chose the government to be a principal source of benefits to the firm (e.g., tax concessions, grants, favourable regulations, etc.).

Gallagher was both persistent and personally charming. Alastair Gillespie, minister of energy, mines and resources between September 1975 and June 1979, described Gallagher's persistence as follows:

> He learned the technique of gaining access by learning the habits of ministers. He would come down to Ottawa and I don't think he would make a decision about when he was going to go back to Calgary. If he had come down to see some people and they were on his list, he would stay until he had done so. He was very purposeful about it. I can remember on one occasion coming into my office at 8:30 in the morning and who was sitting in a chair in my outer office but Jack Gallagher. He didn't have an appointment. How does a minister coming in at 8:30 a.m. say "no" to a man who says he just wants ten minutes of your time? (Lyon 1983, 53)

Gallagher was businesslike in his use of his target's time, and he was thoroughly prepared. Wining and dining with plenty of social conversation was not his approach. Mutual advantage rather than friendship was the basis for Gallagher's exchanges with influential people in government. The president of one of Dome's subsidiaries put the matter this way:

> I have never seen Jack lobby in the normal sense. I have never seen him take people out to dinner and that sort of stuff. He is a very austere guy. The idea of sitting down and chitchatting and having dinners with people just would never appeal to him. He used to jam visits with so many people into a day that it was really an efficient trip. He would line all these appointments up — it was all bang, bang, bang from one guy to the next, ministers and deputies. I have seen him take a half-hour or shorter period with a minister and try to cram as much information of a factual nature into that period as he can. Jack is on a first-name basis with a lot of them, but I have never seen any close friendships at work. (Lyon 1983, 54)

Gillespie observed: "He would be very businesslike and he always had a reason for wanting to see you and you always felt that what he had to say was worth listening to — and that, of course, was part of his magic. People didn't turn him down, because they knew he had something interesting to talk about" (Lyon 1983, 53).

Gallagher understood the imperatives of the political and bureaucratic systems. Gillespie noted:

> He probably understood better than almost any other businessman how the government worked and what the government's objectives

were. He always had a very positive suggestion: "Here is a way of gaining your objectives." (Lyon 1983, 53)

Gallagher's technique was quiet and simple — and devastatingly effective. He always had something to offer the policy-makers: a tidbit of intelligence, an idea, a policy initiative that would be helpful to those in the seats of power. Almost incidentally, it would also be helpful to Dome. He never stalked in angrily and told them their plans were hogwash — in the manner, for example, of one abrasive Calgary oilman who needlessly infuriated Liberal MPs at a Commons committee hearing by insisting on referring to the National Energy Program. (Lyon 1983, 55)

Gallagher had an uncanny ability to align Dome's interests with those of the government (even if some of the government's objectives were not publicly articulated). He was "a visionary whose latent desire to develop Canada's Arctic frontier happily coincided with a growing awareness in Ottawa of the country's vast unexplored riches" (Lyon 1983, 51).

Gallagher made helpful suggestions — a slight change in direction here, a modification there, a tax concession perhaps — and assured them that Dome, ultra-nationalistic Dome with big red maple leaves plastered on its ships, would be only too happy to lead the charge in the direction that Ottawa wanted the oil industry to run. (Lyon 1983, 55)

With respect to the exploration of the Beaufort Sea, long a dream of Gallagher, Dome was perfectly situated when the OPEC oil shocks in 1973 and 1979 created great pressures on Canada to become energy self-sufficient. Lyon put it this way: "Private ambition nestled comfortably alongside the National Interest. Ottawa wanted to know — indeed, was desperately anxious to learn — what riches the Beaufort might contain, and obliging Jack Gallagher would find out for them. At a price" (1983, 57).

In addition to trying to find petroleum "elephants" on federal lands, Dome's work in the high Arctic served to assert Canada's claim to sovereignty over the Northwest passage and beyond.

Gallagher, by taking a longer-run and politically sensitive view of Dome's relationship to the federal government, was able to be part of a mutually beneficial exchange of information with senior policy advisors. For example, the then deputy minister of energy (and later deputy minister of finance) Thomas Shoyama saw Gallagher as a "helpful and enthusiastic Canadian nationalist" (see also Foster 1984, 46–48). Lyon continues:

Shoyama also regarded Gallagher as a valuable window on the energy industry, conveying to federal bureaucrats his view of the

Alberta oil industry and those of the Alberta government. Shoyama found it useful to ask, "What do you think of this, Jack?" And, since the Calgary oilman was a frequent visitor to New York, "How are the Americans viewing the situation in Canada, Jack?" In return, Gallagher quizzed the mandarins at EMR in Ottawa on their views of OPEC or intelligence emanating from the International Energy Agency. (1983, 54)

Dome Petroleum's political contributions were miniscule for a corporation of its size. In 1981, for example, Dome gave $1800 to the Liberal party and $769 to the Conservatives. One of its subsidiaries, Dome Mines, gave $1000 to each of the two main parties, while TransCanada Pipe-Lines gave $1800 to the Conservatives and nothing to the Liberals (Lyon 1983, 56). (For the contributions of other oil companies, see chapter 10.)

Frequency of contact and persistence were also the hallmarks of Dome's approach to government relations. Bill Richards, the president of Dome, was Marc Lalonde's first visitor from the oil industry after he became minister of energy, mines and resources on March 31, 1980. In the months that followed, both the chairperson and the president of Dome became persistent visitors to Lalonde's office. In light of the enormous amount of Dome's floating-rate debt, the federal government offered terms to Dome in September 1982 that would have seen it acquire over 40 percent of the shares for $500 million in convertible debentures. Dome did not accept the federal government's offer *and* an identical offer from the banks. Rather, it has sought — successfully so far — to restructure its finances without the help of the government.

In the end, did Dome's close relationship with the federal government help it when it got into severe financial trouble? Lyon puts it this way:

> The intriguing question is whether the favor Dome did Lalonde has been reciprocated. Did it have any bearing on subsequent actions by Ottawa in helping avert the company's bankruptcy? The likelihood is that it did not; Lalonde may have felt a personal political debt to Dome, but by the time the "bail-out" was complete, a new energy minister, Jean Chrétien, was dictating Ottawa's terms. Chrétien is in no sense beholden to Dome — to which the severity of the bail-out deal bears eloquent witness. In the end, when Dome *really* needed help from Ottawa, to an extent even greater than it had required previously, it received not a warm handshake but a back-handed slap to the face. (1983, 63)

It may have been that the closeness of Dome to the federal government caused it to rely too heavily on its policies. Dome — at its peril — ignored the dynamic and ephemeral nature of politics.

It is obvious that without Lalonde's NEP, Dome would never have contemplated the HBOG takeover. Unfortunately for Dome, political debts have no collateral, their value being dependent on volatile public moods, the expediency of the moment, and the shifting of personalities. (Lyon 1983, 63)

5.0 THE STRATEGIC USE OF THE CONCEPT OF THE PUBLIC INTEREST IN LOBBYING

Even if the "abolitionists" are correct (recall section 6 in chapter 4) that the public interest is an empty concept, the fact remains that it is widely used. The fact that virtually all interest groups couch their appeals (demands) in terms of the public interest suggests that all believe that policy makers and those persons who influence them believe the concept to be important. Emotionally, the normative content of the phrase remains strong, although operationally the phrase is used largely as an *ex post facto* rationalization for decisions made on other grounds.

5.1 Enlarging the Scope of the Conflict

Schattschneider suggests that "a political conflict among special interests is never restricted to the groups most immediately affected. Instead, it is an appeal (initiated by relatively small numbers of people) for the support of vast numbers of people who are sufficiently remote to have a somewhat different perspective on the controversy" (1960, 27). In other words, pressure-group politics involves the socialization of conflict in which "losers" in other fora seek to alter outcomes by involving others in the conflict. Private power relationships are modified when the scope of conflict is enlarged in the political arena. Schattschneider states that "everything we know about politics suggests that a conflict is likely to change profoundly as it becomes political. . . . Everything changes once a conflict gets into the political arena — who is involved, what the conflict is about, the resources available, etc." (1960, 37). This observation follows from his argument that "the most important strategy of politics is concerned with the scope of the conflict" (1960, 3) — that is, the ability of the immediate combatants to involve more of the audience in their dispute. In fact, he sums it up by saying that "one possible synthesis of pressure politics and party politics might be produced by describing politics as the socialization of conflict" (1960, 39).[39]

Hodgetts emphasizes that "for practical purposes and especially in a pluralistic democratic community we are left, then, not with a public interest, but with any number of interests pursued by many 'publics' " (1981, 219–20). The practical task facing policy makers is to identify those interests that deserve to be recognized and legitimized in government policy. In effect, those interests that are served by public policy actions are *ipso facto* labelled as being in the public interest. Government (both politicians and public administrators) becomes the "arbitrator, conciliator, and definer of the interests to be fostered, placated, rewarded or penalized through public policy" (Hodgetts 1981, 221). The object of the game for interest groups, therefore, is to make their case sufficiently appealing that they are able to win from policy makers the imprimatur that what they want is "in the public interest." They seek to have their claims validated by having them embodied in government action. Private desires are thereby transformed into public policy.

In operational terms, the decision to legitimize certain interests by incorporating them into a public policy action necessarily amounts to making basic value choices. These choices will usually involve one or more of the following:

- focusing on the present versus the future (present consumption vs. future consumption based on present savings);
- improving costs or conferring benefits on the many versus the few (i.e., many public programs effectively redistribute income or consumption opportunities from the many to the few);
- trade-offs among desirable outcomes and among "deserving" individuals/groups; and
- trade-offs between means and ends.

The dilemma lies in the use of the extensive, legitimate, coercive powers of the state, in the name of the public interest, for the largely exclusive benefit of a relatively few people able to organize to advance their interests. Organization is important in the political arena, for it is by this means that most interests are articulated, focused, and represented in the bargaining process. It is true that a political entrepreneur may be able to develop a constituency among those with a common but unorganized interest, but he or she will have to rely on his or her ability to signal to its members that he or she is advancing their interests and they will have to offer their political support in exchange. There is an interesting point here. This situation may be less subject to the conventional free-rider effect whereby an individual can obtain a benefit even without contributing to its creation, for without the votes of the members of the unorganized interest group, the political entrepreneur will not be able to stay in the legislature. Each individual, however, will find it hard to believe that his or her one vote could make the difference in whether the political entrepreneur who represents him or her will stay in office.

5.2 Transforming Private Interests into the Public Interest

The negative connotations associated with private interests (pecuniary, narrow, self-interested, benefiting only a few, secular) require that groups couch their demands for government action in terms more pleasing to their fellow citizens. The advancement of a private interest must be justified; that is, it must be accepted by others as being appropriate and worthy of recognition by the state. Therefore, the self-interest of the group must be made to seem to serve other nobler ends and be sufficiently acceptable to others that they will be held to be in the public interest and ratified by government action.

5.2.1 Cloaking Self-Interest

There is a need to cloak naked self-interest in the rhetoric of the public interest for several reasons. First, it avoids what is widely considered to be unseemly behaviour. The direct pursuit of one's self-interest through government action simply violates the norms of those segments of the community that actively participate in the policy process. An interest group could not justify its demands for a certain policy action by simply saying that its members would like the additional income that would as a result accrue to them. It smacks too much of the "boarding house reach," although, as we shall see, there are some pecuniary private interests whose advancement is widely seen to be in the public interest. The failure here to call a spade a bloody shovel is a form of prudery, but that does not make it any the less real. Disguising the importance of one's own interest by using the appropriate rhetoric is simply an act of hypocrisy that is universally accepted and expected.

Second, if claims on the state were made directly and overtly in terms of the self-interest of those making them, the need for politicians to make hard choices would be manifest. The clash of interests would be exposed. If all conflicts of interest were made clear and the battle joined, government would become overloaded and unable to function. From a systematic point of view, it is necessary to disguise, diffuse, and ignore some conflict situations. The rhetoric of the public interest ameliorates conflict and hides from the regular losers (the weakly organized and unorganized interests) the fact that they are regular losers.[40] The term *the public interest* in itself suggests that the unrepresented public (namely the mass of the people) are being made better off because of particular policy decisions. Therefore, to expose the Hobbesian struggle for advantage is to increase future conflict when the regular losers recognize their plight. Reluctant losers have a tendency to try to "spoil the game." Symbolic gestures are necessary if the game is going to continue in much the same way. Dissidents must be brought into the fold.

Third, private interests must be cloaked in public interest rhetoric to gain support from other groups (or at least disarm their opposition). The prospect of positive externalities landing in their lap may make another group willing to support the proposed action. Again, the term *the public interest* has the connotation of everyone benefiting in some measure at least. The fact that the original proponents of a policy change stand to gain $1000 per person while the other beneficiaries get at most

10 cents each, not to mention the plight of the big losers, will not be played up.

5.2.2 From Sow's Ear to Silk Purse

For special interests to be successful in having their claims legitimized with the stamp of public approval, they must transform their private interests into what is perceived to be the public interest. In some cases, this process could be likened to turning a sow's ear into a silk purse. How is this done? It is done largely by the assertion that when the group's claims are properly understood, it will be seen that they are in the public interest or at least not inconsistent with it. Here are a few of the arguments or appeals that are made in this context:

1. *"Everyone Benefits":* The argument is made that there is, in effect, a common interest to be served in validating the group's claims because everyone will benefit. The interest group's objective is to show that the beneficiaries of a public policy it is seeking are far more numerous than its own membership. The theme is "something for everyone." An effort will be made to gloss over the fact that even if the benefits are widely distributed, they are usually most unevenly distributed.

An obvious example of this argument is that of the property developer seeking a zoning variance from a local government in order to build a major office complex. He or she will argue that a whole variety of individuals stand to benefit if the concession is granted and the project goes ahead. There will be jobs for construction workers and for the employees of the many direct and indirect suppliers of materials and services. The multiplier effect will be emphasized and almost certainly exaggerated. It will be argued that the tax base of the city will be enlarged, reducing the pressure on other taxpayers. Every person working in the complex will enjoy the new facility more than they did the older buildings it replaced. The developer will claim that all (or many) local residents will feel a surge of pride when they see the completed building. It will prove that the downtown core is growing and is as modern as any city in the country. And on it goes — the arguments will be limited only by the imagination of the developer's public relations firm. The gist, however, is to convey the idea that the project has benefits far beyond an increase in the shareholders' wealth. A simple self-interested act is reconstructed into the claim that, in the words of McDonald's, "We do it all for you."

2. *"Particularly Deserving People Benefit":* In every society there are some groups that are widely perceived as more worthy or deserving of special consideration in matters of public policy. Canadians, Herschel Hardin (1974) argues, have a strong redistribution ethic institutionalized in various public policies. He points to the large array and great size of federal-provincial transfer payments designed to reduce regional

disparities in the provision of public services. But the redistribution ethic goes far beyond these transfers.

In effect, the idea that some individuals or groups are more deserving than others means that not all private interests are perceived as selfish or primarily self-interested in contradistinction to "the public interest" in the sense of interests that are widely shared. For example, arguments by individuals or interest groups which demand government action in the name of the public interest based on an actual or potential loss of jobs, the loss or potential loss of an accustomed social and economic position, and threats to national unity or cultural identity tend to find a positive response among policy makers. In other words, a public program that is designed to protect the jobs of workers in a particular industry or region is seldom construed as merely advancing the pecuniary interests of the workers involved. This is true, remarkably, even if representatives of the workers are advocating the public program. So we are told that it is in the national interest to impose "voluntary" quotas[41] on Japanese cars entering Canada to preserve the jobs of autoworkers in Ontario and Quebec even though those workers already have wage rates well above the national average. Very clearly, the private interest of the autoworkers not only outweighs the private interests of car buyers (and dealers selling Japanese cars), but is also deemed to be a public interest.[42]

Which groups are seen as deserving special consideration? Very broadly, it is often those people who are labelled as "disadvantaged." The particular subcategories of those widely perceived as deserving vary over time. Indeed, some groups work hard to convince their fellow citizens that they are disadvantaged and therefore have a moral claim to more of life's good things than they are now getting. Currently, our sympathies in terms of public policy extend in varying degrees to:

- "the poor" (this category is often defined in terms of certain regions, or occupations);
- "the handicapped";
- native people;
- women (e.g., single women with children); and
- some minorities, particularly those that are economically marginal.

An excellent example of a public policy decision very strongly shaped by consideration for "the poor" was that by the CRTC regarding CNCP Telecommunications' application to compete with Bell Canada and BC Tel in long-distance public telephone service. The application was rejected largely because competition would have meant lower long-distance rates but higher rates for local, basic telephone service. Eight "antipoverty, social-issue, pensioners and labour organizations" have formed the Coalition for Affordable Telephone Service. They believe that "the preservation of the affordable, accessible telephone to be the number one goal of public policy."[43] According to the chairperson of the CRTC, "This could have serious implications for many telephone subscribers — some simply would no longer be able to afford basic telephone service [and this] also could seriously threaten the principle of universality of telephone service in Canada." The chairperson, at his press conference, stated: "I want to assure Canadians that the Commission would not make decisions which would jeopardize the principle of universal accessibility to telephone service at an affordable price."[44] In other words, regardless of how much the majority of telephone users (households spend a yearly average of $200 on long-distance and $132 on local service) stand to benefit from competition and changes in the relative price of local and long-distance services, the fact that a small percentage of subscribers may not be able to afford higher local rates means that the status quo is to be preserved. The tip of the tail is to wag the entire dog! (More generally, see Globerman & Stanbury 1986.)

There are other groups that do not properly fall into the disadvantaged category, but are nevertheless treated as meriting special consideration. The most obvious group consists of farmers. Agriculture policy in Canada redistributes massive amounts of income from consumers and taxpayers to farmers despite the fact (unknown to most Canadians and vigorously denied by farmers) that the average net wealth of farm households is about three times the national average.[45]

Interest groups wishing to use this argument to advance their claims must appreciate several points. First, tastes in redistribution change and there are regional differences in the ranking of the deservingness of particular groups. Obviously, the interest group does not want to try to advance the cause of a group of people who are no longer high priority. Second, there is often a large gap between the public rhetoric concerning the moral worth of certain groups and the actual amount of redistribution that is effected by public policy. This is an area where symbolism is important. One wants to provide evidence of sensitivity without actually "going too far." Third, it should be appreciated that quite small benefits to the more deserving can camouflage vastly greater benefits to other groups. The outstanding example is rent control. In Ontario, for example, controls are justified as being necessary to ensure that low-to moderate-income households can obtain "decent, affordable" rental housing. Analysis indicates that 60 to 70 percent of the gross benefits of controls in the form of rent savings go to nonpoor households (see Stanbury & Vertinsky 1985).

3. *"Hitch Your Wagon to a Star"* or *Appealing to Emotionally Powerful Symbols or Themes:* It is evident that certain themes or concepts — which, like fashions, come and go in official favour — catch the government's fancy (presumably because they also resonate with important groups of voters) and are widely used to justify a range of government actions. The astute interest group associates its cause with these themes and tries to show that by acceding its demands the government will

promote those themes already widely accepted as being in the public interest. This point is emphasized by government relations consultant Bill Lee:

> "If you are seeking a grant, loan or a bail-out, the worst thing you can do is talk about the impact on your profits." . . . Instead, he suggests, talk in terms of "jobs lost, technology enhancement missed, R and D (research and development) not established, trade enhancement not occurring." Stress the public interest. If you can link your cause to a broad policy priority such as job creation, Canadian content in manufacturing, or some other "motherhood" issue, the experts say your prospects of getting along with Ottawa will soar. (Quoted in Black 1982, 9)

Below are examples of the themes that are highly evocative in policy making.

- *Exports:* For some reason, a policy change that generates another $1 worth of exports is more highly valued than one that would generate another $2 or $3 of domestic sales. It may be that many Canadians believe that the ability to export is an indication of an economy's virility. In any event, the promotion of exports is a totem in Canadian society so strong that the most tenuous linkages between what an interest group really wants and its beneficial impact on exports are easily accepted. For example, business groups have argued — so far successfully — that virtually no mergers should be prohibited so that Canadian firms can grow to world scale and hence be better able to compete with American, European, and Japanese giants in foreign markets (Stanbury 1985b). This argument was even trotted out when Zellers bought Fields Stores; The Bay bought Zellers and Simpsons and a major interest in Simpson-Sears; and then the Thomson interests acquired control of The Bay. We were assured that without such growth by merger, Canada's export potential would be impaired. The fact that none of the department stores sells anything abroad (except perhaps a few mail orders) was ignored.

  In general, quite extraordinary amounts of public money (subsidies, tax expenditures, soft loans) may be obtained for the purpose of increasing exports. Studies of these schemes reveal that the public funds often exceed the estimated present value of new exports generated. An excellent example is the case of the Bombardier contract to build subway cars for the City of New York. The estimated value of the concessionary financing plus other forms of government assistance to Bombardier may exceed the value added of the subway cars actually made in Canada because about one-half the value added for the project — at the insistence of the buyer — had to be created in the U.S.[46] This project was also labelled as high technology, a theme to which we now turn.

- *High Technology*: This is one of the latest and catchiest phrases. It is argued that through high technology Canada can cease to be a nation consisting of "hewers of wood and drawers of water." High technology is perceived as the embodiment of the future, and virtually any activity can be linked to this code word, which opens government coffers and justifies any type or size of government activity. For example, the Scientific Research Tax Credit, we were told, would create a flowering of new R & D activity notably in "high tech" areas. What started out as a vehicle to assist the faultering star of Silicon Valley near Ottawa (Mitel), which had received large amounts of government funds, was supposed to cost about $100 million in tax revenues foregone. Less than two years later, the estimated cost to the treasury is some $2.6 billion.[47] The sad part is that there is very little high-tech output to show for this vast expenditure of public funds.

    What passes for a "national industrial strategy" in Canada is a curious mixture of (1) subsidies, quotas, tariffs, and other forms of assistance to declining and fundamentally uncompetitive industries (e.g., shoes, clothing, textiles, shipbuilding), and (2) various subventions to what are described as high-technology activities (Watson 1983). For example, the federal government spent over $2 billion in the early 1980s subsidizing Canadair (the Challenger business jet) and de Havilland (the Dash 7 and 8 turboprops). During the peak period of the subsidies, the cost per person-year of employment maintained exceeded $100 000. A senior public servant close to the scene indicated that even if the losses were double or treble those experienced, the cabinet would not have shut down the operations. In the same vein, the two heavy-water plants in Cape Breton in 1984/85 were subsidized to the tune of over $130 000 per person-year of employment of which the average employee received about $35 000.[48]

- *National Unity*: Under Pierre Trudeau in the 1970s and early 1980s this theme became a centrepiece and justification of a very wide range of federal policies. The shoe manufacturing industry argued successfully — taking their cue from federal cabinet ministers — that unless tariff and import quotas were maintained or increased and unless large "industrial incentive grants" were made to Quebec-based shoe firms, the national fabric would be rent by separatists. Quebecers would be able to argue with conviction that "federalism didn't pay" and that the rest of Canada didn't care about them. (It is remarkable how esteem for Quebec and the French fact in Canada has been measured largely in terms of large explicit and implicit transfers from other regions to Quebec via federal policies.) National unity, we were told, required legislated bilingualism and the acceleration of francophones into many visible positions in the federal government. Now the Mulroney government, after breaking the historical hegemony of the Liberal party in Quebec, emphasizes that national reconciliation and consensus require that even more public resources be devoted to Quebec.[49] Strategically, by tacitly and overtly proclaiming their marginality to Canada, Quebecers have been able to dominate the rationale of federal policy making for almost two decades.

With this theme as with the others, the object of the interest group is to show or to appear to show that what it wants contributes to these socially approved national objectives. In a sense, these themes represent arguments that have been "pre-sold." By linking itself to these approved themes, the interest group is able to advance its own private interests in the name of the public interest.

- *Equity/Fairness*: One of the most evocative appeals under the rubric of the public interest is that of "fairness" and "equity." The power of the appeal is based on the idea that in a democracy it is not possible to have too much equality. Differences of almost any kind are extremely hard to justify. The assumption of equality in all things (not just fundamental political rights) is the status quo that must be refuted (or quietly and conveniently ignored in an act of hypocrisy that resolves uncomfortable contradictions). Berlin argues that "no reason need be given for an equal distribution of benefits — for that is 'natural' — self-evidently right and just, and needs no justification, since it is in some sense concerned as being self-justified" (1961, 131). Intuitively, many people believe that the idea of "justice" is based on equality of treatment. While it is easy to logically refute this proposition, it has a strong popular appeal. From equality of basic rights, we have moved a long way to the idea of equality of opportunity and are now moving to the idea of equality of results.

De Tocqueville, writing over 150 years ago, noted that the spread of equality in terms of basic political rights made people more aware of other aspects that differentiate them from one another: "When everything is more or less level, the slightest variation is noticed. Hence the more equal men are, the more insatiable will be their longing for equality."

The demand for equal treatment or "equity" can be used by interest groups in a host of ways. For example, once Ottawa committed itself to large-scale financial help to build a convention centre in one large city, it was virtually inevitable that every city would eventually get a comparable grant. Equity required that the "feds" help every city wanting a convention centre — even after several have been built, thereby ensuring that subsequent centres would lose even more money than their predecessors.

Similarly, regional economic development subsidies, tax breaks, and other federal benefits based on such criteria as high unemployment rates, and lower average incomes often spread to regions or projects that don't meet the criteria. Why? Because, say the proponents of such regions and projects, fairness requires that the largesse be spread around — regardless of the original criteria. Provincial politicians are masters in using the equity argument to get more from Ottawa when they spot what they believe is a "special deal" for another province.

The beauty of the words *fairness* or *equity* is that they evoke a strong normative response in most people (who wants to be labelled as acting unfairly or treating people inequitably?), and they are nebulous. This means that a very wide range of arguments can be made in their name. For example, the Canadian Bankers' Association (1985a, 3) brief on the April 1985 Green Paper, *The Regulation of Canadian Financial Institutions*, argued, on the basis of public opinion polls the CBA commissioned, that "Canadians clearly want *all* financial institutions, including the chartered banks, to participate fully in changes to the Canadian financial system." The CBA also argued that "balanced treatment of financial institutions, including banks, means equitable treatment for all Canadians because banks are the major financial institutions serving Canadians, wherever they may live." The CBA pursues its equity argument by saying that "it is important to ensure that some Canadian communities are not, in effect, favoured over others; that any restructuring of the financial system benefits the greatest possible number of consumers." Now for the punch line: the CBA states that "the achievement of this objective requires equal broadening of powers for all financial institutions at the same time."

Elsewhere, the CBA (1985b) argued that the proposed changes, if implemented, would give rival institutions (e.g., trust companies) an advantage over the existing chartered banks. The CBA says that more competition is fine, but there must be "a level playing field." Therefore, by stressing this clever phrase and fairness to consumers, the CBA is trying to change the terms of the debate over a new regulatory framework away from such matters as increasing competition, the prevention of conflicts of interest, and the protection of the soundness of financial institutions to the matter of the fairness of the proposed changes. It should be noted that other financial institutions wishing to compete with the banks say that without important constraints on the scope of the banks' activities, the latter will be able to use their great size and advantages to enter new areas and dominate them. In other words, both sides are demonstrating that what is fair is in the eye of the beholder.

• *Jobs:* In a country that for the past decade has never had the national unemployment rate below 7 percent (between 1982 and 1985 unemployment averaged over 11 percent), it is not surprising that any action that is believed to create jobs will find considerable political support. Moreover, some provinces chronically suffer unemployment rates far above the national average. For example, in 1984 the national average was 11.3 percent, but the unemployment rate in Newfoundland was 18.8 percent, in New Brunswick 14.9 percent, in B.C. 14.7 percent, and in Quebec 12.8 percent.

Canadian governments have been willing to use large amounts of public money in an effort to create or maintain jobs. For example, the federal government was spending over $130 000 per person-year to keep the heavy-water plants in Cape Breton in 1984 and 1985. In November 1985 Quebec and the federal government agreed to pay up to $110 million in interest on the first $200 million of loans for a $300-million automobile assembly plant to be built by Hyundai in Bromont, Quebec. The Korean automaker, whose cars now enter Canada duty-free, agreed to employ 1200 people by 1990. Compared to the heavy-water plants, the subsidy per job seems modest. Much less modest was the more than $2 billion the federal government poured into Canadair Ltd., maker of the Challenger executive jet, over the past five years or so. The object was to keep some 4000 employees on the job. In other words, maintaining each job may have cost taxpayers some $200 000. In expressing his concerns in the fall of 1985 about the effects of free trade, Ontario premier David Peterson referred to a government study that estimated that well over 200 000 manufacturing jobs would be lost in Ontario if Canada entered a free trade agreement with the U.S.

In each case it was argued that it was in the public interest to spend the taxpayers' money to maintain or create jobs.[50] Moreover, advocates of these large direct and indirect subsidies argue that for each job created or maintained at least two other jobs will be indirectly created or maintained. The point is that the cry of more jobs is good politics — even if the cost to the treasury is many times the transfer payments that would be made to the unemployed.

4. *Play Down the Pecuniary Benefits to the Advantaged*: The rich and powerful evoke little overt public sympathy, although there is no dearth of hired hands anxious to make a case on their behalf. As capacious as it is, it will be hard to stretch the concept of the public interest to include government actions whose central purpose is the enrichment of those widely perceived to be well-off. (Some argue that this is precisely what the Reagan administration has done.) For example, it is necessary to play down the fact that a group is engaged in a direct assault on the treasury or on their fellow citizens' wallets with the help of government regulation. In 1985 dairy farmers were pressing for an increase in the $300 million in annual cash subsidies they receive (indirect subsidies are several times this amount). They did not simply argue that this should be done because they would like the cash. Instead, we were told that their costs of production have risen and it is only fair that they be compensated. We were told also that other regulated prices have been raised — why should farmers be treated differently? We were also told that the incomes of dairy farmers are low. And so on.

Recently, the Reichmann family, prior to its takeover of Gulf Canada and subsequent sale of part of its assets to Petro-Canada, obtained a tax ruling regarding the value of the assets of certain refineries to be acquired in the deal. The result was a saving of $111 million in income taxes.[51] The effect of this cabinet decision was to give a family whose net wealth exceeds $1 billion some $111 million in public money. Not surprisingly, this part of the transaction was not played up by the Reichmanns or by the government — it took a request under the Access to Information Act to bring the facts to light in the media. What was played up was the assumed benefit of Canadianization of one of Canada's largest oil companies and the fact that a crown corporation would now have a much larger number of retail outlets scattered throughout the country.

The moral, then, is clear. In trying to transform private interests into the public interest, play down the pecuniary benefits of the proposed government action accruing to those already perceived as well-off. Instead, trumpet the benefits (tangible and intangible) that accrue to those groups and individuals widely deemed to be deserving of special consideration. The fact that the former may greatly outweigh the latter can be concealed with only a modicum of skill.

5. *"Do No Harm"*: Governments, like doctors, are expected to function according to the cardinal principle of "do no harm." In other words, the intent of government intervention is to make people better off, but in any event, not make them worse off. This principle is often evoked by interest groups seeking to block or modify a proposed government action. For example, the farmers and other residents of a river valley that is supposed to become the bottom of a large lake behind a new hydro-electric dam can argue with some force that they should not be made worse off as a result of a government decision to allow the dam to be built. The problem is not just a matter of paying the fair market value of the resident's property plus the moving and resettlement costs. There is the disruption itself – important intangibles ranging from the loss of the view to changes in patterns of friendship.

In general, Canadians implicitly place a large value on the status quo. People are effectively given "rights" in their present economic and social positions, particularly where they are middle class/middle income or above. While the redistribution of income through certain government policies is tolerated, the loss of accustomed position associated with other types of actions is widely condemned. The ethic is that there should be no losers — more specifically, no reluctant losers. Therefore, it is in the public interest to alter the public decision so as to reduce the number of big losers (particularly if they are highly vocal) or to diffuse losses more widely so that they can be effectively ignored.

Another example of the "do no harm" axiom is the practice of using "grandfather" clauses in many types of occupational regulation. When an occupation becomes certified or licensed, the current practitioners who do not meet the newly established educational or training require-ments are still allowed to carry on because it is deemed unfair to take away their livelihood in the process of regulating the occupational group. In the case of pollution regulations, existing plants that are old and do not meet the new regulations are often left alone or have only to meet less stringent standards than plants that will be constructed in the future.

The most extreme application of the "do no harm" principle would require that only those public policies that produce Pareto-superior outcomes would be acceptable (i.e., those in which some people gain and everyone else is no worse off than they were before). This would rule out — if compensation were not allowed — the enormous set of policy actions in which there are both winners and losers and where the sum of the gains exceeds the sum of the losses in some widely accepted sense.

6.0 REGULATING LOBBYING

The regulation of lobbying, broadly defined, in the Canadian context has been approached from two different directions. The first involves proposals to require paid lobbyists to be registered so that who is representing whom can be determined by the targets of their lobbying efforts.

The second approach has involved the writing of conflict-of-interest guidelines for ministers, MPs, senators, and senior public servants governing their behaviour while in office and after they leave office. Of particular concern is the situation where a former senior public servant or former cabinet minister lobbies his or her former department shortly after leaving the government payroll.

6.1 First Attempts

There have been only desultory efforts to regulate lobbying by the federal government. Tex Enemark, when he was executive assistant to the federal minister of consumer and corporate affairs, drafted a resolution at the 1970 Liberal party national convention calling for the registration of lobbyists. The resolution passed. His minister, Ron Basford, then requested that legislation be drafted, but he moved to another department before it could be introduced. This effort was prompted in part by the enormous pressure exerted by the Pharmaceutical Manufacturers Association a few years earlier (Lang 1974; Harrison 1978c). In 1969 NDP member Barry Mather introduced a private member's bill that would have required lobbyists to be registered. Like most private member's bills, it died on the order paper.

In 1976 the late Walter Baker, a Conservative MP, introduced a private member's bill to require the registration of lobbyists — anyone receiving payment for attempting to exercise influence on legislation before Parliament or on the outcome of decisions within the administrative responsibility of a minister.[52] Baker said the public register "would reveal who the lobbyist is, on whose behalf he is working, and for how long." According to the Ottawa *Citizen*, Baker's bill was prompted by the firm of Reisman and Grandy, acting as consultants for Lockheed Aircraft, which was seeking the contract for a fleet of long-range patrol aircraft from the Department of National Defence worth some $900 million.[53] Reisman was the former deputy minister of finance and Grandy was the former deputy minister of industry, trade and commerce. Both had retired from the government in the spring of 1975.

6.2 Conflict-of-Interest Guidelines

The 1976 "Conflict of Interest Guidelines" for former senior public officials was prompted by the Reisman-Grandy affair. They were originally intended to be mandatory, but in April 1977 they were stripped of their sanctions (Harrison 1978e). Harrison concludes that

> in the final analysis, the public's protection lies in the integrity of the public service and its masters. "I think the system is to a degree self-regulating," says Ernest Steele [a former senior official, then head of the Canadian Association of Broadcasters]. "We have a public service in this country whose integrity is really very high. I think that's the ultimate defence." (1978e)

The conflict-of-interest guidelines issued by Prime Minister Trudeau in April 1978 stated: "A former office holder must not, within the relevant time period, lobby for or on behalf of any person or commercial corporation before any department or agency with which he was employed or with which he had a direct and substantial official relationship during the period of two years prior to the termination of his employment."[54] The ineffectiveness of these guidelines became apparent the next year. Newspaper columnist Frank Howard noted:

> On August 13, the former deputy minister [of Supply and Services, Jacques DesRoches] whose employment terminated July 30, becomes president of the Air Industries Association of Canada, lobbyists for the aerospace industry in Canada [which sells about one-quarter of its output to the Department of National Defence].
>
> According to a recent article in the *Globe and Mail* which featured an interview with DesRoches, the air industry sells about 25 per cent of its production to defence.
>
> The chief procurement agent for the government, in defence and other purchases, is the department of Supply and Services. The "relevant time period" referred to in the guidelines is one year.
>
> Despite all this, the DesRoches case has not come before the senior personnel directorate of the Privy Council Office which is supposed to be the guardian of the guidelines.
>
> PCO officials give two reasons for this: firstly, the former office-holder himself is supposed to take the initiative in raising the issue, and DesRoches has not done this, and, secondly, the guidelines were

under review at the time of the DesRoches departure, so it was not clear whether the old Liberal guidelines would still apply. In fact the review of guidelines just completed [states that they] only apply to elected officials. But as far as anyone at PCO is concerned, there's no real problem in the DesRoches case unless the former DM himself raises the issue. "After all," said one PCO official, "that's what the guidelines are for, to protect the individual public servant."[55]

In mid-1978, following the disclosure that the former minister of finance, Donald Macdonald, was sitting on the board of McDonnell-Douglas, one of the companies bidding on the estimated $2.3-billion contract for new fighter planes, the Edmonton *Journal* argued that lobbyists should be registered "so the public knows just who is trying to influence whom."[56]

Toward the end of the 256-day Conservative government of Joe Clark, Jean Pigott, the prime minister's advisor on human resources, stated that the federal government was in the process of setting up a central registry of lobbyists and special interest groups. Pigott said that the list already contained 1500 multipurpose, single-issue interest groups, cultural groups, and others.[57]

6.3 Quebec City Lobbyists Request Registration

In Quebec City, on behalf of other professional lobbyists, Dominique Boivin requested in late 1982 that their status be officially recognized by the national assembly. Boivin argued that "lobbying is a dynamic element of our democratic system" and that it allows "the demands and expectations of groups to be conveyed more correctly and to be understood in their best context."[58] He and his colleagues were seeking to become registered in the same way that their counterparts in the U.S. have been for many years. Boivin noted that legislative lobbying is not subject to any law in Canada; hence it is not officially recognized.

It is interesting to note that, like many other occupational groups, lobbyists apparently believe they can raise their status by gaining official recognition. And such recognition can be gained by becoming regulated. In other words, individuals who are now free of regulation, and who frequently argue on behalf of their clients that government should not create more rules and regulations to hamper the private sector, are themselves seeking to become regulated. No wonder politicians have difficulty interpreting such conflicting signals.

6.4 Robinson's Bill

In May 1980 W. Kenneth Robinson, the Liberal member for Etobicoke-Lakeshore, obtained First Reading for his private member's bill C-495, "An Act respecting the registration of lobbyists." Debate on Second Reading did not occur until January 19, 1983. Robinson said that the intention of his bill was "to make the public aware and provide for public scrutiny of the individuals and organizations that hope to influence Government policy and legislation. This would also allow the civil service, with whom many lobbyists deal, to know who they are really talking to and why."[59] In his bill a "lobbyist" was defined as

> any person who attempts to influence, directly or indirectly
> (a) the introduction, passage, defeat or amendment of any legislation or budgetary estimates before either House of Parliament, or
> (b) a decision to be taken on any matter coming within the administrative jurisdiction of a Minister of the Crown, whether or not that matter has come or may come before either House of Parliament for legislative action.[60]

Under Robinson's bill, lobbyists would be required to be registered with the clerk of the Parliaments and to provide the following information:

> (a) his name and business address,
> (b) the name and business address of each person by whom he is employed or retained as a lobbyist, and
> (c) a description of the subject matters in reference to which he is so employed or retained.[61]

This information would have to be provided at the beginning of each calendar year and each time the lobbyist acquired a new client. The registry was to be open to any MP, senator, or accredited member of the parliamentary press gallery. Failure to register was to be punishable by a fine of up to $100 per day. It should be noted, however, that only those lobbying for payment (which was broadly defined) would be required to register. This means that individuals representing themselves or an organization would not be required to register. It is surprising, in light of Robinson's point about ensuring that public servants are aware of who is representing whom, that they would not be entitled to inspect the registry. Note that under the bill, lobbyists were to be provided with an identification card by the clerk of the Parliaments. Perhaps public servants could ask to see the identification card of those apparently seeking to influence them.

During the course of the debate on Second Reading, Robinson emphasized that his bill was not designed to restrict lobbying, but rather to ensure that the targets of their efforts "should know on whose behalf they are acting and making representations." He praised lobbyists for their efforts at providing another source of feedback in government programs:

> Lobbyists are able to provide legislators with feedback on the actual operation of Government programs in the field. As we already know

there is usually a discrepancy between bureaucratic theory and the practical application of Government programs. The sooner the Government is able to gain insight into the effects of any given program, the sooner it will be able to act upon that information.[62]

Robinson was strongly supported by Walter Baker, the Conservative MP for Nepean-Carleton, who had twice previously introduced a private member's bill to require the registration of lobbyists. Baker emphasized the need to "recognize the legitimacy of the function but let us ensure not only that right is done, or that justice is done but that it appears to be done."[63] Baker expressed his concern about the decline in the public's trust of basic institutions, including Parliament. The maintenance of that trust requires that the advocates of policy actions "declare their interest" but they need not indicate how much money they receive for their representations. Baker acknowledged there could be some difficulties in defining who was a lobbyist in operational terms.

Ian Deans, the NDP member for Hamilton Mountain, said both he and his party supported the concept embodied in the bill. He emphasized that the purpose of such a bill is not to discourage public input to MPs, senators, or the cabinet. He then said that such a bill

> may make it easier for the public to participate. They will be better able to judge the arguments advanced by certain, and sometimes high-priced, individuals who put forward the position of a particular vested interest but fail to identify that party. I think members of the public would be less likely to be influenced if they fully understood that the person making the argument to Government was a lobbyist paid to do so. From that point of view I think the Bill is valuable.[64]

Deans felt that there was a "need to show that it is legitimate to be a lobbyist but, more important, there is a need to show that certain people in the country in fact exercise considerably more influence than others, even though they are faceless and frequently nameless . . . [with the bill] we would at last be able to see the faces and names of those who exercise power behind the scenes."[65]

The NDP member was at some pains to distinguish what might be called the "professional" from the "amateur" lobbyist:

> There may be someone living in Vancouver who has a very strong sense of miscarriage of justice in a particular issue. He or she may, together with some friends, pay the expense of coming to Ottawa to visit various Members of Parliament to express a concern. Such people are not lobbyists in the sense of the word to which this legislation refers. Indeed they are lobbyists inasmuch as they are lobbying Members to gain favour for their points of view. We are not talking about these kinds of people. We are talking about per-

sons sitting in offices somewhere in high-rise towers. Not only are we talking about them, but about those who make the trip for considerable remuneration or at someone else's expense to present a well thought-out brief which pays little attention to other matters than that it must be done in a professional and very technically correct manner.[66]

Deans even named two prominent government relations consultants in indicating at whom the bill was directed: "We are talking about the Bill Lees and the Bill Nevilles [recall Figure 9-1] of the world and the others moving in and out of the circle of Government, lurking behind the scenes in the halls, carefully sidling up to people at lunch and whispering in their ears."[67]

What seems surprising is that experienced members of all parties should imply so strongly that they currently have difficulty in knowing which interests are being represented by the people they see in their offices, in committee meetings, and in other contexts. What is wrong in asking them whom they represent and are they being paid to lobby on their behalf?

Deans raised some practical questions about who would be required to register: "How would we deal with associations? How would we register them? Whom would we register officially? Would we make a provision for others to represent them? If so, at what cost if at all? Would they all have to register? . . . Would we register law firms? There are many legal firms which take on substantial lobbying efforts."[68]

6.5 The Gillespie-Lalonde Affair

In February 1983 the former minister of energy, mines and resources (EMR) (between September 1975 and May 1979), Alastair Gillespie, was accused of violating the conflict-of-interest guidelines issued by the prime minister in October 1976.[69] The particular guideline in question stated that former ministers and senior officials for two years following their departure from office "must not . . . lobby for or on behalf of any person or commercial corporation before any department or agency with which he was employed or with which he had a direct and substantial official relationship." Although lobbying is not defined in the guidelines, in his covering letter the prime minister wrote that "to use one's former position . . . to influence public servants is objectionable, but to have an intimate knowledge of the machinery of government and an acquaintance with public servants is not." In April 1980 Prime Minister Trudeau issued a revised set of conflict-of-interest guidelines that included the same two-year "cooling off" period for former ministers. In addition, they contained a directive to current ministers: "In any official dealings with former office holders, ministers must ensure that they do not provide grounds or the appearance of grounds for allegations of improper influence, privileged access or preferential treatment."

After the scandal broke, it was revealed that beginning in December 1980 Alastair Gillespie, as head of a consortium determining the feasibility of establishing a plant in Nova Scotia to convert coal to liquid fuels, began contacts with senior officials in his former department (EMR) to obtain a grant to study the prospects for such a plant. Under the consortium agreement, Gillespie put up $25 000 while his five corporate partners — including Petro-Canada — put up $300 000 each. If the project moved beyond the feasibility study stage, Gillespie could be bought out for $250 000. Under certain conditions, he would be paid $750 000 for his interest. On April 4, 1981, a joint federal–Nova Scotia grant of $1 million was approved in principle for the consortium's work following the recommendation of the minister of EMR, Marc Lalonde. On June 3, 1981, the two-year cooling-off period provided in the guidelines expired. On September 25, 1981, Lalonde signed the financing agreement and it was made retroactive to June 30, 1981, because the consortium had already spent some of the money.

After a Canadian Press story on February 16, 1983, outlining Gillespie's involvement in the consortium's efforts to get the grant, a storm broke in Parliament. Opposition members demanded that Lalonde resign. Deputy Prime Minister Allan MacEachen described Trudeau's guidelines as "just that, guidelines . . . they are up to the conscience of the individual." After denying that Lalonde knew about the consortium and Gillespie's participation in it before September 1981, the prime minister was soon forced to admit Lalonde knew about the Gillespie deal in January 1981 — before the cooling-off period had expired.

Gillespie denied that he or his consortium at any time "sought privileged access or preferential treatment." He said, however, he was aware of the guidelines and that he respected them. He said that the consortium paid him a retainer of $30 000 per year plus $600 a day that averaged about $40 000 per year. Opposition members charged that the agreement between the governments and the consortium had to be reworked several times and that the criteria had to be expanded to accommodate the consortium's request for funds.

Lalonde held fast and the Liberals rallied around him. The government defeated an opposition motion to have the Commons Committee on Privileges and Elections consider the case in light of the conflict-of-interest guidelines. Then in July 1983 the prime minister announced the appointment of Mitchell Sharp and Michael Starr, both former ministers, as co-chairmen of a task force to look into conflict-of-interest guidelines for ministers, their staff, and public servants. However, it was made clear by the prime minister that the inquiry should "not be a study of past conduct."[70] This prompted the Ottawa *Citizen* to ask in an editorial, "Why bother? If the prime minister wants to free his political friends from their moral obligations, he should have the courage to do so himself. He need not bother with the task force sideshow."[71]

The task force reported in May 1984 just before the Liberals resigned and went to the polls, only to be defeated by Brian Mulroney and the Conservatives on September 4, 1984.

6.6 The Mulroney Government's Initiatives

In late August 1985, Prime Minister Brian Mulroney stated he would introduce tougher conflict-of-interest guidelines for legislators and public servants and also introduce new legislation to regulate lobbyists.[72] He said that industry lobbyists and representatives of foreign governments will have to be registered. "We will have a bill that will govern their behaviour, the remuneration and their interests," he said, so that civil servants will know with whom they are dealing at all times, whom they represent, and who is paying them how much.[73]

On September 9, 1985, the prime minister tabled in the House a set of "tougher" conflict-of-interest guidelines, which he said promised "a new day of trust and confidence."[74] They would have prevented, for example, the appointment of ministers' relatives (e.g., John Crosbie's sons) to government jobs. The prime minister said his new guidelines broadened and clarified the rules about jobs taken after departure from government. For example, former ministers would not be expected to have dealings with their former departments for two years, while the cooling-off period for bureaucrats was set at one year.[75] Also on September 9, Mulroney announced that a lobbyist registration bill would be coming soon.

On December 19, 1985, the minister of consumer and corporate affairs, Michel Côté, released a discussion paper on the regulation of lobbyists.[76] The minister said that the government had not changed its stand on the issue and that he personally favoured legislation, rather than a code of conduct or guidelines, to register individuals and groups seeking to influence government policy. On December 16, Côté had said that legislation would be introduced before December 20 when Parliament adjourned. Four months later it was not introduced.

In releasing his discussion paper, Côté acknowledged that he had received many representations from those who might be subject to legislation regarding lobbyists. While not committed to specific provisions, Côté said that any new scheme would be based on the following four principles:

- there should be public disclosure of information about paid lobbyists "to help lift the shroud of mystery that surrounds lobbying";
- registration requirements should leave no doubts about who should and should not register;
- procedures adopted "should not unduly impede their access to public office holders"; and
- administrative requirements should be kept simple.

A House of Commons committee studied the discussion paper in the spring of 1986 and legislation was expected by the summer. It is obvious that there are problems with defining "lobbying" and related terms. In addition, it is clear that many lobbyists and their clients do not want their relationship to be made public. The process by which the regulation of lobbyists is to be achieved itself reflects the ability of lobbyists to influence policy making.

Would public registration of lobbyists be helpful? At least we would have some idea of who is (officially) working for whom in seeking to influence government policy. Sawatsky quotes Tex Enemark, formerly an Ottawa consultant and principal deputy minister, and president of the Mining Association of British Columbia for four years, as saying: "I'm not sure it's possible to regulate it very well. But I think it would be a good idea if it were clear what people's interests were. In the cocktail circuit in Ottawa a public servant may be talking to a lawyer and doesn't realize exactly that he's on the circuit for a purpose" (1983).

Enemark argues that "anybody who is in the business of either making representations to government, or if more than 35 per cent of his income comes from advising people in how to make representations to government, ought to simply be registered with a list of his clients. So at least you have some idea of who's who" (Sawatsky 1983).

NOTES

1. *Globe and Mail*, March 23, 1983, p. 11.
2. Linda Diebel, "Moores rewriting rules of lobbying, critics say," Vancouver *Sun*, July 27, 1985, p. A9.
3. See Michael Harris, "Ex-premier still controversial in private-sector incarnation," *Globe and Mail*, July 22, 1985, pp. 1–2.
4. Ibid., p. 1. For a rather different approach, see the description of Kissinger Associates in *Time*, February 17, 1986, p. 20; and Lenny Glynn, "The Sovereign State of Kissinger Inc.," *Report on Business Magazine*, July/August 1985, pp. 60–64.
5. Michael Harris, "Tory-owned consulting firm shows clout in Fisheries switch," *Globe and Mail*, June 28, 1985, pp. 1, 8.
6. Diebel, op. cit.
7. "No lobby fees needed for access, PM says," *Toronto Star*, June 28, 1985, p. F12; "Access to Tory Ministers is free PM says amid furor over fee," *Globe and Mail*, June 28, 1985, p. A8.
8. Ibid.
9. Michael Harris, "Moores defends his directorship at Air Canada," *Globe and Mail*, July 23, 1985, p. 5.
10. Ibid.

11. See the *Globe and Mail*, September 6, 1985, p. 1, and September 7, 1985, p. 1.
12. Ibid., March 23, 1983, p. 11.
13. Recall the discussion in chapter 4 regarding how "problems" can become policy issues.
14. John Gray, *Globe and Mail*, October 25, 1980.
15. This is not always the case: "In my experience, a very important factor is the information they [lobbyists] convey, much of it gossip. This is often vitally important to the civil servant, who wants to know, for example, which deputy minister is presently dissatisfied with his assistant deputy minister, or what job opportunities there might be for him in and out of government" (Roman 1978, 215).
16. *Globe and Mail*, January 29, 1985, p. B2.
17. More generally, see Dann (1980).
18. See House of Commons Standing Committee on Finance, Trade and Economic Affairs (1982).
19. See John Ferguson, "The bankers will win despite current fiasco," Vancouver *Sun*, September 14, 1985, p. H8.
20. We note that in 1985 during the course of the CRTC's hearings on CNCP Telecommunications' application to enter the long-distance voice telecommunications market, both CNCP and the Communications, Electronic, Electrical, Technical and Salaried Workers of Canada (an intervenor) used advocacy ads to try to advance their position. A copy of one of the latter's ads can be found in chapter 12.
21. *The Public Sector*, February 25, 1980, pp. 5–6.
22. Generally, see Adelson et al. (1985) and Baetz and Thain (1985, chap. 17).
23. CFIB, *Mandate*, no. 87, 1981, pp. 1, 4. A copy can be found in Baetz and Thain (1985, chap. 17).
24. Baetz and Thain (1985, 344).
25. Keith Spicer, "Budget-bashing Bulloch is blunt," Vancouver *Sun*, March 24, 1982, p. A4.
26. Adelson et al. (1985, chap. 3).
27. Roderick McQueen, "Time to bite the Bulloch," *Maclean's*, February 22, 1982, p. 44.
28. "How lobby groups fared in MacEachen's new budget," *Financial Post*, July 17, 1982, p. 5.
29. Adelson et al. (1985, chap. 3).
30. Spicer, op. cit.
31. Ibid.
32. CFIB, *Mandate*, no. 97, 1981, pp. 1, 3.
33. *Globe and Mail*, March 20, 1985, p. B21.
34. See, for example, Diane Francis, "Nine families said to control stock worth 46% of value of the TSE 300," *Toronto Star*, March 19, 1985, pp. A1, A15; and Jack McArthur, "Answers are frighteningly few on

impact of runaway conglomerates," *Toronto Star*, March 20, 1985.

35. See *Atlantic Sugar Refineries et al.* v. *The Attorney General of Canada* (1980) 16 C.R. (3d) 128; and Reschenthaler and Stanbury (1981).

36. *Globe and Mail*, January 29, 1982.

37. Letter to the editor, *Globe and Mail*, June 8, 1983, p. 7.

38. John Gray, *Globe and Mail*, October 25, 1980.

39. Schattschneider argues that "it is probably a mistake to assume that pressure politics is the typical or even the most important relation between government and business. The pressure group is by no means the perfect instrument of the business community. What does big business want? The winners in intrabusiness strife want (1) to be let alone (they want autonomy) and (2) to preserve the solidarity of the business community" (1960, 41). The latter means keeping peace within the business community by supporting all business people who have conflicts with government and other organized interests, e.g., labour.

40. The perception of costs and benefits can be manipulated by the way that interest groups deal with them. For example, opportunity losses are perceived by few people to be as salient as costs in the form of reduction from one's current position; i.e., people are loss avoiders and are quite insensitive to the failure to obtain a potential benefit. Costs that are concentrated are more likely to cause an adverse reaction than the same total cost that is widely dispersed. On the benefit side, it is possible to create intangible symbolic benefits by clever propaganda. Most people fail to appreciate the time value of money, so that large absolute benefits that will only occur well into the future may be made to seem valuable as similar benefits occurring in the near future.

41. See Stanbury and Fulton (1984).

42. This behaviour is also quite consistent with the federal Liberal party, then in power, basing its action on placating marginal voters in southern Ontario.

43. *Financial Post*, September 14, 1985, p. 13.

44. CRTC Press Release, August 29, 1985.

45. See Forbes, Hughes, and Warley (1982) and Forbes (1985).

46. See "A bonanza for Bombardier," *Maclean's*, May 31, 1983, p. 43; "Canadian taxpayers save N.Y. commuters a nickel a day," *Vancouver Sun*, June 2, 1982, p. B5; "A subway collision over export credits," *Business Week*, June 14, 1982, pp. 30-31; "U.S. plans new probe of Bombardier's MTA deal," *Globe and Mail*, July 20, 1982, p. B5; "Bombardier loan called waste," *Globe and Mail*, July 17, 1982, p. 4; and "U.S. Treasury chief approves Bombardier deal," Ottawa *Citizen*, July 14, 1982, p. B3.

47. See Linda McQuaig, "Research credits cost $2.6 billion," *Globe and Mail*, January 29, 1986, p. A8. More generally, see Giles

Gherson, "Tax credit party gives Ottawa costly hangover," *Financial Post*, July 6, 1985, p. 4; "Scientists are worried by research tax credit," *Globe and Mail*, June 11, 1984, p. 14; "Ottawa faces four years of SRTC: Ouch," *Financial Post*, January 12, 1985, p. 13; and Peter Ladner, "While the getting was good," *Canadian Business*, February 1985, pp. 88–95.

48. See Government of Canada, *Estimates*, 1984/85.

49. See, for example, "The French fact and the Tories," *Maclean's*, September 9, 1985, pp. 6a, 6c, 6d; and "Mulroney at a crossroads," *Maclean's*, September 2, 1985, pp. 8–9. An excellent example of a "Quebec versus English Canada" contretemps concerned the closing of the Gulf Canada refinery in Montreal. See, for example, Graham Fraser, "Quebecers close ranks on refinery," January 11, 1986, p. A9; Richard Cleroux, "Gulf sale controversy threatens to explode into full-blown crisis," *Globe and Mail*, January 13, 1986, p. A5; "Another Tory leaves the fold," *Maclean's*, January 13, 1986, p. 8; Jamie Lamb, "PM writhing in darkening nightmare," Vancouver *Sun*, January 15, 1986, p. A4; and "Tory problems in Quebec," *Maclean's*, January 20, 1986, pp. 6–7.

50. See "The high cost of jobs in Cape Breton," *Maclean's*, December 2, 1985, pp. 26, 28.

51. See Christopher Waddell, "Petrocan deal to cost millions in lost taxes," *Globe and Mail*, August 11, 1985, pp. B1, B5. See also "Gulf avoided $1-billion in taxes, Turner says," *Globe and Mail*, October 2, 1985, pp. 1–2.

52. "MP proposes bill to list lobbyists," Ottawa *Citizen*, April 8, 1976, p. 3; and Orland French, "Lobbying's no whisper word to Baker," Ottawa *Citizen*, April 9, 1976, p. 33.

53. " 'Cooling off' time on government contacts urged for ex-PS," Ottawa *Citizen*, March 26, 1976, p. 31; W. A. Wilson, "Trudeau government has set low standard of conduct," Ottawa *Journal*, March 29, 1976, p. 5; "Right of ex-deputy ministers dealing with government questioned," Ottawa *Citizen*, March 24, 1976, p. 19; "Ex-mandarins' business links raise eyebrows in Parliament," Ottawa *Citizen*, March 26, 1976, p. 4; and "Former mandarins protest outcry," *Financial Post*, April 3, 1976, p. 5.

54. *Conflict of Interest Guidelines* (Ottawa: Prime Minister's Office, 1976).

55. Ottawa *Citizen*, August 8, 1979, p. 2.

56. "Know thy lobbyist," Edmonton *Journal* editorial, June 3, 1978.

57. "Ottawa setting up lobbyist registry," *Globe and Mail*, November 21, 1979, p. B17.

58. "Quebec lobbyists pressing members for official status," *Globe and Mail*, December 28, 1982, p. 8.

59. House of Commons, *Debates*, January 19, 1983, p. 22010.
60. Bill C-495, "An Act respecting the registration of lobbyists," First Reading, May 2, 1980.
61. Ibid.
62. House of Commons, *Debates*, January 19, 1983, p. 22011.
63. Ibid.
64. Ibid.
65. Ibid.
66. Ibid.
67. Ibid.
68. Ibid.
69. See, for example, Mary Janigan, "Uncommon scent of scandal," *Maclean's*, March 7, 1983, pp. 14–15; "Deal over energy generates heat," *Maclean's*, February 28, 1983, p. 11; "Reputation of integrity a precious asset: Lalonde," *Globe and Mail*, February 25, 1983, p. 9; "Gillespie defends his role in obtaining federal funds," Vancouver *Sun*, February 18, 1983, p. C11; Giles Gherson, "Conflict rules need fresh scrutiny," *Financial Post*, March 5, 1983, p. 9; Jamie Lamb, "A strange type of accountability," Vancouver *Sun*, February 24, 1983, p. A4; Richard Gwyn, "Lalonde at bay: he must resign," Vancouver *Sun*, February 25, 1983, p. A5; Jeff Sallot, "Gillespie's energy dealings outlined in documents," *Globe and Mail*, February 25, 1983, p. 8; and Jeff Sallot, "Countdown to conflict-of-interest debate," *Globe and Mail*, February 24, 1983, p. 7.
70. "Gov't may relax rules on conflicts," Ottawa *Citizen*, July 8, 1983, p. 3.
71. Ottawa *Citizen*, July 9, 1983, p. 16.
72. Ian Mulgrew, "PM promises to take wraps off Ottawa," *Globe and Mail*, August 23, 1985, pp. 1, 2.
73. Ibid.; and Tom Barratt, "Mulroney vows patronage rules," Vancouver *Sun*, August 23, 1985, p. A14.
74. Charlotte Montgomery, "PM introduces tougher rules to prevent conflict of interest," *Globe and Mail*, September 10, 1985, pp. 1–2.
75. *Globe and Mail* editorial, September 25, 1985, p. 6.
76. See "Ottawa backs down on lobbying controls," Vancouver *Sun*, December 20, 1985, p. C7; Hugh Winsor, "Lobbying delays plans for legislation on lobbyists," *Globe and Mail*, December 20, 1985, p. A5; David Oxtoby, "Ottawa prepares disclosure rules for lobbyists," *Financial Times*, January 13, 1986, p. 10; Charlotte Montgomery, "Mulroney's proposed reforms run into resistance," *Globe and Mail*, February 11, 1986, p. A9; and Minister of Consumer and Corporate Affairs, *Lobbying and the Registration of Paid Lobbyists: A Discussion Paper* (Ottawa, 1985).

10

Corporations and Political Contributions

1.0 INTRODUCTION

Money, it is said, is the mother's milk of politics.[1] Traditionally, at least prior to the Election Expenses Act of 1974, corporations were the largest teat from which milk flowed to finance the Liberal and Progressive Conservative parties in Canada. In this chapter I examine a number of questions concerning the financing of the three main federal political parties in Canada in the period 1974 to 1984. Particular emphasis is placed on the role of corporate contributions, particularly large ones, as a source of revenue for the Liberal and Conservative parties in this period, which included three general elections.

Section 2 sketches some of the key characteristics of the methods of financing political parties in Canada prior to the 1974 changes in federal legislation. Section 3 outlines the critical characteristics of the rules governing contributions and expenditures by federal parties and candidates.

Among the questions that are explored in this chapter are the following: Have nonelection expenditures by the Liberals, Tories, and the NDP increased more rapidly than election campaign expenditures that are limited by statute? Have they outpaced inflation? Are the parties, in effect, substituting nonelection expenditures for constrained election outlays in an effort to improve their organizational effectiveness and hence win more seats? These matters are addressed in section 4.

Also in section 4, I examine the various sources of party revenues, which consist almost entirely of contributions. Has the generous tax credit — worth $75 on a contribution of $100 — had the effect of increasing the number and economic importance of contributions from individuals, hence making the Liberals and Tories less dependent on contributions from corporations? Has the requirement that all contributions of $100 or more in cash or kind be disclosed made corporations (or individuals) less willing to make large contributions?

Note: I am deeply indebted to Karyn MacCrimmon for her careful work as research assistant on the data on the parties' revenues and expenditures, and to the staff of the chief electoral officer in Ottawa for data.

Section 5 focuses on the role of large contributions by both individuals and corporations. Do a few decision makers have the potential power to influence party policies by giving or withholding large donations? Do large contributions from business firms come almost entirely from large firms or is size not a critical determinant? Among the top 200 nonfinancial enterprises, for example, are political contributions proportionate to the size of the firms? Do foreign-owned firms donate less to Canadian parties, perhaps because their parents practise a form of extraterritoriality? For example, corporations in the United States cannot make contributions directly to parties or candidates, although they may do so through political action committees (see Jacobson 1985; Alexander 1983; Drew 1983).

I also examine the extent to which interest groups of various types are important sources of political contributions. Public choice theorists, notably Downs (1957), argue that parties exchange the promise of favourable policies if they form the government for political support, most notably political contributions. Recall chapter 4.

Section 7 discusses the question of whether there are gaps in the legislation regarding the financing of parties and candidates in Canada. Section 8 addresses the sensitive issue of campaign contributions and political corruption. What is the line, for example, between legitimate campaign contributions and those designed to obtain special access or influence in matters of public policy? Section 9 grapples with the problem of developing a policy concerning campaign contributions for business firms in Canada.

2.0 POLITICAL CONTRIBUTIONS PRIOR TO THE ELECTION EXPENSES ACT OF 1974

Despite a paucity of information in the public domain prior to the federal Election Expenses Act, scholars have sought to document how political parties raised and spent their funds.[2] One of their principal conclusions is that prior to the 1974 legislative reforms, both major parties were almost totally dependent on contributions from large corporations: "Until the 1960s, only 4% of Canada's population contributed individually to federal parties, and 90% of all campaign monies received reputedly came from the financial power centres of Toronto and Montreal" (Stevenson 1982, 25). A survey of voters in the mid-1960s revealed only about 5 percent of the respondents were solicited for political contributions (Meisel & Van Loon 1966, 42).

Except for the period 1908 to 1930, corporations in Canada have been free to donate as much as they wish to political parties. Even during the ban "there were several loopholes . . . and enforcement was non-existent" (Stevenson 1982, 34).[3] Indeed, corporations have been encouraged to make political contributions directly to parties and candidates in Canada

— in contrast to the U.S. where such contributions have long been prohibited. In Canada, unions were prohibited from making political contributions only between 1920 and 1930. In both cases, the rationale for
the legislation was the same: to prevent shareholders' and union members' money from being used for political purposes of which they may
not approve.

Paltiel has described the heavy reliance on corporate donations prior
to the Election Expenses Act of 1974 as follows:

> The centralized corporations and financial institutions located in
> Toronto and Montreal provide the bulk of funds needed by the
> major parties. . . . There are only a handful of these large con-
> tributers — hundreds rather than thousands. For the 1972 election
> half the funds raised in Ontario by the Liberal Party were collected
> personally by the chairman of the party's Treasury Committee from
> 90 large corporations. (1975, 182)

"In the Liberal Party of the 1960s, election-year contributions were
as high as $100,000 from a single source" (Stevenson 1982, 31). Corpo-
rations were the source of such contributions. This was at a time when
party spending on elections was less than $3 million. It was then the
practice of major corporate contributors to give 60 percent to the party
in power and 40 percent to the opposition (Paltiel 1970). The federal
Liberal party's longtime corporate fund raiser, Senator John Godfrey,
applied a formula of 0.2 percent of a corporation's profit in election
years. Therefore, for every $1 million in profit, the corporation was
expected to donate $2000 (Stevenson 1982, 31–32). In off-election years,
the major parties have tended to ask for 20 percent or 25 percent of
what the firm had given in election years.

In the "bad old days," how did the major federal parties obtain political contributions from business? Whitaker asserts that in the period
1946 to 1958 "there is no reason to believe that the contract levy system initiated . . . in the late 1930s was abandoned as the Government
[Liberal] party grew older in the comfortable exercise of power. Indeed
there is, on the contrary, every reason to believe that it was extended
and made more comprehensive and efficient" (1977, 199). The increase
in government intervention in the economy also produced greater
amounts for party "bagmen" who usually were (and are) prominent
business people and lawyers. See Figure 10-1. In time, a number were
appointed to the Senate (e.g., John Godfrey, John Aird, Richard Stanbury, Armand Daigle, and Louis Gelinas). Whitaker (1977, 201) states
that the Liberals were able to raise and spend two to three times as much
as the Conservatives in 1957 — some $6 million to $7 million, which he
admits is a ballpark estimate. However, even these estimates do not
include "the very considerable contributions in kind rather than in cash
which had become available to the Government party" (Whitaker 1977,

Figure 10–1
THE BAGMEN AND CORPORATE POLITICAL CONTRIBUTIONS

John Godfrey is a senator, appointed to the upper chamber in 1973 by a grateful Prime Minister Pierre Trudeau. He is a senator because he is a good bagman; he has raised money, lots of money, for the Liberal party's election campaigns. . . . He was expected to retire from the field after the last election in 1974, but he raised an astonishing $1.5 million on his own from 90-odd firms and was deemed too valuable to let go. Besides, he says, "I despise people who get appointed to the Senate and then just quit. I want to do my duty" (Urquhart 1978).

His duty is to the Liberal party. For this election [1979] his canvass has been pared to just 35 firms but they are traditionally the party's biggest donors and he will be asking them to contribute $50,000 each. The pitch will come over drinks at the club, in the executive suite or even over the telephone. Godfrey's approach will be simple and direct: You don't have to like Trudeau and the Liberals, but in the interest of democracy and free enterprise you should support them. He will suggest a donation of $2000 for every $1-million the firm makes in profits. Few will turn him down. . . . But, when they are asking for money, they try to avoid mentioning politics except in the broadest terms. "Don't talk politics," an instruction sheet for Liberal bagmen advises bluntly. "Leave it to the politicians. Introduce yourself properly and explain why you are canvassing. Discuss free enterprise, etc. Corporations should accept responsibilities the same as citizens. Shareholders' best interests are being furthered by supporting free enterprise" (Urquhart 1978).

The bagmen do, however, serve as a conduit of business opinion back to their parties. During the 1974 election, for example, when things were going badly for the Conservatives, Robert Stanfield met with his party's bagmen in Toronto. He came under attack for everything from his advocacy of wage-price controls (a "socialist" policy, said one bagman) to his failure to come out against the capital gains tax. For Stanfield, it was a tougher session than any press conference he endured during the campaign. . . . "When I was in charge of raising money in Ontario for the 1968 federal election," says Godfrey, "all canvassers were instructed to approach prospective donors on the basis that giving a donation was merely being a good corporate citizen, and there was nothing in it for anyone, that they were merely supporting the democratic process and that they should give equally to the party in power and the official opposition. . . . It is extremely rare, he says, to encounter a donor who expects a direct return for his contribution. "Since I became involved in 1968, I can only recall four instances in which a prospective donor stated that what he might give would be influenced by some action, legislative or otherwise, which he wanted the government to take. I can recall how startled these gentlemen were when I told them forcefully and in no uncertain terms that the Liberal party was not for sale, the government was not for sale, and that was not the basis upon which the Liberal party raised or accepted money." . . . A further constraint on the bagmen has been imposed by Trudeau. He has established an annual ceiling on corporate donations of $25,000 or $50,000 in election years. Explains Trudeau: "We don't want to be indebted to any small number of large corporations." The ceiling, in effect, applies to the Conservatives as well, because few companies will give more to one party than the other. While a ceiling of $25,000 a year can add up to $100,000 over a four-year period, the self-imposed restraint has put a crimp in the style of the bagmen, who are used to receiving that much or more in one lump

Figure 10–1 (continued)

during an election campaign. (Reproduced from Ian Urquhart, "The Bucks Stop Here: Behind Every Great Leader Is an Equally Great Bagman," *Maclean's*, May 15, 1978, pp. 446-44)

. . . Among the first people [Godfrey] consults before phoning his "clients" is Hal Jackman, Toronto financier and chairman of Empire Life Insurance Co. Jackman, three times unsuccessful as political opponent to former finance minister Donald Macdonald, is Godfrey's opposite number in the Conservative party, the quiet power behind the purse strings. Most companies give the same amount to Grits and Tories, so Godfrey and Jackman prevent price cutting by settling in advance what to ask. Once agreed, they sometimes drive off to meet prospects together, Godfrey says. How much they collect won't emerge until next year, in reports filed by the parties and published by the chief electoral officer. The big banks, as a group, are the handsomest donors at $20,000 or $25,000 apiece to each of the old-line parties. . . . Paul Klie, Liberal campaign co-ordinator in Ontario, says two or three firms sent cheques "with strings attached" in the last campaign; they were sent back. (Reproduced from *Maclean's*, February 4, 1980, p. 36)

204). Of particular importance were the services provided by the advertising agencies who made up their out-of-pocket expenses by generous contracts for advertising by government departments and agencies. This practice appears to continue today.[4]

The activities of the Union Nationale in Quebec under Maurice Duplessis provide an example of the antithesis to the present method of financing federal political parties in Canada. Quinn points out that "the party never made a public appeal for funds, never took up a collection at a political meeting, had no revenue from membership fees or the sale of party literature and yet it was able to spend an estimated three to four million dollars in every election campaign" (1975, 75). This amount not only dwarfed expenditures by the opposition parties, it was more than that spent by any party in Ontario. It was about equal to that spent by the Tories during the 1949 federal election.

The Union Nationale raised its money in three principal ways, according to Quinn (1976, 74-75). First, contributions were actively solicited from businesses that had government contracts of any sort. Successful firms, in effect, paid kickbacks to the party. Second, the discretionary power over the granting and renewal of liquor licences was used to raise funds. Owners were requested to contribute based on what the party thought the traffic would bear. Third, as the party in power, the Union Nationale solicited and obtained large donations from companies in the natural resource sector, as these firms were heavily dependent upon government policy for their success. Failure to cooperate could result in the loss of tax concessions and strict enforcement of various types of regulations, including labour laws.

It was these excesses that stimulated the Parti Québécois to bring in one of the most stringent election-financing laws in Canada. It provides, among other things, that only individuals may legally contribute to parties and candidates. Obviously, this dramatically alters the role of corporations in financing political activities.

Referring to the general election of July 8, 1974, the last before the new, far-reaching legislation came into effect, Paltiel states that efforts to determine revenues and expenditures by parties and candidates "is seriously hampered by ignorance. . . . The most serious difficulty is the refusal of party and public officials to supply information which neither law, custom, nor practice has required of political parties, or party fund-raisers and spenders" (1974, 184). While the expenditures declared by candidates was $10.7 million, Paltiel (1974, 185) put the total at $35 million when national, regional, and provincial associations are included. This figure, however, did not include the imputed value of free broadcasting time provided by the crown-owned CBC.

Paltiel (1974, 190–91, 194–95) states that "the National Treasury Committee of the Liberal Party of Canada . . . raised approximately $6.2 million for the 1974 general election." While the bulk of the funds were raised in Ontario and Quebec, teams of canvassers worked in B.C., Manitoba, and Saskatchewan. In Alberta, Senator Harry Hays "operated as [a] 'lone wolf' exploiting . . . extensive business contacts." Paltiel emphasizes that "the principal targets of these groups and individuals were the national offices of national and multi-national corporations." He notes that the amount of money raised in Quebec was less than half the amount spent in that province. The Conservatives' comparable committee raised $3.9 million also largely from corporate sources. The NDP's federal election fund raised only $372 000 of which $235 000 came from trade unions. This importance of corporate donations was reduced after the Election Expenses Act of 1974 came into effect.

3.0 THE NEW RULES OF THE GAME IN 1974

The Liberals enacted the most far-reaching electoral finance legislation in the nation's history effective August 1, 1974, after the general election of July 8 that returned them to power after twenty months of minority government. The Election Expenses Act took the form of amendments to the Elections Act, the Income Tax Act and the Broadcasting Act. How did it come about? Stevenson explains that "five election campaigns between 1957 and 1965 had strained party funds to the breaking point and increasing reliance on costly television advertising compounded the problem" (1982, 10). In 1964 the federal government appointed a special Committee on Election Expenses, the Barbeau Committee, "to advise on the best practicable way to set enforceable limits to expenditures in election campaigns." It reported in October 1966. Many of its recommendations were eventually implemented in 1974. However, the 1968 federal election intervened and in 1970 a House of Commons Special Committee on Election Expenses was appointed to study the problem. Following its report, in May 1972 new legislation was introduced, but it was not until January 1974 that it was passed. This was said to be partly due to the aftermath of the Watergate affair in the U.S. The new Election Expenses Act did not apply to the 1974 election.

With the Liberals forming a minority government, the NDP was able to influence the legislation markedly. The NDP insisted on disclosure of the names of contributors of more than $100 in cash or kind; it reduced the requirements for candidates' eligibility for reimbursement; it increased the relative size of the tax credit for small donors; and it obtained an exclusion for "volunteer labour" from election expenses (Stevenson 1982, 12). The most important elements in this legislation and subsequent amendments are now described.

3.1 Party Registration and Agency

Political parties have been recognized as legal entities since 1970. The 1974 legislation required the appointment of a chief agent and auditor responsible for filing information with the chief electoral officer. Only a candidate or person authorized by a party may incur election expenses. The act, however, specifically exempted interest groups or individuals who engage in advertising during election campaigns provided they are promoting discussion of public policy and as long as they do not align themselves with a specific party or candidate. An amendment to the Canada Elections Act (Bill C-169), passed in October 1983, removed these exemptions and resulted in a successful constitutional challenge.[5]

3.2 Spending Limits

The 1974 legislation provided that each registered party could spend on election expenses no more than 30 cents for each elector in each riding in which it had an official candidate in the sixty-day period prior to election day. This provision was modified in October 1983 by "indexing" the maximum allowable expenditure by the increase in the Consumer Price Index (CPI). Each year, effective April 1, the chief electoral officer must publish a fraction (F) based on the following formula: F = (average CPI during the previous January to December)/88.9, where the CPI is based on 1981 = 100, and 88.9 was the average CPI in 1980. Note that the 1983 amendment had the effect of indexing the spending limit from 1980, the year of the previous federal election. For the 1984 general election, F = 117.2/88.9 = 131.83, where the average CPI for 1983 was 117.2. Therefore, each registered party was allowed to spend 39.55 cents for each voter on the preliminary voters list in each riding that it had a candidate. If a party ran a candidate in all 282 ridings, its maximum allowable election expenditures in 1984 was $6.393 million. The party campaign expenditure limit, however, excludes volunteer labour and grants by the parties to candidates.

Candidates are also subject to a spending ceiling. It was originally set at $1 per elector for the first 15 000 plus $.50 for the next 10 000 plus $.25 for each elector in excess of 25 000. In the 1980 general election this limit averaged $27 000. This ceiling was also indexed in October 1983 in the same way as the limit on party expenditures — see above. Seidle and Paltiel (1981, 265) point out that if the limit had been allowed to keep pace with inflation between 1974 and 1980 it would have been set at about $43 000. In 1968 it was estimated that the average amount spent by candidates was $15 000 (Stevenson 1982, 56). J. P. Boyer argues that "conceptually, it seems odd to allow limitless funds to go into a political system and then try to restrict what comes out. Such an approach appears to belie human nature and ignore the realities of Canadian campaign practices" (1979, 177).[6]

3.3 Advertising

Under the Broadcasting Act as amended in 1974, radio and television stations must make available up to 6.5 hours of prime time for paid advertising by the parties during the election campaign. This time is allocated among the parties by the CRTC according to a formula based on the number of seats held and the party's popular vote. In 1984, for example, the Liberals were allocated 173 minutes, the Tories 129 minutes, the NDP 69 minutes, and other parties 46.5 minutes. The 1974 act also set a maximum of 6.5 hours on advertising in the electronic media during the four weeks immediately preceding election day. No such limit applies to other media (e.g., print), although expenditures must stay within the party's or candidate's limit.

In addition to "purchasable time" in the 1984 election, the radio and TV networks were required to allocate the following free-time periods:

Radio		*Television*	
• CBC-AM English	2 hours	• CBC English	3.5 hours
• CBC-AM French	2 hours	• CBC French	3.5 hours
• Radiomutuel	1 hour	• CTV	3.5 hours
• Telemedia	1 hour	• TVA	1 hour

3.4 Reimbursement of Campaign Expenses

All candidates who receive at least 15 percent of the votes cast and who comply with the requirements for submitting their report on election expenses are entitled to be reimbursed for a part of their election expenses by the federal government. The formula established in 1974 set the reimbursement as the sum of (1) the cost of a first-class letter to all electors;

(2) $.08 for each of the first 25 000 electors, and (3) $.06 for every elector above 25 000. However, in October 1983 this formula was changed
to pay to candidates one-half of their actual expenses (not to exceed 50
percent of the maximum allowable expenses) provided that the candidate obtained 15 percent of the votes cast and had filed the appropriate
forms with the chief electoral officer.[7]

In the 1984 federal election the average riding had 59 200 voters.
Therefore, the maximum allowable expenditure for a candidate in the
average-sized riding was $37 637. Hence, a candidate obtaining 15 per-
cent of the votes would be reimbursed for $18 819, if he or she spent the
maximum allowable amount on the campaign. Registered parties were
entitled under the 1974 legislation to be reimbursed by the federal government for one-half the standard *media* costs (not production costs) of
radio and TV ads up to the maximum allotted number of minutes. This
provision, which obviously favoured the electronic over the print media,
is quite important because in the 1979 and 1980 general elections the
three main parties spent about one-half of their total election expenditures on radio and TV advertising.[8] In 1983 this provision was changed
to a reimbursement of 22.5 percent of the maximum-allowed party
expenditures.

The amount of the reimbursement is given in Table 10-2 below.

3.5 Disclosure

Under the 1974 legislation, every registered party must submit a detailed
statement of revenues and expenditures annually. Candidates must do
the same after a by-election or general election. The name of every person or organization who has donated $100 or more in cash or in kind to
the party or to a candidate must be reported. While these lengthy lists
are available for public inspection at the office of the chief electoral
officer and may be obtained on request, only summary data are published in the CEO's report on each general election. See Chief Electoral
Officer (1979, 1980, 1984).

3.6 Tax Credits

In addition to reimbursing parties for electronic media advertising and
reimbursing candidates for a substantial fraction of their campaign
expenses, the federal government (really taxpayers in general) provides
a tax credit (deduction against taxes payable, not income) as follows:[9]

- 75 percent of amounts contributed up to $100, plus
- 50 percent of amounts contributed between $100 and $550, plus
- 33.3 percent of amounts contributed exceeding $550 — up to a total
  tax credit of $500.

Therefore, the maximum credit ($500) is achieved with a donation of $1150. There is no statutory limit, however, on the total amount a person or corporation can give to a party or candidate, but the amount is not deductible for income tax purposes.

4.0 PARTY REVENUES AND EXPENDITURES, 1974–84

In this section I examine the following questions:

Q1: Have nonelection expenditures by the three main federal parties in both election and nonelection years grown more rapidly than election expenditures and the rate of inflation?

Q2: Despite the Election Expenses Act of 1974, do contributions by corporations still account for a very large fraction of the total revenues of the Liberal and Conservative parties at the federal level in Canada?

Q3: Has the structure of the tax credit for political contributions (and more sophisticated direct-mail fund raising) resulted in a rapid growth in the number of individual contributors and a decline in the importance of big donations from individuals?

4.1 Nonelection Expenditures

One of the major effects of the 1974 Election Expenses Act has been the public disclosure of much more information about the revenues and expenditures of all federal political parties. Table 10-1 indicates that the growth in party nonelection expenditures (i.e., those excluding expenses during election campaign periods) has been very substantial between 1974 and 1984. In 1974/75 (the first twelve-month period), the Liberals and Tories spent $1.96 million and $1.60 million respectively. In 1984 the Liberals spent $12 million while the Tories spent $20.8 million. The NDP's expenditures in 1975 (the first full year for which we have data) were $2.57 million while in 1984 they were $7.41 million. The growth in nonelection expenditures for all parties exceeded the rate of inflation; that is, between 1975 and 1984 the CPI and the Gross National Expenditure (GNE) deflator increased 2.1 times, while expenditures by the Liberals, Tories, and NDP increased 6.1, 13.0, and 2.9 times respectively.

It should be noted, however, that nonelection expenditures have not grown steadily since 1974. For example, Liberal expenditures in 1977 were more than double those in 1974/75, but in 1979 they were only two-thirds of the 1977 level. Nonelection expenditures by the Liberals were in the range of $5.1 million to $6.3 million in nominal terms between 1978 and 1983 (except for 1979), so it was not until 1984 that

Table 10–1
MAJOR PARTIES INCOME AND EXPENDITURES, 1974–84
($ thousands)

Period	Liberals Income	Liberals Expend.	Progressive Cons. Income	Progressive Cons. Expend.	NDP Income	NDP Expend.
1974					1 437[d]	1 270[d]
	2 217[a]	1 963[a]	1 721[a]	1 597[a]		
1975			1 203[c]	889[c]	2 580	2 570
	5 823[b]	4 707[b]				
1976			4 084	3 497	2 281	2 315
1977	4 587	4 187	3 774	4 233	3 006	3 105
1978	5 018	5 283	5 465	5 470	3 401	3 514
1979	6 302	2 771	8 376	5 083	4 741	4 678
E		3 913		3 845		2 190
R	718		794		496	
1980	6 218	5 769	7 564	4 923	6 101	5 992
E		3 846		4 407		3 086
R	910		978		677	
1981	5 592	5 116	6 950	7 542	6 003	6 491
1982	6 746	5 497	8 521	8 521	7 108	6 837
1983	7 736	6 277	14 767	10 338	8 669	8 009
1984	11 598	11 999	21 979	20 777	10 513	7 407
E		6 293		6 393		4 731
R	1 416		1 438		1 064	

[a] 1/8/74 to 31/7/75   12 months
[b] 1/8/75 to 31/12/76   17 months
[c] 1/8/75 to 31/12/75   5 months
[d] 1/8/74 to 31/12/74   5 months
E = general election campaign expenditures
R = reimbursement of election expenses by federal government, i.e., one-half the allowed outlays on electronic media for advertising in 1979 and 1980 and 22.5% of total permitted party election expenses in 1984.
Income = contributions plus other income, e.g., interest. In some years for the Liberals and the PCS "other income" was reported as a deduction from "other expenses."

Source: Calculated from *Report of the Chief Electoral Officer Respecting Election Expenses, 31st General Election, 1979*; annual returns filed by the parties with the CEO, 1979–84; and *Report of the Chief Electoral Officer Respecting Election Expenses, Thirty-Third General Election, 1984.*

such expenditures doubled to $12 million. In the case of the Tories, nonelection expenditures were between $4.2 and $5.5 million between 1977 and 1980. They then began to increase steadily in 1981 and 1982. However, the largest increases took place in 1983 when expenditures reached $10.3 million and in 1984 when they rose to $20.8 million. In other words, the Tories were able to treble their annual rate of non-election expenditures between 1981 and 1984 even though 1984 was an election year, requiring the party to raise an additional $6.3 million — the legal limit on such expenditures.

These data on nonelection expenditures suggest that, on the basis of recent trends, the three main parties at the federal level are now spending much more in constant dollars on their organizational activities outside campaign periods than was the case even five years ago. This trend is most noticeable for the Tories, but it is also the case for the Liberals. The trend is least obvious for the NDP.

Second, the data in Table 10-1 suggest that constraints on election campaign expenditures ($6.393 million in 1984 if a party fielded a full slate of candidates) have resulted in the substitution of party expenditures outside the designated campaign periods where expenditures are only limited by the party's ability to raise funds.

Third, growing party expenditures have been matched by the ability of all parties to raise much more money in recent years. (Perhaps the cause and effect should be reversed; the growth of nonelection expenditures is limited only by a party's ability to raise money.) The strongest example is that of the Tories, who in the election year of 1984 raised $22 million (and spent over $27 million on election and nonelection expenses). In contrast, in 1980 (also an election year) the Tories raised $7.6 million and spent a total of $9.33 million. All parties are making extensive use of direct-mail campaigns aimed at the individual donor who can write a cheque for $100 but only end up paying $25 after the effect of the tax credit (see Table 10-5). At the same time, the Liberals and Tories are continuing to actively solicit much larger contributions from corporations, while the NDP focuses its efforts on trade unions for larger donations. Yet it is the NDP that has received the largest donations in recent years from an individual.[10]

4.2 Election Expenditures

Election expenditures by the three main federal parties increased by 75 percent between the 1979 and 1984 general elections; those by all candidates increased by 66 percent — see Table 10-2.[11] By comparison, annual nonelection expenditures by the three parties increased by 221 percent between 1979 and 1984. However, election expenditures rose slightly more than the rate of inflation: the CPI and GNE deflator increased by 52 and 51 percent respectively between 1979 and 1984. Between 1974 and 1983 the legal maximum on both party and candidate expenditures was not indexed to the rate of inflation. However, when the maxima were indexed in October 1983, they were indexed from 1980. Therefore, increases in total party and candidate expenditures in the future, assuming both spend to their legal limits, will depend upon the general rate of inflation.[12]

While party and candidate election expenditures are limited, they are also, as noted in section 3, subject to reimbursement by the federal government. In the case of the three major parties, reimbursement

Table 10–2
GROSS AND NET EXPENDITURES BY PARTIES AND CANDIDATES ON FEDERAL GENERAL ELECTION CAMPAIGNS, 1979, 1980, and 1984
($ thousands)

Expenditures by		1979 ($)	1980 ($)	1984 ($)	Increase 1984/1979 (%)
• Parties	Conservative	3 845	4 407	6 389	66
	Liberal	3 913	3 846	6 293	61
	NDP	2 190	3 086	4 731	16
	Total	9 948	11 339	17 413	75
• Candidates	Conservative	6 016	5 680	10 726	78
	Liberal	6 186	6 074	9 447	53
	NDP	2 665	2 987	4 479	68
	Total	14 867	14 741	24 652	66
Reimbursement from federal government to					
• Parties	Conservative	794	977	1 438	81
	Liberal	718	910	1 416	97
	NDP	496	677	1 064	115
	Total	2 008	2 564	3 918	95
— as a % of party expenditures		20.2	22.6	22.5	
• Candidates	Conservative	2 868	2 871	5 117	78
	Liberal	3 594	3 656	4 081	14
	NDP	1 671	1 886	1 917	15
	Total	8 133	8 393	11 115	37
— as a % of party expenditures		54.7	56.9	45.1	

Source: *Report of the Chief Electoral Officer Respecting Election Expenses, 1979; 1980; 1984* (Ottawa: CEO).

amounted to 20.2 percent of the total campaign expenditures in 1979, 22.6 percent in 1980, and 22.5 percent in 1984. For the candidates of these parties, reimbursement amounted to 54.7 percent of total expenditures in 1979, 56.9 percent in 1980, but dropped to 45.1 percent in 1984. This reflects the change in the formula described in section 3.

With respect to Question 1 we can say that noncampaign expenditures in both election and nonelection years have grown more rapidly than campaign expenditures in election years. The reason why the latter have barely outpaced inflation between 1979 and 1984 is the statutory limit on such expenditures, although as the data in note 12 make clear, party expenditures for the Liberals and Tories only became binding in 1984.

Table 10–3
ANALYSIS OF PARTY ELECTION EXPENSES, 1979, 1980, and 1984
($ thousands)

Expenditure Category		1979 $	1979 %	1980 $	1980 %	1984 $	1984 %
Print Advertising	PC	267	7.0	578	13.1	207	3.2
	Lib	576	14.7	403	10.5	763	12.1
	NDP	315	14.4	426	13.8	154	3.3
Radio	PC	939	24.4	652	14.8	1236	19.3
	Lib	563	14.4	579	15.1	1069	17.0
	NDP	248	11.3	233	7.6	495	10.4
Television	PC	1539	40.0	1876	42.6	1758	27.5
	Lib	1295	33.1	1613	41.9	1695	26.9
	NDP	771	35.2	1167	37.8	1158	24.5
Total Advertising	PC	2745	71.4	3106	70.5	3201	50.1
	Lib	2434	62.2	2595	67.5	3527	56.0
	NDP	1334	60.9	1826	59.2	1806	38.2
Travelling	PC	632	16.4	639	14.5	3201	17.7
	Lib	691	17.7	421	10.9	881	14.0
	NDP	233	10.6	378	12.2	146	3.1
Other Expenses	PC	468	12.2	662	15.0	2058	32.2
	Lib	788	20.1	830	21.6	1885	30.0
	NDP	623	28.4	882	28.6	2779	58.7
Total Expenses	PC	3845	100	4407	100	6389	100
	Lib	3913	100	3846	100	6293	100
	NDP	2190	100	3086	100	4731	100

Source: Tabulations from data provided by the Chief Electoral Officer 1979, 1980, 1984.

Table 10-3 indicates that advertising expenditures, both electronic and print, account for a large portion of total election expenditures by the three largest federal parties. In the 1979 and 1980 elections, the Conservative party spent 70 percent of its total expenditures on advertising. For the Liberal party, the comparable fractions were 62.2 and 67.5 percent respectively, while those for the NDP were 60.9 and 59.2 percent. In the latest general election (1984) all parties spent a reduced fraction of their campaign expenditures on advertising: 50.1 percent for the Tories, 56.0 percent for the Liberals, and only 38.2 percent for the NDP. The decrease was attributable to lower expenditures, in proportionate terms, on print and television advertising. See Table 10-3. Other data (Chief Electoral Officer 1984, 11) indicate that for Liberals, Tories, and NDP, "National Office Expenses" accounted for 17.2, 9.7 and 24.9 percent of total election expenses respectively in 1984.

The rapid growth of nonelection expenditures, particularly since

1981, suggests that the three major parties are becoming "professional-ized" and that they are substituting nonelection expenditures in elec-tion and nonelection years for election expenditures that are limited by law. This is true, albeit to a lesser extent, of the NDP, which even in 1984 only spent 74 percent of its legal limit as a party. (Its candidates only spent 37.8 percent of their limit on a combined basis.) It may be that the raising and spending of much larger sums by the major parties is indicative of greater competition among them. The recent sharp growth in nonelection spending, particularly by the Tories and Liberals, may also be attributable to new and improved methods of fund raising, notably direct mail. Unfortunately, publicly available data do not indicate what fraction of party expenditures go toward fund raising.[13] In any event, the critical point is that for the three main federal parties, nonelection expenditures have become "big business" in the past few years.

4.3 Sources of Contributions

I now test Questions 2 and 3 set out above. As noted in section 2, leading scholars of political finance prior to the reforms of 1974, on the basis of admittedly imperfect information, have stressed the importance of cor-porate contributions, particularly large contributions, as the primary source of revenues for the federal Liberal and Conservative parties. While no precise data are available on the fraction of party revenues provided by corporations prior to the Election Expenses Act of 1974, it probably exceeded 75 percent for the Liberals and Tories.

4.3.1 Contributions to Parties

Table 10-4 provides data on the sources of contributions to the three main federal parties between 1974 and 1984. It indicates that corpora-tions[14] have accounted for about one-half of total contributions to the federal Liberal party since 1974. However, there has been considerable year-to-year variation. For example, in 1979, an election year, the ratio was 74.3 percent and in 1982 it dropped to 41.3 percent. In seven of the ten years between 1975 and 1984, the Tories' reliance on corporate con-tributions was less than that of the Liberals. For example, in 1982 and 1983 the Tories received only 27.5 and 34.2 percent of their total contri-butions from corporations. But note that in the election years of 1979, 1980, and 1984, the ratios for corporations were 59.9, 57.8, and 52.0 percent respectively.

One of the effects of the Election Expenses Act of 1974 was an initial reduction in large corporate donations, which now had to be disclosed. For example, in 1974 after the act came into effect only seventeen cor-porations gave $10 000 or more to the Liberal party. There was even a fear of an organized boycott when Canadian Pacific and Inco, tradi-tionally large donors, refused to contribute.[15] The pause proved to be temporary, but the reluctance of foreign-owned firms, particularly those

Table 10–4

SOURCES OF CONTRIBUTIONS TO THE MAJOR POLITICAL PARTIES, 1974–84

Year and Party		SOURCE (% distribution)					Total ($ 000)
		Individuals	Corporations & Commercial Organizations	Trade Unions	Provincial Organizations[5]	Other	
1974	Lib	*	*	*	*	*	*
	PC	*	*	*	*	*	*
	NDP[1]	89.4	1.0	9.3	n/a	0.3	1 437
1975	Lib[2]	51.4	46.2	*	n/a	2.4	2 149
	PC[3]	45.8	51.8	0	n/a	2.4	2 794
	NDP	80.2	5.6	14.2	n/a	*	2 580
1976	Lib[4]	52.8	46.0	*	n/a	1.2	5 599
	PC	48.9	49.3	0	n/a	1.8	3 907
	NDP	80.4	4.2	15.3	n/a	0.1	2 206
1977	Lib	44.9	51.8	*	n/a	3.3	4 424
	PC	49.2	48.6	*	n/a	2.2	3 545
	NDP	77.3	6.6	15.2	n/a	0.9	2 861
1978	Lib	44.0	52.1	*	n/a	3.9	4 780
	PC	49.6	49.0	0	n/a	1.4	5 363
	NDP	78.3	6.4	15.0	n/a	0.3	3 259
1979(E)	Lib	22.7	74.3	*	n/a	3.0	5 221
	PC	38.0	59.9	*	n/a	2.1	8 376
	NDP	59.2	3.7	37.0	n/a	0.1	4 597
1980(E)	Lib	36.7	60.0	*	n/a	3.3	6 218
	PC	40.2	57.8	—	n/a	2.0	7 564
	NDP	46.2	1.6	27.9	19.3	0.1	6 101
1981	Lib	41.2	53.1	*	n/a	5.7	5 095
	PC	62.2	37.0	0	n/a	0.8	6 950
	NDP	47.0	18.2	8.6	35.8	6.0	6 003
1982	Lib	52.3	41.3	0.1	n/a	6.3	6 104
	PC	60.8	27.5	0	n/a	11.7	8 521
	NDP	53.1	2.0	6.7	32.9	5.3	7 108
1983	Lib	44.8	48.6	*	n/a	6.6	7 285
	PC	64.5	34.2	0	n/a	1.3	14 108
	NDP	57.7	0.5	7.3	31.1	3.4	8 669
1984(E)	Lib	49.1	50.6	*	n/a	0.3	10 553
	PC	48.0	52.0	0	n/a	0	21 145
	NDP	39.5	0.5	20.5	30.0	9.5	10 513

E = election year
* Included in 1975; see notes 2 and 3.
[1] 1/8/74 to 31/12/74   Lib = Liberal Party
[2] 1/8/74 to 31/7/74   PC = Progressive Conservative Party
[3] 1/8/74 to 31/12/75   NDP = New Democratic Party
[4] 1/8/75 to 31/12/76   n/a = not applicable
[5] Includes contributions from individuals, trade unions, and some businesses to provincial organizations then transferred to the federal party.

Sources: Calculated from *Report of the Chief Electoral Officer Respecting Election Expenses, 31st General Election, 1979*; and annual returns filed by the parties with the CEO, 1979–84.

owned in the U.S., was (and is) hard to overcome (Wearing 1981, 226). So much so that "a prominent, Conservative fund-raiser acknowledged that 'the parties have worked together to explain the law to U.S. subsidiaries' " (Stevenson 1982, 33). Because the parent firms were forbidden to make political contributions (which now take the form of donations to the numerous political action committees [Jacobson1985; Alexander 1983]) the subsidiaries found it hard to believe that not only was such activity legal in Canada, but it was encouraged in the Income Tax Act and by the political elite. For example, the chairperson of IBM ruled out contributions of $25 000 in election years and $5000 otherwise by IBM Canada, arguing that it was a misuse of American shareholders' money to contribute to Canadian parties when it was illegal to make comparable contributions in the United States (Stevenson 1982, 32).

A 1977 survey of 700 firms with more than 100 employees by the Institute for Political Involvement found that among larger firms (over 500 employees) the 1974 Election Expenses Act has resulted in the same size of political contribution for 79 percent of the firms (n = 314). Almost 5 percent of these firms contributed more and 3 percent contributed less. The comparable figures for smaller firms (n = 375) were 83, 8, and 7 percent respectively (IPI 1978, 9).

In the case of Canadian-owned firms (both large and small), 10.2 percent said they contributed less after the 1974 legislation as compared with 9.7 percent of subsidiaries of foreign companies. The survey found 78.3 percent of Canadian firms gave the same amount and 8.5 percent gave more as compared with 85.2 and 3.2 percent respectively for subsidiaries of foreign firms.

For the Liberals and the Tories, contributions from individuals are the only other major source of party revenue. For the Liberals, donations from individuals outweighed those from corporations in three of the ten years between 1975 and 1984 — see Table 10-4. For the Tories they were more important in five of the ten years. In fact, in 1981, 1982, and 1983, the Tories raised over 60 percent of their contributions from individuals. As we shall see in Table 10-5, it is the Tories who have been the most successful in using direct-mail techniques to raise money from individuals. They have also been more successful in raising the number of corporate contributors (see Table 10-8 below).

The NDP, not surprisingly, obtains very little money from corporations.[16] Rather it has relied primarily on individual donations and, to a lesser extent, on contributions from trade unions. From 1974 to 1978, unions provided about 15 percent of the party's funds, and as Table 10-4 indicates, this fraction increased sharply in 1979 and 1980, both election years. Since 1981, the federal NDP indicates that over 30 percent of its total contributions came from several provincial party organizations (in B.C., Alberta, Manitoba, Ontario, New Brunswick, Nova Scotia, and the Yukon). The result is that contributions by individuals directly to the federal NDP have declined from 77 to 80 percent of all contributions between 1975 and 1978 to 39.5 percent in 1984.

Perhaps the most extraordinary change in the way the three main parties raise contributions has been the Conservatives' ability to raise about one-half their funds from many individuals, most of whom give less than $100.

The federal Election Expenses Act of 1974 and similar provincial statutes (Boyer, 1978a, 1979) amount to a "democratization of the political influence system" (Osborn 1975, 88) in which members of groups formerly outside that system are being drawn in by means of subsidized campaign contributions. A longtime Tory fund raiser remarked on the increased identification that contributions by the "average guy" bring: "When you contribute money, there's no question that your interest heightens to some degree. You feel more a part of the situation when you've made a tangible contribution. Your identification with the party heightens. There's bigger commitment" (Stevenson 1982, 28).

At the same time, the broadening of the base of party and election financing, in the words of a well-known Liberal MP, "also provided a way out for the larger corporations who were really starting to feel the pinch and who really felt that they ought not to be in this business of donating money anymore, if only because of the interconnection between Government and business" (Stevenson 1982, 24).

Table 10-5 indicates that in 1983 and 1984 the Tories were able to tap more individual donors than the NDP by a substantial margin. Moreover, the Tories have been able to obtain significantly greater average contributions from their donors ($109 vs. $52 in 1984, and $92 vs. $76 in 1983).[17]

The average donation by individuals to the Liberals, on the other hand (with the exception of 1981), has been larger than those to the Tories. The largest difference was in 1984 when the Liberals averaged $178 per individual donor versus $109 for the Tories. However, the Tories generated donations from 93 199 individuals in 1984, compared with only 29 056 for the Liberals. In 1983 the comparable figures were 99 264 and 33 649 respectively. The greater ability of both the Tories and the NDP to tap individuals for donations than the Liberals is well illustrated by the fact that in 1977 the Liberals and Tories received donations from 21 063 and 20 339 individuals while the NDP benefited from 60 169 individual contributors; yet in 1984 the Liberals had increased the number of individual contributors by only 38 percent over 1977, the NDP increased theirs by 33 percent, while the Tories had increased theirs by 358 percent.[18]

4.3.2 Contributions to Candidates

Table 10-2 indicates that during election campaigns the *candidates* of the two main federal parties spend substantially more than do their par-

Table 10–5
NUMBER AND AVERAGE SIZE OF CONTRIBUTIONS BY INDIVIDUALS
TO FEDERAL PARTIES, 1974–84

Individual Contributions		Liberal Party	Progressive Conservative Party	New Democratic Party
1974	number	9882 [a]	6423 [a]	27 910[b]
	average	$112	$99	$46
1975	number		6594 [d]	58 889
	average		$98	$35
		25 870[c]		
1976	number	$114	23 409	56 142
	average		$82	$32
1977	number	21 063	20 339	60 169
	average	$94	$86	$37
1978	number	22 350	35 615	67 133
	average	$94	$75	$38
1979(E)	number	13 025	34 952	63 655
	average	$91	$91	$43
1980(E)	number	17 670	32 720	62 428
	average	$141	$98	$52
1981	number	24 735	48 125	56 545
	average	$85	$90	$51
1982	number	27 968	52 694	66 665
	average	$114	$98	$57
1983	number	33 649	99 264	65 624
	average	$97	$92	$76[e]
1984(E)	number	29 056	93 199	80 027
	average	$178	$109	$52[f]

E = election year
[a] 1/8/74 to 31/7/75
[b] 1/8/74 to 31/12/74
[c] 1/8/75 to 31/12/76
[d] 1/8/75 to 31/12/75
[e] If the $453 365 donation of Irene Dyck is eliminated, the average was $69.
[f] If the $215 767 donation of Irene Dyck is eliminated, the average is $49.

Sources: *Report of the Chief Electoral Officer Respecting Election Expenses, 1979; 1980; 1984*
          (Ottawa: CEO).

ties, while the amounts are similar for the NDP. What are the important sources of contributions to candidates by party? For Conservative candidates as a whole, individuals have accounted for 43.4, 37.7, and 41.6 percent of the total in the 1979, 1980, and 1984 elections respectively. The comparable fraction for Liberal candidates was somewhat lower:

Table 10–6
SOURCES OF CONTRIBUTIONS TO ALL CANDIDATES IN THE GENERAL ELECTIONS OF 1979, 1980 and 1984

Election	Party	Indivi-duals	Business & Commercial Organiza-tions	Unions	Political Orgs. and Registered Parties	Other	Total (%)	Total Contribu-tions ($ 000)
1984								
	PC	41.6	39.6	0*	17.1	1.7	100	11 335
	Lib.	28.4	27.6	0*	41.5	2.4	100	8 392
	NDP	43.2	1.6	13.4	38.7	3.1	100	3 724
1980								
	PC	37.7	31.2	0*	29.3	1.8	100	5 888
	Lib.	34.6	28.2	0*	35.2	2.0	100	6 293
	NDP	38.2	1.7	17.5	29.6	3.0	100	2 674
1979								
	PC	43.4	33.9	0*	20.5	2.2	100	6 086
	Lib.	26.8	22.2	0*	48.3	2.7	100	6 558
	NDP	35.2	1.4	18.2	42.2	2.9	100	2 307

PC = Progressive Conservative
Lib = Liberal
NDP = New Democratic Party
* = less than 0.1%

Source: Computed from the *Report of the Chief Electoral Officer Respecting Election Expenses, 1979; 1980; 1984* (Ottawa: CEO).

26.8, 34.6, and 28.4 percent respectively. One might expect, therefore, that Liberal candidates were more dependent on donations from business. This was not the case. Table 10-6 reveals that corporate donations to Liberal candidates were a smaller fraction of their total contributions than they were for Tory candidates. For example, in 1984 Tory candidates obtained 39.6 percent of their funds from corporations while their Liberal counterparts obtained 27.6 percent of their funds from business. For Liberal candidates, the largest single category of contributions was that of "political organizations and registered parties," that is, provincial and federal party organizations. In 1984, these accounted for 41.5 percent of Liberal candidates' contributions. In 1979 the figure was 48.3 percent. Tory candidates' dependency on party sources appears to have declined over the past three elections — from 20.5 percent in 1979, to 29.3 percent in 1980, to 17.1 percent in 1984.

NDP candidates have to offset their virtual absence of contributions from business by relying more heavily on trade unions (who have provided 13 to 18 percent of contributions) and provincial and federal party organizations, which accounted for 30 to 42 percent of total contributions over the past three general elections.

4.3.3 Conclusions Regarding Questions 2 and 3

Question 2 asked whether corporations still account for a very large fraction of the total revenues of the two leading parties at the federal level. If by "very large fraction" we mean three-quarters or more (or even two-thirds), then we must answer the question in the negative. The data in Table 10-4 indicate that between 1975 and 1984, corporations accounted for 41.3 to 60.0 percent (with the exception of 1979 when they accounted for 74.3 percent) of contributions to the Liberal party and from 27.5 to 59.9 percent for the Conservative party.

With respect to Question 3, dealing with the growth in the number of individual contributors, the data in Table 10-5 make it clear that all three major parties have been successful in increasing the number of contributions from individuals since the 1974 Elections Expenses Act. The Conservatives have been the most successful in terms of both the rate of growth in the number of contributors and in the absolute number of contributors as of 1984. However, the Tories did not surpass the NDP in terms of the total number of individuals contributing until 1983. In terms of the average size of contributions from individuals, both the Liberals and Tories have consistently outperformed the NDP by a large margin.

Regarding the importance of large contributions from individuals we cannot as yet provide an answer. This issue will be addressed again in the next section.

5.0 THE IMPORTANCE OF LARGE CONTRIBUTORS, INDIVIDUAL AND CORPORATE

In George Orwell's *Animal Farm* all the animals were equal, but some were more equal than others. So it is with political contributions. While contributions from all individuals and firms are welcomed by the Liberal and Conservative parties, large donations from both are the most warmly welcomed. In this section I try to answer the following questions:

Q4: Has the requirement that all contributions in excess of $100 be publicly reported reduced the willingness of corporations to make large donations to the federal Liberal and Conservative parties?

Q5: Are political contributions by large corporations usually the same to both the federal Liberal and Conservative parties? (The old rule-of-thumb was said to be 60 percent to the party in power and 40 percent to the leading opposition party.)

Q6: Are virtually all large contributions ($10 000 and over) to the federal Liberal and Conservative parties made by the largest enterprises (e.g., the *Financial Post 500*)?

Q7: Among the largest corporations (e.g., the top 200 nonfinancial corporations), are political contributions to the federal Liberal and Conservative parties approximately proportionate to their sales?

Q8: Among the largest corporations (e.g., the *Financial Post* top 200), do foreign-owned firms contribute less to political parties than do those owned by Canadians?

5.1 Large Contributions by Individuals

As documented above (Tables 10-4, 10-5), the three main federal parties are now quite dependent upon annual contributions from tens of thousands of individuals. Despite the growth in the number of individuals making contributions to all the main parties in Canada, do a few individuals who make large donations account for a significant fraction of the total amount of contributions from individuals?

This is not easily determined. While all donations, whether in cash or kind, over $100 must be publicly reported, it is necessary to go through from 13 000 to 99 000 names of individuals for each of the three major parties for each year since 1974 to obtain a comprehensive answer on the frequency and size of large contributions. Instead, I defined a large contribution as one of $2000 or more and searched the returns filed by the Liberals and Conservatives for 1983 and 1984. A donation of $2000 amounted to some 20 times the average in those years except for the Liberals in 1984 (11.2 times). On the other hand, the net after-tax cost of a $2000 donation is $1500 after the maximum tax credit of $500 is taken into account. This is not a terribly burdensome amount for upper-middle-income Canadians. In 1984, average income per household was $35 853, while 26.8 percent of households had an income of $45 000 or more.[19]

The Conservative party received donations of $2000 or more from 45 individuals in 1983 and from 278 in 1984. The comparable figures for the Liberals were 38 and 28 respectively. See Table 10-7. Only two individuals in 1983 and five in 1984 made a large donation to both parties. The largest single donations were as follows:

	To Liberals	To Conservatives	To NDP
1983	$10 000 (3)	$15 000 (1)	$453 365 (1)
1984	10 000 (2)	50 000 (2)[20]	215 767 (1)

It should be noted that most of the large donations were in the range of $2000 to $2999. In 1983 the Conservatives received only 9 donations of $3000 or more from individuals, while the Liberals received 20. In 1984 the comparable figures were 79 and 6 respectively. The average donation of those making contributions of $2000 or more to the Tories was $2978 in 1983 and $3906 in 1984. For the Liberals, the comparable figures were $3758 and $3150.

Table 10–7

SIZE OF LARGE CONTRIBUTIONS BY INDIVIDUALS TO THE LIBERAL AND CONSERVATIVE PARTIES, 1983 and 1984

($2000 and over)

Size Category	Conservatives		Liberals		Both Parties	
	1983	1984	1983	1984	1983	1984
$ 2 000– 2 999	36	199	18	22	0	0
3 000– 3 999	3	25	8	1	0	0
4 000– 4 999	1	12	3	0	0	1
5 000– 9 999	4	24	6	3	1	3
10 000–19 999	1	9	3	2	1	0
20 000–49 999	0	7	0	0	0	1
50 000 +	0	2	0	0	0	0
Total	45	278	38	28	2	5
Average (large contributions)	$ 2 978	$ 3 906	$ 3 758	$ 3 150	$6 266*	$4 666*
Average (all individual contributions)	$ 92	$ 109	$ 97	$ 178	n/a	n/a
Total number of individual contributors	99 264	93 199	33 649	29 056	n/a	n/a
Total amount of individual contributions ($ 000)	9 106	10 142	3 262	5 181		
Large contributions as a % of all indiv. contributions	1.5%	10.7%	4.4%	1.7%		

* = average per contributor per party; therefore, the average total contribution per contributor
 is double the amount indicated.
n/a = not applicable

Source: Tabulation by the author from the annual returns filed by the parties with the Chief
 Electoral Officer.

Large contributions ($2000 or more) from individuals do not account for a major fraction of all contributions from individuals. For the Tories, such contributions amounted to 1.5 percent of all contributions from individuals in 1983 and 10.7 percent in 1984. For the Liberals, the comparable data are 4.4 and 1.7 percent. In passing, I note that the unusually large donations to the NDP by Mrs. Irene Dyck amounted to 9.1 and 5.2 percent of the party's donations from all individuals in 1983 and 1984 respectively.[21]

In summary, neither major party is heavily dependent on a small number of individuals' personal contributions. Even in 1984, a banner year for Tory money raisers, only 42 individuals gave the party more than $5000 and only 18 gave it more than $10 000. These sums are not so large or so frequent that the Conservative party could not do without them if their donors sought favours in exchange for their contributions. Therefore, with respect to the role of big individual donors in Question 3, we can say that they are few in number and do not account for a major share of contributions from individuals. Because of the absence of data on their role prior to 1974, we cannot say whether their importance has increased or decreased over time.

5.2 Contributions from Corporations

The Conservatives have been successful in sharply increasing the number of firms in recent years from whom it has obtained political contributions — from 5011 in 1980 to 9432 in 1982 to 21 286 in 1984. However, the Tories had over 8000 business contributors in 1978, not an election year, as compared with only 5111 in 1980, an election year. In fact, the Tories had 5720 business donors in 1976, the first twelve-month period for which we have data for the party under the 1974 legislation. Although the Tories have expanded their base of business contributors since 1980, they have not been able to increase the average donation in either constant or nominal dollars. For example, the average in 1983 was $232 compared with from $327 to $394 between 1976 and 1978. See Table 10-8.

The Liberals' business base grew much more slowly in recent years — from 4420 contributors in 1980 to 5652 in 1982 to 6494 in 1984. The last figure for an election year was smaller than the previous year (7536). Moreover, the Liberals were able to tap as many corporations in 1977 as they did in 1982. What is more remarkable is that in the election years of 1979, 1980, and 1984 their total number of business contributors actually fell in comparison to the previous year. However, the average contribution to the Liberal party has been consistently greater than that to the Conservatives. See Table 10-8. But in recent years the Tories have more than made up the difference by having a much larger number of business contributors.

For both parties, there is clearly an "election year effect" present in the past three elections. The average size of business contributions more than doubles over the previous year (unless like 1979 it was also an election year).

From the evidence in Table 10-8 we can answer Question 4 in the negative. Clearly, the number of corporations willing to make donations to the two main federal parties has increased quite dramatically in the past five years — for the Tories in particular, who enjoyed an increase

Table 10–8

CORPORATE CONTRIBUTIONS TO THE LIBERAL AND CONSERVATIVE PARTIES, 1974–84

	Liberal Party		Prog. Conservative	
	Number*	Average	Number*	Average
1974				
	2 418[a]	$ 413	2 034[a]	$479
1975			1 301[b]	364
1976	5 150[c]	500	5 720	337
1977	5 672	404	4 370	394
1978	5 021	496	8 040	327
1979(E)	3 736	1 037	7 691	653
1980(E)	4 420	844	5 011	872
1981	6 039	448	7 312	352
1982	5 652	446	9 432	310
1983	7 536	352	18 067	232
1984(E)	6 494	822	21 286	517

* From 1974 to 1979 the number is the sum of "private corporations" and "public corporations." It excludes "unincorporated organizations." From 1980, the category is "business and commercial organizations."

E = election year
[a] 1/8/74 to 31/7/75
[b] 1/8/75 to 31/12/75
[c] 1/8/75 to 31/12/76

Source: Tabulation by the author from *Report of the Chief Electoral Officer Respecting Election Expenses, 1979; 1980; 1984* (Ottawa: CEO).

of 325 percent between 1980 and 1984. For the Liberals, the increase between 1980 and 1983 was 70 percent (the number fell slightly in 1984). Since any contribution of $100 or more must be publicly reported, the evidence indicates that more corporations are willing to make contributions, including large contributions.

How important are large contributions from corporations? For the purposes of analysis I defined a large contribution from a corporation (or other commercial organizations such as partnerships of professionals) as being $10 000 or over. The federal Conservative party received 43 such contributions in 1983 and 198 in 1984. The average value of these large contributions was just over $18 000 and $22 000 respectively — see Table 10-9. The Liberal party obtained such large contributions from 45 corporations in 1983 and 113 in 1984. The average value of these contributions was just under $20 000 and $21 000 respectively.[22]

Twenty-eight corporations in 1983 and 89 in 1984 donated $10 000

Table 10–9

SIZE OF LARGE CORPORATE CONTRIBUTIONS TO THE LIBERAL AND
CONSERVATIVE PARTIES, 1983 and 1984

($10 000 and over)

Size Category	Conservatives		Liberals		Corps. Contributing to both Liberal and PC parties	
	1983	1984	1983	1984	1983	1984
10 000–14 999	23	94	24	51	0	0
15 000–19 999	4	27	5	21	0	0
20 000–29 999	7	35	3	19	14	38
30 000–49 999	8	25	12	14	3	17
50 000–99 999	1	14	1	8	10	26
100 000 ı	0	3	0	0	1	8
Total	43	198	45	113	28	89
Average (large contributors only)	$18 154	$22 032	$19 976	$20 976	$21 027*	$23 337*
Average (all business contributors)	$ 232	$ 517	$ 352	$ 822	n/a	n/a
Total no. of business and commercial contributors	18 067	21 286	7 536	6 494	n/a	n/a

* average per party
n/a = not applicable

Sources: Tabulations by the author from reports filed by the parties with the Chief Electoral
Officer; and *Report of the Chief Electoral Officer Respecting Election Expenses, 1984*
(Ottawa: CEO).

or more to both the Liberal and Conservative parties. Their average
donation per party was higher than those firms that gave to only one
party (Table 10-9).

Contributions of $10 000 and more accounted for 16.2 percent of the
value of all corporate contributions to the Tories in 1983 and 39.6 percent in 1984. For the Liberal party, although fewer in number, they
were even more important — accounting for 25.4 and 44.4 percent of
total corporate contributions in 1983 and 1984 respectively (Table 10-
10). Put another way, in the election year of 1984 the 198 largest corporate donations to the Tories and the 113 largest to the Liberals accounted
for some two-fifths of all corporate contributions.

The largest single corporate contributions in 1983 and 1984 were as
follows:

To Liberals

1983 $ 51 958 (Canadian Pacific Ltd.)
1984   78 822 (Power Corp.)

To Conservatives

1983 $ 50 000 (Canadian Pacific Ltd.)
1984   150 000 (Candor Investments Ltd.)

The three largest contributors to both parties on a combined basis in 1983 were as follows: Canadian Pacific Ltd. ($101 958), Imasco Ltd. ($66 669), and Brascan Ltd. ($62 400). In 1984 the top three on a combined basis were Candor Investments ($150 000), Bank of Montreal ($150 000), and Royal Bank ($150 000).

It seems fitting that Canada's second-largest firm (in terms of revenues) should be the largest single contributor to both parties in 1983.[23] In 1984 well-known Tory businessman and former Tory candidate Ste-

Table 10–10

DEPENDENCE OF THE FEDERAL LIBERAL AND CONSERVATIVE PARTIES ON LARGE CORPORATE AND INDIVIDUAL CONTRIBUTORS, 1983 and 1984

	Progressive Conservatives		Liberals	
	1983	1984	1983	1984
• Number of individual contributors ≥ $2000	45	278	38	28
• Total large contributions by individuals	$134 000	$1 085 868	$142 804	$88 200
• % of all *individual* contributions	1.5%	10.7%	4.4%	1.7%
• Number of corporate contributors ≥ $10 000	43	198	45	113
• Total contributions by corporations	$781 000	$ 4 362 000	$899 000	$ 2 370 000
• % of all corporate contributions	16.2%	39.6%	25.4%	44.4%
• Total party income	$14 767 000	$21 979 000	$7 736 000	$11 598 000
• Large individual and corporate contributions as a % of total party income	6.2%	24.8%	13.5%	21.2%

Source: Tables 10–7, 10–9.

phen Roman directed $200 250 to his party from two corporations that he controls: Denison Mines ($100 250) and Roman Corp. ($100 000). It is interesting to note that the largest single donor to the Tories in 1984, Candor Investments, is not listed in the *Financial Post 500* or among any of its other specialized categories.

Because individuals and corporations each accounted for roughly one-half of the total contributions to both the Liberal and Conservative parties in 1983 and 1984 (recall Table 10-4), it is desirable to combine large contributors in both categories to see if the parties are heavily dependent upon a very few patrons for their support. In 1984 the Tories obtained one-quarter of their total income from the 278 largest donations by individuals and the 198 largest donations by corporations. The federal Liberals received 21.2 percent of its total income from only 28 individuals and 113 corporations in 1984 (Table 10-10). The dependency on large contributions was much less in 1983, which was not an election year.

Do corporations that make large contributions give to both major parties? The data in Table 10-11 indicate that in 1983 almost two-thirds of the large contributors to each of the parties also made a large contribution to the other major party. In 1984, an election year, 79 percent of the firms making a large contribution to the Liberals also made one to the Conservatives. The reverse was less frequent; only 45 percent of large corporate contributors to the Conservatives also made a large donation to the Liberals.

Of the 28 corporations that made a large donation ($\geq$ $10 000) to both parties in 1983, 18 gave roughly the same amount (± 10 percent) to both parties, while 7 gave at least 10 percent more to the Liberals than the Tories and 3 gave at least 10 percent more to the Tories than the Liberals. In 1984, 50 of the 89 corporations making a large contribution to both parties gave roughly the same amount (± 10 percent) to both parties. Perhaps sensing that the Tories would form the next government, 24 of the 89 large contributors gave at least 10 percent more to the Tories than the Liberals, while 15 favoured the Liberals more than the Tories (Table 10-10). In 1984, of 198 large contributors to the Tories, 109 did not also make a large contribution to the Liberals and of those that did (89), 24 gave at least 10 percent more to the Tories.

These results indicate that corporations that make large political contributions (in this case $10 000 and over) do not give essentially the same amount to the two parties most likely to form a government. Moreover, these data would also contradict the older observation that large donors (particularly large corporations) tend to divide their political contributions 60:40 between the party in power and that in opposition respectively. More evidence with respect to Question 5 is provided in subsection 5.3 below.

Table 10–11
ANALYSIS OF LARGE CORPORATE CONTRIBUTIONS TO THE LIBERAL AND PROGRESSIVE CONSERVATIVE PARTIES, 1983 and 1984
($10 000 and over)

	1983		1984	
	Liberals	PCS	*Liberals*	PCS
Total number of contributions to one or more parties:	45	43	113	198
Average contribution	$19 976	$18 154	$20 976	$22 032
Total ($ 000)	899	781	2 370	4 362
Corporations contributing to only one party:				
Number	17	15	24	109
Average contribution	$15 616	$15 771	$15 374	$20 271
Total ($ 000)	265	237	369	2 210
Corporations contributing to both parties:				
Number	28	28	89	89
Average contribution	$22 624	$19 430	$22 486	$24 188
Total ($ 000)	633	544	2 001	2 153
Contributors contributing same amount to both parties ($\pm$10%)	18		50	
Contributors contributing more than 10% more to the Liberals than to the PCS	7		15	
Contributors contributing more than 10% more to the PCS than to the Liberals	3		24	

Source: Tabulated by the author from the annual returns filed by the parties with the Chief
Electoral Officer.

5.3 Contributions from Large Corporations

Business firms in the *Financial Post 500* (the 500 largest nonfinancial enterprises ranked by sales) accounted for 49 percent of the number of large contributions ($10 000 and over) to both the Liberal and Conservative parties in 1983. They accounted for 54 percent of the large contributions to the Liberals in 1984, but only 38 percent (76 of 198) to the Tories in 1984 (Table 10-11). Even if we add to the largest 500 nonfinancial enterprises the largest 100 private corporations, largest 100 financial corporations, largest 100 subsidiaries, the 100 "most promising" (i.e., smaller but growing corporations), and several other smaller

Table 10–12
CORPORATE POLITICAL CONTRIBUTIONS $10 000 OR OVER BY VARIOUS FINANCIAL POST CATEGORIES, 1983 AND 1984

Financial Post Category	Total Number of Firms in Category	1983		1984	
		Liberal	PC	Liberal	PC
Nonfinancial corp.					
1–100	100	17	19	39	40
100–500	400	5	2	22	36
Private Corp.	100	0	0	1	1
Financial Corp.	100	7	7	10	12
Subsidiaries	100	1	2	4	6
Tomorrow's Cos.	100	0	0	2	1
Life Insurers	25	1	1	2	2
Accounting Firms	20/25	0	2	5	5
Investment Dealers	15	0	1	3	3
Advertising Agencies	15	0	0	1	0
Law Firms	10	0	0	2	1
Total	985/980	31	34	91	108
Number of contributors of ≥$10 000 not in FP categories		14	9	22	90
Total contributors ≥ $10 000		45	43	113	198

Source: Tabulation by the author from the annual returns filed by the parties with the Chief Electoral Officer and the *Financial Post 500* for 1984 and 1985, which are based on 1983 and 1984 data.

categories (Table 10-12), we find that a significant portion of large contributions apparently come from much smaller firms. In 1983, 31 percent of large contributions to the Liberal party came from firms outside the ten *Financial Post* categories; for the Tories it was 21 percent. In 1984 the comparable figures are 19 and 45 percent respectively. In other words, almost one-half the contributions of $10 000 or more to the Conservatives in 1984 did not come from the largest 500 nonfinancial enterprises in Canada or from the largest firms in nine other categories. Therefore, we are led to answer no to Question 6.

Let us look at the "participation rate" among firms in some of the *Financial Post*'s categories. First, even in 1984, a banner year for large corporate contributions, only 40 percent of the top 100 nonfinancial enterprises in Canada gave $10 000 or more to the Liberal party and/or the Conservative party. Among the next 400 largest only 5.5 percent made a large donation to the Liberals, while 9 percent made such a donation to the Tories.

Among the 100 largest financial corporations (including the banks), only 10 made a large donation ($10,000 +) to the Liberals in 1984, while 12 made a large donation to the Tories. The five largest chartered banks were standouts in this regard in both 1983 and 1984:[24]

	To Liberals		To Conservatives	
	1983	1984	1983	1984
• Bank of Montreal	$30 000	$75 000	$30 000	$75 000
• Bank of Nova Scotia	30 000	70 000	30 000	70 000
• Canadian Imperial Bank of Commerce	31 500	70 000	30 000	70 113
• Royal Bank of Canada	30 103	75 000	30 000	75 000
• Toronto-Dominion Bank	30 101	70 466	19 147	70 187

These contributions suggest the limit on contributions established by Pierre Trudeau no longer applies.[25] The contrast to the contributions of other financial institutions is obvious:

	To Liberals	To Conservatives
• Canada Trust	$15 000	$23 000
• First City Financial (& First City Trust)	15 000	37 750 + 12 500
• Royal Trust	14 253	12 282
• National Bank of Canada	30 020	0
• North West Trust	0	15 000
• Western Capital Trust	0	10 100

There was a fairly high participation rate among the largest accounting firms. Five of the top 25 gave $10 000 or more to both the Liberals and the Tories in 1984:

	To Liberals	To Conservatives
• Clarkson Gordon	$20 421	$16 822
• Coopers & Lybrand	39 204	39 022
• Ernst and Whinney	15 000	62 108
• Peat Marwick Mitchell	30 829	30 454
• Thorne, Riddell	19 720	25 812

Previous research indicated that oil companies, like the big banks, were an important source of funds for the Liberal and Conservative parties.[26] I found this to be the case as well, as these data on large contributions in 1984 indicate:

	To Liberals	To Conservatives
• Canadian Occidental Petroleum	$30 000	$30 000
• Gulf Canada	26 200	25 000
• Hiram Walker Resources	15 000	0
• Husky Oil	27 500	23 458

	To Liberals	To Conservatives
• Norcen Energy Resources	10 969	10 521
• Nova, an Alberta Corp.	25 903	25 000
• Suncor Inc.	12 412	15 632
• Union Oil Co.	20 000	25 500
• Canadian Superior Oil	0	18 000
• Carter Oil and Gas	5 000	10 000
• Chevron Canada Ltd.	0	26 600
• Home Oil Co.	0	12 726
• Ranger Oil	0	26 600
• Walker-Home Oil	0	10 688

It is very important to appreciate the number of very large oil companies (and their rank on the *Financial Post 500*) that did *not* make a large contribution to either of the two main parties:

#5 Imperial Oil Ltd.	#31 Total Petroleum (North America) Ltd.
9 Texaco Canada Inc.	37 Dome Petroleum Ltd.
10 Shell Canada Ltd.	55 Amoco Canada Petroleum
14 Petro-Canada (a federal crown corporation)	60 Mobil Oil Canada
	68 Ultramar Canada Inc.

To put the oil companies' contributions in 1984 into perspective, it should be appreciated that the five largest banks gave $360 466 to the Liberals as compared with $172 984 from nine oil companies. The five banks gave $360 300 to the Tories in 1984 as compared with $269 725 from thirteen oil companies.

Among nonfinancial firms in Canada, a position in the *Financial Post*'s top 200 is a good indicator of large size. For example, the list for 1984 (based on 1983 sales) indicates the size of the companies demarking the size cohorts in Table 10-13:[27]

#1	General Motors of Canada Ltd.	$16 298 million
51	Inco Ltd.	1 901
101	Dominion Textile Inc.	878
151	United Co-ops of Ontario	538
200	Canadair Ltd.	376

The data in Table 10-13 enables one to compute "participation rates" in terms of both large ($10 000 +) and small (under $10 000) political contributions in 1983 and 1984 for the top 200 firms in Canada. Our broadest generalization is that in these two years about one-half of all the firms in the top 200 made a political contribution to either or both main parties. In 1983, 47.5 percent of the top 200 gave to the Liberals, while 51.5 percent gave to the Tories. In 1984, an election year, 47 percent gave to the Liberals and 56 percent gave to the Tories.

Table 10–13
POLITICAL CONTRIBUTIONS BY FIRMS IN THE FINANCIAL POST 500 TO THE LIBERAL AND CONSERVATIVE PARTIES, 1983 and 1984

Financial Post Rank*	1983				1984			
	Liberal Party		Conservative Party		Liberal Party		Conservative Party	
	≥ $10 000	< $10 000	≥ $10 000	< $10 000	≥ $10 000	< $10 000	≥ $10 000	< $10 000
1– 50	10	15	12	14	21	4	20	6
51–100	7	20	7	24	18	11	20	12
101–150	2	18	0	19	8	16	12	15
151–200	0	23	0	27	4	17	4	23
201–300	3	DK	1	DK	5	DK	10	DK
301–400	0	DK	0	DK	4	DK	7	DK
401–500	0	DK	1	DK	1	DK	3	DK
Total	22	76**	21	84**	61	48**	76	56**

* Nonfinancial corporations as ranked by sales.
** Total for firms in the top 200 only.
DK = Don't know, as only the top 200 firms were analyzed for contributions under $10 000.

Source: Same as Table 10–12.

In terms of large contributions, the data in Table 10-13 reveal a major difference between nonelection and election years. In 1983, 9 percent of the top 200 made a large contribution to the Liberals, while 9.5 percent made one to the Conservatives. In 1984, however, these percentages rose to 25.5 and 28 percent respectively. I note, however, that the largest contributions in an election year came at the expense of the frequency of smaller ones. That is, an election year did not increase the top 200's overall rate of participation in making contributions to the two main parties. In 1983, 38 percent of the top 200 firms made a contribution under $10 000 to the Liberals, while 42 percent made such a contribution to the Tories. In 1984, an election year, the comparable figures were 24 and 28 percent respectively.

The data in Table 10-13 do not indicate very large variations in the overall participation rate by size cohort within the top 200 in 1983 and 1984. For example, in 1983 one-half the top 50 made a contribution to the Liberal party and 52 percent made one to the Conservatives. Among firms in the 151–200 cohort, the comparable figures were 46 and 54 percent respectively. In 1984, across the four cohorts, the percentage of firms giving to the Liberals was 40 to 58 percent, while the percentage giving to the Tories ranged from 52 to 64 percent.

The participation rate in terms of large contributions is much lower for firms ranked from 201 to 500 on the *Financial Post* list. In 1983 only 1 percent of such firms made a large donation ($10 000 +) to the Liberals and 0.67 percent made such a donation to the Tories. However, the election year effect was present for these smaller firms. Three percent made a large donation to the Liberal party in 1984, while 6.7 percent made one to the Conservatives. See Table 10-13.

Of those firms among the top 200 that made any political contributions in 1984, only a small fraction gave to only one of the leading parties. Only 4 percent of the firms giving to the Liberals did not also make some contribution to the Tories. However, 15.2 percent of the top 200 firms that gave to the Tories gave nothing to the Liberals. Among the cohort of firms ranked 151 to 200 this ratio was 25.9 percent. See Table 10-14.

Table 10-14 also reveals that even in an election year, the great majority of political contributions by large firms (i.e., those in the top 200) are not that large:

Contribution in 1984	To Liberals	To Conservatives
under $5000	26.5%	26.8%
$5000–9999	22.2	23.4
$10 000–14 999	24.2	20.5

In other words, only 27.4 percent of contributions to the Liberals by firms in the top 200 were $15 000 or more, while 29.3 percent of those

Table 10–14

SIZE DISTRIBUTION OF POLITICAL CONTRIBUTIONS BY FIRMS IN THE FINANCIAL POST TOP 200, 1984

Size of Contribution	Ranking								Total	
	1–50		51–100		101–150		151–200			
	Lib	PC	Lib	PC	Lib	PC	Lib	PC	Lib	PC
0– 999	1	1	1	2	2	2	2	3	6	8
1 000– 4 999	0	1	3	5	7	6	10	10	20	22
5 000– 9 999	3	4	7	5	7	7	5	10	22	26
10 000–14 999	5	3	11	9	5	8	3	3	24	23
15 000–19 999	6	3	1	4	2	1	1	1	10	9
20 000–29 999	4	5	6	5	0	1	0	0	10	11
30 000–49 999	5	8	0	2	1	1	0	0	6	11
50 000–99 999	1	1	0	0	0	0	0	0	1	1
100 000 +	0	0	0	0	0	1	0	0	0	1
Total	25	26	29	32	24	27	21	27	99	112
Number of contributions only to party indicated	2	3	0	3	1	4	1	7	4	17

Source: Same as Table 10–12.

made to the Tories were of this size. (Recall that in 1984 about one-half the firms in the top 200 made no contribution to either party.)

A more detailed analysis of the political contributions in 1984 of the top 100 nonfinancial enterprises in Canada is presented in Table 10-15. Forty-six percent and 42 percent of the firms made no political contributions to the Liberal or Conservative party respectively — even in an election year. Of those making a donation, 15 gave the Liberals less than $10 000 and 18 gave the Tories less than $10 000. Some of the contributions were very small when the size of the firms involved is taken into account. Recall that the firms in the top 100 had revenues in 1984 from $879 million to $16.3 billion. For example, 8 of the donations to the Liberals and 12 to the Tories were $5000 or less. On the other hand, 16 firms gave the Liberals $20 000 or more and 21 gave the Tories $20 000 or more.

Did the old rule of thumb of giving 60 percent of a firm's total political contributions to the party in power and 40 percent to the opposition party hold in 1984 for firms in Canada's top 100? It no longer holds. Fifteen firms gave the Tories 50 percent more than they gave to the Liberals, who formed the government until September 1984, while for only four firms was the reverse the case. Some extreme examples of "un-

Table 10–15
ANALYSIS OF POLITICAL CONTRIBUTIONS BY FIRMS IN THE
FINANCIAL POST TOP 100, 1984

Category	Liberal Party	Conservative Party
• No contribution	46	42
• Contribution:		
— under $10 000	15	18
— $10 000–19 999	23	19
— $20 000 and over	16	21
	54	58
• Contribution *only* to the party indicated	2	6
• Number of contributions to the other party more than 50% greater than to to the party indicated	15	4

Source: Same as Table 10–12.

balanced" major corporate political donations to the two major parties in 1984 were the following:

	To Liberals	To Conservatives
Canadian Tire	0	$36 000
George Weston	$15 000	35 000
Consolidated Bathurst	7 000	22 000
Nabisco Brands	20 285	35 500
Seagram Co.	15 597	30 240
Hiram Walker Resources	15 000	0

Among the top 200 nonfinancial enterprises in Canada, are political contributions roughly proportionate to size? Recall Question 7. I have addressed this question for 1983 and 1984 in relation to sales or revenues of firms in four cohorts within the top 200.[28] The measure of the relative size of political contributions is the number of cents in contributions per $1000 of revenues of the median firm in each size cohort. The results reported in Table 10-16 suggest quite clearly that the "proportionality hypothesis" should be rejected for both parties in both years. The data indicate that, proportionately, firms in the top 50 give less than those ranking from 51 to 200. For example, in 1983, firms in the top 50, on average, gave 33 cents per $1000 of revenue (or sales) of the median firm to the Liberals and 31 cents to the Tories. However, in the next three cohorts (in descending order), firms gave 60, 60, and 55 cents to the Liberals and 67, 40, and 55 cents per $1000 of revenue to the Tories in 1983.

In 1984 contributions in relation to revenues were higher to both par-

Table 10–16
POLITICAL CONTRIBUTIONS OF FIRMS IN THE FINANCIAL POST TOP 200, 1983 and 1984

Year and Party	Financial Post Rank			
	1–50	*51–100*	*101–150*	*151–200*
1983 — Liberals				
No. ≥ $10 000	10	7	2	0
No. < $10 000	15	20	18	23
Total $	279 388	179 859	73 693	50 141
Average $	11 176	6 661	3 685	2 180
Contributions per $1000 of revenues* (cents)	33	60	60	65
1983 — Progressive Conservatives				
No. ≥ $10 000	12	7	0	0
No. < $10 000	14	24	19	27
Total $	266 259	233 469	47 418	59 017
Average $	10 241	7 531	2 496	2 186
Contributions per $1000 of revenue* (cents)	31	67	40	55
1984 — Liberals				
No. ≥ $10 000	21	18	8	4
No. < $10 000	4	11	16	17
Total $	507 407	316 183	173 050	102 732
Average $	20 296	10 903	7 210	4 892
Contributions per $1000 of revenue* (cents)	59	93	104	109
1984 — Progressive Conservatives				
No. ≥ $10 000	20	20	12	4
No. < $10 000	6	12	15	23
Total $	567 246	377 426	316 502	136 015
Average $	21 817	11 795	11 722	5 038
Contributions per $1000 of revenue*			170	
(cents)	63	100	116**	112

* cents per $1000 of revenue of the "median" firm in the cohort, i.e., #25, #75, #125, #175.
** 116 without the largest contribution of $100 250 in this cohort.

Source: Same as Table 10–12.

ties, presumably because it was an election year. (Recall Tables 10-8 and 10-13.) With respect to the Liberals, firms in the 151–200 cohort gave, on average, in proportionate terms, 85 percent more than those in the top 50 (109 vs. 59 cents per $1000 of revenue of the median firm). Firms in the two intermediate cohorts also gave substantially more in proportionate terms.

Average contributions to the Tories in 1984 increased as a fraction of sales of the median firm from 63 cents per $1000 of revenue for the top 50 to 100 cents for those firms ranked 51 to 100 on the *Financial Post* list. Because of one very large contribution in the 101–150 cohort, the average amount of contributions per $1000 of revenue of the median firm was 170 cents while it was 112 cents for the firms ranked 151 to 200.

On the basis of the foregoing analysis, we answer Question 7 in the negative. However, more detailed calculations relating average contributions to the average volume of sales (or assets or profits) of all the firms in each size cohort might fail to reject the proportionality hypothesis. The same thing may occur if a more complex multivariate analysis were used.

5.4 Political Contributions in Relation to the Ownership of Large Corporations

I now examine Question 8, derived from the previous findings of Wearing (1981, 201–5), based on the contribution to the Liberal party of the 122 largest financial and nonfinancial firms in Canada in 1978. He provided evidence showing that foreign-owned firms in Canada donate less frequently and in small amounts to political parties. Only one-quarter of the wholly foreign-owned firms made any contribution to the federal Liberals in 1978, and the average donation was just over $3900. One-half the firms where foreigners had a majority interest donated, and their average donation was just over $7100. Large Canadian-owned industrial firms donated an average of $11 000, and over 70 percent of firms in the category made a donation. This ratio was 82 percent for Canadian-owned financial institutions that contributed an average of about $9100 each. The big contributors, over $10 000 and over $20 000, were disproportionately domestically owned firms.

Table 10-17 shows the average size of corporate contributions to both the Liberal and Conservative parties in 1983 and 1984 for the 200 largest nonfinancial enterprises in Canada. Financial enterprises were ignored because in virtually every case no foreigner can own more than 10 percent of the voting shares. Three ownership categories are distinguished: domestically owned firms; foreign ownership of 50 to 99 percent of the firm; and 100 percent foreign-owned firms.

If we divide the results into eight cells (firms ranked 1–100 and 101–200,

Table 10–17

AVERAGE POLITICAL CONTRIBUTIONS AMONG THE TOP 200 ENTERPRISES IN CANADA IN RELATION TO OWNERSHIP, 1983 and 1984

Financial Post Rank		1983 Liberals			1983 Conservatives			1984 Liberals			1984 Conservatives		
		D	F 50-99	F100	D	F 50-99	F100	D	F 50-99	F100	D	F 50-99	F100
1-50	no.	22	1	2	23	2	1	22	1	2	23	2	1
	avg.	$12 064	$12 662	$ 864	$10 571	$9 518	$4 086	$21 371	$26 200	$5 527	$22 578	$12 641	$22 681
51-100	no.	16	5	6	20	5	6	17	7	5	19	7	6
	avg.	$ 7 544	$ 7 507	$3 604	$7 231	$7 104	$8 948	$10 716	$14 194	$6 931	$12 618	$14 956	$ 5 498
1-100	avg.	$10 161	$ 8 366	$2 919	$9 009	$7 794	$8 253	$16 727	$15 695	$6 530	$18 072	$14 442	$ 7 953
101-150	no.	11	3	6	10	4	5	13	7	4	16	7	4
	avg.	$ 4 321	$ 4 484	$2 119	$2 883	$1 830	$2 254	$ 7 994	$ 6 697	$5 564	$14 137	$ 5 678	$12 640
151-200	no.	15	2	6	20	1	6	15	2	4	19	3	5
	avg.	$ 1 976	$ 930	$3 107	$1 907	$2 648	$2 597	$ 5 048	$ 7 074	$3 214	$ 4 649	$ 6 000	$ 5 935
101-200	avg.	$ 2 969	$ 3 062	$2 613	$2 232	$1 994	$2 441	$ 6 416	$ 6 780	$4 389	$ 8 986	$ 5 775	$10 026

D = domestically owned firms, i.e., foreign ownership 0–49% as indicated by the *Financial Post*.
F50–99 = foreign ownership from 50 to 99% of the firm as indicated by the *Financial Post*.
F100 = 100% foreign owned as indicated by the *Financial Post*.

Source: Tabulation by the author from the annual returns filed by the parties with the Chief Electoral Officer and the *Financial Post 500* for 1984 and 1985, which are based on 1983 and 1984 data.

by two parties, by two years), we find that in only three of the cells did the hypothesized relationship with respect to the average size of donations hold; namely, that Canadian-owned firms (D) gave more than did firms where foreigners own a majority of the shares (F50–99), which in turn gave more than wholly foreign-owned firms (F100). The clearest case that supports Wearing's finding is among the 100 largest firms that gave to the Tories in 1984. The average for Canadian-owned firms was $18 072, while that for majority foreign-owned firms was $14 442. Wholly foreign-owned subsidiaries gave an average of only $7953.

In four of the eight cells, the average donation of F50–99 and F100 corporations combined was not significantly different from the average of Canadian-owned firms in the same cell. For example, in 1983 the average donation to the Conservatives by 30 Canadian-owned firms in the 101–200 cohort was $2232. The average in the same cohort for 16 firms with 50 to 100 percent foreign ownership was $2301.

In summary, according to the data in Table 10-17, Wearing's hypothesis should probably be rejected, although in a minority of instances the data support it.

5.5 Contributions by Interest Groups

Public choice theorists, notably Downs (1957), argue that political parties "sell" the promise of policies favourable to particular interest groups in exchange for political support from those groups. One of the most important types of support consists of contributions to parties and candidates, hence Question 9:

Q9: Do interest groups make very substantial contributions to those political parties and candidates believed to have a reasonable chance of forming a government in Canada?

While interest groups are important sources of political contributions in the U.S., particularly through the use of political action committees,[29] I found that interest groups were unimportant sources of contributions to either the Liberal or Conservative parties in 1983 and 1984 — despite the fact that the *Directory of Associations in Canada* lists approximately 11 000 associations of all types (Land 1984).

Indeed, in 1984, an election year, the total value of contributions to the Liberals by 81 interest groups (defined broadly to include trade unions, government organizations, as well as trade, professional, and ethnic associations) was $32 454. This amount was less than one-half the contribution of any of the five largest chartered banks. Only 5 contributions were $1000 or more. The Tories in 1984 received only $12 920 from some 27 interest groups; only 3 of these contributions exceeded $1000.[30] See Table 10-18.

In comparing the 39 associations contributing over $100 to the Liberals to the Tories' list of contributors over $100, only four associations were found to have contributed over $100 to both parties in 1984.

In 1983, the Liberals received $12 469 from 30 interest groups. Only one contribution exceeded $1000. Of the 39 associations giving over $100 to the Liberals in 1984, only 8 had given over $100 in 1983.

The larger contributions by interest groups to both parties in 1984 has an interesting pattern. Almost all of the trade associations gave only to the Liberals, while the reverse was the case for professional bodies. Ethnic groups, including Indian bands, gave exclusively to the Liberals. See Table 10-18.

Particularly surprising was the small number and small size of political contributions by trade associations. The only one of note was that of the Pharmaceutical Manufacturers Association of Canada. Its contributions were as follows:

	1983	1984
To Liberals	$3 000	$3 900
To Conservatives	3 375	3 595

PMAC's contributions in both years were the largest by any interest group (excluding individual corporations) to both parties. Its arch rival, the Canadian Drug Manufacturers Association, did not contribute over $100 to the Liberals or Tories in 1983 or 1984. This is surprising in light of the fact that both associations have been locked in a desperate struggle over the compulsory licensing provision in the Patent Act for several years. PMAC was trying to have the provision removed, while CDMA wanted it retained.[31]

In summary, the evidence for 1983 and 1984 is unequivocal: interest groups as such, as distinct from individual corporations, do not constitute an important source of political contributions. In 1984, an election year, the total of their contributions was less than any one of the five big chartered banks.

6.0 POLITICAL RESOURCES OTHER THAN CAMPAIGN CONTRIBUTIONS

Some of the most valuable resources — other than campaign contributions — to assist in election campaigns are those available only to the party in power acting as the government of the day. It can spend public money in ways that result in partisan advantages. These techniques include the following:

6.1 Government Advertising

In the months preceding an election campaign, it is common to observe an increase in government advertising designed to connect the party in power to the beneficial actions of the government. For example, the

Table 10–18
CONTRIBUTIONS TO POLITICAL PARTIES BY VARIOUS INTEREST GROUPS, 1984

Interest Group	Liberals ($)	PCs ($)
Business/Trade Associations:		
• Association of Canadian Advertisers	373	—
• Assoc. of Canadian Distillers	400	163
• Brewers Assoc. of Canada	722	—
• Business Council on National Issues	400	—
• Canadian Chamber of Commerce	400	—
• Canadian Construction Assoc.	400	
• Canadian Federation of Independent Business	400	—
• Canadian Manufacturers' Assoc.	400	—
• Canadian Recording Industry Assoc.	200	504
• Canadian Shipbuilding & Ship Repairing Industry Assoc.	—	1000
• Canadian Soft Drink Assoc.	208	—
• Canadian Textile Institute	400	—
• Canadian Trucking Assoc.	400	—
• Dominion Marine Assoc.	400	—
• Mechanical Contractors Assoc.	—	170
• Pharmaceutical Manufacturers Assoc. of Canada	3900	3595
• Toronto Construction Assoc.	651	—
Professional Groups:		
• Canadian Chiropractic Assoc.	500	500
• Cdn. Assoc. of University Teachers	800	—
• Assoc. Médicale du Québec	—	498
• Canadian Association of Optometrists	—	163
• Canadian Medical Association	—	815
• Eastern Ontario Chiropractic Assoc.	—	1800
• Ontario Medical Association	—	375
Other Interest Groups:		
• Campbell River Band Council	1000	—
• Canadian Jewish Congress	800	—
• Canadian Polish Congress	404	—
• International Fund for Animal Welfare (Cdn.)	2400	—
• Labourer's International Union of North America	1075	
• National Indian Brotherhood	800	—
• Montreal Lake Indian Band	595	—
• Conne River Indian Band	1336	—
• Fédération de francophones Hors Québec	800	—
• St. Boniface Hospital	792	—
• X-Kalay Foundation (Man) Inc.	595	—

Source: Tabulated by the author from the returns of the parties filed with the Chief Electoral Officer.

Conservative MP for Western Arctic wrote to the chief electoral officer after the last general election with the following complaint:

> The attached brochure entitled "We're in it Together," published by the Government of Canada, was circulated throughout the Northwest Territories during the election campaign. It was an insert in the 20th July, 1984 edition of *News/North* and was also an insert in other local papers at or about the same time. The brochure is in Liberal party colours and was evidently designed to complement and be part of the Liberal party campaign.

The MP condemned this practice for three reasons:

> Firstly, it is a charge against all taxpayers including many of whom may not wish to help finance a party campaign. Secondly, it appears to be a mechanism for circumventing the rules governing the election expenses, and thirdly, it gives an unfair advantage to members of the incumbent party. The practice ought to be prohibited by law. (Chief Electoral Officer 1984, 77)

6.2 Order-in-Council Appointments

It is common practice in Canada to appoint party loyalists to order-in-council positions, that is, those at the discretion of the cabinet. (However, one can go too far and create an adverse public reaction, as the last-minute appointments of Liberal prime ministers Pierre Trudeau and John Turner in 1984 indicate.)[32] The number and scope of order-in-council appointments are enormous. "There are at least 3,500 order-in-council appointments that can be made by the Prime Minister, and about 500 are such high-level jobs as ambassadors, judges, deputy ministers and heads of key government agencies" (MacGregor 1985, 11). It has been reported that the federal cabinet controls some 4500 appointments.[33]

Between October 1984 and mid-June 1985, the federal Tories filled some 1200 posts — largely with the party faithful. Officials within the Prime Minister's Office receive nominations from ten provincial advisory committees on appointments. These are fed into a national advisory committee on patronage appointments. They then go to the Cabinet Committee on Priorities and Planning, but the final decision rests with the prime minister (MacGregor 1985, 10). *Maclean's* describes the background of Joan Price-Winser, Canada's new consul-general in Los Angeles: "Although the socially prominent 59-year-old Montrealer had had little experience in paying jobs, Price-Winser did serve the Tories faithfully through eight elections as a campaign organizer, and she helped run the Mulroney hospitality suite at the 1976 Conservative leadership convention in Ottawa" (MacGregor 1985, 10).

The federal Liberals were particularly solicitous toward former candidates when they were in power:

In the first nine years of the Trudeau government, 160 of the appointments approved by cabinet went to former Liberal candidates or their spouses. At least 50 of the judges appointed by Trudeau were Liberal candidates. More? At least eight members of the Immigration Appeal Board had been Liberal candidates; at least 17 members of the Unemployment Insurance Commission boards of referees; at least 12 members of the Canadian Pension Commission; at least four members of the Parole Board.

When B.C. voters in the 1972 election defeated 10 Liberal MPs, the Trudeaucrats promptly fixed up seven of them with jobs. If the voters repudiated them, then the voters must be wrong. The government must correct that error. Of the 29 men that the prime minister appointed to his first cabinet in 1968 (only four are left), 14 of them have been rewarded with safe appointments.[34]

Order-in-council appointments are also important to provincial governments. As a lame-duck premier, Frank Miller made more than 350 order-in-council appointments in the two months between his election and the defeat of his minority government.[35] (The Ontario cabinet has some 3500 positions it can award.) Party affiliation can be important even in civil service appointments in the Maritimes:

In Nova Scotia, Ron Russell, the minister in Tory Premier John Buchanan's cabinet responsible for Nova Scotia's Civil Service Commission, admits that party affiliation plays a role in nearly 300 appointments that the cabinet makes and in the as many as 1,000 civil service hirings a year. "If I knew of a position and I was going to recommend somebody," said Russell, "seven times out of 10 that person would be a member of the Conservative party." (MacGregor 1985, 15)

6.3 Other Methods

1. Political benefits may flow from the careful targeting and timing of new expenditures programs in marginal ridings in the few months prior to election date. An outstanding example of this type was the $2.4-billion Special Recovery Program to create 100 000 new jobs announced by the Liberals in the budget of April 1983. According to *Maclean's*, the government drafted more than 100 press releases and erected 164 large signs ($1300 each) and over 400 smaller ones at project sites. The funds were not uniformly distributed:

Quebec, with 74 of its 75 seats held by Liberals, has received the lion's share of the program money (an estimated $639 million).

Ontario's share is substantial (an estimated $301 million). The Maritimes were well cared for ($309 million), but the western provinces, with the exception of British Columbia ($137 million), did not do so well (only $166 million in total).[36]

External Affairs Minister Allan MacEachen's riding alone received $40 million in project funds, prompting the leader of the opposition to say that Cape Breton Island "may soon sink under the weight of federal dollars."

This type of activity might be described as politically expedient decision making recognizing the room for discretion accorded to the cabinet and its individual members. Others may view it as a type of collective bribe using public funds. Noonan (1984, 704) distinguishes between political expediency and bribes. He emphasizes that "political expediency" carries with it political accountability and that "it is supposed, not unreasonably, that perceptions of political advantage by the accountable officeholder will often coincide with what is the public good." On the other hand, in the case of a bribe, "there is no accountability but to the briber."

2. It may be very helpful for electoral purposes to raise the visibility of MPs and cabinet members of the party in power by more travel, more speeches, more policy announcements — all of which are backed up by large-scale communications efforts of government departments.[37] This involves a larger number of publicly funded official functions that act as an excellent substitute for electioneering. Indeed, in some instances "just doing the public's business" is the best method of campaigning. Ministers can be seen to be "above the rough and tumble" of partisan competition: they can aspire to the title of "statesman" rather than "grasping politician."

3. The Westminster model of government provides an enormous number of opportunities for ministers to exercise their discretion. As an election approaches, they can give the greatest weight to short-run political considerations in exercising their discretion, which always amounts to a decision as to "who gets what" from government.[38] The exercise of discretion can go so far as to amount to the selective enforcement of statutes and regulations.

6.4 Understanding Patronage

Patronage must be placed in the broader context of maintaining political parties and financing electoral campaigns. Parties and individual politicians need resources to run for office. Campaign contributions include the donation of services such as loyalty and support for the party and its nominees, particularly when the party is not in power. Some "contributors" do not want to be "paid" for their efforts and support.

Indeed, for the party or politician to try to do so would violate the norms of some supporters. These people can be rewarded through a variety of nonpecuniary means by being given "inside" information, by expressions of appreciation and regard, by personal contact with leading figures in the party, by informal access when problems do arise, or by emphasizing the collaborative effort of achieving a goal — electing an individual or getting the party into office.

A strong web of human relationships are woven by reciprocity, a powerful social norm — see section 8.2 below. It is perfectly natural that individuals who work for a candidate and/or party, and who remain loyal in the face of electoral defeat, should expect to be rewarded in some way when it is possible to reward them with more than a pat on the back (which is also important). The *quid pro quo* need not be contemporaneous; it need not be of equivalent value; nor is it necessary to reward every individual who provides political help. But rewards must be offered to those who have aided the party in the past and are perceived by others as deserving of a reward. Without such inducements, few contributions to the organization will be forthcoming in the future. It is unrealistic to expect that by satisfying affiliative needs, by being personally grateful, and by offering esteem, a politician or party can command the loyalty and support of those who are willing to support it with more than their vote.

The party in power can use the resources of the state to favour its own, and it is argued that it can do this without sacrificing the level of job competence. The fact is that filling many public jobs is a matter of "satisficing"; that is, it consists of choosing the first acceptable candidate who is also a supporter or at least neutral toward the party in power. "Competence is the key," says one Tory. "Some of these appointees have no political color. Others are political, but they have to be competent."[39] Former Liberal cabinet minister Robert Kaplan explains the tradition of patronage appointments in Canada:

> There is an area where I think it's important for the government to have political confidence in the people to whom it is giving government business. . . . Where competitive bidding doesn't work, where developing the image of the government doesn't work, where price competition is not a factor, patronage has been the traditional Canadian method of awarding work in those areas. . . . The Liberals did it and the Conservatives are doing it now.[40]

In May 1984 then opposition leader Brian Mulroney vowed that "there'll be jobs for Liberals and NDPs too after I've been Prime Minister for 15 years and I can't find a living, breathing Tory in the country."[41] As prime minister, he is well on his way to keeping his promise.

George Washington Plunkitt was a leader in the Tammany Hall organization in New York for many years straddling the turn of the century.

While this was the "golden age" of machine[42] or boss politics, his views on party loyalty, patronage, and ingratitude in politics are highly relevant today. Loyalty was the first article in Plunkitt's creed — a personal loyalty to people who have helped you in the past and will support you in the future. As he saw and practised it, a politician gets his or her constituents jobs and other forms of government aid; they show their gratitude by voting for him or her or for those he or she supports.

The essence of Plunkitt's politics — and still the basis of all political organizations — was reciprocity or the exchange of favours. Not only is the individual to be loyal to the party, but the party is to reward its supporters. Plunkitt agreed with his strongest opponents on one thing: "When a man works in politics, he should get something out of it" (Riordon 1948, 52). Patronage, in Plunkett's view, is absolutely necessary to maintaining a viable political organization: "I acknowledge that you can't keep an organization together without patronage. Men ain't in politics for nothin'. They want to get somethin' out of it" (Riordon 1948, 51).

Obviously, not everyone agrees that patronage is a necessary evil in politics. Columnist Don McGillivray argues that "patronage is like weeds in the garden." While one can never be rid of them completely, they have to be fought on a continuous basis: "But if we quit fighting, the garden will soon be overrun with weeds and the political system with nepotism and cronyism. Reducing patronage to a minimum isn't going to leave the party system without grease or glue or cause it to wither away."[43] Finally, McGillivray argues, participation in politics not only should not be, but is not, simply a question of offering tangible rewards using the public purse:

> To say that people only work for political parties because they hope to profit personally by a turn at the public trough is to take an excessively cynical view of things. Thousands of Canadians contribute work and give money to political parties with no thought of a government job. What sustains them? They believe in their cause. They see themselves as the good guys, the forces of right and reason. They believe the other parties are bad for the nation or province.[44]

7.0 GAPS IN THE LEGISLATION?

Despite the 1974 reforms of federal election expenses legislation (and subsequent amendments), there remain a number of areas not covered by the expenditure limits, disclosure requirements, and so on. As a result, both parties/candidates and donors have "more room" in raising and spending money for political purposes than the previous discussion of the 1974 reform legislation would suggest.

7.1 Personal Benefits

Some politicians accept personal benefits in kind from wealthy individuals or from corporations. Examples are not hard to find. In October 1984 Prime Minister Mulroney and his family enjoyed a Florida vacation at the home of Paul Desmarais who controls Power Corporation, a major conglomerate.[45] The *Globe and Mail* questioned Mulroney's judgment: "Mr. Desmarais is bound to have many economic ties with the federal Government. Should the Prime Minister indebt himself to any such individual, even in full public view?"[46] This move by Desmarais shows his agility in forming political alliances. He has long been thought to be close to senior Liberals, including Pierre Trudeau when he was prime minister. Moreover, Desmarais is related by marriage to Jean Chrétien. It is said that he was one of the main financial backers of Mulroney's unsuccessful but most expensive campaign for the Tory leadership in 1976.[47]

In 1965 Prime Minister Lester Pearson used the French West Indies vacation home of David Rockefeller, whose cousin's bank in Canada (the Mercantile) was about to be affected by legislation then pending in the House of Commons. We know also that Alberta premier Peter Lougheed accepted free tickets from CP Air to enjoy a winter vacation in Hawaii with his family. Several federal and provincial cabinet ministers have been slightly embarrassed when it was revealed that they had flown in corporate jets to vacation spots or during the course of their work.[48]

Whitaker, in his book on the organization and financing of the Liberal party between 1930 and 1958, notes that "there was no shortage of wealthy businessmen who felt it worthwhile, for whatever reason, to become financial benefactors of leading Liberals" (1977, 197). A succession of Liberal prime ministers — W. L. Mackenzie King, Louis St. Laurent, and Lester Pearson — received gifts in cash or in kind, or annuities to enable them to assume the rigors of high office. The largest donation to finance Lester Pearson's "modest annuity" came from the McConnell sugar interests in Montreal. It appears that this industry enjoyed "the somewhat curious immunity . . . from prosecution under anti-combines legislation throughout both the St. Laurent and Pearson administrations" (Whitaker 1977, 197). More recently, a group of business people, who wished to remain anonymous, paid some $250 000 to construct an indoor swimming pool for Prime Minister Trudeau adjacent to the prime minister's official residence.

As Liberal leader and premier of Nova Scotia, Gerald Regan received between $6000 and $13 200 annually from a special trust fund over a fifteen-year period. The payments were to supplement his official salary.[49] Friends and officials of the federal Progressive Conservative party collected some $300 000 from wealthy individuals and corporations to

create a trust fund for Claude Wagner when he left a judgeship to re-
enter politics in 1972. Income from the fund was used to supplement
Wagner's income. The then leader of the party, Robert Stanfield, denied
knowledge of the fund prior to newspaper reports in November 1975.
The irony is that Brian Mulroney, who with Wagner also unsuccessfully
contested the Tory leadership in 1976, may well have helped to raise the
money for the trust fund.[50]

7.2 Leadership Campaigns

There are no government controls over expenditures on campaigns to
become party leader, although recently the parties have established limits
— for example, in the 1984 race to replace Pierre Trudeau the Liberals
set a limit of $1.6 million for each candidate. The Conservative party in
Ontario set a limit of $500 000 on spending by candidates running to
succeed Frank Miller.[51] When David Peterson won the leadership of the
Ontario Liberal party in 1982, the limit was $75 000, although Peterson
spent about $100 000. The financing of such campaigns is important
for several reasons. The first is the old adage that it may be cheaper and
more effective to obligate a politician early in his career. A leadership
campaign may be the first time a "comer" has need of large sums from
contributors. He or she may be grateful years later to those whose money
put him or her into power. Second, there may be greater loyalty to early
backers than to "johnny-come-latelys" who scramble to get on the bandwagon of an obvious winner.

As importantly, the cost of leadership campaigns has risen far more
rapidly than the Consumer Price Index. In the 1976 Conservative leadership campaign, candidates spent from $153 000 to $343 000 each.
The winner, Joe Clark, spent $168 353, while Brian Mulroney is believed
to have spent $343 000. He did not file a financial statement.[52]

The 1983 federal Progressive Conservative leadership race saw candidates spend several times the amount spent in 1976. Brian Mulroney,
Joe Clark, and John Crosbie's campaigns each cost about $1 million.
Peter Pocklington spent $235 000 on a precampaign speaking tour and
another $730 000 on the official campaign. David Crombie spent about
$325 000. The race left Mulroney with debts of about $200 000, while
John Crosbie owed some $260 000 and Joe Clark finished with debts of
$175 000.[53]

In the 1984 Liberal party leadership campaign, both John Turner
and Jean Chrétien spent very close to the $1.6-million limit established by
the party. Third-place finisher Donald Johnston spent almost $900 000.
John Roberts spent $550 000; Mark MacGuigan, $475 000; and John
Munro, $625 000. While candidates had to identify donors of more than
$500, the amounts did not have to be reported.[54]

Columnist Orland French described the rising cost of leadership campaigns in Ontario as follows:

> When William Davis won the leadership in 1971, $100,000 would buy a respectable campaign. A contender could spend that amount, or less, and not be accused of running a campaign on the cheap. . . . This time around, candidates are talking casually of spending anywhere from $500,000 to $750,000. One candidate told me, before he declared his intention to run, that he expected the winner would have to spend $1-million.[55]

Moreover, in the race to replace William Davis as leader of the PCs in Ontario, the party decided it would not require the candidates to reveal the names of their contributors. "Why?" asked Orland French.

> Too difficult to keep track of, says party president David McFadden. Too hard to figure out the cost of donated services. . . . It's treated as a private matter, as in a private club. But we really do have a right to know. People out there, with more private and corporate money at their disposal than most of us, are quietly stuffing it into the pockets of their favorite candidates and saying, "Go for it." What's in it for them? What do they expect to gain if their candidate makes it?[56]

French argued that "disclosure won't help us read their minds, but it might give us some clues."

7.3 Nonelection Expenditures by Parties

There are no limits on expenditures by parties *outside* the official election campaign period. Nonelection spending is becoming much more important in Canada. The federal chief electoral officer reports that in 1984 the Progressive Conservative party collected more than $21.9 million in contributions and spent some $20.8 million. In contrast, the Liberals raised $11.6 million in contributions and spent about $12 million. (Newspaper reports state that the Liberal party was $3 million in debt in mid-1985.)[57] The NDP collected $10.5 million in 1984 but spent only $7.4 million. Therefore, in 1984 the three main parties spent over $41 million on nonelection expenditures. Less than one-half of this amount ($17.4 million) was spent *directly* on the general election of September 4. Recall Tables 10-1 and 10-2.

There is some degree of substitutability between expenditures during campaigns and those between campaigns in that an extensive and sophisticated party organization financed from unrestricted funds is likely to be more effective during the legally defined campaign period. In other words, electoral success is no longer simply a product of the campaign itself, but depends in part on the organizational work carried out year in and year out. Wearing's (1981) analysis of the federal Liberal party makes it clear that in the 1960s and 1970s the party's machinery was allowed to atrophy between elections. It seems clear from the expenditure data of all three major parties that party organization is being institutionalized. More full-time employees are being hired, and more elaborate communications systems and programs are being put in place. The result will be the increased importance of fund raising to each of the parties. In short, political money will become a major issue on the public policy agenda in the future.

The federal Liberal party has recently established a "leader's club" for large contributors. Members obtain newsletters and attend meetings along with 100 to 200 others with the leader where their views are solicited. In making this move, the Liberals were following the Progressive Conservatives' "500 Club," which is based on a minimum contribution of $1000. Using this technique, the PCs say they raise over $2 million per year. The approach has been so successful that local chapters have been formed across Canada. The Liberals state that their efforts are aimed at "business and professional people, key supporters across the country, who are willing to come on and get involved at a certain level."[58]

In the summer of 1985 the Ontario Liberal party offered $1000 memberships in the Liberal Economic Advisory Forum "that will guarantee occasional direct access to the Premier. This regrettable invention has been joined by fundraising cocktail parties at anywhere from $150 a ticket to $2,000, depending upon which Liberal Cabinet luminary will be there. . . . Invitations tend to reach individuals and groups that might be affected by the minister in attendance, an unsubtle tithe on doing public business."[59] When federal minister of communications Marcel Masse resigned suddenly in September 1985, he had to cancel a fundraising dinner. It was described as "one of those increasingly controversial 'paid access opportunities' where guests are invited to dine and trade talk with a politician in exchange for a donation to the politician or his party."[60]

Both the federal Liberals and Tories have sought to broaden the base of their fund raising. As we have seen, the Tories have been somewhat more successful in reducing their dependence upon large contributions from wealthy individuals or from corporations. One of the keys to the PCs' ability to both raise more money than the Liberals over the past few years and increase the fraction raised from small contributors has been their success with direct-mail solicitations. See Table 10-5. For example, in March 1984, just after Prime Minister Trudeau announced his resignation, the Tories' direct-mail campaign included a plastic membership card for all contributors of $25 or more. They would become sustaining members of the PC Canada Fund. The solicitation letter stated that "nearly 75% of all the funds our Party raises come from private individuals like you who are willing to commit $100 or $50 to [the] PC Canada Fund. Unlike the Liberal[s] and NDP who obtain a large part of their funding from special interest groups, we are truly a grass-roots Party." The appeal referred to the likelihood of an election in the near future and stated that "we must begin immediately to set aside the substantial campaign funds we will need to defeat the Liberal/socialist alliance." The letter concluded with this request: "Please consider an extra-generous donation today."

Only two months after their smashing electoral victory on September 4, 1984, the federal PCs mounted another national direct-mail appeal. In the letter, the party president stated:

> I know that many citizens may think that their support is needed only at election time. Frankly, nothing could be further from the truth. In addition to providing valuable research, communications and on-going services, the Progressive Conservative Party must also continue to fund vital operations that help set the tone and policy that are essential to providing good government. By becoming a Sustaining Member of the PC Canada Fund, you can go beyond your personal vote and play a vital role in the shaping of government decisions and putting effective ideas to work.[61]

Appeals like this apparently did not much move Brian Mulroney. In 1984 he did not make a contribution to the party and in 1983 he donated only $495. In contrast, in 1984 Liberal leader John Turner donated $2372 to his party and NDP leader Ed Broadbent gave $1600 to his.[62]

7.4 "Third Party" Campaigns

In October 1983, by unanimous vote, with only a forty-minute debate, Parliament amended the Canada Elections Act (Bill C-169) so as to prohibit the incurring of election expenses by third parties (i.e., other than registered political parties) during an election campaign.[63] The previous legislation, enacted in 1974, exempted those people who promoted views, held by themselves or a nonpartisan association to which they belonged, on an issue of public policy, and those who were acting "in good faith" (i.e., not trying to circumvent the legislation). The objective was to ensure that a candidate with wealthy friends who spent money on his or her behalf would not have an advantage over one without such friends. It was a way to prevent "end runs" around the statutory limit on campaign expenditures by candidates and parties.

Because the two exemptions were open to abuse, Parliament eliminated them, although as the *National Citizens' Coalition* case made clear, little evidence could be provided of such abuse.[64] Hence, no one was able to print, publish, or distribute an advertisement, handbill, or placard during an election campaign unless it was authorized by a registered party or candidate. And the penalties upon conviction were harsh — a fine of up to $5000.

In amending the 1974 legislation in October 1983, Parliament was obviously limiting free speech. But was it doing so in violation of the 1982 Charter of Rights and Freedoms? The National Citizens' Coalition thought so and brought an action in the Supreme Court of Alberta in January 1984 seeking to have sections 70.1(1) and 72 of the Canada Elections Act declared unconstitutional. They won their case.[65]

Mr. Justice Medhurst ruled that the amended sections amounted to a restriction on the freedom of expression and that they must meet the tests set out in section 1 of the charter. That is, the crown must show that the ban is a "reasonable limit," that is, "prescribed by law," and that it can be "demonstrably justified in a free and democratic society." The judge held that in weighing the individual's right of freedom of expression and an effective system of electing MPs, "fears or concerns of mischief that may occur are not adequate reasons for imposing a limitation. There should be actual demonstration of harm, or a real likelihood of harm to a society value before a limitation can be said to be justified." He held that the limitation on freedom of expression "has not been shown to be reasonable or demonstrably justified in a free and democratic society."[66]

Following this decision, any person or nonpolitical organization or association may incur election expenses during the campaign period to directly promote or oppose a registered party or candidate. Section 70.1(1) now has no legal force and effect. Nonparty groups are now able — unlike the candidates and parties — to spend without limit. Nor do they have to account for their sources of revenue (contributions) or their expenditures.

> The way is clear for peace groups, unions, feminists, corporations, those urging changes in the abortion laws and anyone else with a message to buy advertising to urge the election or defeat of candidates and parties in the Sept. 4 election.
>
> There will be no prosecutions under disputed sections of the election laws that are supposed to restrict campaign advertising by lobbyists and special interest groups, federal sources said yesterday. "We are going to have a free debate and free market of ideas in this election campaign," predicted Colin Brown, founder of the National Citizens' Coalition lobby group that first challenged the restrictions in court. . . . Mr. Brown's 30,000-member lobby group hopes to raise $700,000 to spend on advertising during the election. The coalition, often described as a right-wing lobby, advocates "more freedom through less government."[67]

The chief electoral officer proposes that new legislation be enacted to control such activities. The essence of his proposals is that nonpolitical organizations would be free to contribute funds or services to official candidates and parties. They could either register as a party and nominate candidates or they could obtain written authority from candidates or parties to incur election expenses on their behalf and those expenses would be chargeable against the maximum allowable expenses of the candidate or party. The purpose of these proposed amendments is to close the loophole created by the *National Citizens' Coalition* case while avoiding any violation of the 1982 Charter of Rights and Freedoms. Thus, nonpolitical organizations could speak out for or against registered parties and/or candidates, but their expenditures would be subject to the existing constraints.

The leading academic writer on election financing, K. Z. Paltiel, argues that if nonparty advertising is allowed, "the whole thing becomes uncontrollable" (quoted in Stevenson 1982, 63). His view is echoed by Professor J. C. Courtney, who testified in the *National Citizens' Coalition* case:

> Were special interest groups or individuals free to participate in the electoral process totally without constraints, they would enjoy advantages not otherwise available to the political parties. The fact is that the respective roles and responsibilities of political parties and special interest groups are different. Political parties are electorally accountable for their acts, which is one of the ways in which the term "responsible government" is given meaning in a parliamentary system. Generally every three or four years political parties are held to account by the electorate. By definition, special interest groups are necessarily different. They have more narrowly-defined interests, goals and memberships than political parties and, in the final analysis, they are not electorally responsible for their activities.[68]

But why should interest groups, particularly if they are independent of parties and candidates, not be permitted to spend money supporting certain policies, candidates, and parties during election campaigns? Paltiel suggests that they should be excluded but only during the official campaign period. During that time, in his view, the issue should be "just between the parties and the voters." The problem is that the party in power has enormous discretion over when an election is called. The exclusion of interest groups from the campaign period makes more sense when the election day is set by statute. Then, it may reasonably be argued, preventing nonparty groups from advertising their views during the six to eight weeks of the campaign is a restriction analogous to the restriction on print and broadcast advertising in the forty-eight hours immediately before the polls open.

With the law as it is — no controls on nonparty advertising — there is the possibility that U.S.-style political action committees (see Malbin 1980, 1984) could be formed to raise funds to support particular policies, candidates, or parties without reference to the parties or candidates. But it is not clear how effective such expenditures would be if disowned by the party/candidate they are designed to support. Moreover, voters may react negatively, viewing lavish interest-group campaigns as being in violation of the spirit of the 1974 reforms.

7.5 Tax Deductible Status and Political Activity

The minister of national revenue announced at the end of May 1985 that the government would introduce legislation to allow registered charitable organizations to retain their tax deductible status even if they used some of the funds collected to attempt to influence public opinion and government policy. Previously, the courts had held that such activities were "political" and were incompatible with the tax-exempt status of registered charities.[69] This could open the door to more direct political activity by interest groups, including single-issue groups such as pro- or anti-abortion groups or environmental groups.

8.0 POLITICAL CONTRIBUTIONS AND POLITICAL CORRUPTION

8.1 Defining Political Corruption

What is political corruption? How can we distinguish legitimate campaign contributions from bribes or other forms of corruption? James Q. Wilson provides a useful definition of political corruption: "Corruption occurs whenever a person, in exchange for some private advantage, acts other than as his duty requires" (1974, 30).[70] V. O. Key (1974, 23) defines political graft — his term for corruption — as the abuse of power for personal or party profit.[71] Power attracts corruption, and the natural locus of corruption is where discretionary power resides. Those persons in the political system who have the power to say yes or no to the initiatives of private individuals or companies are the natural targets of those who seek to advance their interests by corrupt or legitimate means.

     Bretton acknowledges that "realistically, in its simplest form, corrupt money seeks to secure economic advantages for its donor. . . . the aim of corruption is to secure access to policy and decision-making" (1980, 190). But, it should be noted, corrupt money usually complements rather than substitutes for legitimate channels of contact and influence.[72] Precisely because this is the case, it is most difficult to detect and restrict by legislation. Money is used to reinforce a group's effectiveness in using institutionalized means of access and influence.

     Corruption is also hard to identify because what is deemed to be corruption "requires consideration of the prevailing norms governing public conduct, morality, generally the standards of public service" (Bretton 1980, 191).[73] For example, is large-scale, systematic patronage in the form of order-in-council appointments and in the award of contracts for professional services that we find at the federal level political corruption? Should the term be limited to illegal acts, that is, bribery and influence peddling?

Wilson (1974, 31) emphasizes that corruption in Western democracies is most odious when cash is exchanged for a political advantage (contract, vote on a piece of legislation, the exercise of discretion in the administration of a public program). However, other types of exchanges in political markets are not so perceived, for example, log-rolling, ticket balancing, and making political appointments. The fact is that the exchange of favours consisting of services in kind are much less frequently condemned. This may be because such exchanges are seldom contemporaneous, because they are less explicit, because they are part of the process of compromise necessary to make democratic political processes work, and because unsophisticated observers believe that the individuals involved do not *personally* benefit from the exchanges in a direct fashion.

The point is that the public can understand a payment of $5000 in small bills by a contractor to a public official in order to obtain a government contract worth $300 000, but finds it hard to understand the nonpecuniary benefits of gaining, holding, and exercising power for its own sake. People fail to appreciate that politicians' egos — the desire to do the Lord's work on a large scale — can result in vastly greater expenditures of public funds. Two cabinet ministers who agree to vigorously support each other's initiatives can bring about two major programs that are expensive, inefficient, and of benefit only to a fairly small number of each minister's constituents. One has to think only of the fact that new federal expenditures in Prime Minister Mulroney's own riding in 1985/86 will exceed the all-new programs announced for Western Canada.[74] Such behaviour is not perceived as any form of corruption, but as "smart politics."

Most Canadians believe that their governments are relatively free of corruption. Yet one can point to major scandals in which business provided funds in return for past or future favours. One thinks of the Pacific Scandal of 1874, which nearly ruined Canada's first prime minister, and the Beauharnois scandal of 1931 in which the federal Liberal party accepted a large donation ($700 000) from a hydro-electric enterprise in exchange for a lucrative concession.[75] However, it was not until 1979 that the first charge of influence peddling was laid when a Fredericton lawyer was charged with nine counts of the offence. Some $28 200 was collected for the provincial PC party or local associations between 1970 and 1974 by the man acting as a fund raiser and claiming he had influence with the government.[76] He was convicted in 1980.

Recently, the most famous charge of bribery and influence peddling involved former federal Liberal cabinet minister Bryce Mackasey. However, he was discharged at a preliminary hearing.[77] In 1983 prominent fund raisers in Nova Scotia were convicted of "taxing" the recipients of government contracts and the suppliers of the monopoly provincial liquor stores to raise funds for the provincial Liberal party.[78]

Patrick Boyer (1979, 176) points out that

> the provisions of the *Criminal Code* which prohibit bribing public officials have given rise to a number of other cases, the most notorious of which involved Robert E. Sommers, who in the late 1950s, when Minister of Lands and Forests of British Columbia, accepted bribes from H. Wilson Gray, Pacific Coast Services Ltd. and Evergreen Lumber Sales Ltd. The conviction for offering bribes, accepting bribes, and for conspiracy to commit these offences was upheld on appeals to both the British Columbia Court of Appeal and the Supreme Court of Canada, and Sommers became "the first cabinet minister in the Commonwealth to be jailed for corruption in office" (Bruton et al. 1964, 19).

However, it should be noted that the Social Credit party succeeded in retaining Sommers's seat in the subsequent election. Generally, see Sherman (1966, chap. 7).

In the winter of 1964–65 a "welter of squalid scandals" erupted in the Liberal government of Lester B. Pearson. These included a rather unusual purchase of furniture by Maurice Lamontagne, an advisor to the leader of the opposition and later a cabinet minister (Gwyn 1965, 6, 16). There were also charges of bribery against Yvon Dupuis, minister without portfolio, who it was said accepted $10 000 to facilitate the obtaining of a licence for a racetrack in his riding. Dupuis was the first federal minister to resign and face bribery charges (Gwyn 1965, 63, 95).

8.2 The Importance of the Norm of Reciprocity in Politics

The ambivalence about various types of exchanges in political markets stems from the pervasiveness and power of the norm of reciprocity. Indeed, sociologist Alvin Gouldner argues:

> Contrary to some cultural relativists, it can be hypothesized that a norm of reciprocity is universal. As Westermarck stated, "To require a benefit or to be grateful to him who bestows it, is probably everywhere, at least under certain circumstances, regarded as a duty." A norm of reciprocity is, I suspect, no less universal and important an element of culture than the incest taboo, although similarly, its concrete formulations may vary with time and place. (1961, 171)

In the same vein, Noonan states: "Reciprocity is in any society a rule of life and in some societies at least it is *the* rule of life. . . . The recipient is bound by the receiving" (1984, 3).

The reciprocal character of many transactions remains regardless of

its size, the imprecision as to what is expected in return, the timing of
the reciprocation, or the indirectness with which the exchange is carried out. Elizabeth Drew points out the symbiotic relationship between
politicians and interest groups with money in her study *Politics and
Money*: "The candidate's desperation for money and the interests' desire
to affect public policy provide a mutual opportunity. When the possibility of mutually beneficial exchanges exists, it will become a fact" (1983,
4).

The power of the norm of reciprocity is illustrated by the statements
of one of the partners of the new advertising agency named by the
Mulroney government as the federal government's agency of record. He
said he proposed to donate part of the profits to the Conservative party
for use in Quebec. The minister responsible for the government's advertising contracts emphasized that this was a personal decision and that
"it was never a condition of the contract that any funds be returned to
the party." The issue here, it was suggested, is not the profitability of the
federal contract as such, but rather the possibility of greater private
sector business, as the new advertising and public relations firm would
be seen as having an "in" with the government.[79]

8.3 Distinguishing Bribery from Political Contributions

Because reciprocity is such a powerful norm, does it mean that political
campaign contributions are inherently suspect even if they are made in
accordance with the law?[80] Noonan argues that this will be the case
because of the difficulty of distinguishing bribes from legitimate contributions: "Bribery is an act distinguished from other reciprocities only if
it is socially identified and socially condemned. The exchange of favours
with a power holder is otherwise like other reciprocal transactions in the
society. A bribe is not distinguished from other ways of eliciting a benevo-
lent response" (1984, 3-4). He points out that "The [ancient] Greeks
did not have a word for bribes because all gifts are bribes. All gifts are
given by way of reciprocation for favours past or to come" (1984, 687).
Noonan defines a bribe as "an inducement improperly influencing the
performance of a public function meant to be gratuitously exercised"
(1984, 3).[81]

Noonan distinguishes between campaign contributions, bribes, and
gifts. He argues that gifts declare an identification between the giver
and the recipient and that legitimate campaign contributions are of a
similar character:

> Campaign contributions are imperfect gifts because they are usu-
> ally not set in a context of personal relations; they are intended to
> express a limited love — an identification with a cause. They are
> not wholly the recipient's — their purpose is restricted. They are
> given in response to work done or expected to be done. They are

not tips because they are not given to low-level employees but to those who if elected must exercise discretion in public affairs. They do not express or create overriding obligations, that is, there is no absolute obligation on the part of the contributor to recognize past work by the candidate; and there is no absolute obligation on the part of the candidate to do the work the contributor expects. Absence of absolute obligation creates one difference between contributions and bribes. Size is thus a relevant characteristic. A large contribution can create an overriding obligation; its proper name becomes bribe.

Contributions normally differ from bribes in a second way. They are not secret. They are given openly. They are recorded and reported. Above a very small amount, they are given in a traceable form, not in cash. They are not disguised or laundered. The difference between secrecy and non-secrecy bears on accountability. The contributor acknowledges that he stands with this candidate. The candidate acknowledges that he takes this contributor's money. Voters know with whom the candidate identifies. Political accountability is preserved. . . . Campaign contributions can be bribes, as successful prosecutions have established. Cash and secrecy are today the normal badges of criminality. But contributions can also be distinct from bribes, meant not to manipulate an officeholder but to identify with him and the cause he supports. No doubt in close cases the motivations of contributor and candidate are morally significant; it is not surprising that moral lines should depend on motivation. The entire set of laws on campaign contributions can be read as an effort, clumsy surely but persistent also, to reinforce the moral line already in existence between bribes and contributions. (1984, 696–97, 698)

Bretton (1980, 174) distinguishes between "seeing" and "blind" monetary inputs to the political system. The former, a "high-powered flow of money," is seeing "by dint of the knowledge and skills it can attract or buy." On the other hand, "blind contributions are made by the relatively uninformed, the average citizen, the well intentioned who contributes without a clear conception of why and for what the money is being spent, or what concrete results might be expected." Bretton argues that "sophisticated money can re-assess the efficacy of a contribution following a failure and re-direct its energy accordingly."

In his careful analysis of campaign contributions, Noonan was not able to establish a *functional* difference between campaign contributions and bribes: "All that was shown were governmental efforts, usually clumsy, half-baked, and ineffective, to channel contributions, publicize them, and limit their amounts and origins. Lines were drawn between contributions and bribes. Each line was arbitrary. . . . The system presently in force [in the U.S.] is simply one of licensed bribery" (1984, 688–89).

Yes, the lines are arbitrary, but that is the case in many other situations where society has defined certain acts as crimes. One has only to think of speed limits. What is it about 41 km/h that is criminal while 40 km/h is not? The difference lies only in definition in a statute. True crimes are characterized by a mental element of evil intent (*mens rea*). "Real crimes are sins with legal definitions," in the words of Lord Devlin. In the case of a bribe, what is being condemned is the "gift" of money specifically for the purpose of perverting the judgment of a public official. This has long been proscribed in moral terms. Speaking to Moses after having delivered the ten commandments, God said, "You shall not take shohadh [offerings to an official], which makes the clear-eyed blink and the words of the just crooked" (Exod. 23:6–8). The intent of the briber is to influence the public official to the benefit of the briber in a way that would not occur in the absence of the bribe.[82] What is defined as improper behaviour is inherently a community standard, not an exogenous moral absolute. We must recognize, however, that a good deal of hypocrisy is involved in determining what is or is not acceptable political behaviour.[83] Often the difference is a triumph of form over substance. Although the moral and legal rules change over time, those who wish to play the game must be able to identify the line that separates tolerated behaviour from that which results in social, political, or legal sanctions. One of the more interesting conundrums relates to the putative distinction between the role of campaign contributions in facilitating access to key political decision makers and that in influencing outcomes.

8.4 Paying for Access or Buying Influence?

It is frequently argued that the purpose of campaign contributions is access, not influence. Even the Bible notes that "a gift (mattana) opens the door to the giver and gains access to the great" (Prov. 18:16). Eight years before the 1974 reforms, Paltiel (1966) states that "clearly, *quid pro quos* have been sought [by large contributors]; our Royal Commission reports are replete with this information. But certainly what most givers want, whether they give large or small amounts at the local or party level is *access* to decision makers at various levels."[84] In his description of campaign financing prior to the 1974 act, Osborn summarizes previous work on the reasons why some businesses make large donations to political parties as follows:

> Although many businessmen use platitudes such as "supporting the democratic system," it seems clear that the givers' need is to guarantee access to decision-making at various levels. Despite the fact that we are uncomfortable in admitting it, money does buy favors

— at the lowest level, it buys concessions, dispensations, and specific acts of patronage; at the higher levels, it "stabilizes the field for corporate activity." (1975, 86)

Do large contributions create obligations that require special access? In the words of one Conservative MP, "I'm not sure we [the parties] became beholden to them [large donors], but we know we would tap them and we knew we had to look after them" (Stevenson 1982, 33). In his view, any sense of obligation to big donors has changed since 1974 by reason of the party limits on contributions, public disclosure, and the increased importance of individual contributions.

Dalton Camp, long a Conservative party insider, has described the role of corporations — largely headquartered in Toronto — in funding the Liberal and Conservative parties as follows:

Money is the imperative of party politics and the ways and means come largely from Canada's corporate donors, most of whom are found within a bagman's walk through the canyons reaching out from Bay and King [the heart of the city's financial district]. But more than that: almost all the provincial parties are wards of the same principal officers whose contributions, judiciously meted out, represent the proxy title of their shareholders to a political system to be saved from socialism. (1979, 91)

Money, however, does not "buy" specific policies favourable to corporate donors. The relationship is less direct and more complex. Camp states:

Yet it would be merely gauche to assume that Toronto money subjects the parties to corporate dominance. Such may be a suitable mythology for the gullible (and harmless, even if believed) but the reality is more subtle. Toronto money merely maintains access to the parties, keeping open essential lines of communications, corporate hotlines, so to speak, to the right ears at appropriate times. For the wise donor, the financing of the political system may very well be a duty and an obligation to the system, but it is, as well, insurance against the unlikely — such as the ascendancy of socialism — or against occasional political aberration, a Walter Gordon budget, say, or a Carter report on tax reform. When such contingencies arise, the price for access is modest indeed. (1979, 91)

In general, however, Camp argues that "the influence of big business . . . upon the politicians and parties is most often nugatory." This is so because "mature politicians secretly believe board chairmen and company presidents to be political cretins and would as soon take their advice as harken to a herd of mandrills" (1979, 92).[85]

But why should corporations, other interest groups, or individuals pay for access to a public official at all? It is argued that such payments are merely a way of rationing the official's scarce time but do not influence outcomes once access is gained. Elizabeth Drew quotes a "key Senate Democratic aide" as follows: "A member of Congress's time is very limited. Who do they see? They'll certainly see the ones who gave the money. It's hard to say no to someone who gave you five grand" (1983, 77).[86] In the case of Canada, the analogy could be made to cabinet ministers, but not to backbenchers even of the party in power.

Is access to key politicians all that campaign contributions provide? Gaining access is surely the first measure of influence on the political process, and its purpose is to have the opportunity — usually in an informal meeting — to try to persuade the legislator to do or not to do somthing, the effect of which is beneficial to the interest group. The focus of these efforts at persuasion is the provision of information This point is emphasized by an experienced legislative aide in Washington: "Obviously the most important factor in establishing the legislative outcome is the information that the members are acting upon. Clearly, this has to be viewed in the context of members overburdened with demands on their time. So a little bit of information will carry a member a long way" (quoted in Drew 1983, 77–78).

The role of persuasion is more important on the many issues that do not involve moral principles or on ones that do not have a large, direct impact on those constituencies that the government or particular ministers consider important.

In Noonan's (1984, 689) view, the idea that large contributions only provide access, and do not directly influence policy, is a transparent pretense. Where such payments are large, secret, and variable, rather than small, open, and uniform, they are "accompanied by the tacit understanding that the attention bought will be favourable. Access payments of this sort are bribes." Special access connotes the chance to have one's problems considered in a way which does not follow normal channels (Gibbons 1976, 7). And Bretton argues that "the key to corruption is access. To be influenced, the public official must be accessible to the corrupter" (1980, 198).[87]

8.5 Politicians' Knowledge of Political Contributions

Politicians, particularly cabinet ministers, make much of the fact they are not directly involved in fund raising and do not know the identity of the major contributors to their own campaigns or party. For example, the press secretary of Pat Carney, minister of energy, mines and resources, said that the minister was not aware of the identities of her campaign donors in the 1984 campaign. (She raised $67 323 of which $7700 came from companies involved in the oil and gas business.) Aides to other ministers made the same claim.[88] Despite such protestations, it would be naive to suggest that cabinet members in Canada are unaware of who are the large contributors to their party and to their own campaigns. We should recall that under the reforms in the 1974 legislation the name of every contributor of more than $100 must be reported to the chief electoral officer and published by him or her. Even if the ministers' knowledge is *ex post*, the strong norm of reciprocity makes it difficult to believe that major contributors will not able to benefit in some degree in their future contacts with the politicians.

While the 1974 legislation reduced the reliance on corporate donations for the two major parties, corporate gifts of $50 000 still occur in noticeable numbers. When a corporation makes a large donation, the following things occur: (1) its senior executives have a personal contact with a high party official, which in the future may be used as a point of access in making contacts with cabinet ministers; (2) senior party officials are made aware of the enterprise's generosity (only the first $1150 benefits from the maximum tax credit of $500) — two facts can hardly hurt the firm when it makes contact with those officials to obtain information or an introduction to the right people in the executive (both political and bureaucratic).

9.0 BUSINESS POLICY CONCERNING POLITICAL CONTRIBUTIONS

9.1 Various Motivations and Public Policy

Individuals, interest groups, and corporations make contributions to parties and candidates for a wide variety of reasons:

- to support basic democratic values, which require competitive political parties;
- to facilitate access to top-level decision makers;[89]
- as a token of esteem for a particular candidate they admire;
- as an acknowledgment for a service rendered sometime in the past;
- for the promotion of a specific legislative program, or in the expectation of receiving government contracts;[90]
- to create a climate of opinion favourable to the donor's interests;
- to maintain the prevailing class structure;
- for specific ideological objectives that are embedded in certain public policies (e.g., gun control; anti-abortion laws);
- as a form of "insurance" against possible actions with severe negative consequences for the donor — at the extreme this could be interpreted as a form of blackmail; or
- to create goodwill and to establish a sense of obligation for no current purpose, but that will be drawn upon in the future.

In a given instance, it may be all but impossible to fathom the intent of the donor in making a political contribution.

In Canada, the major parties argue that "good corporate citizenship" behooves business firms to make political contributions (Stevenson 1982, 35). Since 1974 business has been encouraged to do so by a federal tax credit that makes the net cost of a $1150 contribution only $500. However, *all* donations over $100 must be reported to the chief electoral officer and reported publicly. It has been argued that "the tax credit system also makes it impossible for corporations to write-off large cash, services or goods donations on their income tax returns. This was designed to discourage further corporate gifts" (Stevenson 1982, 41). At the same time, trade unions are required to disclose donations in kind exceeding $100. However, the 1974 legislation excluded "volunteer labour" from election expenses at the insistence of the NDP.

Recent approaches to combating the general problem of conflict of interest in Canada rely heavily upon the instrument of disclosure, and are based on the idea that if a politician's interests are potentially known to all those who deal with him or her, the problem of conflict of interest is reduced. But is it? Or does this approach convert a moral or legal problem into one that is to be judged in the court of public opinion on election day? More generally, see Starr and Sharp (1984).

9.2 Ideals versus Realities

The issue of how money is raised to finance candidates and political parties will always remain a difficult one in a society in which democratic ideals clash with certain "realities." These include the following:

- The operation of political parties and election campaigns requires substantial sums of money even where constraints are imposed on what may be spent by candidates and parties during campaigns. Parties need funds for three main purposes: to fight election campaigns; to maintain a viable political organization between elections; and to provide research and advisory services for the party's leadership and members (particularly for the parties in opposition).

- In recent years the three major parties have built more elaborate and formal organizations. Large-scale, ongoing organizations staffed by professionals require substantial sums of money. In 1984, an election year, for example, election expenses amounted to only one-half of the three parties' total expenditures during the year. Fund raising has become a more sophisticated, specialized activity within each of the major parties, with an emphasis on direct-mail solicitation.

- Wealth and economic power are highly concentrated in Canada. In other words, not everyone has the same economic stake in the system and those that have a larger stake generally have a greater capability of advancing their interests in political markets. Recall the discussion in chapter 4.

- The size and scope of the public sector are so great that it is capable of influencing the economic position of members of many interest groups in a significant fashion. Recall the analysis in chapter 3.

- Rent-seeking behaviour has become endemic in Canada, and campaign contributions are merely another method of increasing the odds of obtaining a benefit from government.
- Small (hence disinterested) contributions — even with the generous tax credit — can only generate about one-half the funds presently raised by the three major parties.
- Within government, power is concentrated in the cabinet; for example, cabinet has a monopoly over the supply of new legislation and makes more than 4000 order-in-council appointments to a great variety of positions, ranging from deputy minister to members of the various harbour boards.

There is, therefore, a strong symbiotic relationship between the politicians and parties that need money to gain and retain office and those that have a large stake in the system that can be strongly affected by decisions made by politicians and by those persons over whom politicians have control.

While the two main parties encourage contributions from business, they believe that equal-sized donations be made to both the Liberals and the Tories. The two main parties appear to set their own limits on the size of individual contributions so as to prevent the appearance of becoming too indebted to one source, although the limits set in the mid-1970s were exceeded in 1984. (Apparently, the NDP does not follow this practice.) The parties want businesses to make contributions each year, not merely in election years, although larger amounts in election years are deemed to be desirable. The parties make it clear that they will not accept contributions subject to any conditions regarding what the party and/or candidates will or will not do in exchange for the contribution.

The reforms of 1974 have the curious side-effect of making it logically impossible for politicians to claim that they don't know who has contributed money to their campaigns or party. Since all donations in cash or kind (except volunteer labour) over $100 must be publicly reported, everyone knows who received how much from whom. (As we have noted, this seldom applies to leadership campaigns or to personal gifts to individual politicians.)

The argument that political contributions are useful only in ensuring access is both naive and hypocritical. The issue is not really access as such — it is not too difficult for heads of corporations or other interest groups to meet with cabinet ministers and senior public servants to deal with policy issues that directly affect them. The heart of the matter involves the following points. First, large contributions may facilitate access to top political decision makers. Second, large contributions may gain *additional* contacts with senior politicians over and above those arranged through official channels. More contacts may increase the likelihood of persuading the targets to the business's point of view. Third, large contributions may result in off-the-record meetings in which both parties can be more direct and make arguments that cannot be made officially.

Fourth, large contributions are likely to make politicians more attentive to the arguments of those who make those contributions. This stems from the powerful norm of reciprocity. People instinctively want to try to return a favour, and cabinet ministers have usually sufficient discretionary power to help those who have helped them without the suggestion they have done anything improper. It is true that the president of any of the 500 largest firms in Canada will be able to obtain a meeting with a minister and his or her officials on a problem that concerns the firm whether or not the firm has made a substantial political contribution. Why? Because those who wield power in government are necessarily sensitive to those who have power in the private sector. The heads of Canadian Pacific and Bell Canada represent 120 000 and 108 000 employees respectively. Even the fiftieth-largest business employer in Canada had some 11 000 employees in 1984.[91] The economic reach of the largest conglomerates (e.g., Brascan)[92] is simply enormous.

What substantial political contributions do is to establish a link between the firm and senior party officials and through them to cabinet ministers. Such contributions indicate to ministers that the corporation understands the practical aspects of political life, even if it gave the same amount to the opposition. The simple fact is that the minister, necessarily aware of the contribution, will find it very difficult to treat such corporations in *exactly* the same way as those who did not make such contributions. In any event, it appears that voters do not have high opinions of the morality of their elected representatives.[93]

9.3 Corporate Policy[94]

In 1977 the Institute for Political Involvement surveyed 2000 firms in Canada having more than 100 employees. The institute obtained 703 responses suitable for analysis and found that slightly more than one-half the firms communicated directly with political leaders at the federal level (53.2 percent) and with civil servants (55.3 percent) (IPI 1978, 5). Further, large firms (over 500 employees) were more likely to have made direct representations to the federal government than smaller firms.

Yet 49.6 percent of the larger firms and 71.5 percent of smaller firms in the sample (n = 322 and 369 respectively) had no policy on political involvement. Only 34.8 percent of large and 19.8 percent of small firms had a policy of facilitating political involvement (e.g., encouraging employee participation, leaves of absence for those running for office, and candidate meetings on company premises). The survey also found that while 87 percent of the firms had received requests for financial contributions, 36.1 percent had a policy of making no contributions to a party under any circumstances and 44.1 percent had the same policy concerning candidates. Fifty-two percent of the firms in the sample made financial contributions only to certain parties (7.1 percent gave to all parties), and 46.2 percent gave only to certain candidates (3.1 percent gave to all making a request) (IPI 1978, 8).

Crown corporations (84.6 percent) and the subsidiaries of foreign companies (62.0 percent) were much more likely to have a policy of *not* making financial contributions to political parties. The comparable fraction for public Canadian corporations, private Canadian corporations, and subsidiaries of Canadian companies were 25, 21, and 29 percent respectively (IPI 1978, 8).

Fifty-three percent of the companies surveyed made nonfinancial contributions to a party depending on the party and/or the nature of the request. The comparable figure for candidates was 56 percent. Twenty-eight percent of the firms made it a policy *not* to grant nonfinancial requests to parties or to candidates (IPI 1978, 7).

From the corporation's perspective, political contributions should be viewed as part of the overhead associated with its government relations function. They should be made without strings or even the expectation that they will indirectly provide the company with benefits. Rather, they should be made to ensure that the company has "covered all the bases" in dealing with a government. Contributions might be rationalized as a form of "insurance" against discriminatory treatment by politicians. (It should be emphasized that senior bureaucrats generally resent the obvious use of "political pull" by corporations or other interest groups, i.e., where political considerations override what they feel are well-established policy guidelines designed to ensure consistency and equitable treatment of all those subject to a policy.) Contributions fill a potential gap in a company's political credentials that may become of some significance in those many decision situations where politicians necessarily exercise discretion.

Therefore, I propose that corporations adopt the following approach to political contributions:

1. The company's policy toward political contributions should be adopted by a resolution of its board of directors. It should be administered by the president and/or CEO. The policy should be public.[95]
2. The company should make equal annual contributions to the federal Liberal and Progressive Conservative parties. Double this contribution in election years subject to the upper bounds established by the parties. (The NDP neither desires nor deserves financial support from business, as it is basically philosophically hostile to business interests.)
3. The amount of the annual contributions should be roughly related to the size of the enterprise's business activity in Canada. An analysis

of contributions by other enterprises in recent years could be used to establish a rule-of-thumb formula (i.e., as a percentage of assets, sales, or profits. Recall Table 10-16).

4. The contributions should be increased every two or three years to reflect inflation.

5. Companies should be very leery of making contributions to individual candidates. This will require a more complex set of policy decisions to determine which individuals receive how much on what basis (e.g., to candidates in ridings in which the company has major facilities). In general, no matter how careful a company is in making such contributions, it will inevitably create some hard feelings. Moreover, there are good reasons why companies should concentrate on supporting parties rather than individual candidates. First, there are fairly tight limits on campaign expenditures by candidates and it is not too hard for candidates to raise the necessary funds. Second, the federal government now reimburses candidates for one-half of their campaign expenditures. Third, while party expenditures are limited during campaign periods, they are not limited at any other period. Fourth, the parties make transfers to some individual candidates, and some candidates, able to raise more than they are able to spend, make transfers to the central party coffers.

6. To be seen to have perfectly clean hands, the company should inform the two major parties that there is no need for a bagman to call to collect the contribution. Rather, the company will automatically forward its contribution to the party treasurer in the same month each year. In election years, a second cheque will be sent shortly after the election writ has been issued.

7. The company should provide in its annual report a brief summary of its policy concerning political contributions and indicate its total political contributions each year.

8. On a personal level, individual executives should be entirely free to make or not make political contributions as they see fit.[96]

9. Businesses that are substantial suppliers of goods and services to government have to be aware that they could be the object of a type of extortion by politicians or their associates. For example, after a firm wins a competitive contract, it may be approached by a bagman for the party in power with the suggestion that the firm "show its appreciation" by making a contribution to the party's campaign coffers. A clear policy such as that outlined above should virtually eliminate this type of highly questionable activity.

NOTES

1. This phrase is usually attributed to Jesse Unruh when he was the Democratic Speaker of the California legislature.

2. See, for example, Meisel and Van Loon (1966); Paltiel and Van Loon (1966); Paltiel (1966, 1970, 1974a, 1975, 1976a, 1976b, 1977, 1979a, 1979b); Seidle and Paltiel (1981); Stevenson (1982); Wearing (1981); and Whitaker (1977).

3. For more detail on the early history of such legislation, see Boyer (1979, 1983). Boyer was elected as a Conservative member from Ontario on September 4, 1984.

4. See Stanbury, Gorn, and Weinberg (1983). With respect to the Mulroney government, see "Ex-aide worked free for Wilson before ad contract, House told," *Globe and Mail*, April 23, 1985, p. 4; "Atkins and agency may get contract worth $9 million," *Globe and Mail*, April 23, 1985, pp. 1–2; "Wilson ad deal tip of iceberg," *Globe and Mail*, April 29, 1985, pp. 1, 8; and Roy MacGregor, "The Price of Power," *Maclean's* June 24, 1985, pp. 11–12.

5. See *National Citizens' Coalition* case (1984) 5 W.W.R. 436; "Court strikes down election restrictions," *Globe and Mail*, June 27, 1984, pp. 1–2; and Gordon Legge, "Vindication for lobbyists," *Maclean's*, July 9, 1984, p. 40. The effect of the case is to allow any person or organization other than a registered party to incur any amount of election expenses to directly promote or oppose a registered party or candidate. Moreover, these organizations need not publicly report the names of contributors.

6. Ontario, for example, has a different approach. Under the Election Finances Reform Act of 1975 the following rules regarding campaign contributions and expenditures apply:
   • There is no overall limit on campaign spending.
   • Expenditures on media advertising are limited to 25 cents per voter.
   • Contributions are limited to $8000 in election years and $4000 in nonelection years; this applies to individuals, including the candidate, to unions, and to corporations (note, in Quebec only *voters* can make contributions — hence corporations cannot).
   • All contributions over $100 must be publicly disclosed.
   • Public subsidies are provided to candidates who receive more than 15% of the vote; they amount to 25 cents for each of the first 25 000 voters in the riding and 14 cents for each voter above 25 000. (This usually amounts to $5000 to $6000 per riding.)
   • A substantial portion of the contributions by individuals and corporations is deductible against provincial income tax.

7. In Manitoba, the leader of the opposition Progressive Conservative party has stated that if he becomes premier, legislation providing for reimbursement of candidates' campaign expenditures would be repealed retroactively. See *Globe and Mail*, September 4, 1985, p. 12.

8. Compiled by the author from data in reports of the Chief Electoral Officer (1979, 1980, 1984).

9. The purpose of the tax credit is to stimulate small contributions from a large number of individuals. It has had precisely that effect. Seidle and Paltiel (1981, 276) report that the number of persons and value of tax credit (i.e., in terms of tax revenue foregone) between 1974 and 1979 has been as follows:

	Number of individuals	Value of tax credit to individuals	Value of tax credit to corporations
1974	19 584	$1 273 000	n/a
1976	48 313	2 800 000	$ 465 000
1978	64 547	3 901 000	653 000
1979	92 353	6 111 000	1 213 000

The Department of Finance (1985, 39) indicates that the revenue foregone as a result of the political contribution tax credit for individuals is as follows:

1979	$6 million	1982	$6 million
1980	6	1983	8
1981	5		

10. See *Globe and Mail*, July 13, 1985, p. 4; and the NDP's returns to the chief electoral officer for 1983 and 1984.

11. The campaign expenditures in 1984 need to be put into perspective. When we combine party plus candidate gross expenditures in the 1984 election the total is about $42 million. The 1984 presidential election campaign saw the Republicans and Democrats spend in excess of $200 million. In addition, the campaigns of congressmen and senators cost about the same amount. In the 1984 contest for a North Carolina senatorial seat, Jesse Helms, the incumbent, had a war chest of $13.1 million. His opponent, who lost the race, raised some $7.8 million — making the campaign the most expensive in U.S. history (*Maclean's*, November 5, 1984, p. 29).

12. The chief electoral officer (1979, 1980, 1984) reports that over the last three general elections the three main *parties* are now spending a high percentage of the legal limit of campaign expenditures:

	1979	1980	1984
Liberal	86.2%	84.6%	98.5 %
Conservative	87.7	96.9	99.96
NDP	49.1	68.1	74.0

With respect to all *candidates*, the CEO reports the following ratio of expenditures to the legal limits:

	1979	1980	1984
Liberals	79.8%	77.5%	79.0%
Conservatives	77.6	72.4	89.0
NDP	34.4	38.4	37.8

13. A note in the NDP 1984 return filed with the chief electoral officer

indicates that the party spent $301 000 on fund raising in a year in which its contributions from individuals totalled $4.2 million. While the marginal cost of direct-mail fund-raising techniques is very low (paper, printing, and postage), the average cost probably exceeds 25% of the money raised.

14. The term corporations (or businesses) includes both large and small publicly traded and privately held firms. It also includes "commercial organizations," such as law, accounting, and engineering firms, and federal and provincial crown corporations.

15. See Phil Gibson, "Will party fund reform affect competition policy?" Montreal *Gazette*, March 27, 1975. Senator John Godfrey is quoted as saying: "The potential was always there; a lot of large companies could have banded together and decided not to donate to teach the government a lesson. But it just never happened." Liberal MP Herb Gray noted that the absence of the Election Expenses Act did not prevent his party from tackling "a broad range of social issues that have been strongly opposed by big business," such as the CPP and medicare legislation in the 1960s.

16. In 1984 the NDP reported receiving $51 665 from 280 "business and commercial organizations." See Chief Electoral Officer 1984, 3. In 1985 the NDP in Nova Scotia had a public debate over whether the provincial party should even accept donations from small businesses. See "Small-business donation plan sparks debate in N.S. NDP," *Globe and Mail*, August 19, 1985, p. 3.

17. Wearing (1981, 233) provides some information on the size distribution of contributions by individuals to the Liberal party in 1978 (not an election year):

under $100	81.6%
$100–$999	17.7
$1000–$4999	0.7

18. If we compare political party financing for the years 1974, the last election under the old rules, and 1980, the second election since the passage of the Election Expenses Act, we find that the number of individuals who made donations to the political parties was substantially higher in 1980 than in 1974 (9882 to the Liberals; 6423 to the Tories; and 27 910 to the NDP). The average contribution was $112, $99, and $46 respectively in 1974. However, the proportion of campaign contributions from individuals (relative to contributions from corporations or unions) did not increase substantially. In fact, it decreased for both the Liberals and the NDP. In 1974 the Liberals received 48.6% of their contributions from corporations, while the Tories received 61.7% from that source. By current standards, total contributions were quite modest: $2.15 million to the Liberals, $1.66 million to the Conservatives, and $1.50 million to the NDP. (See Stewart 1982, 359–60; Stevens 1976, 6.)

19. Statistics Canada, *Income Distributions by Size in Canada, Preliminary Estimates* (Ottawa: Cat. no. 13-206).

20. The number in parentheses indicates the number of persons giving the largest donation. It may be that both of these contributions were from the same individual. The Conservatives' return indicates $50 000 from W. W. Siebens and $50 000 from W. Siebens.

21. By way of comparison, I note that in 1972 W. Clement Stone, owner of an insurance company, gave the Richard Nixon campaign over $2 million. Almost $17 million was raised from only 124 individuals and $1.7 million came from persons later appointed as ambassadors (Drew 1983, 1, 9).

22. Wearing's (1981, 233) data for the Liberal party in 1978 shows that for all corporate donors, the 41 who gave more than $10 000 contributed 28% of all corporate donations and the average donation for these "big givers" was $16 946. In 1979 (an election year), ten major corporations, including the five major Canadian banks, accounted for 11% of all corporate contributions to the Liberals and Tories (Sheppard 1980, 2). The Canadian penchant for cartelization can also be found in political fund raising: "In the 1980 general election, leading fund raisers . . . reputedly agreed in advance on how much to ask certain top [corporate] contributers to donate to their respective parties in order to prevent 'price-cutting' " (Stevenson 1982, 49). See also Figure 10-1.

23. The largest firm in 1983 and 1984 in terms of revenues was General Motors of Canada, 1983 revenues of $16.3 billion as compared with $14.6 for Canadian Pacific. See *Financial Post 500*, Summer 1984 and Summer 1985.

24. The five major chartered banks have a history of major political contributions to the two main parties as the following data indicate:

	To Liberals	*To Conservatives*
1979	$254 190	$251 587
1980	250 184	250 000
1981	148 708	190 483

(*Canadian Labour*, June 1983, 5)

25. When the Election Expenses Act was passed in 1974, the federal Liberal party, apparently with the urging of Prime Minister Trudeau and the agreement of its "bagmen," began the practice of limiting corporate donations to $50 000 in election years and one-half that amount in other years (Stevenson 1982, 31). The prime minister is quoted as saying, "We don't want to be indebted to any small number of large corporations." See Ian Urquhart (1978, 44).

26. See *Maclean's*, February 7, 1976, p. 47; *idem*, May 7, 1979, p. 25; and *Canadian Labour*, June 1983, p. 5.

27. As is obvious even from this listing, the *Financial Post 500* includes

federal and provincial crown corporations as well as cooperative organizations, including the wheat pools. Stanbury (1985f, 25) found that in 1983 some 39 federal and provincial crown corporations were reported or should have been included in the *Financial Post 500*. Among the top 200 he counted 21 crown corporations. Data in chapter 3 indicate that 40 crown corporations were reported or should have been included in the *Financial Post 500* based on 1984 revenues. The number in the top 200 was 21.

28. Obviously, a multivariate model would have been preferable — one taking into account such other variables as ownership (foreign vs. domestic), industry, contributions to the other party, and so on. While work is under way on such a model, it seemed useful to undertake a weaker test of the hypothesis.

29. In the U.S., Alexander (1983, 367) notes that political action committees (PACs) "are allowed to give up to $5,000 to federal candidates per election — $10,000 if the maximum is given for primary and general elections combined — as opposed to $1,000 per election for individuals." At the end of 1980 there were 1204 corporate, 297 labour, and 574 trade, membership, and health PACs. The number of corporate PACs was only 433 at the end of 1976. Together the PACs raised $137.7 million and spent $131.2 million during the 1979–80 electoral cycle (Alexander 1983, 367). These amounts should be compared to the cost of electing a Congress ($239 million) and the president ($275 million) in 1980 (Alexander 1983, 1). Drew (1983) explains how corporations and other interest groups are able to circumvent the legal limits on political contributions.

Jacobson (1985, 11) reports that between 1974 and 1982 the average value of contributions to candidates for the House of Representatives increased from $61 100 to $222 600. Individuals accounted for from 59 to 73% of total contributions to such candidates between 1974 and 1982. PACs accounted for from 17% (1974) to 31% (1982). The average value of contributions to candidates for the Senate increased from $455 500 in 1974 to $1 771 200 in 1982. Individuals accounted for 76% of such contributions in 1974 and 81% in 1982. PACs contributed 11% in 1974, 21% in 1980, and 18% in 1982.

Jacobson (1985, 10) notes that the total number of PACs registered with the Federal Election Commission grew from 608 in 1974 to 3371 in 1982. Adjusted for inflation, PAC contributions to congressional candidates have more than trebled between 1974 and 1982. "Corporate PAC contributions increased 460%, and their relative share of PAC donations grew from 20 percent to 33 percent over this period. Donations from trade associations and other (usually ideological) groups almost kept pace."

30. To obtain these figures, a research assistant had to review the 21 286

entries in the category "business and commercial organizations."

31. See "Generic drug makers losing in cut-throat lobbying battle," *Globe and Mail*, July 3, 1985, p. 4; "Drug lobby feverish," *Financial Post*, April 26, 1980, p. 16; "Large drug manufacturers have patent on discontent over act," *Financial Post*, May 5, 1984, pp. 28–29; Baetz (1983); Gorecki and Henderson (1981); Dan (1982); "Firms say generic drugs target of a 'slur campaign,' " *Globe and Mail*, October 16, 1984, p. 5; "Côté leans toward costly shift in drug licencing," *Globe and Mail*, June 21, 1984, p. 5; "Under the sugar coating," *Globe and Mail*, April 25, 1984, p. 13; and "Why consumers may soon be paying more for drugs," *Financial Post*, March 5, 1983, pp. 1–2. More generally, see Eastman (1985).

32. See, for example, "Patronage on the installment plan," *Maclean's*, July 9, 1984, p. 9; "Turner gives 18 Liberals plush posts," *Globe and Mail*, July 10, 1984, pp. 1–2; Giles Gherson, "Liberal patronage plums turn into rotten apples," *Financial Post*, December 29, 1984, p. 51; and James Rusk "Mackasey tops patronage income list," *Globe and Mail*, August 4, 1984, p. 5.

33. Vancouver *Sun*, June 19, 1985, p. A7.

34. Allan Fotheringham, *Maclean's*, May 7, 1979, p. 64. More generally, see "Losers and winners occupy list of Liberal appointments," *Globe and Mail*, June 13, 1977, p. 25; and Hugh Winsor and Dorothy Lipovenko, "Patronage: The Trudeau Government says thanks," *Globe and Mail*, June 13, 1977, pp. 1–2. See also Probyn and Proudfoot (1978).

35. Shortly after they took power replacing the PCs, the Liberals under David Peterson began replacing Tory appointees with persons allied to the Liberals. See John Cruikshank, "Ontario Liberals take time to replace Tory appointees," *Globe and Mail*, August 6, 1985, pp. 1–2.

36. *Maclean's*, February 6, 1984, pp. 6–7.

37. See, for example, "Liberal's spending on staff quadrupled, figures show," Vancouver *Sun*, December 5, 1984, p. A12.

38. An excellent example is the decision of the minister of fisheries to allow the transfer of a fishing licence after meeting with the boat's owner. Previously, senior public servants recommended that the transfer not be made because it did not meet the guidelines relevant to such cases. See Michael Harris, "Tory-owned consulting firm shows clout in Fisheries switch," *Globe and Mail*, June 27, 1985, pp. 1, 8.

39. Calgary *Herald*, November 13, 1984, p. A5.

40. "Patronage a tradition, Liberal says," Vancouver *Sun*, June 8, 1985, p. A2. See also "Power and access," *Globe and Mail*, October 8, 1985, p. 6.

41. Quoted in Jamie Lamb, "Still plenty of pork in the barrel," Van-

couver *Sun*, February 5, 1985, p. A4. See also MacGregor (1985) and *Maclean's*, October 21, 1985, pp. 14–15.

42. On machine politics in Canada, see Reid (1976) and Quinn (1976).

43. Don McGillivray, "Don't patronize the patronage system," Vancouver *Sun*, May 13, 1985, p. D12.

44. Ibid.

45. See, for example, David Hatter, "Desmarais opts for other dreams," *Financial Post*, July 6, 1985, p. 15.

46. *Globe and Mail*, October 24, 1985, p. 6.

47. *Maclean's*, February 23, 1976, p. 15.

48. Corporations, however, must find it hard to compete with the government's executive jets, which ministers use too much at such high costs per trip; it is not uncommon for a minister to spend $10 000 to $20 000 on a flight that would cost $400 to $1500 (first class) on Air Canada and that would arrive at about the same time as the government jet.

49. *Maclean's*, March 31, 1980, p. 16.

50. Ibid., February 23, 1976, pp. 14–15.

51. See *Globe and Mail*, September 10, 1985, p. 7.

52. *Maclean's*, June 28, 1976, pp. 17–18.

53. Ibid., October 3, 1983, p. 16.

54. *Globe and Mail*, August 31, 1984, p. 5.

55. Ibid., November 12, 1984, p. 7.

56. Ibid., October 23, 1984, p. 7.

57. Ibid., June 3, 1985, p. 9.

58. *Globe and Mail*, May 3, 1985, p. 10; and Vancouver *Sun*, May 3, 1985, p. A12. Elizabeth Drew (1983, 49) notes that in the U.S. the major parties have established special clubs for large contributors. For example, one established by the Democrats charges individuals $5000 a year and corporations $15 000 a year in contributions. Big givers are rewarded with meetings with important politicians. The organizer of this club was frank in saying what the members get for their contributions: "Access. Access. That's the name of the game. They meet with the leadership and with the chairmen of the committees. We don't sell legislation; we sell the opportunity to be heard."

59. "Power and access," *Globe and Mail*, October 8, 1985, p. A6.

60. "Masse move unplugs fund-raiser," *Globe and Mail*, September 28, 1985, p. 3.

61. Just how a contribution of $50 or $500 would permit the donor to "play a vital role in the shaping of government decisions" is not clear.

62. *Globe and Mail*, July 13, 1985, p. 4.

63. In April 1984 Conservative leader Brian Mulroney said his party's support for the amendment was a mistake that he proposed to rectify: "I didn't see it and I don't think anyone in caucus saw it. That

one got past us. . . . We're working hard to make sure it is changed" (*Globe and Mail*, April 3, 1984, p. 4). The Tories favoured new legislation that would permit individuals to speak out but restrict lobby groups from supporting or opposing parties or candidates. The crown argued that the ban was not on individuals speaking out, but only on spending money to aid or oppose parties or candidates (*Maclean's*, April 30, 1984, p. 26).

64. See *National Citizens' Coalition* case (1984) 5 W.W.R. 436, pp. 446–47.

65. See *Globe and Mail*, June 27, 1984, pp. 1–2.

66. *National Citizens' Coalition* case (1984) 5 W.W.R. 436, p. 453.

67. *Globe and Mail*, July 12, 1983, pp. 1–2. The NCC's court challenge cost the 30 000-member organization about $300 000. The ads the NCC proposed to run were to urge the sale of Petro-Canada, the entrenchment of private property rights in the Constitution, a balanced budget within three years, and the end to indexed pensions for politicians and public servants. Colin Brown, the president of NCC, argues his group is not like a traditional lobby group, i.e., "some outfit with the ability to go up to Ottawa, put an arm around a cabinet minister and sweet talk him into doing something for his client." Brown states that NCC never supports a particular party or candidate but rather tries to get information to the public so they can try to influence MPs or ministers (*Financial Post*, July 21, 1984, p. 28). The NCC has, however, made personal attacks on Pierre Trudeau and several of his ministers — see chapter 12.

   The NCC commissioned a Gallup poll in March 1984 which served as the basis for its planned $700 000 ad campaign during the 1984 federal election. The poll, according to the NCC, indicated a majority supported the association's position that Petro-Canada should be sold to the private sector and the NEP be dismantled. A majority also supported entrenchment of property rights in the Constitution, balancing the federal budget over three years, and eliminating indexed federal pensions for MPs and public servants (Vancouver *Sun*, July 11, 1984, p. B2).

68. *National Citizens' Coalition* case, (1984) 5 W.W.R. 436, p. 438.

69. Vancouver *Sun*, June 3, 1985, p. A11.

70. Gibbons defines political corruption as "the use of a public office in a way that forsakes the public interest, measured in terms of mass opinion, elite opinion or both, in order that some form of personal advantage may be achieved at the expense of the public interest" (1976, 5). In the same vein, Bretton (1980, 188) states: "Corrupt practice can . . . be defined as application of money, or of monetary equivalents, with intent to induce an official [elected or appointed] to violate his duty and/or induce or bring about malfunction of essential aspects of the democratic process." Using this

definition, he concludes that " 'corrupt' money is not significantly different from money that is not 'corrupt.' " I disagree. Surely the issue is not that the two forms of money are identical, it lies in the matter of intent. Money can be donated to political parties or candidates with no intention of "buying influence" or even access. For example, it can be given anonymously, purely out of friendship or admiration for an individual or to support a "cause" that cannot have a pecuniary benefit to the donor.

71. V. O. Key (1974, 23–28) identifies six general types of political graft:
- bribery;
- extortion, i.e., where a public official demands a benefit for him or herself or his or her party in order to provide a public benefit to an individual or company or to not use the power of government to harass someone;
- "state-bribery" — this is Key's term for the use of government resources for individual or party benefit, e.g., patronage;
- political discrimination in the formulation and administration of legislation, i.e., the targeting government activity so as to benefit particular individuals or the party in power directly or indirectly;
- discrimination in the administration of the service functions of government for political advantage; and
- "auto-corruption," i.e., where public officials enrich themselves or their party by using their position to deal with themselves in another guise, e.g., selling public property to a company that is a front for the officials.

For another typology, see Gibbons (1976).

72. Susan Rose-Ackerman (1978) emphasizes that bribery is only one way to influence a government's behaviour. The others include
- following the rules carefully and imaginatively so as to obtain the objectives sought;
- friendship, family ties, personal loyalty, i.e., making use of personal connections inside government; friends, even friends of friends, are usually treated differently than strangers by virtually everyone, and government is no exception;
- the arts of persuasion and supplying of information i.e., lobbying;
- the legal system — this can range from a writ of mandamus requiring an official to perform his or her legal duty to a case before the highest court, challenging the constitutionality of a piece of legislation;
- efforts to influence the next election, i.e., support the opposition in the hope they will get elected and when in office will be more willing to see things your way; and
- threats — these may range from bluffing (e.g., going to court, "going public") to illegal threats to use violence.

73. See "Tanaka's journey to court," *Maclean's*, October 17, 1983, pp. 44–45; and "The 'Flick Affair' Unravels," *Maclean's*, January 7, 1985, p. 52. More generally, see Gibbons and Rowat (1976) and Gardiner and Olson (1974).

74. See, for example, "A riding reaps its reward," *Maclean's*, July 22, 1985, p. 12.

75. See Berton (1976) and Donovan and Winmill (1976) respectively. More generally, see Gibbons and Rowat (1976).

76. *Financial Post*, April 14, 1979, p. 18.

77. See Montreal *Gazette*, August 26, 1983, pp. A1, A2.

78. Senator Irvine Barrow and businessman Charles MacFadden, in raising money for the Liberal Party of Nova Scotia, claimed to have special influence with the government of Premier Gerald Regan. Between late 1970 and late 1978 some $3.7 million was collected from more than 200 companies. The crown alleged that 23 companies were party to an influence-peddling scheme. Distillers and brewers were subject to "toll-gating." For example, Oland Breweries paid 2 cents per case or about $40 000 per year while the Liberals were in power. The opposition Tories received $2500 per year (*Maclean's*, April 18, 1983, pp. 23–24). MacFadden and Barrow were convicted and fined $25 000 each for influence peddling. The other defendant, J. G. Simpson, who pleaded guilty, paid a fine of $75 000 in April 1982. During the trial two distillers (who paid as much as 50 cents per case) stated that MacFadden was a "green light" or "lobbyist" who could assist them in getting their products listed. The trial judge said Simpson had raised $500 000 while Barrow and MacFadden raised $93 000. The president of Acres Consulting Services of Toronto testified that the fund raisers asked his firm to contribute from 3% to 5% of its fees from government contracts. This amounted to one-half his profits. He had never run into a similar request in other provinces. The BNA Act prohibits someone convicted of a felony or an "infamous crime" from holding a seat in the Senate. MacFadden retired as vice-president of National Sea Products, one of the largest fish processors in Canada. See *Globe and Mail*, May 12, 1983, p. 24, and May 13, 1983, p. 3.

79. *Financial Post*, January 12, 1985, p. 3. See also "Tory-linked firm cleared on contract," Vancouver *Sun*, March 30, 1985, p. A11; David Hunter, "Patronage plagues Tories," *Financial Post*, May 4, 1985, p. 18; Tim Naumetz, "Atkins' ad agency may get contract worth $9 million," *Globe and Mail*, April 23, 1985, pp. 1–2; and Charlotte Montgomery, "Ex-aide worked free for Wilson before ad contract, House told," *Globe and Mail*, April 23, 1985, p. 4.

80. In the U.S., the exchange of campaign contributions by lobbyists for at least tacit promises of support for particular legislative proposals by legislators or candidates is well documented by Elizabeth

Drew (1983). The role of political money has become so important
in the electoral process that "the processes by which Congress is supposed to function have been distorted" (1983, 2). Politicians need
more and more money to run for office. That money comes largely
from interest groups anxious to see that their members benefit from
the actions of government or at least are not hurt by government.
Drew (1983, 3) quotes one Washington lobbyist who says that "we're
reaching the point where legislators make decisions only after thinking about what this means in terms of money that will come to them
or go to their opponents."

81. In the U.K., a House of Commons resolution in 1685 defined as "a
high crime and misdemeanour," "the offer of money or other advantage to a Member of Parliament for the promoting of any matter
whatsoever to be transacted in Parliament." In the U.S., it was
not until 1853 that it was a crime to bribe a congressman. And it
was not until the 1920s that the first cabinet-level official (Albert
Fall) was convicted of bribery (in the Teapot Dome scandal).

82. Rose-Ackerman (1978, chap. 2) shows that in an ideal system of
knowledgeable and concerned voters where politicians trade off gains
in personal income against the probability of re-election, corruption is the *only* way special-interest groups could influence political
outcomes. More realistically, she shows that

> if voters are poorly informed about issues, the legislators know
> little about constituents' tastes, interest groups no longer need
> rely on bribery to gain legislative advantage. Instead, they can
> contribute to a politician's campaign fund in return for legis-
> lative support on issues of concern to the group. Thus, politi-
> cians may be less corrupt when the public has poor information,
> but special interests may be even more influential in the deter-
> mination of policy. Furthermore, interest groups now have other
> options open to them besides campaign contributions to poli-
> ticians. They can also try to "educate" either politicians or voters
> to obtain support for their positions. (1978, 55)

Where voters are apathetic about political issues rather than ill-
informed, the provision of information will have little impact on
electoral outcomes. In this case, politicians will focus on dividing
the pay-offs provided by interest groups — the only persons interested in policies and their distributive consequences — between personal enrichment and the "purchase of votes."

83. Bretton (1980, 186) goes so far as to argue that wherever money
goes, corruption is sure to follow. But what is and what is not corrupt is largely a matter of perception, which might suggest that the
term political corruption, like "unauthorized" political behaviour,
should be used only in quotation marks. In his view, "Any distinc-

tion between propriety and impropriety in politics, as in economics
is not only bursting with ambiguity, it is meaningless."

84. In addition, Paltiel (1966) suggests that large donors may wish to
define the parameters within which decisions are made, and this
helps to explain the often heard appeal for funds to preserve the
"two party" system. In his view, full disclosure of the sources of political funds makes clear the origins of the policies and frees the party
from the charge of hidden manipulation.

85. If Camp is referring to the likely quality of *political* advice tendered
by senior business people, he is probably correct. Camp, however, is
wrong if he means that business people cannot influence a government to provide specific benefits to their firm or industry or that
they cannot be a force to be reckoned with in the formation of public opinion. And it is public opinion that is the coin in which politicians deal. Policies stem little from ideology or ideals, but from a
firm sense of what actions will gain or retain political support.

86. Justin Dart, a longtime financial backer of Ronald Reagan and a
member of his "kitchen cabinet," claims that in a dialogue with
politicians, they hear you a little better with a little money. Senator
Daniel Inouye is quoted as saying much the same thing: "The fact
remains that when someone gives you a thousand or two thousand
dollars he expects that door to be open to him — and he gets a little
preferential treatment." And in the same vein business executive
Ira Corn (1981, 466–67) states that "fortunately or unfortunately,
in politics, 'being heard' often means cash." He also says that "those
who help [a politician] financially in his election efforts have a better chance of being heard after the election is over." Corn argues
that "because a corporation's leaders can join with others and contribute $5000, or whatever, to the congressman [via Political Action
Committees] just like labor can, the business leader becomes an
important tangible supporter, rather than an unspoken persona non
grata because of failure to put up real money." Some 700 of the
largest 1000 U.S. corporations had set up PACs by 1981. Many more
were formed since then. While this might imply that political contributions can "buy influence," Corn denies this. He does, however,
argue that corporate PACs "mean that a more even handed attitude
is likely on the part of the politician [between business and labour]."
More generally, see Alexander (1983) and Jacobson (1985).

87. It should be noted that when a politician or party accepts large
campaign contributions from corporations or other interest groups,
they may do so to concentrate their obligations and thereby leave
them unobligated on what they feel are more important issues. In
other words, in order to do the Lord's work on issue A one may have
to make a pact with the devil concerning issue B.

88. Vancouver *Sun*, February 20, 1985, p. A16.

89. Writing in the early 1960s, a former national organizer for the Liberal party emphasized that "nobody who holds office or hopes to hold office can ignore his benefactors." Moreover, large donations speeded access to the powerful:

    Any citizen of Canada can lay his views before the prime minister or the leader of the opposition but, human nature being what it is (and these men are human), a man whose firm donates $25,000 or $50,000 to a political party every election is likely to get through to the party leader a lot faster than somebody the party never heard of. (Scott 1961, 67)

90. Do campaign contributions result in government contracts? *Le Devoir* says an investigation it conducted shows 54 companies hired by a federal crown corporation responsible for redeveloping Quebec City's old part poured more than $140 000 into federal Liberal election coffers during the past three years. The average amount contributed each year by the companies was more than three times the average contribution from private Canadian corporations during that period, the newspaper said. The 54 companies were among 106 contractors and subcontractors hired by Canada Mortgage and Housing Corporation through a subsidiary called Vieux-Port de Québec to renovate the harbourfront, beginning in 1981. Almost all the directors of the agency have some direct ties with the Liberals, *Le Devoir* reported. In the past five years, total federal funding for renovation work on the provincial capital's harbourfront has almost trebled to more than $115 million from $42 million originally estimated. More than $90 million of that was spent without any control by Parliament, said *Le Devoir* (Vancouver *Sun*, August 8, 1984, p. B3).

91. *Financial Post 500*, Summer 1985, p. 108.

92. See Rod McQueen, "The Bronfman empire's reach," *Maclean's*, May 6, 1985, pp. 42–43; Paul Goldstein, "2nd Bronfman empire expands horizons," *Globe and Mail*, July 21, 1984, pp. B1–B2; and Richard Spence, "Edper's astounding reach," *Financial Post*, January 9, 1984, pp. 1, 8.

93. In interviews with 2562 electors in 1974, for example, "the authors found more than half of all the general comments about politics were negative in tone and that an astounding 78 per cent of comments relating to politicians were similarly negative." Some 36% of a 1966 sample of voters thought that "political favoritism" and "corruption" in Ottawa were increasing. In 1974 the fraction was 42%. A similar fraction did not know of an MP they admired. However, a 1977 survey of Ontario voters found that "respondents who had actively participated in partisan politics (by giving money, attending party rallies, displaying campaign symbols, canvassing and so

on) were more likely than others to express confidence in politicians" (*Parliamentary Government* 1, no. 1 [October 1979]: 6–8).

More recently, a national survey of 2038 adults in 1984 found that 42% of the sample believed that federal and provincial legislators are not "honest and sincere." Only 9% agreed that politicians are honest, while 44% "somewhat agreed" that politicians are honest. There were some interesting differences across the provinces. While 51% of Quebecers did not believe their elected representatives were "honest and sincere," only 35% of Ontario residents were of this view (*Toronto Star*, December 19, 1984, p. A14). More generally, see Adams 1984.

94. One of the very few previous efforts in this area is Osborn (1975).
95. The Institute for Political Involvement notes: "Considerable ambivalence pervades the whole issue of financial (as well as non financial) contributions to political parties and candidates. This uncertainty surrounding the function and role of contributions in Canadian politics has not been clarified, in the minds of business managers, by the election expenses acts" (1978, 24).

The institute argues for an explicit statement regarding political contributions in each company's policy concerning its involvement in the political process: "The inclusion of political contributions as a policy component is based on the need for a company to be concerned with the long range political environment. The policy must have critical regard for the alternatives to the party in power as well as the current government party" (1978, 27).

96. The IPI's recommendation is as follows: "The policy should be confined to company political contributions, rather than the contributions of individual employees. However, the company could utilize its various communications facilities to acquaint employees with how the election expenses acts treat such individual contributions for tax purposes" (1978, 28).

11

Business and the
News Media

1.0 INTRODUCTION

The news media are the principal source of the public's information about business. For example, a survey of 2000 adults in the United States in 1982 found that the most important source was TV newscasts (60 percent), followed by newspapers (44 percent), radio (31 percent), and business publications (only 16 percent) (Corrado 1984, 84). Thornton Bradshaw, the former CEO of RCA, has emphasized the importance of the media for business:

> The media are as important to the survival of corporations as they are to the survival of our democracy. . . . Corporations will survive only if people approve of what they do. What people think they do is largely shaped by the media. Public acceptance must be earned by doing the right things, but people must think that corporations are doing the right things. (1981, p. xxv)

Chapter 6 focused on the news media as a source of information in the context of issues management. This chapter explains how a business organization can deal with the news media in its efforts to influence public policy in terms both of specific issues and of how government and the public perceive the organization. This requires that business people understand how the news media function as complex business organizations, their objectives, and the constraints under which they operate. Such understanding must precede efforts to use the media to try to shape public opinion and government policy. Success in both endeavours requires that a business organization be able to communicate to the public and government (bureaucrats and politicians) a credible corporate vision that positions the organization in both the economic and political marketplaces (Corrado 1984, 5). The long-run survival of any organization requires that its behaviour be acceptable to public opinion. And public opinion, in turn, is shaped by what people read or hear in the mass media.

Note: This chapter is co-authored with four of my M.B.A. students: Norm Couttie, Susan Jones, Surjeet Rai, and Jeff Richmond.

We begin by offering some reasons why the mass media are important to business organizations. We then discuss the pervasiveness of the print and electronic media in Canada. In section 3 we examine some of the critical characteristics of the media: the concentration of ownership, the regulation of electronic media, media as business organizations, and the role of different media outlets. We also examine the important question of whether the media are biased toward business. Section 4 focuses on the effective use of the media in government relations. Some detailed suggestions are given regarding how to handle an interview with a reporter.

2.0 IMPORTANCE OF THE MASS MEDIA

2.1 The Power of the Media

The mass media, television in particular, have the power to influence the basic value system of society, to both shape values and mirror public opinion, thereby affecting how people think. The mass media can set the agenda for public discussion, create pressure for action or nonaction, and press for accountability. Frequently, the priorities of the media, stemming from the media's quest for audiences and profits, become the priorities of the public. Reporters are aware of the power of the mass media.[1] Clive Cocking remarks that reporters

> know how easy it is to harm the personal and professional lives of people they write about — and how often it happens. They are also well aware of, shall we say, how *imprecise* journalism is as a craft. Reporters see it every day in how events get dramatized, conflicts exaggerated, how arguments are strengthened by selective use of facts, how impressions are created by judicious use of quotes — and how often error creeps in. . . . it's just the way it is with journalism. (1980, 169)

A public issue may grow out of a major news event, but it may also arise from a mounting number of minor incidents. The news media define public issues and sometimes create them where none existed before. The press has always been a source of ideas for the legislative agenda and also, effectively, a source of pressure on politicians, by reflecting at least certain segments of public opinion. The *Globe and Mail* reflects the views of a different segment of society than does the *Toronto Sun*. What is on the public mind — what people are thinking and talking about — is commonly equated with what is widely reported in the news media. For example, a study of public opinion in Canada from 1960 to 1978 found that public perceptions of the most important problems facing the country were related not only to the actual incidence of unemployment or inflation, but also to newspaper headlines (Kent et al. 1981, 138).

When a story is featured on the front page of a newspaper or on TV, the public, newspeople, and politicians alike tend to regard it as a matter of interest to the public. But a subject that is big in the news may not be what is important to political and economic leaders. Truly important news may strike readers or viewers as dull, too complex, too remote, or too abstract even if its importance is recognized. Newspeople constantly seek to differentiate each day's events, and in so doing form priorities for public discussion and action. At the same time, their own sense of what is trivial and what is significant is shaped by what opinion surveys tell them about the public's interests, preferences, and concerns (Bogart 1972, 58).

Overall, the news media determine what gets recorded as well as what is reported. In the process of selecting the news, the media are performing a "gatekeeping" function in that they influence the flow of information. Furthermore, through the selection process and by the way news is "processed," the media can effectively become advocates of particular views in their reporting activities (over and above their editorial role). In short, the media function as filters of information by means of the various overlapping roles as recorders, advocates, and gatekeepers (Bartha 1984b, 11).

2.2 Sources of Political Power of the News Media

Siegel argues that the mass media's *political* power stems from five major sources as follows:

1. *Provision of Basic Political Information*: The media are powerful because they provide basic information; they survey the society, including the political sphere, and transmit a continuous account of politics that includes warning signals about threats and dangers on the national and international scene, thus preparing the public for future developments. Another example of media power stemming directly from their function as providers of information is that they make people famous, with persons singled out for newspaper or TV coverage receiving public recognition; this is called the "status conferral" role. Furthermore, persons who are "well-informed," largely through the media, are often regarded as influential, becoming important message carriers and image shapers for their friends on political matters.

2. *Political Linkage*: . . . The media are the major link between the public and the government. The nature of this linkage shapes in part the public's involvement in the political process and helps to define the "democratic nature" of the governmental system. The free flow of political communications is one of the major building blocks — perhaps the most important — in democratic

societies. If voters are to make rational choices in elections they must have meaningful information and discussion of public issues; they depend on the media for this information and discussion.

3. *Agenda Setting*: The media do not transmit all the news that they have collected and that is made available by the press services; they are selective. In choosing and displaying news, editors and others who help shape media content must take into consideration the resources at their disposal, time factors and space considerations. Not only do the media describe the events of the political world as the editors perceive them, but they also pick and choose the events they regard as important. In effect they prepare the news menu, thus deciding the issues of the day that are to receive public attention. This is referred to as the agenda-setting function of the media. . . .

4. *Editorial Offerings*: . . . In newspapers this is especially visible in the form of editorials, background stories that discuss political issues and their merits, columns by political columnists, interpretive stories and political cartoons. What emerges is persuasion. The "ideological" perspective is not limited to editorial pages in newspapers and the commentaries of the broadcast press, as journalists often argue, but also shapes the general content of the media; selection of stories and pictures and the prominence of display. The persuasive power is directly related to the correlation function of mass communications; the media help to put the vast amount of information they collect into a "meaningful picture," and provide a support structure for a point of view.

5. *Influence on Political Actors*: Politicians recognize only too well the impact mass communication can have in generating public opinion, and as a result pay close attention to the coverage of politics and the editorial views expressed in the media. Consequently, the media influence politicians themselves. (Siegel 1983, 14–15)

2.3 Media Outlets

The Canadian news media are pervasive and highly developed technically as part of one of the most advanced communications systems in the world (Desbarats 1984, 77). Despite the great distances and costs involved, most Canadians have a wide variety of radio and television services, probably more than any other country (Stewart 1983, 20). There are currently 722 AM and FM radio stations and 250 television stations in Canada (CRTC, *Annual Report*, 1983/84).

The Canadian press consists of 116 daily newspapers with a total daily circulation of 5.5 million (Fletcher & Taras 1984, 203). In addition, there are about 850 weekly community newspapers in Canada, with a combined weekly circulation of 3.3 million (Lem 1983, p. R8). Canada has two weekly business journals, the *Financial Times of Canada*, with a circulation of 105 000 and the *Financial Post*, with a circulation of 190 000 (Noble 1985, p. B6). As well, there are 700 specialized business publications in Canada, with more than 7 million readers monthly in industry, commerce, and the professions (Fiber 1983a, p. R8).

The Communication Research Centre's national readership study indicates that nine out of ten Canadians read daily newspapers in the course of a week, and 79 percent of the population read at least one community newspaper each week (Kubas 1981, 11). Television, however, is the most pervasive medium — 98 percent of Canadian households have at least one working television set, with an average of 1.6 sets per household. Virtually all of the English-language population can receive a CBC-owned or -affiliated station and a CTV affiliate, while 70 percent can also receive at least one independent English-language station (Hoskins & McFadyen 1982, 348).

The average Canadian adult (18 +) spends 25.2 hours per week watching television and 19.1 hours per week listening to radio,[2] but only 53 minutes per day reading a newspaper (Kubas 1981, 12). The frequency and duration of viewers' exposure to TV is such that the average viewer spends more time watching television than doing anything other than sleeping and working (Gale & Wexler 1983, 15). The importance of the electronic media is emphasized by Siegel:

> Broadcasting, and especially TV, is generally perceived as the most important sector of the Canadian mass media in shaping public opinion today. Canadians appear to put greater trust in broadcast news than in what they read in the newspapers. A national Gallup Poll in 1978 found that if there are conflicting reports of an event, Canadians will believe television rather than the printed press. (1983, 32)

By way of illustration Table 11-1 indicates the scope of the circulation of the major dailies and the size of the audience for both local and national television shows in Canada.

2.4 Specialized Media

The business press is a widely diverse group of publications ranging from general business magazines to financial newspapers through to highly specialized trade and professional journals. These publications for the most part depend on a limited advertising base. A recent study by the Canadian Business Press showed a circulation average of 15 000 to 16 000 copies for business periodicals (Fiber 1983a, p. R3).

Maclean Hunter and Southam Communications, both of Toronto, dominate the business press with close to 100 of the 700 publications.

Table 11-1
SIZE OF READERSHIP/AUDIENCE OF MAJOR DAILIES/TV PROGRAMS IN CANADA

The Top 10 Daily Newspapers	*Weekday Circulation*
Toronto Star	503 313
Globe and Mail	328 201
Le Journal de Montréal	322 563
Toronto Sun	248 184
Vancouver Sun	231 611
Montreal Gazette	197 120
La Presse	187 276
Ottawa Citizen	184 340
Winnipeg Free Press	179 395
Edmonton Journal	158 899

Source: *Canadian Advertising Rates and Data*, May 1985.

SIZE OF TELEVISION AUDIENCE
(age 12+, March 1985)

• CTV national news (11 p.m.)	1 327 000	
• CBC "The National" (10 p.m.)	1 114 000	
• CBC "The Journal" (10:30 p.m.)	868 000	
• Local early news (6 to 7 p.m.)		
— BCTV — Vancouver	213 000	(18+)
— CHCH — Toronto	220 000	(18+)
— CFCF — Montreal (Eng.)	300 000	(18+)
• CTV — largest entertainment shows		
— "The People's Choice Awards"	2 800 000	
— "Magnum P.I."	2 057 000	
— "Knight Rider"	1 833 000	
— "Riptide"	1 801 000	
— "Scarecrow and Mrs. King"	1 722 000	
• CBC — largest entertainment shows		
— "Dallas"	1 993 000	
— "Walt Disney"	1 282 000	
— (Early national news)	1 245 000	
— "Remington Steele"	1 140 000	
— "Fifth Estate"	1 132 000	

Source: Bureau of Broadcast Measurement, *Report*, March 1985.

Between these two and the numerous single-publication houses are middle-sized companies such as Wadham Publications of Toronto with 15 business publications and Sandford Evans Communications of Winnipeg, also with 15 publications (Fiber 1983a, p. R8).

The country's two weekly financial newspapers, the *Financial Post* and the *Financial Times of Canada*, along with the *Globe and Mail*'s "Report on Business," have been competing vigorously for circulation and trying to appeal to new readers.[3] However, Diane Francis, a well-known business writer with the *Toronto Star*, states:

> *The Financial Post*, *Financial Times*, and *Report on Business* are not newspapers; they're trade papers. They talk in a form of jargon which is boring; it's grey, there are no pictures, no controversy. Most of the reporters run around and do rewrites of Dow Jones wire copy and put their bylines on it. They print press releases verbatim, intact: they don't do any big pictures or trend pieces. (Quoted in Cohen & Shannon 1984, 34)

Recent increased business coverage in the daily press, the birth of a host of regional business publications and at least two national business magazines (*Your Money* and *Report on Business Magazine*), as well as a variety of recent TV specials on money and corporate behaviour,[4] have further increased competition and indicate that business is currently in good favour with the media. The new crop of business shows and magazines reflects the media's understanding that business is of increasing interest to ordinary people. The recessions of 1974 and the 1980s have aroused people's economic fears, while at the same time causing them to become disillusioned with politics and institutions (Brown 1985, 7). Cohen and Shannon argue:

> The public hungers for knowledge of the economy as reflected in the spectacular marketing successes of expanded business sections in many North American newspapers. Yet consumers of economic news and media alike agree that the picture they receive in the press is often a distorted one, lacking in substance, but most importantly, missing a framework that places the facts in context. (1984, 31)

Specialized trade periodicals sell to advertisers a vehicle with which to reach a relevant audience. Trade periodicals are aimed at people who influence a purchasing decision and have an interest in the subject matter of the publication. The industry recognizes six readership catezgories — agriculture, the professions, merchandising, marketing, technical, and institutions. Within these lie a broad range of periodicals.[5] With few exceptions (mainly in the financial area) these publications are distributed at no charge to the target readership.[6] Publishers are therefore careful to monitor the effectiveness of their circulation in reaching the relevant audience (Fiber 1983a, p. R8).

3.0 CRITICAL CHARACTERISTICS OF THE MEDIA

3.1 Concentration

Canada is basically a nation of one-paper, or at least one-publisher, towns. In fact, all cities in North America, with the exception of multimillion population centres, are one-paper towns (*Business Life*, November 1980, p. 18). While the number of newspapers has not changed much over the years, the number of cities in Canada and the U.S. featuring directly competing daily newspapers has declined sharply. In 1908 there were 130 Canadian dailies, but by 1980, of the 117 dailies, there was competition in only seven cities (Toronto, French-speaking Montreal, Winnipeg, Calgary, Edmonton, Quebec City, and St. John's).

The trend to large-scale corporate ownership began as early as 1920 and accelerated in the decade between 1970 and 1980 (Kent et al. 1981, 8). Chains accounted for 77 percent of the circulation of daily newspapers published in Canada in September 1980, an increase from 58 percent ten years earlier (Kent et al. 1981, 12). By 1983 twelve groups owned 89 percent of the country's 116 dailies, and the six largest controlled 80 percent of the circulation (Fletcher & Taras 1984, 203). News gathering was dominated by the Canadian Press (CP) wire service founded in 1917 as a national cooperative and owned collectively by the major chain-dominated daily newspapers. Set up as a clearing house for news gathered by Canada's dailies, CP has provided an effective and inexpensive mechanism for exchanging news among member papers and for bringing in up-to-date foreign news. All newspaper members are obliged to supply news of their areas to CP, which selects, rewrites, and condenses the material and then disseminates it to members and clients (Cumming, Cardinal & Johansen 1981, 11). CP expanded along with its members and remains today the primary source of nonlocal news for all but the largest Canadian dailies. Increasingly it uses its own reporters to cover major stories within Canada. It has few foreign correspondents, however, and continues to import foreign news from the world's major news services. CP relies heavily on American sources — primarily its U.S. counterpart, the Associated Press.

Radio and television newsrooms, most of which lack the resources to do significant news gathering on their own, rely on similar sources. Two CP subsidiaries, Broadcast News (BN) and Press News, supply much of the news and feature material used by Canada's private broadcasters as well as the CBC. They in turn rely on CP and the major international news services to establish their news priorities. (Only the CBC makes a real effort at independent foreign coverage.) The French media rely on these same sources, with a heavy dose of material from Agence-France-Presse (AFP), the Paris-based service (Fletcher & Taras 1984, 197). As of

January 1985 the Canadian Press became the *only* Canadian general supplier of news to all sectors of the news system. Though on the surface the media seem to present many competing voices, in reality CP dominates the supply of news to daily print outlets and to broadcasting.

In 1981 the Royal Commission on Newspapers found some evidence that concentration of ownership[7] resulted in a loss of diversity of opinion; however, little definitive evidence was found indicating that monopoly and conglomerate ownership reduced editorial quality or that owners interfered to protect their own interests. The commission found that newspapers in competitive situations were more likely than those in monopoly situations to make editorial endorsements of political candidates at all levels of government, as well as present a wider range of political comment. This evidence suggests that competition does increase editorial vigour (Kent et al. 1981, 139).

Chain owners of daily newspapers may also control community newspapers, radio and television stations, periodicals, and major interests outside the media. Besides ownership of more than forty daily newspapers, Thomson Newspapers of Toronto owns fourteen community newspapers, most of them in Ontario, with others in Western Canada and one in New Brunswick (Lem 1983, p. R8). In New Brunswick, the K. C. Irving interests own all five English-language dailies plus a radio station, television station, regional magazine, and book-publishing company.[8] In Saskatchewan the two major dailies and important broadcast outlets are owned by a single group (Fletcher & Taras 1984, 204).

Interlocking media and industrial interests in Canada are very common. In addition to newspapers, the Thomson interests include oil and gas, retailing (The Bay, Simpsons, Simpson-Sears, and Zellers), insurance, travel, and trucking. Power Corporation, one of three groups that own all but two of the French-language dailies in Quebec, is involved in many economic activities unrelated to the media (Fletcher & Taras 1984, 203). The potential for conflict of interest in terms of advertising and editorial decisions where there is a close relationship between articles, news items, and the media owner's business interests, according to Robert Fulford (1977, 12), seems obvious.

3.2 The Electronic Media and Its Regulation

The number of broadcast outlets increased sharply between 1970 and 1980. The number of radio stations grew from 382 to 617, and the number of television stations from 79 to 127 (Thompson 1980, 50). In March 1984 there were 754 AM and 786 FM stations in Canada, of which 410 and 312 respectively were originating stations (CRTC, *Annual Report*, 1983/84).

Some 700 cable TV systems are now licensed to operate in Canada, and over 60 percent of households in Canada have cable TV. As a result of this, about one-quarter of the mainly English-speaking population have twelve or more channels to choose from; about three-quarters have five or more; leaving one-quarter with four or less, all but a few of whom have at least two (Stewart 1983, 20).

Although the number of outlets in each area of the country has been regulated by the CRTC, the future prospects of cable, satellites, and pay TV threaten to further fragment the Canadian audience. Some media observers see Canada not moving toward a concentration of mass media, but toward diversity or "narrowcasting" resulting from attempts by publishers and broadcasters to serve smaller and smaller submarkets of specialized audiencies (Thompson 1980, 50).

Public regulation of broadcasting (radio and television) is extensive (Boyle 1983). The Broadcasting Act includes the following objectives for the broadcasting system: Canadian ownership and control; varied programming; and programming of high standard, using predominantly Canadian creative resources. The federal government objectives for the electronic media have also included the provision of coast-to-coast services in both official languages, contributing to the development and maintenance of Canadian cultural identity, and the promotion of national unity. Both public and private broadcasters are expected to contribute to these goals, and the CRTC is required to implement them. In an attempt to fulfill their objectives, the CRTC has proclaimed Canadian-content regulations for both radio and television, and required cable systems to give priority to Canadian stations (Fletcher & Taras 1984, 199).

Between July 1982 and May 1985 the CRTC was directed to refuse licence renewals to TV stations owned by newspaper companies in the same market, unless the denial would not be in the public interest or would cause the owner "exceptional or unreasonable hardship."[9] The commission, in fact, never refused to renew a licence under the Liberals' cabinet directive. However, the CRTC did rule that the Irving interests, which own the CBC affiliate (with seven rebroadcasting stations) in Saint John, New Brunswick, and all five English-language daily papers in the province, were ineligible for renewal of their licence. However, the Irvings were given until January 1986 to comply. The Irvings took the government to court, and the Conservatives repealed the general directive because, they said, it had served its purpose.

The Canadian-content guidelines have had little effect in increasing the exposure of Canadian audiences to Canadian shows and stimulating the program-production industry. Despite regulations, 75 percent of all Canadian viewing time is taken up with U.S. shows (Trebilcock et al. 1981, p. II-28). Private broadcasters have often claimed that Canadian-content regulations should be based, not on quantity, but on quality of Canadian production. It is not clear, however, how "quality" is to be defined precisely enough for regulation (Stewart 1983, 22).

3.3 Media Companies as Businesses

Private companies in the newspaper or broadcasting industry are motivated by the pursuit of profit, which is largely dependent on advertising
revenue. Of overwhelming significance is the proposition that the media are in the business of selling audiences to advertisers. The purpose
of the medium is to capture audiences to subject them to commercial
messages. For example, advertisers provide 80 percent of a daily newspaper's revenue and all of a radio or TV station's revenue. If all audiences are valued equally by advertisers, then the greater the size of the
audience, the higher the price advertisers are willing to pay for commercial exposure. Hence, revenue-maximizing behaviour entails an emphasis on editorial content or programming that maximizes audience
size. If all articles/programs cost the same to produce or purchase, this
conduct will also maximize profits (Hoskins & McFadyen 1982, 348).
(This is not true of specialized print media that are largely dependent
on subscriber revenues.)

The media have the highest average profit of any sector of the
Canadian economy. Rates of return for Canadian daily newspapers
have been well above the returns on capital in most industries. In 1978
the return on net assets employed in the newspaper industry was 25
percent, and 26 percent for the private broadcasting industry (Kent et
al. 1981, 84).[10]

In 1980 about three-quarters of all television viewing in Canada
was of American programs (appearing on both American and Canadian stations); about 19 percent was of Canadian programs; and
about 5 percent was of foreign programming other than American
(Stewart 1983, 28). Though Canadians show a strong preference for
U.S. entertainment programs, they generally prefer Canadian docu-
mentaries and news shows (Fletcher & Taras 1984, 199). The question
is — why is this so?

The amount of American TV programming that is easily and cheaply
available to Canadian stations explains the dominance of such programs
in part. More importantly, people use television most of the time for
entertainment rather than for intellectual or cultural enrichment. Generally, more intellectually demanding programs are enjoyed by older
viewers. The great majority of American programs in Canada are en-
tertaining, and are enjoyed by a disproportionately large number of
young viewers. In contrast, the majority of prime-time Canadian-
produced programs are more demanding, drawing their audiences from
among older, better-educated people representing a smaller potential
audience (Stewart 1983, 29). Thus, with 100 percent of revenues arising
from advertising, the incentive for showing U.S. programming in Canada is very strong (Hoskins & McFadyen 1982, 348).

3.4 A Particular View of the World?

In the process of attracting audiences to sell to advertisers (or in the case of the CBC, to convince Parliament of its worth), the media, it is argued, also sell a view of the world: "The media . . . define what is normal and respectable in society, what is debatable and what is beyond discussion by decent, respectable citizens" (Westell 1977, 73). Many reporters see themselves as guardians of the public interest, particularly vis-à-vis powerful and entrenched groups such as big business (Westell 1977, 32). For the media, predictability is boring. Conflict, real or imagined, is useful to create excitement, drama, and readability (Hughes 1979, 73).

While each medium has its own special requirements, they all tend to prefer the immediate, the personal, and the concrete to long-term social debate or abstract ideas. Media consumers are conditioned to accept these standards, making it difficult for messages that do not fit the media mould to be heard.

For example, in order to reach a mass audience, a daily newspaper must be a mixture of news and entertainment. The mixture varies from paper to paper depending on the type of reader sought. Also, the news itself must be written to a formula that emphasizes drama, surprise, and conflict, although these elements vary from paper to paper (Cocking 1980). In the writing of the news, the story of the event is almost always inverted, so the result becomes the beginning of the story. The process that leads to the result appears, if at all, as secondary news. This makes for simplicity, but not for understanding, and is done by newspapers to make the news readable. As a result, interpretation and analysis is very difficult, often preventing the reader from forming his or her own opinion (Westell 1982b, 47).

The economic realities of the mass media mean that "hard news" (information shorn of editorial comment) has to compete with entertainment in the battle to maintain the size of the audience. Because size is the most important determinant of revenues, the result is an effort to make the news more like entertainment. Don Hewitt, executive producer of "60 Minutes," one of the most popular "soft news" or "feature journalism" shows, has stated that "our purpose is to make information more palatable and to make reality more competitive with make believe" (quoted in Corrado 1984, 85). A. V. Westin, an ABC vice-president, notes:

> The evening news is not the highest form of journalism. It is partly an illustrated headline service and partly a magazine. And, yes, it is part show business, using visual enticement and a star system to attract viewers. Television news can function best when it is regarded by its viewers as . . . important yet . . . adjunct to the newspapers. When I read statistics that show most Americans get most of their

news from television, I shudder. I know what we have to leave out.
(Quoted in MacDougall 1980)

3.5 Role of Different Media

In English Canada, the *Globe and Mail* testifies to the influence of the
role of the newspaper as the agenda setter for other media — more than
90 percent of media executives read it regularly. *Le Devoir* plays a similar role in the French-speaking community (Kent et al. 1981, 138). These
dailies set the basic day-to-day news and public affairs agenda for the
electronic media. For example, a major story often begins in the *Globe
and Mail*. It goes out overnight on the CP wire, hits radio and TV by
morning, and may reappear in the afternoon during Question Period in
the House of Commons. It goes from there via TV cameras to the local
and national prime-time evening TV news, while the *Globe* and other
print media are preparing the next day's agenda (Fulford 1984, 10).

The newspaper cannot compete with the electronic media in terms of
immediacy, but it can treat the news in more detail and in greater depth.
The target market for the newspaper determines its format, the style, as
well as the content of the news. Some dailies with a national outlook,
such as the *Globe and Mail*, will give a banner headline to national or
international politics, while local dailies will emphasize news that is most
important to their municipality. (The most obvious example is the *Toronto Star*'s obsession with things in Metro Toronto.) The tabloids (which
have been called newspapers for people who don't read) tend to blow up
the most spectacular news item. (The *Toronto Sun* is the leading example and is the most financially successful tabloid in Canada.) In terms of
content, the tabloid calls for concise, superficial treatment of the news,
while a national daily will contain more detailed analysis. In all, the
editorial content of a newspaper depends not only on the characteristics
and limitations of the paper itself but also on the available space and
on the decisions and objectives of management.

The business press functions to keep business and professionals up to
date in a rapidly changing, technology-oriented business world. The
specialized trade journals engage in analysis and debate. When dealing
with complex issues, these elite publications serve as a channel for technical information and viewpoint among a select leader group (Westell
1982b, 47).

Radio broadcasters operate with a large measure of independence,
but programming is shaped by the desire to appeal to a very narrowly
defined target audience. Radio is a personal medium with the unique
capacity to work in the theatre of the mind. Unlike television, radio
attracts audience loyalty to stations, not programs (*Marketing*, February 6, 1984).

The CBC is the only national radio broadcaster in Canada. According to Westell (1982, 47), CBC radio provides more first-class journalism than any other medium in Canada. While private radio places heavy emphasis on local news, local and network programs are closely intermingled on CBC Radio. In terms of information versus entertainment types of programming, the CBC-AM network emphasizes news and information along with some classical and popular music. On the other hand, CBC-FM puts heavy emphasis on classical music, with background information emphasizing the arts and sciences. In contrast, private radio is mainly confined to popular music, with brief newscasts in the context of quite narrowly prescribed formats (Stewart 1983, 24).

By the nature of the medium, television is better suited to capture high drama and transmit emotional experience than it is to present detailed information and explain complex issues (MacDougall 1980, 9). Television news focuses on events that are timely, accessible, politically significant, dramatic, and visually interesting, and involve individuals rather than abstractions. Nevertheless, television is regarded by most Canadians as being the most influential, believable, fair and unbiased medium, as well as the medium that keeps them most up to date (Kubas 1981, 25).

Television not only reflects the needs of the audience, but contributes greatly to the image of the world upon which the audience depends. Society is both the source and the receiver of the message, and the TV medium is the interpreter. Television crosses social, religious, generational, and class lines in an unprecedented manner (Fletcher & Taras 1984, 194).

On television, everything must be understood by everyone (Fulford 1984, 10). Television news responds to a profound need — it reduces the chaos of the day into something approaching order. TV tries never to bore its audience with too many details; yet television manipulates information better than any other medium. TV news stories are more persuasive than their newspaper equivalents because they appear to make good sense, and reporters appear to be completely in control. The style of TV reporting makes us believe we have been told the whole story. In reality, the use of themes, angles, and editing techniques makes events fit the practical circumstances of news production rather than the reverse.

3.6 Are the Media Biased against Business?

The common complaint of business is that media coverage is inaccurate, misleading, superficial, and biased. The business community argues that the media usually fail to provide knowledgeable and skillful reporters to deal with business issues and that the media are hostile and biased against business. On the other side, the media blame business for not being more open and accessible, and for being more interested in the pursuit of profits than in objective and accurate media coverage. ("They want us to be cheerleaders, not reporters.") Although there is some evidence to support both arguments, further investigation suggests that the conflicts typically arise by virtue of each party's respective functions.

What are the bases of conflict between the news media and business organizations? Corrado offers a number of possible explanations:

"I'm boss"	Business people, especially senior managers, are used to having their way. "Just run it the way I sent it in, Sonny."
Reporters as labour	Reporters view business people as labour views management, since most reporters are salaried employees of a large news organization.
The business of business	Management feels its primary responsibility is to shareholders and not to the public, à la Milton Friedman.
Too many bottom lines	Businesses report profits in confusing ways. Reporters don't understand nuances and report figures simplistically.
You're hiding something	The business bureaucracy and its reluctance to divulge information makes reporters suspicious that someone is trying to hide something.
Two different worlds	Reporters need immediate access to high-level officials for comments on issues. Corporate officials aren't used to such demands.
Medium distortion	The media, especially television, are apt to try and show things visually — especially confrontation. Reasoned arguments are not often interesting. TV reporting is not a clear channel of communication, but by its very nature distorts, according to Marshall McLuhan. Newspaper reporters tend to distort by arranging facts and processing information according to the inverted pyramid system.
Priorities	Business people judge stories by their effects — good or bad — on business and assume that if the story is harmful to their business, the reporter must have intended to do damage. But reporters and editors judge a story on whether it is interesting and significant, not by its effect on business. (1984, 79–80)

Businessman William C. Cates of the Argyle Research Corporation spoke for many of his colleagues when he said that with daily newspapers, radio, and television, "there's always a subliminal anti-business tone. That's because every cub newscaster knows that business is evil and must be taxed more and more if not destroyed" (*Dun's Review*, March 1976, p. 31).[11] Reporter Clive Cocking states that "the normal journalistic reaction is not to praise but to criticize" (1980, 111). In the subculture of reporters, to write favourably of people and events is to be perceived as perverse or "gutless." To do so regularly is perceived as harmful to one's career.

The feelings of antibusiness bias are not totally unfounded (Rubin 1977). The following excerpt is one of a number of complaints that were presented to the CRTC by the Committee for Improved Business Reporting, a private sector group, on the occasion of the CBC's application for licence renewal:

> On April 12, 1978 the *Fifth Estate* program aired a 20-minute segment about Canada's sugar refining industry. Of eight people interviewed, one represented the sugar refining industry. The entire program was a condemnation of Canada's sugar industry and current government policies. The one person interviewed as a sugar spokesman was the president of B.C. Sugar who later pointed out to the CBC that less than one minute of a two and one-half hour interview was used, and it was edited to show him in a negative light. The program interviewer . . . also took the unusual step of changing the wording and tonal inflection of one question in a re-taping, which was substantially different from the original question asked of the president. When aired, the president's response paled in comparison to the question. The program discussed at length the Eastern Canadian refiners, using the government's chief witness in a combines trial which is not yet resolved before the courts. Although it was made clear to the CBC that spokesmen were available from the sugar companies and food industry, the *Fifth Estate* chose not to interview them. (Hughes 1979)

This example does not question the accuracy of the reporter's findings but serves to illustrate the media's power in deciding on how an issue will be presented. However, the real substance of the adversarial relationship between media and business is not based solely on such flagrant misuse of media coverage, but on a collision between different objectives.

It is argued that journalists see themselves as having the dual responsibility of providing information to the public as well as providing feedback to the administrators of public institutions from the public. Their loyalty is to finding the truth (Aronoff 1979). Cohen and Shannon suggest that the news media have two roles: to give the public enough facts to make intelligent decisions; and to function as an agent of change — to challenge people in all kinds of ways (1984, 30). Simons and Califano write: "To the businessman, too often the antagonism boils down to this — business builds up; the media tears down. To the media, too often the antagonism boils down to this — business always hides its wrongdoing; only the media penetrates this stone wall" (1979, as cited in Corrado 1984, 74).

Thus, much of what business perceives as media bias is nothing more than a conscientious reporter trying to find the "truth" when dealing with an issue he or she feels the public should know.

> The antagonism grew louder during the seventies as the media, reflecting changing public opinion, began treating business more and more like a public institution instead of a private one. People began realizing that business decisions had tremendous impact on their health and well-being, the quality of their lives, what their kids watched on TV, and on the health of children yet unborn.
>
> As the media grew more demanding, business leaders were unprepared to discuss their decision making or its impact on the media or the public. The media, used to the give-and-take of dealing with government and politicians, found business people defensive, antagonistic, and hidden behind their corporate doors. Business people, on the other hand, found out the media were very powerful, that they sometimes got things wrong, and that controversy sells newspapers. (Corrado 1984, 74)

The tension, however, does not arise solely from the reporter's investigation of the issue but from what constitutes the "truth." Just as it is unlikely that two witnesses will describe a car accident in precisely the same way, so it is unlikely that business people will accept a reporter's account of their comments as accurate. (See Figure 11-1.) As in the example of the accident, it is not so much the witness's (or media's) wish to be biased, but rather a matter of vantage point. Business is right in the middle of the action, with access to most if not all of the relevent information, while journalists stand on the outside looking in, receiving little or no information. Since business distrusts the media's objectivity, it is unlikely to provide sufficient information, thus maintaining the cycle where journalists report negatively about business organizations because they feel it has something to hide and business becomes more secretive for fear of further negative exposure.

Another criticism that business people put forth is that much of the media's bias against business is a result of the media's need for sensationalism. They feel that headlines and TV reports are excessively simplified in order to catch the attention of readers. In general, they feel that television news strives to compete with entertainment shows for ratings, and not being "entertainers," they are afraid to face the camera.

> MIT Professor Edwin Diamond terms today's newscasts "disco news," with young-looking people, high noise levels, flashing lights, the "Eyewitness" brand of information/entertainment. Industry professionals sometimes call this approach "Newszak," a term for an

Figure 11–1
HOW NOT TO USE THE MEDIA
(a case of shooting oneself in the foot)

In the summer of 1982 Dome Petroleum was "bailed out" by a proposed infusion of money by the federal government and by the restructuring of Dome's enormous ($1.4 billion) debts to the banks (see Foster 1984). One of Dome's major creditors was the Canadian Imperial Bank of Commerce (CIBC). Some Dome shareholders were angry about the proposed restructuring, and they launched a class-action suit. Their lack of gratitude riled Russell Harrison, chairperson of CIBC. Rod McQueen explains how Harrison sought to use the media to explain his point of view:

> The world needed to be told a few things, Harrison decreed, and he summoned as his chosen instrument Paul Taylor, an earnest young reporter for the *Globe and Mail* "Report on Business." For an hour that Monday afternoon, they sat opposite each other at one end of Harrison's plush office, with a coffee table between them. Harrison played coy about the actual negotiations, but he was clear on one count: the shareholders should be ecstatic about the bail-out, in which Ottawa and the four banks had agreed to buy up to $1 billion in Dome debentures. He was even clearer about where their praise should be directed. "The common shareholders should get down on their knees and thank God that we came to an agreement," Harrison told Taylor. "If we hadn't done this, their shares would have been worthless now. The shareholders would have been out of their minds not to go along with it. Their only hope rests with us controlling the company." He pointed out that bankruptcy would have meant that shareholders had nothing, although he admitted that the Canadian banks as a group had made a mistake by lending Dome more than half of its $7.4-billion debt. "Do you realize what bankruptcy would have done to Canada? The credit of the Canadian banking system — and the Canadian government itself — would have been in question." . . .
>
> Throughout the interview, Harrison was jovial, even jubilant, but Taylor was uncomfortable, surprised by Harrison's comments. "To me," says Taylor, until then a Commerce account-holder, "he seemed removed from the realities. I decided if that's the way the chairman is, I wanted out." Since the *Globe* deposited his pay directly into a Commerce account, he couldn't pull out entirely, but he did decide to withdraw the full amount each pay-day and transfer his business to the Royal. Taylor returned to the office about five that afternoon, too late to write his bombshell story for Tuesday's editions.
>
> Meanwhile *Toronto Star* financial reporter Diane Francis had also been phoning Harrison regularly with interview requests. At one o'clock on Tuesday, October 5, she gave up on the polite route through the public relations department and spoke to Harrison's secretary, saying that she just had one pointed question for Harrison: "What was the bank's internal per-share value for Dome?" Harrison, who must have wondered what had happened when the story he gave Taylor the day before failed to appear, seized upon Francis as his new mouthpiece. Within three minutes after she'd hung up the phone, she was the surprised recipient of a call from Harrison. Their telephone conversation lasted twenty-five minutes. Harrison was in a snit, and the quotes he gave to her were even juicier than those he'd given Taylor the day before.

Figure 11–1 (continued)

"Shareholders had absolutely nothing," he said. "They shouldn't be suing me, they should be sending me flowers. As for 'poor old Dome' being under pressure, 'poor old Dome' held a gun to our heads. There's never been a company that's done as much harm to our country and its credit rating internationally as this company." He charged that Dome was adept at playing one bank off against another for loans and, as a result, competition for the company's business got out of hand. "There was a queue. It was a disease; everybody thought it was Christmas."

Harrison reserved his toughest shot, however, for the U.S. banks, which held most of the $3.7 billion owed by Dome to foreign lenders. "A pile of loans out of all this mess were unsecured. I don't think we were too bright in getting in so deeply, but they were downright stupid." . . .

Both newspapers carried the stories the following day, Wednesday, October 6, and Harrison immediately telephoned Francis. He began the conversation by blustering: "I don't want a retraction printed because that would do more harm than good." As if he could just phone and get one, thought Francis, as she pressed for details. He remarked on the story's accuracy, except for the comments about U.S. bankers. Countered Francis: "I have it in my notes." "Just because you have it in your notes doesn't mean I said it," he shot back. He went on to say that someone at the bank was phoning all the major U.S. banks to tell them that he had been misquoted. In at least one case, that just piqued their interest. The person phoned at Manufacturers Hanover in New York, for example, rushed to obtain a copy of the *Star* to see what was being disavowed.

For all Harrison's denials, his friends said that the quotes sounded an awful lot like him. Still, bank analysts at the brokerage houses were stunned at the baldness of his comments and Harrison became the butt of editorial cartoons. Other bankers, even months later, would close their eyes in despair. Typical was Glenn Bumstead, secretary of the Toronto-Dominion Bank, Dome's second-largest Canadian creditor, at $1 billion. . . .

"He is an outspoken and intemperate man." (McQueen 1984, 54–56)

Source: McQueen (1984, 54–56).

essentially entertainment program presented in a news format. The first generation of TV news journalists — the Cronkites, Chancellors, Severeids — were newspaper and wire service trained. Today's generation of TV news journalists have only a television background. They tend to follow the "story" model of journalism — telling a story that people enjoy or relate to their own lives — as opposed to the "information" model that sticks to the facts. (Corrado 1984, 84.)

Television demands short, crisp, personalized, visual, and dramatic material to meet the demands of its audience. The brevity of TV reports and their tendency to emphasize drama and conflict at the expense of information make TV a poor vehicle for many types of business news (Desbarats 1984, 87). A show such as CBS's "60 Minutes" demonstrates that controversy creates interest, which in turn increases the viewing audience.[12] Business people fear that they cannot be effective in stating their company's policy and practice, and if they appear on television, they risk the chance of having their statements distorted via editing or they will heighten any controversy rather than diminish it.

Business images on television are projected almost solely in the nonentertainment context of news and public affairs. One study found that these images were predominantly neutral or negative. Business is frequently associated with bad news, and business people, especially those working in big business, are often depicted as greedy, somewhat immoral, and unethical (Gale & Wexler 1983, 34).

In addition, television as a mode of communication is fast moving. Often business spokespeople are given twenty or thirty seconds to express their company's concerns or refute allegations. However, because executives feel this is not sufficient time, they often decline to appear. The consensus in the business community is that, given the public's general mistrust of business, reports on business issues, seldom longer than two or three minutes, cannot adequately convey the complexities. To try to respond in a short "clip" would likewise be inadequate, thus validating the public's mistrust. The counterargument is that business must realize this is the nature of the medium and that its importance in disseminating information cannot be ignored. This means that business spokespeople are going to have to summarize things briefly to get their point across on TV — or leave the field open to their critics.[13] In short, it is better to learn to play the game effectively than risk not being heard at all.

3.7 Reporters Lack Training

A study commissioned by the American Management Association called "Business Media Relationship: Countering Misconception" reached two major conclusions: first, that journalists agreed in equal numbers with corporate executives that the media is generally antagonistic toward the business community; and second, that the majority of journalists and business executives believe that when business reporting is inaccurate it is because of sloppiness rather than bias. Business people attribute this "sloppiness" to the fact that business stories are often assigned to general news reporters. Responsible news executives recognize and admit that, generally speaking, their journalists are weak in reporting the news of business. They explain how in the crush of events and the need to meet deadlines, editors and producers of TV and radio alike often require general-assignment reporters to investigate an unfamiliar area.

Global TV's anchorman Peter Trueman has said that "most people don't understand much about economics and I include myself in that condemnation." Peter Desbarats, now dean of the School of Journalism at the University of Western Ontario and formerly a well-known TV and newspaper reporter, has said: "Everything that I had picked up about economics and business, I just picked up on the run as a working journalist. [I] became sufficiently glib . . . that it sounded like I knew something, but I was always aware that I was treading on very thin ice" (quoted in Cohen & Shannon 1984, 31, 32). In the same vein, Desbarats has observed that

> most newspapers simply have failed to maintain a system capable of absorbing and interpreting information from an increasingly complex world and producing it for readers who require enlightenment almost as much as they need accurate data. As anyone with special knowledge in any field knows, coverage of his own area of expertise by the news media is almost always incomplete, inaccurate, misleading, and frequently destructive. My own experience working with the Royal Commission on Newspapers revealed that the news media, even in coverage of their own field, are often guilty of sloppy reporting, bad judgement, and slapdash analysis. (1983, 13)

CP reporter Gordon McIntosh argues that because journalists are often recruited directly out of university, "this makes for an elitist point of view, because these reporters tend to identify more with business; they don't see things that appeal to the common person." On the other hand, media critic Barrie Zwicker argues that "general news reporters, trained to look for the human side in any story and less hamstrung by the economic indicators that seize their financial-page colleagues, are proving to be the more able chroniclers, not only of social, but of economic change" (quoted in Cohen & Shannon, 1984, 33, 35).

Thus, there is a continuous debate as to who is responsible for the weak reporting. On one side, business argues that journalists should be trained to understand basic economics and some of the realities of running a business. This understanding would, in turn, facilitate communication between the parties, as they would be able to "speak the same language," thus putting an end to inadequate or erroneous coverage. The media's counterargument is that any weak reporting is a result of business's failure to provide information in concise and understandable language. This argument revolves around the reporter's self-concept as a skilled communicator whose function is to translate the jargon of a specific industry into terms that readers or listeners can understand (McGillivray 1979). Reporters feel that if they were to express themselves in jargon that only business understands, they would have abandoned their roles as communicators.

Journalists argue that if there is a problem with their "translations," it is a result of executives' unwillingness to supply information, put it into context, and explain how it relates to the individual citizen. Without such help, reporters are forced to interpret what they are given or dig up on their own. Then they may be accused of misinterpreting the story or not presenting all arguments. Reporters also argue that even if all reporters were "knowledgeable," this is unlikely to solve the problem of inaccurate reporting. The nature of the various media is such that in order to meet deadline, time, and space constraints, information must be left out or simplified. This inevitably results in reduced accuracy and quality. Clearly, if reporting is inadequate and confused, business people must take some of the blame. Not only do they not understand the workings of the media and the constraints placed on journalists, they are often evasive or unavailable when issues arise.

3.8 Are Media-Business Relations Improving?

The above arguments notwithstanding, business-media relations are believed to be improving. Although concerns of bias and lack of training of reporters are still prevalent, the general consensus is that with increased education for business in how to deal with the media and media's growing knowledge of business, the quality of business reporting has improved and as a result has lessened the animosity between the two. A survey of 550 Canadian business leaders, media representatives, and public relations officers conducted for Public and Industrial Relations Ltd. of Toronto suggests that there has been an improvement in the quality of business coverage in the media: 61 percent said the coverage is much better than it was five years ago; 70 percent said they considered business reporting to be "accurate" or "fairly accurate"; some 80 percent of the CEOs responding said they had been interviewed by the press in the past year and more than half considered the results "satisfactory."

> However, many perceived Canadian business stories in general to be biased, oversimplified and lacking in insight. On the other side, senior members of the press gave a generally poor rating to corporate leaders on the quality of the information flow they provide about their businesses.
> Only 44 per cent said it was "fair," while 37 per cent felt that it continued to be "poor," or "very poor." Only 19 per cent of the press representatives sampled said major companies are doing a "good" or "very good" job in supplying the media with adequate information about their business activities. (Fiber 1983b, p. B4)[14]

While business-media relations may be improving, there is evidence of growing distrust of the media by the general public.[15]

4.0 EFFECTIVE USE OF THE MEDIA IN GOVERNMENT RELATIONS

The first question that must be asked is, Why has business been relatively ineffective in using the media? Most of the current literature suggests that there are basically three reasons, which we now discuss.

4.1 Reasons for Business's Ineffectiveness with the Media

4.1.1 Adversarial Relationship

Much of the problem can be explained by the adversarial relationship that usually exists between business and the media (discussed in the previous section). Executives often feel at a disadvantage when talking to a reporter who is quite skilled at asking provocative questions. They are defensive, thinking that the interviewer is always "out to get them" and put them on the spot. They are constantly afraid of being misquoted or having their remarks taken out of context and are, therefore, often reluctant to talk to the media. The problem is that most business people don't understand how the news media function as complex organizations. They don't realize that the media has a product to sell, just like business, and that the reporter is just looking for content that will stimulate and captivate his or her audience. The reporter's employer has to cope with the daily reality of being in the business of selling audiences to advertisers.

Business as an institution can more effectively use the media as a vehicle for relaying information to the public, government, or other interest groups if it does not have an adversarial relationship with the media.

4.1.2 Ineffective Communication

Another major problem is that business people are often unskilled at effective communication. Until recently, most corporate presidents have been chosen more for their ability to manage than their ability to articulate the corporation's perspective in public. Other actors in the environment, especially politicians and interest-group leaders, are generally better communicators and thus can get their point across more effectively. This may be attributable to the fact that most politicians have the type of educational background that encouraged their communications skills, while most business people have a finance or accounting background, which may not have prepared them for media communications. Politicians also get more chances to practise their communications skills.

4.1.3 Ineffective Information Gathering

Government usually only takes strong action against a firm or industry if it feels that it will be supported by current public opinion (e.g., the NEP in 1980). It spends considerable resources monitoring its environment with such tools as public opinion polls. This does not seem to be the case for business, although a few trade associations are making more use of them. (Recall the example of the Import Auto Dealers Association polls noted in chapter 8.) Whether it be due to a lack of resources or simply a lack of interest, business is not as attuned to prevailing public opinion. Consequently, their actions tend to be mostly reactive — putting out fires and responding to politicians' initiatives or the charges of other interest groups. By adapting this crisis-oriented approach, executives are inviting negative feedback.

In summary, in order to make more effective use of the media, business people must become more familiar with how the media business works, and better skilled at communicating with the public and government via the media. They also must monitor their environment more closely and be willing to take a more active role in influencing public opinion. Arthur Sulzberger, publisher of the *New York Times*, is quoted in the following advice regarding corporate communications:

1. *Get out front.* Business leaders need to be just that — leaders. The public perceives them as "the bland leading the bland." Sulzberger argues against the "faceless official spokesman" and for visibility of top corporate leaders, although he points out vulnerability often follows renown.
2. *Stop talking jargon.* Jargon is a problem [for business]. But it is also a problem for the press, which needs to understand business jargon in order to report it more accurately.
3. *Go look for complaints.* [Sulzberger] suggests that most people don't believe business claims about its products but that almost half of the people who complain to companies are satisfied with the responses they get.
4. *Do some complaining yourself.* Business as much as anyone else has a right to be heard, says Sulzberger, and it ought to take advantage of opportunities to speak out. "News is not only what happens but what people think has happened and what values they attach to what has or has not taken place." Tension between the press and government is "healthy," he contends, with business and journalism sharing certain values: both are pro-opportunity, proconsumer, proprofit and profreedom. (Corrado 1984, 91)

We now detail a positive strategy for being more effective with the news media.

4.2 Establishing a Good Working Relationship[16]

The media have considerable power with which to influence business and to influence public opinion concerning business. A story giving exposure to some negative aspect of a business may affect profits adversely, while a positive story can have the opposite effect. The media can be one of business's greatest resources because they can be used to "create an environment more favourable to what they perceive to be their direct interests" (*Business Week*, January 22, 1979). Therefore, it is critical that business learn how to develop a good working relationship with the media. There are several things that business people can do in order to achieve this goal:

4.2.1 Keep Lines of Communication Open

As discussed in chapter 6, one of the keys to business's success in a political environment is the careful monitoring of public opinion. Some business executives live in a rather isolated environment, often associating only with other business people, even in their personal lives. Journalists, on the other hand, are constantly coming in contact with people from all walks of life — the farmer, the union member, the activist, the CEO, and the politician. Therefore, what they talk and write about often typifies the attitudes of the general public. Because of this, journalists are an important source of information for business people as well as an important vehicle for them to get their own ideas across. Business must, therefore, keep the communication lines open to the media, thus maintaining an ongoing dialogue rather than making contact only in times of crisis. The objective is to gain the respect of the media and to increase their knowledge of one's company and industry. As it is inevitable that a major part of a business organization's contact with the news media will occur in the context of a crisis (e.g., strike/lockout, major change in government policy with adverse consequences for the organization, a change in an exogenous economic variable), it is essential that business has good working relations with the media. (If you want your car to start quickly and run well in an emergency, it is advisable to have regular tune-ups, change the oil, check the fan belt and make sure the tires have plenty of tread. All of these actions should be done on a preventative basis, not when the crisis occurs.)

Some governments have been particularly successful in this area, and some of their tactics could be used equally well by business. For example, the Ontario government ran a series of breakfast meetings where different members of the press gallery were invited to meet with the politicians on an informal basis. This was deemed to be good public relations and gave the reporters a chance to get some insight into the current policy issues. Business could do the same thing by making its senior executives available not only to the media, but also to leading academics and special interest groups. This could be done informally at lunches, dinners, or in the context of special seminars in the company/industry.

4.2.2 Educate Journalists

As most journalists do not come from a business background, they sometimes cover business stories very superficially. (There are obvious exceptions, notably business and economics reporters or columnists who have specialized in the area for some time.) Business should make more effort to provide interviews and briefings so that the media would become more aware of the nature of the business environment in a noncrisis situation. Business could also support programs to send journalists back to school to learn basic business and economic concepts. But the best strategy for a firm or trade association is to provide useful information about the organization/industry on an ongoing basis. Most of this information will not result in a story immediately. But as with lobbying, it is the exchange of information that builds up credibility and increases the chances that reporters will be evenhanded in their treatment of the organization.

While press releases and other "canned" briefing material are referred to by journalists as "Gainsburgers" or "puppy chow," they can in fact be very useful as inputs to reporters. Given the pressure of deadlines, the normal human propensity to take the easy way out, and the fact that the material is usually factual and relevant, it is not surprising that chunks of such material are used by news reporters. Therefore, spokespersons for business organizations should make use of such "handouts" and ignore the snide remarks. A large fraction of what is defined as news, in the sense of what is reported, consists of statements by spokespersons of major organizations, media events staged to obtain coverage, and handouts. Pierre Berton has put it this way:

> Handout journalism . . . dominates the media in Canada. I don't mean that everything you read, see, or hear is the result of a printed handout. I mean that much of it arrives, more or less unsolicited, at the media's doorstep. Only a small part of what we receive as "news" is the result of a tough-minded, hard-nosed investigation by aggressive journalists. . . . Ours is a secretive country; investigative reporting is expensive, time-consuming, often fruitless, sometimes unpopular. (1983, 25–26)

4.2.3 Make the Reporter's Job as Easy as Possible

One of the key ways to cultivate a good relationship with the news media is to make the reporter's job as easy for him or her as possible. In its media relations policy, AT&T, for example, emphasizes cooperativeness, "quotability," and confidence (Corrado 1984, 83). To make the reporter's job easy, business must develop a better understanding of how the news media functions. It is important to realize that the reporter is usually under time pressure (sometimes the story must be filed within the hour) and is looking for an interesting story with audience appeal. If certain information is needed, help him or her find it. Have photos available of personnel, new products, and other news events. When dealing with radio or television, prepare brief audio or video clips that emphasize the major points. Prepare a summary statement in nontechnical language. Make senior people available for interviews as often as possible, and advise journalists of any newsworthy events going on inside the organization. Use as spokespersons those individuals who understand the constraints under which the news is produced and can "deliver the goods" both authoritatively and concisely.

4.2.4 Don't Play Favourites

The ideal approach in making contact with the news media is to try to talk to reporters who have a reputation for fairness as well as an understanding of the industry and its relations with government. At the same time, it is important to remember never to play favourites. Never consistently give one reporter a story before anyone else because that approach is likely to backfire in the end. After all, since other reporters have a great deal of control over what is said and written about you, it is not wise to slight them. Try to be fair to everyone. For the same reason, never issue press releases so that one medium always gets them first (i.e., TV, radio, etc.).

4.2.5 Never Take Advantage of the Media

The media can be a valuable resource for business, and it must never be abused. If reporters feel they are being "used," they will resent it, and they have significant power to strike back over the longer term. For example, some companies knowingly release misleading information in an attempt to obtain publicity for their position. Others call press conferences when they really have nothing of substance to say. Very quickly the company will lose credibility with the media — it will be ignored even when it does have something genuinely worthy of media attention.

4.2.6 Dealing with Bad News Properly

All business organizations will have to deal with bad news. Arthur Sulzberger, publisher of the *New York Times*, said, "I would never suggest that good news is no news, but I would suggest that bad news is often big news." He went on to note that "our job is to give the reader accurate information he can use about what is important and what interests him." He acknowledged that in doing this the news media has taken on special responsibilities: "to get to the root of truth, the freedom to crticize, the freedom to goad and stimulate every institution in our society, including our own" (as quoted in Corrado 1984, 79).[17]

From the perspective of the business organization, the first type of bad news is that associated with sudden events such as strikes or accidents. The call for information usually comes as a surprise, and you are often not totally prepared to answer the reporter's questions. The best thing to do is be calm and say that you will call him or her back. Then find out the facts, compose a public statement, and release it to the appropriate media as soon as possible.

Attempts to stonewall an issue that is perceived as affecting the public automatically spurs efforts by the press to "get something" on the company and arouses public suspicions. It's like Br'er Rabbit playing with the tar baby — the more you try to avoid the problem, the deeper you get into it. Furthermore, the firm runs the risk that the press will go to other, less credible, sources and start running hearsay and circumstantial information filled with innuendo. In these kinds of situations, the press positions itself as guardian of the public interest, and the firm finds itself on the wrong side of the issue. (Corrado 1984, 81)

The impact of bad news is smallest if it is given to the media as quickly and directly as possible. This is because most news reporting is at least daily, which means that today you are news and tomorrow you will have been forgotten. Therefore, it is best to lay all the facts out for the reporter as quickly as possible.

The second type of bad news is the sort you can plan for, such as a plant closing. It is always important to notify the employees first rather than letting them read about it in the papers. Then call a news conference. After a general statement and question period, it may be useful to allow each reporter a short interview alone with the company spokesperson.

4.2.7 Dealing with "Errors"
Business executives read stories about their company that they don't like. If the story is factual but they just don't like the interpretation, there is little they can do but grumble to themselves. However, if there is an error of significance, they are totally justified in calmly calling and explaining the error to the reporter. Newspapers are generally reluctant to print corrections, but they may rerun the story in its correct form. If this fails, writing a letter to the editor is another alternative. Getting corrections made on the broadcast media, especially television, is extremely difficult.

4.2.8 Getting Your Story Covered
The best way to get your story into the media is not usually through the network news shows — unless you are the CEO of a major corporation. If you have something to report that affects the local community, the local news shows may be the best bet. An example would be a new product line that creates local jobs. The best approach is to call the local-assignment editor and stress visual opportunities and the importance of the matter to the local community. Local talk shows are a possibility, especially if you have a local angle on a national story. Always try to figure out what audience you want to target. This will guide you in your selection of media. If your story has national importance, get in touch

with the major wire services, as they are the ones most of the major dailies rely on for information.

An interesting approach was used by a group of businesses that got together to sponsor a half-hour business television program called "Everybody's Business." They hoped to give the public a better understanding of the capitalist system by doing profiles on CEOs and reviewing the week's business news. A more detailed checklist for the development of a public information campaign is contained in Figure 11-2.

Figure 11–2
DEVELOPING PUBLIC INFORMATION CAMPAIGNS

I. Establishing Objectives
  A. *Legitimacy.* Does the organization have the authority to pursue the objectives?
    1. Is the campaign related to the organization's mission? If so, how?
    2. Is the campaign mandated by law?
  B. *Specificity.* Are objectives adequately described so that progress toward and achievement of the objectives can be determined?
    1. Are the objectives quantitative?
    2. Are the objectives qualitative?
  C. Relationship with cost and other program objectives
    1. Have the objectives been developed with adequate knowledge and consideration of program cost and costs associated with the problem?
    2. Have the objectives been developed with adequate knowledge and consideration of other program objectives?
  D. What are the objectives?
    1. Agency recruiting.
    2. To educate and/or modify behavior such as high blood pressure and smoking.
    3. Promotion of government objectives such as pollution control and sale of savings bonds.
    4. To inform or advise such as those eligible for Federal assistance.
II. Planning the Campaign
  A. Targeting
    1. The more precisely the intended audiences are identified, the better will be the specific messages based on audience knowledge, attitudes and behavior, and media habits. Has the intended audience been adequately determined?
      a. Should the audience be general?
      b. Should the audience be a narrow segment of the population?
      c. Can selected audiences be prioritized?
    2. How was the target audience established?
      a. How was the prevalence of the problem determined?

Figure 11–2 (continued)

B. Timing
   1. What should the lifespan be?
      a. Should the campaign be finite or continuous?
      b. If continuous, at what level of effort?
   2. Have incremental steps or milestones been established?
C. Budgeting
   1. What is the basis of resource estimates?
      a. Based on budget constraints?
      b. Based on amount of effort needed?
D. Campaign methods
   1. Is there a strategy developed which specifies a coordinated approach for each segment of the target audience?
   2. Will alternative strategies, concepts, and approaches be pretested in the planning steps? If so, how?
   3. What media will be used?
      a. What products will be used for each media?
      b. How has it been determined that the selected media and product will be successful?
   4. What other communication efforts will be used?
      a. Intermediary channels such as community and professional organizations.
      b. Education channels.
   5. Will other interpersonal approaches, such as workshops and seminars, be used?
   6. Have the potential barriers to effectiveness been identified and countermeasures planned?
   7. Is an outside contractor being used to support the campaign? If so, why?
      a. What is the nature and cost of contractor support?
E. Availability of similar information
   1. Has there been an effort to determine if materials and products are already in existence?

III. Monitoring and controlling campaigns
   A. Is there in-process feedback on the campaign?
   B. Where does control reside?
      1. Public affairs management?
      2. Program management?

IV. Campaign effectiveness evaluation
   A. Is there a planned evaluation effort?
      1. What is the nature and extent of the evaluation of goal achievement and adequacy of campaign strategies?
      2. Are any forms of product testing planned?
   B. What are the major external influences and how have they been accounted for?
   C. How is effectiveness evaluation tied into feedback information for campaign control?

Source: Government Accounting Office, 1979 (as reproduced in Corrado 1984, 191–92).

4.3 Organizing to Deal with the Media

Gollner (1984) suggests that one of the key challenges facing business in the near future will be to "increase management's capabilities to anticipate and monitor emerging social and political forces." A properly organized company can use the media to try to influence public response to issues as they arise (Corrado 1984). In order to be effective at doing this, it must have a properly structured communications program in place. Some of the elements of such a program are outlined below.

4.3.1 Organizational Structure

The top public affairs person should report directly to the CEO (Corrado 1984, chap. 1). Unfortunately, until recently, most senior public affairs people have had backgrounds in accounting or law and only got the job because of seniority (or because it was the only senior position available). Companies are now beginning to realize that they should be using an experienced communications professional. Some companies, being too small to justify having a separate public affairs department, can make use of the several consulting firms that specialize in helping companies with their communications programs.

The public affairs department should set out clear goals and a list of current shortcomings. It is crucial to have top management's support in this area, and its input should be solicited when compiling a list of all the target audiences that the firm wants to reach (e.g., shareholders, general public, customers, interest groups, various levels of government). Then all the possible forms of communication should be listed (e.g., annual meetings, press releases, advertising, feature stories, etc.). From this information, the company can decide which audiences are currently being well served and which are not. Thus, management gains an overview and can identify shortcomings that should be looked after in the coming year.

4.3.2 Monitoring the Environment

It is important for business to have an efficient news and information gathering system — recall chapter 6. Monitoring the various forms of media can act as an early warning system, allowing the company to get a handle on budding social and political issues. Monitoring has traditionally been the responsibility of the public relations department, but companies are beginning to feel that the task should be performed by staff and line managers as part of their regular job.

Some firms have set up in-house media relations programs. They do media-content analysis by scanning news, editorials, features, wire services, video, etc. A value is then placed on issues according to the amount of media coverage they receive. They also scan other forms of media put out by thought leaders, academics, and activists (e.g., publications, newsletters, conferences, position statements).

4.3.3 Educating Operating Managers

It is very important to increase the public affairs skills and knowledge of the company's *operating* managers. Seminars should be held that explain to employees how to deal with the media. Internal communications can be used to inform and educate management. These can take the form of monthly or bi-monthly summaries of all the news stories about the company or industry. The public affairs department at Mobil Oil Canada, for example, distributes such bulletins on a daily basis to all employees. This gives management, especially those who have to deal with the press, an idea of what the company's public image is and what the current issues are. Some companies issue public communications guides to their employees. For example, Getty Oil hands out a credit-card–size media-response card to all of its executives so that they can carry it wherever they go.

Some companies are building public relations sections into their management-training programs. For example, Noranda Mines conducts a one-day broadcast-training seminar. Executives are put in front of television cameras and lights and are then peppered with questions designed to put them on the spot. This is intended to train them in public speaking and in handling radio and television appearances. It teaches them how to stay out of trouble and at the same time get a positive story across.

4.4 How to Handle the Media Interview[18]

Previous sections of this chapter have shown how important it is for business to use the media effectively, both as a source of information and as a vehicle to convey its own ideas to the other actors in the environment. Studies have shown that over 75 percent of Canadians rely on the electronic media as their main source of information (Best 1980, 15). Since the personal interview plays such a large role in most television and radio news shows, it is very important that business people learn how to prepare themselves for an interview and how to conduct themselves when talking to the media. Although we concentrate on the electronic media, most of the points that follow are also pertinent to the other news media. (See Figure 11-3.)

Figure 11–3
MEETING THE PRESS

There are four distinct phases in preparing for a media interview: Attitude, advance preparation, execution, and critique.

ATTITUDE

It is important to realize that in an interview, especially a TV interview, the skills of the person asking the questions are probably sharper than the subject. The interviewer

Figure 11–3 (continued)

doesn't know more about the topic but most likely knows more about conducting interviews. The interview subject is on the interviewer's turf, even if it's in the subject's office. Nevertheless the interviewee should be enthusiastic for the cause and believe in the company and in what it does. He or she should reflect the company's credibility.

ADVANCE PREPARATION

It seems obvious, but not everyone realizes how important it is to prepare for an interview. . . . A skilled manager, when faced with an upcoming interview, will brainstorm with associates every possible tough question that might arise. . . . The mock interview is a moment for total candor on everyone's part. One associate should ask tough questions, while another times the response if preparing for TV. . . .

Another technique for preparing is to write down some very negative and uncomfortable things about the firm or its policies in one column, then draft a list of favorable things in the other column and try to work out ways of "bridging" from one column to the next.

By all means, the interview subject should have a clear idea of the points he or she wants to make. Statistics, anecdotes, and examples to highlight these points should be in mind.

EXECUTION

When talking to a reporter, the subject of off-the-record comments frequently arises. Most experts advise against *any* off-the-record remarks. Yet the system is used every day. The "capital" of off-the-record remarks is Washington, D.C., where there are even degrees of off-the-record statements:

- "Off the record" — Reporters cannot use the information given to them.
- "Background" — Reporters can use the information but can't name the source (an administration official suggested today. . . .).
- "Deep background" — Reporters can use the information but can report it on their own authority only (it appears that no missiles will be sent to . . .).

. . . There are times when it is necessary to go off the record, to clarify a point or to maintain credibility with a reporter. It is not wise to do so unless there is a trusting relationship between the subject and the reporter.

CRITIQUE

This is the final phase of the interview process. If a record of what's been said has been made with video or audio tape (some newspaper reporters audio tape their interviews), it should be examined to see how one might have done a better job. It is a good idea to ask associates to go over their impressions as well of how the interviewee came across. Decide what should be worked on for the next interview and work on the skill. If somebody "sticks you good" during the interview or does a hatchet job in editing, complain to his or her boss, but do so in a reasoned, well-documented manner. There are organizations, . . . that arbitrate complaints concerning bad press coverage. Then there's always the option of spending thousands of dollars on an ad to complain about the coverage. The best bet, however, is to complain to the interviewer's boss.

Source: Corrado (1984, 93, 94, 96).

4.4.1 Initial Contact

If you are approached and asked for an interview, it is important to remember that you are under no obligation to talk to the reporter. Your rights are protected by both the CRTC Act and the Broadcasting Act. However, as discussed earlier, it is often in the best interest of business-media relations to grant as many interviews as possible. Assuming you decide to actually go ahead and talk to the reporter, there are several things that you should try to find out before the interview takes place.

When initial contact is made, find out who is actually going to be conducting the interview, who else is going to be interviewed for the same story, where and when the interview will take place, and when it will be broadcast or published. Many business executives prefer to have the interview conducted in their office because they feel more comfortable there than in a television studio. Try to find out what angle the reporter is following and in what context your comments will be used. If you don't feel that you are well enough informed to do the interview, you have every right to insist that the reporter talk to your company's most capable spokesperson instead.

Try to assess the individual reporter's training, interests, and background with respect to your industry. The company public affairs department should be able to help on this matter. It is obviously better to deal with a reporter who is fairly familiar with your line of business. If this is not the case, it is a good idea to prepare a brief synopsis in nontechnical language and give it to the reporter to look over before the interview.

4.4.2 Know Your Audience

When planning your responses to likely questions, remember that there are two audiences that you are addressing: the reporter and the readers/viewers/listeners. The reporter wants newsworthy stories with audience appeal. He or she is under time pressure to meet deadlines, to make stories interesting to a wide audience, and competitive pressures to "scoop" rivals.

The second audience can be broken down into several categories. For example, are you communicating to a specialist reading a technical journal or a family watching the evening news? Either way, it is important to express your message in terms that your audience will understand. Try to tie your message to your audience's interests whether they be social, financial, or human interest. Think of ideas that they will find interesting and appealing. One suggestion is to use anecdotes and examples. Statistics can also be useful as long as they are understandable.

Where possible, it is a good idea to talk from the viewpoint of the audience's interest rather than the company's. For example, rather than saying, "We cannot afford the increase that the union is asking for," it would be better to say, "If we give a wage increase, we will have to pass it on in the form of higher prices to our customers, and this is something that we do not want to do" (Burger 1975). However, at the same time, don't attempt to appear totally unself-interested — the public is skeptical and probably will not buy it. Also, it is best to speak in personal terms where possible. This reminds the audience that corporations are not "impersonal monoliths in which no one retains his individuality or has any individual responsibility" (Burger 1975).

4.4.3 Structure Your Statement

It is important to make your statements concise and to the point. Television news is largely a matter of headlines and brief visuals. With complex business issues, business people are accustomed to having an entire meeting to make their point. Now they must do it in roughly half a minute or it will end up on the cutting-room floor. They must therefore practise using short, crisp statements in order to get their message across succinctly and credibly. "Quotability" appears to be a function of three elements: the ability to be brief and to the point; the capacity to transform specialized knowledge into issues and language that can be widely understood; and a gift for putting one's points in evocative and interesting language, that is, making memorable phrases.

One useful technique to make sure you get your points across is to structure your statement like an inverted funnel or pyramid. Make the most important point right at the beginning and emphasize it (e.g., "The most important point is . . ."). This will help the harried editors identify your main message. Most business executives are used to leading up to the main conclusion/recommendation with a series of background statements. When dealing with the media, it is better to state the main point first and then follow it up with your arguments. Psychological tests have shown that people will remember, assimilate, and comprehend your message better this way. Also, there is less chance that your main point will be edited out. Another useful hint to help avoid having your main message edited out is to sandwich it between interesting, attention-getting opening and closing statements.

4.4.4 Understanding "Off the Record"

Remember that there is no dividing line between informal conversation and the start of the official interview. It is practical to assume that anything that you say can be printed unless you can get written agreement from the reporter. Consider the example of a former federal cabinet minister

> who confidently defended his department's position on environmental issues in an interview with a reporter. After the interview was over, and he was showing the reporter to the door, the cabinet minister was asked if he thought the environment groups opposing government policy were off base. "Between you and me, I think

they're right on," the minister replied. . . . It was the minister's final, off-the-cuff [and what he believed was off the record] remark that made the headlines.[19]

The moral? Never treat any encounter with reporters as a casual chat over the backyard fence.

Reporters generally do not like to agree to the "off the record" condition because it means that even if they get the information somewhere else, they can not use it. Corrado notes that in Washington, D.C., there are even degrees of off-the-record statements:

- "Off the record": Reporters cannot use the information given to them;
- "Background": Reporters can use the information but can't name the source (an administration official suggested today . . .); and
- "Deep background": Reporters can use the information but can report it on their own authority only (it appears that no missiles will be sent to . . .). (1984, 96)

Two points are important. First, not every reporter knows the subtleties of these three categories and it is hard for the spokesperson of a business organization to be able to do so. Second, it is not wise to go on and off the record in the course of an interview or briefing unless there is a trusting relationship between the spokesperson and the reporter.

Sometimes you will not be able to reveal certain information requested of you. If there is information that you simply cannot give out (e.g., legal reasons, proprietary data), it is better just to say so and explain why than it is to play dumb. Otherwise, it is like an admission of guilt.

4.4.5 Be Honest — Even If It Hurts

It is always best to be candid and answer questions sincerely. Tell the truth even if it is embarrassing. The public understands that everyone makes an occasional mistake. (To err is human, to forgive is divine.) However, they are not likely to tolerate dishonesty. If you are caught in a lie, both the public and the media are very unlikely to forgive and forget. If your organization plans to be around for years, the credibility of its spokespersons is its most valuable asset in dealing with the news media. Therefore, acknowledge the true situation and try to put it in as positive a context as possible. Also, never exaggerate. Understatement, after it is "checked out," builds credibility. If you cannot answer a question, do not try to bluff your way out of it; just say, "I don't know." But where there is time to do so, offer to find out the answer if it concerns your organization. Then follow up. Remember that it is not wrong to indicate there are areas that you cannot discuss, at least at that time. "No comment" is different from "I don't know," and this difference can be made understandable to the interviewer and the audience.

4.4.6 Try to Be Proactive

An interview should not consist of an executive merely reacting to the reporter's questions. It can be used to make one's own important points. A useful technique is called "bridging." This is where the executive answers the reporter's question briefly, makes a general statement, and then states one of his or her own ideas. For example, if asked, "Is it true that your company has resisted unionization?" the executive might respond with something about collective-bargaining elections and then proceed to point out how many jobs his company has provided in the community (*Business Week*, January 19, 1981). Bridging is particularly useful when you are asked a question that reflects negatively on your company. It takes practice to become good at this technique. One way is to write out a list of all the things in the company that make you feel uncomfortable (e.g., pollution, hiring of minorities). Then write out some of the company's good points. Finally, practise "bridging" between the items on the two lists. (See Figure 11-4.)

Figure 11–4
INTERVIEW TECHNIQUES

---

1. **The "set-up."**   A long preamble precedes a question, sometimes loaded with misinformation or a "when did you stop beating your wife" question.

   Example
   "Considering the low regard that people have for the oil industry, how do you, as a major oil company chief executive, expect people to believe you're not ripping them off?"

   Solution
   There are two schools of thought on how to deal with this problem. One is to break in politely to challenge the premise. (By the way, don't nod your head when the question is being asked . . . it makes viewers think you agree with what's being said.) The second approach is to wait until the question is finished, then go back and knock down the preface: "Yes, it's true that some people don't think much of our business, or business in general, but in fact, our profits have been flat for the last two years. . . ." or simply: "What you've said is just not true. Let's look at the figures. . . ."

2. **"Either . . . or."**   The interviewer poses two unacceptable alternatives.

   Example
   "Either you're naive, or you're protecting someone higher up. . . ."
   Another example: "Now were those irresponsible statements due to ineptness or greed?" or "Are you for or against takeovers?"

   Solution
   One solution is to answer the question directly: "Neither. The real issue here is. . . ." and move to the points you want to make. Or you can just ignore the trap and respond the way you want to.

Figure 11-4 (continued)

3. **Irrelevancy.** In this situation, you are called upon to answer a question in an area unrelated to your own. The problem is that you can end up being quoted out of context. The memorable remark of Jimmy Carter in the *Playboy* interview about lusting in his heart is a classic example of what can happen when you get into an area far afield of your own, as it were.

Example
"Mr. Jones, besides being marketing director of Widgets Unlimited, you're also on the Youth Commission. Do you think the drinking age should be lowered?"

Solution
You might simply remark that your youth commission believes in supporting the laws in existence, then launch into some information regarding the good works of the commission.

4. **The empty chair.** In this situation, the interviewer quotes an opponent or person with a different point of view who has criticized your view but is not present.

Example
"Mr. Nader has said that your product is a health hazard and should be recalled immediately." or "Congressman X says your industry is notorious for price-fixing. . . ."

Solution
You can respond simply "I haven't seen those remarks." or "I don't understand in what context those remarks were made." or "I can't believe the Congressman said that, but I believe the facts will show. . . ." You should make sure not to attack an opponent who is not present.

5. **The broadside.** This is the "ad hominem" argument, in which you are attacked directly.

Example
"You're a polluter, aren't you?" (or a liar, or racist, or redliner, etc.)

Solution
The best advice: deny it straight out, if it's not true; or be candid if there's some truth in it: "We previously did have a pollution problem, but in the last two years we've licked it," or "Redlining has no place in our loan operations."

6. **Let's pretend.** This technique involves the interviewer asking a hypothetical question, a "What if . . ." question.

Example
"What if gasoline goes up to two dollars a gallon. Should the government take over the oil companies then?"

Solution
Politicians are constantly asked these types of questions. The best advice is to demur and move to the point you want to make: "I think such a question is pure speculation. I think our real problem is conservation. . . ."

Figure 11–4 (continued)

7. **Inconsistency.** If you or your organization has changed opinions or policies over time you might be asked about that change.

Example
"Your firm issued a press release previously, indicating that you would not leave this community and move to Arkansas. . . ." or "You previously stated that there were absolutely no health problems with your new drug. . . ."

Solution
You should clearly explain the reasons for the change, whether it was due to a change in policy or circumstances. "Our intentions have always been to maintain a plant in this community. However, the difficult economic conditions nationally and the flood of competing imports have forced us to consolidate operations. . . ." or "Our research until recently indicated that our new drug had sufficient safeguards. . . ."

8. **No comment.** "No comment" is not the same as "I don't know." "No comment" can be stated a number of ways. If you don't know, you don't know.

Example
"Is it true your company is considering buying our local TV station?"

Solution
If the answer is "No comment," it can be done smoothly: "Our firm has a history of attempting to expand into many new areas. We look at over five hundred companies a year for possible acquisition. But it's a major decision in every case and one in which there must be consensus within the company. There has been no decision at this time about buying your local TV station."

* See also "Learning to Shine on TV," *Business Week*, January 9, 1981, pp. 114–16; and Jack Hilton and Mary Knobloch, *On Television! A Survival Guide for Media Interviews* (New York: AMACOM, 1980).

Source: Corrado (1984, 94–95).

If you are asked a direct question, you are expected to give a direct answer. In general, avoid answering with a simple yes or no. This is not interesting to the reporter, so he or she will probably provoke you to try to get you to elaborate. It is better for you to amplify your point until you have said what you want to say, possibly using the bridging technique described above.

4.4.7 Dealing with Errors

Executives are obviously concerned about errors occurring in the final story when it is broadcast or published. Although interviewers do not have control over editing what they said, most reporters are receptive to a request to read back the article for factual accuracy before it goes to print. In a broadcast interview, if the reporter makes an erroneous statement, correct him or her immediately. Never hesitate to contradict or to ask questions of the interviewer. If a question is ambiguous, ask for clarification. If it is based on a false premise, point that out firmly but politely. If the interview is being taped and you are asked a tough question, it is perfectly reasonable for you to request that the tape be stopped while you compose your thoughts. This way you can make sure that your response contains the information that you wish to convey to your audience. If you were to try and answer spontaneously, you might say something inaccurate that you would later regret. Often a reporter will confront you with what he or she claims to be the "facts" — but you have never heard of them. If you are uncertain, indicate that you have not seen the original study, statement, etc. (See Figure 11-4.) It is always a good idea to tape the interview for your own record. It could be useful for convincing your own management that what appeared on television wasn't necessarily all that was actually said in the interview.[20]

4.4.8 Personal Appearance Matters

Television interviews are different than those for newspapers in one major way. A newspaper reporter acts as a buffer between you and your audience. He or she interprets, synthesizes, and condenses your remarks into the final form that is published. On television, the viewers actually see and hear you, although tapes are usually edited. They can tell whether you are nervous or confident. Try to talk to the interviewer rather than the camera, except in the rare instance when you are making an appeal to your audience (or if you are on a phone-in show). On television, surveys have shown that the audience will remember how you looked much longer than what you said or how you said it (Barnes 1983). Try to avoid defensive body language and distracting mannerisms. Practising with video equipment can provide valuable training in this area. (Recall Robert Burns's line about the value of seeing ourselves as others see us.) Dress appropriately and do not wear flashy jewelry. Many consultants suggest that wearing dark suits is too typical of "big business." The audience might be more receptive if you looked more relaxed, personal, and hard working by appearing in your shirtsleeves.

4.4.9 Control Your Temper

It is very important to control your temper during an interview. This is especially true of television when you are in full view of the audience. It is a medium that exaggerates emotion. Do not treat the reporter as an adversary — remember, you probably know much more about the topic than he or she does. At the same time, do not be arrogant or falsely humble; just be confident while at the same time respecting the journalist's competence. Always try to be relaxed and talk in an informal, conversational tone. If a reporter interrupts you, he or she is usually not being rude — but simply may not be satisfied with your answer. Never repeat hostile questions, even to deny them. The reporter's question will not show up in the article, just the executive's answer. Therefore, if you do not use hostile words, none will appear in print. Recall W. L. Mackenzie King's point that few men in public life have gotten into trouble for things they did *not* say. This point should also be kept in mind when dealing with the broadcast media. Editing can hide the fact that a reporter has put words in your mouth, so you must be very careful about how you respond to hostile questions.

One final very important point to remember is that when giving an interview, you should never be satisfied with your company's performance. What you have done in the past is fine, but you are trying to do better. Once you start patting yourself on the back, you leave yourself open to attack. (See Figure 11-3.)

An interview should be looked upon as an opportunity to get your point of view across before a large audience, not a cause for fear. With practice, business executives can learn how to use the interview as an effective tool with which to influence other actors in their environment, notably government, public opinion, and other interest groups.

NOTES

1. One observer, writing in the *Economist* (May 18, 1985, p. 13), puts it this way: "Journalists, as the man said, do not have responsibility. The trouble is they do not have power, either: what they do have is influence, which is a very different thing." Stanley Baldwin, when he was prime minister of Great Britain, referred to the proprietors of the largest circulation papers as "aiming at power, and power without responsibility — the prerogative of the harlot through the ages." Consider also the views of Peter Newman on the power of the press:

> FREEMAN: Do you feel you exercise power as a journalist? That you can make people's reputations or break them? What exactly is the power of the press?
>
> NEWMAN: The press has influence, not power. We change people's minds. We create the climate in which politicians, businessmen, entertainers are viewed, but we don't ourselves . . . have the power to destroy or create wealth or to implement major policy decisions.
>
> (Freeman 1982, 66)

The power of media owners in Canada is attested to by the Trudeau government's withdrawal of legislation to curb increased concentration in the newspaper industry. See *Globe and Mail*, December 15, 1983, p. 9.

2. TV and radio data from Bureau of Broadcast Measurement, *Report*, Fall 1983. The Neilsen Status Report on Pay TV (April 1984) indicates that subscribers to pay TV age 18 and over spend another five hours per week in front of their TV sets.

3. *Canadian Advertising Rates and Data* (May 1985) indicates the following circulation figures for major business-oriented publications in Canada:

Financial Post	195 775
Financial Times	100 281
Canadian Business	96 789
Executive	52 973
Report on Business Magazine (included for free in the *Globe and Mail*)	328 201
Metro Toronto Business Journal	43 055
Ontario Business	24 000
B.C. Business	19 767

4. These shows include "Venture" (CBC), "Everybody's Business" (Global), and "Marketplace" (CBC) — however, the last show is consumer-oriented.

5. The number of journals and their circulation figures for three specific industries are as follows:

- forest industry: eight periodicals, 73 473 circulation in January 1985;
- metal working: ten periodicals, 171 131 circulation; and
- finance/banking: five periodicals, 70 426 circulation.

   By comparison, the five largest general business publications (*Financial Post, Financial Times, Globe and Mail*'s "Report on Business," Montreal *Gazette* business report, and the *Toronto Star*'s business section) have a circulation of 1 137 643 (CARD, January 1985).

6. See "A debate over 'free' magazines," *Maclean's*, May 27, 1985, pp. 41, 43, which states that "fully 77 percent of the trade and business titles published in Canada are controlled-circulation publications. Bruce Wright, assistant vice-president of Southam Communications, said that controlled-circulation business magazines literally blanket their highly selective market and can be mailed to people holding specific positions in every company within a given industry."

7. Generally, see Thompson (1980).

8. In 1976 the Supreme Court of Canada aquitted the K. C. Irving interests of charges of merger and monopoly under the Combines Investigation Act in respect to their newspaper holdings. See Reschenthaler and Stanbury (1977).

9. See Dan Westell, "Ownership rollback good news for Irvings," *Globe and Mail*, June 4, 1985, p. 4.

10. For more detail on the profitability of the electronic media, see McFadyen, Hoskins, and Gillen (1980).

11. In addition, most executives feel that journalists are suffering from a form of "liberal guilt" (see Lichter & Rothman 1981). They see most journalists as denouncing their middle-class, capitalistic values in the name of the disadvantaged. Business people believe that no matter what they say, their words will be used against them in order to show the exploitative behaviour of big business. This is part of a larger phenomenon of how business is portrayed in fiction. See Gitlin (1984) and Lichter, Lichter, and Rothman (1982). See also Angus Reid, "Don't call us, we'll call you," *Report on Business Magazine*, November 1985, p. 17; and Conrad Black, "Why Does the Press Savage Success?" *Report on Business Magazine*, March 1986, pp. 97–98.

12. See Corrado (1984, 86–88) regarding Illinois Power's experience with "60 Minutes" and its own video-taped response to that program's errors and distortions.

13. See Gary Lamphier, "The journalistic search for the quotable quote," *Maclean's*, April 6, 1981, p. 46.

14. More generally, see Public and Industrial Relations Ltd. (1983).

15. *Time* in its cover story "Journalism Under Fire" (December 12, 1983, pp. 60–81) notes that "public respect for journalism has fallen dramatically [in the U.S.] in recent years. The National Opinion Research Center, which found in 1976 that 29% of the population had 'a great deal of confidence in the press' reports that this year that figure fell to a new low of 13.7%." This figure should be compared to the percentage of the population that "have a great deal of confidence" in medicine (52.3%), in education (29.2%), in television (12.7%), and in Congress (10.2%).

There is plenty of evidence that people think that journalists are rude, accusatory, and cynical. They are said to twist facts to suit their not-so-hidden liberal agenda. They are seen as meddling in politics, harassing business, and invading people's privacy. This is the way *Time* summed up public opinion about the American press. With the greater importance of television news, the media are increasingly seen as remote from the average person — that, and the size of the networks and newspaper chains, generates distrust.

Robert MacNeil of PBS's "MacNeil-Lehrer News Hour" has said that "more and more people have the experience of being interviewed or being at an event that was covered, and they know what they see on the screen is not the way it was" (p. 62). Frank Mankiewicz, an experienced political advisor and executive, put it this way: "Sooner or later everybody will know the dirty little secret of American journalism that the reports are wrong. Because sooner or later everybody will have been involved in something that is reported . . . [and] part of it is always wrong" (p. 67).

The "investigative" impulse to bask in the fame of another Watergate, creates incentives for reporters to believe the worst, to try to find "evil, guiding hands" behind events, and to attack established individuals and organizations. Moreover, the "new journalism" encourages subjectivity in the interests of a higher truth than all of the facts would produce. The most troubling criticism of the press to news executives is that it is arrogant. "Reporters have sometimes lost sight of the fundamental truth that their job is to provide a service to the community rather than to seek the glamour and glory that now often seem to draw people into the craft" (p. 73).

16. For more details see the following sources. Corrado (1984); Arnoff (1979); Atkinson (1981); Burger (1975); Chickering (1982); French (1982); Gollner (1983); Hughes (1979); McDougall (1984); McGillivray (1979b); Munter (1983); Simons and Califano (1977); Standing (1980); and "Corporate Communications: The Battle for Hearts and Minds," *Saturday Review*, September 29, 1979, pp. 16-31.

17. Recently in *Time* magazine (May 27, 1985, p. 77) Thomas Griffith asked whether the media, given its perceived penchant for bad news, has struck the right balance. "Does the news on the air or in print reflect reality?" he asked. Griffiths makes several good points. First, government (and other large organizations) go to great lengths to produce a favourable image by managing the information and "events" they provide for the media. Hence, there is a need for an antidote. Second, much of the world is off-limits to reporters and bad news only filters out slowly and probably incompletely. This suggests that additional effort must be made to obtain such news. Third, the ability of the media to report plenty of bad news is associated with democratic government. Less-free societies tend to use their media to stress the positive features of their governments. Griffith concludes that perhaps news programs and newspapers should carry a notice: "Warning — this is only part of the day's reality."

18. For more details, see Banks (1978); Corrado (1984); Hughes (1979); McDougall (1984); Munter (1983); Burger (1975); Standing (1980); "Learning to Shine on TV," *Business Week*, January 19, 1981, pp. 114-16; Bruce Gates, "Prepare for media interview or beware the results," *Financial Post*, March 30, 1985, p. 17; Rick Blanchford, "Businessmen given tips on how to deal with the press," Ottawa *Journal*, June 18, 1980, p. 27; and "How to Handle the Press," *Newsweek*, April 19, 1982, pp. 90-94.

19. Cited in Bruce Gates, op. cit.

20. Corrado (1984, 86-88) describes how Illinois Power did this for the interviews of its executives by "60 Minutes" and used their own videotape to show distortions introduced by CBS's editing.

APPENDIX TO CHAPTER 11

Characteristics of the Media

1. Important characteristics of *newspapers* as a communications medium are as follows:
   - Anglophones are heavier readers of newspapers than francophones. Conversely, francophones rely more heavily on TV as their most important source of news.
   - When there are conflicting news reports, Canadians will believe television rather than print media.
   - In most markets (which are local/regional) there is only one daily newspaper.
   - Newspapers are generally said to provide the best source of continuous coverage of the local environment.
   - Newspaper reports of news are likely to be more detailed and to offer less opinion content than broadcast reports. Moreover, print reports are "reversible"; readers can go back over what they have read before.
   - Daily newspapers are the media of record, the principal collectors of news, and the suppliers, via the CP wire service, of news input for broadcast outlets.
   - Over 80% of adult Canadians read newspapers, spending an estimated 53 minutes per day doing so (Kubas 1981). While Canadians spend an average of more than three hours per day watching TV, they spend only two hours per week reading books.
   - Both the print and broadcast media appeal to essentially the same adult audience.
   - Newspaper chains dominate both the English- and French-language dailies. In 1982 the leading chains were as follows:

	No.	*% of English Circulation*
Southam	14	33
Thomson	40	26
Torstar	1	11
Maclean-Hunter-Sun	3	8
Other chains	22	8
Independents	26	13

	No.	*% of French Circulation*
Peladeau	2	42
Trans-Canada	4	32
UniMedia	2	16
Independents	3	10

2. Important characteristics of *television* as a communications medium are the following:

- Over 97% of households in Canada have TV, and individuals spend an average of 25 hours per week watching TV (those who have pay-TV spend another five hours per week in front of "the tube").
- There were 1442 stations in Canada in March 1984. However, only 211 were originating stations.
- TV is regarded as the most persuasive medium. It is more vivid and has a greater impact on viewers than do the print media on readers. "Because of film presentation in TV, the audience has the impression that it is getting the news first hand, and this sense of being almost a witness to important events makes television 'believable' " (Siegel 1983, 35). David Brinkley notes that "words lying down are more remote than a person talking in living colour" (Siegel 1983, 34).
- "Politicians hardly get excited when they see the reporter with his notebook. It is the TV cameras that make the politicians take notice: the quick smile appears [as the camera begins to roll]" (Siegel 1983, 34).
- "The economics of broadcasting (1982 revenues of $2.5 billion), in the primary activities of programme creation and transmission, do not reflect its social and political impact" (Siegel 1983, 157).
- Over 60% of households in Canada have cable TV. As of March 1984 the fraction of households with cable TV by province ranged from 31.8% in Newfoundland to 45.2% in Quebec to 65.4% in Ontario to 84.4% in B.C.
- The electronic media in Canada are regulated extensively (Boyle, 1983). Despite more stringent Canadian-content regulations, TV programming is dominated by American-produced material, although the CBC is more successful in presenting Canadian programming.
- "TV is the dominant mass medium for entertainment, information, persuasion, education, advertising, and cultural activity" (Siegel 1983, 175).
- TV is the costliest and most profitable medium.
- TV programming is a mosaic ranging from news, to soap operas, to serious drama, to educational programs.
- Many views and features programs actively compete with entertainment programs.
- With the aid of satellites, TV has been able to "collapse" time and distance. Live, world-wide broadcasts of major events (e.g., Olympic games, summit meetings, hijacking crises) are common.
- Cable TV has vastly increased the number of channels available in most areas of the country. The mass audiences of the major net-

works are threatened by the "narrow-casting" and audience frag-
mentation possible through cable TV and direct broadcast satellites.
Pay TV has yet to make great inroads against "free" and cable TV,
and it now has to compete with low-cost rentals for video recorders
($1 to $3 per day for movies in major cities). One-quarter of households own a video recorder and the fraction is growing rapidly as
its price falls in real terms.

3. Important characteristics of *radio* as a communications medium are
as follows:

- There are about 1.5 radios for every person in Canada (satura-
  tion) and the average Canadian listens to radio 19.2 hours per week.
  Nearly 90% of the population listens to radio.
- Radio is predominantly a Canadian medium. Programming consists primarily of talk and recorded music, both of which are cheap
  to produce.
- It is a fragmented, local/regional medium. In March 1984 there
  were 754 AM and 786 FM stations in Canada, of which 410 and 312
  were originating stations. Three-quarters of advertising revenues
  come from local sources. Except for the CBC English and French
  networks, programming has a local orientation and it is highly dif-
  ferentiated to appeal to specific audience (consumer) segments.
- Radio is mobile — some 93% of automobiles have a radio installed
  in them.
- Listening to the radio is often a secondary activity, e.g., the largest
  audience is between 6:30 and 9:30 a.m. (i.e., wake-up music, news,
  traffic, and weather reports), and during the driving-home period
  (4:00 to 6:00 p.m.).

12

Advocacy Advertising

1.0 INTRODUCTION

In the last decade many business people in Canada perceived that they were operating in an increasingly hostile environment. Under pressure from legislators and regulators, other special interest groups, and public opinion — a consequence of the general increase in politicization of economic decision making — many business leaders experienced both a crisis of confidence and a feeling of weakness in their dealings with government. In their attempt to address these matters, some businesses and trade associations have turned to advocacy advertising in order to accurately and directly communicate their concerns to governments and to various publics with a view to influencing public policy.[1]

Advocacy advertising — which seeks to sell ideas rather than goods and services — is a new tool in the process of business-government relations largely predicated on the assumption that business can influence public policy decision-makers both directly and indirectly by shaping public opinion by means of paid advertising. Such advertising is often used in conjunction with other actions designed to influence policy, notably lobbying. Examples abound: in recent years Canadian Pacific Investments, the Investor's Group, and the major banks have all spent money on a series of advocacy ads. Foreign-owned major oil companies, including Gulf Canada and Imperial Oil[2] (Esso), have launched expensive media campaigns designed to improve their image, advocate specific policies, and respond to attacks. The Nissan Motor Company (Datsun) bought space to argue against the Ontario government's auto rebate scheme, which was limited to domestically manufactured vehicles. After the November 1981 federal budget the Canadian Federation of Independent Business took out a full-page ad in leading newspapers angrily denouncing the proposed changes in tax policy (Adelson et al. 1985).

At the end of this chapter, two institutional or corporate image ads (Examples 1 and 2) and eight advocacy ads are reproduced. Examples 3 to 6 consist of advocacy ads by four trade associations (PMAC, IPAC, Shoe Retailers Assoc., and CFIB). Example 7 is a two-page ad by Gulf Canada, part of the largest group of institutional and advocacy ads ever run in Canada. Example 8 is an advocacy ad by Imperial Oil responding to the allegation that the company and other oil companies had overcharged consumers some $12 billion over more than a decade. Finally, Examples

9 and 10 illustrate the use of advocacy ads by trade unions and by ad hoc groups responding to proposed changes in government policy (Alliance for Canadian Broadcasting).

2.0 THE GROWTH OF ADVOCACY ADVERTISING

Why has there been such a growth of corporate[3] and other forms of advocacy advertising? Stridsberg (1977, chap. 4), on the basis of his international survey, offers several reasons. First, there is the contribution of the adversary culture — such ads were "the almost inevitable product of a young generation of talented, experimental advertising people with strong political commitments" (1977, 44). Second, some advocacy ads have been created in response to global events, for example, the greater importance of such issues as population growth, energy prices, and the Vietnam War. Third, in the U.S., the Arab-Israeli conflict in 1973 and the response of Mobil Oil Corporation[4] pointed the way for other corporations to participate in the debate over energy policy that involved dependence on imported oil versus domestic oil, coal, and nuclear power.

As important as these reasons may have been, Stridsberg's analysis ignores other explanatory factors that may be more important in the Canadian context. There has been a very substantial expansion of regulatory activities by federal and provincial governments in Canada and by state governments in the U.S. in the 1970s (ECC 1979; Stanbury 1980). Corporations and trade associations came to believe that their influence on public policies declined steadily from the late 1960s to the early 1980s. In other words, when traditional lobbying "failed," business sought other tools and techniques of participating in the debate over public policies. In general, in Canada at least there appears to have been a shift in the importance of various approaches of influencing government from less to more publicly oriented methods. In the "golden age" of C. D. Howe (Bothwell & Kilbourn 1979), top executives could deal informally with Howe in person or by telephone.[5] Besides, Howe never made a major move affecting big business without first checking it out with scores of the corporate movers and shakers. When Howe and the St. Laurent Liberals passed from the federal scene, formal lobbying became more important: a number of ministers had to be contacted; briefs had to be written and presented before inquiries and committees; consultative committees were set up; and the detailed work of the trade association professional dealing with public servants became more important.

With the Trudeau era, business found there were new organizational structures in Ottawa and new values (Gillies 1981).[6] Although the government often used rhetoric that upset the business community and introduced or modified scores of programs in the interests of national unity (keeping Quebec in Confederation), the redistribution of income, and regional development, it was actually rather generous to business interests. It provided or maintained protective regulation, generous cash subsidies, and a veritable cornucopia of tax expenditures (Howard & Stanbury 1984). However, foreign investment controls, "tax reform" in 1972, and the National Energy Program in 1980 made business angry — as did the prime minister's musings in 1975 (see Hartle 1976) about the failures of private enterprise and the need for more direct action by government. Trudeau's thinly veiled contempt for business people and obvious disinterest in the economy (until the polls told him he was in trouble — see Gwyn 1981) made Canadian executives feel threatened and unloved. The nostalgia for the "good old days" of C. D. Howe was intense. Moreover, the 1974 amendments to the statutes dealing with the financing of elections and political parties reduced the Liberal and Conservative parties' extraordinary reliance on large contributions from relatively few corporate donors (see chapter 10). While money does not "buy influence" in any simple fashion, it was a way of making sure of an attentive hearing by the top political decision makers.

In short, the old tools and techniques of influencing government were perceived to be wanting. They were not abandoned, but new ones had to be found as business-government relations changed.[7] Advocacy advertising seemed like a potentially valuable technique, although — as with any new technique — there was much learning necessary to use it effectively and efficiently.

3.0 DEFINITION

Stridsberg (1977, 16), after reviewing some nine terms, including cause-and-issue advertising, opinion advertising, public affairs advertising, and advocacy advertising, chooses to use the term controversy advertising for what I have called advocacy advertising. He defines it as "any kind of paid public communication or message, from an identified source and in a conventional medium of public advertising, which presents information or a point of view bearing on a publicly recognized controversial issue" (1977, 18). The advertiser's intention is to have an influence on a matter of recognized public controversy. The results sought range from the correction of factual information, changing the opinions of members of a target audience, the mobilization of supporters, the solicitation of financial contributions, and the passage or defeat of a specific piece of legislation.

Advocacy advertising is designed "to tackle controversial issues and present facts and arguments that project the sponsor in the most positive light and opponents in the most negative" (Sethi 1977, 8). According to Jean Fortier, a former CRTC commissioner, advocacy advertising is "not aimed at selling products or services, but rather to promote opinion. It is not aimed at influencing the consumer's spending choice, but rather his ideological and political choice" (quoted in Hardy 1982, 36).

In summary, advocacy advertising is designed to sell ideas rather than goods or services — those ideas that shape public policies that affect (or may affect) the firm paying for the advertising.

Advocacy advertising is characterized by information selection on the basis of issues determined outside the company, and by the desire to alter the terms and outcomes of a debate that is or is likely to affect the company's fortunes. It involves a course of action, not merely preparing the ground for action. However, some types of ads may be designed more to raise the company's visibility and give it a favourable image than to propose specific action by government.

4.0 DRAWING DISTINCTIONS

It is essential to distinguish advocacy advertising from three other types of advertising: public service advertising, product or service advertising, and corporate image or institutional advertising (Stridsberg 1977, chap. 2).

Public service advertising promotes certain policies or courses of action in what is widely recognized by the public as being the public interest. In the U.S., for example, the Advertising Council recruits professional advertising personnel on a volunteer basis to prepare ad campaigns submitted by various groups (e.g., the Red Cross, the U.S. Forest Service, medical research bodies) on a nonprofit basis.[8] These are supplied to the various media, which are requested to run them without charge for the space or time. It should be noted that in Canada there is no counterpart to the U.S. Advertising Council. What would be public service ads in the U.S. are ads paid for by governments — for example, fasten your seat belt; if you drive don't drink; etc. (See Stanbury et al. 1983)

Stridsberg (1977, 27) notes that public service ads "can easily slip over the line into controversy advertising" where

- the social or economic action advocated is disputed by a significant sector of the population (e.g., ads advocating the use of condoms to prevent venereal disease could be seen by the foes of birth control as unacceptable);
- what is per se a neutral positive kind of activity is viewed in terms of alternative possibilities and the trade-offs involved (e.g., a fight-inflation campaign in the U.K. in 1974 was seen by some as sacrificing the unemployed on the altar of price stability); and
- the "conventional wisdom" advocated by "the establishment" is confronted by the obstinate desire of a large segment of the public to do otherwise (e.g., the countercampaign of the People's Bicentennial Commission against the U.S. Ad Council's ads for the Bicentennial Commission).

Conventionally, we say that regular product or service ads are designed to generate net revenue for their corporate sponsor while advocacy ads are trying to sell ideas. The contrast is between share of market and share of mind. However, as the advertisers of certain products (e.g., alcoholic beverages, tobacco products, proprietary drugs, and even baby formula sold in Third World countries) have found out, the use of the product or service can be disputed by interest groups of various sizes. The focus of their concern can range widely: packaging materials (e.g., fluorocarbons in spray cans), ingredients (e.g., allegedly carcinogenic red dyes), nutritional content (e.g., snack foods with "empty calories"), and product safety (e.g., Ralph Nader and the Corvair).

Corporate image or institutional advertising consists of "signed, paid messages by a company in conventional advertising media [which] seeks to obtain a desired level of public awareness and maximum favorable impression among selected audiences" (Stridsberg 1977, 32). Carefully chosen facts are used to create an impression of the company's activities, moral standards, policies, management style, and expectations. Such advertising, Sethi (1977, 8) suggests, is aimed at "building a good image for the corporation and its management or keeping the corporate name in the public eye." Furthermore, he continues, "it deals with the characteristics of the corporation itself rather than those of its products or services. . . . the focus is on good public relations and the objective is to win friends. . . . institutional advertising is expensively and beautifully produced, is generally dull, bland and self-serving."

The objective of corporate image advertising is to facilitate the activities of the corporation as they may relate to the financial community (raising capital), governments (to generate favourable attitudes among those exercising regulatory discretion over the company), and even the media (to increase the probability of favourable news coverage).

From the corporation's perspective, images are designed: they are what the corporation aspires to more than what it is. The image is what it wants to create in the minds of its target audiences. Such advertising, as Stridsberg points out, "asks no action on the part of its audiences beyond the passive approval and favourable attitudes conducive [to the actions the corporation seeks from the target, e.g., government]" (1977, 33). While advocacy advertising seeks to alter or reinforce opinion, image advertising seeks to create a favourable climate for subsequent action. For example, after changing its name to Nova, An Alberta Corporation in 1981, the Alberta Gas Trunk Line Company spent over $1 million on a three-month advertising campaign designed to erase the popular impression that the company (with 60 000 shareholders) was either a crown corporation or a "foreign-controlled resource monger."[9] The television commercials and print ads focused on Nova's manufacturing, gas transmission, research, oil, petrochemical and pipeline development interests in an effort to convey the company's growth and diversity to its shareholders and the public. Gulf Canada conducted an extensive "corporate advertising" campaign between 1981 and 1985, using both institutional or corporate image ads, and advocacy ads.

Image advertising is not limited to corporate organizations but has also been used extensively by trade associations to clear up popular misconceptions and foster a more positive attitude toward an industry. This was the objective of the Ontario Mining Association's 1981 ad campaign, which cost $98 000. The campaign, which consisted of five ads placed on a rotating basis in twenty-six Ontario newspapers and magazines, was based on the results of a major research study conducted to determine the public's attitude toward the mining industry.[10] The ads attempted to dispel the popular conceptions of the industry being a "dark, dirty and unpleasant" place to work and that the life style in the mining areas of northern Ontario is characterized by isolation and a lack of amenities. The ads were also aimed at extinguishing the perception that the mining industry was bad for the environment, unsafe, and foreign owned.

Another example of this type of advertising by a trade association was the $3-million image-boosting push for life insurance companies undertaken by the Canadian Life Insurance Association (CLIA) in the fall of 1980. Television commercials, as well as full-page ads run in fourteen major daily newspapers, were designed to show that the life insurance business is accessible and responsive to consumer needs.[11]

Advocacy advertising, which is aimed at shaping public opinion on public policy issues and/or at political decision makers, should also be distinguished from the use of ads to deal with takeover bids. Such ads are aimed at shareholders and also provide lucid signals to antitrust authorities. When property developer Robert Campeau attempted a takeover of Royal Trust in 1980, he became the target of a hostile advertising campaign initiated by Royal Trust's senior management. In retaliation, Campeau placed full-page ads in the *Globe and Mail* and the *Toronto Star* answering Royal Trust allegations that his company and he might suffer from incompetence and/or instability. "If Royal Trust Co.'s campaign was uncharacteristically mean and disreputable Campeau's comeback was equally contrived and incomplete," observed one analyst.[12] More recently, the takeover of Consumers Gas by Unicorp in 1985 was marked by a series of full-page ads by both sides aimed at shareholders.[13]

5.0 WHY ARE ADVOCACY ADS NEEDED?

Stridsberg (1977, 20–23) suggests there are three reasons why advocacy ads are needed by corporations:

1. The corporation's constituencies (shareholders, employees, creditors, suppliers) will not tolerate silence in the face of "attacks" by its critics (e.g., so-called public interest groups), government agencies, or by a decline in public opinion.
2. The media are perceived by many companies to fail in their responsibilities; fair, accurate, or complete coverage in a controversy may

not be obtained.[14] One critic argues that business and other "establishment" entities have frequently been the subject of "accusatory
journalism." Others emphasize that the U.S. is an "adversary culture."
Advocacy advertising, therefore, is a way of reaching large audiences
"without the benefit of an editor, writer or commentator." (This ignores
the fact that such ads may themselves inspire controversy in the news
columns or even counter-ads by other interest groups.)

3. Advertisers taking part in public controversy want maximum control over the message and the environment in which it is delivered.
   The "problem" with the news media is very seldom the amount of
   space or time, but the way the issue/information is presented. Cynics argue that big business, unlike some other interest groups, can
   buy space/time to deliver its message in the way it wants, while other
   groups have no comparable resources.

Advocacy ads can serve other purposes and, in general, can be thought
of as another of the tools available to an interest group to influence
public policy directly or indirectly. Where public opinion on an issue is
important, advocacy ads may be a way of reaching a larger audience
(not necessarily every adult) so as to gain support for the advertiser's
position. Such ads can reinforce the representations made directly to
government (bureaucrats and politicians) and create or sustain a climate of opinion appropriate to what the firm or trade association wishes
to achieve. Gulf Canada's long-term objective of its large-scale corporate
advertising campaign (1981–85) was to establish "a public opinion environment where key target audiences recognize that Gulf Canada provides a benefit to the country and therefore, within reason, are prepared
to let the Company do the things it needs to do to survive and/or grow."
See Figure 12-2 below.

6.0 WHEN TO USE ADVOCACY ADS

Advocacy advertising has been posited as an important method for Canadian companies involved in complex problems, such as strikes, environmental conflicts, or concerns about foreign investment, to get their story
across.[15] Hardy points out that advocacy advertising

seems to be appropriate when any or all of the following conditions
pertain:
- the consultation route has collapsed or been shut off;
- there is a considerable audience that is predisposed — hence advocacy gives them ammunition to conduct their own word-of-mouth
  campaign;
- the issues are short-term and/or specific;
- there is positive proaction before an issue is politicized;
- the media have downplayed the full facts and there are hard data
  available. (1982, 37–38)

It is not hard to think of reasonable counterarguments to a number of these propositions. First, advocacy ads are likely to be more useful if they are not used as a last resort in dealing with government (e.g., as Hardy's initial point suggests).[16] Advocacy ads, when they are closer to image or institutional ads, may help influence the general climate in which detailed negotiations are conducted. For some issues, "going public" is one of the last things an interest group wants to do. For others, however, marshalling public opinion may be useful from the outset — it depends on the nature of the issue and the target of the group's actions.

Second, advocacy ads may be necessary on a longer-term basis, not just when an issue is short term or specific. While Gulf Canada began its extensive series of advocacy ads, in part because of fears that it would be "nationalized" by Petro-Canada, it realized that energy policy issues would be high on the policy agenda in varying forms over several years at least. Gulf's object was to raise its visibility and credibility to give it the right to speak out publicly in the debate. It wanted to be seen by the public as a good corporate citizen advocating a responsible and reasonable position not at variance with the public interest (see section 12 below).

Third, an issue may be politicized before a company or trade association is able to identify it, appreciate its significance, and begin to take action (recall the stages of issue development in chapter 6). Hardy's fourth point appears to fail to recognize that in some cases strong public advocacy is needed precisely because an issue has become politicized. For example, such ads can be used to reinforce the fervour of one's supporters and to mobilize them into action.

After an analysis of a number of television and print advocacy ads in the U.S., Gallup and Robinson concluded that viewers and readers are receptive to advocacy commercials and ads if they are direct and to the point, provide information and validation, don't threaten, and acknowledge another point of view.[17]

Nevertheless, the results of advocacy advertising are not directly apparent and the lack of published research on the subject in Canada is noteworthy.[18] Consequently, a debate exists over its effectiveness in shaping public opinion and indirectly influencing public policy decision-makers. Critics argue that going public often implies the organization failed to develop the expected liaisons or backed itself into a "no-win situation" (Hardy 1982, 37). Arguing in public is not only potentially embarrassing to corporate executives, but it increases the risk of backlash in matters dealing with legislators and regulators. A case in point is the ad campaign by the Independent Petroleum Association of Canada (IPAC) in response to the federal government's National Energy Program introduced in October 1980. Responsible for representing the interests of about 350 independent oil and gas companies at both the federal and provincial levels, IPAC was caught off guard by the federal government's massive intervention (Alm et al. 1984). After studying the NEP documents, IPAC realized that prices received by producers would be rolled back, reducing company cash flows by 20 percent, shut-in gas wells would no longer be eligible for the maximum 100 percent exploration write-off, and marginal or "stripper" wells would be more expensive to operate. In short, the budget was viewed by IPAC as a disaster for its member companies. More generally, see Doern and Toner (1985, chap. 6).

With independent producers outraged, IPAC's decision to plan a $200 000 ad campaign quickly followed. The campaign was a compromise between demands for a full-scale "strike," shutting down production on the one hand, and behind-the-scenes lobbying on the other. Anxious to discuss implementation of the energy policy with the minister responsible, IPAC sought a meeting with Energy Minister Marc Lalonde. When it became clear that a discussion with Lalonde would not be forthcoming, IPAC decided to launch its advocacy campaign. The full-page ad, which proclaimed, "Mr. Lalonde, Your Energy Policy Will Harm Canadians," was run on November 17, 1980, in the business section of every major Canadian newspaper. (A similar ad run as part of the same campaign can be found in Example 4.) According to IPAC, the campaign was aimed at four targets: Lalonde, the media, the general public, and IPAC voters.

While the ads proved popular with the IPAC membership and the media, it is not clear whether the campaign made a significant impact on public opinion. What is clear, however, is that by personally attacking Lalonde in public, IPAC lost all credibility in the eyes of the energy minister, who stated: "IPAC is not a very credible association. I've been looking at the stands they've taken over the last one and one half years and I have long ago stopped taking them seriously."[19] Consequently, IPAC did not make any lobbying gains until Jean Chrétien took over the energy portfolio and the group tried a completely different approach (Alm et al. 1984).

The IPAC ads were a specific attack on the NEP, and the use of Lalonde's name brought them onto a personal level. In contrast, the Canadian Petroleum Association, whose members include the foreign-owned integrated companies, took a nonpersonal approach in their 1982 ad campaign against the NEP. That campaign reveals another problem with Hardy's ideas on when to use advocacy ads. Hardy seems to suggest that advocacy advertisements *can* directly influence members of the legislature, but it seems clear, on the contrary, that lobbying backbenchers by means of advocacy advertising is likely to be ineffective. Party discipline limits the effectiveness of lobbying of any kind directed solely at MPs, much less through advertising. Unlike U.S. Congress representatives, MPs are only very rarely allowed to vote their own or their constituents' convictions. In the U.S., however, advertising can be very useful to underscore other lobbying tactics. It should be noted, however, that lobbying directed at government backbenchers may be able to influence cabinet ministers in caucus meetings. In June 1985 lobbying by senior citizens (which did not include advocacy ads), egged on by both opposition parties, achieved a reversal of the Mulroney government's plan to partially de-index old age pensions.[20]

7.0 TYPES OF ADVOCACY ADS AND THEIR POSTURES

On the basis of his extensive review of many examples of advocacy advertisements in a dozen countries, Stridsberg (1977, chap. 3) suggests that three postures emerge in such ads.

7.1 Defence of an Economic or Social Point of View

This type of ad usually takes two forms: (1) the effort to retaliate by justifying or explaining situations in which the corporation (or other advertiser) concedes there are alternative courses of action; and (2) portrayal of the attacked party as "victim."

David Kelley (1982, 81) argues, for example, that many advocacy ad campaigns are unsuccessful — not because companies haven't chosen the right issue or don't speak in a language their audience understands — but because "the critics of corporations have been allowed to set the terms of the debate in which everything concerning business is argued." He says that "accepting this framework is a fundamental mistake." The fundamental framework — which always has business on the defensive — is based on these assumptions according to Kelley:

- the public interest is the ultimate standard by which we are to judge everything, including business;
- since it is founded on the pursuit of material wealth, business has a lower moral value than other activities (notably public sector activities); and
- since it is subject to political controls, a company is a political as well as an economic entity.

Kelley argues that certain rights (to property, to contract, and to economic autonomy) stem not from any cost-benefit analysis, but from the nature of man as an autonomous intellectual being. These rights must be secured first, before cost-benefit analysis can be applied to determine "whether the market [or government] effectively integrates the activities of individuals exercising their rights" (1982, 82). Kelley suggests that rather than being defensive, business enterprises should launch programs in economic education explaining what goes on inside the corporations that compete in the marketplace. "The most important measure, however, is to speak about government interference [or actions advocated by interest groups] in business life in a very personal way" (Kelley 1982, 85). The point is to make the consequences of these actions as specific and as clear as possible in language the public can understand: higher prices; loss of jobs; drop in new investment; and so forth.

7.2 Aggressive Promotion of a Point of View

This approach may be based on the idea that "the best defence is a strong offence."[21] In Stridsberg's words, "The advertiser literally protests against the opposing point of view, and in so doing offers more or less specific alternatives of his own" (1977, 37). Here, a corporation may propose very specific action by government, for example, by endorsing or condemning specific pieces of legislation or government programs. In Canada, Gulf Oil promoted modification of the NEP of October 1980 in a long series of advocacy ads in major daily papers, *Maclean's, Time,* and other print media. See section 12 below and Example 7.

Issue or advocacy advertising can be used to raise the public visibility of what may have been handled as a "technical issue," to use Bartha's (1982) terminology. Ads make senior public servants, politicians, and their advisors (not to mention the firm's own constituents) aware of the company's general position. They back up the more conventional forms of lobbying. As one British executive put it: "This type of communication with the government . . . reinforces our constant dialogue with the government" (quoted in Milmo 1983, 11).

7.3 Establishment of a "Platform of Fact"

This approach to advocacy advertisting is to "permit the advertiser to have a voice in the controversy, and to participate in its resolution." In this case, according to Stridsberg, "the advertisements are factual, do not present demands for action or justification of past events, and rep-

Figure 12–1
POSSIBLE STEPS IN THE ADVOCACY ADVERTISING PROCESS

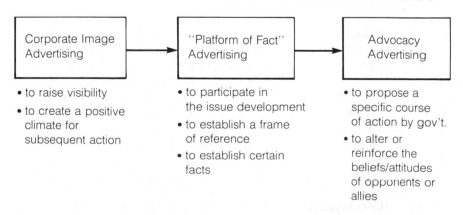

Corporate Image Advertising	"Platform of Fact" Advertising	Advocacy Advertising
• to raise visibility • to create a positive climate for subsequent action	• to participate in the issue development • to establish a frame of reference • to establish certain facts	• to propose a specific course of action by gov't. • to alter or reinforce the beliefs/attitudes of opponents or allies

resent a selection of information intended to put the corporation in a good light" (1977, 38). In effect, a company participates in a public policy issue, but does not overtly advocate specific political actions. Such ads may be close to corporate image advertising, but their objective is different. It is to "create a platform of fact in the public mind, to which reference can be made should the corporation find it advisable to use advertising to communicate to the public at some future date its position in a controversy" (Stridsberg 1977, 38).

Therefore, one may discern three possible steps, which are illustrated in Figure 12-1, in the advocacy advertisement process.

7.4 "Advertorials"

"Advertorials" lie in the twilight zone of print journalism. They are "a themed advertising section in which advertisers buy editorial content" (Elliott 1984, 3). They are attractive because they look like news and have a greater likelihood of being read than regular advertisements. For example, *Penthouse*'s first advertorial in June 1983 drew 886 000 entries for a "dream car" contest. A *Fortune* advertorial on computers in May 1983 generated 42 050 inquiries. In 1983 the *New York Times* generated more than $14 million from advertorials as compared with $91.2 million in revenues from the paper's Sunday magazine. According to Elliott (1984, 36), *Fortune*'s advertorials accounted for 14 percent of the magazine's ad pages in 1983. One of the advantages of advertorials is that the advertiser's message is taken out of the clutter of the rest of the publication, notably the display advertising material. In addition, advertorials may have a longer life with readers than other ads.

Critics, however, see advertorials as a blurring of the traditional separation between editorial content of a publication (the responsibility of the editor) and its paid advertising (the responsibility of its advertisers).

8.0 TARGETS

Stridsberg (1977, 48, 49) points out that advocacy or "controversy advertising is almost never addressed to the so-called 'general public.' It is addressed to narrowly defined segments of the total available audience." (This is in contrast to public service ads, which are aimed at the largest possible audience.) He found from his extensive survey that target audiences differ in terms of the three postures of advocacy ads identified earlier, and that most advocacy ads are not intended to confound attackers but to reach (1) those who support or are likely to support the advertisers, or (2) those most likely to accept and communicate the point of view to others, or (3) those who are uncommitted or most inclined toward passive acceptance of the advertised point of view.

Keim and Zeithaml (1981, 42) argue that communications theory supports the idea that "communication focused at particular audiences will be more effective than those targeted at the general public," in part, because of the heterogeneity of the general public. Several rifle shots will do better than one large shotgun blast. Mass communications must contend with selective exposure, selective distortion, and selective retention, as many individuals have to cope with cognitive dissonance (Festinger 1957). People are most receptive to messages consistent with their interests, values, and existing patterns of belief about how the world works or ought to work.

Targeting is critical also because of the relationship among rationally ignorant voters, the objective functions of politicians, and the role of specialized interest groups. While the potential benefits of voting in terms of the expected value of determining the outcome of any election has declined, the costs of being politically informed have declined. Special interest groups find it worthwhile to inform voters of issues and each party's record on them. Politicians focus more on the behaviour of organized interests who vote than on citizens at large who do not.

Therefore, Keim and Zeithaml (1981, 44) argue, a business firm can operate its own interest group by developing a "natural constituency," namely, among its shareholders, employees, retired employees, suppliers of inputs, and residents of local communities in which it has facilities (see also Grefe 1982). In their view, "Sharply focused advocacy advertising can be an effective way for a business to transform its undeveloped natural constituency into a politically powerful interest group." Hence, the corporation can overcome the rational ignorance problem, reduce the costs of becoming informed politically, and facilitate political action by a substantial group of people on issues in which they have — through the company — a direct stake.

Why is such an approach to advocacy advertising likely to be superior? Keim and Zeithaml (1981, 44) offer several reasons. First, the natural constituents are more likely to be receptive to the company's message. Second, the problem of source credibility is likely to be minimized. Third, this target audience is more likely to be motivated toward political action because of the stake they have in the company's welfare. Fourth, sharply focused advocacy ads are likely to be more cost-effective than a broadside aimed at the general public.

Keim and Zeithaml emphasize that such ads should be factually accurate and noncoercive. The ads should provide information that is appealing, and encourage constituents to become politically active. The proximate target of an advocacy ad may not be the true target. Milmo notes that "Airbus Industrie, the British-European aircraft consortium, featured economic issues in its advertising [in the summer of 1983] in an effort to gain support from government, politicians and trade unions for its new 150-seater A-320 aircraft. Its ultimate target was the state-owned British Airways which was looking to buy 31 medium-bodied aircraft" (1983, 20). Despite the effort to get public opinion and the government behind its sales pitch, Airbus lost out to Boeing.[22]

Even where advocacy ads are designed to influence opponent groups, Stridsberg (1977, 51) argues that the sponsors of such ads often lose sight of their basic targets and in the faulty execution of such ads place them in inappropriate media outlets.

In general terms, the potential target audiences appear to be the following:

- the "natural constituents" of the firm (employees, shareholders, creditors, suppliers, and possibly customers);
- potential influentials in government(s) (i.e., politicians and senior public servants who provide policy advice);
- influentials in the media (Irving Kristol argues that plain-spoken, detailed, factual advocacy ads should challenge reporters' professional integrity);
- influential/"opinion-making" intellectuals and educators (these people are believed to influence others, and where they are not hopelessly committed against the corporation, the views they disseminate may be influenced by advocacy ads); and
- the "socially and politically aware" who take a greater interest in politics and policy issues.

9.0 TYPES OF CREATIVE STRATEGIES

Fox and Calder (1985, 7–8) argue that advocacy ads by business organizations have followed an education model. Such a model is based on business's assumption that "people are hostile toward what they do not understand. It follows that the way to rectify the situation is to educate the public — to inform them of the facts." Business believes that the public's hostility to it — and to other major institutions — is based on recent or current experience with economic conditions. In particular, poor economic conditions (e.g., high unemployment and inflation) make people worse off on average than do good times; hence they "lose confidence in the system." Surveys measuring the level of confidence in business tap an "upwelling of individual and public frustration [with one's own life circumstances], the feeling of being overwhelmed" (Hamilton 1973, cited in Fox & Calder 1985, 10). As Fox and Calder put it: "In good times people place confidence in business and other institutions; in bad times people become less tolerant of the imperfections inherent in every institution. Confidence appears to be closely linked with favourable attitudes toward business but not based on actual business effectiveness."

Their advice is simple: business must recognize that attitudes shaped by economic conditions cannot be overcome by educational campaigns trying to overcome people's ignorance of how the economy works. In any event, business advocacy compaigns — if they are to have a ghost of a chance in difficult times — must "become highly personal in tone. People want to feel confident about their own economic prospects. [Therefore] companies should begin . . . advocacy efforts with their own employees" (Fox & Calder 1985, 11). Outside the company a business must try to convince people that it is working to create a better future.

Stridsberg (1977, chap. 7) provides a useful but nonexhaustive list of creative strategies used in advocacy ads:

- *Factual Correction*: Ads are often reinforced by booklets or toll-free telephone lines providing further information.
- *Immediate Reaction*: Here the ads may be seen as an effort to "nip a problem in the bud" by getting into print within forty-eight hours in a newspaper. While Mobil Oil had a long-running series of advocacy ads every Thursday in the *New York Times*, the content was varied to reflect recent issues. See the discussion of Imperial Oil's ads in response to the Bertrand Report in section 11 below.
- *One-Time Reply*: The object is to provide a single statement "to bring opponents to reason or to rally support sufficient to overcome them." Occasionally, but only occasionally, such a strategy can be a striking success.
- *Warning to Constituents*: Making one's natural potential allies aware of a threat to the corporation so that they may take the action they deem appropriate.
- *Mobilizing Constituent Support*: This strategy goes beyond a warning and seeks to have constituents take political action (e.g., to write legislators).
- *The Association as a Surrogate*: A trade association is used to broaden the base of the campaign and to diffuse possible hostility from other groups or government. One must distinguish ad hoc organizations from well-established ones that usually serve a wider range of functions.
- *Surrogate Spokespersons*: (1) Use of an interview with a highly credible individual (or a speech, editorial, etc.) who agrees with the advertiser's point of view but is independent,[23] (2) use of public opinion data in which the advertiser's position is one of the alternatives posed. (There is a danger here that the target audience will become jaded with self-serving "research events" [see chapter 11].)
- *Direct Counterattack*: In this case, the ad states the opposing view and attacks it — rarely used because of the risks involved.
- *Rational Explanation*: Such ads present both sides of the issue, explains the trade-offs involved, and presents the advertiser's view. This is a difficult strategy to execute.
- *Contribution of Audience Members*: Includes calls for letter-writing campaigns; unfortunately, most people don't want to get involved unless their personal stake in the issue is high and there is a direct threat to it.

- *Information Base*: This strategy is designed to establish a "right to a voice" in the issue and a "platform of fact." The latter type of campaign is "generally characterized by long-term planning, continuity, access to all kinds of media, and a high degree of professionalism in . . . preparation" (Stridsberg 1977, 67). See section 12 regarding Gulf Canada's corporate ad campaign.
- *Generic Controversy and Individual Product Advertising*: Certain types of products may themselves become the source of controversy and it may be necessary to advertise to try to deal with such opposition.

10.0 EXECUTION OF ADVOCACY ADS

Successful advocacy ad campaigns appear to share several elements:

1. *Objectivity*: While the self-interest of the advertiser cannot (and will not be) ignored, effective ads must move beyond sloganeering to a more analytical and broadly based approach.
2. *Credibility*: To be effective any ad must be believable; it must correspond to public and easily available facts. The advertiser must have "clean skirts" — all the details in the ad must "check out" or it will be undermined. Exaggeration can be interpreted as crying wolf. The preferred "tone of voice" is under- rather than overstated.

   One of Gulf Canada's ads came under fire in one newspaper story for being selective and misleading. The ad stated that the company's federal and provincial taxes totalled $597 million in 1981, a figure that included $75 million in deferred taxes. "Although you might have inferred it was paid, I guess we tried to stay away from saying in fact we paid taxes on that basis during the year," said one company spokesperson.[24] This type of overstatement can damage the advertiser's credibility.
3. *Audience Receptivity*: Generally the role of advocacy advertising is to reinforce existing behaviour, not to teach new attitudes or behaviour. Where such advertising is the product of crisis, as is often the case, audience receptivity may be reduced by the fact that the corporation has made no prior efforts to establish its identity with the audience nor to have signalled to the public its ongoing interest in public policy issues. (Recall Figure 12-1 above.) Moreover, advertisers may fail to formulate their advocacy ads in a context and in terms that are seen as relevant by their audience. It is how they define/see the issue that matters, not how top executives think of it.
4. *Definition of Objectives*: It is hard to overstate the need to think clearly about the objectives of advocacy advertising and how they relate to other strategies and company policies. What role/function are such ads to play in the general effort to influence government policy or a particular issue or cluster of issues? Who is the target audience? What

response is the company or trade association seeking? What are the possible adverse consequences?

5. *The Choice of Media*: In choosing the media for advocacy ads on a particular issue, it is advisable to try to identify those who are either likely to be uncommitted or to be like "natural constituents." In some cases, communicating directly with what appears to be "the opposition" will be unavoidable. Stridsberg suggests that "advertising addressed to committed supporters generally takes a defensive or strongly active stance, reinforcing their loyalty and building their enthusiasm and activity. Influentials are more prudently exposed to the 'platform of fact' approach, as a general rule, and not exposed to a higher energy level except in periods of recognized crisis" (1977, 55).

The suitability of different media depends upon a number of factors: audience coverage, cost (total and per thousand), nature of the message, the creative strategy employed, legal or practical constraints on gaining access to particular media, and appropriateness (e.g., possible need for many words to deal properly with the issue or for very rapid response to a dynamic issue — daily newspaper versus preparation of a video commercial).

The fact that the most senior management are closely associated with their company's advocacy advertising largely explains the observed preference for lengthy print ads characterized by long verbal clarifications, the use of the financial pages in daily newspapers — a dignified environment, a desire to present corporate views in an ambience and with the appearance of news (this is most obvious in the case of advertorials), and discomfort with choosing visual illustrations (Stridsberg 1977, 58).

Apparently top executives, as well as many other citizens, believe that the thirty-second TV spot commercial is totally inadequate for a serious exposition of important issues of public policy. See the example of Gulf Canada in section 12 below.

More generally, see the appendix to this chapter for some tips on how to successfully execute an advocacy advertising campaign.

11.0 PURPOSES AND EXAMPLES OF ADVOCACY ADVERTISING

Advocacy advertising focuses on building the legitimacy of the views of its sponsor. It attempts, according to Sethi, "to sustain or change public opinion on long-term fundamental values underlying social and political institutions" (quoted in McDowall 1982a, 21). According to Hardy, "The most frequently expected chain of results is that paid advertisements will lead predisposed members of the public to communicate their wishes to their elected politicians. . . . In return, politicians will pass legislation which will be implemented by regulators in government" (1982, 36). One problem associated with this simple model, however, is that usually the policy process is rather complex and several variables are needed to explain outcomes.

Several distinct rationales for advocacy advertising can be identified in the growing number of advocacy campaigns launched in Canada. The first is the reinforcement of the values and legitimacy of the free enterprise system.

11.1 Defending the Free Enterprise System

The approach taken varies from subtle attempts to buttress the legitimacy of the present economic system to not-so-subtle attacks on state interventionism. The $300 000 ad campaign launched by the Bank of Nova Scotia in August 1982 affords an example of the former approach:[25] it initially featured three full-size newspaper ads aimed at injecting some feelings of optimism into the despair over the economy. Originally, according to the ad agency responsible for the ads, the idea was for a campaign to point out how the bank was assisting people through the difficult economic times. Gradually, however, the themes moved toward an approach that would address people's economic fears, while implying that no change to the economic system (which had seen bank profits soar) was needed.

In stark contrast to the Bank of Nova Scotia's approach are the blatantly hostile ad campaigns against state intervention underwritten by the National Citizens' Coalition. The NEP, inflation, the size of the federal debt, the Constitution, government pensions, the 1981 budget, and even Pierre Trudeau's leftist leanings have all been the subject of the coalition's crusade against socialism at the federal level in Canada. The headlines in their ads have included the following:

- "Do You Believe This Man?" referring to Marc Lalonde, the minister of energy, mines and resources (*Globe and Mail*, June 6, 1981, p. B3);
- "Say It Isn't True, Al!" referring to increases in MPs' pensions (*Toronto Star*, February 23, 1982, p. D7);
- "Top International Magazine [*The Economist*] Slams Trudeau's Policies" (*Globe and Mail*, August 14, 1982, p. 3);
- "Asset or Liability," referring to Pierre Trudeau (*Maclean's*, October 25, 1982);
- "It's Pierre Trudeau's Party . . . And Look Who's Been Invited" (*Globe and Mail*, November 3, 1982, p. B16);
- "Merv Lavign Is Fighting for the Right to Earn a Living: He Needs Your Help" (*Globe and Mail*, March 6, 1985, p. 5); and
- "The Deficit — It's Your Move" (*Financial Post*, April 27, 1985, p. 15).

Another example of this type of approach is the Haughton Group, which has sponsored ads designed to "speak out on the basic values of freedom of enterprise."[26] Since the inception of its ad campaign in 1976, which featured a half-page ad proclaiming, "Mr. Trudeau, you are a national catastrophe," the subjects covered have included inflation, lenient judges, and the repatriation of the Constitution.

Between these two extremes lie efforts such as the 1975 campaign launched by the Investors Group in response to the Royal Commission on Corporate Concentration, which began its work in 1975 and published its *Report* in March 1978. (See Gorecki & Stanbury 1979.) The campaign featured a series of full-page interviews with the chief executive officers of several large companies, including Alcan, Canadian Pacific, Ford, and TransCanada PipeLines. The ads focused on the importance and need for large corporations in the Canadian economy and on the competitive nature of business in Canada; they also stressed the importance of profits to society.

11.2 Overcoming Adverse Public Opinion

A second rationale — overcoming public hostility toward business due to ignorance or misinformation — is one of the most prevalent explanations given, not only for advocacy advertising, but for all institutional advertising. Sethi points out that "surveys and public opinion polls consistently show that the public holds a low image of business and a high degree of misinformation about business activities" (cited in McDowall 1982, 26). The most notable recent example of this type involves the oil industry. The Canadian Petroleum Association (CPA), which represents the oil and oil-related companies including the big multinationals, launched a $4-million advertising campaign in 1981 after a 1980 public opinion poll by Decima Research concluded that over three-quarters of Canadians did not trust the petroleum industry. The purpose of the CPA campaign was to prevent further government intervention in the oil industry by generating voter support for oil companies before the next election. Ian Smyth, executive director of the CPA, commented, "We've learned that some government policy will go where public opinion takes it."[27] See also Doern and Toner (1985, chap. 6).

The campaign, which ran on television, as well as newspapers and magazines, and outlined how government taxes take most of the dollars motorists spend for gasoline, had a heavily factual orientation. (Recall the discussion of the "platform of fact" approach above.) A poll taken three months after the campaign was launched revealed that a majority of respondents trusted oil companies more than they did governments. CPA officials did not claim that the ads alone were behind the opinion shift, but did say that the campaign was effective.[28] (Competing with the CPA at the time was the Department of Energy, Mines and Resources, which had planned an advertising blitz to "dramatically alter the public's perception of the energy situation and thereby change their beliefs." If people, it was thought in EMR, could be convinced to drop energy from their list of major policy concerns before the NEP was announced, the ability of the oil companies, opposition MPs and the media to generate controversy would be reduced.)[29]

11.3 Going Public

Frequently, in attempting to alter public policy, companies lobby to no avail and, convinced that all methods of influence have been exhausted, turn to advocacy advertising in an attempt to generate favourable public opinion for their case. In October 1980, for example, the NEP imposed world oil prices on Canadian-owned ships while exempting the rail and road industries from the implied surcharge. The tax was intended to prevent foreign ships from benefiting from lower Canadian domestic fuel prices, but the government failed to take into account the impact the policy would have on Canadian shipping. In response, the Dominion Marine Association (DMA), which represents twenty shipping companies operating 175 ships under the Canadian flag, branded the government's policy as "discriminatory" and lobbied Ottawa for an easement. "We tried every means of persuading the government that this tax should be uplifted. That didn't work so we made a public appeal," stated Philip Hurcomb, general counsel to the DMA.[30] A full-page, black and white ad was run in the *Globe and Mail*'s "Report on Business" and in *La Presse*. The campaign was the first of its kind for the DMA, which stated that it would consider future ads concerning other problems that government regulations have created for the shipping industry.

11.4 Countering Misleading Information

Counteracting the spread of misleading information by critics is another rationale for advocacy advertising, according to Sethi (quoted in McDowall 1982a, 27). This rationale is aptly illustrated by Imperial Oil's ad campaign in response to the Bertrand report. The director of investigation and research under the Combines Investigation Act, Robert Bertrand, alleged that Imperial and the other oil companies had "ripped off" (in the media's words) the public of some $12.1 billion. These allegations were subsequently spread across newspaper headlines and were accorded top-story status on television and radio news (Baetz 1982). Overnight, negative public attitudes toward the industry soared to 70 percent. However, close examination of the seven-volume report revealed that the $12.1-billion figure was based on a number of unrealistic assumptions (Foster 1982, 260).

Imperial had known for several weeks that a hostile report was in the offing. Immediately following release of the report, it launched it's advocacy campaign with a full-page ad declaring "16,000 people at Imperial Oil take pride in the confidence that Canadians have placed in us over the past 100 years. We will not betray that confidence."[31] See Example 8. The ad appeared in thirty-seven dailies across Canada and was followed up by a second ad that stated: "Allegations of a consumer rip-off by oil companies are going to be examined in a public inquiry. Our response — the sooner the better." Within a few days of the report's release, Jack Armstrong, Imperial's CEO, had filmed a television commercial denying the allegations and welcoming a public inquiry. Although the ad ran for a week on independent and affiliate stations, both the CBC and CTV turned down the commercial on the grounds that it was of an advocacy nature and aimed at trying to change public policy. The refusal is illustrative of a fourth rationale for advocacy ads — rectifying the problem of inadequate access to and bias in the news media. Despite the fact that the networks, without qualification, had featured the $12-billion "ripoff" as a lead item, they effectively refused Imperial Oil the opportunity of a paid rebuttal.

11.5 Participating in the Public Debate on Complex Issues

Finally, business firms use advocacy advertising to fill the need for greater explanation of their views on complex policy issues. Comprehension of complex issues does not necessarily result from inundating the public with highly biased messages using selective information: by providing the public with opposing viewpoints and addressing controversial issues through highly credible and authoritative spokespersons, some companies contribute to the public's education. This rationale is evident in much Canadian advocacy advertising. However, before a company's position on complex issues can be explained, it must "earn the right to speak" on such issues. This is illustrated by the case of Gulf Canada's multi-stage "corporate advertising" program.

12.0 GULF CANADA'S CORPORATE ADVERTISING ACTIVITIES, 1981–85

Gulf Canada Ltd. appears to be the most prolific advocacy advertiser in Canada.[32] It's public affairs budget is one of the largest in the country. Between 1979 and 1984 expenditures were as follows:

- 1979 $2.6 million
- 1980   2.9
- 1981   4.2

- 1982 $4.4 million
- 1983   4.3
- 1984   3.2

In May 1981 the company embarked on a national print campaign with eight ads centred around the theme of Canada's need for new supplies of domestic oil and the role Gulf could play in their development. At that time 60 percent of Gulf Canada was owned by Gulf Oil Corp. of Pittsburgh and 75 percent of its stock was foreign owned. The $3-million campaign represented a tripling of Gulf's estimated 1980 corporate advertising budget, and between 1980 and 1982 Gulf spent over $6.2 million on its advocacy campaign.[33] Bob Fenner, director of Gulf's public affairs unit, commented that the timing of the campaign was "fortuitous," but stated that it was "not a knee-jerk reaction to the NEP or combines [investigation] or anything else."[34]

In 1984, ads sponsored by the company focused on the presentation Gulf made to the Macdonald Commission[35] concerning the future of the Canadian economy. Encouraged by the public response to its advertising efforts proposing "a new approach to consultation among government, labor and business," Gulf Canada published a full-page ad in May 1984 announcing the first issue of *Commentator* magazine.[36]

12.1 Background[37]

Gulf Canada Ltd. began in 1906 as the British American Oil Company with about two dozen employees. By 1984 it had revenues of $5.3 billion (Canada's eleventh-largest nonfinancial enterprise) and about 9000 employees.

In 1981 Gulf Canada began using corporate advertising "in an effort to help Canadians understand both the scope and complexities of Gulf's activities in Canada." The context in which Gulf began its multiyear compaign of institutional or corporate image advertising and advocacy advertising included the following elements: (1) the 1973 oil embargo associated with the Arab-Israeli war resulted in a sharp rise in world oil prices; (2) Canadians were at the time the highest per capita consumers of energy in the world and imported a substantial fraction of their needs; (3) public opinion concerning the international oil companies was characterized as hostile or mistrustful; (4) in October 1980 the federal government launched the NEP, the central goal of which was the "Canadianization" of the petroleum industry; (5) Petro-Canada was created in 1975[38] and soon acquired the Canadian operations of Atlantic Richfield (1977), Pacific Petroleums Ltd. (1978), and Petrofina (1981); and (6) there were rumours in the newspapers that Gulf Canada was a possible acquisition target of Petro-Canada, backed by the federal government's unlimited purse.

12.2 Phase I of Gulf's Campaign

Preparations began in the summer of 1980, and the ads began in May of 1981 and operated through most of 1982. The campaign tested two fundamental assumptions. First, while public opinion against the industry was negative, things weren't as bad as Gulf executives thought they were or as bad as the more vocal critics would have the world believe. Second, people were prepared to listen — that there is a peculiar Canadian sense of fair play. Gulf believed that aside from committed opponents — perhaps 20 percent of the population — other Canadians were prepared to listen provided that the message was reasonable and nonstrident.

Corporate advertising was part of a long-term commitment to a "total corporate communications program. . . . — a complete, orchestrated mix of media contact, government contact, speeches etc."

The content strategy was to portray Gulf as an organization that had made a contribution, could continue to make a contribution, and should be left to operate as a private company. The ads sought to be nonstrident and factual in tone and to associate Gulf with the public interest. The theme of one of the first ads was to quote from an employee of forty-three years: "Gulf people have served Canadians for 75 years. Here's to the next 75."

The target audience was identified as all Canadians 18 years of age and older. The media chosen consisted of daily newspapers in major cities; later a significant portion of the budget was spent on magazines, notably *Time* and *Maclean's*.

The corporate/advocacy advertising campaign began by obtaining the commitment of the president and CEO, John Stoik. He was to be featured in a number of Gulf's ads in the next few years — see Example 7.

The potential themes for the first set of ads were developed in meetings of Gulf senior executives and its ad agency, Straiton, Pearson, Martin & Holman Ltd. "From these meetings, the agency was able to develop statements about Gulf Canada and Canada's energy concerns that were both positive and negative; both public-serving and self-serving. These statements were then tested among a random sample of Canadians to determine which were the most important to them." Gulf also wanted to determine what it was people wanted to know about the company.

Gulf Canada then selected the seven "most interesting" statements from among those tested. These were developed into advertisements for further testing. Before exposure to these advertisements, interviewers asked people to rank Gulf as a company on a semantic differential scale on seven criteria such as, "A good corporate citizen," "Interested in the country's well-being." The interviewees were then shown two completed advertisements and the headlines from five more. Next, they were asked to again rate Gulf Canada on the same list of criteria that they had seen beforehand. Interest in the campaign and the change in attitudes were dramatic. Sixty-one percent of those interviewed said they would look forward to seeing the campaign and seventy-nine percent felt that the advertisements would be informative to Canadians. Of equal importance, positive attitude towards Gulf Canada on the individual criterion improved between ten and twenty percent.

According to Gulf, "This pre-testing effort proved three things. First, there were, indeed, misconceptions about Gulf Canada and a need for communication with the Canadian public. Second, the seven statements selected were right on target. Third, the proposed ads — provided they were informative — would be well received."

Phase I was based on a strategy of "earning the right to speak" on public policy issues, that is, establishing visibility and, more importantly, credibility.

The ads created in this strategy have talked about how new lubricating oils and new Arctic drilling techniques will help Canada attain oil self-sufficiency. They also have talked about how the corporation benefits Canada . . . how 98 cents of every dollar earned is used by Gulf to run its business in Canada and, to answer the question posed on the cover — how Gulf Canada spends $3 billion each year on everything from paper clips to polar bear sentries to run its business in Canada. All of the ads in this strategy were designed to show that, both in its research and development and in its corporate operation Gulf Canada is contributing to the well-being of all Canadians.

John Straiton, whose agency helped create the Gulf Canada institutional advocacy campaign, made the following comments about the campaign in its first two years:

- In the kick-off ad in our Gulf campaign, we quoted the criticism journalists had about Gulf. This started the campaign off with some credibility.
- We talked with 20 or more of Gulf's senior people in the east and the west. Many said they were sick and tired of being seen as a "grey, faceless corporation." We ran an ad with the theme of oil self-sufficiency. John Stoik, President of Gulf Canada, posed with his tomato plants to show he pulls his pants on one leg at a time like the rest of us. And the rest of the executives were presented as human beings in other ads.
- We tested over 40 ideas that came up during our top level interviews; we tested them in Montreal, Toronto and Calgary. One of the ideas that emerged was that "Gulf has a team of experts who have proved they know how to find oil and they should be encouraged to explore for more oil to help Canada achieve oil self-sufficiency." The ad "Oil is found in the minds of men" talks about the Gulf scientists and technicians who know how to look for oil.

- Another idea rated very highly by the public was Gulf Canada's energy efficient building in Calgary. We believe in finding out how messages pull so we bury offers at the end of the text to see what kind of response we get. The ad "We decided to apply the best conservation technology in our new Calgary building" was in the first year of the campaign; it was the most popular in terms of write-in response. (1983, 24–27)

The day after the "Gulf uses 98 cents of every dollar it receives to run its business in Canada" ad ran in major Canadian dailies, it was used by an MP in a House of Commons committee on energy to rebut the testimony of James Laxer on the evils of multinational oil companies in Canada.

In July 1982, Gulf Canada commissioned its first independent benchmark research study. Though its campaign had been running only six months, Gulf learned several very important things. Awareness of Gulf as a corporate advertiser was up. Recall of advertising in magazines rose from 39 percent in January to 47 percent in July. Equally important, on two key issues — "Gulf Canada is run by Canadians" and "Gulf Canada cares about people" — impressions of Gulf were more favourable. This was particularly gratifying to the company because foreign ownership is still an emotional issue with many Canadians. The survey results indicated that this wider acceptance is "probably directly attributable" to Gulf's corporate advertising campaign.

12.3 Phase II of Gulf's Campaign

As experience was gained with the campaign in 1981 and 1982, Gulf Canada's public affairs unit began to modify and set more precise objectives for corporate/advocacy advertising. The fall of 1982 marked the beginning of the second phase; the first ad in this phase appeared at the end of January 1983. Phase II ran until the fall of 1983.

The second strategy involved speaking out.[39]

Advertisements have ranged from a proposal by Gulf Canada's CEO, John Stoik, for "a new approach to government/labour/business dialogue to eliminate confrontation and to speed economic recovery," to a suggestion that the instability of world oil prices may be more opportunity than problem for Canada. These ads in this second strategy were designed to show that Gulf Canada is a responsible and responsive citizen — willing not only to speak out, but also to speak up and propose actions that will help stimulate Canada's economic growth.

The objective in Phase II was to "move Gulf toward ground of its own choosing." The key theme was to advocate greater consultation between government and business with a view to reducing hostility and more particularly to improving economic conditions by getting the economy growing again. This theme was included even in those ads that focused on modifying the NEP — see Example 7.

Because of the strong positive response to the consultation theme, Gulf revamped and repositioned its internal communications magazine *Commentator* to become a major vehicle for external communications. The first issue appeared in May 1984. Its purpose is "to provide a forum in which representatives of the various sectors in Canadian society will be invited to express their views on a particular subject." The first issue, not surprisingly, deals with energy and contains the views of a labour leader, officials of two provincial governments, a pulp and paper industry trade association executive, an investment dealer, and "Gulf Canada's corporate perspective." After three issues, in mid-1985 total circulation was about 30 000.

> In July 1983, research showed that recall of Gulf corporate advertising had increased again. More importantly, the study revealed that more people feel Gulf is a very important company for Canada's future energy self-sufficiency; a company that creates jobs in Canada; is willing to risk lots of money to find oil; is actively exploring for more oil; is good at finding oil and a company that speaks with a reasonable voice on issues relating to energy. Gulf Canada and the agency consider this kind of follow-up research extremely important. "It's always important to re-examine and readjust your priorities and goals," they say. "Conditions change; attitudes change and if you don't keep a watchful eye on your corporate advertising, it can become unfocused. Complacency is always a danger when you're trying to communicate effectively and meaningfully with people."

In Phase II Gulf committed a significant portion of its budget to magazines because people don't get the full story from TV or radio commercials. "Gulf was dealing with complex issues. They simply couldn't be handled by one-liners. With magazines, Gulf believed it could extend its reach to that group of people who were rational . . . who would take time to read and understand . . . who would draw their own conclusions. The informative nature of the campaign and the resultant copy length meant that the advertisements for magazines had to be extended to a two-page spread format. To measure input, several different ads were tested in this format."

Paul Pearson of Gulf's advertising agency has described the creative concepts behind the ads as follows: "We wanted an honest, straightforward editorial look. No glitter. Just the facts. So, all the ads were done in black and white. Full color would only reinforce the opulent oil company cliché." The ads were written so that the full meaning was contained in the headline and subheadline. Every headline was a quote from a Gulf Canada employee. Why? "Because, quite simply, people read quotes," said John Straiton. "The quote makes a statement. The sub-headline expands on it. Together, they offer a digest of the entire ad. . . . Illustrations and captions offer additional information on the subject introduced in the headline. One of them always features the person being quoted. He or she is shown as an ordinary individual doing ordinary things. This reinforces the idea that Gulf is a company of Canadians who are not only employees, but also human beings."

Starch readership figures showed an astonishing 20 to 25 percent read most of the ads. This, for more than 1,000 words of text! Each Gulf Canada ad contains an offer for more information. Since the start of the magazine campaign in 1981, Gulf has received many thousands of letters and requests for information. Many of these letters have required lengthy and thoughtful replies. What's more, when Gulf decided to run an ad quoting from these letters — not one person refused their use.

12.4 Phase III of Gulf's Campaign

Bob Fenner, director of Gulf's public affairs unit, stated:

The third phase began in the fall of 1983 [and continues as of mid-1985] with the decision to escalate the program — escalate in terms of message, frequency and more wide-spread involvement in the PA program of Gulf people. The theme we chose was "Beyond Economic Recovery." We started doing everything more often — media contact, MP dinners, speeches. A key factor in increasing the frequency of speeches has been the so-called "Grassroots" program that has seen people from a variety of departments going out to speak to service clubs, P.D. Days and so on.

The three phases of Gulf's institutional/advocacy advertising campaign were not discontinuous. The "Canada benefits" theme of Phase I was continued in the two subsequent phases. Phase III's "Beyond economic recovery" theme was just an extension of the consultation theme in Phase II.

Bob Fenner has stated that Gulf's general approach in its lengthy ad campaign is "that we were no longer going to sit back and watch other people make history and wait for that history to roll over top us. We were going to mix in the fray." He continues: "Throughout 1984, we worked on [our] obsession with participating in change and helping to shape it. Everything we are doing and saying relates, one way or another, in one time frame or another, to that obsession." Fenner has emphasized that Gulf's ad campaign, which has cost about $2 million per year, is designed to "buy a share of mind" so that the company is able to actively participate in the process of change, particularly with respect to public policy. Fenner indicates that Gulf uses four types of information to measure the effects of its ad campaigns: public opinion research; responses to the ads (letters, phone calls); cost-effectiveness of alternative modes of influencing public opinion; and other measures such as the recognition afforded by *Time*'s brochure on Gulf's corporate advertising.

In 1982 the media plan was concentrated primarily in magazines. In 1983 Gulf's ads continued in *Time* and *Maclean's*, but also were placed in daily papers (as at the beginning of the ad campaign in 1981). In the Toronto area, community newspapers were used as well. In 1984 the same pattern was followed as in 1983, with the exception of the community papers in the Toronto area.

Gulf's ads have resulted in several thousand letters. For example, the ad announcing the first issue of *Commentator* attracted 3700 letters, the ad for the second issue resulted in 4200 letters, and that for the third attracted 3000 letters. Some 95 percent of the letters indicated a favourable response, while only a 79 percent favourable response had been predicted.

12.5 Latest Research on the Campaign

The latest public opinion survey (conducted among readers of *Maclean's* and *Time* in June and July 1984 in Halifax, Calgary, Vancouver, and Toronto), based on 618 completed telephone interviews, indicates the following:

- Gulf is number one — as measured in unaided recall — for communicating about economic development and energy matters (12 percent vs. 6 percent for Petro-Canada and Imperial Oil). Unaided recall has increased steadily since the base year 1979.
- Aided awareness increased slightly in Halifax, Calgary, and Vancouver but was down in Toronto over the 1983 survey.
- Audience evaluation for Gulf corporate advertising remains good: 53 percent rated the ads as "good" or "excellent." Specific recall was good (133 of 618 respondents were able to play back ad messages).
- Perceptions of Gulf have been maintained at the same high levels achieved in 1983. But there was some slippage in earlier messages.
- People who claim recall of Gulf corporate advertising have a higher opinion of the company than those who do not, the difference being in the range of 10 to 20 percentage points. "Among *Time* and *Maclean's* readers there is widespread endorsement for more cooperation between government, business and labour; changes in government energy policies; and reducing confrontations between business and government. Gulf's use of these broad themes has not adversely affected its standing for successful, truthful and reasonable public communications." The research data suggest that "there continues to be considerable opportunity for extending Gulf's corporate personality in terms of being

run by Canadians, reinvesting in Canada, buying from Canadian suppliers, caring about people, and other dimensions that serve to give the Company the standing it deserves."

- More than one-half of the sample said that the following statements fit their impression of Gulf Canada:
  - creates jobs in Canada,
  - actively exploring for new oil and gas in Canada,
  - a very important company for Canada's future energy self-sufficiency,
  - speaks with a reasonable voice on issues relating to energy,
  - does important scientific research in Canada,
  - communicates very well with the public,
  - employs top experts in their Canadian company,
  - puts to work good ideas for conserving energy, and
  - is good at finding new supplies of domestic oil.

Table 12-1

CHARACTERISTICS OF THOSE WHO HAVE RESPONDED TO GULF CANADA'S IMAGE/ADVOCACY ADS, 1982–84

Characteristic	Persons Responding to Gulf's Ads (%)	All Canadians Living in Cities of 1 Million + Population (%)
• Male	91	49
• Age ≤ 25	4	22
≥ 41	57	42
• Business, professional	62	16
• Labour, housewife	2	27
• University graduate or postgraduate education	68	20
• Income over $30 000	69	33
• Worked on a volunteer basis for a political party in the past year	18	10
• Written or telephoned a federal MP or provincial MLA about a public issue in the past year	35	8
• Spent time helping any organization concerned with community issues in the past year.	42	27

Source: Gulf Canada Ltd.

On the other hand, from 20 percent to 24 percent of those surveyed had the following *negative* impressions of Gulf Canada:

— interested only in itself, not in Canada or the public,
— sends most of their profits out of the country,
— foreign ownership prevents them from being good corporate citizens in Canada, and
— cannot believe what they tell us about energy.

The whole matter of Gulf being foreign owned was put to rest in mid-1985 when Olympia and York, an enormous conglomerate owned by the Reichmann family, acquired 60 percent of the shares of the company from Chevron Corp. The latter's parent, Standard Oil of California, had acquired Gulf Canada's parent Gulf Oil Ltd. of the U.S. in the largest-ever merger for some $13.2 billion (U.S.) in 1984.

Figure 12–2
GULF CANADA LTD.'S COMMUNICATIONS PROGRAM STRATEGY

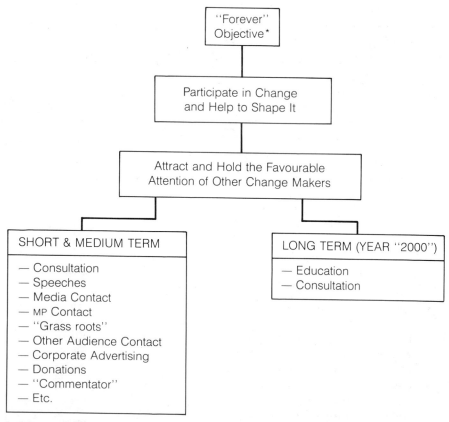

* A public opinion environment where key target audiences recognize that Gulf Canada provides a benefit to the country and, therefore, within reason, are prepared to let the company do the things it needs to do to survive and/or grow.

Table 12-1 is based on Gulf's research of those who have responded to its institutional/advocacy ads in comparison with all Canadians living in centres of one million or more population. Those who have responded could be labelled as "socially and politically aware." They obviously have a much higher interest in public policy issues.

13.0 CONTROVERSIES

Advocacy advertising is or can be controversial.[40] Here are some of the issues that have been raised about it as a vehicle for influencing public policy:

- Border-crossing advertising — for example, where a multinational enterprise advocates its position on foreign investment in a country that is threatening more restrictive measures.
- Significant national differences — Stridsberg argues that it "appears that controversy advertising is less likely to be found in countries where social and economic priorities are ordered through very strong governmental mechanisms" (1977, 87). It is also not apparent where media coverage is deemed to be fair (nonadversarial) and corporations believe they are well integrated into the policy-making machinery.
- Advocacy advertising favours the political interests of those with "deep pockets." It is a form of interest-group representation open only to those with larger financial resources (e.g., a single, full-page ad in the *Globe and Mail* costs about $15 000); hence larger corporations have an advantage in the process of influencing government policy. Moreover, some argue it adds insult to injury for the costs of corporate advocacy ads to be tax deductible. Morris Wolfe argues:

> Advocacy advertising represents a step backwards; it reaffirms the old notion that those who have money are entitled to more freedom of speech than those who don't. The fact is, consumer and other critics usually can't afford to reply in kind. They can only hope that whatever they say in response to advocacy advertising will be sufficiently news-worthy to make it into print or onto the air. . . . As Leonard Brockington, the first chairman of the CBC, put it in 1939: "Above all there should be no preference for wealth. Freedom of speech is not for sale." Of course, freedom of speech has always been for sale, as anyone who has checked the price of a printing press or a TV transmitter knows. But advocacy advertising, which puts the manipulative techniques of product selling in the hands of propagandists, increases the extent to which it is for sale. Governments and the media have it in their power to put a stop to advocacy advertising. It's in the public interest that they do so. (1980, 17–18)

- Whose interests are being advanced in corporate advocacy ads? Where there is a separation of ownership and control, professional managers may be using shareholders' money in ways they would not approve. Advocacy ads may be as much an expression of the egos (or fears) of top executives as they are an efficient/effective vehicle for influencing public policy. Thomas Wetzel, an advertising executive, remarks that advocacy ads are often placed too late: "The issue it is aimed at is so far along in the decision process, the ad really only helps vent the collective spleen in the organization placing it. . . . does the ad really contribute to winning the war or does it just make you feel good?" (1982, 26). Moreover, through such ads the corporation may be taking a political stance that is incompatible with the views of its shareholders.

- Should the media have the right to reject advocacy ads? In Canada, all television commercials are screened by a self-regulatory body (Telecaster Committee of Canada) set up in 1972. In 1982 the committee added "issue and opinion" advertising to the other categories of sensitive commercials, for example, advertising to children and feminine hygiene products.

> Committee policy is that it will rule on acceptability of commercials from governments, corporations, associations, or individuals, when such advertising attempts to sway public opinion on an issue under public debate. "The ability to purchase and pay for commercial time cannot be the only criterion in accepting announcements which present a particular point of view on an issue of public concern, or government, political or social policy," according to a committee announcement. Commercials must be factual, the advertiser identified and the message meet all legal and regulatory requirements.[41]

While the committee has no formal power to reject ads, its recommendations are usually followed. Ultimate authority over what appears on the air rests with the CRTC and the courts.

NOTES

1. Morris Wolfe dates the arrival of advocacy advertising in Canada with the *Globe and Mail*'s full-page ads aimed at business leaders: "How to win acceptance in a world full of critics."

   > One result of the information explosion, says the Globe, "has been corresponding growth in the number of society's self appointed critics." What's needed, Canada's national newspaper advises in a follow-up brochure, is more "corporate vocality." Businesses should buy space in the Globe and tell their side of the story. In case the business world has any doubt whose

side the Globe is on, its publisher, A. Roy Megarry, asserts, "We are enthusiastic supporters of the free-enterprise system — sometimes more so than some segments of the business community." (1980, 17)

Recently the Brewers of Canada (Amstel, Carling O'Keefe, Labatt, Molson, Moosehead, Northern, Pacific Western, Rocky Mountain) began a series of advocacy ads in 1986 designed to hold down or reduce the high and growing level of federal and provincial taxes on beer. See, for example, "Everybody benefits from fair taxation," *Report on Business Magazine*, March 1986; and "A big production number from the Brewers of Canada," *Globe and Mail*, February 16, 1986, p. B4.

2. See generally Gillian Steward, "The Age of Imperialism Comes to an End," *Canadian Business*, August 1982, pp. 61–71; and Peter Foster, "Imperial Rule," *Saturday Night*, November 1982, pp. 28–42. See also, Peter Foster, "Oil majors fight back in media," *Financial Post*, September 5, 1981, p. 14; and in particular Mark C. Baetz 1982 and Robert E. Landry, "Imperial Oil speaks out on the Bertrand Report," in McDowall (1982a, 33–35). The Report of the Royal Commission on Corporate Concentration noted that in 1976

> Imperial Oil Limited ran advertisements with the slogan: "Each year Imperial spends hundreds of millions of dollars on the big, tough, expensive job of developing petroleum supply. . . . If Imperial is to continue to help Canada lessen its oil dependence on other countries the company will have to put even more money to work." This was an advertisement that many advertisers and agencies in Canada viewed as a political statement dealing with an area of public controversy, and which an executive of Imperial's own advertising agency classified as "a prototype of advocacy advertising of the future." Critics of the Imperial Oil advertisements argued that Imperial claimed a profit of only 6 cents on the sales dollar, which is not the way a company should normally report its profits. In 1975, Imperial's rate of return on invested capital was about 12% and on shareholders' equity about 16%, and this is what they reported in their 1975 annual report. Critics further point out that Imperial spent $74 million on exploration in 1975, the same amount they spent in 1972 when their profits were only about 60% of the 1975 profits. (1978, 347)

3. John Straiton points out that "Bell Telephone started image advertising in 1908 — and they talked about creating an individual character for the company. They did not intend it to get subscribers. In 1928 they ran this message 'Telephone Service, A Public Trust' " (1983, 18).

4. See "Mobil Takes on the Media," *International Management*, August, 1981. See also Paul J. Hoernmans, "How Mobil Implemented Its Advocacy Strategy," in McDowall 1982, 50–52.

5. Kruk states:

> Even today, the name C. D. Howe evokes memories in many Canadians of those postwar years, when consultation and partnership between business and government helped fuel an unprecedented era of prosperity and economic nation building in Canada. The continuous consultation of those years also helped to ensure that the development of public policies benefitted from the detailed knowledge and views of the sectors of the economy that would be most affected by them. Those policies were therefore more workable and more broadly supported than they would otherwise have been. Says the Montreal economist Dian Cohen: "Those were years of a very constructive relationship among government, business and labor. In fact the fifties were a golden era for Canada." (1984, 2)

6. Kruk put it this way:

> Regrettably, the traditional dialogue between government and business in Canada diminished. In fact, industry and government appeared to have drifted so far apart by 1981 that former prime minister Pierre Trudeau called them "two solitudes." People in both industry and government feel the breakdown did not occur through design but as the result of numerous social and economic changes in the nation's character. Both sectors agree that a key factor in the decline was the emergence in the sixties and seventies of big government.
>
> Some political scientists explain that this interventionist style of government grew from the response of politicians to constituents who felt that industry and the market place economy had developed some negative aspects — corporate concentration, environmental dangers, workplace hazards and unfair practices toward minorities. Moreover, by the sixties the public had begun to develop a general wariness toward business — and for that matter, toward most institutions — which was, in turn, reflected in the attitudes of numerous government officials. Business felt the consequences: heavier taxes, more regulation, monitoring and intervention, bureaucratic complexity and decision makers who seemed unsympathetic and isolated. More and more, business people felt alienated and mistrustful of government. (1984, 2, 4)

7. Kruk notes that business-government relations began to improve toward the end of the Trudeau era (e.g., Finance Minister Marc

Lalonde's effort) and under the Mulroney Conservative government elected in September 1984:

> In the past year or so, both the Conservatives and Liberals have begun to consult extensively with the business community on everything from taxation policy to the price of natural-gas exports. The department of finance is working hard to make the process of budget creation more open and consultative, and since 1982 the federal ministry of state for economic and regional development has been posting senior civil servants — as federal economic development coordinators — to every provincial capital, partly for the purpose of keeping Ottawa informed about business from coast to coast. (1984, 4)

More generally, see Pitfield (1984).

8. Generally, see Yarwood and Enis (1982), Fox and Kotler (1980), and Lovelock and Weinberg (1983).

9. "What's in a name? For Nova, a cool $2 million," *Canadian Business*, February 1981, pp. 21–22. The total cost of the name was $2 million in media and regulatory expenses. The old name was "old fashioned and far too long" according to a senior executive.

10. "OMA Looks to Improve Image," *Marketing*, April 20, 1981, p. 21.

11. "CLIA Launches a Three-Year, $3 Million Image-Boosting Push," *Marketing*, September 22, 1980, p. 2.

12. Tom Reid, "The Devil's Advocate," *Marketing*, November 15, 1980, p. 54.

13. See Sethi (1977a), Rubin (1977), Lerbinger (1977), and Baram (1977).

14. Wetzel argues: "Another considerable side benefit of long-range issue advocacy advertising is that it can help with media relations. News people often claim that they aren't swayed by this kind of advertising. . . . but it's often easier to get in to see a reporter or an editor when a campaign is elevating an issue than when it is getting no attention at all. And journalists often quote facts during interviews that they could only have gleaned from reading an advertisement" (1982, 27). In Canada, the long-running campaign by the Canadian Pulp and Paper Institute which provides facts on the industry and its role in the economy "triggered a quadrupling of news stories on industry issues" (*Globe and Mail*, October 19, 1983, p. B6).

15. Roy Megarry, editor of the *Globe and Mail*, cited in Reid, op.cit.

16. Edelson notes: "It's easier to raise an industrywide kitty in the face of an attack than a more modest budget to *anticipate* problems. As a noted Washington lawyer once said, 'The best client is a rich man who is in trouble' " (1981, 48).

17. Gallup and Robinson, Inc., "1976 Case Studies of the Effectiveness of 'Public Issue,' 'Advocacy' and 'Economic Education,' Advertising in Magazines and Television," October 1976.

18. The only book on the subject in Canada is McDowall (1982a). However, major advocacy advertisers do pre- and post-testing to determine the effectiveness of their ads. For example, Gulf Canada's series of ads over the past five years increased its unaided recall from 2% in 1979 to 12% in July 1984 according to Bob Fenner, director of public affairs for the company. More generally, see section 12 in the text.

19. Quoted in "Independent Oilmen Hit back at Lalonde," Vancouver *Province*, September 18, 1981. IPAC ran a similar ad on April 14, 1981, after it became clear that Lalonde would *not* meet with IPAC representatives. See also Alm et al. 1984.

20. See *Toronto Star*, June 28, 1985, p. A1; and Vancouver *Sun*, June 28, 1985, p. A1.

21. Wetzel argues that "an organization that names an issue often controls it . . . naming the issue is another way of initiating it" (1982, 26). Adversary groups by making accusations about the misbehaviour of corporations can immediately put them into a defensive/reactive position. Moreover, there may be effectively two sets of rules — one for the advocates of change said to represent the public interest and another more stringent for corporations, i.e., they must be more responsible in their statements and actions than are "protest" groups in the particular. This was certainly the case with respect to the protesters and MacMillan Bloedel in regards to its plans to log Meares Island. See Dusting et al. (1985).

22. In the words of Airbus's advertising agency, "The main message was that Airbus was vital to the future of the European aircraft industry and thousands of jobs in Britain. Though it had political nuances, the advertising was essentially a tactical exercise, publicizing particular issues to achieve a sale" (quoted in Milmo 1983, 2).

23. Wetzel notes that the Edison Electric Institute's efforts to improve the economic health of investor-owned utilities by obtaining more generous increases from regulators made use of the surrogate spokesperson technique: "In one, a former Wisconsin public service director tells why it is important that utilities be made more economically healthy in terms of the national interest. In another, a Harvard professor underlines the argument and in a third, the president of an investment company shows the correlation between a good regulatory climate in specific states and healthy electric utilities" (1982, 27).

24. *Globe and Mail*, December 1, 1982. An executive with Gulf's advertising agency has suggested that the single newspaper story may have originated within the federal government. But he also points out that he was not fully conversant with the meaning of deferred taxes. He emphasizes that the objective of the ad was to tell people in plain words where Gulf's money actually went.

25. "Banking on Better Times," *Marketing*, August 16, 1982, p. 2.
26. "Haughton hits back at government," *Marketing*, November 1980, p. 32.
27. "Advocacy Ads: What the media didn't say," *Maclean's*, January 18, 1982, p. 48.
28. *Globe and Mail*, December 1, 1982, p. 4.
29. See "It's difficult to draw the line between advertising policies and party," *Financial Post*, May 26, 1984. More generally, see Stanbury et al. 1983.
30. "Now Shippers Go Advocacy Ad Route," *Marketing*, October 9, 1981, p. 36.
31. Peter Foster, "Oil majors fight back in the media," *Financial Post*, September 5, 1981, p. 14.
32. *Globe and Mail*, December 1, 1982.
33. *Globe and Mail*, June 3, 1981.
34. Ibid.
35. See Royal Commission on the Economic Union and Development Prospects for Canada, *Challenges and Choices* (Ottawa: Minister of Supply and Services, 1984).
36. *Globe and Mail*, May 25, 1984, p. 9.
37. Most of the material in this section is based on documents provided by Gulf Canada and on *Time*'s "What do paper clips have to do with corporate communications? Gulf Canada Limited: A Corporate Advertising Case History" (no date).
38. For a useful discussion of its origins and growth, see Pratt (1981). More generally, see Foster (1979).
39. Straiton remarks: "After a year of credible, helpful, non-confrontational advertising we feel Gulf has perhaps earned the right to speak out occasionally. The president delivered a speech in B.C. and it received minimal coverage. When we ran this ad based on his proposals for a joint attack on the country's problems, he was called by TV and radio people. Gulf received laudatory phone calls from senior politicians" (1983).
40. See, for example, "Why Close Woodlands and Riverview?" advocacy ad by the Committee for Quality Care, Vancouver *Sun*, January 25, 1986, p. A12; Kim Bolan, "BCGEU criticized for offensive ads," Vancouver *Sun*, January 27, 1986, p. A1; "A bad advertisement," Vancouver *Sun* editorial, January 29, 1986, p. A4; "Ministers criticize union ad," Vancouver *Sun*, January 31, 1986, p. A20; "Handicapped groups criticize BCGEU ads," Vancouver *Sun*, February 11, 1986, p. A3; and "Support a positive solution," advocacy ad by the Committee for Quality Care, Vancouver *Sun*, February 15, 1986, p. A14.
41. Nancy Brown, "Teacher ads cut by Toronto group," Victoria *Times-Colonist*, December 2, 1982.

APPENDIX TO CHAPTER 12

John Straiton on Advocacy Advertising

John Straiton is one of the pioneers and most prominent practitioners of advocacy advertising in Canada. His agency, Straiton, Pearson, Martin & Holman Ltd., has prepared advocacy and institutional ads for such clients as Gulf Canada, Canadian Pulp and Paper Association, Canadian International Paper, and Maclean Hunter. In a recent speech, Straiton (1983) offered the following insights into advocacy advertising:

1. P.R. people often argue that a well placed news release or a press conference will do ten times as much as a paid advertisement. I would agree. . . . [But] when your story has run *once* it is no longer news, even if it's a front-page attention grabber — you get one shot at the reader's mind and it's on to the next sensation. You may reach 20% — even 50% of readers once. One time only. [However] with a well-planned schedule of paid advertising, you can reach over 80% of readers, viewers, not once, but many times over. Paid messages give you *complete* control over what you say, how you say it, and largely, to whom you say it. You choose the battleground.

2. Advocacy Advertising Cannot Perform Miracles.
   (a) It cannot change public opinion overnight. In some industries, petroleum, mining and today, banking, for example, you have to work mightily to overcome public skepticism. You must work consistently, continually, and patiently to edge your way into public confidence. There are people you will never win over.
   (b) If your company or your industry has been lax or insensitive to public attitudes, advocacy advertising will take a long time to show benefit. If your industry or company is not prepared to bring its behavior into line with public perceptions, you might as well save your money — for advocacy advertising will inevitably backfire.
   (c) Advocacy advertising will not make a dramatic effect upon the value of your stock. But it can dispose people favourably to a company or to an industry.

3. Some of the things that advocacy advertising *can* do are the following:
   (a) It can make you *visible*. Too long Canadian businesses have kept a low profile — even no profile. "Never complain — never explain" as Noel Coward said. You are usually more inclined to think well of a person you know than of a stranger.
   (b) Advocacy advertising can work at many levels simultaneously — from opinion-leader to legislator to financier to worker — if it is properly conceived.
   (c) Advocacy advertising can buoy up your employees' attitudes. One of the complaints of Gulf executives was that they were seen as

part of a grey, faceless corporation. When I created advertising for Canadian International Paper, employees were proud when those full page ads told their friends, relatives and customers that they worked for an important, responsible company. The first people to be informed about your advocacy advertising should be your employees.

(d) Good paid messages can affect public attitudes, improve their understanding, and sometimes as a result, their sympathy towards you.

(e) Since public opinion is voter opinion good advocacy advertising can, in the long haul, have some effect on legislation.

4. *Time* Magazine sponsored a study of corporate advertising conducted by Yankelovich, Skelly and White. They studied 5 companies that do *not* do corporate advertising and 5 companies who *do*, to discover the effect upon upper income people (other than government and union leaders). They found a "lift" factor among those doing corporate advertising for: *awareness* (13%), familiarity (22%) and overall impression (34%). This upper income group had an improved regard for the companies doing corporate advertising in certain specific areas.

5. We have learned several things about how to make successful advocacy advertising:

(a) Top level commitment. Unless presidents, chairmen, executive committees support the intent of your messages your campaign will probably fail.

(b) To make successful advocacy advertising you need *credibility*. There are 3 parts to this.
First: Find out what the public believes, through research. Tailor your message to these beliefs.
Second: Find the way to say it believably. This is where the art comes in, where most advocacy campaigns go on the rocks. The choice of a good advertising agency is essential.
Third: Make sure your instincts are right about ads, messages, tone. Here again it is wise to sound out through research, whether people believe advertising. These are — of course — the same steps you would take if you were selling panty hose or spaghetti sauce.

(c) Strengthen your campaign with facts. Make sure your facts are irrefutable — it makes everything else you say more credible.

(d) Choose the right media. If you want to reach the greatest possible number of people and your message is simple — consider television. If your employees are a major audience — T.V. is effective. But make sure you have a couple of million dollars handy. One good commercial can cost over $100,000. For opinion-leaders, business heads, educators, legislators, newspapers and magazines are effective. Newspapers are flexible — you can be in with your message within days — hours if necessary. T.V. is slow and ponderous.

(e) When you can afford it, use large space. In T.V. — consider the two minute commercial. Have the *look* of importance. Starch readership studies show that, for low interest product categories, larger space can increase the *reading* of your message. For instance, banking and financial advertising received 150% more reading in business magazines when it ran in double pages as compared with single pages. A caution about large space — especially in recessionary times — it *can* trigger complaints of extravagance. The 1983 campaign for the Canadian Pulp and Paper Association cost about $.02 per Canadian for the year. Gulf's campaign will cost about $.08 per Canadian for the year.

(f) Sloganeering is not terribly credible.

(g) Whenever possible, *monitor* the effectiveness of your advocacy advertising through readership research, write-in offers, pre and post attitude studies.

EXAMPLES OF INSTITUTIONAL AND ADVOCACY ADVERTISEMENTS

Example 1

NOVA REPORT NO. 1 *A closer look* GAS TRANSMISSION

WE PUT OUR GAS THROUGH COMPUTER SCHOOL

New technology is helping us deliver.

Because we carry more than 75% of the Canadian natural gas marketed each year, were continually working on new ways to make our pipeline system—already one of the most technically advanced in North America—even more dependable and cost-efficient.

That's why were in the process of implementing a new, highly sophisticated computer control system that will distribute our ability to monitor and control the flow of gas within Alberta.

Four computers are being installed in our district offices. And they'll be able to monitor on-site equipment and 'talk' to their big brothers at gas transmission headquarters in Edmonton.

This system, a combination of commercially available hardware and internally modified software that serves our particular purposes, will also increase overall computer capacity to meet our future needs. And it's slated for completion as early as next year.

The net result? Improved service, greater flexibility and a natural gas delivery system thats getting more and more 'intelligent' every day, a process that's making it

possible for us to meet Canada's changing energy needs.

That's something that computes —for us and for Canada.

Gas transmission is what gave us our start in the energy business. And, as we continue to build the future with energy, gas transmission provides us with one of our most important sources of revenue.

NOVA employs more than 1,500 people on this system and provides benefits to communities right across the country in the form of land payments, taxes and the purchase of Canadian-made goods and services.

That's something were proud of because by combining imagination with sound business judgement, were working to keep Canada strong—right into the next century.

We'd like you to take a closer look at what we're doing.

If you'd like to know more about our work in gas transmission or any of the other things were doing to build the future with energy, simply write to us or call our toll-free number. (800) 661-9264.

You'll find wherever energy is involved, were in action.

NOVA

BUILDING THE FUTURE WITH ENERGY

NOVA, AN ALBERTA CORPORATION   P.O. Box 2535, Stn. M, Calgary, Alberta · T2P 2N6

Example 2

There are banks and "near banks." What's the difference?

Because you deposit your money there doesn't make it a bank. There *are* distinctions.

You walk up to the counter holding your cash and passbook. You hand them to the teller who enters the deposit in your book. You've completed a banking transaction.

Where are you? In a bank? Not necessarily.

Here in Canada there are several different kinds of financial institutions competing with each other in the business of banking. Not all of them are banks.

Dealing with money.

You can probably think of many places to put your money: like insurance, the stock market or real estate. And there are plenty of institutions to help you do this.

But the financial institutions which are closest to performing bank-like functions – sometimes called "near banks" – are mainly trust companies (and their associated mortgage loan companies), credit unions and caisses populaires.

The 11 longest-established chartered banks carry on their activities through a 7,400-branch system, one of the most extensive in the world – with one branch for approximately every 3,500 Canadians.

And we also have some 75 trust companies and 3,600 credit unions and caisses populaires with a total of 5,600 banking offices.

What is a chartered bank?

A chartered bank is an institution named in the federal Bank Act and governed by that Act. Banks are closely regulated by various federal government bodies, primarily the Department of Finance, and they're responsive to the Bank of Canada, the government-owned central bank, which regulates credit and currency in the interests of the country's economy.

The "near banks" by and large are under provincial regulation, and are indirectly responsive to Bank of Canada influence.

Banks are like financial "supermarkets".

Before 1954 – when they were first allowed to give some types of mortgages – banks did a relatively limited amount of lending to consumers.

More recently, banks have become full-service supermarkets of financial services, especially with considerable expansion of their mortgage and consumer lending activities.

Though they offer services similar to those provided by banks, trust companies are not a different kind of bank; they're a different type of institution.

Trusts manage people's assets.

Like banks, trust companies make loans. They also take deposits. But what sets them apart from banks is the fact that they are also in the fiduciary business; that is, the managing of people's assets (property and money that we own, measured in

Banks, trust companies and credit unions appear to be the same, but they're not.

dollars and cents) and handling of estates.

If, for instance, you receive an inheritance and don't feel qualified to manage it, you can appoint a trust company as your agent to manage it for you. As the name suggests, you *trust* them to look after your money, to invest it, and to otherwise safeguard your assets.

Most of the loans that trust companies make are in the form of mortgages. In fact, legislation effectively limits the extent of trust companies' non-mortgage lending. And, real estate brokerage has become another very active function of many trust companies.

Banks spread their funds.

Trust companies have more than half of their assets in mortgages, but banks have much more diversified loan portfolios.

By law, banks must quite severely limit the proportion of their lending which goes into mortgages. (Although they may do additional mortgage lending through subsidiaries.) The rest of their money is lent to everyone from your neighbour building a family room, to the local hardware dealer increasing his stock, to a major

Canadian corporation planning a big new venture.

By law, banks cannot offer trustee services. Nor can they act as real estate brokers. And whereas trust companies lend mainly to individuals, banks lend to both corporations and individuals.

Financial Co-operatives.

Credit unions are literally financial co-operatives. While their ownership was originally limited to people with a common bond who might be employees of a particular company, or members of an association or parish, this limitation is disappearing, so it is now often possible for a credit union to accept the membership of other individuals.

A credit union is owned and operated by its members, and is generally restricted to serving those members. A bank is owned by its shareholders and may offer its services to everybody.

Caisses populaires were the first co-operative financial institutions established in North America. Originally set up to provide a source where working people could borrow money at a low rate of interest, they function like credit unions.

Close supervision.

All of these financial institutions are supervised by government authorities. But here, again, there are differences in the rules which are applied.

The chartered banks are probably the most closely regulated and inspected. Banks, for instance, have to keep cash reserves. These funds are largely held by the Bank of Canada, and the banks earn no interest on them. On the other hand, trust companies can and do earn interest on their reserves. And credit unions and caisses populaires can take advantage of favourable tax rules established for co-operatives, while banks are taxed as commercial corporations.

Legislation varies.

Banks are governed by federal legislation. In some instances, banks are subject to provincial legislation. Trust companies can choose to be incorporated federally or provincially. All credit unions and caisses populaires are incorporated provincially.

So, you see, there are differences (as well as similarities) between banks and "near banks".

But they all compete with each other for your business; banks with banks, banks with "near banks", and "near banks" with "near banks". This kind of competition is good for the economy, and it thrives on the differences – and the similarities – between banks and "near banks".

No. 5 in a series of advertisements to help you understand banking better.

Canada's Chartered Banks.

The Canadian Bankers' Association on behalf of

Bank of Montreal · The Bank of Nova Scotia · Toronto Dominion Bank · National Bank of Canada · Canadian Imperial Bank of Commerce
The Royal Bank of Canada · The Mercantile Bank of Canada · Bank of British Columbia · Canadian Commercial Bank · Northland Bank · Continental Bank of Canada
ABN Bank Canada · Bank of America Canada · Barclays Bank of Canada · Continental Illinois Bank (Canada) · Deutsche Bank (Canada)
Hongkong Bank of Canada · Korea Exchange Bank of Canada · National Bank of Detroit, Canada · Swiss Bank Corporation (Canada) · The Bank of Tokyo Canada

Example 3

Canada's Pharmaceutical Industry
Searching Today
for Better Health Tomorrow

New drug discoveries for tomorrow depend on investment in research today . . . . . drug research that is carried out around the world. Canada has a role to play in this research.

The Pharmaceutical Manufacturers Association of Canada represents 66 pharmaceutical companies in Canada. We research, develop, manufacture, and market drug products that save lives, reduce suffering, and improve the quality of life. We are Canada's drug discovery industry. The percentage of sales that we re invest in Canadian drug research and development is 4.5 times greater than the average for all other manufacturing industries in Canada combined. In 1983 the innovative Canadian pharmaceutical industry invested over $100 million in research . . . an investment in Canada's better health for tomorrow . . . . . an investment in our economy today. Canada's pharmaceutical industry creates employment for more than 16,000 Canadians . . . physicians, pharmacists, chemists, pharmacologists, biochemists . . . scientists from Canadian universities.

This worthwhile role of Canada's pharmaceutical industry must continue to grow and keep pace with the rest of the world.

But Canada's pharmaceutical research base is in danger. The rate of increase in drug research expenditure is slowing. Increasingly, firms are importing their finished products instead of manufacturing them in Canada. In the longer term, Canada's participation in the dynamic new field of pharmaceutical biotechnology may suffer.

Why this danger?

Canada's Patent Act enables anyone to obtain a license to copy, import, and market drugs before the patent expires. This is called compulsory licensing. These compulsory licenses are not only unfair to the innovative scientists, but they discourage the research and development of new drugs in Canada.

Why Patents?

Patent rights are critical to the innovative process. Patents are granted to induce public disclosure of an invention. In return the innovator is rewarded by the exclusive use of the invention for a limited period of time.

However, Canada's patent laws deny drug researchers the full patent rights they have in other countries . . patent rights which the Act provides to every other Canadian researcher.

Pharmaceutical research is time consuming; it takes over 10 years on the average to develop a new drug. Pharmaceutical research is expensive: it takes an average of $100 million to research and develop a new drug. The chances for success are slim. For every 10,000 chemical substances created in laboratories only 1,000 are considered promising enough for further investigation. Of these, only **one** will prove a safe and effective therapeutic agent.

Without the patent system the innovator could not justify this investment. Without this investment Canadians would not have benefited from most of today's remarkable drug discoveries.

A Role for Canada

When new drugs are researched or developed in Canada, Canadians benefit even more. Employment opportunities are created for Canadian researchers across the country. When new discoveries and knowledge are developed in Canada, they are available to Canadians earlier. They are used with greater effectiveness and fewer risks.

The pharmaceutical industry wishes to continue its search for excellence and give to all Canadians the most modern drugs at reasonable prices.

We believe you will agree that Canada should continue to play a role in pharmaceutical research and that Canadians should contribute to the worldwide search for new and improved drugs.

For information, please write:

Pharmaceutical Manufacturers Association of Canada
500 1111 Prince of Wales Drive
Ottawa, Ontario
K2C 3T2

Pharmaceutical Manufacturers Association of Canada

Example 4

MR. LALONDE PLEASE LISTEN!

THE NATIONAL ENERGY PROGRAM IS HURTING <u>ALL</u> CANADIANS

CANADIAN JOBS LOST

Jobs being lost are not only those in the Canadian oil and gas industry. The lay-offs in Western Canada have a direct impact on jobs in Central Canada.

How?

· People who work in oil fields buy clothes, furniture, food, cars and appliances, most of which are made in Ontario and Quebec

· The oil and gas companies buy electronics, valves, tools, trucks, steel, paper, compressors, building supplies and hundreds of other products from every province, particularly Ontario and Quebec

· The cut-backs in the oil and gas industry will be felt even more in central Canada than the west

CANADIAN OIL SUPPLY JEOPARDIZED

Canadian oil companies have been forced to slash exploration. Canadian capital and expertise are being driven out of our country

The Result:

· Canada's hopes for oil self-sufficiency by 1990 have been dashed

· Canada's dependence on foreign oil — never a secure source — is being increased

· Canadian taxpayers are paying $400,000 per hour to subsidize oil imports

· The future of our children is being mortgaged by a rising national debt

· The people of Ontario and Quebec will be hurt most — they have more manufacturers, more pension funds, more jobs, more taxpayers than other provinces

MR. LALONDE

Our Canadian Companies — the very ones your National Energy Program was supposed to help — have been devastated by this Program. We asked for a Special Joint Committee of the Senate and House of Commons to examine all the serious far-reaching implications of your program. This request was denied.

We urge you to reconsider. As you, Mr. Lalonde, said in introducing the National Energy Program "it will impinge on almost every sphere of Canadian activity, on the fortunes of every Canadian, and on the economic and social structure of the nation for years to come"

TO CANADIANS EVERYWHERE

If you are concerned about jobs, oil security, Canada's economic future, we urge you to write to the Prime Minister, House of Commons, Ottawa, K1A 0A6, and to the editor of your local newspaper. The future of our country is at stake.

INDEPENDENT PETROLEUM ASSOCIATION OF CANADA

Canadians working for Canada to produce Canadian oil and gas supplies, and jobs
in every region of our country
350 MEMBER COMPANIES

Example 5

QUASH
FOOTWEAR IMPORT
QUOTAS

ALLEGATIONS

The Federal Government must guarantee 50% of the market for domestic shoe manufacturers because the industry only has 40%.

Consumers pay less for shoes because of import quotas.

Canadian shoe manufacturers cannot compete with imports.

Footwear quotas must continue for at least 5 more years so manufacturers can invest in new technology.

The Mulroney Government advocates less protectionism; better relations with our key trading partners, and freer trade.

THE FACTS

■ The Department of Regional, Industrial Expansion (DRIE) confirms that Canadian shoe manufacturers enjoy well in excess of 60% of the market (value terms, 1984).

■ Not according to the Consumers' Association of Canada, and the Competition Policy Branch of Consumer and Corporate Affairs.
■ A quota system generates higher costs for everyone. **Federal Government departments estimate the cost to be over $200 million per year.**

■ The 1985 Canadian Import Tribunal heard evidence that domestic manufacturers are strong and competitive in many areas.
■ In 1981, the Anti-dumping Tribunal found the Canadian Footwear Industry could meet the competition of developed nations and state trading footwear exporters.

■ Footwear quotas have existed for 8 years. Since 1977, some manufacturers have developed new skills and modernized. Federal government programmes helped defray investment costs thus reducing pay-back periods.
■ In 1984, an official of Consumer and Corporate Affairs said before the Tribunal, "If eight years of quotas have not allowed the industry to become competitive, three more years are unlikely to; if they have, quotas are no longer needed. In either case an extension is unwarranted."

■ The focus of international trade retaliation due to shoe quotas will impact upon every region of Canada and many industries.
■ The outcome of the debate on footwear trade policy will determine the direction of the Federal Government regarding protectionism. It will serve as a clear signal to our trading partners and either fuel, or quell, protectionist forces at home and abroad.

In December 1984, the Federal Cabinet endorsed the terms-of-reference of the Canadian Import Tribunal inquiry of the domestic footwear industry. **That mandate called for either an end to quotas in 1985, or a phase-out formula over a period not to exceed three years** (i.e. by November 1988).

Canadian shoe retailers ask the Government to uphold its stated public commitment as expressed in the Tribunal's mandate. We urge the Federal Cabinet to acknowledge the needs of retailers and consumers.

THE CANADIAN SHOE
RETAILERS' ASSOCIATION
representing over 2,200 shoe stores across Canada

2510 YONGE STREET, TORONTO, ONTARIO M4P 2H7 (416) 487-7011

Example 6

The MacEachen budget is not what it seems to be. It is a sly, devious document that nearly fooled us all.

Budget night and the talk is of Robin Hood. Of taking from the rich and giving to the poor. Of closing tax loopholes on fat cats. Of increasing revenue while lowering taxes. And, best of all, only millionaires would feel the pinch and they, after all, can afford it.

The perfect budget. Or is it?

At first blush the news did not seem to be too bad. There was the usual opposition carping, but so what? That is to be expected. Nearly everyone was fooled.

Now, however, the Canadian Federation of Independent Business has had some of the top tax and business minds in the country examine the fine print of an extremely complex document. What they discovered has shocked us all. Only now are we able to see what the results will be from the more than 163 technical amendments that are proposed.

The unanimous conclusion of the best tax experts in the country is – disaster. A disaster for small business, farmers, working Canadians, professionals and the unemployed. In short, the whole economy.

But at this point, most Canadians don't even realize it. Indeed, your Member of Parliament probably does not understand what this budget will do to his constituents.

RECOMMENDED SOLUTION

John Bulloch, President of the Canadian Federation of Independent Business, is calling for delayed implementation of the budget, pending public hearings by The Standing Committee of the House of Commons on Finance, Trade and Economic Affairs. "This budget must not be passed until Parliamentarians have had the opportunity to hear from knowledgeable individuals who, unlike the budget drafters, have to function in the Canadian economy."

This is a wise and prudent direction that can only result in improved legislation. Help us bring it about.

If you agree with us and would like the government to delay its budget legislation and hold hearings on its true effects, then please help us to strengthen the message. Send in the attached coupon and we will deliver it to the Minister of Finance.

Example 7

"How can we get Canada going again? A major impetus could be an orderly energy resource development strategy."

John Stoik
President and Chief Executive Officer, Gulf Canada Limited

Most Canadians seem to agree that a national industrial strategy would help us to sustain economic recovery and help us plan realistically and constructively for a world beyond economic recovery.

But other than agreeing that we want less unemployment, more productivity, a Canadian high technology industry – and that we never again want to relive the last few years – there are many different views of what that strategy should be.

While we ponder the problem, we keep missing opportunities to realize our potential – a potential as great as or greater than that of almost any other industrialized nation.

One step toward an industrial strategy that would sooner or later benefit a majority of Canadians, should be the orderly, long-term development of our tremendous energy resources – particularly oil and natural gas.

However, implementing such a strategy would mean changing some of the rules of the energy resource game – or at least having a game in which the rules don't change half way through the season.

John Stoik

What Canadians want most right now is jobs.

And labour and industry alike desire higher productivity.

One widely-discussed route to these goals is to stimulate new industries such as high technology.

We support this idea.

But Gulf Canada believes that to develop new opportunities, we need strength and growth in the traditional industries upon which much of our economy is built. These have been, and will be for generations, the basic Canadian strengths. They are major users of high technology. They could be bigger users.

The opportunity

Canada has an enormous supply of oil and gas, resources that people at home and abroad will need and use well beyond the year 2000, despite the growth of alternate energy sources.

Exports – not just of crude oil and natural gas, but of finished products – would create jobs and provide valuable foreign exchange.

In the meantime, exploration and development of these resources generates jobs in hundreds of manufacturing and service industries across Canada.

Where high technology is concerned, the petroleum industry spends millions of dollars on electronic equipment, computers and other "high tech" products.

The petroleum industry can provide a major impetus to the Canadian economy. But to maximize the opportunity, we need sensible policies that we can depend upon.

Such policies would have an impact far beyond the immediate and obvious benefits. They would, for instance, send a signal to the international investment community that foreign investment is welcome and needed in Canada.

Canada's oil sands deposits may make us the most petroleum rich country in the world. Unfortunately, the cost of extracting oil from these stubborn deposits is high. New technology must be developed to make these vast reserves available. The investments needed are in the billions. Yet if our governments can give encouragement to industry today, the oil sands can be a source of future wealth that can put Canada in the forefront of oil-producing nations.

And the sooner and more clearly this signal is sent, the better for all of us.

What do we need to do?

Gulf Canada suggests the following policy measures:

1. The indisputable benefits of Canadian oil and gas resource development must be recognized – benefits such as security of supply and the opportunity to develop export markets. A commitment now to oil and gas development will help sustain economic recovery.

2. Canada should take advantage of the decline in international prices to move to world prices for all its domestic oil production.

3. The National Energy Program must be reviewed.

To quote from a study published by the non-partisan C.D. Howe Institute:

"The NEP was introduced to Canadians as a solution to the nation's

energy problems. It promised to unite Canadians and to make them prosper . . . the NEP has proven to be a major disappointment. New energy challenges are emerging that are quite different from those the NEP was designed to deal with . . . A reassessment of Canada's energy objectives is already overdue."

As a start, Gulf Canada recommends the following measures:

– Eliminate the discriminatory aspects of the Petroleum Incentive Payments (PIPs) and introduce an exploration incentive system that treats companies equitably.

– Eliminate the back-in provision that allows the Federal Government to claim, retroactively, 25 percent of discoveries – including Hibernia, discovered before the introduction of the National Energy Program.

– Stimulate industry activity – and thus job creation – by taking less

money out of the industry. Under the current system, money that could be going toward finding and developing new petroleum energy is taxed away before we have a chance to reinvest it. We suggest that the fiscal regime be modified to give the industry a chance to make a greater contribution to Canada's economic recovery.

The need for consultation

Gulf Canada contends that many of the policies that contributed to our recent economic woes were the product of confrontation instead of consultation.

To maintain economic recovery – and to plan realistically and constructively for a world beyond economic recovery – we must foster genuine co-operation among business, government and labour.

To that end, Gulf Canada has proposed new approaches to tripartite consultation. Without such genuine consultation, we may be doomed to go on spinning our wheels, missing opportunities and – at worst – reliving the experience of the last few years.

Our thoughts on these and other subjects were summarized in our submission to the Macdonald Royal Commission on the Economic Union and Development Prospects for Canada.

If you would like a copy, write to:
Bob Fenner
Director – Public Affairs,
Dept. 422N,
Gulf Canada Limited,
130 Adelaide St. West,
Toronto, Ontario
M5H 3R6

GULF CANADA LIMITED

Example 8

Rip-off....? Nonsense!

J. A. Armstrong, Chairman Imperial Oil Limited.

"The allegation of a consumer rip-off will not stand up to an impartial inquiry. In fact, strong competition has helped keep Canadian prices low.

Imperial Oil is certain that it has not broken the law or in any sense been involved with other companies to fix prices.

16,000 people at Imperial Oil take pride in the confidence that Canadians have placed in us over the past one hundred years. We will not betray that confidence".

Example 9

TELEPHONE DEREGULATION

Canada can't afford it.

Canada's telephone system is second to none. A wrong decision by the Canadian Radio-Television and Telecommunications Commission (CRTC) may change that.

CNCP Telecommunications has applied to compete with Bell Canada for long distance service in Ontario and Quebec. Other companies are waiting in the wings. All promise a better deal for the consumer. The facts show otherwise.

Similar «deregulation» has already taken hold in the United States. The result? Costs are way up; service is way down:

- Local phone rates have jumped an *average 37%* since January 1984, with more dramatic increases predicted.

- Overall long distance charges have *risen*, with rates falling mostly between major business centres.

- «Local measured service» is being introduced, a charge for the frequency and length of *local calls*.

- Waits of up to *45 days* for phone installation.

- *Complicated* billing and new phone service charges.

- Basic service priced *beyond the reach* of the elderly, the handicapped, single parent families, students and the jobless.

If you have a telephone, you have a stake in stopping deregulation.

Call your Member of Parliament. Contact us for petitions and more information. Fill out and mail the coupon below (postage free).

To: Hon. Marcel Masse
   The Minister of Communications, House of Commons
   Ottawa, Ontario K1A 0A6

I wish to add my name to those opposing deregulation of Canada's telephone system. We currently enjoy a fair and cost-efficient system that works well for all Canadians. Proposed changes before the CRTC can only undermine our tradition of affordable, universal service.

NAME: (please print): _____ SIGNATURE: _____

ADDRESS: _____

CITY: _____ PROV. _____ POSTAL CODE: _____

COMMUNICATIONS, ELECTRONIC, ELECTRICAL, TECHNICAL AND SALARIED WORKERS OF CANADA

National Office, 141 Laurier Ave. W., Suite 906, Ottawa, Ontario K1P 5J3 (613) 236-6083

Example 10

PICTURE TROUBLE ISN'T TEMPORARY PLEASE DON'T STAND BY!!!

Don't stand by waiting for someone else to fix the trouble: the trouble is the lack of government commitment to Canadian programming.

In 1932 Prime Minister Bennett insisted Canada

"must be assured of complete control of broadcasting from Canadian sources."

In 1952 the Honourable Lionel Chevrier argued that

"it is perfect nonsense to suggest that private enterprise, left to itself, will provide Canadian programming."

In 1968 the Broadcasting Act enshrined the idea that a Canadian broadcasting system should

"safeguard, enrich and strengthen the cultural, political, social and economic fabric of the country."

Nice words but did anybody listen? Seems not when you consider that today, over 75% of television programs aired in this country are American! While we don't question the popularity of these shows, the trouble is they keep pushing Canadian programs off network schedules, reducing the number of opportunities for Canadians to see themselves and their world on television. And that's too bad because what unites a country is a national sense of self.

If you agree that these opportunities shouldn't be lost,

DON'T STAND BY!

Here's what you can do.

1) Write to us. We'll send you information on public broadcasting—what it is, why it's important and how little it *really* costs—plus we'll add your name to our membership; or

2) Write to your M.P., or better still, to Prime Minister Mulroney to ask for a greater commitment to public broadcasting. Send your letters POSTAGE FREE to: The Prime Minister, House of Commons, Ottawa, Ontario K1A 0A6; and

3) Start talking! To friends. To family. To anyone who'll listen about the importance to all Canadians of having a public broadcasting system that's alive and well. If you belong to a club, group, organization or association, ask them to pass a resolution calling for more Canadian programming.

 ALLIANCE FOR CANADIAN BROADCASTING   P.O. BOX 220 STATION 'A' TORONTO, ONT. M5W 1B2

The Association of Television Producers and Directors (Toronto) bringing together individuals and groups across Canada.

REFERENCES/BIBLIOGRAPHY

Aberback, J. *et al.* (1981) *Politics and Bureaucrats in Western Europe* (Cambridge, Mass.: Harvard University Press).

Abrams, Burton A., and Russell F. Settle (1978) "The Economic Theory of Regulation and Public Financing of Presidential Elections," *Journal of Political Economy*, Vol. 86(2), pp. 245-257.

Acheson, Keith (1985) "Economic Regulation in Canada: A Survey," in *Canadian Industrial Policy in Action* (Toronto: University of Toronto Press).

Adams, Michael (1984) "Canadian Attitudes Towards Legislative Institutions," in *Canadian Legislatures: The 1984 Comparative Study* (Toronto: Queen's Printer for Ontario).

Adatia, Amin, Peter Fetisoff, and Peter Taylor (1983) "The Employers' Council of British Columbia" (Commerce 592 paper, April, University of B.C., Faculty of Commerce).

Adelson, Lyle, Helen Becker, Lucy Komori, and Allen Lee (1985) "The Canadian Federation of Independent Business" (Commerce 592 paper, Faculty of Commerce and Business Administration, University of B.C.).

Adkins, Lynn (1978) "How Good are Advocacy Ads?" *Dun's Review*, June, pp. 76-77.

Aitken, H.G.J. (1967) "Defensive Expansion: The State and Economic Growth in Canada," in W.T. Easterbrook and M.H. Watkins (eds.) *Approaches to Canadian Economic History* (Toronto: University of Toronto Press), pp. 193-221.

Albert, Alain (1981) "La Participation Politique: Les Contributions Monetaires aux Partis Politiques Quebecois," *Canadian Journal of Political Science*, Vol. 14(2), pp. 397-410.

Albinski, Henry S. (1973) "The Canadian Senate: Politics and the Constitution," in O.M. Kruhlak, *et al.* (eds.) *The Canadian Political Process*, revised ed. (Toronto: Holt, Rinehart and Winston of Canada), pp. 466-486.

Alexander, Herbert E. (1981) "Corporate Political Behaviour," in Thornton Bradshaw and David Vogel (eds.) *Corporations and Their Critics* (New York: McGraw-Hill), pp. 33-47.

Alexander, Herbert E. (1983) *Financing the 1980 Election* (Lexington, Mass: D.C. Heath).

Alinsky, Saul D. (1971) *Rules for Radicals* (New York: Vintage Books).

Allen, Robert W., *et al.* (1979) "Organizational Politics: Tactics and Characteristics of its Actors," *California Management Review*, Vol. 22, pp. 77-83.

Alm, Ralph, *et al.* (1984) "The Independent Petroleum Association of Canada: An Analysis of Lobbying Techniques" (Paper for Commerce 592, Faculty of Commerce and Business Administration, University of B.C., mimeo).

Alpin, John C., and W.H. Hegarty (1980) "Political Influence Strategies Employed by Organizations to Impact Legislation in Business and Economic Matters," *Academy of Management Journal*, Vol. 23, pp. 438-450.

Alt, James E., and E. Alec Chrystal (1983) *Political Economics* (Berkeley: University of California Press).

Alter, Jonathan (1984) "The Media in the Dock," *Newsweek*, October 22, pp. 66-72.

Altheide, David L. (1976) *Creating Reality* (Beverly Hills: Sage Publications).

Amato, Guy, Steve Hindmarch, Phil Jemielita, and Clark Seadon (1983) "The Sunday Shopping Issue in British Columbia: History, Analysis and How the Retail Merchants Association Sought to Exert Influence" (Commerce 592 paper, April, University of B.C., Faculty of Commerce).

Anderson, Ian (1983) "Lost and Found" (re lobbying for Micmac Indians of Newfoundland) *Saturday Night*, Vol. 98(8), August, pp. 11-14.

Anderson, Robert D. (1980) "The Federal Regulation-Making Process and Regulatory Reform in W.T. Stanbury (ed.) *Government Regulation: Growth, Scope, Process* (Montreal: The Institute for Research on Public Policy).

Anisman, Philip (1975) *A Catalogue of Discretionary Powers in the Revised Statutes of Canada, 1970* (Ottawa: Law Reform Commission of Canada/Information Canada).

Antilla, Susan (1981) "Business' Media Watchdog," *Dun's Business Month*, Vol. 118(4), October, pp. 108-109.

Appleby, Paul H. (1952) *Morality and Administration in Democratic Government* (Baton Rouge: Louisiana State University Press).

Aram, John D. (1983) *Managing Business and Public Policy: Concepts, Issues and Cases* (Marshfield, Mass.: Pitman Publishing Inc.).

Aranson, Peter H., and Melvin J. Hinich (1979) "Some Aspects of the Political Economy of Election Campaign Contribution Laws," *Public Choice*, Vol. 34, pp. 435-461.

Archbold, William D. (1977) "Business Council on National Issues: A New Factor in Business Communication," *Canadian Business Review*, Vol. 4(2), pp. 13-15.

Armstrong, R.W. (1970) "Why Management Won't Talk," *Public Relations Journal*, Vol. 26, November, pp. 6-8.

Armstrong, Richard A. (1980) "Public Issues Management," in R.A. Bucholz (ed.) *Public Policy and the Business Firm* (Washington University, St. Louis: Center for the Study of American Business), pp. 131-144.

Armstrong, Richard A. (1981) "The Concept and Practice of Issues Management in the United States," *Vital Speeches of the Day*, Vol. 47(24), October 1, pp. 763-765.

Aronoff, Craig E. (ed.) (1979) *Business and Media* (Pacific Palisades, Calif.: Goodyear Publishing).

Arrington, Charles B., and Richard N. Sawaya (1984) "Managing Public Affairs: Issues Management in an Uncertain Environment," *California Management Review*, Vol. 26(4), Summer, pp. 148-160.

Arthurs, H.W. (1985) "Law as an Instrument of State Intervention: A Framework for Enquiry," in *Law, Society, and the Economy* (Toronto: University of Toronto Press).

Atkinson, David Scott (1981) "Business Media Relationships Explored," *Marketing*, Vol.86 (40), October 5, p. 30.

Atkinson, Michael (1978) "Policy Interests of Provincial Backbenchers and the Effects of Political Ambition," *Legislative Studies Quarterly*, Vol. 3, pp. 629-646.

Atkinson, Michael (1985) "Parliamentary Government in Canada," in M.S. Whittington and Glen Williams (eds.) *Canadian Politics in the 1980s*, 2nd edition (Toronto: Methuen), pp. 331-350.

Atkinson, Michael, and M.A. Chandler (eds.) (1983) *The Politics of Canadian Public Policy* (Toronto: University of Toronto Press).

Atwood, Margaret (1972) *Survival: A Thematic Guide to Canadian Literature* (Toronto: Anansi).

Aucoin, Peter (1971) "Theory and Research in the Study of Policy-Making," in G. Bruce Doern and Peter Aucoin (eds.) *Structures of Policy Making in Canada* (Toronto: Macmillan of Canada), pp. 10-38.

Auditor General of Canada (1982) *Report of the House of Commons: Fiscal year ended 31 March 1982* (Ottawa: Minister of Supply and Services).

Audley, Paul (1983) *Canada's Cultural Industries: Broadcasting, Publishing, Records and Films* (Toronto: Lorimer).

Auld, D.A.L., and F.C. Miller (1982) *Principles of Public Finance: A Canadian Text*, 2nd edition (Toronto: Methuen).

Austen-Smith, D. (1981) "Voluntary Pressure Groups," *Economica*, Vol. 48, pp. 143-153.

Austin, Ian, and Linda McQuaig (1983) "The Law and Conrad Black," *Maclean's*, February 21, pp. 26-35.

Axel, H. (1980) *Political Activism: The Chief Executive's Role* (New York: The Conference Board, Info. Bulletin No. 71).

Axworthy, Lloyd (1985) "Control of Policy," *Policy Options*, Vol. 6(3), pp. 17-20.

Baetz, Mark C. (1978) "The Business Council on National Issues" (London, Ontario: University of Western Ontario, School of Business Administration, case study).

Baetz, Mark C. (1984) "The Canadian Drug Manufacturers' Association and a Review of Section 41 of the Patent Act" (School of Business and Economics, Wilfrid Laurier University, mimeo).

Baetz, Mark C. (1985a) "Sector Strategy," *Policy Options*, Vol. 6(1), pp. 14-15.

Baetz, Mark C. (1985b) "Imperial Oil and the Bertrand Report," in Baetz and Thain, *Canadian Cases in Business-Government Relations* (Toronto: Methuen), chap. 18.

Baetz, Mark C., and Donald Thain (1985) *Canadian Cases in Business-Government Relations* (Toronto: Methuen).

Baggaley, Carman (1981) *The Emergence of the Regulatory State in Canada, 1880-1939* (Ottawa: Economic Council of Canada, Regulation Reference Technical Report No. 15).

Bagnall, James (1983) "Faster-acting Fira alters way it works," *Financial Post*, October 8, pp. 1-2.

Bain, George (1982) "Parliament Hill Retorts: The Press is Home," *Quest*, Vol. 11(1), March, p. 86.

Bain, George (1985) "Why Canada's Loyal Opposition Should be Disloyal to Itself," *Report on Business Magazine*, March, pp. 17-19.

Baldwin, Elizabeth (1977) "The Mass Media and the Corporate Elite," *Canadian Journal of Sociology*, Vol. 2(1), Winter, pp. 1-27.

Baldwin, John R., *et al.* (1984) "Imports, Secondary Output, Price-Cost Margins and Measures of Concentration: Evidence for Canada, 1979" (Ottawa: Economic Council of Canada, Discussion Paper, April).

Banfield, Edward C. (1955) "Note on Conceptual Scheme," in Martin Myerson and Edward C. Banfield, *Politics, Planning and the Public Interest* (Glencoe, Ill.: Free Press), p. 303.

Banks, Louis (1978) "Taking on the Hostile Media," Harvard Business Review, Vol. 56(2), March-April, pp. 123-130.

Banks, Louis (1981) "The Rise of the Newocracy," Atlantic Monthly, Vol. 247(1), January, pp. 54-59.

Banting, Keith (ed.) (1985a) *State and Society: Canada in Comparative* Perspective (Toronto: University of Toronto Press).

Banting, Keith (ed.) (1985b) *The State and Economic Interests* (Toronto: University of Toronto Press).

Barach, Jeffrey A. (1985) "The Ethics of Hardball," *California Management Review*, Vol. 27(2), Winter, pp. 132-139.

Baradat, Leon P. (1979) *Political Ideologies: Their Origins and Impact* (Englewood Cliffs, N.J.: Prentice-Hall).

Baram, Robert (1977) "Newspapers: Their Coverage and Big Business," in Bernard Rubin (ed.) *Big Business and the Mass Media* (Lexington, Mass.: Lexington Books/D.C. Heath), pp. 135-168.

Barnes, Ken (1983) "We Can Fight Back," *Canadian Banker and ICB Review*, Vol. 90(2), April, pp. 44-49.

Barnet, Sylvan (1976) "How to Organize for Controversy Advertising," *Public Relations Journal*, Vol. 32, November, pp. 23-25.

Barnhill, J.A. (1982) "Issues in Canadian Competition Legislation: Positions of Two Major Associations" (CMA vs. CAC), in S.J. Shapiro & L. Heslop (eds.) *Marketing Canada* (Toronto: McGraw-Hill Ryerson), pp. 175-201.

Barrows, David S., and D.A. Chisholm (1982) "Microelectronics Task Force — Methodology and Findings," *Business Quarterly*, Vol. 47(2), Summer, pp. 28-33.

Bartha, Peter (1977) "Welcome back, partner: there's fresh appeal to an old understanding," *The Review* [Imperial Oil], No. 5, pp. 8-11.

Bartha, Peter (1982) "Managing Corporate External Issues: An Analytical Framework," *Business Quarterly*, Vol. 47(3), Autumn, pp. 78-90.

Bartha, Peter (1984a) "Tuning in on Issues Management," *Canadian Business Review*, Vol. 11(2), Summer, pp. 25-27.

Bartha, Peter (1984b) "Managing Corporate External Issues: An Analytical Framework," in J. Fleck and P. Litvak (eds.) *Business Can Succeed!* (Toronto: Gage Publishing), pp. 9-27.

Bartha, Peter (1985a) "External Relations: An Integral Part of Corporate Decision-Making," in V.V. Murray (ed.) *Theories of Business-Government Relations* (Toronto: Trans-Canada Press), pp. 349-368.

Bartha, Peter (1985b) "Organizational Competence in Business-Government Relations: A Managerial Perspective," *Canadian Public Administration*, Vol. 28(2), pp. 202-230.

Bauch, Dean, Scott Brunsdon, Rich Chechik, Eylin Gilbart, and Frank Keith (1983) "The Cadillac Fairview-Crown Trust Affair" (Commerce 592 paper, April, University of B.C., Faculty of Commerce).

Baxter, Clive (1977) "Lobbying — Ottawa's Fast-Growing Business," in Paul W. Fox (ed.) *Politics: Canada*, 4th ed. (Toronto: McGraw-Hill Ryerson), pp. 206-210.

Beachemin, Guy (1978) "PMAC — Who, What, When, Where, Why?" *Canadian Pharmaceutical Journal*, January, pp. 3-5.

Beck, Stanley M. (1985) "Corporate Power and Public Policy," in *Consumer Protection, Environmental Law and Corporate Power* (Toronto: University of Toronto Press).

Beck, Stanley M., and Ivan Bernier (1983) *Canada and the New Constitution: The Unfinished Agenda*, 2 vols. (Montreal: The Institute for Research on Public Policy).

Becker, Gary S. (1983) "A Theory of Competition Among Pressure Groups for Political Influence," *Quality Journal of Economics*, Vol. 98(3), pp. 371-400.

Beigie, Carl E., and James K. Stewart (1985) "Canada's Industrial Challenges and Business-Government Relations: Toward Effective

Collaboration," in V.V. Murray (ed.) *Theories of Business-Government Relations* (Toronto: Trans-Canada Press), pp. 121-142.

Bejermi, John (1980) *How Parliament Works* (Ottawa: Borealis Press).

Belford, Terrence (1978) "John Bulloch: Crusading on Behalf of the Small Businessman," *En Route* (Air Canada's magazine), April, pp. 26-31.

Belobaba, Edward P. (1985) "The Development of Consumer Protection Legislation in Canada, 1945-1984," in *Consumer Protection, Environmental Law, and Corporate Power* (Toronto: University of Toronto Press).

Benditt, T.M. (1973) "The Public Interest," *Philosophy and Public Affairs*, Vol. 2, Spring, pp. 291-311.

Bentham, Jeremy (1960) *A Fragment on Government and an Introduction to the Principles of Morals and Legislation*, Wilfred Harrison (ed.) (Oxford: Blackwell. First published in 1823).

Bentley, Arthur F. (1935) *The Process of Government* (Bloomington: Principia. First published in 1908).

Ben-Zion, Uri, and Z. Eytan (1979) "On Money, Votes and Policy on a Democratic Society," *Public Choice*, Vol. 27(3).

Berger, Peter L. (1981) "New Attack on the Legitimacy of Business," *Harvard Business Review*, Vol. 59(5), Sept/Oct., pp. 82-89.

Berlin, Isaiah (1961) "Equality," in F.A. Olafson (ed.) *Justice and Social Policy* (Englewood Cliffs: Prentice-Hall).

Bernier, Ivan, and Andree Lajoie (eds.) (1985) *Regulations, Crown Corporations and Administrative Tribunals* (Toronto: University of Toronto Press).

Berry, B.M. (1978) "Origins of public interest groups — Tests of two theories," *Policy*, Vol. 10, pp. 379-399.

Berry, Glyn R. (1974) "The Oil Lobby and the Energy Crisis," *Canadian Public Administration*, Vol. 17(4), pp. 600-635.

Berton, Pierre (1976) "The Pacific Railway Scandal," in K.M. Gibbons and D.C. Rowat (eds.) *Political Corruption in Canada: Cases, Causes and Cures* (Toronto: McClelland and Stewart), pp. 15-18.

Berton, Pierre (1983) "For Immediate Release, Or Handout Journalism," in Barrie Zwicker and Dick MacDonald (eds.) *The News-Inside the Canadian Media* (Ottawa: Deneau Publishers), pp. 25-32.

Best, Dunnery (1980) "Business Image Going on the Air," *Financial Post*, December 13, p. 15.

Biggs, Sam, Leo Cizak, Bruce Drake, and Kirk Spowage (1983) "The CRTC's Pay-TV Decision: The Role of Lobbying" (Commerce 592 paper, April, University of B.C., Faculty of Commerce).

Binkley, Wilfred, and Malcolm Moos (1950) *A Grammar of American Politics* (New York: Alfred A. Knopf). As cited in Theodore J. Lowi (1969) *The End of Liberalism* (New York: Norton), p. 75.

Bird, R.M. (1970) *The Growth of Government Spending in Canada* (Toronto: Canadian Tax Foundation).

Bird, R.M. (1979) *Financing Canadian Government: A Quantitative Overview* (Toronto: Canadian Tax Foundation).

Bird, R. M., and Christopher Green (1985) "Government Intervention in the Canadian Economy: A Review of the Evidence" (Toronto: Institute for Policy Analysis, University of Toronto, March, mimeo).

Bird, T.R. (1982) "Analysis of Impact of Electronic System on Advertising Revenue in Canada," Working Paper (Montreal: The Institute for Research on Public Policy).

Birdzell, L. Earle (1975) "Business and Government: The Walls Between," in Neil H. Jacoby (ed.) *The Business-Goverment Relationship: A Reassessment* (Pacific Palisades, Calif.: Goodyear Publishing), pp. 29-39.

Black, E.R. (1982) *Politics and the News* (Toronto: Butterworths).

Black, Hawley (1982) "Experts call co-operation the key," *Financial Times*, July 12, p. 9.

Blaikie, David (1982) "Hard Sell on the Hill is a $100 million Business," in Paul Fox (ed.) *Politics: Canada*, 5th ed. (Toronto: McGraw-Hill Ryerson), pp. 252-258 (orig. *Toronto Star*, January 20, 1979).

Blair, Cassandra (1984) *Forging Links of Co-operation* (Ottawa: The Conference Board in Canada).

Blair, Cassandra (1985) "The CEO's View of Political and Social Change," *Canadian Business Review*, Vol. 12(1), Spring, pp. 18-20.

Blakeney, Allan (1981) "Goal-seeking: Politicians Expectations of Public Administrators," *Canadian Public Administration*, Vol. 24(1), pp. 1-7.

Blank, Stephen, *et al.* (1982) *Assessing the Political Environment: An Emerging Function in International Companies*, The Conference Board, Report No. 794 (New York: The Conference Board).

Bliss, Michael (1980a) "Rich by Nature, Poor by Policy: The State and Economic Life in Canada," in R.K. Carty and W.P. Ward (eds.) *Entering the Eighties: Canada in Crisis* (Toronto: Oxford University Press), pp. 78-90.

Bliss, Michael (1980b) "Singing the Blues," *Canadian Business*, Vol. 53(9), September, pp. 128-132.

Bliss, Michael (1982a) "The Evolution of Industrial Policies in Canada: An Historical Survey" (Ottawa: Economic Council of Canada, Working Paper).

Bliss, Michael (1982b) "The Battle that Business Lost," *Canadian Business*, Vol. 55(11), November, pp. 48-55.

Bliss, Michael (1985) "Forcing the Pace: A Reappraisal of Business-Government Relations in Canadian History," in W.W. Murray (ed.) *Theories of Business-Government Relations* (Toronto: Trans-Canada Press), pp. 105-119.

Block, Walter (1981) "Profit is Best Measure of Newspapers," *Financial Post*, Vol. 75(34), August 29, p. 9.

Blomqvist, A.G. (1985) "Political Economy of the Canadian Welfare State," in *Approaches to Economic Well-Being* (Toronto: University of Toronto Press).

Bloom, Paul N., and Stephen A. Greyser (1981) "The Maturing of Consumerism," *Harvard Business Review*, Vol. 59(6), Nov./Dec., pp. 130-139.

Blumenthal, Michael (1979) "Candid Reflections of a Businessman in Washington," *Fortune*, Vol. 99(2), January 29, pp. 36-40, 42, 44, 46, 48-49.

Blumenthal, Sidney (1982) *The Permanent Campaign*, rev. ed. (New York: Simon & Schuster).

Boardman, Anthony, *et al.* (1983) "An Overview of Mixed Enterprise in Canada," *Business Quarterly*, Vol. 48(2), pp. 101-106.

Boardman, Anthony, Catherine Eckel, and Aidan Vining (1984) "The Advantages and Disadvantages of Mixed Enterprises: A World Survey." To be published in A.R. Negandi and H. Thomas (eds.) *Research in International Business and International Relations*, Vol. I (Greenwich, Ct.: JAI Press).

Bodenheimer, Edgar (1962) "Prolegomena to a Theory of the Public Interest," in Carl Friedrich (ed.) *The Public Interest* (New York: Atherton), pp. 205-217.

Bogart, Leo (1972) *Silent Politics: Polls and the Awareness of Public Opinion* (Toronto: John Wiley).

Bohn, Glenn (1983) "Power resides beyond reach of public tours," Vancouver *Sun*, September 6, p. A7.

Bon, Daniel L., (ed.) (1981) *Lobbying: A Right? A Necessity? A Danger?* (Ottawa: The Conference Board of Canada).

Bon, Daniel L., and Kenneth D. Hart (1983) *Linking Canada's New Solitudes: The Executive Interchange Program and Business-Government Relations* (Ottawa: The Conference Board of Canada).

Booth, Amy (1984) "Dealers vs. banks: the fight intensifies," *Financial Post*, April 14, p. 4.

Borcherding, T.E. (1983) "Toward a Positive Theory of Public Sector Supply Arrangements," in J.R.S. Prichard (ed.) *Crown Corporations in Canada* (Toronto: Butterworths), pp. 99-184.

Bothwell, Robert, and William Kilbourn (1979) *C. D. Howe: A Biography* (Toronto: McClelland and Stewart).

Boudreau, A.J. (1950) "Public Administration and the Public Interest," *Canadian Journal of Economics and Political Science*, Vol. 16, pp. 371-374.

Bower, Joseph L. (1977) "Effective Public Management," *Harvard Business Review*, Vol. 55(2), March-April, pp. 131-140.

Bower, Joseph L. (1983) *The Two Faces of Management: An American*

Approach to Leadership in Business and Politics (Boston: Houghton Mifflin).

Boyer, J. Patrick (1978a) "The Legal Status of Corporate Political Contributions in Canada Today," *Business Quarterly*, Vol. 43, Spring, pp. 67-76.

Boyer, J. Patrick (1978b) "The Legal Status of Union Political Contributions in Canada Today," *Business Quarterly*, Vol. 43, Autumn, pp. 20-35.

Boyer, J. Patrick (1979) "Legal Aspects of the Corporate Political Contributions in Canada," *Canadian Business Law Journal*, Vol. 3(2), January, pp. 161-192.

Boyer, J. Patrick (1981) "The Corporation in Politics," *Business Quarterly*, Vol. 46(4), pp. 77-86.

Boyer, J. Patrick (1983) *Money and Message: The Law Governing Election Financing Advertising, Broadcasting and Campaigning in Canada* (Toronto: Butterworths).

Boyle, Harry (1983) "The Media Control Institution in Society: Canada and the United States Compared," in B.D. Singer (ed.) *Communication in Canadian Society* (Don Mills, Ontario: Addison-Wesley), pp. 93-100.

Bradshaw, Thornton, and David Vogel (eds.) (1981) *Corporations and Their Critics* (New York: McGraw-Hill).

Brecher, Irving (1983) "Burying Industrial Strategy," *Policy Options*, Vol. 4(5), pp. 19-21.

Brechin, Maryon (1974) "The Consumer Movement in Canada," in V. H. Kirpalani and R. Rotenberg (eds.) *Cases and Readings in Marketing* (Toronto: Holt, Rinehart and Wintston), pp. 141-146.

Bregha, Francois (1981) *Bob Blair's Pipeline: The Business and Politics of Northern Energy Development Projects*, rev. ed. (Toronto: James Lorimer).

Brenner, Steven N. (1979) "Business and Politics: An Update," *Harvard Business Review*, Vol. 57(6), Nov/Dec., pp. 149-163.

Brenner, Steven N. (1980) "Corporate Political Activity: An Exploratory Study in a Developing Industry," in Lee E. Preston (ed.) *Research in Corporate Social Performance* (Greenwich, Ct.: JAI Press), pp. 197-236.

Bretton, Henry (1980) *The Power of Money* (Albany: State University of New York Press).

Brimelow, Peter (1977) "The Shopkeepers' shopkeeper" [re John Bulloch] *Maclean's*, July 11, pp. 51-52.

Brodie, M. Janine, and Bruce D. Macnaughton (1980) "Legislators versus Bureaucrats: The Norms of Governing in Canada," in H.D. Clark *et al. Parliament, Policy and Representation* (Toronto: Methuen), pp. 241-254.

Brooks, Neil (1981) "Making Rich People Richer," *Saturday Night*, July, pp. 30-35.

Brown, Bob, Paul Cooke, and JoAnne Gin (1982) "Canadian Government Involvement in Manufacturing Location Decisions: Volkswagen and Michelin" (Commerce 592 paper, April, University of B.C., Faculty of Commerce).

Brown, Douglas, and Julia Eastman (1981) *The Limits of Consultation: A Debate Among Ottawa, the Provinces and the Private Sector on an Industrial Strategy* (Ottawa: Science Council of Canada).

Brown, Ian (1984) "Why Canadians still won't play the stock market," *Globe and Mail*, April 27, p. 7.

Brown, Ian (1985) "New Darling of the Media: The Biz World," *Globe and Mail*, February 12, p. 7.

Brown, J.K. (1979) *This Business of Issues: Coping with the Company's Environments*, Conference Board Report No. 758 (New York: The Conference Board).

Brown, J.K.(1981) *Guidelines for Managing Corporate Issues Programs*, Conference Board, Report No. 795 (New York: The Conference Board).

Brown, Robert (1976a) "Greater Access to Media," *Editor and Publisher*, November 20, p. 48.

Brown, Robert (1976b) "Shop Talk at Thirty," *Editor and Publisher*, November 20, p. 48.

Brown-John, Lloyd (1981) "The Regulatory Policy Process: The Role of Ontario Trade Unions as Intervenors" (Paper presented at the Canadian Political Science Association annual meeting, Halifax, May).

Brown-John, C. Lloyd (1985) "Comprehensive Regulatory Consultation in Canada's Food Processing Industry," *Canadian Public Administration*, Vol. 25, pp. 70-98.

Bruton, Peter, *et al.* (1964) "Graft Never Hurt a Politician at the Polls," *Maclean's*, Vol. 77, January 25, pp. 18-19, 31-32.

Bryce, George K. (1984) "Rationalizing Regulation," *Policy Options*, Vol. 5(3), pp. 41-44.

Bryden, Kenneth (1982) "Public input into policy-making and administration: The present situation and some requirements for the future," *Canadian Public Administration*, Vol. 25(1), Spring, pp. 81-107.

Bucholz, Roger A. (ed.) (1980) *Public Policy and the Business Firm* (St. Louis: Washington University, Center for the Study of American Business).

Bucholz, Roger A. (1982) *Business Environment and Public Policy* (Englewood Cliffs, N.J.: Prentice-Hall).

Bucovetsky, M. W. (1975) "The Mining Industry and the Great Tax Reform Debate," in A. P. Pross (ed.) *Pressure Group Behaviour in Canadian Politics* (Toronto: McGraw-Hill), pp. 89-114.

Budd, Gary, Janice Downing, Donald McLellan, and J. Reed Pozer (1983) "The Vancouver Stadium Site Controversy" (Commerce 592 paper,

April, University of B.C., Faculty of Commerce) (includes long appendix).

Burch, Phillip H. (1981) "The Business Roundtable: Its Make-up and External Ties," *Research in Political Economy*, Vol. 4, pp. 101-27.

Burger, Chester (1975) "How to Meet the Press," *Harvard Business Review*, Vol. 53, July/August, pp. 62-70.

Burrell, Gibson (1985) "Corporatism in Comparative Context," in V.V. Murray (ed.) *Theories of Business-Government Relations* (Toronto: Trans-Canada Press), pp. 221-241.

Business Council on National Issues (1986) *The Business Council on National Issues, 1976-1986* (Ottawa: BCNI).

Business Life (1980) "Profits and the Press," No. 2671, November, pp. 14-18.

Business Quarterly (1984) "Tea for Three: The New Partnership Between the Arts, Business and Government," Vol. 49(3), Fall, pp. 81-120.

Business Week (1979) "The Corporate Image: PR to the Rescue," No. 2569, January 22, pp. 47-57.

Business Week (1981) "Learning to Shine on TV", January 19, pp. 114-116.

Butler, D., and B. MacNaughton (1981) "Public Sector Growth in Canada: Issues, Explanations, Implications," in M. Whittington and G. Williams (eds.) *Canadian Politics in the 1980s* (Toronto: Methuen).

Cairns, Alan C. (1977) "The Governments and Societies of Canadian Federalism," *Canadian Journal of Political Science*, Vol. 10, December, pp. 694-726.

Cairns, Alan C. (1981) "The Constitutional, Legal, and Historical Background," in H.R. Penniman (ed.) *Canada at the Polls, 1979 and 1980* (Washington, D.C.: American Enterprise Institute), pp. 1-23.

Cairns, Alan (1985) "The Embedded State: State Society Relations in Canada," in *State and Society: Canada in Comparative Perspective* (Toronto: University of Toronto Press).

Cameron, David R. (1985) "The Growth of Government Spending: The Canadian Experience in Comparative Perspective," in Keith Banting (ed.) *State and Society: Canada in Comparative Perspective* (Toronto: University of Toronto Press).

Camp, Dalton (1979) *Points of Departure* (Toronto: Deneau and Greenberg).

Campbell, Colin (1978) *The Canadian Senate: A Lobby from Within* (Toronto: Macmillan).

Campbell, Colin (1983) *Governments Under Stress: Political Executives and Key Bureaucrats in Washington, London and Ottawa* (Toronto: University of Toronto Press).

Campbell, Colin (1985) "Central Agencies in Canada," in Kenneth

Kernaghan (ed.) *Public Administration in Canada: Selected Readings*, 5th ed. (Toronto: Methuen), pp. 112-122.

Campbell, Colin, and George Szablowski (1979) *The Super Bureaucrats: Structure and Behaviour in Central Agencies* (Toronto: MacMillan).

Campbell, Colin, and George Szablowski (1980) "The Centre and the Periphery: Superbureaucrats' Relations with MPs and Senators," in H.D. Clarke *et al. Parliament, Policy and Representation* (Toronto: Methuen), pp. 194-215.

Campbell, Dave, Gail Frose, Dave Parkes, and Lindsay Ryerson (1985) "VIA Rail: A Case Study of Lobbying and Political Decision Making" (Commerce 592 paper, Faculty of Commerce and Business Administration, University of B.C.).

Canada, Department of External Affairs (1983) *A Review of Canadian Trade Policy - A Background Document to Canadian Trade Policy for the 1980's* (Ottawa: Ministry of Supply and Services, Canada).

Canadian Advertising Rates and Data (1985), Vol. 58, January.

Canadian Bankers' Association (1985a) *Financial Services Industry: Responding to the Public Interest* (Toronto: CBA), July.

Canadian Bankers' Association (1985b) *The Regulation of Canadian Financial Institutions: Proposals for Discussion* (Toronto: CBA), July.

Canadian Federation of Independent Business (1981) *A Decade of Action for Independent Business* (Toronto: CFIB).

Canadian Tax Foundation (1985) *The National Finances, 1984-85* (Toronto: Canadian Tax Foundation).

Carmichael, E.A., and J.K. Stewart (1983) *Lessons from the National Energy Program* (Toronto: C.D. Howe Institute).

Carroll, Archie B. (1981) *Business and Society: Managing Corporate Social Performance* (Boston: Little, Brown).

Carroll, Archie B. (1984) "Managing Public Affairs: When Business Closes Down; Social Responsibilities and Management Actions," *California Management Review*, Vol. 26(2), Winter, pp. 125-140.

Carroll, Robert, *et al.* (1983) "The Mining Association of Canada" (Commerce 592 paper, April, University of B.C., Faculty of Commerce).

Cassinelli, C.W. (1962) "The Public Interest in Political Ethics," in Carl Friedrich (ed.) *The Public Interest* (New York: Atherton) pp. 44-53.

Causey, T. F., *et al.* (1976) *Managing the Political Regulatory Environment: A Study of Business Response to the A.I.B.* (London, Ont.: University of Western Ontario, School of Business Administration).

Cavanaugh, Gerald F. (1976) *American Business Values in Transition* (Englewood Cliffs, N.J.: Prentice-Hall).

Caves, R.E., M.E. Porter, A.M. Spence *et al.* (1980) *Competition in an Open Economy: A Model Applied to Canada* (Cambridge, Mass.: Harvard University Press).

Chagall, David (1981) *The New Kingmakers* (New York: Harcourt Brace Jovanovich).

Chan, Chung-Wai, Michelle Couto, and Leslie Ridcock (1985) "An Examination of the Lobbying Efforts of the Pharmaceutical Manufacturers Association of Canada" (Commerce 592 paper, Faculty of Commerce and Business Administration, University of B.C.).

Chandler, Alfred D., Jr. (1980) "Government versus Business: An American Phenomenon," in John T. Dunlop (ed.) *Business and Public Policy* (Cambridge, Mass.: Harvard University Press), pp. 5-6.

Chandler, Alfred D., Jr. (1979) "The Adversaries," *Harvard Business Review*, Vol. 57(6), Nov.-Dec., pp. 88-92.

Chandler, M.A., and W.M. Chandler (eds.) (1979) *Public Policy and Provincial Politics* (Toronto: McGraw-Hill Ryerson).

Chant, D.A. (1975) "Pollution Probe: Fighting the Polluters with Their Own Weapons," in A.P. Pross (ed.) *Pressure Group Behaviour in Canadian Politics* (Toronto: McGraw-Hill Ryerson), pp. 61-68.

Chant, John, and Steve Easton (1985) "Developments in Canadian Financial Markets, 1962 to 1982," in *Post-War Macroeconomic Developments* (Toronto: University of Toronto Press).

Chapman, R.G., and K.S. Palda (1983) "Electoral Turnout in Rational Voting and Consumption Patterns," *Journal of Consumer Research*, Vol. 9, March, pp. 337-346.

Chapman, R.G., and K.S. Palda (1984) "Assessing the Influence of Campaign Expenditures on Voting Behaviour with a Comprehensive Electoral Market Model," *Marketing Science*, Summer, pp. 207-226.

Chickering, A. Lawrence (1982) "Warming up the Corporate Image," *Public Opinion*, Vol. 5(5), October/November, pp. 13-15.

Chief Electoral Officer (1979) *Report Respecting Election Expenses, 1979* (Ottawa: CEO).

Chief Electoral Officer (1980) *Report Respecting Election Expenses, 1980* (Ottawa: CEO).

Chief Electoral Officer (1983) *Statutory Report* (Ottawa: Minister of Supply and Services).

Chief Electoral Officer (1984) *Report Respecting Election Expenses, 1984* (Ottawa: CEO).

Chin, Caroline, Mike McChesney, and Margo Stephens (1982) "Balance Billing: A Study in Negotiation Tactics and Lobbying" (Commerce 592 paper, April, University of B.C., Faculty of Commerce).

Christian, William, and Colin Campbell (1983) *Political Parties and Ideologies in Canada*, 2nd ed. (Toronto: McGraw-Hill Ryerson).

Clark, Hon. Joe (1985) "Business-Government Relations: Opening the System," *Business Quarterly*, Vol. 50(2), pp. 82-85.

Clark, S.D. (1938) "The Canadian Manufacturers' Association," *Canadian Journal of Economics and Political Science*, Vol. 4, pp. 505-523.

Clark, S.D. (1939) *The Canadian Manufacturers' Association: A Study in Collective Bargaining and Political Pressure* (Toronto: University of Toronto Press).

Clarke, H.D., *et al.* (1982) "The Impact of Issues and Leaders in the 1979 Federal Election," *Canadian Journal of Political Science*, Vol. 15(3), September, pp. 517-552.

Clarke, H. D., *et al.* (1984) *Absent Mandate: The Politics of Discontent in Canada* (Toronto: Gage).

Clarke, Larry D. (1985) "The Role of Governments in Changing Government-Industry Relations," *Business Quarterly*, Vol. 50(2), pp. 70-74.

Clarkson, Stephen (1982) *Canada and the Reagan Challenge* (Toronto: James Lorimer).

Clausen, A.W. (1981) "Voluntary Disclosure: An Idea Whose Time Has Come," in Bradshaw and Vogel (eds.) *Corporations and Their Critics* (New York: McGraw-Hill), pp. 62-70.

Cline, C.G., and L. Masel-Waters (1984) "Backlash: The Impact of a Video Case Study on Opinions of AT&T," *Public Relations Review*, Vol. 10, Fall, pp. 39-46.

Close, H.W. (1980) "Public Relations as a Management Function," *Public Relations Journal*, Vol. 36, March, pp. 11-14.

Cobb, Roger W., and Charles D. Elder (1975) *Participation in American Politics* (Baltimore, Md.: Johns Hopkins University Press).

Cochran, Clarke E. (1974) "Political Science and 'The Public Interest'," *Journal of Politics*, Vol. 36, pp. 327-355.

Cocking, Clive (1980) *Following the Leaders: A Media Watcher's Diary of Campaign '79* (Toronto: Doubleday).

Coe, B.J. (1983) "The Effectiveness Challenge in Issue Advertising Campaigns," *Journal of Advertising*, Vol. 12(4), pp. 27-35.

Cohen, Dian, and Kristin Shannon (1984) *The Next Canadian Economy* (Montreal: Eden Press).

Cohen, Andrew, Dan Horigan, Adele Hurley and Ian Smyth (1985) "Community Access to Decision-Making," interviews in *Gulf Commentator*, Vol. 2(1) Spring, pp. 20-27.

Coleman, James S. (1982) *The Asymmetric Society* (Syracuse, N.J.: Syracuse University Press).

Coleman, W.D., and H.J. Jacek (1983) "The Roles and Activities of Business Interest Associations in Canada," *Canadian Journal of Political Science*, Vol. 16(2), June, pp. 257-280.

Collier, Linda (1980) "Advocacy Advertising: An Issue Unresolved," *Canadian Association Executive*, September.

Collison, Robert (1980) "The Idea Peddlers Take Over," *Saturday Night*, Vol. 95(3), April, pp. 16-21.

Collison, Robert (1982a) "Have the Interventionists Lost Their Nerve?" *Canadian Business*, Vol. 55(1), January, pp. 31-36.

Collison, Robert (1982b) "Ottawa's policy entrepreneurs," *Canadian Business*, Vol. 55(1), January, pp. 40-42.

Committee on Economic Development (1979) *Redefining Government's Role in the Market System* (New York: CED).

Comparelli, Peter (1983) "The Lobbyists: Creative loiterers play political street game," Vancouver *Sun*, June 22, p. B1.

Conference Board in Canada (1973) *Policies on Leave for Political Action in Canada* (Ottawa: Conference Board in Canada).

Conference Board in Canada (1985) *Consultation and Budget Secrecy: Reforming the Process of Creating Revenue Budgets in the Canadian Federal Government* (Ottawa: Conference Board in Canada).

Consumer and Corporate Affairs (1984) *Annual Report: Combines Investigation Act for the Year Ended March 31* (Ottawa: Ministry of Supply and Services Canada).

Cook, Frances, Kym Henkee, Peter Moll, and Karen Russell (1982) "The Vancouver Shopping Hours Lobby" (Commerce 592 paper, April, University of B.C., Faculty of Commerce).

Corn, Ira G. (1981) "The Changing Role of Corporations in Political Affairs," *Vital Speeches of the Day*, Vol 47(5), May 15, pp. 463-468.

Cornfield, Michael (1980) "The Press and the Media," *The Public Interest*, No. 59, Spring, pp. 117-125.

Corrado, Frank M. (1984) *Media for Managers* (Englewood Cliffs, N.J.: Prentice-Hall).

Corry, J.A. (1936) "The Fusion of Government and Business," *Canadian Journal of Economics and Political Science*, Vol. 2(3), August (re crown corporations), pp. 301-316.

Coulson, Ron (1980) "Corporate Credibility: What It's All About," *Business Quarterly*, Vol. 45(1), Spring, pp. 71-73.

Courchene, T.J. (1984) "The Citizen and the State: A Market Perspective," in George Lermer (ed.) *Probing Leviathan: An Investigation of Government in the Economy* (Vancouver: The Fraser Institute), chap. 2.

Courchene, T.J. (1985) "The Market System in the Age of Entitlements," *Business Quarterly*, Vol. 50(2), pp. 75-81.

Crane, David (1982) *Controlling Interest: The Canadian Oil and Gas Stakes* (Toronto: McClelland and Stewart).

Cronyn, John B. (1977) "Government Relations and the Changing Role of the Corporation" (E.D. MacPhee Lecture, Banff School of Advanced Management, March 18).

CRTC (1977) *Advocacy Advertising Seminar* (Ottawa: CRTC).

Cullen, R. Allan, and Mike McLoughlin (1983) "The Canadian Ship Building and Ship Repairing Association: An Interest Group" (Commerce 592 paper, April, University of B.C., Faculty of Commerce).

Cummings, C., M. Cardinal, and P. Johansen (1981) *Canadian News*

Service, Royal Commission on Newspapers, Vol. 6 (Quebec: Ministry of Supply and Services Canada).

Cutler, Lloyd (1981) "To Form a Government," *Foreign Affairs*, Vol. 58, pp. 129-144.

Cutler, Maurice (1973) "Watergate: Could It Happen Here?" *Business Quarterly*, Vol. 38, September.

Daminato, Catherine, Gordon Hall, Richard Hatch, Phyllis Hiebert, and Ethel Mallett (1982) "Chrysler Corporation: A Case Study of Government Interaction with the Private Sector" (Commerce 592 paper, April, University of B.C., Faculty of Commerce).

Dan, Leslie L. (1982) "The Drug Industry in Canada: A Position Analysis," *Business Quarterly*, Vol. 47 (3), pp. 62-71.

Dann, Abbie (1980) "New Rules Change the Game, The Bank Act Hearings, 1978-79," *Parliamentary Government*, Vol. 2(1), Autumn, pp 3-8.

d'Aquino, Thomas (1974) "The Prime Minister's Office: Catalyst or Cabal?" *Canadian Public Administration*, Vol. 17, pp. 55-79.

d'Aquino, Thomas (1984) "Political Neutrality is Right," *Policy Options*, Vol. 5(1), January.

Dardenne, Peg (1982) "Corporate Advertising," *Public Relations Journal*, Vol. 38, November, pp. 34-38.

Daves, Stanley M. (1984) *Guiding Beliefs: Managing Corporate Culture* (Cambridge, Mass.: Ballinger Books).

Davis, O.A., and A.B. Whinston (1967) "On the Distinction Between Public and Private Goods," *American Economic Review*, Vol. 57(2), pp. 360-373.

Dawson, H.J. (1960) "An Interest Group: The Canadian Federation of Agriculture," *Canadian Public Administration*, Vol. 3, June, pp. 134-49.

Dawson, H.J. (1963) "The Consumers' Association of Canada," *Canadian Public Administration*, Vol. 6, March, pp. 92-118.

Dawson, H.J. (1975) "National Pressure Groups and the Federal Government," in A. P. Pross (ed.) *Pressure Group Behaviour in Canadian Politics* (Toronto: McGraw-Hill).

Dean, James W. (1982) "Interest Groups, Political Inefficiency and Negative Sum Regulation" (University of Toronto, Faculty of Law, Law and Economics Workshop Series, WSIV-16, March 24, mimeo).

DeLeon, P.H., *et al.* (1982) "How to Influence Public Policy: A Blueprint for Activism," *American Psychologist*, Vol. 37, pp. 476-485.

DeLong, James V. (1982) "How to Convince an Agency: A Handbook for Policy Advocates," *Regulation*, September/October, pp. 27-36.

Demers, L., and D. Wayland (1982) "Corporate Social Responsibility: Is No News Good News? Part 2," *C.A. Magazine*, Vol. 115(2), February, pp. 56-60.

Department of Consumer and Corporate Affairs (1981) "Image Advertising," in *Misleading Advertising Bulletin*, October/December, pp. 3-5.

Department of Finance (1983) *Economic Review, April 1983* (Ottawa: Minister of Supply and Services Canada).

Department of Finance (1985) *Account of the Cost of Selective Tax Measures August 1985* (Ottawa: Minister of Supply and Services Canada).

Derthick, Martha, and Paul Quirk (1985) *The Politics of Deregulation* (Washington, D.C.: Brookings Institution).

Desbarats, Peter (1983) "Truth in Journalism: A Yawning Matter?" in Barrie Zwicker and Dick MacDonald (eds.) *The News — Inside the Canadian Media* (Ottawa: Deneau Publishers), pp. 7-15.

Desbarats, Peter (1984) "News Media: The 'Wild Card' in the Business-Government Shuffle," in Fleck and Litvak (eds.) *Business Can Succeed* (Toronto: Gage Publishing), chap. 5, pp. 76-91.

Desbarats, Peter (1985) "How the Media Operate," *Business Quarterly*, Vol. 50(2), pp. 93-98.

Diamond, Edwin (1975) *The Tin Kazoo: Television, Politics and the News* (Cambridge, Mass.: MIT Press).

Diamond, Edwin, and Stephen Bates (1984) *The Spot: The Rise of Political Advertising on Television* (Cambridge, Mass.: MIT Press).

Dills, Jim (1981) "Local revenue base is still heart and soul of weeklies," *Marketing*, Vol. 86(3), January 19, p. 26.

Di Manno, Rosie (1984) "We'll defend our culture, U.S. told," *Toronto Star*, April 26, pp. A1, A4.

Dimma, William A. (1976) "Government, Business Labour: Some Future Directions," *Business Quarterly*, Vol. 19, Summer, pp. 37-49.

Dizard, John (1977) "Who'll Pay for Bob Blair's Pipeline?" *Canadian Business*, October, pp. 48-52, 102.

Dobell, Rod (1982) "Policy-Planning MPs," *Policy Options*, Vol. 3(4), pp. 33-38.

Dobell, Rod (1984) "Doing a Bennett," *Policy Options*, Vol. 5(3), pp. 6-10.

Dodge, William (ed.) (1978) *Consultation and Consensus: A New Era in Policy Formulation?* (Ottawa: Conference Board of Canada).

Doern, G. Bruce (ed.) (1978) *The Regulatory Process* (Toronto: Macmillan).

Doern, G. Bruce (1983) "The mega-project episode and the formulation of Canadian economic development policy," *Canadian Public Administration*, Vol. 26(2), pp. 219-238.

Doern, G. Bruce (ed.) (1985) *The Politics of Economic Policy* (Toronto: University of Toronto Press).

Doern, G. Bruce, and Peter Aucoin (eds.) (1979) *Public Policy in Canada* (Toronto: Macmillan).

Doern, G. Bruce, and R.W. Phidd (1983) *Canadian Public Policy: Ideas,*

Structure, Process (Toronto: Methuen).

Doern, G. Bruce, and Glen Toner (1985) *The Politics of Energy* (Toronto: Methuen).

Doerr, Audrey (1982a) "The Role of Coloured Papers," *Canadian Public Administration*, Vol. 25(3), pp. 366-379.

Doerr, Audrey (1982b) "Public Administration: Federalism and Intergovernmental Relations," *Canadian Public Administration*, Vol. 25(4), pp. 564-579.

Doerr, Audrey (1982c) *The Machinery of Government in Canada* (Toronto: Methuen).

Dominick, Joseph (1981) "Business Coverage in Network Newscasts," *Journalism Quarterly*, Vol. 50(2), Summer, pp. 179-191.

Donovan, S.J., and R.B. Winmill (1976) "The Beauharnois Power Scandal," in K.M. Gibbons and D.C. Rowat (eds.) *Political Corruption in Canada: Cases, Causes and Cures* (Toronto: McClelland and Stewart), pp. 57-65.

Dorken, H. (1981) "Coming of Age Legislatively: In 21 Steps," *American Psychologist*, Vol. 36, pp. 165-173.

Dowling, Deborah (1982) "The feasibility of political leave," *Financial Post*, March 20, p. 23.

Downs, Anthony (1957) "An Economic Theory of Political Action in a Democracy," *Journal of Political Economy*, Vol. 65, pp. 135-150.

Downs, Anthony (1962) "The Public Interest: Its Meaning in a Democracy," *Social Research*, Vol. 29, pp. 1-36.

Downs, Anthony (1967) *Inside Bureaucracy* (Boston: Little, Brown), chap. 8, "Officials' Milieu, Motives and Goals," pp. 78-91.

Downs, Anthony (1972) "Up and Down with Ecology — the 'Issue-Attention Cycle'," *The Public Interest*, No. 28, Summer, pp. 38-50.

Draper, Dianne (1975) "Environmental Interest Groups and Institutional Arrangements in British Columbia Water Management Issues," in Bruce Mitchell (ed.) *Institutional Arrangements for Water Management* (Waterloo: University of Waterloo), pp. 119-170.

Dreier, Peter (1982) "Capitalists vs. the Media: An Analysis of an Ideological Mobilization Among Business Leaders," *Media, Culture and Society*, Vol. 4.

Drew, Elizabeth (1983) *Politics and Money* (New York: Macmillan).

Driscoll, James W., *et al.* (1979) "Private Managers and Public Myths — Public Managers and Private Myths," *Sloan Management Review*, Vol. 21(1), Fall, pp. 53-57.

Drohlich, Michael L. (1980) "Managing PR Crises through Advance Planning," *Scope*, May, pp. 7-11.

Drucker, Peter F. (1980) *Managing in Turbulent Times* (New York: Harper & Row).

Duke, William E. (1983) "Demystifying the Issues in a World of Transition," *Public Relations Journal*, Vol. 39, August, pp. 17-18.

Dunlop, John T., *et al.* (1979) "Business and Public Policy," *Harvard*

Business Review, Nov./Dec., pp. 85-102.

Dunlop, John T. (ed.) (1980) *Business and Public Policy* (Cambridge, Mass.: Harvard University Press).

Dusting, Tricia, Ann Ellis, Vivien Escott, Vic Johnston, Hanif Patni, and Christine Riek (1985) "Meares Island: A Study of Lobbying Strategies and Tactics" (Commerce 592 paper, Faculty of Commerce and Business Administration, University of B.C.).

Dwivedi, O.P. (ed.) (1982) *The Administrative State in Canada* (Toronto: University of Toronto Press).

Dyson, K. (1980) *The State Tradition in Western Europe* (Oxford: Martin Robertson).

Eads, George (1981) "Picking Winners and Killing Dogs," *Wharton Magazine*, Vol. 6(1) Fall, pp. 33-41.

Eastman, Harry C. (1985) *Report of the Commission of Inquiry on the Pharmaceutical Industry* (Ottawa: Minister of Supply and Services).

Eckel, Catherine, and Theo Vermalen (1984) "Internal Regulation: The Effects of Government Stock Ownership on the Value of the Firm," Working Paper, Department of Economics, Virginia Polytechnic Institute and State University.

Eckel, Catherine, and Aidan Vining (1985) "Elements of a Theory of Mixed Enterprise," *Scottish Journal of Political Economy*, Vol. 32(1), February, pp. 82-94.

Economic Council of Canada (1979) *Responsible Regulation* (Ottawa: Ministry of Supply and Services).

Economic Council of Canada (1981) *Reforming Regulation* (Ottawa: Ministry of Supply and Services).

Economic Council of Canada (1982a) *Intervention and Efficiency: A Study of Government Credit and Credit Guarantees to the Private Sector* (Ottawa: Minister of Supply and Services).

Economic Council of Canada (1982b) *Financing Confederation: Today and Tomorrow* (Ottawa: Minister of Supply and Services).

Economic Council of Canada (1984) *Steering the Course: Twenty-first Annual Review* (Ottawa: Supply and Services Canada), chap. 2, "Government and the Economy."

Edelman, Murray (1964) *The Symbolic Uses of Politics* (Urbana: University of Illinois Press).

Edelson, Alfred H. (1981) "Advocacy Advertising: Issue Ads are Better, but There's Still Room for Improvement," *Advertising Age*, March 30, pp. 47-48.

Editor and Publisher (1977) "Local Angle Interests Most Business/ Financial Editors," August 20.

Ehrbar, A.F. (1978) "Backlash Against Business Advocacy," *Fortune*, Vol. 98(4), August 28, pp. 62-68.

Ehrbar, A.F. (1979a) "Pragmatic Politics Won't Win for Business," *Fortune*, Vol. 99(11), June 4, pp. 76-80.

Ehrbar, A.F. (1979b) "When Your Chief Executive Goes Public," *Public*

Relations Quarterly, Vol. 24, Summer, pp. 6-8.

Eichner, Alfred S. (1983) "The Micro Foundations of the Corporate Economy," *Managerial and Decision Economics*, Vol. 4, November.

Elford, Craig, and W.T. Stanbury (1986) "Mixed Enterprises in Canada," in D.G. McFetridge (ed.) *Canadian Industry in Transition* (Toronto: University of Toronto Press), pp. 261-303.

Elkins, Arthur, and D.W. Callaghan (1981) *A Managerial Odyssey: Problems in Business and its Environment*, 3rd ed. (Reading, Mass.: Addison-Wesley Publishing).

Elliot, Stuart J. (1984) "Advertorials: Straddling a Fine Line in Print," *Advertising Age*, Vol. 55, April 30, p. 3, 36-37.

Emsloff, J.R., and R.E. Freeman (1978) "Managing the External Environment of Business: A Theory of Stakeholder Management," *The Wharton Applied Research Center*, March.

Eppink, D.J. (1981) "Futures Research — Is it Used?," *Long Range Planning*, Vol. 14, April, pp. 33-36.

Epstein, Edwin M. (1972) "Corporations and the Political Imperative," *Business and Society Review*, No. 2, Summer, pp. 54-67.

Epstein, E.J. (1973) *News from Nowhere: Television and the News* (New York: Random House).

Etzioni, Amitai (1984) *Capital Corruption* (New York: Harcourt Brace Jovanovich).

European Institute for Advanced Studies in Management and European Foundation for Management Development (1982) *Facing Realities: The European Societal Strategy Project: Summary Report*.

Ewing, Raymond P. (1980) "Issues, Issues," *Public Relations Journal*, Vol. 36, June, pp. 14-16.

Ewing, Raymond P. (1981) "The Uses of Futurist Techniques in Issues Management," in A. Elkins and D.W. Callaghan, *A Managerial Odyssey: Problems in Business and Its Environment* (Reading, Mass.: Addison-Wesley Publishing), pp. 169-175.

Executive (1978) "Political Contributions — Let Government Pay the Shot," Vol. 20, June, p. 11.

Executive (1982a) "Conversation Canada: Eight Ex-CEOs of Major Corporation Discuss the Direction Government is Taking Their Country and the Private Sector," Vol. 24 (8: 9), August/September, pp. 28-43.

Executive (1982b) "Conversation Quebec: Four CEOs of Montreal-based corporations speak out on PQ nationalism and intervention," Vol. 24(10), October, pp. 26-39.

Fahey, Liam, William R. King, and Vadake K. Naraganon (1981) "Environmental Scanning and Forecasting in Strategic Planning — the State of the Art," *Long Range Planning*, Vol. 14, February, pp. 32-39.

Fama, Eugene F., and Michael D. Jensen (1983) "Separation of Owner-ship and Control," *Journal of Law and Economics*, Vol. 26, June, pp. 301-325.

Faulkner, J. Hugh (1976) "The business/government relationship in Canada," *Optimum*, Vol. 7(1), pp 5-15.

Faulkner, J. Hugh (1982) "Pressuring the Executive," *Canadian Public Administration*, Vol. 25(2), Summer, pp. 240-253.

Fenn, Dan H., Jr. (1979) "Finding Where the Power Lies in Government," *Harvard Business Review*, Vol. 57, Sept.-Oct., pp. 144-53.

Ferguson, James L. (1976) "Business and the News Media — Can We Find a Better Channel?" *Editor and Publisher*, October 23, p. 20.

Ferguson, John (1983a) "TV News is Not for Labour," Vancouver *Sun*, June 27, p. D12.

Ferguson, John (1983b) "Drop Bomb on Friday, then Run, Is Ottawa's Disarming Strategy," Vancouver *Sun*, August 3, p. A16.

Ferguson, Marjorie, Monica Marshal, Diedra McDevitt, and Eric van Soren (1985) "Foreign Banks in Canada: A Study of the Process of Raising the Domestic Asset Ceiling" (Commerce 592 paper, Faculty of Commerce and Business Administration, University of B.C.).

Festinger, Leon (1957) *A Theory of Cognitive Dissonance* (Evanston, Ill.: Row, Peterson).

Fetherling, Doug (1979) "The New Image of Public Relations," *Canadian Business*, Vol. 52(12), December, pp. 78-82, 87, 89, 108.

Fiber, Ben (1983a) "Business Press Targets Decision-makers," *Globe and Mail*, September 12, pp. R3, R8.

Fiber, Ben (1983b) "CEOs Find Media Business Coverage Has Improved," *Globe and Mail*, December 7, p. B4.

Field, M. (1979) "Polls and Public Policy," *Journal of Advertising Research*, Vol. 19(5), October, pp. 11-17.

Fields, J.M., and H. Schuman (1976) "Public Beliefs About the Beliefs of the Public," *Public Opinion Quarterly*, Vol. 40, pp. 427-448.

Fife, Sandy (1983) "Anatomy of a letter-perfect lobby," *Financial Times*, August 8, p. 17.

Financial Times of Canada (1982) "Dealing with Ottawa," July 12, pp. 11-14.

Finkel, Alvin (1979) *Business and Social Reform in the Thirties* (Toronto: James Lorimer).

Finlay, J. Richard (1982) "Toward a Neoenterprise Spirit: The Tasks and Responsibilities of the Public Affairs Function," *Business Quarterly*, October, Special Supplement, pp. 34-42 (originally Vol.43, Summer 1978, pp. 34-42).

Finn, D. (1978) "Why Business Has Trouble with the Media and Vice Versa," *Across the Board*, Vol. 15, February, pp. 55-60.

Finn, David (1980) "Public Invisibility of Corporate Leaders," *Harvard*

Business Review, Vol. 38, November-December, pp. 102-109.

Fiorina, M.P. (1981) *Retrospective Voting in American National Elections* (New York: Yale University Press).

Fisher, John (1976) "Advocacy Advertising — An Evil with a Big Risk," *Marketing*, June 7, pp. 7-10.

Flathman, Richard E. (1966) *The Public Interest* (New York: Wiley).

Fleck, J.D., and I.A. Litvak (eds.) (1984) *Business Can Succeed: Understanding the Political Environment* (Toronto: Gage Publishing).

Fleck, James D. (1985) "The Business Council on National Issues and Canadian International Competitiveness," in V.V. Murray (ed.) *Theories of Business-Government Relations* (Toronto: Trans-Canada Press), pp. 369-381.

Fleming, Brian (1978) "The Prime Minister's Office: A Functional Source of Political Advice," *Hearsay* magazine, Dalhousie University Law School, August.

Fleming, John E. (1980) "Linking Public Affairs with Corporate Planning," *California Management Review*, Vol. 23(2), Winter, pp. 35-43.

Fleming, John E. (1981) "Public Issues Scanning," in Lee E. Preston (ed.) *Research in Corporate Social Performance and Policy* (Greenwich, Ct.: JAI Press), pp. 155-173.

Fletcher, Frederick J. (1981a) "Playing the Game: The Mass Media and the 1979 Campaign," in H.R. Penniman (ed.) *Canada at the Polls, 1979 and 1980* (Washington, D.C.: American Enterprise Institute), pp. 280-321.

Fletcher, Frederick J. (1981b) *The Newspaper and Public Affairs* (Ottawa: Minister of Supply and Services), Vol. 7 of Research Studies on the Newspaper Industry.

Fletcher, Frederick J., and Daphne Taras (1984) "The Mass Media and Politics: An Overview," in Michael S. Whittington and Glenn Williams (eds.) *Canadian Politics in the 1980s*, 2nd ed. (Toronto: Methuen).

Fletcher, Frederick J., and D.C. Wallace (1985) "Federal-Provincial Relations and the Making of Public Policy in Canada: A Review of Case Studies," in *Division of Powers and Public Policy* (Toronto: University of Toronto Press).

Forbes, J.D. (1979) "Influence Groups in Canadian Consumer Policy," *Canadian Marketer*, Vol. 10, pp. 27-32.

Forbes, J.D. (1982) "Institutions and Influence Groups in the Canadian Food System Policy Process" (Vancouver: University of B.C., Faculty of Commerce, Working Paper 842, September).

Forbes, J.D. (1984) "Organizational/Political Dimensions of Consumer Pressure Groups" (Unpublished paper, Faculty of Commerce, University of B.C., March, mimeo).

Forbes, J.D. (1985a) "Organizational and Political Dimensions of

Consumer Pressure Groups," *Journal of Consumer Policy*, Vol. 8, pp. 105-131.

Forbes, J.D. (1985b) *Institutions and Influence Groups in Canadian Farm and Food Policy* (Toronto: Institute of Public Administration of Canada).

Forbes, J.D., and T. Punnett (1985) "Who are the consumer activists?" (Vancouver, B.C.: University of British Columbia, Faculty of Commerce and Business Administration, mimeo).

Ford, Ashley (1984) "Alcan's Delicate Mega-Project," *B.C. Business*, Vol. 12(6), June, pp. 34-40.

Forget, C.E. (ed.) (1984) *La Caisse de dépôt et placements du Québec* (Montreal: C.D. Howe Institute).

Forster, Ben (1979) "The Coming of the National Policy: Business, Government and the Tariff, 1876-1879," *Journal of Canadian Studies*, Vol. 14(3).

Forsyth, Michele, Mary McDonnell, Dan Montgomery, and Aivars Reinfelds (1982) "Massey-Ferguson: Government Aid to a Multi-national" (Commerce 592 paper, April, University of B.C., Faculty of Commerce).

Fort, Rodney D., and John Baden (1981) "The Treasury as a Common Pool Resource and the Development of a Predatory Bureaucracy," in John Baden and R.J. Stroup (eds.) *Bureaucracy vs Environment* (Ann Arbor: University of Michigan Press), pp. 9-21.

Foster, Myles B. (1984a) "The Extent of Government Intervention in Canada" (Ottawa: Department of Finance, May 25, mimeo).

Foster, Myles B. (1984b) "The Growth and Control of Crown Corporations" (Ottawa: Department of Finance, mimeo).

Foster, Peter (1980) *The Blue-Eyed Sheiks* (Toronto: Totem Books).

Foster, Peter (1982a) *The Sorcerer's Apprentices: Canada's Super Bureaucrats and the Energy Mess* (Toronto: Collins).

Foster, Peter (1982b) "Imperial Rule" (re Imperial Oil), *Saturday Night*, Vol. 97(11), November, pp. 28-42.

Foster, Peter (1983) "The Battle of the Sectors," *Saturday Night*, March, pp. 23-32.

Foster, Peter (1984) *Other People's Money: The Banks, The Government and Dome* (Toronto: Totem Books).

Fotheringham, Allan (1984) "Of Greed, Fear and Failure," Maclean's, Vol. 96(50), December 12, p. 72.

Fournier, Pierre (1985) "Consultation in Canada: Case Studies and Perspectives," in *The State and Economic Interests* (Toronto: University of Toronto Press).

Foxall, G.R. (1980) "Forecasting Developments in Consumerism and Consumer Protection," *Long Range Planning*, Vol. 13, February, pp. 29-33.

Fox, Karen, and Philip Kotler (1980) "The Marketing of Social Causes:

The First 10 Years," *Journal of Marketing*, Vol. 44, pp. 24-33.

Fox, Karen, and Bobby J. Calder (1985) "The Right Kind of Business Advocacy," *Business Horizons*, Vol. 28, January-February, pp. 7-11.

Fox, Paul (1982) "Federal Election Expenses Act Aids Parties and Campaign Financing," in Paul Fox (ed.) *Politics Canada*, 5th ed. (Toronto: McGraw-Hill Ryerson), pp. 292-295.

Frank, Dave, Jerry Kaye, and Rob Moore (1985) "An Analysis of How the University of British Columbia Has Sought to Influence Government Funding Decisions" (Commerce 592 paper, Faculty of Commerce and Business Administration, University of B.C.).

Fraser, Alistair (1980) "Legislators and Their Staffs," in Harold D. Clarke *et al.* (eds.) *Parliament, Policy and Representation* (Toronto: Methuen), pp. 230-240.

Fraser, G. (1977) "Out, Damned Slush!" *Maclean's*, Vol. 90, May 30, p. 17.

Frechette, W.D.H. (1977) "The CMA — Spokesmen for Industry," in Paul W. Fox (ed.) *Politics: Canada*, 4th ed. (Toronto: McGraw-Hill Ryerson), pp. 210-212.

Frederick, G.D. (1983) "The State of Private Sector Strategic Planning in Canada," *Long Range Planning*, Vol. 16(3), pp. 40-46.

Frederick, W.C. (1983) "Corporate Social Responsibility in the Reagan Era and Beyond," *California Management Review*, Vol. 25(3), pp. 145-157.

Freeman, Natalie V. (1982) "Student of Power" (re Peter Newman on politicians and businessmen), *City Woman*, Fall, pp. 58-65.

Freeman, R. Edward (1984) *Strategic Management: A Stakeholder Approach* (Marshfield, Mass.: Pitman Publishing Inc.).

French, Orland (1982) "Taking the Press to Lunch," *Globe and Mail*, November 24, p. 7.

French, Richard D. (1979) "The Privy Council Office: Support for Cabinet Decision Making," in Richard Schultz *et al.* (eds.) *The Canadian Political Process* (Toronto: Holt, Rinehart and Winston), pp. 363-394.

French, Richard D. (1980) *How Ottawa Decides: Planning and Industrial Policy-making, 1968-1980* (Toronto: James Lorimer).

French, Richard D. (1985) "Government Without Business: The Parti Quebecois in Power," in V.V. Murray (ed.) *Theories of Business-Government Relations* (Toronto: Trans-Canada Press), pp. 159-180.

Friedland, M.L. (1978) "Pressure Groups and the Development of the Criminal Law," in P.R. Glazebrook (ed.) *Reshaping the Criminal Law* (London: Stevens and Sons), pp. 202-239.

Friedrich, Carl (ed.) (1962) *The Public Interest* (New York: Atherton Press).

Frohlich, Norman (1985) "A Theoretical Framework for Studying Business-Government Relations in the Western Resource Sector"

(Working Paper prepared for the Western Resources Program of the Institute for Research on Public Policy, July).

Fulford, Robert (1977) "You See, the Trouble With Journalism is Journalists," *Saturday Night*, Vol. 92(8), October, pp. 12-14.

Fulford, Robert (1982) "The Personal Journalism of Peter Worthington," *Saturday Night*, Vol. 97(10), October, pp. 13-23.

Fulford, Robert (1984) "The Grand Illusion: Television News Suggests There's Nothing in the World that Can't be Made Comprehensible in Twenty Seconds," *Saturday Night*, Vol. 99, June, pp. 9-10.

Fulton, Jane, and W.T. Stanbury (1985) "Comparative Lobbying Strategies in Influencing Health Care Policy," *Canadian Public Administration*, Vol. 28(2), Summer, pp. 269-300.

Gale, Judy L., and Mark N. Wexler (1983) "The Image of Business in Canadian Produced Television," *Canadian Journal of Communication*, Vol. 9(2), Spring, pp. 15-36.

Gallagher, Kathryn, Ross Hedley, Peter Louis, and Pamela Tobe (1983) "The Whistler Bailout: A Case Study of the B.C. Government's Intervention into the Financially Troubled Whistler Village Land Company" (Commerce 592 paper, April, University of B.C., Faculty of Commerce).

Gans, Herbert J. (1980) *Deciding What's News* (New York: Vintage Books).

Garbett, T.F. (1981) *Corporate Advertising: The What, the Why and the How* (New York: McGraw-Hill).

Gardiner, J.A., and D.J. Olson (eds.) (1974) *Theft of a City: Readings on Corruption in Urban America* (Bloomington: Indiana University Press).

Gardner, Bruce (1981) *The Governing of Agriculture* (Lawrence, Kansas: The Regents Press of Kansas).

Gendreau, Murray, Peter Lam, Patrizia Owen, and Avinash Vaid (1984) "Prostitution in Vancouver's West End: A Community's Approach to Action" (Commerce 592 paper, Faculty of Commerce and Business Administration, University of B.C.).

Gherson, Giles (1983) "Business given another Liberal ear," *Financial Post*, December 17, p. 9.

Gibbons, Kenneth M. (1976) "The Political Culture of Corruption in Canada," in K.M. Gibbons and D.C. Rowat (eds.) *Political Corruption in Canada* (Toronto: McClelland and Stewart).

Gibbons, K.M., and D. Rowat (eds.) (1976) *Political Corruption in Canada* (Toronto: McClelland and Stewart).

Gillies, James (1981) *Where Business Fails* (Montreal: The Institute for Research on Public Policy).

Gillies, James (1982) "The Business-Government Solitudes," *Policy Options*, Vol. 3(1) Jan.-Feb., pp. 6-8.

Gillies, James (1984) "The Parliamentary Imperative," *Saturday Night*, Vol. 99, June, pp. 52-56.

Gillies, James, and Jean Pigott (1982) "Participation in the Legislative Process," *Canadian Public Administration*, Vol. 25(2), pp. 254-264.

Gitlin, Todd (1983) *Inside Prime Time* (New York: Pantheon Books).

Gitlin, Todd (1984) "The Image of Business on Prime Time Television," *California Management Review*, Vol. 26(2), Winter, pp. 64-73.

Glessing, R.J., and W.P. White (1973) *Mass Media: The Invisible Environment* (Chicago: Science Research Associates).

Globe and Mail (1983) "Improvement Detected in Business-Media Links," June 29, p. B6.

Globerman, Steven, and Richard Schwindt (1985) "Business-Government Relations: A Synthesis and Test of Hypotheses," in V.V. Murray (ed.) *Theories of Business-Government Relations* (Toronto: Trans-Canada Press), pp. 243-264.

Globerman, Steven, and W.T. Stanbury (1986), "Changing the Telephone Pricing Structure," *Canadian Public Policy* (forthcoming).

Goffman, Erving (1972) *Strategic Interaction* (New York: Ballantine).

Gold, Harold (1983) "Revitalizing Caucus: Enhancing the Role of Private Members," *Parliamentary Government*, Vol. 4(1), pp. 11-15.

Goldenberg, Allan (1981) "Increased Cost of Sales Calls Make Business Press an Attractive Buy," *Marketing*, Vol. 86(3), January 19, p. 26.

Goldfarb, Martin (1980) "Restraint of Government: What People Want," *Policy Options*, Vol. 1, March, pp. 36-38.

Goldstein, Jonah (1979) "Public Interest Groups and Public Policy: The Case of the Consumers' Association of Canada," *Canadian Journal of Political Science*, Vol. 12(1), March, pp. 137-155.

Goldstein, Tom (1985) *The News at Any Cost* (Toronto: Musson).

Gollner, Andrew B. (1983) *Social Change and Corporate Strategy: The Expanding Role of Public Affairs* (Stamford, Conn.: Issue Action Publications Inc.).

Gollner, Andrew B. (1984a) *Public Affairs in Canada: A Survey* (Montreal: The Institute for Research on Public Policy).

Gollner, Andrew B. (1984b) "Managing Public Affairs," *Canadian Business Review*, Vol. 11(3), Autumn, pp. 29-33.

Gollner, Andrew B. (1985) "The Dynamics of State Intervention," in V.V. Murray (ed.) *Theories of Business-Government Relations* (Toronto: Trans-Canada Press), pp. 57-81.

Good, David A. (1980) *The Politics of Anticipation: Making Canadian Federal Tax Policy* (Ottawa: Carleton University School of Public Administration).

Goodpaster, K.E., and J.B. Mathews (1982) "Can a Corporation Have a Conscience?" *Harvard Business Review*, Vol. 60(1), Jan/Feb., pp. 132-141.

Gordon, Charles (1980) "Canadian Press Wire Backbone of Coverage," Ottawa *Citizen*, January 30, p. 10.

Gordon, Peter (1975) "What's needed is consensus, not confrontation," *Financial Post*, March 22, p. 7.

Gorecki, P.G., and Ida Henderson (1981) "Compulsory Patent Licensing of Drugs in Canada: A Comment on the Debate," *Canadian Public Policy*, Vol. 7(4), pp. 559-568.

Government of Canada, Department of Finance (1980) *Government of Canada Tax Expenditure Account* (Ottawa: Ministry of Supply and Services Canada, December).

Government of Canada, Department of Finance (1981) *Analysis of Federal Tax Expenditures for Individuals* (Ottawa: Ministry of Supply and Services Canada, November).

Government of Canada (1983) "Speech from the Throne to open the Second Session, Thirty-Second Parliament of Canada" (Ottawa: December 7, 1983).

Grafftey, H. (1973) "Who Will Bear the Brunt of Election Expenses?" *Canadian Business*, Vol. 46, September, p. 80.

Graham, Ron (1980) "The Canadian Establishment Meets the CBC," *Saturday Night*, Vol. 95(8), October, pp. 42-51.

Gram, Harold A., and Ronald L. Crawford (1981) *Canadian Management — Response to Social Issues* (Toronto: McGraw-Hill).

Granatstein, J.L. (1966) "Conservative Party Finances, 1939-1945," in K.Z. Paltiel (ed.) *Studies in Canadian Party Finance* (Committee on Election Expenses) (Ottawa: Queen's Printer), pp. 257-316.

Gray, Charlotte (1983) "Friendly Persuasion," *Saturday Night*, Vol. 98(3), March, pp. 11-14.

Green, Christopher (1985) *Canadian Industrial Organization and Policy*, 2nd ed. (Toronto: McGraw-Hill Ryerson).

Green, Mark (1979) *Who Runs Congress?* 3rd ed. (New York: The Viking Press).

Green, Mark, and Norman Waitzman (1980) *The Corporate Lobbies: Political Profiles of the Business Roundtable and the Chamber of Commerce* (Washington, D.C.: Public Citizen).

Green, Mark (1981) "When Corporations Become Consumer Lobbyists," in Thornton Bradsha (and David Vogel (eds.) *Corporations and Their Critics* (Toronto: McGraw-Hill), pp. 5-21.

Greenwald, Carol S. (1977) *Group Power: Lobbying and Public Policy* (New York: Praeger Publishers).

Greer, Harold (1976) "A Criticism of the Hydrogate Report," in K.M. Gibbons and D.C. Rowat (eds.) *Political Corruption in Canada: Cases, Causes and Cures* (Toronto: McClelland and Stewart), pp. 140-143.

Grefe, E. (1981) *Fighting to Win: Business Political Power* (New York: Harcourt Brace Jovanovich).

Gregg, Allan R. (1984) "The Corporation and the Public," in J.D. Fleck and I.A. Litvak (eds.) *Business Can Succeed: Understanding the Political Environment* (Toronto: Gage Publishing), chap. 7.

Griffith, Ernest S. (1962) "The Ethical Foundations of the Public Interest," in Carl Friedrich (ed.) *The Public Interest* (New York: Atherton), pp. 14-25.

Griffith, Thomas (1974) "Must Business Fight the Press?" *Fortune*, Vol. 89, June, pp. 203-214.

Griffith, Thomas (1983) "Why Readers Mistrust Newspapers," *Time*, May 9, p. 60.

Grubel, Herbert (1984) "The Costs of Canada's Social Insurance Programs," in George Lermer (ed.) *Probing Leviathan: An Investigation of Government in the Economy* (Vancouver: The Fraser Institute), chap. 3.

Grunig, E., and D.A. Ipes (1983) "The Anatomy of a Campaign against Drunk Driving," *Public Relations Review*, Vol. 9, Summer, pp. 36-52.

Guither, Harold D. (1980) *The Food Lobbyists* (Lexington, Mass.: Lexington Books).

Gunderson, Morley (1983) *Economics of Poverty and Income Distribution* (Toronto: Butterworths).

Gupta, Anil K., and L.L. Lad (1983) "Industry Self-Regulation: An Economic, Organizational and Political Analysis," *Academy of Management Review*, Vol. 8(3), July, pp. 416-425.

Gustafson, Kerry, Gerret Kavanaugh, Randy Stefanson, and Brian Thomson (1983) "An Analysis of Two Provincial Mining Associations with Particular Emphasis on the Lobbying Activities" (Commerce 592 paper, April, University of B.C., Faculty of Commerce).

Guthrie, Steve, Ivan Hopkins, Susan Dahinten, Jeff Coffey, and Stephen Findlay (1984) "Interest Groups and the Legislation of Agricultural Land Reserves within British Columbia" (Commerce 592 paper, April, University of B.C., Faculty of Commerce).

Guzzardi, Walter J. (1981) "Business is Learning How to Win in Washington," in A. Elkins and D.W. Callaghan, *A Managerial Odyssey: Problems in Business and Its Environment* (Reading, Mass.: Addison-Wesley Publishing), pp. 138-146.

Gwyn, Richard (1965) *The Shape of Scandal: A Study of a Government in Crisis* (Toronto: Clarke, Irwin and Company).

Gwyn, Richard (1978) "Business changes its tune," Ottawa *Journal*, July 13, p. 7.

Gwyn, Richard (1981) *The Northern Magus* (Toronto: Totem Books).

Gwyn, Richard (1982) "A committee of MPs bows before the banks," *Vancouver Sun*, August 3, p. A6.

Gwyn, Sandra (1980) "Yesterday's Princes: The Bleak Future for Unemployed Cabinet Ministers," *Saturday Night*, Vol. 95(1), January/February, pp. 18-23.

Hackett, Robert (1983) "Is T.V. News Biased Against Labour?" *Canadian Labour*, May, pp. 12, 14.

Hadekel, Peter (1977) "Newsroom Power Pull Sheets Quebec Dailies," Vancouver *Sun*, October 26, p. A19.

Hamdi, Ramsay D., Dieter W. Jentsch, and John C. Yip (1983) "The British Columbia Institute of Agrologists: A Study in Lobbying Organization and Activity" (Commerce 592 paper, Faculty of Commerce and Business Administration, University of B.C.).

Hamilton, W.M. (1983) "Beating Government to the Punch," *Policy Options*, Vol. 4(1), pp. 6-7.

Handler, E., and J.R. Mulkern (1982) *Business in Politics* (Lexington, Mass: D.C. Heath).

Hanley, John W. (1981) "Monsanto's 'Early Warning' System," *Harvard Business Review*, Vol. 59(6), Nov/Dec, pp. 107-122.

Hannigan, John A. (1983) "Ideology, Elites, and the Canadian Mass Media," in B.D. Singer (ed.) *Communications in Canadian Society* (Don Mills, Ont.: Addison-Wesley Publishers), pp. 55-61.

Happy J., and J.P. Kyba (1983) "Business Attitudes Toward Employee Involvement in the Canadian Political Process" (Toronto: Institute for Political Involvement, mimeo).

Hardin, Herschel (1974) *A Nation Unaware: The Canadian Economic Culture* (Vancouver: J.J. Douglas).

Hardin, Russell (1982) *Collective Action* (Baltimore: Johns Hopkins University Press).

Hardy, Kenneth G. (1982) "Time to be Heard on Advocacy Advertising," *Canadian Business Review*, Vol. 9(1), Spring, pp. 35-39.

Harris, P. (1982) "Pressure groups and protest," *Politics*, Vol. 9(1), pp. 111-120.

Harrison, Fred (1978) "Lobbyists act as Canada's unofficial opposition," *Saskatoon Star-Phoenix*, August 9, 1978, p. 10; "'Somebody' Lobbyist reach government ears," August 10, 1978, p. 5; "Government yields to business pressure," August 12, 1978, p. 14; "Proposal to control lobbies dies under study," August 24, 1978, p. 5.

Hartle, D.G. (1976) "On Prophets and Power: A Comment on the Prime Minister's Revelations," *Canadian Public Policy*, Vol. 2(2), pp. 249-256.

Hartle, D.G. (1978) *The Expenditure Budget Process in the Government of Canada* (Toronto: Canadian Tax Foundation).

Hartle, D.G. (1979) *Public Policy Decision Making and Regulation* (Montreal: The Institute for Research on Public Policy).

Hartle, D.G. (1982) *The Revenue Budget Process of the Government of Canada* (Toronto: Canadian Tax Foundation).

Hartle, D.G. (1984) *The Political Economy of Residential Rent Control in Ontario* (Toronto: Ontario Commission of Inquiry into Residential Tenancies) Research Study No. 12.

Hartle, D.G. (1985) "The Theory of Rent Seeking: Some Reflections," *Canadian Journal of Economics*, Vol.16(4), pp. 539-554.

Hay, J. (1980) "Election '80: The $6 Million Gong Show," *Maclean's*, Vol. 93, February 11, p. 36.

Hay Associates Canada Limited (1982) *The Decade Ahead: Current and Emerging Trends in Canada* (Toronto: Hay Associates, January).

Hay Associates Canada Limited (1983) *Report to Opinion Leaders* (Toronto: Hay Associates, January).

Hay Associates Canada Limited (1984) *Navigating Uncharted Waters: Canada's Next Ten Years, Report to Opinion Leaders* (Toronto: Hay Associates, February).

Hay Management Consultants (1985) *Canada's Future: Coping with New Realities: Report to Opinion Leaders* (Toronto: Hay Management Consultants).

Hayes, David R. (1983) "A Word from the Wise," *Globe and Mail*, February 12.

Hehner, Eric (1985) "Growth of Discretions — Decline of Accountability," in Kenneth Kernaghan (ed.) *Public Administration in Canada: Selected Readings*, 5th ed. (Toronto: Methuen), pp. 341-350.

Heintzman, Ralph (1983) "The Political Culture of Quebec, 1840-1960," *Canadian Journal of Political Science*, Vol. 16, pp. 3-59.

Held, Virginia (1970) *The Public Interest and Individual Interests* (New York: Basic Books).

Helm, Lewis M., *et al.* (eds.) (1981) *Informing the People* (New York: Longman).

Henderson, Hazel (1981) *The Political Reconceptualization* (New York: Anchor/Doubleday).

Henry, J.S. (1980) "From Soap to Soapbox: The Corporate Merchandising of Ideas," *Working Papers for a New Society*, Vol. 7, May-June, pp. 55-57.

Henry, William A. (1983) "Journalism Under Fire," *Time*, December 12, pp. 60-81.

Herman, Edward S. (1981) *Corporate Control, Corporate Power* (New York: Cambridge University Press).

Herring, E. Pendleton (1936) *Public Administration and the Public Interest* (New York: McGraw-Hill).

Hess, Stephen (1981) *The Washington Reporters* (Washington, D.C.: The Brookings Institution).

Hillman, A.L. (1982) "Declining Industries and Political Support Protectionist Motives," *American Economic Review*, Vol. 72, December, pp. 1180-87.

Hobbing, Enno (1972) "Business Must Explain Itself," *Business and Society Review*, No. 3, Fall, pp. 85-86.

Hockin, Thomas A. (ed.) (1977) *Apex of Power*, 2nd ed. (Scarborough: Prentice-Hall).

Hockin, Thomas A. (1985) "Towards Improved Capabilities and Tactics in Business-Government Relations in Canada" (Paper presented at the conference on Theories of Business-Government Relations, York University, Toronto, April 26, 27).

Hodgetts, J.E. (1981) "Government responsiveness to the public interest: has progress been made?" *Canadian Public Administration*, Vol. 24(2), pp. 216-231.

Hoffman, David (1975) "Interacting with Government: The General Public and Interest Groups," in Donald C. McDonald (ed.) *Government and Politics in Ontario* (Toronto: Macmillan), pp. 270-292.

Hogg, Peter W. (1985) *Constitutional Law of Canada*, 2nd ed. (Toronto: Carswell).

Holcomb, J. (1980) "Anticipating Public Policy: An Interest Group Approach," *Public Affairs Review*, Vol. 1.

Hoskins, D.G., and S. McFadyen (1982) "Television Programming in Canada and the U.K.," *Canadian Public Policy*, Vol. 8(3), Summer, pp. 347-357.

Hossie, Linda (1983) "Jancis Andrews: Antiporn Activist," *Chatelaine*, September, pp. 63, 187-193.

House of Commons Standing Committee on Finance, Trade and Economic Affairs (1983) *Report on Bank Profits* (Ottawa: Minister of Supply and Services).

Howard, J.L., and W.T. Stanbury (1984) "Measuring Leviathan: The Size, Scope and Growth of Governments in Canada," in George Lermer (ed.) *Probing Leviathan: An Investigation of Government in the Economy* (Vancouver: The Fraser Institute), chap. 4 and Appendix.

Howarth, E. Michael (1983) "Association Management Firms: A Viable Alternative?" *Canadian Business Review*, Vol. 10(4), pp. 23-25.

Hughes, Frank (1983) "Green Policies" (re green parties), *Policy Options*, Vol. 4(6), pp. 34-36.

Hughes, S.F. (1979) "The Reporter and the Businessman: The Need for New Understanding on Both Sides," *Business Quarterly*, Vol. 44(4), Winter, pp. 73-78.

Hunter, Robert (1980) "The War Within Greenpeace," *Saturday Night*, Vol. 95(8), October, pp. 36-40.

Hurst, J.W. (1970) *The Legitimacy of the Business Corporation in the Law of the United States, 1780-1970* (Charlottesville: University of Virginia Press).

Hutchinson, George (1980) "Canadian anti-combines law consistently impotent," London *Free Press*, December 2, p. A7.

Hutchison, George (1980) "Unelected Rulers," London *Free Press*, December 1, pp. 1, 2, A11.

Institute for Political Involvement (1978) *A Report on the Prospects for Increased Involvement of Business People in the Canadian Political System* (Toronto: IPI).

Irvine, William (1982) "Does the Candidate Make a Difference? The Macro-Politics and the Micro-Politics of Getting Elected," *Canadian Journal of Political Science*, Vol. 15, December, pp. 755-782.

Isenberg, Seymour (1980) "Can you spend your way into the House of Commons?" *Optimum*, Vol. 11(1), pp. 29-39.

Isenberg, Seymour (1981) "Spend and win? Another look at federal election expenses," *Optimum*, Vol. 12(4), pp. 5-15.

Islam, Nasir (ed.) (1983) *Dealing with Governments in Canada: A Seminar Report* (Ottawa: KGD Communications).

Islam, Nasir, and Sadrudin A. Ahmed (1984) "Business Influence on Government: A Comparison of Public and Private Sector Perceptions," *Canadian Public Administration*, Vol. 27(1), Spring, pp. 87-101.

Jackson, R.J., and M. Atkinson (1974) *The Canadian Legislative System* (Toronto: Macmillan).

Jackson, R.J. and M. Atkinson (1980) *The Canadian Legislative System*, 2nd ed. (Toronto: Macmillan).

Jackson, Robert (1982) "Unmasked: the lobbyists," Vancouver *Sun*, March 4, p.5.

Jackson, Gary, Paul Langton, Muktar Rahemtulla, and Ron Tarves (1983) "The British Columbia Teachers' Federation: An Analysis of the Organization and Lobbying Techniques" (Commerce 592 paper, April, University of B.C., Faculty of Commerce).

Jacobson, Gary C. (1978) "The Effects of Campaign Spending in Congressional Elections," *American Political Science Review*, Vol. 72(2), pp. 469-471.

Jacobson, Gary C. (1980) *Money in Congressional Elections* (New Haven: Yale University Press).

Jacobson, Gary C. (1985) "Money and Votes Reconsidered: Congressional Elections, 1972-1982," *Public Choice*, Vol. 47(1), pp. 7-62.

Jacoby, Neil H. (ed.) (1975) *The Business-Government Relationship: A Reassessment* (Pacific Palisades, Calif.: Goodyear Publishing).

James, D.R., and M. Soref (1981) "Profit Constraints on Managerial Autonomy," *American Sociological Review*, Vol. 16, pp. 1-18.

Janigan, Mary (1984) "A Liberal Dose of Patronage," *Maclean's*, February 13, pp. 24-25.

Jensen, Michael C. (1981) "Business and the Press," in Bradshaw and Vogel (eds.) *Corporations and Their Critics* (New York: McGraw-Hill), pp. 50-60.

Jensen, Michael J., and Richard S. Ruback (1983) "The Market for Corporate Control," *Journal of Financial Economics*, Vol. 11, pp. 5-50.

Jessen, Sabine, C.F. Smart, W.T. Stanbury, and I.B. Vertinsky (1983) "Response of the B.C. Forest Industry to the Province's Timber Pricing Proposals" (Case prepared for the Max Bell Foundation's

Program on Business-Government Relations, York University, mimeo).

Johnson, Jon (1983) "Issues Management — What Are the Issues?" *Business Quarterly*, Vol. 48(3), Fall, pp. 22-31.

Johnson, Pat (1981) "Lights, Camera, Action — the Dreaded TV Appearance — How Some Are Coping," *Financial Times*, Vol. 70(8), July 20, p. 16.

Johnston, Donald (1985) "Government and Business: A Liberal Perspective," in Rea and Wiseman (eds.) *Government and Enterprise in Canada* (Toronto: Methuen), pp. 58-64.

Johnston, Richard (ed.) (1985) *Public Opinion and Public Policy in Canada* (Toronto: University of Toronto Press).

Jones, L.R. (1985) "Will Deregulation Give Business More Influence over Government Decision Making?" *Canadian Business Review*, Vol. 12(1), Spring, pp. 35-39.

Jupp, Alex (1980) "A Tyro M.P. Collides with the Process," *Executive*, Vol. 22(5), May, pp. 46-50.

Kahle, Roger (1977) "Opinion Leader Attitudes on Media-Business Relations," in Bernard Rubin (ed.) *Big Business and the Mass Media* (Lexington, Mass.: Lexington Books/D.C. Heath), pp. 169-185.

Kalt, Joseph P. (1981) *The Economics and Politics of Oil Price Regulation: Federal Policy in the Post-Embargo Era* (Cambridge, Mass.: MIT Press).

Kalt, Joseph P., and Mark A. Zupam (1984) "Capture and Ideology in the Economic Theory of Politics," *American Economic Review*, Vol. 74, June, pp. 279-300.

Kampelman, Max (1978) "The Power of the Press: A Problem for Our Democracy," *Policy Review*, Fall.

Kane, T. Gregory (1980) *Consumers and the Regulators: Intervention in the Federal Regulatory Process* (Montreal: The Institute for Research on Public Policy).

Karass, Chester L. (1970) *The Negotiating Game: How to Get What You Want* (New York: Thomas Y. Crowell).

Karass, Chester L. (1974) *Give and Take: The Complete Guide to Negotiating Strategies and Tactics* (New York: Thomas Y. Crowell).

Karpat, George (1982) "Society Promoting Environmental Conservation: Environmental Lobbying in the 1970s" (M.B.A. Major Paper, May, University of British Columbia, Faculty of Commerce).

Kau, J.B., and P.H. Rubin (1982) *Congressmen, Constituents and Contributors* (Boston: Martinus Nyhoff).

Kau, J.B., and P.H. Rubin (1979) "Self-Interest, Ideology, and Log Rolling in Congressional Voting," *Journal of Law and Economics*, Vol. 22, October, pp. 365-384.

Keim, Gerald D. (1981) "Foundations of a Political Strategy for Business," *California Management Review*, Vol. 23, Spring, pp. 41-48.

Keim, Gerald D., and Valerie Zeithaml (1981) "Improving the Return on Advocacy Advertising," *Financial Executive*, Vol. 49, November, pp. 40-42.

Keim, Gerald D., Carl Zeithaml, and Barry Baysinger (1984) "New Directions for Corporate Political Strategy," *Sloan Management Review*, Vol. 25(3), pp. 53-63.

Kelley, David (1982) "Critical Issues for Issue Ads," *Harvard Business Review*, Vol. 60(4), July-August, pp. 80-87.

Kelly, Donald W. (1974) "The Development of a New Textile Policy for Canada: A Case Study of Government-Industry Relations in Canada" (Unpublished D.B.A. thesis, Harvard University).

Kennedy, Leslie W. (1983) *The Urban Kaleidoscope: Canadian Perspective* (Toronto: McGraw-Hill Ryerson).

Kent, T., B. Spears, and L. Picard (1981) *Report of the Royal Commission on Newspapers* (Ottawa: Ministry of Supply and Services Canada).

Kernaghan, Kenneth (1976) "Policy, Politics and Public Servants: Political Neutrality Revisited," *Canadian Public Administration*, Vol. 19, pp. 432-456.

Kernaghan, Kenneth (ed.) (1983) *Canadian Public Administration: Discipline and Profession* (Toronto: Butterworths).

Kernaghan, Kenneth (ed.) (1985a) *Public Administration in Canada: Selected Readings*, 5th ed. (Toronto: Methuen).

Kernaghan, Kenneth (1985b) "Inter-governmental Administrative Relations in Canada," in Kernaghan (ed.) *Public Administration in Canada: Selected Readings*, 5th ed. (Toronto: Methuen), pp. 152-168.

Kernaghan, Kenneth (1985c) "Power and Public Servants in Canada," in Kernaghan (ed.) *Public Administration in Canada: Selected Readings*, 5th ed. (Toronto: Methuen), pp. 258-266.

Kernaghan, Kenneth (1985d) "Power, Parliament and Public Servants: Ministerial Responsibility Re-examined," in Kernaghan (ed.) *Public Administration in Canada: Selected Readings*, 5th ed. (Toronto: Methuen), pp. 280-288.

Kernaghan, Kenneth (1985e) "Pressure Groups and Public Servants in Canada," in Kernaghan (ed.) *Public Administration in Canada: Selected Readings*, 5th ed. (Toronto: Methuen), pp. 308-323.

Kernaghan, Kenneth (1985f) "The Public and Public Servants in Canada," in Kernaghan (ed.) *Public Administration in Canada: Selected Readings*, 5th ed. (Toronto: Methuen), pp. 323-330.

Kernaghan, Kenneth (1985g) "Judicial Review of Administrative Action," in Kernaghan (ed.) *Public Administration in Canada: Selected Readings*, 5th ed. (Toronto: Methuen), pp. 358-373.

Kesselman, Jonathan R. (1977) "Non-business Deductions and Tax

Expenditures in Canada: Aggregates and Distributions," *Canadian Tax Journal*, Vol. 25(2), March-April, pp. 160-179.

Keynes, John Maynard (1932) *Essays in Persuasion* (New York: Harcourt).

KGD Communications (1983) *Dealing with Governments in Canada: The Canadian Lobbyists Handbook* (Ottawa: KGD Communications).

Khemani, R.S. (1986) "Extent and Evolution of Competition in the Canadian Economy," in D.G. McFetridge (ed.) *Canadian Industry in Transition* (Toronto: University of Toronto Press), pp. 135-176.

Kieran, W. (1969) "Lobbying," *Executive*, Vol. 11(4), April, pp. 33-37.

Kierans, Tom (1984) "Commercial Crowns," *Policy Options*, Vol. 5(6), pp. 23-29.

Kierans, Tom, and W.T. Stanbury (eds.) (1985) *Papers on Privatization* (Montreal; The Institute for Research on Public Policy)

King, Stephen (1981) "Conflicts Between Public and Private Opinion," *Long Range Planning*, Vol. 14, August, pp. 90-105.

Kirby, M.J.L. (1980) *Reflections on the Management of Government in the '80s*, The 1980 Alan B. Plaunt Memorial Lecture (Ottawa: Carleton University).

Kirby, M.J.L., H.V. Kroeker, and W.R. Teschke (1978) "The Impact of Public Policy-Making Structures and Processes in Canada," *Canadian Public Administration*, Vol. 21(3), Fall, pp. 407-417.

Kirby, Sen. Michael (1985a) "Government Policy Development and Resource Allocation Process," *Gulf Commentator*, Vol. 2(1), Spring, pp. 8-11.

Kirby, Sen. Michael (1985b) "Restructuring the Atlantic Fishery: A Case Study in Business-Government Relations," *Business Quarterly*, Vol.50(2), pp. 115-118.

Klein, Ted, and Fred Danzig (1974) *How to be Heard: Making Media Work for You* (New York: Macmillan).

Klepper, M. (1981) "A TV Interview Need Not be a Lynching," *Wall Street Journal*, December 28, p. 8.

Kniewasser, A.G. (1982) "Fighting for the Private Sector," *Executive*, Vol. 24(5), May, pp. 55-65.

Koch, A., and S. Labovitz (1976) "Interorganizational Power in a Canadian Community: A Replication," *Sociological Quarterly*, Vol. 17, pp. 3-15.

Kome, Penney (1983) *The Taking of Twenty-Eight: Women Challenge the Constitution* (Toronto: Women's Press).

Kome, Penney (1985) *Women of Influence: Canadian Women and Politics* (Toronto: Doubleday Canada).

Kornberg, Allan, and William Mishler (1976) *Influence in Parliament: Canada* (Durham, N.C.: Duke University Press).

Kornberg, Allan, and H.D. Clarke (eds.) (1983) *Political Support in*

Canada: The Crisis Years (Durham, N.C.: Duke University Press).

Kotler, Philip (1982) *Marketing for Non-Profit Organizations* (Englewood Cliffs, N.J.: Prentice-Hall).

Kotler, Philip, and Ronald Turner (1981) *Marketing Management* (Scarborough: Prentice-Hall).

Kraus, Sidney, and Dennis Davis (1976) *The Effects of Mass Communication on Political Behaviour* (University Park: Pennsylvania State University).

Kristol, Irving (1974) "The Corporation and the Dinosaur," *Wall Street Journal*, February 14, p. 20.

Kristol, Irving (1975) "On Corporate Capitalism in America," *The Public Interest*, No. 41, pp. 124-141.

Kristol, Irving (1978) *Two Cheers for Capitalism* (New York: Basic Books).

Kruk, Gerry (1984) "Renewing the Dialogue," *Imperial Oil Review*, No. 4, pp. 2-6.

Kubas, Leonard, *et al.* (1981) *Newspapers and Their Readers* (Ottawa: Minister of Supply and Services) (Research Studies on the Newspaper Industry).

Kubas, Leonard (1981) "Hard Facts Paving Road into the 1980s," *Marketing*, October 13.

Kwavnick, David (1972) *Organized Labour and Pressure Politics* (Montreal: McGill-Queen's University Press).

Labreche, Julianne (1980) "The Quiet Persuaders of Parliament Hill," *Financial Post Magazine*, November 29, pp. 33-34, 39-40, 42.

Labreche, Julianne (1981) "The Good Guys of Parliament Hill: Five Politicians Wield a Big Stick for Small Business," *Financial Post Magazine*, May, pp. 33-40.

Lambert, Richard A., and David F. Larcker (1985), "Golden Parachutes, Executive Decision-Making, and Shareholder Wealth," *Journal of Accounting and Economics*, Vol. 7, April, pp. 179-208.

Lamphier, Gary (1981) "The Journalistic Search for the Quotable Quote," *Maclean's*, April 6, p. 46.

Land, Brian (1984) *Directory of Associations in Canada*, 5th ed. (Toronto: Micromedia Limited).

Lande, Richard (1984) "Freeing Cross-Border Freight," *Policy Options*, Vol. 5(6), pp. 61-62.

Lane, Edgar (1964) *Lobbying and the Law* (Berkeley: University of California Press).

Lane, John, *et al.* (1982) "The Canadian Federation of Independent Business" (Commerce 592 paper, Faculty of Commerce and Business Administration, University of B.C., April).

Lang, Ronald W. (1974) *The Politics of Drugs* (Lexington, Mass.: Saxon House/Lexington Books).

Langford, John W., and Kenneth J. Huffman (1983) "The Uncharted Universe of Federal Public Corporations," in J.R.S. Prichard (ed.)

Crown Corporations: The Calculus of Instrument Choice (Toronto: Butterworths), chap. 4.

Lapham, Lewis H. (1981) "Gilding the News," *Harper's*, July, pp. 31-39.

Laver, Michael (1981) *The Politics of Private Desires: The Guide to the Politics of Rational Choice* (Harmondsworth: Penguin Books).

Lawrie, N. J. (1976) "The Canadian Construction Association: An Interest Group and Its Environment" (Unpublished Ph.D. dissertation, University of Toronto, 1976).

Laxer, James, and Anne Martin (1976) *The Big, Tough Expensive Job: Imperial Oil and the Canadian Economy* (Don Mills: Musson).

Leavens, Kathy, Alex Muir, and Rosalinda Rimmer (1983) "Consumers' Association of Canada" (Commerce 592 paper, April, University of B.C., Faculty of Commerce).

Lee, William (1972) "The Executive Function: The Ministerial Assistant's View," *Quarterly of Canadian Studies*, Vol. 1(1) Winter.

Lefever, Ernest, *et al.* (1983) *Scholars, Dollars, and Public Policy* (Washington, D.C.: American Enterprise Institute).

Lem, Gail (1983) "Stable Readership is Key to Strength of Weeklies," *Globe and Mail*, September 12, p. B8.

Lemco, Jonathan, and Peter Regenstreif (1985) "Less Disciplined MPs," *Policy Options*, Vol. 6(1), pp. 32-33.

Lenoski, Gerald (1977) "Ministerial Staffs and Leadership Politics," in Thomas A. Hockin (ed.) *Apex of Power*, 2nd ed. (Scarborough, Ont.: Prentice-Hall), pp. 165-175.

Lerbinger, Otto (1977) "Corporate-Media Relations," in Bernard Rubin (ed.) *Big Business and the Mass Media* (Lexington, Mass.: Lexington Books/D.C. Heath), pp. 63-95.

Lermer, George, and W.T. Stanbury (1985) "The Cost of Redistributing Income by Means of Direct Regulation," *Canadian Journal of Economics*, Vol. 28(1), pp. 190-207.

Levitt, Theodore (1968) "Why Business Always Loses," *Harvard Business Review*, Vol. 46, pp. 81-89.

Lewis, David (1972) *Louder Voices: The Corporate Welfare Bums* (Toronto: James Lewis & Samuel).

Lewis, Jefferson (1976) "Our Man in Ottawa: Taking on the big guys on behalf of you and me" [re Andrew Roman], *Weekend Magazine*, January 31, pp. 4-8.

Lewis, Robert (1977) "The hidden persuaders: Guns don't make laws, but gun lobbies damn well do," *Maclean's*, June 13, pp. 40b-40i.

Lewis, Robert (1982) "Ottawa's power brokers," *Maclean's*, May 24, pp. 20-28.

Lichter, Linda S., *et al.* (1982) "How Show Business Shows Business," *Public Opinion*, Vol. 5(5), October/November, pp. 10-12.

Lichter, S. Robert, and Stanley Rothman (1981) "Media and Business Elites," *Public Opinion*, October/November, pp. 42-60.

Lilley, Wayne (1981) "Tricks of the horse trade" [re negotiating], *Canadian Business*, August, pp. 33-40.

Lippman, Walter (1955) *Essays in the Public Philosophy* (Boston: Little, Brown).

Lipset, Seymour Martin, and William Schneider (1978) "How's Business: What the Public Thinks," *Public Opinion*, July/August, pp. 41-47.

Lipsey, R.G. (1984) "Can the Market Economy Survive?" in George Lermer (ed.) *Probing Leviathan: An Investigation of Government in the Economy* (Vancouver: The Fraser Institute), chap. 1.

Liston, D. (1980) "Politics, Government and Company Planning: The New Perspective," *Long Range Planning*, Vol. 13(5), October, pp. 57-64.

Littlejohn, Edward (1980) "Implications of the Changing Role of Business in Society for Management Education: An Executive Viewpoint," in Rogene Bucholz (ed.) *Public Policy and the Business Firm* (St. Louis, Washington University, Centre for the Study of American Business), pp. 175-190.

Litvak, I.A., and C.J. Maule (1974a) "Interest Group Tactics and the Politics of Foreign Investment: The Time-Reader's Digest Case Study," *Canadian Journal of Political Science*, Vol. 7, December, pp. 616-629.

Litvak, I.A., and C.J. Maule (1974b) *Cultural Sovereignty: The Time and Reader's Digest Case in Canada* (New York: Praeger, 1974).

Litvak, I.A. (1979) "The Ottawa Syndrome: Improving Business-Government Relations," *Business Quarterly*, Vol. 44(2), Summer 1979, pp. 22-29.

Litvak, I.A. (1981) "Government Intervention and Corporate Government Relations," *Business Quarterly*, Vol. 46(3), Autumn, pp. 47-54.

Litvak, I.A. (1982) "National Trade Associations, Business-Government Intermediaries," *Business Quarterly*, Vol. 47(3), Autumn, pp. 34-42.

Litvak, I.A. (1983) "Lobbying Strategies and Business Interest Groups," *Business Quarterly*, Vol. 48(2), Summer, pp. 42-50.

Litvak, I.A. (1984) "Canadian Business — U.S. Government Relations," *Business Quarterly*, Vol. 49(3), Fall, pp. 35-42.

Litvak, I.A. (1985) "The Canadian Softwood Lumber Coalition: A Case Study," *Business Quarterly*, Vol. 50(2), pp. 99-104.

Lorsch, Jay, and Gordon Donaldson (1983) *Decision Making at the Top: The Shaping of Strategic Direction* (New York: Basic Books).

Lovelock, Christopher, and B.C. Weinberg (1983) *Marketing for Public and Nonprofit Managers* (New York: John Wiley).

Lowery, Sharon, and M.L. DeFleur (1983) *Milestones in Mass Communication Research: Media Effects* (New York: Longman).

Lowi, Theodore (1964) "American Business, Public Policy, Case Studies and Political Science," *World Politics*, Vol. 16(4), July, pp. 677-715.

Lowi, Theodore (1970) "Decision Making vs. Policy Making: Toward an Antidote for Technocracy," *Public Administration Review*, Vol. 30, May/June, pp. 314-325.

Luhman, N. (1979) *Trust and Power* (New York: Wiley).

Lusterman, Seymour (1981) *Managerial Competence: The Public Affairs Aspects*, Conference Board Report No. 805, (New York: The Conference Board).

Lyon, Jim (1983) *Dome: The Rise and Fall of the House that Jack Built* (Toronto: Macmillan).

MacCready, Douglas J. (1984) *The Canadian Public Sector* (Toronto: Butterworths).

MacCrimmon, Kenneth R. (1983) "Essence of Strategy: Ends, Means and Conditions" (Vancouver: University of British Columbia Press, Faculty of Commerce and Business Administration, mimeo).

Macdonald, H. Ian (1975) "The Public Interest and the Private Sector," (E.D. MacPhee Lecture, Banff School of Advanced Management, March 14).

Macfarlane, David (1980) "The Accidental Tycoon" [Ken Thomson], *Saturday Night*, Vol. 95(8), October, pp. 23-35.

MacGregor, R. (1979) "Who Pays How Much to Whom," *Maclean's*, Vol. 92, May 7, p. 25.

MacGregor, Roy (1985) "The Price of Power" [re patronage], *Maclean's*, June 24, pp. 10-16.

MacIntosh, Robert M. (1978) "Three Solitudes: Business, Government and Academe" (E.D. MacPhee Lecture, Banff School of Advanced Management, March 17).

MacLaren, Roy, Chairman (1976c) *How to Improve Business-Government Relations in Canada* (Ottawa: Report to Minister of Industry, Trade and Commerce, September).

MacLaren, Roy (1976b) "Firefighting or a Systematic Relationship?" *Business Quarterly*, Vol. 41(4), Winter, pp. 46-52.

Maclean's (1984) "The PACs elude control," May 14, pp. 35-36.

Magaziner, Ira, and Robert Reich (1983) *Minding America's Business: The Decline and Rise of the American Economy* (New York: Vintage Books).

Magnusson, Warren, and Andrew Sancton (eds.) (1983) *City Politics in Canada* (Toronto: University of Toronto Press).

Malbin, M.J. (ed.) (1980) *Parties, Interest Groups and Campaign Finance Laws* (Washington, D.C.: American Enterprise Institute).

Malbin, M.J. (ed.) (1983) *Parties, Interest Groups and Money in the 1980 Election* (Washington, D.C.: American Enterprise Institute).

Malbin, M.J. (ed.) (1984) *Money and Politics in the United States* (Chatham, N.J.: Chatham House).

Malcolm, Andrew (1985) *The Canadians* (Toronto: Fitzhenry & Whiteside).

Mallory, J.R. (1967) "The Minister's Office Staff: An Unreformed Part of the Public Service," *Canadian Public Administration*, Vol. 10, pp. 25-34.

Malvern, Paul (1985) *Persuaders: Lobbying, Influence Peddling and Political Corruption in Canada* (Toronto: Methuen).

Manzer, R. (1969) "Selective Inducements and the Development of Pressure Groups; The Case of the Canadian Teachers' Associations," *Canadian Journal of Political Science*, Vol. 2(1), March, pp. 103-117.

Marketing (1983) "Use of CEO as 'performer' only in special situations," Vol. 88, May 9, p. 2.

Marks, F. Raymond, with Kirk Leswing and Barbara A. Fortinsky (1972) *The Lawyer, the Public and Professional Responsibility* (Chicago: American Bar Foundation).

Marsh, D. (1976) "On joining interest groups: An empirical consideration of the work of Mancur Olson, Jr.," *British Journal of Political Science*, Vol. 6, pp. 257-271.

Marsh, D. (1978) "More on joining interest groups," *British Journal of Political Science*, Vol. 8, pp. 380-384.

Martin, Paul E. (1984) "Why and How to Privatize," *Policy Options*, Vol. 5(2), pp. 22-25.

Maslove, Allan M. (1981) "Public Policy, Tax Expenditures, and Distribution" (Unpublished monograph, School of Public Administration, May, mimeo).

Maslove, Allan M., and Herbert O'Heron (1985) "Federal and Provincial Revenue and Expenditure Patterns" (Ottawa: Study for the Royal Commission on the Economic Union and Development Prospects for Canada, mimeo draft).

Mathews, R.L. (ed.) (1982) *Public Policies in Two Federal Countries: Canada and Australia* (Australia: Centre for Research on Federal Financial Relations, Australian National University).

Mathias, Philip (1971) *Forced Growth: Five Studies of Government Involvement in the Development of Canada* (Toronto: James Lorimer).

Mathewson, F., and R. Winter (1985) *Competition Policy and Vertical Exchange* (Toronto: University of Toronto Press).

Matthews, B. (1983) "Talk is Not Cheap," *Financial Post Magazine*, September 1, pp. 27-28.

McBride, S. (1983) "Public Policy as a Determinant of Interest Group Behaviour: The Canadian Labour Congress' Corporatist Initiative," *Canadian Journal of Political Science*, Vol. 16(3), September, pp. 501-517.

McCall-Newman, Christina (1982) *Grits: An Intimate Portrait of the Liberal Party* (Toronto: McClelland and Stewart), pp. 175-238.

McCallum, John (1983) "Government Involvement in the Future Business World," *Business Quarterly*, Vol. 48(3) Autumn, pp. 15-20.

McCallum, John, and Andre Blais (1985), "Government, Special Interest Groups and Economic Growth," in *Responses to Economic Change* (Toronto: University of Toronto Press).

McClelland, D.C., and D.H. Burnham (1976) "Power is the Great Motivator," *Harvard Business Review*, Vol. 54, March-April, pp. 100-110.

McClosky, Herbert, and John Zaller (1985) *The American Ethos: Public Attitudes Toward Capitalism and Democracy* (Cambridge, Mass.: Harvard University Press).

McCormack, Thelma (1983) "The Political Culture and the Press of Canada," *Canadian Journal of Political Science*, Vol. 16(3), pp. 451-472.

McCormick, Peter (1983) "Politics after the Landslide: The Progressive Conservative Caucus in Alberta," *Parliamentary Government*, Vol. 4(1), pp. 8-10.

McCoy, Charles S. (1985) *Management of Values: The Ethical Difference in Corporate Policy and Performance* (Marshfield, Mass.: Pitman Publishing Inc.).

McDougall, A.K (1984) "Advocacy: Getting Business Views Across," in *Ninety Seconds to Tell it All: Big Business and the News Media* (Illinois: Dow Jones-Irwin).

McDowall, Duncan (ed.) (1982a) *Advocacy Advertising: Propaganda or Democratic Right?* (Ottawa: Conference Board in Canada, May).

McDowall, Duncan (1982b) "And Now a Word from Our Sponsor: Ottawa Turns to Advocacy Advertising," *Canadian Business Review*, Vol. 9(3), Autumn, pp. 29-32.

McDowell, Edwin (1979) "Corporate Communications: The Battle for Hearts and Minds," *Saturday Review*, Vol. 6(19), September 29, pp. 16-20.

McEwen, Daniel (1981) "Straight Talk: Tips to Help You Survive a Broadcast Interview," *Quest*, Vol. 10(4), August, pp. 42b-42d.

McFadyen, Stuart, Colin Hoskins, and David Gillen (1980) *Canadian Broadcasting: Market Structure and Economic Performance* (Montreal: The Institute for Research on Public Policy).

McFetridge, D.G. (1985) "The Economics of Industrial Policy: An Overview," in *Canadian Industrial Policy in Action* (Toronto: University of Toronto Press).

McGillivray, Don (1970) "Lobbying at Ottawa," in Paul Fox (ed.) *Politics: Canada*, 3rd ed. (Toronto: McGraw-Hill Ryerson; first published in 1964), pp. 163-175.

McGillivray, Don (1979a) "Are Media Anti-Business?" Montreal *Gazette*, September 17, p. 19.

McGillivray, Don (1979b) "Business and the Media: Necessary Tension," Ottawa *Citizen*, September 17, p. 51.

McGillivray, Don (1983) "Finance Department Trying to Limit Press

Freedom," Vancouver *Sun*, April 14, p. F8.

McGrath, James, Chairman (1985) *Report of the Special Committee on Reform of the House of Commons* (Ottawa: Queen's Printer, June).

McGrath, Phyllis S. (1976) *Managing Corporate External Relations: Changing Perspectives and Responses* (New York: The Conference Board).

McGrath, Phyllis S. (1977) *Action Plans for Public Affairs*, Conference Board, Report No. 733 (New York: The Conference Board).

McGregor, Deborah (1982a) "Ottawa seeks truce with small business," *Financial Times*, March 1, p. 7.

McGregor, Deborah (1982b) "Business lobby splits on strategy: Debate centres on confrontation," *Financial Times of Canada*, March 22, pp. 1-2.

McHugh, Drake (1982) "The Image Makers," *Canadian Petroleum*, Vol. 23(6), June, pp. 78-82.

McIntosh, Gord (1984) "Leaky Lavelle" (re head of Auto Parts Mfg. Assoc.), *Metro Toronto Business Journal*, November, pp. 34-36.

McKercher, Will (1980) "Government and the Drive Towards Centralized Control (Business Caught in the Middle)," *Business Quarterly*, Vol. 45(4), Winter, pp. 37-43.

McKie, Craig (1977) "Some Views on Canadian Corporatism," in C. Beattie and S. Crysdale (eds.) *Sociology Canada: Readings*, 2nd ed. (Toronto: Butterworths).

McLeod, J.T. (1976) "The Free Enterprise Dodo is No Phoenix," *Canadian Forum*, Vol. 56(663), August, pp. 6-13.

McMenemy, John (1977) "Influence and Party Activity in the Senate: A Matter of Conflict of Interest?" in Paul W. Fox (ed.) *Politics: Canada*, 4th ed. (Toronto: McGraw-Hill Ryerson), pp. 454-461.

McMenemy, John (1982) "Business Influence and Party Organizers in the Senate Imperil the Independence of Parliament," in Paul Fox (ed.) *Politics: Canada*, 5th ed. (Toronto: McGraw-Hill Ryerson), pp. 541-548.

McMillan, Charles J., and Victor V. Murray (1983) "Strategically Managing Public Affairs: Lessons from the Analysis of Business-Government Relations," *Business Quarterly*, Vol. 48(2), Summer, pp. 6-12.

McNulty, P. (1978) "Public Side of Private Enterprise: A Historical Perspective on American Business and Government," *Journal of World Business*, Vol. 13, Winter.

McQuaid, Kim (1981) "The Roundtable: Getting Results in Washington," *Harvard Business Review*, Vol. 59, May-June, pp. 114-123.

McQuaig, Linda (1985) "Big Business' Soft-Talking Lobbyist," *Report on Business Magazine*, March, pp. 68-72.

McQueen, Rod (1978) "Interview with W.O. Twaits Co-chairman, the Business Council on National Issues," *Maclean's*, July 24, pp. 4,6,7.

McQueen, Rod (1982) "Time to bite the Bulloch," *Maclean's*, February 22, p. 44.

McQueen, Rod (1984) *The Money Spinners* (Toronto: Totem Books).

McQueen, Rod (1985) "Canada Warms Up to U.S. Business," *Fortune*, Vol. 111(5), March 4, pp. 114-120.

Meekison, J. Peter (ed.) (1977) *Canadian Federalism: Myth or Reality* (Toronto: Methuen).

Meisel, John (1974) "Elite Accommodation in Canadian Politics," *Canadian Forum*, Vol. 54, May-June, pp. 44-46.

Meisel, John, and Richard Van Loon (1966) "Canadian Attitudes to Election Expenses 1965-1966," in K.Z. Paltiel (ed.) *Studies in Canadian Party Finance* (Committee on Election Expenses) (Ottawa: Queen's Printer), pp. 23-146.

Migue, Jean-Luc (1979) *Nationalistic Policies in Canada: An Economic Approach* (Montreal: C.D. Howe Research Institute), chap. 5, "The Economics of Protectionist Policy Choices," pp. 54-70.

Milbrath, L.W. (1965) *Political Participation* (Chicago: Rand McNally).

Miles, R.H. (1980) "Causal Texture of Organizational Environments," in *Macro-Organizational Behaviour* (Glenview, Ill.: Scott, Foresman and Co.), pp. 189-218.

Miller, L.M. (1984) *American Spirit: Visions of a New Corporate Culture* (New York: William Morrow & Co.).

Milmo, Sean (1983) "Knock'em, sock'em U.K. Ads All the Rage," *Business Marketing*, Vol. 68, November, pp. 10-11, 20-21.

Mintzberg, Henry (1983), *Power in and Around Organizations* (Englewood Cliffs, N.J.: Prentice Hall).

Mishler, William (1978) "Nominating Attractive Candidates for Parliament: Recruitment to the Canadian House of Commons," *Legislative Studies Quarterly*, Vol. 3(4), November, pp. 581-599.

Mitnick, B.M. (1980) *The Political Economy of Regulation* (New York: Columbia University Press).

Moe, T.M. (1980) *The Organization of Interests* (Chicago: University of Chicago Press).

Moe, T.M. (1981) "Towards a broader view of interest groups," *Journal of Politics*, Vol. 43, pp. 531-543.

Monmarquette, Claude (1985), "Economic Rationality and Political Behaviour in Canada," in *Responses to Economic Change* (Toronto: University of Toronto Press).

Monypenny, Phillip (1953) "A Code of Ethics for Public Administration," *George Washington Law Review*, Vol. 21, pp. 423-44.

Moore, David G. (1980) *Politics and the Corporate Executive* (New York: The Conference Board, Research Report No. 777).

Morningstar, Helen J. (1977) "The Consumers' Association of Canada: The History of an Effective Organization," *Canadian Business Review*, Vol. 4(4), Autumn, pp. 30-33.

Morris, Seymour (1980) "Managing Corporate External Affairs," *Management Review*, Vol. 69(3), March, pp. 49-53.

Morschauser, J. (1976) *Public Issues, Private Interests* (New York: The Conference Board).

Moskowitz, Milton (1981) "Who Said 'Profit'? — Getting Rid of a Dirty Word," in F.D. Studivant and L.M. Robinson (eds.) *The Corporate Social Challenge* (Homewood, Illinois: R.D. Irwin Inc.), pp. 95-98.

Moss, Laurence A.G. (1982) *The Canadian Business Environment in the 1980s* (Menlo Park, Calif.: SRI International, May).

Moyer, Mel S. (1982) "The Controversy over Electronic Point-of-Sale Systems," in S.J. Shapiro and L. Heslop (eds.) *Marketplace Canada* (Toronto: McGraw-Hill Ryerson), pp. 233-255 (re use of a public advisory committee by Ontario Ministry of Consumer and Commercial Relations).

Mueller, Dennis C. (1979) *Public Choice* (London: Cambridge University Press).

Mueller, Dennis C. (ed.) (1982) *The Political Economy of Growth* (New Haven, Conn.: Yale University Press).

Muller, Nathan J. (1978) "Single Interest Political Groups: Antidote to Apathy," *Political Action Report*, Vol. 2(10), October.

Munter, Mary (1983) "How to Conduct a Successful Media Interview," *California Management Review*, Vol 25(4), pp. 143-150.

Murphy, Kevin (1985) "Corporate Performance and Managerial Remuneration," *Journal of Accounting and Economics*, Vol.7, April, pp. 11-42.

Murphy, Thomas P. (1974) *Pressures Upon Congress: Legislation by Lobby* (Woodbury, N.Y.: Barron's Educational Series).

Murray, Edwin A., Jr. (1982) "The Public Affairs Function: Report on a Large-Scale Research Project," in Lee E. Preston (ed.) *Research in Corporate Social Performance and Policy* (Greenwich, Ct.: JAI Press), pp. 129-155.

Murray, Michael A. (1975) "Comparing Public and Private Management: An Exploratory Essay," *Public Administration Review*, Vol. 35, July/August, pp. 364-71.

Murray, V.V., and C.J. McMillan (1983) "Business-Government Relations in Canada: A Conceptual Map," *Canadian Public Administration*, Vol.26(4), pp. 591-609.

Murray, V.V. (ed.) (1985) *Theories of Business Government Relations* (Toronto: Trans-Canada Press).

Nadel, Mark V. (1975) "The Hidden Dimension of Public Policy: Private Governments and the Policy-Making Process," *Journal of Politics*, Vol. 37, pp. 2-34.

Nagelschmidt, Joseph (ed.) (1982) *The Public Affairs Handbook* (Washington, D.C.: Amacom).

Naisbitt, John (1982) *Megatrends* (New York: Warner Books).

Nash, Laura L. (1981) "Ethics Without the Sermon," *Harvard Business Review*, Vol. 59(6), pp. 79-90.

Navarro, Peter (1984) *The Policy Game: How Special Interests and Ideologues Are Stealing America* (New York: John Wiley and Sons).

Nelson, F.A., and R.L. Heath (1984) "Corporate Public Relations and New Media Technology," *Public Relations Review*, Vol. 10, Fall, pp. 27-38.

Neufeld, E.P. (1982) "Industrial Policy in Canada in the 1980s," *Western Economic Review*, Vol. 1, December, pp. 14-33.

Neville, William (1984) "How Government Decides," in Fleck and Litvak (eds.) *Business Can Succeed* (Toronto: Gage Publishing), pp. 28-45.

Neville, William (1985) "Government Policy Development and Resource Allocation Process," *Gulf Commentator*, Vol. 2(1), Spring, pp. 12-15.

Nevitte, Neil, and Roger Gibbins (1984) "Neo-conservatism: Canadian Variations in an Ideological Theme," *Canadian Public Policy*, Vol. 10(4), pp. 389-394.

Newman, O. (1981) *The Challenge of Corporatism* (London: Macmillan).

Newsweek (1982) "How to Handle the Press," April 19, pp. 90-94.

Nielsen, Richard P. (1983) "Strategic Planning and Consensus Building for External Relations — Five Cases," *Long Range Planning*, Vol. 16(6), pp. 74-81.

Nierenberg, Gerald I. (1973) *Fundamentals of Negotiating* (New York: Hawthorne).

Nisbet, Robert (1975) "Public Opinion versus Popular Opinion," *The Public Interest*, Vol. 41, Fall, pp. 166-192.

Niskanen, William A. (1976) "Bureaucrats and Politicians," *Journal of Law and Economics*, Vol. 18(3), pp. 617-643.

Noble, K. (1985) "Financial Post Targets Against Times," *Globe and Mail*, March 20, p. B6.

Noelle-Neumann, E. (1974) "The Spiral of Silence: A Theory of Public Opinion," *Journal of Communication*, Vol. 24(2), Spring, pp. 43-57.

Nolan, Joseph T. (1975) "Protect Your Public Image with Performance," *Harvard Business Review*, Vol. 53, March-April, pp. 135-142.

Nolan, Joseph T. (1981) "Business Beware: Early Warning Signs in the 80s," *Public Opinion*, April/May, pp. 14-17, 57.

Nolan, Joseph T. (1985) "Political Surfing When Issues Break," *Harvard Business Review*, Vol. 63(1), January/February, pp. 72-81.

Noonan, John T. (1984) *Bribes* (New York: Macmillan).

Nord, Douglas C. (1980) "MPs and Senators as Middlemen: The Special Joint Committee on Immigration Policy," in H.D. Clarke *et al. Parliament, Policy and Representation* (Toronto: Methuen), pp. 181-194.

Norman, Adler (1971) "The Sounds of Executive Silence," *Harvard*

Business Review, Vol. 49, July/August, pp. 100-105.

Norrie, Ken (ed.) (1985) *Fiscal Federalism* (Toronto: University of Toronto Press).

Northey, Margo (ed.) (1981) *Politics and the Mass Media* (Montreal: Reader's Digest Foundation).

Novak, Michael (ed.) (1978) *The American Vision: An Essay on the Future of Democratic Capitalism* (Washington, D.C.: American Enterprise Institute).

Novak, Michael (ed.) (1979) *The Denigration of Capitalism: Six Points of View* (Washington, D.C.: American Enterprise Institute).

Novak, Michael (1982) *The Spirit of Democratic Capitalism* (New York: Simon and Schuster).

Nozick, Robert (1974) *Anarchy, State and Utopia* (New York: Basic Books).

Offe, Claus, and Helmut Wiesenthal (1979) "Two Logics of Collective Action," *Political Power and Social Theory*, Vol. 1, pp. 67-115.

Oliphant, Peter, *et al.* (1985) "An Emperor's Clothes" (regulating telephone rates), *Policy Options*, Vol. 6(1), pp. 16-20.

Olley, Robert E. (1977) "The Canadian Consumer Movement: Basis and Objectives," *Canadian Business Review*, Vol. 5(4), pp. 26-29.

Olsen, Dennis (1980) *The State Elite* (Toronto: McClelland and Stewart).

Olson, Mancur (1965) *The Logic of Collective Action* (Cambridge, Mass: Harvard University Press).

Olson, Mancur (1982) *The Rise and Decline of Nations* (New Haven, Conn.: Yale University Press).

Ontario Public Interest Research Group (1976) "The Dryden Story" and "The Reed Story," *Last Post*, Vol. 5(8), December, pp. 33-38, 38-40.

Ontario Select Legislative Committee (1976) "The Hydrogate Affair," in K.M. Gibbons and D.C. Rowat (eds.) *Political Corruption in Canada: Cases, Causes and Cures* (Toronto: McClelland and Stewart), pp. 117-139.

Ornstein, Michael D. (1980) "Assessing the Meaning of Corporate Interlocks: Canadian Evidence," *Social Science Research*, Vol. 9, pp. 287-306.

Osberg, Lars (1981) *Economic Inequality in Canada* (Toronto: Butterworths).

Osborn, David (1975) "Business and Political Donations: A Framework for Decision," *Business Quarterly*, Vol. 40(1), Spring, pp. 86-89.

Ostry, Sylvia (1980) "Government Intervention: Canada and the United States Compared," *Policy Options*, Vol. 1, March, pp. 26-31.

Owen, Brian (1976) "Business Managers' Influence [or Lack of Influence] on Government," *Business Quarterly*, Vol. 41(3), pp. 58-69.

Page, B.I., and R.Y. Shapiro (1983) "Effects of Public Opinion on Policy," *American Political Science Review*, Vol. 77(1), March, pp. 175-190.

Pal, Leslie (1985) "Simple Access," *Policy Options*, Vol. 6(3), pp. 24-27.

Palda, K. Filip, and K.S. Palda (1985) "Ceilings on Campaign Spending: Hypothesis and Partial Test with Canadian Data," *Public Choice*, Vol. 45, pp. 313-331.

Palda, Kristian S. (1973) "Does Advertising Influence Votes? An Analysis of the 1966 and 1970 Quebec Elections," *Canadian Journal of Political Science*, Vol. 6(4), pp. 638-655.

Palda, Kristian S. (1975) "The Effect of Expenditure on Political Success," *Journal of Law and Economics*, Vol. 86(2), pp. 245-257.

Palda, Kristian S. (1985) "Does Canada's Election Act Impede Voters' Access to Information?" *Canadian Public Policy*, Vol. 11(3), pp. 533-542.

Paltiel, K.Z. (ed.) (1966) *Studies in Canadian Party Finance* (Committee on Election Expenses) (Ottawa: Queen's Printer)

Paltiel, K.Z., Howat P. Noble, and Reginald A. Whitaker (1966) "The Finances of the Cooperative Commonwealth Federation and the New Democratic Party, 1933-1965," in K.Z. Paltiel (ed.) *Studies in Canadian Party Finance* (Committee on Election Expenses) (Ottawa: Queen's Printer), pp. 317-404.

Paltiel, K.Z., and R.J. Van Loon (1966) "Financing the Liberal Party, 1867-1965," in K.Z. Paltiel (ed.) *Studies in Canadian Party Finance* (Committee on Election Expenses) (Ottawa: Queen's Printer), pp. 147-256.

Paltiel, K.Z. (1970) *Political Party Financing in Canada* (Toronto: McGraw-Hill).

Paltiel, K.Z. (1974a) "Campaign Financing in Canada and Its Reform," in H.R. Penniman (ed.) *Canada at the Polls* (Washington, D.C.: American Enterprise Institute), pp. 181-208.

Paltiel, K.Z. (1974b) "Party and Candidate Expenditures in the Canadian General Election of 1972," *Canadian Journal of Political Science*, Vol. 7(2), pp. 341-352.

Paltiel, K.Z. (1975) "Campaign Financing in Canada and its Reform," in H. Penniman (ed.) *Canada and the Polls: The General Election of 1974* (Washington: American Enterprise Institute), pp. 181-208.

Paltiel, K.Z. (1976a) "Federalism and Party Finance," in K.M. Gibbons and D.C. Rowat (eds.) *Political Corruption in Canada: Cases, Causes and Cures* (Toronto: McClelland and Stewart), pp. 193-203.

Paltiel, K.Z. (1976b) "Election Expenses," in D.J. Ballamy, J.H. Pammet, and D.C. Rowat (eds.) *The Provincial Political System* (Toronto: Methuen), pp. 161-177.

Paltiel, K.Z. (1977) *Party, Candidate and Election Finance*, Study No. 22 for the Royal Commission on Corporate Concentration (Ottawa: Minister of Supply and Services).

Paltiel, K.Z. (1979a) "Canadian Election Expenses Legislation: Recent Developments," in H. Thorburn (ed.) *Party Politics in Canada*, 4th ed. (Scarborough, Ontario: Prentice-Hall), pp. 100-110.

Paltiel, K.Z. (1979b) "The Impact of Election Expenses Legislation in Canada, Western Europe and Israel," in H.E. Alexander (ed.) *Political Finance* (Beverly Hills: Sage Publications), pp. 15-39.

Paltiel, K.Z. (1982) "The Changing Environment and Role of Special Interest Groups," *Canada Public Administration*, Vol. 25(2), Summer, pp. 198-210.

Pammett, Jon, and B. Tomlin (eds.) (1984) *The Integration Question: Political Economy and Public Policy in Canada and North America* (Toronto: Addison-Wesley).

Panitch, Leo (ed.) (1977a) *The Canadian State: Political and Economic Power* (Toronto: University of Toronto Press).

Panitch, Leo (1977b) "The Role and Nature of the Canadian State," in Panitch (ed.) *The Canadian State: Political Economy and Political Power* (Toronto: University of Toronto Press), pp. 3-27.

Panitch, Leo, (1977c) "The Development of Corporatism in Liberal Democracies," *Comparative Political Studies*, Vol. 10(1), April, pp. 61-90.

Panitch, Leo (1979) "Corporatism in Canada?" in Schultz, Kruhlak, and Terry (eds.) *The Canadian Political Process*, 3rd ed. (Toronto: Holt Rinehart & Winston), pp. 53-72.

Pappin, J. Maureen (1976) "Tax Relief for Political Contributions," *Canadian Tax Journal*, Vol. 14(3), May-June, pp. 298-305.

Pare, Paul (1978) "Political Involvement: From a Necessary Evil to a Management Skill," *Canadian Banker and ICB Review*, Vol. 85, October, pp. 55-59.

Park, Mike, Cathie Ross, Bill Franklin, and Jennifer Sydenham (1983) "The Lobbying Activities of the B.C. Federation of Labour" (Commerce 592 paper, April, University of B.C., Faculty of Commerce).

Parliamentary Government (1980a) "Round Table: Is Lobbying MPs Worth the Effort?" Vol. 2(1), Autumn, pp. 9-12.

Parliamentary Government (1980b) "Access to Parliament: Politics is Everybody's Business," Vol. 2(1), Autumn, pp. 3-15.

Parliamentary Government (1980c) "The MP as Broker: Business/Labour/Government Relations," Vol. 2(1), Autumn, pp. 13-15.

Parliamentary Government (1982) "Commons Committee Witnesses: A Process of Enlightenment;" "The Committee Track Record: A Limited Pay Off;" "Ontario: Rights of Committee Witnesses," Vol. 3(4), Autumn, pp. 3-14.

Partridge, John (1982a) "Slugging it out for the little guy" (re CFIB), *Canadian Business*, Vol. 55(2), February, pp. 30-37, 91 et seq.

Partridge, John (1982b) "Tough cop at the OSC," *Canadian Business*, Vol. 55(8), August, pp. 42-47.

Partridge, John (1985) "Steel Makes a Stand" (re U.S. protectionism), *Report on Business Magazine*, May, pp. 52-59.

Patridge, P.H. (1971) *Consent and Consensus* (London: Macmillan).

Peacock, Alan (1978) "The Economics of Bureaucracy: An Inside View," in *The Economics of Politics* (London: Institute for Economic Affairs), pp. 119-129.

Pearce, Michael R., and Alan R. Greer (1982) "Ontario Rusty Ford Owners' Association vs. Ford Motor Company of Canada — The Activists' Version," in S.J. Shapiro and L. Heslop (eds.) *Marketplace Canada* (Toronto: McGraw-Hill Ryerson), pp. 32-58.

Peers, Frank W. (1969) *The Politics of Canadian Broadcasting, 1920-1951* (Toronto: University of Toronto Press). (See his second volume published in 1980.)

Peltzman, Sam (1976) "A Theory of Government," *Journal of Law and Economics*, Vol. 19(2) pp. 211-41.

Perham, John (1981) "New Company Watchdog," *Dun's Business Month*, Vol. 118(6), December, pp. 88-89.

Pertschuk, Michael (1982) *Revolt Against Regulation: The Rise and Pause of the Consumer Movement* (Los Angeles: University of California Press).

Peters, G. (1977) "Insiders and outsiders: The politics of pressure group influence on bureaucracy," *Administration and Society*, Vol. 9, pp. 191-218.

Peters, H.R. (1982) *Foundations of Mesoeconomics and Structural Policy* (Bern and Stuttgart: Verlag Paul Haupt).

Petryszak, N.G. (1980) "The Nature of the Canadian Television Audience — A Case Study," *Canadian Journal of Communications*, Vol. 7(2), pp. 50-71.

Pfeffer, Jeffrey (1981) *Power in Organizations* (Marshfield, Mass.: Pitman Publishing Inc.).

Phidd, R.W., and G.B. Doern (1978) *The Politics and Management of Canadian Economic Policy* (Toronto: Macmillan).

Phillips, Kevin (1979a) "Corporate and Trade Association Public Affairs," *Business and Public Affairs*, Vol. 1(4), April 15.

Phillips, Kevin (1979b) "Business and the Media," *Business and Public Affairs*, Vol. 1(5), May 1.

Pigott, Jean E. (1980) "Lobbyists: Canada's Fifth Estate," *Canadian Business Review*, Vol. 7(4), Winter, pp. 30-32.

Pinard, Maurice, and Richard Hamilton (1982) "The Quebec Independence Movement," in Colin H. Williams (ed.) *National Separation* (Cardiff: University of Wales Press), pp. 203-233.

Pipes, Sally, and Michael Walker (1984) *Tax Facts 4: The Canadian Consumer Tax Index and You* (Vancouver: Fraser Institute).

Pitfield, Michael (1980) "Reflections on Politicians by a Bureaucrat" (Toronto: Institute for Political Involvement, March 5, speech).

Pitfield, P.M. (1984) "Closing the Government-Business Gap," *Canadian Business Review*, Vol. 2(2), Summer, pp. 21-24.

Podhoretz, Norman (1981) "The New Defenders of Capitalism," *Harvard Business Review*, Vol. 59(2), March/April, pp. 96-106.

Porter, Michael E. (1980) *Competitive Strategy* (New York: The Free Press).

Post, James E. (1979) "The Corporation in the Public Policy Process — A View Toward the 1980s," *Sloan Management Review*, Vol. 2(1), Fall, pp. 45-52.

Post, James E. (1985) "Assessing the Nestle Boycott: Corporate Accountability and Human Rights," *California Management Review*, Vol. 27(2), Winter, pp. 113-131.

Post, James E., *et al.* (1982) "The Public Affairs Function in American Corporations; Development and Relations with Corporate Planning," *Long Range Planning*, Vol. 15(2).

Post, James E., *et al.* (1983) "Managing Public Affairs: The Public Affairs Function," *California Management Review*, Vol. 26(1), Fall, pp. 135-150.

Postlewaite, G. (1978) "The PMAC Public Relations Program: Patching a Tattered Image", *Canadian Pharmaceutical Journal*, January, pp. 8-11.

Pottle, Neil (1983) "The Canadian Oil and Gas Industry's Attempt to Influence Government Policy, Part II" (Commerce 592 paper, April, University of B.C., Faculty of Commerce).

Pratt, Larry (1976) *The Tar Sands: Syncrude and the Politics of Oil* (Edmonton: Hurtig).

Pratt, Larry (1981) "Petro-Canada," in Allan Tupper and G. Bruce Doern (eds.) *Public Corporations and Public Policy in Canada* (Montreal: The Institute for Research on Public Policy), pp. 95-148.

Presthus, Robert (1971) "Interest Groups and the Canadian Parliament: Activities, Interaction, Legitimacy and Influence," *Canadian Journal of Political Science*, Vol. 4, December, pp. 444-460.

Presthus, Robert (1973) *Elite Accommodation in Canadian Politics* (Toronto: Macmillan of Canada).

Presthus, Robert (ed.) (1974a) "Interest Groups in International Perspective," in *The Annals of the American Academy of Political and Social Science*, Vol. 413, May.

Presthus, Robert (1974b) "Interest Group Lobbying: Canada and the United States," *Annals of the American Academy*, Vol. 413, May, pp. 44-57.

Presthus, Robert (1974c) *Elites in the Policy Process* (London: Cambridge University Press).

Presthus, Robert (ed.) (1977) *Cross-National Perspectives: United States and Canada* (Leiden: E.J. Brill).

Preston, Lee E. (1985) "Business Government and the Public Interest: The Search for Meso-Economic Policy," in V.V. Murray (ed.) *Theories of Business-Government Relations* (Toronto: Trans-Canada Press), pp. 293-308.

Preston, Lee E., and James E. Post (1975) *Private Management and Public Policy* (Englewood Cliffs, N.J.: Prentice-Hall).

Priest, Margot, W.T. Stanbury, and Fred Thompson (1980) "On the Definition of Economic Regulation," in W.T. Stanbury (ed.) *Government Regulation: Scope, Growth, Process* (Montreal: The Institute for Research on Public Policy), pp. 1-16.

Priest, Margot, and Aron Wohl (1980) "The Growth of Federal and Provincial Regulation of Economic Activity, 1867-1978," in W.T. Stanbury (ed.) *Government Regulation: Scope, Growth, Process* (Montreal: The Institute for Research on Public Policy), pp. 69-149.

Prince, Michael J. (1979) "Policy Advisory Groups in Government Departments," in G. Bruce Doern and Peter Aucoin (eds.) *Public Policy in Canada* (Toronto: Macmillan), pp. 275-300.

Prince, Michael J., and J.A. Cherrier (1980) "The Rise and Fall of Policy Planning and Research Units: An Organizational Perspective," *Canadian Public Administration*, Vol. 23(4), pp. 519-541.

Privy Council Office (1981) *The Policy and Expenditure Management System* (Ottawa: PCO, March).

Privy Council Office (1985) "The Policy and Expenditure Management System," in Kenneth Kernaghan (ed.) *Public Administration in Canada: Selected Readings*, 5th ed. (Toronto: Methuen), pp. 192-202.

Probyn, Stephen (1977) "The Selling of the Pipeline: The Losers Tried to Sell Ottawa on What Was Needed, Bob Blair Won by Selling Them What He Knew They Wanted," *Canadian Business*, Vol. 5(4), October, pp. 54-56, 104-105.

Probyn, Stephen, and Scott Proudfoot (1978) "Inside Ottawa's Patronage Machine," *Quest*, Vol. 7(7), November, pp. 26-27, 32-39.

Pross, A. Paul (ed.) (1975a) *Pressure Group Behaviour in Canadian Politics* (Toronto: McGraw-Hill Ryerson).

Pross, A. Paul (1975b) "Canadian Pressure Groups in the 1970s: Their Role and Their Relations with the Public Service," *Canadian Public Administration*, Vol. 18(1), pp. 121-135.

Pross, A. Paul (1976) "Pressure Groups," in D.J. Bellamy et al. (eds.) *The Provincial Political Systems: Comparative Essays* (Toronto: Methuen), pp. 132-146.

Pross, A. Paul (1981) "Pressure Groups: Talking Chameleons," in M. Whittington and G. Williams (eds.) *Canadian Politics in the Eighties* (Toronto: Methuen), pp. 287-311.

Pross, A. Paul (1982a) "Governing Under Pressure—The Special Interest Groups—Summary of Discussion," *Canadian Public Administration*, Vol. 25(2), Summer, pp. 170-182.

Pross, A. Paul (1982b) "Space, Function and Interest: The Problem of Legitimacy in the Canadian State," in O.P. Dwivedi (ed.) *The Administrative State in Canada* (Toronto: University of Toronto Press), pp. 107-129.

Pross, A. Paul (1982c) "The Canadian Public Service and the Special Interest State," in O.P. Dwivedi (ed.) *The Administrative State: Canadian Perspectives* (Toronto: University of Toronto Press).

Pross, A. Paul (in process) *Group Politics and Public Policy* (Toronto: Oxford University Press).

Protheroe, David R. (1980) *Imports and Politics* (Montreal: The Institute for Research on Public Policy).

Public Affairs Council (1968) *Dollars and Sense*, rev. ed. (Washington, D.C.).

Public and Industrial Relations Limited (1983) *The Coverage of Business News: A Study of Opinion Among Chief Executive Officers, the Media and Public Relations Practitioners* (Toronto: PIR Limited).

Qualter, Terence H. (1983) "Propaganda in Canadian Society," in B.D. Singer (ed.) *Communications in Canadian Society* (Don Mills, Ont.: Addison-Wesley Publishers), pp. 176-187.

Quinn, Herbert F. (1976) "Quebec: Corruption Under Duplessis," in K.M. Gibbons and D.C. Rowat (eds.) *Political Corruption in Canada: Cases, Causes and Cures* (Toronto: McClelland and Stewart), pp. 66-80.

Raiffa, Howard (1982) *The Art and Science of Negotiation* (Cambridge, Mass.: Belnap Press of Harvard University Press).

Rasky, Frank (1984) "Other People's Money," *Canadian Business*, Vol. 17(10), October, pp. 55-60.

Ratner, R.S. (1984), "Lobbying the Senate," *Canadian Parliamentary Review*, Vol. 7(1), Spring, pp. 8-11.

Rea, K.J., and J.T. McLeod (1976) "The Changing Role of Government and the Drift Toward Corporatism," in Rea and McLeod (eds.) *Business and Government in Canada*, 2nd ed. (Toronto: Methuen), pp. 334-325.

Rea, K.J., and Nelson Wiseman (eds.) (1985) *Government and Enterprise in Canada* (Toronto: Methuen).

Reford, Robert (1983) "The BCNI: Senior Voice of Business in Canada," *Canadian Business Management Development*, Vol. 2, August 15, pp. 373-377.

Reich, Robert (1981) "Regulation by Confrontation or Negotiation?" *Harvard Business Review*, Vol. 59(3), May/June, pp. 81-93.

Reich, Robert (1983a) *The Next American Frontier* (New York: Penguin Books).

Reich, Robert (1983b) "Why Democracy Makes Economic Sense," *The New Republic*, Issue 3596, December 19, pp. 25-32 (review of Mancur Olsen, *The Rise and Decline of Nations*).

Reid, Escott M. (1979) "The Saskatchewan Liberal Machine before 1929," in H. Thorburn (ed.) *Party Politics in Canada*, 4th ed. (Scarborough, Ontario: Prentice-Hall), pp. 21-32.

Reid, Leonard N., *et al.* (1981) "Does Source Affect Response to Direct

Advocacy Print Advertisements?" *Journal of Business Research*, Vol. 9(3), pp. 309-319.

Reinfelds, Aivars (1982) "Prince Albert Pulp Co.; Athabasca Forest Industries: An Attempt at Economic Diversification by the Government of Saskatchewan" (Commerce 592 paper, April, University of B.C., Faculty of Commerce).

Renfro, William L. (1980) "Forecasting the Impact of Public Policies," *Long Range Planning*, Vol. 13, August, pp. 80-89.

Reschenthaler, G.B., and W.T. Stanbury (1977) "Benign Monopoly? Canadian Merger Policy and the K.C. Irving Case," *Canadian Business Law Journal*, Vol. 2(2), pp. 135-168.

Reschenthaler, G.B., and W.T. Stanbury (1981) "Recent Conspiracy Decisions in Canada: New Legislation Needed," *Antitrust Bulletin*, Vol. 26(4), pp. 839-869.

Reschenthaler, Gil, Bill Stanbury, and Fred Thompson (1982) "Whatever Happened to Deregulation?" *Policy Options*, Vol. 3(3), May/June, pp. 36-42.

Research Branch, Library of Parliament (1970) "Pressure Groups in Canada," *The Parliamentarian*, Vol.51(1), January, pp. 11-20.

Reuber, Grant L. (1978) "Government by Ear-Stroking," in William Dodge (ed.) *Consultation and Consensus: A New Era in Policy Formulation?* (Ottawa: Conference Board of Canada), pp. 3-11.

Reuber, Grant L. (1981) "Business and Government: Some Lessons for Each Other" (Speech to the Men's Canadian Club of Ottawa, November 12).

Reuber, Grant L. (1982) "Better Bureaucracies," *Policy Options*, Vol. 3(5), pp. 11-14.

Richards, J., and L. Pratt (1979) *Prairie Capitalism: Power and Influence in the New West* (Toronto: McClelland and Stewart).

Riordon, William L. (1948) *Plunkitt of Tammany Hall* (New York: Alfred A. Knopf).

Ritchie, Ron (1973) "Business-Government Relationships: Can We Create a More Effective Instrument for Socio-Economic Planning?" *CA Magazine*, Vol. 102(6), June, pp. 26-29.

Ritchie, Gordon (1983) "Government Aid to Industry: A Public Sector Perspective," *Canadian Public Administration*, Vol. 26(1), pp. 36-46.

Rivington, Lynda (1983) "Sanctum/Sanctorum: The Role of Caucus," *Parliamentary Government*, Vol. 4(1), pp. 3-7.

Robertson, Gordon (1983) "The Deputies' Anonymous Duty," *Policy Options*, Vol. 4(4), July, pp. 11-13.

Robertson, Gordon (1985) "Public Policy and Business: Some of the Problems of the 'Eighties," *Business Quarterly*, Vol. 50(2), pp. 66-69.

Robinson, Joan (1983) *Economic Philosophy* (Harmondsworth: Penguin Books, 1983; originally published in 1962).

Rogers, Byron (1977) "Federal Government Response to Consumerism and the Consumer Movement in Canada: A Critical Review" (Ottawa: Dept. of Consumer and Corporate Affairs, September, Occasional Papers of the Consumer Interest Study Group No. 2).

Roman, Andrew (1978) "Comments" (on the paper by W.T. Stanbury) in W.A.W. Neilson and J.C. McPherson (eds.) *The Legislative Process in Canada: The Need for Reform* (Montreal: The Institute for Research on Public Policy), pp. 208-217.

Rose-Ackerman, Susan (1978) *Corruption: A Study in Political Economy* (New York: Academic Press).

Ross, Alexander (1977) "How to Join the March to the New Politics," *Quest*, Vol. 8, February, pp. 40-42, 44, 46, 48 (re Canadian Federation of Independent Business).

Ross, Donald K. (1973) *A Public Citizen's Action Manual* (New York: Grossman Publishers).

Ross, Irwin (1976) "Public Relations Isn't Kid-Glove Stuff at Mobil," *Fortune*, Vol. 94(3), September, pp. 106-111.

Ross, R.S., and M.G. Ross (1981) *Understanding Persuasion* (Englewood Cliffs, N.J.: Prentice-Hall).

Ross, Val (1981) "Cancelled due to lack of interest," *Maclean's*, July 6, pp. 42-43 (re public interest groups).

Ross, Val (1983) "The Empire Strikes Back," *Maclean's*, April 4, p. 37-52.

Rothman, Stanley, and S. Robert Lichter (1982) "Media and Business Elites: Two Classes in Conflict?" *Public Interest*, Vol. 69, pp. 117-125.

Rothschild, K.W. (ed.) (1971) *Power in Economics* (Harmondsworth: Penguin Books).

Rousseau, H.P. (1983) "The Dome Syndrome: The Debt Overhanging Canadian Government and Business," *Canadian Public Policy*, Vol. 9(1), March, pp. 37-52.

Roussopoulos, D. (ed.) (1973) *The Political Economy of the State* (Montreal: Black Rose Books).

Rowley, C. K. (1978) "Market 'Failure' and Government 'Failure,' " in C.K. Rowley (ed.) *The Economics of Politics* (London: Institute for Economic Affairs).

Rowley, J.W., and W.T. Stanbury (eds.) (1978) *Competition Policy in Canada: Stage II, Bill C-13* (Montreal: The Institute for Research on Public Policy).

Royal Commission on the Economic Union and Development Prospects for Canada (1985), *Report*, 3 vols. (Ottawa: Minister of Supply and Services Canada).

Royal Commission on Financial Management and Accountability (1979) *Final Report* (Ottawa: Minister of Supply and Services, Canada).

Rubin, Bernard (ed.) (1977a) *Big Business and the Mass Media* (Lexington, Mass.: Lexington Books/D.C. Heath).

Rubin, Bernard (1977b) "Advocacy, Big Business and Mass Media," in B. Rubin (ed.) *Big Business and the Mass Media* (Lexington, Mass.: Lexington Books/D.C. Heath), pp. 1-62.

Rubin, Jeffery, and Bert Brown (1975) *The Social Psychology of Bargaining and Negotiation* (New York: Academic Press).

Rumsfeld, Donald (1979) "A Politician-Turned-Executive Surveys Both Worlds," *Fortune*, Vol. 100(5), September 10, pp. 88-92, 94.

Rush, J. (1980) "A booming trade at the ear of government," *Globe and Mail*, October 25, p. 11.

Rush, Michael (1979) "Committees in the Canadian House of Commons," in J.D. Lees and M. Shaw (eds.) *Committees in Legislatures: A Comparative Analysis* (London: Martin Robertson), pp. 191-241.

Salisbury, Robert (1968) "The Analysis of Public Policy: A Search for Theories and Roles," in Austin Ranney (ed.) *Political Science and Public Policy* (Chicago: Markham Publishing).

Salter, Liora (ed.) (1981) *Communication Studies in Canada* (Toronto: Butterworths).

Samuelson, Paul A. (1972) "The Businessman's Shrinking Prerogatives," *Business and Society Review*, No. 1, Spring, pp. 36-38.

Sanders, Douglas (1983) "The Indian Lobby," in Keith Banting and Richard Simeon (eds.) *And No One Cheered: Federalism, Democracy and the Constitution Act* (Toronto: Methuen), pp. 301-332.

Sasges, Michael (1984) "National Newspapers Spend Bucks to Lift Circulation," Vancouver *Sun*, November 16, p. F7.

Saumier, Andre (1983) "Business Lobbying," *Canadian Public Administration*, Vol. 26(1), pp. 73-79.

Savoie, Donald J. (1983) "The Minister's Staff: The Need for Reform," *Canadian Public Administration*, Vol. 26(4), pp. 509-524.

Sawatsky, John (1983) "Power plays: How the lobby system works," Montreal *Gazette*, May 28, p. B5.

Schattschneider, E.E. (1960) *The Semi-Sovereign People* (New York: Holt Rinehart & Winston).

Schatz, H. (1983) "Consumer interests in the process of political decision-making," *Journal of Consumer Policy*, Vol. 6, pp. 381-395.

Schiele, R. (1975) "Don't be so afraid of political action," *Canadian Business*, Vol. 48(11), November, p. 39.

Schmertz, H. (1984) "Why Banks Should Take a Public Stand on Issues," *Bank Marketing*, Vol. 16, September, pp. 20-23.

Schroeder, Hal (1983) *Corporate Social Performance in Canada: A Survey* (Lethbridge: University of Lethbridge).

Schubert, Glendon A., Jr. (1957) "'The Public Interest' in Administrative Decision-Making: Theorem, Theosophy, or Theory?" *American Political Science Review*, Vol. 51, pp. 346-368.

Schubert, Glendon A., Jr. (1960) *The Public Interest* (Glencoe, Ill.: Free Press).

Schultz, George P. (1979) "The Abrasive Interface," *Harvard Business Review*, Vol. 57(6), Nov.-Dec., pp. 93-97.

Schultz, Richard (1977) "Interest Groups and Intergovernmental Negotiations: Caught in the Vise of Federalism," in Peter Meekison (ed.) *Canadian Federalism: Myth or Reality*, 3rd ed. (Toronto: Methuen), pp. 375-396.

Schultz, Richard (1979) *Federalism and the Regulatory Process* (Montreal: The Institute for Research on Public Policy).

Schultz, Richard (1980) *Federalism, Bureaucracy and Public Policy* (Montreal: McGill-Queen's University Press).

Schultz, Richard, *et. al.* (eds.) (1979) *The Canadian Political Process*, 3rd ed. (Toronto: Holt Rinehart and Winston).

Schultz, Richard, and Alan Alexanadroff (1985) *Economic Regulation and the Federal System* (Toronto: University of Toronto Press).

Schumpeter, Joseph (1949) *Capitalism, Socialism and Democracy* (New York: Harper).

Schwartz, Mildred A. (1978) "The Group Basis of Politics," in J.H. Redekop (ed.) *Approaches to Canadian Politics* (Toronto: Prentice-Hall), chap. 15, pp. 323-346.

Schwartz, Tony (1981) *Media: The Second God* (New York: Random House).

Scott, D.B. (1981) "Choo Choo, the Liberals' Other Turner," *Quest*, Vol. 10(8), December, pp. 55-61.

Scott, J.R. (1961) "Political Slush Funds Corrupt All Parties," *Maclean's*, Vol. 74(18), September 9, pp. 13, 67-70.

Scotten, Clifford (1982) "Big [Government] is Bad," *Policy Options*, Vol. 3(5), pp. 28-29.

Seidle, F. Leslie, and K. Z. Paltiel (1981) "Party Finance, the Election Expenses Act, and Campaign Spending in 1979 and 1980," in H. R. Penniman (ed.) *Canada at the Polls, 1979 and 1980* (Washington, D.C.: American Enterprise Institute), pp. 226-279.

Seligman, Daniel (1979) "The Politics and Economics of 'Public Interest' Lobbying," *Fortune*, November, pp. 44-45.

Sethi, S. Prakash (1976) "Issue-Oriented Corporate Advertising: Tax Treatment of Expenditures," *California Management Review*, Vol. 19(1), Fall, pp. 5-13.

Sethi, S.Prakash (1977a) *Advocacy Advertising and Large Corporations* (Lexington Mass.: D. C. Heath).

Sethi, S. Prakash (1977b) "Business and the News Media: The Parade of Informed Misunderstanding," *California Management Review*, Vol. 19(3), Spring, pp. 52-62.

Sethi, S. Prakash (1977c) "Advocacy Advertising and the Multinational Corporation," *Columbia Journal of World Business*, Vol. 12(3), Fall, pp. 32-46.

Sethi, S. Prakash (1979) "Institutional/Image Advertising and Idea/Issue

Advertising as Marketing Tools: Some Public Policy Issues," *Journal of Marketing*, Vol. 43(1), January, pp. 68-78.

Sethi, S.Prakash (1981) "Serving the Public Interest: Corporate Political Action Strategies for the 1980s," *Management Review*, Vol. 70, March, pp. 8-11.

Sexty, Robert W. (1984) "The Ideology of Canadian Business and the Prevalence of Public Enterprise" (Paper presented at the Michigan State University, Canadian-American Business Development Forum, June 3-5, mimeo).

Seymour-Ure, Colin (1974) *The Political Impact of the Media* (London: Constable).

Shaw, Gillian (1982) "Names in News Reap Newspapers," Vancouver *Sun*, December 18, p. A10.

Shepherd, J.J. (1981) "Hidden Crown Corporations," *Policy Options*, Vol. 2(2), pp. 40-42.

Shepherd, J.J. (1983) "Government Aid to Industry: A Private Sector Perspective," *Canadian Public Administration*, Vol. 26(1), Spring, pp. 47-45.

Sheppard, Robert (1980) "Who's Who of Political Donors Unveiled," *Globe and Mail*, July 11, pp. 1-2.

Sher, Melvin (1977) "Ottawa Heeds Protests Over Patent Law," *Canadian Business*, July, pp. 23-29.

Sherman, Paddy (1966) *Bennett* (Toronto: McClelland and Stewart).

Shifrin, Leonard (1982) "The Administrator Responds to Public Response?" *Optimum*, Vol. 13(1), pp. 93-95.

Siegel, Arthur (1983) *Politics and the Media in Canada* (Toronto: McGraw-Hill Ryerson).

Silberman, Jonathan, and Gilbert Yochum (1980) "The Market for Special Interest Campaign Funds," *Public Choice*, Vol. 35, pp. 75-83.

Silbert, Dave (1983) "Local Journalists Eaten by Politicians — A Case Study That the Kent Commission Didn't See," *Content*, April-May, pp. 4-24.

Silk, Leonard, and Mark Silk (1980) *The American Establishment* (New York: Basic Books).

Simeon, Richard (1962) *Federal-Provincial Diplomacy: The Making of Recent Policy in Canada* (Toronto: University of Toronto Press).

Simeon, Richard (1974) *Federal-Provincial Diplomacy: The Making of Recent Policy in Canada* (Toronto: University of Toronto Press).

Simeon, Richard (ed.) (1979) *Confrontation and Collaboration: Intergovernmental Relations in Canada Today* (Toronto: The Institute of Public Administration of Canada).

Simeon, Richard (1982) "Fiscal Federalism in Canada: A Review Essay," *Canadian Tax Journal*, Vol. 30(1), Jan-Feb., pp. 41-51.

Simeon, Richard (1985) *The Political Economy of Canadian Federalism, 1940 to 1984* (Toronto: University of Toronto Press).

Simon, William E. (1979) *A Time for Truth* (New York: Reader's Digest Press).

Simons, Howard, and J.A. Califano, Jr. (1979) *The Media and Business* (New York: Vintage Books).

Simpson, Jeffrey (1980) *The Discipline of Power* (Toronto: Personal Library).

Simpson, Jeffrey (1985) "How Old Pols Turn a Profit," *Report on Business Magazine*, October, pp. 40-46.

Slatter, Stuart S.P. (1980) "Strategic Planning for Public Relations," *Long Range Planning*, Vol. 13, June, pp. 57-60.

Smiley, Donald V. (1964) "Public Administration and Canadian Federalism," *Canadian Public Administration*, Vol. 7, September, pp. 371-388.

Smiley, Donald V. (1970) *Constitutional Adaptation and Canadian Federalism since 1945* (Ottawa: Information Canada).

Smiley, Donald V. (1971) "The Structural Problem of Canadian Federalism," *Canadian Public Administration*, Vol. 14(3), pp. 326-343.

Smiley, Donald V. (1980) *Canada in Question: Federalism in the Eighties*, 3rd ed. (Toronto: McGraw-Hill Ryerson).

Smiley, Donald V. (1981) "Freedom of Information: Rationales and Proposals for Reform," in John D. McCamus (ed.) *Freedom of Information: Canadian Perspectives* (Toronto: Butterworths), pp. 1-21.

Smith, Adam (1937) *An Inquiry into the Nature and Causes of the Wealth of Nations*, edited by Edward Cannan (New York: The Modern Library; originally published in 1776).

Smith, D.G., B.D. Hendry, L.M.J. Chipman, and Alan Chappelle (1984) "Project Wolf: An Analysis of Lobbying Effectiveness" (Commerce 592 paper, April, University of B.C., Faculty of Commerce).

Smith, Larry (1980) "Getting Your Way with a Bureaucrat," *Canadian Business*, September, pp. 104-105, 110-112, 131.

Smith, Larry (1981) "Ethical ways of using politicians for profit," *Canadian Business*, Vol. 54(2), February, pp. 129-132.

Smith, Lee (1976) "Business and the Media," *Dun's Review*, Vol. 107(3), March, pp. 31-34.

Smith, Lee (1981) "Why Does the Public 'Hate' Profits?" in F.D. Sturdivant and L.M. Robinson (eds.) *The Corporate Social Challenge* (Homewood, Illinois: R.D. Irwin Inc.), pp. 99-102.

Smith, Roger S. (1979) *Tax Expenditures: An Examination of Tax Incentives and Tax Preferences in the Canadian Federal Income Tax System* (Toronto: Canadian Tax Foundation).

Smith, Seymour (1979) "How to Plan for Crisis Communication," *Public Relations Journal*, March, pp. 17-18.

Sonnenfeld, Jeffery (1981) *Corporate Views of the Public Interest* (Boston: Auburn House Publishing Co.).

Special Senate Committee on Mass Media (1970) *The Uncertain Mirror* (Ottawa: Queen's Printer).

Spence, Richard (1980) "Do Corporate Ads Work? Little Evidence to Say They Do in Canada," *Financial Times*, December 15, p. 10.

Stanbury, W.T. (1972) "Changes in the Size and Structure of Government Expenditures in Canada, 1967-1968" (Unpublished Ph.D. dissertation, University of California at Berkeley, Department of Economics).

Stanbury, W.T. (1977) *Business Interests and the Reform of Canadian Competition Policy, 1971-1975* (Toronto: Carswell/Methuen).

Stanbury, W.T. (1978) "Lobbying and Interest Group Representation in the Legislative Process," in W.A.W. Neilson and J.C. McPherson (eds.) *The Legislative Process in Canada: The Need for Reform* (Montreal: The Institute for Research on Public Policy), chap. 6, pp. 167-207.

Stanbury, W.T. (1979) "Definitions of 'the Public Interest'," Appendix D in D.G. Hartle *Public Policy Decision Making and Regulation* (Montreal: The Institute for Research on Public Policy), pp. 213-218.

Stanbury, W.T. (ed.) (1980) *Government Regulation: Growth, Scope, Process* (Montreal: The Institute for Research on Public Policy).

Stanbury, W.T. (1982) "Changes in the Use of Governing Instruments in Canada" (Faculty of Commerce and Business Administration, University of British Columbia, unpublished paper, August).

Stanbury, W.T. (1984a) *The Normative Bases of Rent Regulation* (Toronto: Study prepared for the Commission of Inquiry into Residential Tenancies, September).

Stanbury, W.T. (1984b) *The Normative Bases of Government Action* (Toronto: Ontario Commission of Inquiry into Residential Tenancies, September).

Stanbury, W.T. (1985a) "How Rent Controls Came to Ontario: A Public Choice Perspective," *Ryerson Lectures in Economics* (Toronto: Ryerson Polytechnical Institute).

Stanbury, W.T. (1985b) "Half a Loaf?: Bill C-29, Proposed Amendments to the Combines Investigation Act," *Canadian Business Law Journal*, Vol. 10(1), February, pp.1-34.

Stanbury, W.T. (1985c) "The Politics of Canadian Competition Policy, 1976-1985" (Vancouver, B.C.: Faculty of Commerce and Business Administration, unpublished manuscript).

Stanbury, W.T. (1985d) "A Framework for the Analysis of Business-Government Relations," in Mark Baetz and Donald Thain (eds.) *Canadian Cases in Business-Government Relations* (Toronto: Methuen), chap. 1.

Stanbury, W.T. (1985e) "The Psychological Environment of Business-

Government Relations in Canada," *The Business Quarterly*, Vol. 50(2), Summer, pp. 105-114.

Stanbury, W.T. (1985f) "Government as Leviathan: Implications for Business-Government Relations," in V.V. Murray (ed.) *Theories of Business-Government Relations* (Toronto: Trans-Canada Press), pp. 15-55.

Stanbury, W.T. (1986) "Changing Canada's Competition Law: Analysis of Bill C-91" (Faculty of Commerce and Business Administration, University of B.C., April, mimeo).

Stanbury, W.T., and Fred Thompson (1980) "The Scope and Coverage of Regulation in Canada and the United States: Implications for the Demand for Reform," in W.T. Stanbury (ed.) *Government Regulation: Scope, Growth, Process* (Montreal: The Institute for Research on Public Policy), pp. 17-67.

Stanbury, W.T., and G.B. Reschenthaler (1981) "Reforming Canadian Competition Policy: Once More Unto the Breach," *Canadian Business Law Journal*, Vol. 5(4), pp. 381-437.

Stanbury, W.T., and Fred Thompson (1982a) *Regulatory Reform in Canada* (Montreal: The Institute for Research on Public Policy).

Stanbury, W.T., and Fred Thompson (1982b) "The Prospects for Deregulation in Canada: Political Models and the American Experience," *Osgoode Hall Law Journal*, Vol. 20(4), December, pp. 678-720.

Stanbury, W.T., and Susan Burns (1982) "Consumer and Corporate Affairs: Portrait of a Regulatory Department," in G. Bruce Doern (ed.) *How Ottawa Spends Your Tax Dollars, 1982* (Toronto: Lorimer), pp. 173-216.

Stanbury, W.T., and George Lermer (1983) "Regulation and the Redistribution of Income and Wealth," *Canadian Public Administration*, Vol. 26(3), pp. 386-401.

Stanbury, W.T., G.J. Gorn, and C.B. Weinberg (1983) "Federal Advertising Expenditures," in G.B. Doern (ed.) *How Ottawa Spends: The Liberals, the Opposition Parties and National Priorities* (Toronto: Lorimer), chap. 6.

Stanbury, W.T., C.F. Smart, and I.B. Vertinsky (1983) "Government Relations at MacMillan Bloedel Ltd.: The Emergence of a New Function" (Case prepared for the Max Bell Foundation's Program on Business-Government Relations, York University, mimeo).

Stanbury, W.T., and Jane Fulton (1984) "Suasion as a Governing Instrument," in Allan M. Maslove (ed.) *How Ottawa Spends 1984: The New Agenda* (Toronto: Methuen), pp. 282-324.

Stanbury, W.T., and Peter Thain (1986) *The Origins of Rent Regulation in Ontario* (Toronto: Ontario Commission of Inquiry into Residential Tenancies).

Stanbury, W.T., and I.B. Vertinsky (1986) *Rent Regulation: Design*

Characteristics and Effects (Toronto: Commission of Inquiry into Residential Tenancies).

Standing, James (1980) "Business and the Press: How to Improve Relations," *Business Quarterly*, Vol. 45(2), Summer, pp. 87-90.

Starr, Michael, and Mitchell Sharp, Co-Chairmen (1984) *Ethical Conduct in the Public Sector: Report of the Task Force on Conflict of Interest* (Ottawa: Ministry of Supply and Services Canada, May).

Statistics Canada (1983) *Annual Report of the Minister of Supply and Services Canada Under the Corporations and Labour Unions Returns Act, Part 1 — Corporations 1980* (Ottawa: Minister of Supply and Services).

Steed, Judy (1983) "Power and the process man," *Globe and Mail*, September 24, p. 10.

Steinberg, Charles S. (1975) *The Creation of Consent: Public Relations in Practice* (New York: Hastings House).

Steiner, George A., Harry and Else Kunin (1981) "The New Class of Chief Executive Officer," *Long Range Planning*, Vol. 14(4), pp. 10-20.

Steiner, George (1983) *The New CEO* (New York: Macmillan).

Stepney, Peter, Dan Price, Doug Ruffle, and Neil Charleson (1985) "South Moresby: A Clearcut Decision?" (Commerce 592 paper, Faculty of Commerce and Business Administration, University of B.C.).

Stevens, Geoffrey (1976a) "An Oversight Perhaps?" *Globe and Mail*, February 11, p. 6.

Stevens, Geoffrey (1976b) "The Blue-Ribbon Committee," *Globe and Mail*, June 25.

Stevens, Robert (1980) "Lobbyists: a Big Cog in Ottawa Economy," *Ottawa Journal*, May 8, p. 29.

Stevenson, Anna B. (1982) *Canadian Election Reform: Dialogue on Issues and Effects* (Toronto: Ontario Commission on Election Contributions and Expenses).

Steward, Gillian (1981) "Big Oil Listens," *Energy*, October, pp. 10-14.

Steward, Gillian (1982) "The Age of Imperialism comes to an end" (re Imperial Oil) *Canadian Business*, Vol. 5(8), August 1982, pp. 61-71.

Stewart, W.B. (1980) "Canadian Social Systems and Canadian Broadcasting Audiences," in B. Singer (ed.) *Communications in Canadian Society* (Don Mills: Addison-Wesley).

Stewart, Walter (ed.) (1980) *Canadian Newspapers: The Inside Story* (Edmonton: Hurtig).

Stewart, Walter (1981) "In Praise of Politicians, How to tell the good guys from the bad," *Quest*, December, pp. 61-69.

Stewart, Walter (1982) "Paying the Poplollies," in Paul Fox (ed.) *Politics Canada*, 5th ed. (Toronto: McGraw-Hill Ryerson), pp. 359-360.

Stewart, Walter (1983) "The Royal Canadian Oil Farce," *Quest*, Vol. 12, October, pp. 35-42d.

Stimulus (1984) "The Business Press Was Hit Hardest by the Largest of All Media but After Two Years of Losses, Publishers Are Cautiously Optimistic," June, pp. 23-25.

Stoik, John L. (1985) "The Role Government Has Played in the Past — The Role It Ought to Play in the Future," *Business Quarterly*, Vol. 50(2), pp. 86-89.

Stoltz, Volker (1983) " 'Conflict PR' in the Formation of Public Opinion," *Public Relations Quarterly*, Vol. 28, Spring, pp. 28-31.

Straiton, John S. (1983) "Advocacy Advertising in Recessionary Times" (Speech to the Canadian Pulp and Paper Association, Montreal, Quebec, February 2, mimeo).

Straiton, John S. (1984) *Of Women and Advertising* (Toronto: McClelland and Stewart).

Streeck, W. (1983) "Between Pluralism and Corporatism: German Business Associations and the State," *Journal of Public Policy*, Vol. 3, pp. 265-284.

Strong, Maurice (1984) "The Necessary Private-Public Mix," *Policy Options*, Vol. 5(6), pp. 6-12.

Stroup, Margaret (1980) "Issues Management," in R.A. Bucholz (ed.) *Public Policy and the Business Firm* (Washington University, St. Louis: Center for the Study of American Business), pp. 145-152.

Stubbart, Charles (1982) "Are Environmental Scanning Units Effective?" *Long Range Planning*, Vol. 15(3), June, pp. 139-145.

Stridsberg, Albert (1977) *Controversy Advertising* (New York: Hastings House).

Subcommittee on Administrative Practice and Procedure of the Committee of the Judiciary, U.S. Senate (1978) *Sourcebook on Corporate Image and Corporate Advocacy Advertising* (Washington, D.C.: USGPO).

Sutherland, S.L., and G. Bruce Doern (1985) *Bureaucracy in Canada: Control and Reform* (Toronto: University of Toronto Press).

Swimmer, Eugene (1984) "Six and Five," in Allan M. Maslove (ed.) *How Ottawa Spends 1984: The New Agenda* (Toronto: Methuen), pp. 240-281.

Tafler, Sid (1983) "Pushing the 'right' ideas," *Globe and Mail*, December 10, p. 8.

Tait, Janice (1981) "Women Looking for Leverage," *Policy Options*, Vol. 2(3), pp. 54-56.

Tardi, Gregory (1984) "The Reach of Government," *Policy Options*, Vol. 5(2), pp. 33-34.

Tarschys, Daniel (1975) "The Growth of Public Expenditures: Nine Modes of Explanation," *Scandinavian Political Studies*, Vol. 10, pp. 9-31.

Task Force on Conflict of Interest (1984) *Report: Ethical Conduct in the Public Sector* (Ottawa: Minister of Supply and Services Canada, May).

Taux, Andrew (1985) "The High Cost of Failing to Deregulate," *Report on Business Magazine*, October, pp. 102-108.

Taylor, Charles (1982) *Radical Tories: The Conservative Tradition in Canada* (Toronto: House of Anansi).

Taylor, M.G. (1960) "The Role of the Medical Profession in the Formulation and Execution of Public Policy," *Canadian Journal of Economics and Political Science*, Vol. 26(1), February.

Taylor, M.G. (1978) *Health Insurance and Canadian Public Policy* (Montreal: McGill-Queen's University Press).

Thain, D.H. (1970a) "The Coming Crunch in Federal Government-Business Relations," *Business Quarterly*, Vol. 35(3), Autumn, pp. 22-34.

Thain, D.H. (1970b) "The Key Issues in Federal Government Business Relations," *Business Quarterly*, Vol. 35(4), Winter, pp. 25-37.

Thain, D.H. (1979a) "The Mistakes of Business in Dealing with Politics and Government," *Business Quarterly*, Vol. 44(3), Autumn, pp. 16-54.

Thain, D.H. (1979b) "Mistakes of Government in Dealing with Business," *Business Quarterly*, Vol. 44(4), Winter 1979, pp 20-29.

Thain, D.H. (1980) "Improving Competence to Deal with Politics and Government: The Management Challenge of the 80's," *Business Quarterly*, Vol. 45(1) Spring, pp. 31-45.

Thain, D.H. (1981) "Canada's Management Crisis," *Business Quarterly*, Vol. 46(4), pp. 61-75.

Thain, D.H., and M. Baetz (1979) "Increasing Trouble Ahead for Business Government Relations in Canada," *Business Quarterly*, Vol. 44(2), Summer, pp. 56-65.

Thain, D.H., and M.C. Baetz (1982) "Will Canadian Business Leaders Meet the Parti Quebecois Challenge?" *Business Quarterly*, October Special Supplement, pp. 43-57.

Thomas, David (1981) "Nationalists in the Boardrooms," *Maclean's*, December 7, pp. 54-56.

Thomas, Paul (1983) "Practicable Reforms for Parliament," *Policy Options*, Vol. 4(1), pp. 18-22.

Thomas, Philip S. (1980) "Environmental Scanning — the State of the Art," *Long Range Planning*, Vol. 13, February, pp. 20-28.

Thompson, D.N. (1980) "Reshaping Canadian Newspaper Markets," *Business Quarterly*, Vol. 45(4), Winter, pp. 48-56.

Thompson, D.N. (1983) "The Canadian Pharmaceutical Industry: A Business-Government Failure," *Business Quarterly*, Vol. 48(2), Summer, pp. 32-35.

Thompson, Fred, and W. T. Stanbury (1979) "The Political Economy of

Interest Groups in the Legislative Process in Canada," in Schultz, Kruhlak, and Terry (eds.) *The Canadian Political Process*, 3rd ed. (Toronto: Holt Rinehart and Winston), pp. 224-249.

Thompson, Fred, and W.T. Stanbury (1984) "The Comparative Politics of Regulation: A Contingency Theory of the Function of Interest Groups in the Legislative Process," in Fred Thompson (ed.) *Regulatory Regimes in Conflict* (Lanham, Md.: University Press of America), pp. 81-102.

Thompson, Fred, and W.T. Stanbury (1984) "Looking Out for No.1: Incumbency and Interest Group Politics," *Canadian Public Policy* Vol. 10(2), pp. 239-244.

Thompson, Mark (1982) "Fig Leaf Politics: The Influence of Labour on Trade Policy in Canada" (Paper presented at the Conference on Domestic Groups and Foreign Policy, Carleton University, June 9-11).

Thompson, Tony (1985) "Advertising's New Men Cut Themselves In," *Report on Business Magazine*, October, pp. 96-100.

Thorburn, H. G. (1964) "Pressure Groups in Canadian Politics: Recent Revisions to the Anti-Combines Legislation," *Canadian Journal of Economics and Political Science*, Vol. 30(2), May, pp. 157-174.

Thorburn, H.G. (1985) *Interest Groups in the Canadian Federal System* (Toronto: University of Toronto Press).

Thurow, Lester (1981) *The Zero-Sum Society* (Harmondsworth: Penguin Books).

Tilley, Kenneth G. (1977) "Ministerial Executive Staffs," in Paul W. Fox (ed.) *Politics: Canada*, 4th ed. (Toronto: McGraw-Hill), pp. 409-414.

Time (1983) "What do paper clips have to do with corporate communications? Gulf Canada Limited, A Corporate Advertising Case History" (Toronto: Time).

Time (1983) "Journalism Under Fire," December 12, pp. 60-81.

Tisdall, Charles W. (1980) Communicating in the Doubting 80s," *Business Quarterly*, Vol. 45(3), Autumn, pp. 82-87.

Tolchin, Susan J., and Martin Tolchin (1983) *Dismantling America: The Rush to Deregulate* (Boston: Houghton Mifflin).

Traves, Tom (1979) *The State and Enterprise: Canadian Manufacturers and the Federal Government, 1917-1931* (Toronto: University of Toronto Press).

Traves, Tom (1985) "Business-Government Relations in Canadian History," in Rea and Wiseman (eds.) *Government and Enterprise in Canada* (Toronto: Methuen), pp. 8-19.

Trebilcock, M.J. (1981) *The Choice of Governing Instrument: Some Applications* (Ottawa: Economic Council of Canada, Regulation Reference Technical Report No. 12), chap. 2.

Trebilcock, M.J., and D.G. Hartle (1982) "The Choice of Governing

Instrument," *International Review of Law and Economics*, Vol. 2, pp. 29-46.

Trebilcock, M.J., D.G. Hartle, J.R.S. Prichard, and D. Dewees (1982) *The Choice of Governing Instrument* (Ottawa: Minister of Supply and Services).

Trebilcock, M.J. (1985) "The Political Economy of Business Bail-Outs in Canada," in R. Hill and J. Whalley (eds.) *Domestic Policies and the International Economic Environment* (Toronto: University of Toronto Press).

Trebilcock, M.J., *et al.* (1986) *The Political Economy of Bailouts*, 2 vols. (Toronto: University of Toronto Press).

Trebuss, A. Susanna (1981) *Defining the Strategic Environment: An Analysis of Organizational Perspectives* (Ottawa: The Conference Board in Canada, Executive Bulletin No. 15, February).

Trueman, Peter (1980) *Smoke and Mirrors* (Toronto: McClelland and Stewart).

Truman, David B. (1971) *The Governmental Process: Political Interests and Public Opinion*, 2nd ed. (New York: Alfred A. Knopf).

Tuchman, Gaye (1978) *Making News: A Study in the Construction of Reality* (New York: The Free Press).

Tuerck, David G. (ed.) (1978) *The Political Economy of Advertising* (Washington, D.C.: American Enterprise Institute).

Tullock, Gordon (1983) *Economics of Income Redistribution* (Hingham, Mass.: Kluwer Boston).

Tuohy, Carolyn (1981) "The Struggle for Professional Power," *Policy Options*, Vol. 34 40, March/April, pp. 34-40.

Tupper, Allan (1983) "Bill S-31 and the Federalism of State Capitalism" (Discussion Paper #18, Institute of Intergovernmental Relations, Queen's University).

UBC Information Services (1984) "How to Deal with the Media," *UBC*, January 26, mimeo.

United Nations (1981) *1979/80 Statistical Yearbook*, 31st issue (New York: United Nations).

Urquhart, Ian (1978) "The Bucks Start Here: Behind Every Great Leader Is an Equally Great Bagman," *Maclean's*, May 15, Vol. 91(10), pp. 44b-44p.

Useem, Michael (1984) *The Inner Circle* (London: Oxford University Press).

Usher, Dan (1985) "The Growth of the Public Sector in Canada," in *Responses to Economic Change* (Toronto: University of Toronto Press).

U.S. House of Representatives, Campaign Finance Study Groups, Committee on House Administration (1978) *An Analysis of the Impact of the Federal Election Campaign, 1972-1978* (Washington, U.S. G.P.O.).

Vamos, Mark N. (1984) "Does Madison Avenue Control Our Minds?" *Business Week*, No. 2871, December 3, pp. 11-13.

Vance, Stanley (1983) *Corporate Leadership* (New York: McGraw-Hill).

Van Dam, A. (1976) "Government and Business: Bringing the Two Together," *Canadian Business*, Vol. 49(10), October, pp. 87-88.

van den Haag, Ernest (ed.) (1979) *Capitalism, Sources of Hostility* (Washington, D.C.: Heritage Foundation).

Vanderbok, W.G. (1977) "Legislators, Bureaucrats, and Canadian Democracy: The Long and Short of It," *Canadian Journal of Political Science*, Vol. 10, pp. 615-624.

Van Loon, R.J. (1981) "Stop the music: the current policy and expenditure management system in Ottawa," *Canadian Public Administration*, Vol. 24(2), Summer, pp. 175-199.

Van Loon, R.J. (1983) "The Policy and Expenditure Management System in the Federal Government: The First Three Years," *Canadian Public Administration*, Vol. 26/2, pp. 255-284.

Van Loon, R.J. (1985) "Kaleidoscope in Grey: The Policy Process in Ottawa," in M.S. Whittington and Glen Williams (eds.) *Canadian Politics in the 1980s*, 2nd ed. (Toronto: Methuen), pp. 412-433.

Van Loon, R.J., and M.S. Whittington (1981) *The Canadian Political System: Environment, Structure, and Process*, 3rd ed. (Toronto: McGraw-Hill Ryerson).

Veilleux, Gerard (1980) "Intergovernmental Canada: Government by Conference? A Fiscal and Economic Perspective," *Canadian Public Administration*, Vol. 23(10), pp. 33-53.

Vernon, Raymond (1974) *Big Business and the State* (Cambridge, Mass.: Harvard University Press).

Vining, Aidan (1983) "Provincial Ownership of Government Enterprise in Canada," *Annals of Public and Co-operative Economy*, Vol. 54(1), March, pp. 35-55.

Vining, Aidan, and Robert Botterell (1983) "An Overview of the Origins, Growth, Size and Function of Provincial Crown Corporations," in J.R.S. Prichard (ed.) *Crown Corporations: The Calculus of Instrument of Choice* (Toronto: Butterworths), chap. 5.

Vining, Aidan (1984) "Public Sector Enterprises in Canada," in *Public Enterprises in International Perspective* (Hyderabad: Institute of Public Enterprise).

Vogel, David (1978a) *Lobbying the Corporation: Citizen Challenges to Business Authority* (New York: Basic Books).

Vogel, David (1978b) "Why Businessmen Distrust Their State: The Political Consciousness of American Corporate Executives," *British Journal of Political Science*, Vol. 8, pp. 45-78.

Waldie, Ken G. (1985) "The Evolution of Labour-Government Consultation on Economic Policy," in Craig Riddell (ed.) *Labour-Man-*

agement Co-operation in Canada (Toronto: University of Toronto Press).

Walker, Dean (1982) "Fighting for the Private Sector," *Executive*, Vol. 24(5), May, pp. 55-65.

Walker, Dean (1984) "Lobbyists Isn't a Four Letter Word," *Executive*, Vol. 26(3), March, pp. 30-32.

Wallace, D.C. (in press) "The Kent Commission: The Fourth Estate Under Attack," in R.B. Byers (ed.) *Canadian Annual Review of Politics and Public Affairs* (Toronto: University of Toronto Press).

Wallace, D.C., and Fred Fletcher (eds.) (1985) *Canadian Politics Through Press Reports* (Toronto: Oxford University Press).

Ward, Norman (1972) "Money and Politics: The Costs of Democracy in Canada," *Canadian Journal of Political Science*, Vol. 5(3), pp. 335-347.

Ward, Peter (1982) "The Ottawa Runaround," *Business Life*, Vol. 9, Spring, pp. 42-49.

Watson, Jack (1982) "Let's Get It Right," *Volume Retail Merchandising*, Vol. 33(2), February, p. 3.

Watson, W.G. (1981) "Old Wine in Old Bottles" (clothing and textiles) *Policy Options*, Vol. 2(4), pp. 14-19.

Watson, W.G. (1983) *A Primer on the Economics of Industrial Policy* (Toronto: Ontario Economic Council).

Watson, W.G. (1984) "Freshening the Debate" (over industrial policy), *Policy Options*, Vol. 5(3), pp. 54-58.

Ways, Max (1972) "Business Needs to Do a Better Job of Explaining Itself," *Fortune*, September.

Wearing, Joseph (1981) *The L-Shaped Party: The Liberal Party of Canada, 1958-1980* (Toronto: McGraw-Hill).

Weaver, Sally M. (1982) "The Joint Cabinet/National Indian Brotherhood Committee: a unique experiment on pressure group relations," *Canadian Public Administration*, Vol. 25(2), Summer, pp. 221-239.

Weick, Karl E. (1984) "Small Wins: Redefining the Scale of Social Problems," *American Psychologist*, Vol. 39(1), January, pp. 40-49.

Weidenbaum, Murray L. (1977) *Government, Business, and the Public* (Englewood Cliffs, N.J.: Prentice-Hall).

Weidenbaum, Murray L. (1986) *Business, Government and the Public*, 3rd ed. (Englewood Cliffs, N.J.: Prentice-Hall).

Weidenbaum, Murray L., and Robert De Fina (1978) "The Cost of Federal Regulation," Reprint No. 88 (Washington, D.C.: American Enterprise Institute).

Wessel, Milton R. (1976) *The Rule of Reason: A New Approach to Corporate Litigation* (Reading, Mass.: Addison-Wesley).

Westell, Anthony (1977) *The New Society* (Toronto: McClelland and Stewart).

Westell, Anthony (1980) "The Press: Adversary or Channel of Communication," in H.D. Clarke *et al.* (eds.) *Parliament, Policy and Representation* (Toronto: Methuen), pp. 25-34.

Westell, Anthony (1982a) "Political Trends: Is Canada Turning Right?" *Canadian Business Review*, Spring, pp. 31-35.

Westell, Anthony (1982b) "Quality News and Views," *Policy Options*, Vol. 3(4), July/Aug., pp. 47-49.

Western Miner (1981) "Plain Speaking Is Needed if Business and Industry Are to Communicate Properly About Public Concerns," August, pp. 54-57.

Weston, Greg (1983) "Trudeau and the Press Play Cat and Mouse Games," Vancouver *Sun*, April 2, p. A6.

Wetzel, Thomas H. (1982) "The Case for Issue Advocacy Advertising," *National Underwriter* (Life and Health Insurance Edition), Vol. 86, August 13, pp. 52-53.

Whalen, Hugh (1961) "The Peaceful Coexistence of Government and Business," *Canadian Public Administration*, Vol. 4, March, pp. 1-15.

Whitaker, Reginald (1977) *The Government Party: Organizing and Financing the Liberal Party of Canada, 1930-1958* (Toronto: University of Toronto Press).

White, Roderick (1984) "Handicapped Gamesmen" (crown corporation managers), *Policy Options*, Vol. 5(3), pp. 33-36.

Whittington, Les (1981) "Lobbying Ottawa: It can be relatively easy if you know all the rules," *Financial Times*, June 22, pp. G1, G13.

Whittington, M., and G. Williams (eds.) (1985) *Canadian Politics in the Eighties*, 2nd ed. (Toronto: Methuen).

Wicker, Tom (1975) "Who Elected the Press?" in *On Press* (New York: Viking Press), chap. 9, pp. 161-187.

Williams, Blair (1980) "The Para-political Bureaucracy in Ottawa," in H.D. Clarke *et al. Parliament, Policy and Representation* (Toronto: Methuen), pp. 215-230.

Wilson, Ian (1982) "Environmental Analysis," in K. Albert (ed.) *Business Strategy Handbook* (New York: McGraw-Hill).

Wilson, James Q. (1968) "Corruption Is Not Always Scandalous," *New York Times Magazine*, April 28, as reprinted in J.A. Gardiner and D.J. Olson (eds.) *Theft of a City: Readings on Corruption in Urban America* (Bloomington: Indiana University Press, 1974), pp. 29-32.

Wilson, R. (1974) "Special Report on Community Newspapers: Weeklies Coming of Age," *Marketing*, Vol. 89, September 10, pp. 9-13.

Wilson, V. Seymour (1971) "The Role of Royal Commissions and Task Forces," in G. Bruce Doern and Peter Aucoin (eds.) *The Structures of Policy Making in Canada* (Toronto: Macmillan), pp. 154-178.

Wilson, V. Seymour (1981) *Canadian Public Policy and Administration* (Toronto: McGraw-Hill Ryerson), chap. 13, "The Bureaucracy and

Its Publics," pp. 383-422.

Winn, Conrad (1985) "Ministerial Roles in Policy Making: Vote-Seeker, Shaman and Other Incarnations," in *Industrial Policy* (Toronto: University of Toronto Press).

Winsor, Hugh, and Dorothy Lepovenko (1977) "Patronage: The Trudeau Government Says Thanks," *Globe and Mail*, June 13, pp. 12, 25.

Winter, J.P., *et al.* (1982) "Issue-Specific Agenda-Setting: The Whole as Less than the Sum of the Parts," *Canadian Journal of Communication*, Vol. 8, January, pp. 1-10.

Wissema, G. (1981a) "Futures Research—Is It Useful?" *Long Range Planning*, Vol. 14, April, pp. 29-32.

Wissema, G. (1981b) "Issues Management: Preparing for Social Change," *Chemical Week*, Vol. 129(18), October 28, pp. 46-51.

Wolfe, Morris (1980) "The Case Against Advocacy Advertising," *Saturday Night*, Vol. 95, December, pp. 17-18.

Woll, Peter (1974) *Public Policy* (Cambridge, Mass.: Winthrop Publishers).

Wollencroft, Timothy B. (1982) *Organizing Intergovernmental Relations* (Kingston: Institute of Intergovernmental Relations, Queen's University).

Women Rally for Action (1976) *The Rally Story* (Vancouver).

Wood, John (1978) "East Indians and Canada's New Immigration Policy," *Canadian Public Policy*, Vol. 4, pp. 547-567 (interest-group lobbying).

Woodward, Michael, and Bruce George (1983) "The Canadian Indian Lobby of Westminster," *Journal of Canadian Studies*, Vol. 18(3), Fall, pp. 119-143.

Wyckham, Robert J. (1982) "The Life Cycle of Consumer Protection in British Columbia," in S.J. Shapiro and L. Heslop (eds.) *Marketplace Canada* (Toronto: McGraw-Hill Ryerson), pp. 32-58.

Yarwood, Dean L., and Ben. J. Enis (1982) "Advertising and Publicity Programs in the Executive Branch of the National Government: Hustling or Helping the People?" *Public Administration Review*, Vol. 42, January/February, pp. 37-46.

Yates, Douglas (1982) *Bureaucratic Democracy: The Search for Democracy and Efficiency in American Government* (Cambridge, Mass.: Harvard University Press).

Yudof, Mark (1983) *When Government Speaks: Politics, Law and Government Expression in America* (Berkeley: University of California Press).

Zalesnick, A., and M.F.R. Ket De Vries (1975) *Power and the Corporate Mind* (Boston: Houghton Mifflin).

Zussman, David (1982) "The Image of the Public Service in Canada," *Canadian Public Administration*, Vol. 25(1), Spring, pp. 63-80.

Zwicker, Barrie, and Dick MacDonald (eds.) (1983) *The News: Inside the Canadian Media* (Ottawa: Deneau Publishers).

INDEX